Contents

THE
NEWS MACHINE

HACKING

THE UNTOLD STORY

James Hanning

with

Glenn Mulcaire

London

GIBSON SQUARE

First published by

Gibson Square

Tel: +44 (0)20 7096 1100

info@gibsonsquare.com
www.gibsonsquare.com

ISBN 978-1908096951
Available as an e-book

Printed and bound by CPI Group (UK) Ltd, Croydon, CR0 4YY

1

Not a Word

For a long time, very little was known for certain about the phone-hacking scandal surrounding News International. It even barely intruded on the nation's radar that some grubby, soulless guy and an accomplice on the News of the World had been sent to prison, for eavesdropping on members of the royal household. Bad business, thought those who did hear about it. But they were punished, so presumably any problem had been nipped in the bud. The problem was that within weeks of the two men's conviction, the person paying their wages, who resigned over the affair, had become one of the future Prime Minister's closest confidants.

To some this was vindication of the move-along-nothing-to-see stance taken by the paper. To others, it smelt, raising ever louder questions of who knew what. The story was to develop into what Labour MP Tom Watson predicted would be Britain's Watergate. He had some understanding of the authority and responsibility that goes with being an editor, it invited suspicion. The insertion of Andy Coulson into the heart of the opposition was smooth enough, but was remarkable for the opportunism shown by those who brought it about. The more that emerged, the more surprising that shame-lessness. The courts have gone some way towards apportioning blame. This book seeks to look at how the *News of the World* got to such a state, and what happened subsequently.

Many have had or will have their say in court. Some have been believed, some not. The one person at the heart of it all, though, has said next to nothing since his arrest on 8 August 2006. When Glenn Mulcaire did apparently say something publicly, his words were drafted by his lawyer. Maybe he had something to say for himself after all?

But, surely, we all know Glenn Mulcaire is the crook whose dirty work caused all the phone-hacking trouble? People may argue about who asked him to do this or that, or what their motivation might have been, but the immutable fact at the bottom of it all was that Mulcaire was an unscrupulous and greedy private investigator who cared nothing for his victims' privacy or feelings? A man who sat in a south London trading estate systematically trawling through the phone, mortgage and medical records of hundreds of people surely wouldn't have the audacity to claim motives other than the lowest, sleaziest and most reprehensible? Yet almost nobody knows what has been going on in Glenn Mulcaire's mind in the years since he was first arrested. It has suited too many people for him not to speak. The phone hacking scandal became both a blame game and a study in deniability. Mulcaire, initially a beneficiary of both, became a victim of both. The more guilty people who said they knew nothing, the more Mulcaire must have been responsible. Because he was unable to speak without risking enormous legal and financial claims against him, all the more filth was piled at his door.

Mulcaire and Clive Goodman both 'took one for the company' in 2007 and pleaded guilty, when more senior people at *News of the World* escaped charges (for the time being, as it turned out). He was dismissed as a lawless rogue, yet his bosses knew his work was responsible for winning awards for his newspaper.

To meet Mulcaire is to be surprised, however, and to know his story is to get a feel for how part of an industry worked. How a public appetite for salacious stories, light and heavy, put so much pressure on those responsible for churning them out that the news machine that they were operating simply went up in smoke. Journalism is full of decent people who start off wanting to make the world a better place but who find themselves steered off course by the demands of the market place. They like the idea of holding the powerful to account and standing up for the downtrodden, but are confronted by a public more interested in Miley Cyrus and Cristiano Ronaldo's latest conquest than poverty and global warming. So an accommodation has to be reached.

Nowhere did this accommodation with the real world go more spectacularly wrong than in the case of Glenn Mulcaire. It may surprise those who read about the 6,000 people claimed to have been victims of Mulcaire's eavesdropping that he too signed up to work for the *News of the World* with good intentions. The streetwise investigator, the man David Blunkett wanted to rot in hell, the dab hand at low-level blagging and company searches, had wanted to use his talents for the general good.

Specifically, from the age of 17, he had wanted to be a private detective and help catch criminals. As he grew into the profession, through bread-and-butter company searches, garnished with some light blagging, he believed the details of his painstaking work could be used in the public's interest. His work was indeed scrutinised by the police, eventually, but not as he had intended. On 7th December 2011 he was arrested for the second time and, again, put on trial, for the unlawful interception of voicemails. By this time, the *News of the World's* disregard for the law had become directly responsible for the re-writing of the entire rule book of British press regulation. His story, then, is also the story of the modern media.

How did this come about? What sort of man can call himself God-fearing and public-spirited yet behave in a way that leads directly to the disgrace and closure of one of the landmarks of British journalism, putting a bomb underneath not only the media as whole, but the political and police system as well? That is one of the questions this book seeks to answer, calling for the first time on extensive evidence from Mulcaire himself.

It will also look at Mulcaire's involvement in the case of Milly Dowler, the story of the kidnapped and later murdered Surrey schoolgirl that turned the phone hacking saga from a hiccup in media regulation to a national outrage. It will show how Mulcaire 'stood up' one of the biggest scoops of the decade. How he helped ferret out some of the country's most dangerous sex offenders. It will ask David Cameron some hitherto unasked questions about how he could have hired Andy Coulson, editor of the *News of the World* within weeks of the phone hacking scandal first exploding.

Most of this came as a surprise to me. It took me about four years to get to meet Glenn Mulcaire. I had become increasingly interested in the phone hacking scandal and, from my position as comment and then deputy editor of the *Independent on* Sunday had sought to nudge the story on, while of course acknowledging the groundbreaking work of Nick Davies of the *Guardian*. As the story grew from modest beginnings, I found I had got to know some of those involved. If another paper broke a story, I had a rough idea who to call to check its accuracy or otherwise. I tried to sort the wheat from the chaff, and could occasionally break the odd bit of new ground myself, but as time went on and with others having six times as many outlets as a Sunday paper, the returns on my efforts grew more marginal. All the same, increasingly, the person editors wanted to hear about was the elusive figure of Mulcaire. He remained the big catch.

Yet he wouldn't come out to play. I had written to him, as I'm sure hundreds of journalists had done, but it seemed his silence had been bought. The 'out-of-control' investigator who had served 6 months in prison was having his legal fees paid by News International. Lawyers piled up the private claims for breach of privacy against him, hoping to lever him away from his protectors, but News International were paying his legal fees (even if no one, seemingly, told Rupert Murdoch) and he seemed impregnable. Meanwhile, the legal process continued, with lawyers lining up to demand he name his controllers at News International. Its executive Rebekah Brooks told the Old Bailey in March 2014 that her organisation planned to oppose such court orders because they felt Mr Mulcaire was an 'unreliable witness'. 'Financially and reputationally we did not want that to happen... the view was he could say anyone or anything,' she said.

2

Almost Two Decades
of Spreading Rot
The News Story that Grew and Grew

As Glenn Mulcaire remained frustratingly elusive, I often wondered who is this mysterious, purportedly feral figure at the centre of the rot that appears to be spreading from the media to the police and the highest political circles in the country? Those few people who knew him were highly protective. He was said to be a good Catholic family man. 'Glenn's all right,' they would say, as in 'you should know the full story – it's very different from what you'd think.'

It was ever more intriguing, although when I finally got to know him I would occasionally have to correct any sympathy for him. He had, after all, peddled tittle-tattle and sleaze for a very comfortable living, invading the privacy of countless people and helped drag my profession – of which I've always been unfashionably proud – to the bottom rank in public esteem.

As I understood it, he had played a part in eavesdropping on a blamelessly homosexual unmarried MP. In accusing football boss Gordon Taylor of having an affair with the PFA's in-house solicitor, when, his lawyer later pointed out, he was consoling her after the death of her father. And in generally helping build and feed an increasingly ravenous public appetite for inconsequential celebrity nonsense. Who is to say what he might have got up to – with computers, bank accounts and so on – that wasn't in his files?

My frustration mounted as a great many journalists, cynically or innocently, said investigative sleaze wasn't really a story. The sophisticated view – which I struggled to share – was that self-regulation meant a more than respectable amount of self-interest and 'light touch' regulation: if corners have to be cut in order to get to the truth, then let them be cut. No bones were broken, and the greater good had been served.

It's a view I would have happily shared, except this wasn't about noble-cause corruption. If every now and then an investigator had to be used and sailed close to the wind legally in the cause of writing a proper public interest story, fine. But as often as not this was about fishing expeditions – the indiscriminate, lawless trawling of the deep in the hope of picking up a soggy fag end. Being given an inch is one thing. Taking a mile is another.

After Andy Coulson was appointed to work alongside David Cameron in May 2007, the more implausible the official version seemed to me to be becoming and the greater the number of perfectly decent public figures there were prepared to believe it. The only thing that would trump their conviction would be some hard facts from the people who had done it. Yet not only Mulcaire but many in the organisation seemed to have ditched their normally assiduous dedication to disseminating the truth.

He was the story, yet he was unattainable. One figure who was prepared to talk to me – eventually – was a roguish former showbiz reporter called Sean Hoare. He had worked hard and played even harder in the service of the *Sun*'s and the *News of the World*'s features desks. There was very little Sean wouldn't do either for his own gratification or to get a story for his paper. Many were the lost weekends with major-league rock stars, parts of which would then appear subsequently in one of the red tops. The phrase rough diamond doesn't begin to do Sean justice; but in his early 40s his wild man life style was beginning to catch up with him. At one point his doctor gave him 2 days to live and friends were never quite able to gauge just how ill he was.

By mid-2007, Sean was an angry man without a job. He had left the *News of the World*, having fallen out badly with Andy Coulson, with whom he had shared many an adventurous evening in the past. Coulson felt that Sean's excesses were getting the better of him and, to put it as neutrally as possible, he decided to place his professionalism ahead of blind loyalty to Sean, by this time in serious need of treatment for an addiction to alcohol. Sean's resentment was heightened when his friend Clive Goodman ('an absolute gentleman', in Sean's words) was sent to prison and sacked by the *News of the World* for his part in the hacking of the royal phones, the scandal that saw Glenn Mulcaire go to prison. Coulson's behaviour had the effect of isolating Goodman and Mulcaire, portraying them as rogue operators. Sean's sense of decency and justice – more finely honed than he would admit, or than the bosses' caricature of him would suggest – was appalled. He knew better than anyone that redtop journalism was a rough and tumble world, and he had few pious pretensions about it. So when he saw someone he had regarded as one of his kind, a tabloid scuffler, and a treacherous one, alongside the leader of the Opposition, he was affronted. 'What's he doing up there?' he would fume. 'He sent my mate to prison. It's just wrong.'

His marriage was checkered and for all his desire to 'get clean', his friends still needed a lot of convincing that he had beaten his demons. But the Sean I met in 2010 was a pretty convincing one. Before our appointment, he was anxious to satisfy himself that there would be 'no funny business'. He wanted me to promise I would not have hidden cameras or microphones – that our encounter was not just off the record, it was 'not for use'. He had evidently forgotten that most of the broadsheet press can't afford 'funny business'. (Read that as you will, but we did manage to recompense him for his train the fare from Watford.) We met in Kensington, near my office, and had a modest half of something non-alcoholic, I think, but we chatted for ages. This was not a man obviously seething with rage at having been stitched up by his former mate. Nor did he seem to particularly want revenge on behalf of Clive Goodman, although that was a part of it. More, he was rather more coolly aware that an entire industry had taken a wrong turn, and that it needed putting right. Nobody could be in any doubt that he was telling the truth, it seemed to me, and he genially recited tales of monstrous intrusion that now seems to belong to another era.

It wasn't as if Sean had had a Damascene conversion one day, more that as time went on, the party was grinding to a halt. Of course this had much to do with his own health (which led increasingly, tragically, to him being edged towards the party's exit) but also a sense that he owed it to his wife Jo and to the world to get a bit more real. In short, it was time to sober up, but that didn't prevent him enjoying going over old ground. He had tales of how News International executives would hack into the computer system of their rivals to get access to their list of upcoming news stories. This was ultimately the cheat's way of conducting business, the sort of homework-stealing sneakery that earns nothing but contempt in the school yard. Yet in the world of the red top, it was all part of the game. There was no limit on lying and cheating, as long as you got the story.

Sean was a News International man through and through. He lived for the story, but demanded entertainment on the way. So he and his co-conspirators were invariably in the thick of the action if there was a showbiz opening or an after-gig party. He had worked on Bizarre, the training ground for up and coming showbiz journos who wanted to catch the proprietor's eye. Andy Coulson, Rav Singh, Dominic Mohan and Piers Morgan all worked there. It was a testing ground, to test not only a reporter's talent but also their endurance.

Sean knew how to play the system. He was one of many who would tell his boss he needed a certain amount of cash for a story. If the source ends up receiving a rather smaller proportion of that figure, who was to know if the reporter had trousered a commission on the way through? When source protection was vital, it would be counterproductive for the left hand to know too much about what the right hand was doing. But this didn't just work occasionally. It was systematic.

As for the dark arts, Sean was in the thick of it. It was casual, routine. On a quiet day, he would be asked to do a bit of 'finger-fishing' to see what X or Y had been up to. He talked of a 'hack off' between two journalists, to see which one could crack the hardest (most secure) voicemails. Sean, a selfless encourager of young talent, was proud to report that the winner was a protégé of his who went on to occupy a senior position. He used to report, almost absent-mindedly, as if everyone knew, how executives would be forever trying to listen in to one another's voicemails. Partly, he said, they were trying to pinch one another's stories, and partly, if – to put it more decorously than perhaps they would – they were checking on one another's fidelity. Rebekah Brooks (as she then wasn't) and Andy Coulson were to the fore in that category.

But the main purpose of what one journalist tagged a 'handy little trick' was stories. One tale, quite possibly apocryphal, involved somebody having a row in a restaurant with Heather McCartney, later the wife of Beatle Paul, after which the one-legged campaigner left a message on the person's voicemail, the gist of which was 'Don't you ever call me Hoppy again.' The message, wouldn't you know it, was picked up by the red-top papers and shared between them, none wanting to be alone in offending the girl friend of so revered a figure at the height of his happiness with her. It was only after extensive legal threats on a Saturday afternoon that the papers were forced to pull the story.

Another of Sean's tales concerned the breaking of the story about Sven-Goran Eriksson's relationship with Ulrika Jonsson. He and a colleague had hacked the phone of one of them, and had managed to establish they were having an affair. They reported this to the office early one week, where ecstatic *News of the World* editor Andy

Coulson declared the story a certain 'splash' for Sunday, congratulated them on their scoop and told them to take the afternoon off. This they chose to spend celebrating their catch. The problem was, they bumped into a reporter from the *Mirror*, to whom Sean's colleague could not help boasting. The *Mirror* reporter thought the tale too good to wait till Sunday, so reported it to his bosses, satisfied himself of its truth (you may well ask how) and the *Mirror* stole the story, running it in the '3am Girls' column on a Thursday. Andy Coulson's reaction at having such a tale stolen from under his nose does not need to be guessed at.

Sean was torn. He wanted the truth about the extent to which redtop stories were driven by titbits picked up from celebrities' phones to come out, but he was reluctant to go public about what he knew, knowing that he might face a charge himself. The police – who had taken their cue from Prime Minister David Cameron and the Press Complaints Commission – were struggling to believe, let alone prove, the extent of the wrongdoing. The House of Commons Culture, media and sport committee, which included the redoubtable Tom Watson, spent several months looking into the matter, concluding that it was 'inconceivable' that no senior executive knew what had been going on, but admitting it had not been able to lay a glove on Andy Coulson.

This was an affront to anyone who knew the truth, but even the anarchic Sean was disinclined to sacrifice his freedom and his family's peace of mind, recently restored by Sean's apparent return to health, in the cause of press regulation. He fumed quietly to friends, and expressed an earnest hope that the truth would come out. Then, one day in September 2010, he went on Radio 4's PM programme and alleged that phone hacking was 'endemic' at the paper and that the Prime Minister's press spokesman had asked him to hack phones to acquire stories. To most senior staff on the red top papers, it was a childish statement of the bleedin' obvious, but nobody had had the courage to say it publicly.

So now the dam seemed likely to break. Surely others would come forward? News International bosses had been warned that Andy Coulson choosing to take a job in Downing Street would attract yet more fire to David Cameron's decision to appoint him. Surely, now, that judgment would be confirmed?

In the following months, more did emerge. Yet Mulcaire was still the story. Sean's stories were highly entertaining, but he felt he had said his piece. The police did go to see him, but would only interview him under caution that he might himself be subject to arrest. There were to be no deals. Sean was scandalised, but trapped. His wife Jo had only recently reclaimed him from alcohol dependency. The last thing she wanted was him up on a criminal charge.

Yet still Mulcaire wouldn't play ball.

My paper had run the only ever interview with him on 19 July 2009, conducted by Peter Burden, a Shropshire-based journalist who had written a book about *News of the World*'s excesses. Burden had got to know Mulcaire, visit his home in Cheam and gain his trust sufficiently for Mulcaire at least to speak to him. The investigator was coy about his plans, but was clearly in a bad way financially. The treasures that Mulcaire had to offer were not forthcoming. He had lost an enormous amount, but he still had much more to lose. He knew too much about people the police had not even interviewed. Too many people were threatening legal action against him, and he was reliant on News International to help pay his legal bills. Far from receding into the past, the scandal was growing, dogging his escape from it and rehabilitation.

Peter Burden was in pole position with Glenn and occasionally we would speak to exchange gossip. Burden was astonishingly brave, placing on his website flagrant allegations of misconduct by senior people at the *News of the World* which had such a deafening ring of truth that Wapping could only ignore them. Such was the power of the News International lawyers these people generally got away with it – in that the mainstream media failed to air his allegations. Burden had been trying unsuccessfully to persuade Mulcaire to collaborate on a book. Mulcaire had had tentative conversations with a former colleague, who planned to write a racy account of goings-on at the paper, but the deal never got off the ground. Legal concerns trumped any amount of money he might have made from such a venture. Peter Burden also sought to persuade Mulcaire into print, and they reached an agreement, binding for a year, that he would write 'the inside story'. Yet that project also ran into the sand. Burden had other fish to fry and Mulcaire's heart evidently wasn't in it. Plus, publishers were still wary of a book involving a convicted criminal which would doubtless make a number of contentious allegations against some very powerful people.

In late 2012, I was told by Peter Burden that Mulcaire was willing to meet. I wasn't sure what he intended, but to someone with an unhealthy interest in the hacking scandal, any meeting was welcome. We met at Starbucks in Victoria station that autumn. When I arrived at the busy coffee bar, Glenn, gangling, tanned and fashionably dressed, was skittering about nervously. I was to learn that's how he often is, but he was in a high old state. He affected friendliness but kept looking over my shoulder and his. He was convinced we were being watched, at very least, and that I was somehow pulling a fast one. I said something crass about how I had waited a long time to meet him. He mumbled something and asked to see my mobile. He asked me if I would take the battery out. Only that way could he be sure I was not – or somebody else was not – using it as a recorder or transmitter. I know now that he also used an electronic device to check whether I was 'wired', with a recording device.

I would like to say it was not long before he came to trust me. In fact, a year later and about15 meetings on, he was still asking me to remove the battery from my phone. Yet we had progressed. I had a bit more of a grasp of how he was feeling and how misunderstood he felt. I think he gathered that I had no axe to grind, nor any political line to push. I just wanted to get to the bottom of who knew what and how it had all come about.

By this time, Operation Weeting, the police investigation headed by Deputy Assistant Commissioner Sue Akers, was well into its stride. Prosecutions were looming. Would that suit Mulcaire or not, I wondered. Having served time, surely he would not be required to do so again? Maybe he would be required to be a witness, I thought.

In any event, it was not clear where our acquaintance was going. He had failed to overcome the legal and financial obstacles to writing a book, and was in all probability prevented even from giving an interview. Anything of interest would almost certainly risk prejudicing the court cases. I had the impression from a friend that Peter Burden had pretty much given up hope of collaborating with him, and was myself coming to think my interest in Glenn was no more than voyeuristic on my part.

But as we spoke, it became clear how fired up he was, and the more time we spent together, the more I came to feel how real his frustration was. He just seemed to want his story told, clearly and factually, without frills and embellishment. Why, he demanded, had nobody sought his side of the story?

I was hard pressed to explain this. Surely everybody wanted to hear his story, contaminated though he was as a source? He knew the answers as to who had ordered the infringement of the privacy of thousands of people. Wasn't that something my profession wanted to know about? Evidently not, or not on terms that he thought suitable.

It would be a surprise if someone so well versed in the culture of the grubbier end of the newspaper business didn't seek to make as much money as possible from an exclusive. Glenn knew that a lot of people wanted to hear his story, but a lot of powerful, well resourced people didn't. It would take a pretty large cheque to cut that Gordian knot. And he needed such a cheque badly. He had not had proper, sustained work since he was sent to prison.

While one might be sympathetic to someone who knew he had done wrong, had served his time and wanted to turn things around, it was all academic to my mind. My newspaper has never been in the business of paying hefty sums for exclusives, and one or two of its freelance contributors will testify that it feels a bit of a bonus to be paid at all. The idea that our cheque book might be able to fight off the competition to land one of phone hacking's biggest fish was absurd. But we do try to treat stories thoughtfully and credit our readers with an appetite for more than the sex lives of soap stars. And, for any ultra-cynics who might be reading this, at its very lowest, we can't afford private investigators.

And there was another big no-no. Mulcaire was soiled goods. How could he expect to make money from a scandal in which he was a leading participant? Media standards may have declined, and infamy may be the new celebrity, but this would surely be a new low. Besides, a coach and horses had been driven through the press' rules, but one rule at least stood: the media should not enable criminals to profit from their crimes.

Whether Mulcaire was aware of this or not, I do not know. Certainly it had not featured in our conversations about his previous dalliances with those wanting to do a book deal (though they must all have been aware of it). I seemed to be the last person on the dance floor. If anyone was to do a book with him, it was me. (I of course credit myself with a valiant-for-truth persistence in wanting to see the story through – others will put it down to an obsessive and impractical interest in a toxic topic.) So it fell to me to tell Mulcaire that whatever else happened, he would not be allowed to make any money from telling his story. Again, there would be 'no funny business'. If he wanted someone to help present his version of events, I was interested, but, given the low base from which his public credibility was starting, I would need a pretty free hand. He discussed the issue with his wife Alison, and came back to say he understood the situation. (At a later stage, the subject of money was raised again briefly, but again dismissed.)

He wanted the right to be listened to. I said I hoped I could offer that at least, but that he could not expect me to do his PR for him. I would be the reporter of his take on things, but not be an advocate for his position. I told him I would need to be able to ask him any questions I wanted, and he should answer them to the best of his ability and above all truthfully. I said I would be a sympathetic sceptic, and insist on being able to check his version with other sources, to the extent that that was possible. If I ever had any reason to doubt he was telling the truth, the game was off.

We seemed to be getting somewhere. We were both keen the book should not be about Murdoch-bashing, or redtop-bashing. He renounced any thought of making money more easily than I expected. He had come to distrust journalists as a breed, so what he wanted was a fair crack of the whip. He believed that I, in harness with my newspaper, would give him that.

3

'I Don't Think
I Should Know More about This'

News International's first few versions of what happened in the phone hacking affair bore very little resemblance to the subterranean truth. An enormous number of lies were told to sustain the fiction that only two people were in on the law-breaking. It was to take several years before anything approaching the full picture was to appear, and by the time it did, the entire centre of gravity of the privacy versus right-to-know balance had shifted.

That small media story, about a couple of barely known sleuths, was to herald the end of an entire approach to popular journalism. Where popular newspapers had always pushed the boundaries, and however many times they were thrown out of the 'last-chance saloon', they seemed to know that their trade would continue to be self-regulated. So the same mindset lived on, one which essentially saw 'getting the story' as the legitimator of any behaviour. While this wasn't true in all cases, the bigger the story, the greater the latitude afforded the journalist. So among their peers, the journalist who got the big story was rarely criticised, few questions were asked, and the sanctity of source protection meant that plenty else never came to be scrutinised. Editors would be accustomed to saying 'I don't think I should know any more about this', although in the end, in the company of the smallest handful of confidants, they would have to inform themselves sufficiently if, in the worst of cases (a writ), they were required to answer for their actions.

Journalists are by nature inquisitive and acquisitive, and the rise of the cult of celebrity (in part created and fed by the press surely) in a highly competitive market meant more than ever that stories were the only currency that mattered. Greater and greater demands would be placed on journalists and more and more outlandish schemes would be devised to find them. In the old days, Fleet Street's smoke-filled bars used to brim with raucous, irreverent middle aged men in raincoats telling rakish tales of how they cut a corner, slipped a security guard a fiver, impersonated a teacher, guard or relative of 'the victim' in order to get the story and file it for the London edition by deadline time. Of paramount importance would be the getting of the story, but it may not be too romantic to think that a degree of implicit peer pressure was applied by the opinion of fellow journalists. A degree of cunning was always acceptable and if shared among long-time colleagues, admired. But possibly an ethos of what was considered acceptable would play some role. Harold Evans, former editor of the *Sunday Times* and for many an essential guide to journalistic practice and ethics, used to have a rule for journalists considering taking a liberty with the truth or otherwise crossing the boundaries of defensible practice, supposedly with some greater goal in mind. He would tell them to ask themselves if – when they came to write their story – they would be willing to tell the reader what they had done. In other words, would they be confident that the reader would say 'that's Ok – I can quite see why (s)he did that, and it was in the public interest to do so because an important truth has been revealed.' It may just be that anticipated peer disapproval in the bars of EC4 used to play some small part in policing some of Britain's more unruly Grub Street scribes.

But in the age of celebrity and sophisticated eavesdropping, just having a roguish attitude, a few trusted sources and recycling copy from the news agencies wasn't enough. Boundaries had to be pushed, and technology offered plenty of scope for the imaginative to subvert the rules.

The Leveson inquiry heard the claims of Steven Nott, a sales manager based in South Wales, who in 1999 tried to alert people to the fact that anybody could listen in to somebody else's voicemails as long as they had the PIN number, which was usually on a factory setting and therefore easily known. He contacted the *Daily Mirror*, who told him they were keen on the story, sat on it and in the end never ran it. He then went to the *Sun*, but they didn't bite either. Subsequent events lead him to believe senior executives on the papers knew full well the significance of what he was saying. Either they knew already, or they used it to their advantage. 'It didn't take me long to realise what I had done. I couldn't believe I was so stupid to tell a national newspaper how to get hot news for free just by hacking into someone's phone,' he said. (Nott believes that was how phone-hacking took off, although others have different views.)

Mobile phone scanners, of the sort that had picked up the mobile conversations between Prince Charles and Camilla Parker-Bowles on the one hand, and Princess

Diana and James Gilbey on the other, were extensively used during the analogue age. According to one *News of the World* reporter, they were a vital tool in knowing about the movements of the royals, particularly at weekends: 'The photographers could listen in to the royal protection officers at Highgrove and other country estates because they were the only ones on the airwaves, discussing how to get Diana or whoever out and where they were going. Many staffers and freelancers had them in their kitbags in the 1990s. I remember playing with one in an editor's office.' Seemingly, the royal protection officers had no idea.

In February 1997, the *News of the World* ran a story about Phil Davies, a celebrated rugby player, having an extra-marital affair. Tape recordings of the pair proving the existence of the relationship were 'inadvertently picked up by radio hams', or so the paper said. The reporter in question, Paul McMullan, recalls: 'It was the first time the lawyers told us to be careful with recorded mobile phone stuff.... I spent a whole week disguising the source of the story; we all did for 10 full years before Clive went to jail. Everybody knew this was an executive direction coming from either legal or editorial departments to be careful about writing their story so as as not to reveal their source.' Despite admitting that the news was based on three distinct phone calls, the paper was flagrant in tweaking the law's tail. At the end of the article were the words: 'It is illegal to intercept phone calls intentionally, but not if found at random.' As if all three calls had been picked up by chance.

Journalists have of course always known the value of being able to eavesdrop. But only recently had the technology become so easily available. It enabled journalists not just to discover unsuspected truths in an instant, but also to provide clinching evidence, even if it wasn't adducible in the writing of the story, or admissible in court. Some celebrities were wise to their vulnerability, and took precautions, but many did not. One victim was the former manager of Scotland's national football team, Craig Brown.

As the Euro 2000 tournament in Belgium and the Netherlands drew to a close, the *News of the World* marked the occasion by peering into his personal life. On 2nd July, the paper was able to report that 'former Radio One beauty' Louise Port, 23, was having a secret affair with him, even though 'faithful lover Phyllis Kirk is still waiting at home for him'. It revealed that he had attended two games with her although he hardly ever ventured out of his room in the Holiday Inn on the outskirts of Amsterdam, possibly because he was with Louise. The story continued in customary redtop style, detailing what the couple ordered for room service and tormenting the language with a series of painful football metaphors (he wanted to 'make sure he wasn't caught offside with Louise' by colleagues and had escaped fellow pundits to make 'a few plays of his own and analyse a different set of positions upstairs'). The story spoke gloatingly about how 'Louise thinks she's in love', suggesting this was unwise given Brown's famously roving eye. Helpfully, a 'close friend' of the couple was on hand to talk freely about the minutiae of their relationship.

So how had the paper got the story? He had just passed his 60th birthday, but if senescent inactivity was beckoning, he wasn't rushing to greet it. The previous year the *News of the World* revealed Craig was seeing Ayr church elder Phyllis Kirk and teacher Lynda Slaven at the same time. 'Neither woman was aware he was two-timing them,' the paper clarified. 'Then the bombshell news emerged that the frisky football father figure was seeing a THIRD woman – district nurse Allison Brown.' If ever a man had form and might be good for a headline, it was Brown.

The features desk's Paul McMullan, who was in Amsterdam at the time and was well experienced in the ways of news reporting, was given the job and told, as he had been many times before: 'Make it work'. This is a familiar phrase to many reporters, used to being briefed on a story whose source does not want to be identified and they don't need to know. In this case, says McMullan, it was not source protection that was the issue but the fact that some of the evidence had been uncovered unlawfully. The proof, acquired surreptitiously, was not usable.

McMullan rang the office, saying 'I am never going to be able to prove they are shagging.' 'They said 'we are running this', just write it.' McMullan just needed to get Brown talking and acknowledge the bones of the story to avoid a subsequent libel claim. 'Make it work' meant what it said, and few questions would be asked as long as the reporter produced the goods. The confirmation might not be a straight 'Yes, it's true', but might come in the form of an off the record admission (possibly from 'a friend'), or tell-tale pictures, or an implicit acquiescence. McMullan duly obliged, and the office provided the rest. 'I think the "close friend" quotes were taken from the tapes of mobile phone messages back at the office,' remembers McMullan. Thus the paper had a classic story from next to nothing. It had been based on a hunch, that Craig Brown's libido was undimmed, and was backed up by a spot of 'finger-fishing' and an assured piece of foot-in-the-doormanship by a reporter.

On other occasions, the (usually) women in question were less innocent, and would record their own conversations with their lover, with a view to selling the stories to the papers. In such cases, there may be a degree of premeditation, which on occasion would, in extreme cases, invite speculation as to the women's true motivation.

And the journalists, of course, loved the chase. Journalism may be a vocation for many, and some become addicted to story-getting as if it were a drug. The more prominent the piece, the bigger the high; the greater the approbation of the bosses, the more gratifying the reluctance of congratulations from competitors and the unspoken 'how did (s)he get that?' And while a glow remains for a few days, the hunger to repeat the trick is constant. Success breeds success, but it also breeds desire. The thrill of writing a news story which surprises, subverts, challenges, changes the bigger picture and above all cannot be ignored by colleagues and competitors is immense. What greater vindication could there be for someone who enters the profession (hypocritically or not) with the words 'the people have a right to know' emblazoned on their minds?

Of course, life couldn't go on without friendly contacts on 'the other side', in parliament, medicine, law or wherever, but journalistic machismo requires that these are regarded as purely means to an end. They are, of necessity, treated with confidentiality. This is of course as it should be, although the protection of a source can be used to hide the fact that, for all the bluster and omniscience, a reporter only has one contact on a given topic, knowledge of whose prejudices might slant a boss against his story.

When onto that 'given' is transposed an unprecedented reader interest in celebrities (and a keenness of those celebrities to exploit this insatiable appetite), a ferocious circulation battle and the availability of hitherto unimagined technology with which to snoop, the pressure on journalists is greater than ever.

Stealing ideas off competitors was the least of it. Paul McMullan recalls how the *News of the World* used to pay someone £500 to acquire the *Sunday Mirror*'s news list every week. 'We knew who had the list and there would be a weekly meeting between the person on the *Sunday Mirror* and our person, and often I would get tasked with writing up whatever story they had. Actually the person in question only received £300 a week. The *News of the World*'s intermediary was creaming off £200 a week, which went into his pocket. When Piers Morgan moved to the *Mirror* he sacked the person who had been passing over the list.'

The *News of the World* always kept abreast of the burgeoning technological possibilities. If another paper was getting the big stories, the bosses wanted to know why. If the dark arts were involved, then Wapping would have to up its game. If it found itself lagging its competitors, soon enough a senior figure from management would crack the whip and push the straggler to the front of the pack. On occasions, staff were hired from other papers for their proficiency in the dark arts, and Sean Hoare cheerfully admitted he was one. News International doesn't do laggards. In its last 10 years it reached new levels of bombast and success. And with the *Times*, the *Sunday Times* and the *Sun* in the same stable, it ensured that the Murdoch world view was well represented on the nation's news stands. It also made Murdoch a figure to be feared, both in journalism and public life.

As mentioned earlier, newspaper journalists are inclined to enjoy the raucousness of office life – the heartless banter, the default cynicism and facetiousness, the finding out of secrets, the labour-saving short cuts and the glib, 'I wasn't born yesterday' knowingness. And under the cover of macho callousness, there is often a camaraderie and a commonly held (but rarely articulated) view that when all is said and done, the job of exposing bad people is a worthwhile one, and most of the people in it do it for decent, or at least defensible, reasons.

But the *News of the World*, the paper that used to claim 'All human life is here', lost sight of much of that. Its ethos was corrupted by unmeetable demands and a culture of bullying. Sean Hoare on the features desk, as we have seen, couldn't take the pressure, although his own temperament made him an unsuitable candidate to try. Matt Driscoll, a football writer on the paper, was eventually awarded £792,736 in compensation for being the victim of 'a consistent pattern of bullying behaviour'.

One reporter recalls the change in the atmosphere at the paper, 'They promoted halfwits and liars. One executive in particular was vile on a daily basis. He loved making you miserable. Plus there were others who didn't have the contacts or the ability. Hacking phones was just a tool to them that made their lives easier. All of them were terrified of Rebekah [Brooks]. They just wanted snippets to tell Rebekah.' And Rebekah would pass them on to Rupert Murdoch, or so journalist Michael Wolff asserts, not that Murdoch, presumably, or Brooks, a jury has found, would have known the source of the gossip.

It became a machine, losing sight of the 'human life' and spitting out those who didn't shape up. The fear of being spat out made more and more journalists do things they 'did not go into journalism' to do. Indeed, the closure of the paper can be traced back from the start of hacking scandal to Clive Goodman – under mounting pressure from his bosses – taking a risk on a story about the royal princes. Newspapers are always high-wire acts to an extent, but with hindsight the degree of pressure that prevailed suggested something was likely to give. One journalist with over 10 years on the paper said its closure as a result of phone hacking was a bit like Al Capone being caught for tax evasion. 'It was routine, and really wasn't that big a deal in the scheme of things – I never imagined something as trivial as that would bring the paper down,' he said.

Hand in hand with the ultra-competitiveness of the red tops was the widespread reliance on private investigators. Their use by journalists had reached a height unimagined by most readers, it is fair to assume, by the late 1990s. It would be extremely unfair to tar all private investigators with the brush of criminality. Many are highly reputable, discreet, professional and honourable, and are to the fore where the regulation of their trade is concerned. Those were generally wary of journalists, who they saw as inclined to print rather more of a story than was discreet, and for a private investigator, discretion was all. 'Most PIs wouldn't work for the media,' one of their number remembers. 'They just wouldn't trust them.'

But others were willing to work with the media, and the work was extensive if not particularly creative. Much of it was routine tracing of individuals or companies, finding of phone numbers and so on, sometimes legally, sometimes not. They had the contacts and knowhow to provide such information, so they would be used, simply, as a labour-saving device by newspapers. The provision of this kind of information was not held in high esteem in the investigators' higher echelons, but it was regarded as invaluable and harmless by the papers. And those who commissioned it tended to do so unchallenged by their bosses, and certainly by their employees. As one for *News of the World* reporter put it: 'No reporter sitting in a car on a story that most of Fleet Street is chasing who gets a call from the desk and is told to go to a certain address is going to say, "Where did you get that address? Are you sure it was legally acquired?"'

In some cases, though, the work was more sophisticated. On occasions the difficult bits of a journalist's trade got farmed out to private investigators, so that the scribes in the office were active only at the beginning of the story (the acquiring of a piece of gossip) and the end, the writing it up. The erection of a buffer between the writer and the fact needing to be discovered or verified suited everyone – the investigator was paid to dig up the nugget without too many questions being asked as to how he had done so, and the journalist got the kudos of his colleagues. One well established former business journalist cheerfully admits to his extensive use of private investigators. 'You would have been mad not to do it,' he said. 'Everyone else was doing it. In a competitive world, not to use PIs was unthinkable. Apart from anything else, it saved so much time.'

The body responsible for overseeing the protection of personal and professional data is the Information Commission. In November 2002 it acquired a warrant to investigate the premises of a private investigator, John Boyall. It became clear that he had been misusing data from the Police National Computer. It was a source of stories for journalists, but one to which they were not supposed to have access. Two inquiries followed as a result of the raid. One, called Operation Motorman, was run by the Information Commissioner, and the other, Operation Glade, conducted by the Metropolitan Police.

The Information Commissioner later described the sort of work that was being performed:

> The 'suppliers' almost invariably work within the private investigation industry: private investigators, tracing agents, and their operatives, often working loosely in chains that may include several interme-diaries between the ultimate customer and the person who actually obtains the information. Suppliers use two main methods to obtain the information they want: through corruption, or more usually by some form of deception, generally known as 'blagging.' Blaggers pretend to be someone they are not in order to wheedle out the

information they are seeking. They are prepared to make several telephone calls to get it. Each call they make takes them a little further towards their goal: obtaining information illegally which they then sell for a specified price. Records seized under search warrants show that many private investigators and tracing agents are making a lucrative business out of this trade.

Having raided the Hampshire home of one investigator, Steve Whittamore, in early 2003, the Commission's 'Operation Motorman' found 305 (mostly newspaper) journalists had asked for over 13,000 pieces of information, over 11,000 of which almost certainly involved breaking the Data Protection Act. The total value to Whittamore was over half a million pounds.

The Whittamore records were broken down into files, known colloquially by their colour. In the 'Blue Book', which detailed Whittamore's dealing with the Murdoch newspapers, were over a thousand instances of his services being used. The files do not in themselves prove unlawful behaviour, and much of the work was clearly lawful. In fact, the figure of a thousand is comparatively small, but it is known the Murdoch papers also used other investigators.

Whittamore was just the point of contact. He had a range of sources in key positions who were able to furnish him with the data his clients needed. He had sources at the Department of Work and Pensions, the Driver and Vehicle Licensing Agency, British Telecom and elsewhere, all anxious to help. As Nick Davies reported in his landmark book *Flat Earth News*, 'These sources, scattered across some of the state's biggest databases, appeared to be peddling their information through at least ten different private investigators, former police officers and petty criminals, who knew each other and worked with each other, swapping contacts and making deals together in their corner of the information black market.'

In early 2005, two investigators, Boyall and Whittamore, pleaded guilty to breaches of the data protection act, while the other two, a Wandsworth-based former police officer and a police press officer, admitted committing misconduct in public office (i.e. procuring confidential police data from the Police National Computer). It is a mark of the scant importance the authorities attached to this topic that the four were given conditional discharges. The press barely covered the story.

Though taken for granted in parts of the media, the extensive use of investigators remained unknown to the public. The findings above, and the rest of the Information Commissioner's report, were not published until some time later.

Publicly, of course, the *News of the World* remained beyond reproach. In March 2003, its former editors Rebekah Brooks and Andy Coulson gave evidence to the House of Commons media select committee. Brooks, seemingly unaware of the law, let slip that: 'We have paid the police for information in the past, and it's been....' Coulson butted in confidently: 'We operate within the code and within the law and, if there is a clear public interest, then the same holds for private investigators, subterfuge, video bags, whatever you want to talk about…' Labour's Chris Bryant pointed out that paying police officers is illegal. Coulson said 'As I said, within the law.' He too seemed either not to know the law or be indifferent to it.

Journalists divide themselves into two essential categories: news people and features people. News people go out, attend press conferences, ask difficult questions to politicians, break bad news to concerned parents, explain motorway pile-ups and generally report hard facts. Features people deal with life's softer, frothier side, expressing opinions, building up conceits, interviewing and often promoting celebrities. They sometimes fancy themselves as being more writerly than their news counterparts, for which they are regarded as belonging in 'the shallow end'. To the more hard-bitten in news, features people are not quite proper journalists, too reliant on help from PR people to get their pages filled, though news people too are hugely reliant on being given press releases and spoon-fed 'the story' by those paid to steer the coverage. Features people, it is said, do not understand that news is something someone doesn't want printed, and that innuendo, opinion and frivolous and ill-sourced gossip are emphatically not news. All newspapers need a bit of both. There's nothing to beat a big news story speedily, comprehensively and digestibly handled, but a stylishly written take on a subject we all thought we knew well, can convey something equally valuable.

Successful newspapers knew not to ignore their readers' interest in who was going out/going on holiday/taking drugs/cavorting on a beach/getting drunk at a premiere with whom. Kelvin Mackenzie, editor of the *Sun* from 1981 to 1994, was a towering figure in popular journalism. He had a knack of touching a public nerve. He was often brutal and raucous, but this was usually mitigated by humour. There are countless stories of 'Kelvin' (as he is known to everyone) going over the top, perhaps the gravest of which was his paper's front page headlined 'The Truth', which reported that many of those who died in the Hillsborough football disaster had been drunk, thieving and urinating on one another, a calumny Liverpool has never forgiven. More entertainingly, he once told the Prime Minister, John Major, who had called meekly to ask how he planned to cover something in the next day's paper, that he was planning to pour 'a large bucket of shit' over him.

He did not worry too much where the story came from or (within reason, and this was before the days of hacking) how it was acquired, as long as it ended up being interesting or funny. The paper he ran was Murdochism at its bawdiest. The proprietor loved it. Whereas many editors in the Murdoch stable felt their boss breathing down their neck, even from the other side of the Atlantic, Mackenzie enjoyed a great deal more latitude. He was free to make mistakes, and though he often did, Murdoch knew Mackenzie needed to be given his head.

The floor of a Kelvin-run office was not a place for sensitive souls. He once shouted across a busy news room to a reporter who he believed was having an affair with one of the secretaries on the *Sun*: 'Oi! I don't want you dipping your pen in the company ink!' He fitted the age of the bully-boy, barrow-boy perfectly, and although not ideally suited to marginally more reflective, liberal times, he exerted a big influence on many careers.

Three talented young journalists in particular learned their trade from the Kelvin textbook. Piers Morgan's first job in journalism was with the *South London News*, but he was recruited by Mackenzie from the *Streatham and Tooting News*, and became editor of the *Sun*'s pop column Bizarre. He had clearly caught Rupert Murdoch's eye and in 1994, at just 29, he was made editor of the *News of the World*.

Andy Coulson started his working life on the *Basildon Echo* and in 1988 moved to the *Sun*, where he worked with Piers Morgan. He fell out with Kelvin Mackenzie, and moved to the *Daily Mail*, but soon came back and took up the editorship of Bizarre in 1994. Rebekah Brooks joined the *News of the World* in 1989 as a secretary, and became a feature writer on the magazine before long.

Kelvin set the standard at that time, and the unconstrained bravado with which he edited became a template. 'They all thought they could emulate Kelvin, but Kelvin was unique,' says one well seasoned News International insider. 'They saw what Kelvin did, and the degree of freedom that Rupert gave him, and they decided they wanted some of it,' says another.

'The people under Kelvin all knew they were being fast-tracked,' says another old hand. 'They knew they'd succeed, and they had seen how Rupert was prepared to indulge the successful. Failure wasn't an option at a company like that. They were big businesses, market leaders, given every chance to succeed. The only question was... they would win, but by how much?'

The trio were often photographed together, and were clearly enjoying themselves. The first to achieve editor status was Piers Morgan, who in 1994 took the chair of the *News of the World* in his late twenties, becoming the youngest national newspaper editor for over 50 years. This was Murdoch publicly announcing that he backed talent, and, as his subsequent career has shown, Morgan is a highly charismatic journalist. His Wikipedia entry reports that he 'quickly gained notoriety for his invasive, thrusting style and lack of concern for celebrities' privacy'. That his judgment can go awry is not in doubt, but he had bucket loads of the Mackenzie chutzpah.

Paul McMullan remembers the Morgan editorship: 'The culture of the *News of the World* was dominated, when I first started, by Piers Morgan.... He was young and in my opinion very talented, but with youth clearly came inexperience and his reckless determination to get a story at all costs is something that set the trend. To be fair, this was the spirit of the day. This was 1994-5. Diana was still alive and it was all good fun. A car chase in St Tropez or through the streets of Paris was something that was done with a smile and a wave. It hadn't yet taken that darker turn.'

In the event Morgan didn't stay long at the *News of the World*. A variety of reasons – to do with those lapses of judgment – have been offered for Morgan leaving the paper, but the truth is not complicated. At the end of 1995, the *Mirror*, always fighting to keep out of the *Sun*'s shadow, came calling. It knew that Morgan, though young and learning his trade as an editor, was likely to be restless. The job that anyone who sought to emulate Kelvin – who, incidentally, was to have his voicemails intercepted later – was editorship of the *Sun*. And Morgan calculated that, while the daily paper was the next logical step in his career, there were a fair few people ahead of him in the queue. He told a colleague at the time: 'It will take me an age before I'd get a chance to edit the *Sun*.'

So Morgan headed across to the *Mirror*, where he was treated like royalty by the management. In the best sceptical tradition, journalists are inclined to express doubt about the success of their peers. For every journalist who applauds Morgan's success at the *Mirror*, there are several who say he 'bought' circulation. One who has watched his career closely says: 'He had 11 months of growth, because so many of the resources of the *People* (the *Mirror*'s stable-mate) had been poured into the *Mirror*, which was doing well as it came up towards being sold. Piers was on the cover of the prospectus. He got what he wanted.'

His reign there was characterised by trouble-making, for better or worse. He had to apologise for a tasteless headline before England's crunch football game against Germany in 1996 ('For you, Fritz, the European Championship is Over!'), and survived allegations of impropriety when he bought £67,000 worth of shares that two of his financial journalists had tipped. He was censured by the Press Complaints Commission, although this did not noticeably dent his self-belief.

As Morgan progressed, so too did his friends Andy and Rebekah. Coulson was on the Bizarre column from 1994 where Sean Hoare was his deputy. The pair enjoyed countless high-octane nights of mischief on the town, and before Sean died he recounted great many of them, some for the sake of entertainment, others because he was aggrieved at the way some colleagues and himself had been treated by the management. It would be otiose to rehearse what would have gone on when two well paid men-about-town got together in the company of highly-paid showbiz personalities, but the pair certainly knew how to work hard and play hard.

While of the three Piers Morgan was the most obviously talented, Rebekah Brooks's ascent was no less inevitable. Five years after turning up at Wapping as a secretary on the magazine (as a 'keen, likeable young girl', recalls a colleague), in 1994 she was made features editor of the *News of the World*. She had become an expert in 'buy-ups', the forking out of money for a particularly sensational story, an arena in which her likeability could be deployed with enormous effect. One of her first successes as features editor was a five-page exclusive interview with footballer Paul Gascoigne, for which she paid between £50,000 and £80,000. It was classic *News of the World* fare, in which Gascoigne admitted 'I've been a violent bastard and a coward and I want the world to know it'. 'Paul is a friend,' explained Brooks at the time. 'He rang me and asked me to see him. Then he poured out his heart.'

One person who worked with Rebekah at that time was Paul McMullan, her deputy, known as Mucky to his colleagues for his willingness to do pretty well anything to get the story. While careful not to make allegations against Brooks, he does point to her inexperience. 'She'd never done an investigation or barely written a news story,' he says. 'She was quite sweet in those days. She knew she was out of her depth and would rely on other people to make her shine. And, funnily enough, it was because she was so hopeless, we wanted to protect her as our boss when we would find out she didn't know what she was doing.'

Brooks's tendency to bring out the protective side in men is a constant in her career. Many speak of someone seemingly anxious for approval, and her apparent vulnerability drove her to work all the harder to impress. A former *News of the World* reporter told *Vanity Fair* magazine: 'She was going at 150 all day…. She was very intense. I thought she was a very insecure woman, actually, desperate for a lot of love and attention…. I was quite friendly with her at some point, as friendly as anyone can get with her, and in her quieter moments she would say, "No one loves me; I'm in a battle here." But even then, she was careful. Even out drinking after work, 'she did not get pissed, ever. She never let her guard down…. She'd get you to do things…. She had this charisma, this magnetic attraction…. She would praise to high heaven, make you feel like you were on top of the world. It was only afterwards that you realized you were manipulated.'

It was not only Paul Gascoigne who was impressed by her. News International executive chairman Les Hinton had also fallen under her spell. As subsequent controversies were to show, the cementing of the pair's relationship was to prove a crucial moment in the company's history. Rupert Murdoch always enjoyed being a hands-on proprietor, but there were limits to what even he could keep his eye on. As one senior figure at the company said: 'The business had got so big and Rupert had to trust someone. The company's first total manager was Les Hinton. Editors always reported to Les. For a prospective editor to succeed, they had to be endorsed by Les. Rupert was very keen to have people validated, and Les liked Rebekah.'

Hinton admired her ability to convert ideas into stories in the paper. She was adept at impressing her bosses, and could show a necessary toughness. In a 1997 memo she wrote to the paper's feature writers: 'The editor and I are very concerned at the standard of the (ideas in the) features list. This morning it was appalling, as it has been for the last few weeks. Some of you are highly experienced and highly paid, however the level of stories and ideas on the schedule would not even make the *Basildon Bugle*, never mind a national newspaper. Some of you are young and have just joined the desk yet I can see no evidence of any effort or enthusiasm which warrents (sic) your posi tion on the biggest selling tabloid.'

The success that Piers Morgan was enjoying at the *Mirror* was worrying the owners of the *Sun*. The *Mirror* was giving youth its chance, and some felt News International should be doing the same. Change was in the air, although *Sun* editor Stuart Higgins was resisting anything too radical. So when the deputy editor's chair became vacant, it was a chance for the management to nudge the tiller in their direction.

Higgins and Hinton were not close and Hinton, Murdoch's right-hand man, wanted changes that Higgins was resisting. At News International, such situations tend not to endure. Before long, the writing was on the wall, and was made all the clearer when in January 1998 Hinton insisted on making Rebekah Brooks Higgins's deputy. Higgins resisted her because he thought she lacked experience and would seek to take the paper away from its natural readership. Brooks wanted, she said later, to make the *Sun* 'less blokey'. In a man's world, which News International's red tops very much were, that would have been an achievement indeed. Les Hinton knew her desire to get rid of 'Page Three', the daily picture of a topless woman, was doomed to failure, and told her if she persisted it would put unnecessary obstacles in her way. She stopped lobbying for it, and it seemed to do the trick.

At Brooks' 30th birthday party in late May 1998, according to media pundit Roy Greenslade, 'Hinton made a speech which all but anointed Brooks as Higgins's successor while Higgins, barely concealing his dislike for Brooks, indicated that he knew he was about to go.' But there was, unusually, disagreement between Hinton and Murdoch as to who should succeed Higgins, Murdoch worrying that Brooks lacked experience. In the end, the job went to David Yelland, deputy editor of the *New York Post* and a former City page editor at the *Sun*.

Yelland set about redesigning the *Sun* in a mildly more cerebral direction. This was a matter of degree, admittedly, but he wanted to reposition the paper and lead it away from the excesses of 1980s bombast, while retaining its sense of humour. Brooks was as disappointed as might be expected of someone who felt she had been promised the job, and did not disguise her disappointment well. She, like Piers Morgan before her, felt the *Sun* was the big prize, and to have a man for whom she had limited respect being given the job ahead of her was hard to take.

But being passed over for the *Sun* was to prove a mere hiccup. In May 2000, Les Hinton got his way. Phil Hall, at the helm of the *News of the World* for five years, was sacked to make way for Brooks. At 32, she had arrived.

One of the least publicly understood aspects of what went wrong at the *News of the World* was the fact that the paper's commanding heights were taken over by a new breed. Phil Hall had had extensive news experience in the 1980s and 1990s at the *People*, as both as an executive and a reporter, so had the wherewithal to be able to judge the truth and weight of a story. Even he, though, was considered by some of the reporters to have initiated a tendency towards a more feature approach of the paper.

The Morgan-Brooks-Coulson trio were certainly more oriented towards features than news. One News International veteran who sneaked a look at Brooks' contacts book was shocked: 'They're *all* PR people!' There were other grumblings, too. One reporter was appalled at Brooks getting the editor's job. 'She was totally out of it and unconnected with the day to day running of her office. She was dismal as an editor, the worst editor I ever had. She shouldn't have been there.'

There are few more damaging phrases, in a trade where professionalism is perhaps surprisingly highly rated, than 'not a proper hack'. Brooks seemed to acknowledge her own lack of news experience by appointing Andy Coulson as her deputy. Coulson, she felt, possessed the harder edge that would complement her strengths in softer, 'human interest' stories – although, in truth, Coulson's main redtop experience was also in features. The pair's sexual relationship, which emerged well over a decade later, had begun by that point, and it seems Brooks had high hopes for it, notwithstanding Coulson's marriage. And professionally she wanted to help him, being conscious that he was not highly rated by the companies' bosses. 'There was a feeling at the time that Andy wasn't editor material,' says one senior figure. 'They just weren't sure about him.' In Brooks' early years in the editor's chair, she was also able to count on the guidance of her mentor Les Hinton, with his lifetime's experience in newspapers behind him.

The senior person in the office full-time with the real news 'edge' was Greg Miskiw. He was old-school *News of the World*, having reputedly said of his work: 'That is what we do – *we* go out and destroy other people's lives'. He was the master of many a vintage sting, often in harness with his friend and fellow Ukrainian émigré Alex Marunchak. But Miskiw was on the cusp of his 50th birthday, an old-school smoker and drinker redolent of the age of naughty vicars, busty blondes, dodgy scout-masters and massage parlours. He was seen as something of a dinosaur amid this keen young features-oriented regime brought up on soap stars and MTV.

Nonetheless, whatever else he was, Miskiw was 'a proper hack'. He believed in robust, the-people-have-a-right-to-know journalism, and had a certainty about what he and the paper had been doing. For all his unforgiving exterior, he was in the main supportive of his staff, nurturing them, bringing them on with the chance of writing up the potentially big stories, having a laugh and not sending them on wild-goose chases (always a plus for weather-beaten reporters). He enjoyed the muscle the *News of the World* could bring to bear to a story – the clout of the paper's credibility, the outnumbering of rivals in reporter strength on a big story, the ability to out-pay. The claim to be 'a proper hack' requires a toughness of mind, and Miskiw had plenty of that, possibly to excess.

'He had very little sympathy for the people we wrote about,' says one of his former reporters. He was a prodigiously hard worker, totally absorbed by his work. He and Murdoch's *News of the World* were a good match.

Christine Hart, a private investigator and journalist who worked with and had a relationship with Miskiw, wrote a novel, *In for the Kill*, which contained a fictionalised account of her links with the paper. She said: 'Executives on the paper didn't really care about the subjects of stories. They used to enjoy the hunt of people they could screw over. They became 'non-people' and the execs used to talk openly about 'the kill'. There seemed to be an indifference. There was something really dark about Greg.'

'Greg and Clive [Goodman, his deputy] just couldn't do the new celebby stuff they wanted,' remembers another staff member. 'To the new regime, they were a couple of old gits, and they were put under enormous pressure as a result. They had not only been passed over for promotion, they hadn't even been considered for the top jobs. It must have been really difficult for them.' That pressure was felt across the office, and passed downwards.

4

Dr Evil
The Family Man

Barrister Robert Jay described phone hacking as Mulcaire's 'sole way of being, his industrial activity… what he lives for, to hack into voicemails'. Clive Goodman said he was 'well known for cracking impossible stories often involving communications'. Journalist Nick Davies called him 'a brilliant blagger'. David Blunkett said he hoped Mulcaire would rot in hell.

Who was this man, who first appeared on the *News of the World*'s full-time payroll soon after Rebekah Brooks's appointment as editor? Mulcaire ascribes to himself the name 'Dr Evil', in ironic reference to how little known and understood he believes himself to be by those who know only what some News International executives have wanted them to know.

He was born in September 1970 into swinging London's most switched-on area of privilege, Chelsea. But his parents were of unpretentious background, and the capital's juxtaposition of extreme wealth and modest means were perhaps at their most pronounced in the streets around Kings Road. The Mulcaires were from the entrenched urban poor of SW10's World's End estate rather than the fashionable bohemian rich of Sloanedom.

Glenn's father was, in the language of the day, a dustman, a rogue of the old school and endowed with caricature Irish attributes, starting with the nickname Paddy (it was really Michael) and extending to a 'top of the mornin' bonhomie and a fondness for socialising. Though brought up in a family of tailors in Thurles, County Tipperary, in Ireland, he was a fount of local SW6 knowledge and someone whose exterior cheery manner would be called upon to help his clients lay his hands on the occasional unconsidered trifle. While convention would not have had him down as an obvious soulmate of Chelsea's better-heeled folk, and those who remember him say he was something of a ducker and diver, he is remembered as obliging and hardworking. He is believed never to have had a day off sick in 40 years, and was once featured on BBC1's Nationwide programme, describing him as 'the fastest dustman in the West'.

He was capable of great feats of entertainment. One party trick was to bounce a golf ball on the head of a golf club for minutes on end, a trick he owes to his heritage among Ireland's hurling champions. Another was seemingly to swallow a lit cigarette and smoke it internally, the smoke blowing out of his ears before he would disgorge it again, still lit. And on an evening out he would still be going strong at 4 a.m., singing his heart out and amusing his friends.

One residence on his beat was no less than Buckingham Palace, which, around the time of Glenn's birth, brought with it concerns about the possible terrorist risk from Irish extremists. Glenn's father's unambiguous Irish accent and loyalty towards the nation of his birth suggested that perhaps he was not someone to be allowed behind the Palace Gates. A number of police checks were felt necessary before he was allowed to be one of the few Irishmen to do the Palace bins.

Another home on his dustcart's route was that of Lady Aitken, mother of Jonathan Aitken, later MP and junior minister in the Thatcher government. Pempe, as she was known, was of the patrician cast of mind that likes to think it treats 'the staff' as equals, or something approaching it. Strong-willed and entertaining, she would invite Paddy Mulcaire for a frequent chinwag and, in the best Ealing Comedy tradition, the pair got along hilariously, neither imaging why their backgrounds should prevent them enjoying the other's company. Paddy recalls the occasions with affection, remembering that his host was not above getting out the whiskey at 9.30 in the morning to fortify his efforts on the cart.

On one occasion he and his colleagues came across a pheasant that one of Chelsea's better-heeled residents had left out. Paddy picked it up and, before loading it into the cart, proceeded to kick the lifeless bird across the street with his colleagues. The house's owner came out and shouted: 'Oi, that's my supper you're playing with!' The bird had been left out to hang, but Paddy had assumed it was surplus to requirements, and there was talk of disciplinary action. The heresy they had committed was forgotten a day or two later when Paddy handed back the pheasant, cleaned up and restored to some sort of presentability. If they had broken a taboo, Paddy was not going to allow the owner to have all the moral high ground. He insisted on reminding the gentleman which of them had actually killed the bird. After he lost his job, he was given a redundancy payoff, but a number of his celebrated clients rallied round to endorse his case, including solo round the world yachtsman Sir Francis Chichester.

But while Paddy Mulcaire was the gregarious public face of the family, at home things were different. He was not demonstrative, and could be distant and uncommunicative. He preferred not to be called 'Dad'. And when, much later in life, Glenn was sent to prison, his father chose not to visit him there.

Paddy could also be violent, towards Glenn, his brother Stephen and Glenn's mother Eileen, an ultra-correct, respectful, dutiful Geordie. Of the two parents, she was the quiet home influence, who insisted her two boys' good behaviour and simple courtesies (as do Glenn's own children nowadays). She had a proud degree of military history in her family, her father having served in the Irish guards and the War Office. She had been a professional ballroom dancer and later a window dresser at Peter Jones. She suffered from a rare bone deficiency in her youth and, during a difficult time in her marriage, had a serious eating disorder. Her weight dropped to five and a half stone and one Christmas day nearly died. On several occasions Glenn had to go and stay with his mother's sister, Rosie Harvey (to whom he remains very close), at her house on nearby Burnaby Street during his mother's bouts of illness.

She was the one who in greatest measure passed on to Glenn a commitment to the Catholic faith. He attended first Servites Primary School on Fulham Road and then St Thomas More, a Catholic secondary school between Sloane Street and Sloane Avenue in Chelsea which traditionally imbued a respect for authority, hierarchy and honesty. He would serve at mass from the age of 11 to

15 at our Lady of Dolours, Fulham Road. On one occasion, at the age of 11, he was selected from his class to recite the whole of Gideon, the Old Testament tale of the Mighty Warrior who was tasked by God to reclaim and free the people of Israel. He was also selected from among his classmates to wave to the Pope John Paul II at Victoria station, when he visited in 1982. His form teacher Mrs Feeney wrote in his school report in March 1983: 'Glenn is a well-mannered, responsible and caring member of my form. Totally reliable, he can carry out tasks honestly and efficiently. He participates fully in the classroom and represents the school at football and swimming. His work is satisfactory but more care is needed with presentation in all subjects. I believe that Glenn could do much better if he organised himself in a self-disciplined way.'

Mulcaire remains close to his mother, but he has no hesitation in saying that the person who most influenced him was his brother Stephen, 10 years his elder. For a start he was a 6 foot 3 inches tall 'gentle giant', who was constantly checking that his sibling was keeping out of trouble. As the youngest printing manager estate agents Hamptons had ever had, teetotal Stephen, a product of the London Oratory, was someone for Glenn to look up to in all senses.

Stephen's own enthusiasms included a devotion to Chelsea Football Club, which in his teens he followed to home and away games. The club was then suffering a drop in its fortunes, but perhaps to compensate, its fans were keen to make their mark off the field. This manifested itself in a continuation of violence at football grounds, not curtailed until the arrival of CCTV cameras and after the Heysel and Hillsborough disasters. Though no boot boy, Stephen was never intimidated by the threat of violence and would insouciantly savour the highly charged games with his friends. Young Glenn found the whole theatre of it an inviting spectator sport, but rarely got the opportunity. 'I used to want to go along just to watch the fights,' he says now, recalling his sense of fear at the thought.

Chelsea games were as testosterone-charged as any. One day, at the age of 8, he sneaked away from home and unknown to his parents managed to get himself into Chelsea's ground for a game against West Ham, whose fans were notoriously violent. A series of fights broke out as the West Ham fans sought to 'take the Shed' (i.e. achieve the impossible by displacing the home fans), with a terrified but still inquisitive young Glenn looking on open-mouthed. As Glenn gawped at the sheer aggression, he found his entire body being lifted vertically. It was Stephen, who had grabbed him by the scruff of the neck and picked him up. 'What the hell are you doing here?' he asked as he was marched the 5 hundred yards to the Mulcaires' home. It was Glenn's guardian angel, who knew the difference between childish mischief and putting oneself in serious danger. Stephen never told their parents what Glenn had been up to, but he knew when to take the side of safety. On two other occasions, Glenn, frustrated by tensions at home, ran away. Stephen, though sympathetic and protective in the face of their angry father, read the riot act to his headstrong sibling, patiently explaining that flight was no answer to anything.

Within a season or so of that West Ham game, Glenn

and Stephen went to a Chelsea match against Spurs, when the away fans looked as if they would overwhelm a hopelessly under-resourced line of police and trample through one of the more genteel parts of Chelsea's ground and hem in the home fans. As angry Spurs fans swarmed towards the flimsiest of temporary barriers, the unflappable Stephen registered the danger, and turned to his young brother in a state of near panic. 'If they come through, you go down there and get onto the pitch. You'll be safe down there,' he said. It was a tender moment between two young men at an age when most young men think first of advertising their masculinity and autonomy. 'How he could be so unselfish at a moment like that?" asks Glenn now.

At home, too, Stephen was Glenn's protector. Paddy was inclined to be aggressive (more than once he threw a Radio Rentals television out of the window, and Glenn recalls his father hitting Stephen with a broom handle). On one occasion Paddy hit Glenn across the back with a bicycle inner tube. Stephen turned on his father and told him with some menace: 'Don't ever do that again.' He didn't.

Paddy, though, was capable of great generosity towards his sons, and brought Glenn an expensive car when he (Paddy) was made redundant. His love was shown in ways that the young Glenn could find embarrassing. When Glenn was playing football, Paddy's enthusiasm would get the better of him and he would swear and shout abuse at the opposition on the touchline, way beyond the accepted just deserts of easily embarrassed adolescents. He was also not above the odd terminological inexactitude in order to get what he wanted. Glenn remembers being ushered onto the team bus of the New York Cosmos football team to shake the hand of two of soccer's greatest ever players, Johann Cruyff and Franz Beckenbauer, a treat most schoolboys would kill for. 'I think my dad told the man on the door I had a terminal illness,' he recalls apologetically. 'That was the sort of thing he did.' Paddy recalls simply: 'It did the trick, though, didn't it?'

On another occasion, Paddy bought a snooker table from Harrods, which he took home to World's End on the No 11 bus. In most people at most times, this would normally be merely eccentric, but Paddy's Tipperary tones at a time of heightened terrorist concern caused some consternation and suspicion.

Looking back, Glenn says he was brought up 80 per cent by his brother Stephen and twenty per cent by his mother. 'My father must be in there somewhere,' he says, 'I suppose my willingness to really graft came from my dad.' In some other respects he was not everybody's idea of an enlightened role model. In hindsight, it seems as if Stephen was something of a family safety valve and an emotional load-bearer.

So what happened on 19th September 1981 was shattering for the Mulcaire family in even more ways than one might have imagined. Stephen travelled up the M5 to watch his beloved Chelsea in a match at Shrewsbury. As he and four friends travelled home on a stormy night in an estate car from the game, their car went into a skid and hit a tree. Stephen, in the middle of three on the back seat, had no seatbelt. Four of the young men were taken to intensive care. Three were to emerge alive, but Stephen, his neck broken, never did. He was 21.

In many respects the family never recovered. Glenn, just 11, was too upset to go to the funeral, although his mother would not have allowed him to witness such grief in any case. Over time Paddy's idiosyncracies became yet more pronounced, and for years Eileen barely went out and suffered a series of major eating disorders. She contemplated suicide, and even thought of taking Glenn with her, as it were, but pulled herself back, remembering some curiously prophetic instructions from Stephen, about Glenn: 'Make sure you look after him.' Glenn says now, simply: 'Stephen would never have forgiven her.' It would be glib to surmise what impact the loss of such a young life would have on a young sibling, but proud tears come readily to Glenn's eyes when he remembers him. 'He was my mentor, my idol. I think about him every day.'

Indeed, it is a loss to which Mulcaire still frequently refers, unprompted. Psychologists are inclined to say that those who lose a parent young in life are often highly motivated achievers, having been taught an early lesson in life's brevity, and Stephen's death may have compounded Glenn's drive and willingness to work hard. Not that he had seemed destined for a drifter's life. His vibrant curiosity would surely have seen to that, but in his teenage years he showed a striking willingness to commit and throw himself into whatever he was doing.

Just as striking, given the infamy he was later to acquire, was his out-of-hours work. In modern parlance, there does appear to have been something of 'an ethic' to Glenn's teenage years, and he spent much of his free time working for the benefit of others. He worked for some time at the Chelsea Boys' Club. A youth-club leader, Teus Young, identified leadership qualities in the young

Mulcaire. He recalls: 'He was excellent at interacting with young people, especially underprivileged kids. Some people just have that quality, and he showed it in organising, planning, helping them to work as a team, in offering one to one support. He was always a strong character, and a fantastic support to me in the boys club. Maybe it comes naturally in some people, but he certainly had it. He commands respect. Leadership came out of him. He was an excellent organiser and planner. I'm not saying he wasn't a cheeky bugger too, with lots of aggression and a strong tackler, but definitely bright.'

He was a better than ordinary footballer, and had trials with several clubs. He was on Chelsea's books at one point, being named Under-16 player of the year and lauded by Chelsea's controversial then chairman Ken Bates, being told he would 'go far'. Two of his contemporaries Jason Cundy and Frank Sinclair, did go far in football, becoming first team regulars for the Premiership team and playing in the same sides as Ruud Gullitt and Gianluca Vialli. Mulcaire showed leadership qualities and conviction as a player, and no little measure of self-confidence. But he fell out over an issue of tactics with a Chelsea coach Gwyn Williams, and was asked to leave, because, Williams believed Mulcaire had an attitude problem. To this day, Mulcaire, though agreeing that he can be stubborn, insists Williams was in the wrong. ('We lost a South East Counties trial game 3-1 because of him. I was proved right. He was playing two players out of position. I was totally vindicated, and the other players all knew it, but Williams hated having to listen to feedback and took against me,' he will explain, at greater length than the casual reader may be anxious to know.) Williams told Mulcaire he would never play for a London team again.

At the age of 17 he won a Community Sports Leaders Award for his work in local boys' clubs. He applied to join the SAS 23rd Territorial Army regiment, but was selected for the 14th Inc Duke of York, passing the entrance tests creditably. But there was a problem. He had been so anxious to sign up that he had lied on his application form, and had been found out when it was compared with his National Insurance documents. He was still only 17, and was rejected as too young, being told 'you are too young to die'. But he had impressed his examiners, who sought to steer him towards an area that best suited his abilities.

He was advised to visit another military person who gave him direction as to how he might cater for his interest in other ways. He prefers not to elaborate on who exactly was advising him. He immersed himself in the world of intelligence gathering, doing a course in forensics, graphology, medicine, first aid and so on. It was at this point he says he learned the argot of 'Humint' (human intelligence, i.e. human sources), 'elint' (electronic intelligence) and 'comms' (communications). He tends to be evasive when the subject comes up nowadays. 'I don't want to sound like Johnny English,' he says, but it was clearly a world that absorbed him.

He spent some time working part-time at Harrods, and is proud to say that he served Walt Disney, selling him a jumper, only realising who it was when he presented his credit card. He is prouder still to recall that the film maker sent a letter, complete with Mickey Mouse logo, thanking the shop for their help and for its obliging service. He also earned money to pay for his courses by working as a youth worker and play leader at Park Walk School on King's Road.

Having acquired some proficiency in research techniques, he was asked to attend a job centre and give a reference number for a job advertising 'investigators needed'. He attended a series of interviews in Hammersmith Chambers and was asked to start work the following Monday.

The company in question was Worldwide Investigations, a large intelligence gathering company, and he describes his work as 'tracing and tracking at corporate and criminal level', plus a bit of credit work and due diligence. His work there also included research for two of their subsidiaries, Unitel and Argen. These companies worked discreetly and never talked about their clients. Mulcaire did a good deal of low-key sleuthing for the two subsidiaries, including equity searches and 'paper trails'.

Argen was an intriguing company. It had been set up in 1968 by a man called John Fairer Smith (born Aug 1939, died 1999), reputedly a former member of MI5 and the South African police who returned to his native UK and set up the investigations company. He was later named in parliament and accused of political and economic espionage, his particular task being to subvert British attempts to undermine the racist regimes of South Africa and Rhodesia. For some time he was the controller of Norman Henry Blackburn, who was sentenced to five years in prison after being caught stealing cabinet papers dealing with Rhodesian sanctions. Argen widened its client base enormously (and its most recent iteration is unrecognisable from its earlier existence), employing many former spies and special forces personnel, specialising initially in protection against the then burgeoning threat of terrorism (in the late 70s he was quoted as saying 99 per cent of his clients were on an IRA hit list, and many others were PLO targets). It opened offices around the world and later became adept at more general business intelligence.

It was a world Mulcaire thrived in. Even after the period of working for pro-apartheid clients, Argen continued to attract some unwelcome publicity. But having several spies on its payroll meant its ethos was highly discreet and intelligence-oriented. And it taught Mulcaire to see the information derived from research as a good in itself. It was not the investigator's job to question the client's motives or lifestyle, although, happily by this time there was probably less reason to do so. A great deal of Argen's work was for the government, and specifically for Serious Fraud Office and MI5. In 1993 Mulcaire also started work for First Legal Financial Services, in Milner Street in Chelsea, and then, in 1995, for LRI Research and Intelligence.

This was to prove a crucial move in his career. The company was run by an investigator called John Boyall. As we have seen, Boyall was later the subject of an Information Commission raid in 2002, which gave rise to the exposure of much of the information-gathering business. In the 1980s, Boyall had run a team of three or four women doing tracing jobs on a small scale. From the basement office in Croydon of Legal Research and Intelligence, he presided over a small team of data-gatherers. To the fore among these was a man called

Andy Gadd. Mulcaire and Gadd did the bulk of the legwork in Boyall's operation, and were used extensively by a variety of newspapers. Their work was largely formulaic, but they were reliable and discreet and gave no cause for discontent among their clients.

During the 1990s, the *News of the World* had also been using the services of Christine Hart. She was also a forceful and resourceful journalist who brought a fresh eye to some of the more mundane work of the private investigator. Personally she found little excitement in the routine unearthing of telephone numbers, company searches, blagging of information from the Police National Computer, and sought to bring a more creative – and possibly more empathetic – eye to the knottier issues that confronted her clients. She did a certain amount of humdrum work for news editor Greg Miskiw (turning around numbers and so on) until, after an office party, she started having an affair with him. The relationship, facilitated by the fact that her flat was a few hundred yards from the *News of the World*'s office in Wapping, was largely based on their work together, and she says in hindsight it was unlikely to endure, not least because of Miskiw's relentless drive, hunger for work and sleeplessness. She also felt that, to a degree at least, she was not getting the credit she deserved inside the paper.

The relationship came to an end, though Miskiw and Hart remained friendly – again, in part, because it suited them to do so for professional reasons. Greg Miskiw, who had an insatiable hunger for new wheezes and methods of uncovering information, found John Boyall, though still in his late 40s but something of a senior figure in the world of private investigation, fascinating.

'John Boyall used to be known as Goldfinger for his high living,' says Hart, who got to know Boyall extremely well. 'Goldfinger was always on the lookout for new devices and ways of putting people under the spotlight. He was a real spy who had worked for [intelligence firm] Hakluyt and the big boys like G3. He had good MI6 contacts.'

Miskiw suggested that he, Boyall and Hart go out for dinner. Miskiw, as ever under pressure from his bosses, seemed preoccupied during the meal, at a swish restaurant near Piccadilly, but was agog at what Boyall had to say. 'Greg used to enjoy the spy business and was impressed by John Boyall's money – property in Aspen and skiing lifestyle paid for by his investigation work,' says Hart. ' Boyall impressed him hugely, and could see there was a vast amount his tradecraft could bring to the *News of the World*. The paper had been using an assortment of investigators, including Jonathan Rees, but it was clear that Boyall had a huge amount to offer. It was agreed that Boyall should sign up with the paper, although it was not going to be cheap.

The relationship worked well, initially at least. Greg Miskiw, Clive Goodman, Neville Thurlbeck and others would all avail themselves of Boyall's expertise, mostly put into practice by Mulcaire or Gadd. Miskiw found himself being increasingly taken with this young man Mulcaire. Although much of the tracing work was low-key and routine, Miskiw was impressed by Mulcaire's ingenuity and obliging nature. Increasingly Miskiw would go direct to Mulcaire and when Miskiw and Boyall fell out in late 2001, Miskiw was reluctant to sever the connection. Then Miskiw had an idea. Why pay Boyall's high rates? Why not hire the man who had learned so much from him for roughly half the price – and put him on an exclusive contract? So that is what he did.

With one exception, Mulcaire had not been unhappy working for Boyall, who had responded positively to his request for his own office at the company's premises in Croydon and provided him with a company Saab. But he had had to stand his ground to win that respect. Boyall's employees were paid by the customary Pay As You Earn arrangement. But one day the boss announced that everyone was to be regarded as freelance and was to make their own tax arrangements. It meant accountants and extra costs for the employees. Mulcaire was not happy, and remembers leading the staff over the road to the pub. After a while, Boyall appeared in the pub and announced that anyone who doesn't come back is sacked. Mulcaire recalls being the only one who stayed in the pub. Peace eventually broke out.

But when the offer came to have 'his own gig' with so celebrated an outfit as the *News of the World*, what could be better? Mulcaire was perfectly aware that as a private investigator he was a long way from being the finished article, but it was a brilliant opportunity. It also meant a more than doubling of his salary and it put him firmly on life's escalator. 'Generally John Boyall always treated me personally pretty well,' recalls Mulcaire, who acknowledges that he was anxious to 'get on' in life. (For some time after Boyall was frozen out of the *News of the World*, he pursued the paper for substantial unpaid bills. However, he was always confident that the matter could be resolved without needless publicity, and in the end, the paper's management gave way and Boyall was paid.)

Mulcaire's move was a big step for a man of barely 30.

Some greybeards felt he had been promoted too fast. After all, he had no training in journalism, and he was unregistered as an investigator. They felt most of his work had been humdrum and routine. 'Miskiw was delighted when he signed Mulcaire,' says Christine Hart. 'He didn't really care about people, although he had a thing about Glenn Mulcaire and what he could do for the paper. But Mulcaire was very green and Miskiw was using him. People in the investigation business regarded Mulcaire as just a tracer, and tracers are supposed to stay in the backroom and not have clients of their own. Miskiw cynically took Mulcaire and told him not to flash his money around, for example, which made Mulcaire think he'd arrived in a world of mystique and mystery, but actually I thought it was just condescending to say that.' Under pressure to save money, Miskiw was doing just that while giving a young man, anxious to impress, his head. For that, Mulcaire owed him a great deal.

Miskiw regarded Mulcaire as rather less of an investigator than Mulcaire did himself. For Miskiw, Mulcaire was a useful in-house blagger, or tracer, of the sort PI firms tend to have on call, who was willing to turn his hand to anything. As Christine Hart, who is sympathetic to what happened to Mulcaire, says of tracers, 'they are usually young people or misfits and they are taught format lies to access different things. As far as Greg was concerned Glenn was a tracer. But Greg rated Glenn because he could do everything, and most 'blaggers' can only do a few blags.'

When he signed up with the *News of the World*, he was ecstatic. He looks back now with an almost painful sense of achievement. 'I was so proud of joining that team. It had done great, really great work in exposing people who needed exposing. It was one of the biggest papers in the world, part of one of the most powerful newspaper groups in the world, and was standing up for and entertaining decent people against corruption.'

Judging solely by the stories in the papers, it is easy to write off Mulcaire as a mere 'chancer' who learned a few tricks and got over-promoted as a result. But his accomplishment at inveigling himself into people's trust made him an ideal candidate to bring in news stories, to help feed a news machine rather than being just any old cog. Certainly he is extremely adept at what might candidly be called dishonesty.

For professional ends, a number of techniques would continually re-present themselves as useful. One was to call an office and get the call rerouted so it looked to the ultimate recipient as if it was internal. Similarly, once that was achieved and the person believed they were talking to a colleague in another department, he would seek to make them believe he was reading the same internal computer file as the person he was talking to. He says Vodafone were the easiest, with BT being a bit harder. 'If they think you're reading it ahead of them, you need no more confirmation than that,' he says. 'Then you say the screen has frozen, and can you check something. If they say 'I'll call you back', you've had it. You need it there and then. It's smash and grab, but you need to be very gentle. You have to execute the plan with confidence, but you'll only get one chance.'

Two stories illustrate his capacity for building trust and then exploiting it. They rest on a metaphor of opening a door, putting a wedge under it and then returning later to gain entry. The first relies on one of the participants being a smoker and requires an ability to react quickly to unforeseen developments, but the gist is clear. Asked by the office to establish if a hospital patient has a particular ailment, Mulcaire would take a 'white coat approach'. 'You have to look as if you belong wherever you go,' he says. 'You never inch into a situation because then you stand out as not belonging.' One trick is to go out of hospital doors outside which people are smoking, muttering 'I'll have a quick one before I go in'. Then, he says, note the name on the badge of one of the doctors, turn and go back in. The next day you check BMA records (then obtainable using a suitable pretext), then ring and check if someone is able to obtain the hospital number that identifies a particular patient (ditto).

'Then, one day when you know that doctor is off, you breeze in with his name badge, taking big files which look like case notes,… wait near reception, making marks on the files… wait till the receptionist goes for a cigarette and follow her out. If she happens to know the person (which he says happens very infrequently), he'd say 'I'm not him, we have the same name, but I'm the new, improved one'. Made contact, cheap joke, and then say 'I must be getting back.'

Then, back in Mulcaire's office, with a CD playing the low chatter of background office noise, he would ring the receptionist.

M: 'Hi, my name's [false name]. I expect you're frantic.'
Receptionist: 'Yes but how can I help?'

M pretends to recognise the voice, reminding her that they had met during a cigarette break. He would then reiterate that he didn't want to be a nuisance and needed to be quick.

M: 'My PAS system has frozen and I urgently need some details on a patient…' Mulcaire gives the details, she finds them.

M: 'What medical number comes up?' She gives it.

M: 'And which consultant is dealing with her?… I thought it would be him, let me give him a quick call while you're on.' He pretends to dial. 'Hi, Dr X. You're about to go into theatre? Oh, I'm sorry, but, just quickly, could you wire over some records of one of your patients. Actually it would be easier to get them verbally from the front desk. I'm onto them at the moment.'

Receptionist: 'Yes I heard all that. Ok I'll read what it says.' She reads out details, brief episode details, diagnosis and prognosis.

M: 'Thanks very much.'

Then, to check, he pretends to be the consultant and rings the hospital back, establishing his bona fides by giving the patient's medical number and few details. He says he'll be transferring notes over to them.

M: 'Oh, one other thing, what prescriptions is she on?'

If the answer is consistent with the presumed illness, he has confirmed the story.

Another 'blag' that Mulcaire cites as being fairly 'bog-standard' is the method of getting details of a phone subscriber's 'Friends and Family' list on their phone account. 'Back in 2002 – until journalists started doing it, when they tightened it up – it was comparatively easy. Once you've got the land line, you could get Friends and Family, though not everyone registered them. You'd ring BT posing as the subscriber, and make two calls. The first would ask when the next bill is.

M: 'Do you know how much it is, we're panicking'.

Call centre: 'Oh, it's about £300. Ok, thanks, bye.'

Then you ring later, a second time, again as the subscriber.

M: 'Is it ok to pay by cheque, not direct debit?'

Call centre: 'Yes, that's fine thanks very much…'

M: 'One other thing, can I add another number to my friends and family?'

Call centre: 'Sorry, you're full at the moment.

M: 'Really, oh dear, what have I got at the moment?'

Call centre: 'You've got X, X….'

The key to getting access is gulling the person on the phone into assuming that if you know about the size of the bill, when it's due and so on, you must be who you say you are. It's a technique that no longer works, apparently, as security at phone companies has been considerably improved.

In any event, Mulcaire's mindset – ambitious to provide for his family, morally driven, and socially con- servative – made him well-suited to the type of work Miskiw was looking for. To Mulcaire's mind, Miskiw shared his view of what they were trying to do. 'Greg was never that keen on the celebrity nonsense', he remembers. 'Operationally he was always keener on the greater good stuff.' Feeling he had 'arrived' professionally, at the end of 2000 Mulcaire and wife Alison decided to upgrade, moving, with the help of a £1200-a-month mortgage, from their 3-bedroom flat in Battersea to a 4-bedroom semi-detached house in the affluent village of Cheam. Mulcaire had no inclination towards being a journalist, but he had the skills to make a more than decent living as an investigator. He had found his metier.

The fact that someone so accomplished in deceit might have 'a good side' doesn't fit the settled narrative. The intriguing question is, though, where did Mulcaire himself draw the line? Mulcaire remembers that when he worked for John Boyall he was regarded as being always 'one step ahead of the law'. He took it as read that the state does not have a monopoly in defending the public good. It's an assumption that says the forces of light have many faces, including his. (Whether that view can legitimately extend to contravening the state's edicts and breaking the law is another matter.)

Apart from good manners, rectitude is a strong theme in Mulcaire's makeup and the idea of living by a code is important to him. His upbringing had given him a striking trust in those in authority over him, though his mother was inclined to warn him not to allow people to take advantage of him. ('Don't let them use your brain,' she would say.) He has a faith in those in authority exercising a pastoral duty of care. The way he was later abandoned by his former employers would enrage anyone, but having the paternalistic assumptions of the Catholic Church in his blood must have compounded that disappointment.

He makes no claims to sainthood and is reluctant to throw stones at those who breach Catholic morality. But he strongly resists public hypocrisy. However, he also rejects the idea that he was on any kind of moral crusade with his work for *News of the World*. That, he says, would put him into a very different category. Besides, he acknowledges the power of the money he was earning. Any pretence that that didn't have a major role in his thinking would be absurd.

On the specific subject of deceit, his mother brought him up to believe that 'you can have honesty about your dishonesty, but if you're a liar you're a liar'. Thus dishonesty itself was not a wrong if it was used in the cause of good, a notion presumably most spies and even the odd politician and journalist would endorse. Small wonder that Mulcaire's mother was so aggrieved when the judge in 2007 said he was dishonest. The trickery he used in his work, pales, he says, against the deceitfulness of certain journalists. 'The way they would seek to trip each other up and protect their story at all costs – not for source-protection reasons but for petty careerist ones – was a real eye-opener.' 'They would lie and cheat on each other to a degree that astonished me,' he says.

5

RIPA

'When I started, I didn't do much hacking.' The words of Glenn Mulcaire don't fit with the narrative to which his bosses were wedded for a long time. He had been portrayed as the out-of-control rogue who no one knew about, but by the time of the court case, when the facts emerged, things had changed.

There was a substantial refinement of the argument. In early 2014, the judge reported that there were in total 5,600 notes written by Mulcaire. Of these, 2,200 had one name from several *News of the World* executives written on the top left corner. Just 600 were from Rebekah Brooks' time as editor (2000-2003), and of those around 50 were duplicates. A police witness had earlier reported that from that period only 12 contained unquestionable evidence of a phone having been hacked. Among those targeted were TV presenters Amanda Holden and Ulrika Jonsson, singer Charlotte Church and former TV presenter John Leslie, then at the centre of rape claims. Another was TV presenter Natalie Pinkham, who, at the age of 24, was rumoured to be going out with Prince Harry, then just 17.

Mulcaire remembers the Brooks period as one of working on some pretty weighty issues. Intercepting phone messages was the least of what he got up to at the time. Besides, he says, 'I was never actually asked to hack a phone – it wasn't much use, in that terrorists tend not to leave a voicemail message saying "we're putting the bomb at so-and-so."'

Rebekah Brooks had appointed Andy Coulson as her deputy because she felt he was better placed to handle more heavyweight stories. But she also wanted the paper to be more campaigning, a frequent claim of editors around the time of their appointment – but not always one that is delivered. Brooks, though, for all her 'shallow end' background, meant it. After contemplating putting Mazher Mahmood or Paul McMullan in charge, she brought back Greg Miskiw, until recently the news editor, from the US to head an investigations team, which was, perhaps a little grandiosely, to be the equivalent of the *Sunday Times*'s celebrated Insight team. As with Coulson, Brooks felt the seasoned Miskiw's hard edge complemented her own 'Features' outlook. On the surface at least, the pair got on personally better than it suited her later to acknowledge. Occasionally she would turn up for a drink with the reporters in Wapping with him, although privately Miskiw was at a loss to explain how someone with so little news experience could become an editor. Though they were cut from very different cloth, her deployment of him to this specialist role made a certain amount of sense. The same can be said of Miskiw's hiring of Glenn Mulcaire, who he had persuaded to leave John Boyall at LRI Research and who he signed up on an exclusive contract.

Some felt Mulcaire was a boy being asked to do a man's work and seemed to be the main beneficiary of the paper's wish to cut costs. He was considerably cheaper than working through Boyall, though he lacked Boyall's experience and urbanity. Boyall, though, was more than displeased when he learned that a man he had trained up had left him to work for the *News of the World*. One associate of Boyall remembers: 'Boyall then told me he was his office boy who he had trained up in bog standard tracing. He was livid they had plucked out his boy and cut him out of the equation to get the stuff he had trained him to do on the cheap. Boyall was going to take him down.'

But Miskiw was delighted with his hire. He would coo happily about how adept Mulcaire was at triangulating and pinging, the technique of identifying somebody's whereabouts through their mobile phone. And soon a big project presented itself for Mulcaire to get his teeth into. What gave Brooks's first two months in the editor's chair huge impetus and focus was the disappearance of 8-year-old Sarah Payne, on the evening of 1 July 2000 near the home of her paternal grandparents in West Sussex. A nationwide search began, and 16 days later her body was found in a field near Pulborough, about 15 miles away. It emerged later that her murderer was Roy Whiting, who had been convicted in 1995 of abduction and sexual assault and released having served only three-fifths of his 4-year sentence, despite a psychiatrist's fears that he would offend again. Whiting had been interviewed by the police the day after Sarah Payne had disappeared, but he was not charged until some weeks later.

It was a monstrous case, the sort of incontestable affront to decency that newspapers love to reflect and amplify for their readers. The fact that a sex offender known to the police could move into an area and commit so foul a crime would give rise to both righteous anger and media exploitation.

Rebekah Brooks wanted to do more than echo her readers' horror. She wanted to take a stand and get the law changed, to enable parents to know if a paedophile was living in their neighbourhood. Deputy features editor Paul McMullan had recently been sent to Worthing to write a feature about the Scout movement and the precautions it had had to take to ensure that no unsuitable adults came into contact with children. To that end, the movement compiled a list, mainly from newspaper cuttings, of known sex offenders. In a display of ingenuity (often referred to euphemistically as 'journalistic enterprise') typical of both McMullan and his paper, not only did he dutifully take notes but he helped himself to the entire list. 'It was unique, no one else had it,' says McMullan. 'It's the sort of blag we should have been proud of.'

The list was passed on, via Greg Miskiw, to Glenn Mulcaire, and over successive Sundays in July, the paper published pictures of 49 individuals who had committed sex offences, proclaiming that 'Everyone in Britain has a child sex offender living within one mile of their home'. The campaign gave vent to a lynch mob mentality, but concentrated the national debate on the wisdom or otherwise of existing policies. It also boosted sales by 95,000. The overall effect was hard to calculate, but in one case a paediatrician had to flee her house, having been mistakenly identified as a paedophile. ('Not one of mine,' insists Mulcaire, who used to get his information via probation services, benefit agencies and National Insurance numbers. 'We used to look only at the individual, not any labels anyone attached to them')

To the original list were soon added more names (Mulcaire believes there were over 500). He doesn't know where they came from, other than that Greg Miskiw provided them, but they gave rise to extensive coverage in the paper. Someone who knew Brooks well at that time says Brooks self-identified very strongly with abducted children, 'although she got a bit scared of the things she stirred up', he said, struck by Brooks' gift for striking on campaigns that were both admirable and commercially rewarding. 'It was a cynical campaign to start with, but she then got properly friendly with Sarah Payne and saw it as her job to speak up for these people.' In the end, even Sarah Payne's mother (Sara) became a little uncomfortable with the effect the campaign was having.

Certainly, and unsurprisingly, Rebekah Brooks, according to friends, had several wobbles as the heat of the campaign rose. Greg Miskiw, as befits an old-school news hound, was positively brutal in his professionalism. A reporter called him at the weekend to say that her husband had been named as a paedophile in the paper and that he had driven off, saying he was so humiliated he was going to kill himself. The reporter was in tears at the thought, and asked Miskiw's advice. Miskiw, with the certainty of 'a proper hack', was the embodiment of pressure under fire. 'They never actually do it,' he said. 'He won't though, will he?' He didn't.

It is a period Mulcaire looks back on with particular pride. 'I loved what I did there, all the Sarah's law stuff. It was really worthwhile. Rebekah didn't want Greg there, he wasn't her sort of person at all, I gathered, in being too old school for her, but together we did some great stuff.' He was not asking himself questions about the rights and wrongs, and most of his work didn't seem to require that. To his mind, making life hard for paedophiles and keeping the police up to the mark was unassailably the right thing to do. There was always a greater good to protect, and if breaking the law was the only way to locate and catch a child abuser, then it was worth doing.

Beyond work, things were going well, too. The family was growing, and his football was thriving. Although the management of his beloved Wimbledon FC had decided to move the club to Milton Keynes, he and many fans decided to stay put, forming AFC Wimbledon, which started its life in Premier Division of the Combined Counties League. On 17 July 2002 he scored the new club's first ever league goal at Hayes Lane against Bromley, a spectacular volley still available on YouTube. The glory was to be short-lived as he retired due to injury soon afterwards, but that goal lives vividly in the memory.

At work he was helping to break some big stories, so had good reason to feel in demand. He was on good money, although a former colleague says that on a paper used to throwing its money around on 'celebrity buy-ups' and the like, he sold himself short: 'Glenn was very naïve. He had no idea what a story was worth, or how valuable it was to the paper. He provided them with stuff worth a huge amount more than £100,000 a year.'

While listening in to live phone conversations (by means of a scanner, for example) was unambiguously illegal, the advantage of phone hacking, until 2000 at least, was that it was not explicitly illegal, or so many were inclined to believe. But that year the government brought in the Regulation of Investigatory Power Act (RIPA), which said that interception of communications was only lawful if used in the interests of national security or to prevent or detect serious crime. Effectively only branches of the state were in a position to make such a claim, and controversially there was no provision for a 'public interest defence' for journalists seeking to expose wrongdoing. But the change in the law went broadly unnoticed by journalists. Most had little need to pay any attention, some didn't know of the change, and others knew but simply ignored it. Which category Andy Coulson fell into when he told a House of Commons Select committee in 2009 that his paper 'did not use subterfuge of any kind unless there was a clear public interest in doing so,' is an open question.

Mulcaire's assumptions about his 'dual track' approach – sniffing around celebrities but mitigating it by doing serious investigations – was working to his satisfaction in his early years on the paper. At that time, he says it didn't occur to him that what he was doing was unlawful in any event (which some would say speaks volumes for his inexperience at that time).

If it was a matter of finding those who had abducted Milly Dowler or Sarah Payne or Holly Wells and Jessica Chapman, it wasn't an issue. He had operated in a world where some private investigators regarded regulation as optional and where what could be done discreetly tended to stay below the radar, legal or otherwise, so it was not hugely salient. But now, in any event, working at Rupert Murdoch's huge global company News Corporation, he took it for granted that lawyers were on top of everything that went on. Why else, he says, would he have kept such extensive notes? They are now cited as evidence of industrial levels of criminality, but initially they were an aide-memoire for his researches, a way of keeping track of his taskings. Would anyone keep thousands of sheets of paper lying around in his office if he realised they were one-way tickets to jail?

A cynic would say it was a measure of the paper's arrogance that it also afflicted Mulcaire, leading to his getting sloppy. More wizened souls in the world of private investigation would say that real PIs don't keep records. They could be incriminating. Or at least, they don't keep the sort Mulcaire kept. But he says he placed his trust in his employers, and whenever he asked, he was told: 'It's Ok, it's in the public interest' or 'it's a privacy issue, not a legal one'.

One of the most devastating weapons in Rebekah Brooks' armoury was her capacity to get on with the people who mattered. There are countless examples of her 'victims', level-headed men and women who have been targeted and left helpless by one of her charm assaults. It is one of the reasons she rose so fast, and PMs Tony Blair and David Cameron fell hook, line and sinker.

Brooks had a capacity for doing what was wanted and making the recipient an offer they couldn't refuse, not in a Mafioso sense, but simply in a way that had the effect of bestowing an obligation of guilt and gratitude. And of course she was able to deploy this gift for ingratiation in a way that furthered her own, and her company's, journalistic ends. An outstanding case of this came in late 2002 when a strike of Britain's fire service was threatened.

The 'New Labour' government, having by the

admission of some of its senior figures spent its first term in office consolidating rather than reforming, was anxious to push through a programme of public-service reforms. Tony Blair was later to remark that he 'still bears the scars' of his attempts to realise these reforms, and he met with a good deal of resistance from people who felt it was no job of a Labour government to make life more challenging for millions of union members.

Yet any thought of reform in one area, the fire services, was challenged by the fact that many of its employees felt seriously under-rewarded. Ministers attempted to tie in earnings (and the offer of an independent pay review) with the modernising of practices, but the Fire Brigade dug its heels in and was demanding a 40 per cent pay rise, which would have taken the basic pay to £30,000 a year. It was a moment of some militancy, with Bob Crow, general secretary of the Rail, Maritime and Transport Union, pitching in fraternally. He expressed concern that 'inferior appliances and poorly trained operatives will be used in place of the usual highly trained fire-fighters and that this could put the safety of my members and the travelling public at risk,' he said. The threat of a national fire-fighters' strike, the first for 25 years, was a very real one. 'We seriously rocked the government,' recalls one member. 'They had been very arrogant about how they were going to brush us aside, but we offered them much more resistance than they expected. They were really shaken.'

The FBU was led by Andy Gilchrist, an old-style, rabble-rousing union boss. He was a charismatic match for Deputy Prime minister John Prescott, who was old enough to feel scarred by what union militancy could do to a Labour government's capacity to govern. He offered a rise of 11 per cent over two years, but demanded that the union enter into negotiation, which Gilchrist rejected. His members were balloted in October and the first strike took place in early November, with more threatened. The TUC and other unions were supportive. In response, the government deployed the army to help minimise the damage.

Gilchrist recalls his public prominence rising that autumn. He remembers a degree of personal animosity towards him that September, but it was not until the strike started that he felt he was coming under particular scrutiny. He had been used to journalists waiting outside his house in order to have a word with him, and then leaving. Now he was finding people hanging around, apparently not needing to speak to him at all, merely to keep an eye on him. 'I was being followed, that was a given,' he recalls. One day he decided he had had enough of a young man who simply wouldn't leave, so he reported him to the police, who took him to Walton police station. He believes the man, who admitted waiting around outside Gilchrist's house, was working for South East News agency.

Some days later, Duncan Milligan, the FBU's chief handler of the media, got a call from a friendly journalist, warning him that the *News of the World* was pursuing a story about Gilchrist's personal life. We now know that Glenn Mulcaire had been given his details, and the investigator had been put on his case on 4th December. It seemed Wapping was taking no chances, in that both papers seemed to have the union leader on their radar. Gilchrist was later to say that the *Sun* had 'always known where I was going to be', which he 'could never understand'. The phone number of his wife and two colleagues were also found in Mulcaire's files.

'I think they wanted to hear him say "I'll be along later and I'll bring the coke and the hookers," says a colleague, 'but of course that wasn't going to happen.' But there was something in Gilchrist's past. Four years earlier, married with two children, he had begun an affair with Tracey Holland, a rep for the FBU in Wrexham, while at a conference in Mid Wales. The affair seems to have been pursued when work commitments enabled it to, but fizzled out after 12 months. It was in itself unremarkable and, having ended several years earlier, did not seem to reach the usual exacting, marmalade-dropping standards of the *News of the World*.

Just as Mulcaire was deployed, three weeks before Christmas, it began to look as if the threatened strike was off. And at about the same time, the story seemed to go away. One Saturday passed, during which Gilchrist expected to be told the story would run the following day, but the call never came.

On 13th January 2003, Rebekah Brooks moved from the *News of the World* into the editor's chair at the *Sun*. Rupert Murdoch announced that David Yelland had had 'five fabulously successful years' as the *Sun*'s editor, which wasn't quite how his bilious critics saw it. Murdoch said Brooks had 'proven her talent as a great campaigning editor' and he was 'confident she will triumph at the *Sun*'.

Six days later, with the threat of a strike now reignited, a reporter pushed an envelope through Gilchrist's front door. It contained a mocked-up front page reporting in excited detail the fireman's affair. But the paper in question was not the *News of the World* but the *Sun*.

The reader was spared few details of the affair, the reporting of which was a textbook of salacious prurience. With the help of a £25,000 cheque, accepted after much persuasion, Tracey Holland had poured out the details to the paper. She had been taken to a hotel by the paper while the story developed, where she supplied it with the details. Not only did the '31-year-old brunette fall for his charms', but the pair had enjoyed a 'torrid affair' and 'marathon sex sessions', Gilchrist having 'got his fireman's pole out six times a night'. More than that, Gilchrist was dubbed a 'cheat and a liar' by Tracey, who seemingly hadn't known that he was married with children. And, presumably to the delight of his political opponents, Tracey even ventured a view on his suitability to lead the union into another day's strike, happily due to take place the day after the exposé appeared. 'How can the thousands of men and women have any trust in him after this?' she asked. 'Personally, I am against the strike. A 40 per cent rise is an insult to ordinary people.'

Only now, at his moment of greatest influence, was Gilchrist's love life considered of public interest. The story could not have been better timed to maximise its political impact. 'There is no doubt in my mind it was political,' says Duncan Milligan. 'The attacks on Andy fitted absolutely the political profile of the *Sun*. The *News of the World* had barely covered the fireman's strike and it wasn't of that much interest, but getting Andy like that in the *Sun* suited the government perfectly. I have no evidence for this, but I would not have been astounded if someone in government had said to the Murdoch papers that January: "If you have any dirt on

Gilchrist, please throw it now.'"

How much Mulcaire had to do with the eventual story is not clear, but it is an episode that reflects something of Brooks' determination. The tale appeared to follow her. It also reflects an unresolved watershed issue: how much is a public figure's domestic life 'fair game' for lawful scrutiny?

Another high-profile victim of the *News of the World* was Home Secretary David Blunkett, whose private life came to eclipse his role as a minister and he was forced to resign. Blunkett had been made Home Secretary after the election of 2001, having performed creditably as Education and employment secretary in the first Blair administration.

Blunkett's personal life came to the attention of the *News of the World* at around the time the paper was exposing the antics of Boris Johnson, then editor of the *Spectator*. Johnson, married with children, had had an affair with Petronella Wyatt, also a journalist, and their on-off relationship had kept *News of the World* readers on tenterhooks for months. That, too, had been nailed down by Mulcaire. 'It was a "passively probing"' exercise. I was watching Boris for months, as instructed. I remember the breakthrough, which was a really intimate message that he left.' The affair reflected Johnson in a poor light, and when he denied to his party leader's emissary that it had even taken place, he had to resign as front bench arts spokesman.

One of Johnson's colleagues on the magazine was an American, Kimberley Fortier, its publisher, who had married the publisher of *Vogue*, Stephen Quinn, in 2001. Fortier was as famously vivacious as Johnson was ambitious, and her open and engaged manner attracted the attention of a number of middle-aged men. Blunkett, it seems, was among those mightily smitten, and the pair began their affair two months after Blunkett was made Home Secretary, in 2001. His marriage had ended in the late 1980s, and he was spoken of as a possible future leader of the party, should Gordon Brown's rivalry with Tony Blair end his chances. This sense that he was man in the know made him all the more attractive to journalists anxious to stay on the inside track.

Rebekah Brooks was one of those who sustained a professional friendship with Blunkett, although those who worked with him recall his keenness for the boundaries to remain clear. Given what was to transpire, and the fact that one of her newspapers was to hasten the end of his spell as Home Secretary, this is worthy of some attention. Someone who knows them both well says they had more than admiration for Tony Blair in common. 'Rebekah and he were robust in their view of life. They were both a bit outsider-y…. She played down her middle class roots under Labour and played them up under the Tories. She was non-university educated and would often crash through the constitutional barriers, which could cause problems. She was self-made to a degree and shared the same sense of humour as Blunkett. They are both alpha characters.'

Blunkett wanted the *News of the World* on his side, not least because he was regarded as being on the right of his party and needed as many allies as he could find. Gratifyingly for him, most of Blunkett's policies did win the support of Brooks' readers. One insider said people would support them 'if they were explained properly, which we hoped they would be and generally were, but there was also a tension, a degree of implied threat, that things might sour if we didn't do as she wanted.' Blunkett did indeed resist what Brooks wanted on Sarah's Law, a source of pride which those who expect politicians to have minds of their own might find surprising.

When Brooks moved to the *Sun* in January 2003, if anything, they had even more contact than before. Blunkett attended the *Sun*'s annual police bravery awards, and the pair would meet for other dinners. But civil servants who worked with him tell how punctilious Blunkett was about observing constitutional proprieties, and how anxious he was to prevent his private life impinging on his public duties. It is a mark of the emotional tangle into which he fell that those proprieties came to be forgotten, causing him to resign from cabinet twice.

It was reported in court that just 13 people knew about Blunkett's relationship with Fortier. One was Kath Raymond, who was in a relationship with Les Hinton, executive chairman of News International, although there is no reason to think she had been indiscreet. Quite when, or how, Brooks got to know about the targetting of Blunkett's private life is unclear, although she insists she knew nothing until a few days before her part-time lover Andy Coulson, then at the helm of the *News of the World*, published the story. In late July, Blunkett had attended Ross Kemp's birthday party with Brooks. It was a period of some distress for the minister as Fortier was seeking to break off their relationship.

Glenn Mulcaire had had Blunkett under scrutiny since January 2004, and started off by listening in to Fortier's voicemails. 'Greg [Miskiw] and Neville [Thurlbeck] were super confident there was something there,' remembers Mulcaire. 'It was a particularly sensitive case. One false move and the whole thing could have fallen down. We had to be ready for them, in case we were rumbled, so we had a "spoof" plan in place, whereby if we were caught we would be able to give the impression of having been involved but then gone away and given up, while actually maintaining them under surveillance. Spoofing is a very important part of an investigator's tradecraft, to allow the target to drop their guard and get them to go back to behaving normally.'

Mulcaire doesn't know where the original tip about Blunkett's affair with Fortier came from. Some believe that because Boris Johnson was under scrutiny, and he was known to be prone to straying, a belief grew that maybe he was having an affair with Fortier. (There has never been any evidence for this.) Some close to the former Home Secretary believe the Blunkett connection was a bonus that fell into the *News of the World*'s lap when they were looking for Johnson's lovers.

Mulcaire doubts this very much. He says he was tasked specifically to look at Johnson. If anyone was to infer some connection other than the Blunkett-Fortier one, that would be for a journalist to do, rather than him.

He also says that there would have been a free-for-all among journalists in the office hacking Johnson's phone. 'Once I had given them the PIN number, they would all have been having a go. It would have gone on 24/7 for as long as they could, until something changed, like the target changing their PIN or whatever, in which case they would come back to me and ask for a reset to be done.'

Thus it is indeed conceivable that the tip came from hacking, but not on Mulcaire's part, he insists. Another theory exists that Blunkett had fallen out with senior figures in the defence establishment, but that too is doubted by people close to him.

The details of the affair (and Fortier's decision to end it) are painful to behold, and the brutality of the intrusiveness that revealed it uncomfortable. To help ensure the story didn't leak out, *News of the World* reporters spoke of it in code, referring to the couple as Noddy and Big Ears. The second week of August was to be a fateful one. It seems that that was the week the *News of the World* decided to dash for the line, having worked for eight months on the story. The court was told of a note sent by Mulcaire, saying 'need to triangulate calls, build up a call profile make sure it stands up on its own'. On the same day, the court was told, phone billing records showed contact between Andy Coulson, the editor at the time, and *News of the World* reporter Neville Thurlbeck and then with Rebekah Brooks, by then editor of the *Sun*.

The following day, according to one press report at least, Blunkett contacted Fortier to tell her that the *News of the World* knew about the affair. It is tempting to think Rebekah Brooks had alerted him, but she told the court she knew nothing for several more days. She may have wanted to warn her friend of a coming storm. On the other hand, had she done so it might have jeopardised the writing of her lover Andy Coulson's story. (It was claimed in court that at that period in the relationship the pair were close). How she would have felt about that can only be guessed at. Certainly the matter caused some upset between Blunkett and Fortier, who each blamed the other for the relationship becoming public knowledge.

On Friday 13th, Andy Coulson went to Sheffield to confront Blunkett. On the same day, Coulson spoke to Brooks on the phone for 81 seconds, something the editor of a Sunday paper would normally be unlikely to do to a daily counterpart. Coulson told the Home Secretary 'People know about this affair. I'm not saying it is an open secret, but people are aware of it.' He said he was 'extremely confident of the information' but did not admit that it was partly based on voicemail messages left by him on Fortier's phone. Blunkett tried to insist on not confirming or denying the story, saying he had always drawn a line between the public and the private. Coulson told Blunkett that if he doesn't run the story, someone else will. 'You are Home Secretary and I don't think you can use your right to privacy to bat back an accusation that you have had an affair with a married woman'. But he said he was prepared to publish the story, omitting the woman's name, an extraordinary concession in normal circumstances, and doubly so given that her identity was not in doubt. Nonetheless Coulson wanted confirmation. 'You're asking me to say "Yes, I'm having a relationship with a married woman."' Again Blunkett refused to discuss his private life, but did admit: 'I am very happy to confirm that Kimberly is a close friend of mine (and that) we have seen a lot of each other over the past three years....' Normally that would not have been sufficient, but given the recorded proof, Coulson felt he had enough.

There was nowhere for Blunkett to go. The story was heading for the front pages. Blunkett's special adviser Huw Evans told the Old Bailey that he spoke to Andy

Coulson shortly before the exposé appeared, asking him what evidence he had to justify the story. 'I remember his reply and the tone of his voice, which was flat and unequivocal. He was absolutely certain that the story was accurate and he was going to run it. I remember at the time remaining puzzled as to why he would be so certain.' There was no discussion about not using Fortier's name, which under normal circumstances a paper would.

Rebekah Brooks told the court: 'I think Andy told me that he had the Blunkett story late on Saturday', she said. 'He must have told me he wasn't naming her, or when he told me he might not have said he knew the name.' She said she couldn't remember how the *Sun* got the name, later saying it had become evident from reading old gossip columns, such as Ephraim Hardcastle in the *Daily Mail*.

At the end of the week, he flew to Italy, dining with the 'extremely understanding and helpful' Tony and Cherie Blair, staying with the Strozzi family (whose ancestors had kick-started Machiavelli's career), near San Gimignano. The *News of the World* duly published its article on Sunday August 15 2004. On the same day there were 12 'contact events' between Coulson and Brooks. She also spoke to Huw Evans, David Blunkett's special adviser. Brooks was very matter of fact, saying the story was too big not to run. As to the lover's name, she claimed in court 'I just remember having to get it out of Huw Evans', later amending her position, telling the court she had said: '"We are going to name Kimberly tomorrow" and he didn't say "Kimberly who?"' Nobody in Blunkett's office was surprised she had the name.

Fortier was named in the *Sun* on Monday 16th,

although the paper cited little evidence for the story and had no evident confirmation of it, on or off the record, from Blunkett or his office. The following day, it also emerged that she was pregnant (by an unspecified father, later shown not to be Blunkett), something that also features in Mulcaire's recordings.

Brooks was torn between her professional friendship with Blunkett and her professional obligation to her newspaper group. As the *News of the World*'s managing editor Stuart Kuttner was to say later, using a phrase journalists everywhere will recognise as the acknowledging of a paper's not-to-be-crossed party line: 'I think we rather liked David Blunkett.' Brooks sought to sugar the pill by decreeing this was not a resigning matter, and by reflecting that the relationship was a true love affair, rather than a grubby fling. She felt bad enough to ask Blunkett's special adviser Huw Evans how he was taking things, reassuring him about the sympathetic editorial (written by Kuttner) the paper would be running and otherwise seeking to mitigate what had happened to him. It is surely not unfair to place in the same 'this-is-business-not-personal' category the (estimated) £100,000-a-year column he began writing for the *Sun* soon afterwards and the secret award of approaching £400,000 in compensation for having his phone messages hacked, in May 2011.

That was a long way from being the end of Blunkett's brush with the media. In late November 2004 it was reported that Blunkett was the father of Fortier's 2-yr-old son William, and the following month an official report confirmed that the child's nanny had received quicker treatment than would have been expected had the father not been the Home Secretary. Blunkett resigned as a result. After the 2005 election he returned to office as Secretary of State for Work and Pensions, and began a friendship with Sally Anderson, an estate agent who later passed on details of that association to a newspaper.

That friendship also aroused the interest of the *News of the World*. Glenn Mulcaire was deployed, and he recorded messages of Blunkett attacking the 'hyenas' of the press. On another message, he said: 'They're real bastards. They're doing it for money and they're doing it for themselves. It's a sick world.' And in another: 'Someone very, very close has done a really phenomenal piece of work on destroying both our lives at this moment in time and it's vile. 'Whoever it is I hope they rot in hell.' It was said that Mulcaire would be awarded a huge bonus if he could produce evidence that Blunkett was having a relationship with her. The investigator was overheard on one tape uttering the words, 'Just say 'I love you' and it's 25 grand.' Mulcaire's memory is that he was indeed offered an incentive. 'I wouldn't have randomly picked that figure… that was the figure they mentioned to me as what they'd give me if they stood it up. They used to promise all sorts of bonuses, to keep your mind on the job, but actually I don't remember ever receiving any.'

In November 2005, Blunkett resigned from government for the second time, over a conflict between his political and private interests. Like the Gilchrisst story, the Blunkett case might have been designed as a test case for journalism students seeking to compare the competing weight of privacy versus the public right to know. The personal life of a divorced man might be

thought his own affair, except that his two ministerial res-
ignations show how much his judgment had been
affected by those 'private' matters. But was the intercepting of his voicemails excusable in the public interest?
Could it ever be, maybe if he was suspected of doing
something criminal or dangerous?

'I don't wince at what I did at all,' says Mulcaire, who
is fervent in asserting that he was the agent to the
newspaper's principal. 'They know there is something in
the bag... it is my job to be professional and do the investigation... it's not my job to decide what is a story...
otherwise I'd be a journalist, and I wasn't paid to write
stories.... There has to be a chain of command... it's the
journalist's call as to whether it's a story, and the *News of
the World*'s call as to whether it was legal. They had the
biggest legal team. That was an assumption I made – it
was part of my own governance.... I was proud to be
part of a company that did the right things. I was proud
to work for that paper, and I was proud to be the only
investigator on the paper ever to have been put on
contract. I felt protected by the legal department, one of
the biggest anywhere. I was part of the Murdoch elite,
which felt great... the *News of the World* had a huge
circulation and was doing great work... I loved what I
was doing.'

One of the claims against Mulcaire, made by the BBC
on 25 June immediately after the 2014 trial but echoing
something that had emerged at the Leveson enquiry, is
that he was responsible for breaching the government's
witness protection programme. The very idea suggests a
dastardly degree of indifference to the safety of someone
who the police felt it necessary to protect. And the raid

on Mulcaire's property provided the police with evidence that he had intruded into the privacy of one of the 'Bulger killers'.

The murder of two year old James Bulger in Bootle in 1993 was one of the most shocking cases in recent criminal history. While out shopping in the New Strand shopping centre in Bootle, young James had wandered off. He was abducted, tortured and murdered by two ten-year-old boys, Jon Venables and Robert Thompson. His body was found on a railway line four miles away.

The case attracted enormous publicity. Everybody is familiar with how young boys can behave mischievously, but this cruelty and indifference to suffering provoked countless articles about the nature of evil and what gave rise to it. The judge said the boys were capable of 'unparalleled evil and barbarity'. The pair became the youngest convicted murderers in modern English history. They were sentenced to custody until they reached adulthood, initially until the age of 18.

A series of political judgments raised then lowered their tariff. The Lord Chief Justice Lord Woolf declared, on the basis of expert reports, that 'these young men are genuinely extremely remorseful about the crime which they committed and the effect which it must have had on James's family.' The pair appeared to pose little risk to the public. 'They have worked hard in pursuing their education and, given their circumstances, have considerable achievements to their credit. All those who have reported on them regard the risk of their re-offending as being low.'

In January 2001, another judge declared they were to be given false identities and enabled, as far as anyone can in such a situation, to start again. The judge said the manager of the secure unit where one boy had been living had received hate mail which threatened: 'To the vermin who killed Jamie Bulger, we don't forget, we will get the job done.' Denise Fergus, Jamie Bulger's mother, was quoted as saying that 'mothers like me will be after their blood', and his father, Ralph Bulger, as saying: 'I will do all I can to try my best to hunt them down.' The pair were released in June 2001, and were required to maintain contact with their appointed social workers, but they were to attempt to reintegrate themselves into normal society. The judge had the *News of the World*'s 'name and shame' campaigns on paedophiles explicitly in the judge's mind when she issued strict instruction that the press were not to find and expose the young men.

It was another classic touchstone issue. Those who believed that attempted rehabilitation was the only possible option ('it's a test of our humanity') against those who were sceptical than any such thing could work, or deserved to work. The police, after all, were a bunch of bunglers, or so it was claimed, so, without robust scrutiny, how could we be sure the public was safe? While outing the pair would be clearly in breach of the law, the redtop papers saw it as their duty to nibble away at the edges. The menacing words 'we know where you live' did not need to be spelled out.

That month the *News of the World* reported on how the mother of one of them and her daughter visited an off-licence 'near the new home' to prepare for his homecoming. 'They looked like an ordinary mum and daughter, dressed in denim skirts.'

The *Independent* reported the *News of the World*'s story

like this: 'A tiny detail, of course, and of no help to a vigilante by itself; but combined with other similarly tiny details, combined with the previous week's issue and combined with Sunday's scandalously provocative headline 'Dead Man Walking' over a story about Venables, it is hardly encouraging restraint. Stuart Kuttner, managing editor of the *News of the World* was interviewed on the Today programme last Saturday in the absence of the seemingly pathologically shy Rebekah Brooks. He justified the *News of the World* telling its readers in which region the two teenagers would be living on the grounds that 'It is of enormous public interest because the taxpayers are funding their future lives. The information that was given was too blurred for anyone to home in on them.'

The *News of the World* promised: 'Whether they are at college, with girlfriends, perhaps working with unwitting colleagues, we shall do all in our power to watch over them.' [This], of course, can only mean 'publish information about' so we can expect months if not years of headlines on 'the woman in love with a killer' 'the teacher whose prize student is a monster' and so on. Each one will put another piece in the vigilante's jigsaw.

There continued to be reasons to think the boys had gone off the rails. The idea that their rehabilitation might be unsuccessful, that the clever-clogs 'experts' had been wrong, fed the pair's awful fascination all the more. 'There was an issue of public safety, and to see whether their own welfare was being given a higher priority than that of the wider public's,' is how Mulcaire remembers it. Liberal sensitivities were all very well, but for a robust free press, leaving 'the experts' to do their work was not enough. Could the politicians, notorious for trying to please their own supporters, really be trusted to hold the boffins to account? Child killers were in a category of their own and any threat to the public needed to be flagged up. The fact that it sold newspapers was given.

In this, the most delicate of stories, Mulcaire admits he played a central role in finding one of the boys. He was accused of breaking the law by subverting Mappa, the government programme which arranges for a person to be given a new identity.

In fact, he completely denies this, and puts it all down to the skills of his trade. 'There was no breach,' he says. 'Whatever your politics, this was a case where we had to be incredibly careful,' he remembers. 'But there was no breach of Mappa [Multi Agency Public Protection Agency], and I don't remember any interception of phone messages in that case.' His memory of the issue is hazy, perhaps unsurprisingly, and he has no access to his papers on the subject, but he has no doubt there was a legitimate public interest in keeping the pair under scrutiny. 'There was a heightened concern around this individual.'

In November 2004, the *News of the World* reported that Bulger's mother Denise Fergus had come face to face Robert Thompson, by then 21, a couple of months earlier, and been 'paralysed with fear'. She said: 'I recognised his podgy face and evil eyes in an instant. I wanted the right to know what he looks like. To know where he is. I wanted to rush up to him and scream, "Why did you kill my child?" Yet I was turned to stone paralysed with hatred.'

It is easy for liberal prejudice to disapprove and to

condescend to the anger of a vengeful mother. Yet 'sophisticated' opinion can claim no vindication (and nor can any other). It was to emerge that one of the boys, Jon Venables, had had an unsuitable relationship during his teen years which seemingly had not been known about by those responsible for him. Later he had to return to prison. He had a considerable appetite for child pornography, and in the early 2000s was having a relationship with a woman who had a five-year-old child. Did the woman in question know about his past? Or his unhealthy tastes? Here, the *News of the World* would say, was the justification for its work. Without such scrutiny, those who think they know best probably don't, the argument goes.

Similar considerations came up when it became known that highly respected author Gitta Sereny was writing a book about Mary Bell, who, as a child, had strangled two smaller children (aged four and three) in 1968. She had been released in 1980, and was the subject of a similar injunction. By collaborating with the book, and being paid for it, she opened herself to the charge of invading her own privacy, and of inviting others to do so.

Mulcaire says, 'As far as I remember the [*News of the World*] investigations unit put a lot of cold cases on the grid. I think we had had a tip that the daughter didn't know the mother's history [before her birth]. The girl was approaching the age of 18 and was pregnant and needed to be told. We identified where she was, where she was working. There was a lot of passive probing to make sure we had the right person, and we eventually reached stage 3 – 'eyes on' – whereby we did discreet surveillance. These people live to have control, but in this case, when they are being watched, they have no control.'

Mulcaire recalls sitting down with Bell herself, and eating fish and chips with her. He is reluctant to elaborate as to what exactly was said, but he is adamant that he performed a public service when he confronted her. 'I put fear of God into her. The blood fell from her face when I spoke to her. She didn't answer, she was in total shock. She was terrified of being exposed, but I explained, if we were going to expose you we wouldn't be talking to you... Greg [Miskiw] knew all about it. Nobody knew where she was, but I found her. Greg let me do it... with a reporter crashing it, it often goes very wrong.'

Because Mulcaire has no access to the relevant files, he cannot be certain of the timing. But it may be that the decision by Dame Elizabeth Butler-Sloss in 2003, to award Mary Bell and her daughter a high court injunction guaranteeing lifelong anonymity, was in part the result of Mulcaire's approach. Certainly, the judge said press intrusion would amount to 'further psychological abuse'.

Again, for Mulcaire, there was no question they were doing good work in the public interest. 'I know we talked about it a lot. 'Should we do this, should we do that? Greg was very much into doing the right thing. Actually I don't know if a story ever came out of it. From my own point of view, the fact that we were marking someone's card was good enough for me.' Asked if it was up to the press to decide in a sensitive case like this, Mulcaire is adamant. 'Oh come on. Look at Baby P... Would you trust the social services? And if it's bad now, what would it have been like then?'

Both cases were absolutely on the *News of the World*'s

home, taboo-busting patch. What is striking is that it is clear in Mulcaire's notes, and was therefore available to the police, that he had the phone numbers of police officers who worked on the witness protection scheme. Further, Mulcaire says he was questioned by the police on the matter, of a sort which the authorities usually take extremely seriously, following his arrest in both 2006 and 2011, yet the matter did not lead to a charge.

In May 2004, the *Mirror* ran a series of pictures of British soldiers of the Queens Lancashire Regiment apparently torturing an Iraqi detainee. One image showed a soldier seemingly urinating on a hooded prisoner, while in another he was being hit with a rifle. The pictures came amid stories of allegations that British troops had been abusing prisoners, so as a story their time had come. The pictures were described by one military pundit as 'a recruiting poster for al-Qaida'. Morgan, whose brother was serving in Basra at the time, had had the pictures in his office safe for some days, musing on their authenticity, before deciding he would go for broke and print them on 1st May.

But the pictures were not entirely convincing, and a lot of people believed them to be fakes. The problem was proving it. Mulcaire was tasked by Greg Miskiw, news executive at the *News of the World,* to get to the bottom of the story. Somehow Miskiw had acquired the names of the soldiers in question. He handed them over, and asked Mulcaire to do the rest. By reference to the soldiers' mobile phones, he was able to confirm that the purported torturers had been in the UK at the time the pictures were taken. In other words, they couldn't have been in Iraq, and the pictures were fakes. If ever there was a case of trying too hard, this was it. *Mirror* editor Piers Morgan was required to fall on his sword, though he maintained that even if the story his paper had run was not true, there was a more general truth behind it, in that, he insisted, British troops were indeed abusing prisoners.

Mulcaire believes he was the first person to establish the pictures were phony, although the *News of the World* records do not support this idea. It is possible, he says, that the proof he provided was used either in another paper in the Murdoch group, or conceivably used to help the Ministry of Defence nail the perpetrators. 'If you'd lost a daughter or a son, you'd want to know who had done that,' says Mulcaire. 'There's no doubt it was my information in my mind and Greg's that it was my information that proved they were fakes. We proved it by triangulation and pinging, but I don't know what use my work was put to. Greg always used to cite it as being responsible for Morgan losing his job.'

Perhaps the biggest headline story of Glenn Mulcaire's career was the tale of David Beckham, national heartthrob, golden boy and family man, and his relationship with a 'stunning brunette', Rebecca Loos, in Madrid. Beckham's wife Victoria was at home in London while David was with his adoring public, playing football for the world's richest football club Real Madrid. The story fell into the category of genuinely big story, exposing the clean-cut, loyal, image of Beckham, which brought him around £10m a year in sponsorship deals, as a sham.

Loos, decidedly middle class and sophisticated by the standards of redtop football exposés, was employed as a nanny-cum-fixer for the Beckhams. She and Beckham were naturally spending a lot of time together, and the first hints that she and Beckham were enjoying one another's company a little too much came in September 2003, when, as the *News of the World* put it, 'the lonely England captain was enjoying female company and the bright lights of Madrid while wife Victoria was 800 miles away in London'. The pair were captured on grainy footage, laughing and drinking together. The bare-shouldered girl 'was being really flirtatious', according to one of the paper's ever-reliable 'onlookers'. Sometimes newspapers persuade one of those in an affair to lure their partner to go to a certain location in order to be photographed by a newspaper. But these pictures do not suggest that. There was no sign that Loos knew the photographers were there, nor that she planned to sell her story.

The Sunday before, the paper had put a story on its front page announcing 'Posh & Becks in marriage crisis', which centred on Victoria's concern about her career and her desire stay in London, having originally said she would move with him and the children to Madrid. Given what is now known, it is fair to assume that Beckham had been under some pretty close scrutiny up till that point, but his personal security was fairly resilient and there had seemed little of note to report in any case. Loos was not identified in the story about the flirtatious drink, but she would not be nameless for long.

The fact that a much admired footballer like Beckham was alone in a hot and glamorous city and had been spotted in the company of an attractive single woman was more than enough to arouse the *News of the World*'s interest. The story went a bit quiet as Glenn Mulcaire set about his work. Six months later, Beckham's world exploded. The *News of the World*, with the boldness and conviction which were its hallmarks, announced its prey. 'Beckham's secret affair' shrieked the headline. 'Lonely star beds aide caught in THAT club pic. Wild romps and txt sex behind Posh's back. The story you thought you would never read.' Chief reporter Neville Thurlbeck, whose by-line appeared on the piece, detailed encounters between the pair stretching back to December. The detail of the relationship, which clinched the prize of scoop of the year at the press awards for that year, was unarguable.

The news story had so far developed along familiar lines. The paper has always been a beneficiary of 'ring-ins', members of the public calling to say that something has happened and it may be that this one began like that. News executives got on the case. The information was given to Mulcaire, who set about it with his customary alacrity. Once the story had been verified (most of the hard data being provided by Mulcaire, but with a lot of consultation at head office), Rebecca Loos got wind of the paper's interest. She decided that if the story was to come out, she might as well make the most of it, and Max Clifford, broker of kiss and tell stories par excellence, later convicted of a string of indecent sexual assaults. 'The deal was done after the *News of the World* were onto Rebecca,' remembers someone who was close to events. 'They had been harassing her. Her father called Max Clifford asking if he could help. It was done very quickly, about two weeks before the story appeared. She hadn't set out to have an affair or sell her story.' But the paper was not going to throw away a tale as big as this.

The 'standing up' of the story had been hugely protracted. In any such tale, the word of the person having the affair is not enough. A celebrity can simply lie and deny a true story, and the newspaper has to produce irrefutable evidence. This was Mulcaire's job. Details of texts sent between the pair appeared in the paper. Surely that said enough? No. It might be claimed that somebody else had sent the texts, maybe as a joke. Why would a happily married celebrity do such a thing?

Mulcaire had to prove that Beckham had been in possession of his phone, and alone, when the texts were sent. Beckham's entourage were of course aware that their boss was a figure of huge interest for the popular press, and had sought to take commensurate precautions. Paul McMullan has been reported as saying of Mulcaire: 'He was hacking masses of phones. We reckoned David Beckham had 13 different SIM cards, and Glenn could hack every one of them.' 'Proving that that number and that phone was in someone's pocket at a given time is enormously difficult,' says Mulcaire. 'We needed to prove it finally, and we knew Beckham had lots of numbers, and two phones close to one another tell their own story.'

To Mulcaire, this was an enormous challenge. 'It was a puzzle not a mystery,' as he often says. Each time Beckham switched his SIM card, Mulcaire was able to follow him, a source of some professional pride to him. Through pinging and call analysis, he was able to identify Beckham's movements. The footballer's space for wriggle room was shrinking, but despite the mountain of evidence, the need to be totally certain of the facts made some people at Wapping uncomfortable. If you take on a nationally adored icon, you need your ducks in line. Was

Mulcaire, seen by some as young and keen but inexperienced, up to it? Emphatically so, said news executive Greg Miskiw, who, Mulcaire recalls, said he would resign if Mulcaire's view was wrong.

It was decided they should go for it, notwithstanding the risk of a complete public denial from the other side. A lot of reputations were on the line. It was no time for faint hearts. As with the Blunkett story, they were confident the story was true, and that they had sufficient evidence to prove it. The problem was whether the use of that evidence would be proof of having broken the law. It was a judgment call for an editor: a footballer's desire to keep his friendship secret versus an editor's need to keep his methods secret.

It is one of the great ironies of the episode is that although Glenn Mulcaire was largely responsible for confirming the story, he believes the Beckhams could have fought harder to oppose the paper. 'If I'd been the Beckhams, I would have called the paper's bluff. I would have denied it outright and demanded to see all the evidence. The paper would have had to show the proof. It is true that Neville [Thurlbeck] was babysitting Rebecca, and that she was by that stage signed up and giving evidence to support the story, but that wouldn't necessarily have been enough to swing it. Her word wouldn't have been enough. They conceded too soon. In my view the key that clinched it was the pinging and the call analysis.'

There was indeed a denial of sorts from the Beckham camp. The player himself was quoted as saying: 'During the past few months I have become accustomed to reading more and more ludicrous stories about my private life. What appeared this morning is just one further example.' As the *Daily Mail* pointed out at the time, 'It was noticeable, however, that he failed categorically to deny any kind of sexual relationship with his former assistant.'

Gerard Tyrrell, Beckham's lawyer, had been tipped off by a source in the world of investigation as to how the paper had satisfied itself of the truth of the story, as well as the investigator they were using, Glenn Mulcaire, and had been among those advising Beckham to keep changing his SIM cards. There followed a major legal wrangle. One source close to the story believes that the *News of the World* came to an arrangement with the Beckhams, which effectively drew a line under the issue. Some years ago the author of this book asked the legal department of the *News of the World* what had happened to the Beckhams' writ. He was told the matter had been resolved. The paper was not notably critical of the player subsequently.

Many suspected that Australian model Elle Macpherson also reached an accommodation with the paper after she was named as one of the original victims of phone hacking in the 2006 trial. She and a number of her associates were known to have been targeted, and in the approximately 30 mentions of Macpherson in the paper in the following years, about half were neutral and half were laudatory, a remarkable strike rate. Any such arrangement was denied, and no independent evidence has been found at Wapping to endorse such a claim.

6

Fishing for Headlines

By 2004 Mulcaire had established his position as a key provider to *News of the World* of electronic data and stander-up of stories from a legal point of view. He says now with great pride that he only deals in facts, and he was building a capacity for picking the wheat from the chaff. Having gained a regular berth and the confidence of some, at least, of his employers, he was feeling reasonably established. Though the *News of the World* 'Special Investigations' department had by now been disbanded, he was able to tell himself that all the celebrity stuff was just a means to an end. In other words, he remained convinced that in the end his skills were being put to a worthwhile cause. It was a delusion, he now recognises, not least caused by his head being turned by the status implied by being on a contract worth well over £100,000 a year.

But at the paper, things were changing. His chief protector, Greg Miskiw, left the London office of the paper to work for it in Manchester. Miskiw had always guarded his asset jealously. 'We always knew Greg had someone who could get stuff, but we were never allowed access to him,' remembers one reporter. The problem was that a lot of people thought they knew as much about the dark arts as Mulcaire, and many were hacking phones for themselves. Why did they need Mulcaire? Without Miskiw, Mulcaire needed someone to explain and defend him in the office, and there were plenty who felt his presence was unnecessary and expensive. Researchers and technology were being sacrificed to help pay for Mulcaire's salary, or so it was claimed.

The arrival of new staff compounded the pressure generally. The new recruits cranked up the pressure on the subordinates all the further. It is the job of news editors to challenge the natural human laziness which can afflict newspapers, to demand more, to make reporters ask the unaskable questions, to push the boundaries, to demand longer and longer hours. Sometimes the news rolls in like the tide. It just happens. At other times, as Fleet Street facetiousness has it, you have to 'make it up'. Only very rarely is this literally true, of course (whatever some might believe), but the demands of filling pages can be relentless.

Some news editors can keep the pressure up yet retain the trust and respect of their reporters, sometimes helped along with the occasional drink, friendly lunch or 'jolly'. Others soon win a reputation for hard-heartedness and cold-bloodedness. Neither counts for much as long as the bosses higher up the chain feel the stories are coming in. *News of the World* royal reporter Clive Goodman told the Old Bailey later that the atmosphere while Andy Coulson was editor was 'competitive, fast and quite bullying and menacing – there was an extreme drive for results… if a reporter did not deliver he would be hauled over the coals'. Goodman said this atmosphere came from the top of the paper, 'from Andy', although in court later Coulson denied being a bully.

Vanessa Altin, a former reporter on the paper, told Lord Leveson: 'I was proud that the paper would pursue stories of national interest without fear or favour and we remained the number one selling English speaking newspaper in the world for many years. I worked there happily until 2004 when I returned from maternity leave to discover a new regime had taken over. The newsdesk …. [was] obsessed with sensational celebrity gossip. I was often asked to insert sensational words and sentences which I knew to be inaccurate or blatantly false. They even demanded I fabricate direct quotes and put them in my copy. My refusal led to several years of intense bullying and unreasonable demands in an attempt on their part to force me to quit.

At the same time they started to employ more inexperienced graduate trainees who would do as they were told without question – leaving me in an unpopular minority. I went into the London office and raised my concerns directly with Andy Coulson – who dismissed them out of hand and said he had complete confidence in the newsdesk.'

That newsdesk was not warmly regarded by many of the reporters. Certainly Glenn Mulcaire was wary of it. The reputation for toughness came in part from a desire to stop the skimming, the widespread abuse of the readily available cash, from which reporters were inclined to trouser a commission. But the demands were constant. Previously, the likelihood was that Mulcaire would be called upon to execute specific, surgical tasks. But as time went on, the jobs became more numerous and the net was cast ever wider.

For better or worse, Mulcaire now saw himself as an

investigator. On good days, this would involve a search to right a wrong – the finding of a kidnapped child, the tracking down of a terrorist, the confronting of a drug dealer. And on others he was a hired hand, an instrument of his bosses' whims, being their eyes and ears rather than establishing facts. In these instances, he would feel no obligation to approve or disapprove of his task and merely churn out the product. This, after all, is the requirement placed on countless employees in most walks of life, he points out.

The category of 'fishing expeditions' grew enormously. These were the indiscriminate trawling of the private lives of (mostly) celebrities, in the hope of catching them doing something worth intruding into. Some time in 1994 (from his memory) Mulcaire met two news executives.. Mulcaire went along for what he took to be a run-of-the-mill session, imagining there would be amicable discussion of a new contract, but he came away worried.

The bosses did not give the impression of wanting to make friends. It may be that they were keener on both Andy Gadd, who signed up with the paper in late 2004 (and with whom Mulcaire had worked in the 1990s under John Boyall) and Jonathan Rees, recently released from prison following his conviction for planting cocaine on an innocent woman, who were also by now doing work for the paper. Anyway, they said they wanted to continue the process that had gone before, with an increased emphasis on celebrities.

Hacking by reporters in the office was seen as a cheap and effective way of getting stoires, but, as someone who worked with Greg Miskiw specialising in in-depth investigations, Mulcaire was decidedly seen as less good value for money. Although he could turn material around quickly, his preference was for longer-term, bigger subjects, which inevitably meant they were more expensive. The use of private investigators was regarded by some reporters as, simply, cheating, and the fact that they cost the company a lot of money – not normally the number one concern of some expenses-happy newshounds – just added to the resentment against the PIs.

Looking back, that restaurant meeting was something of a watershed, a taster of what was to come. 'Nothing serious like the public interest was discussed,' recalls Mulcaire. 'I just didn't like them. They seemed like plastic people to me.' Mulcaire cannot recall exactly when, but says either at that meeting or on the phone later, he was told 'If you don't want to do it, we'll get one of the thousands in who will.' It was a pretty bald assertion that if he thought things had changed, he had seen nothing yet. 'I was caught in no man's land. Either they would make me overwork and make me crack or they would max out on everything they could get. I was boxed in.'

It was a key period in the life and death of the *News of the World*. The Murdoch-owned papers had always had a sense of their own place and importance in the national arena. Some would say they behaved as if they owned the place. Certainly there was an assuredness about what they could do, who they could get access to and so on. If there was mischief to be made, they would push the boundaries, but in a way leavened by humour or populist brilliance. Now the goals were being redefined to keep the machine fed. Asked about it some years later, a very senior *Sun* reporter, hugely respected by his peers – and no stranger to the occasional need to cut corners in the interests of getting a story – turned his palms upwards and raised them as if in a 'stand up' gesture and said 'They just lifted it up and up and up'.

A reporter from the paper recalled the changed climate in the office, which ran counter to the old newsdesk machismo. 'Coulson was inexperienced and had to rely on PI's to stand stories up, which was really expensive and shouldn't have been necessary,' he said. 'The old school way of doing stuff was to sit outside in a van, watching people, sometimes for days, even if it does mean having to poo in a plastic bag.' Another describes how in the past there had been a discreet way of using blaggers and private investigators: 'There wasn't much we couldn't get, in terms of phone numbers, addresses, records and so on. It was Ok when it was done judiciously, but then the halfwits turned up and they went and put it all in the paper.' Another says: 'They didn't have contacts or ability. Doing the phones was a tool which made their lives easier. And they used to say things like 'Wouldn't it be good if Kylie was having an affair with so-and-so', and then they'd try to make it come true.' Yet another reporter mentioned: 'There was no care involved. It was all onwards and upwards, don't look back, smash and grab stuff. There was no feeling that you should bother about looking after contacts. They just wanted results.'

After four comparatively productive and worthwhile years, Mulcaire felt himself to be deluged with requests on stories big and small. In looking back, he refers to this period as 'the spike', spraying the room with imaginary machine gun fire. 'It was relentless,' he remembers. This increase in volume may have been down simply to the newsdesk's insatiable drive, but Mulcaire sensed that he was being tested. Could he deliver on so many requests? Would he crack under the pressure? Although generally 'user-friendly' and obliging, Mulcaire would on occasions ask about the purpose of certain taskings.

The mounting pressure took its toll on Mulcaire. He was working enormously long hours, drinking to excess, suffering from anxiety disorder and panic attacks, and was prescribed with beta blockers and Prozac. Some executives would refer to him as 'Mr Grumpy', because of the occasional question why such-and-such a job needed doing. On other occasions he would be asked to do a job that somebody else had failed to perform, thus rendering it more difficult. 'That used to really aggravate me. Why hadn't they asked me in the first place? I also used to complain about my contract, and whether it would be renewed. Plus, it was the volume of stuff they were asking me to do. I used to work long days, often 15 hours, from Tuesdays to Fridays, and then be off with the kids at the weekend, and free on Monday. But gradually – and quite apologetically, actually – they wanted me to do stuff on Mondays, so they'd be ready for Tuesday morning conference. And then they started wanting me doing stuff on Saturdays as well, when I used to do training with AFC Wimbledon's Junior Dons and reserve team.' Mr Justice Saunders later referred to an email Mulcaire sent, asking his bosses to lighten the load.

But whereas in his early days of working for the paper he would show an interest in the stories that were being worked on, latterly, under the weight of tasks given him by the ever-more demanding news desk, he became more and more of a production line. 'I was getting asked to do something on average about every ten minutes. The phone barely stopped ringing,' he remembers. Mostly the sort of things he was asked to do related to stories of little interest to him personally, usually the private lives of soap stars or other celebrities. One lawyer familiar with Mulcaire's activities said in 2013 as the trials approached: 'I didn't think I'd ever say this, but I now feel a bit sorry for Glenn Mulcaire. From what I understand, he started out doing the sort of work that traditionally public-spirited newspapers do, and under the weight of what he was asked to do he became completely institutionalised and stopped asking questions.'

In the course of preparing this book, Mulcaire on several occasions discussed how it could be that so many shockingly intrusive cases could have come to pass. How could anyone defend invading the privacy of, for example, the mother of a 22-year-old girl who has been stabbed by a jealous boyfriend just hours before? How unfeeling does a journalist have to be to excuse that in the name of the trade? It is a question to which Mulcaire has become inured, possibly through a sense of self-protection. He was accused of deleting the voicemails of Milly Dowler, a claim which left him tearful, sleepless and frustrated at his inability to answer the claims. If his role in that case is clearer now than it was, what about those other cases for which News International has had to pay out substantial damages. How does he explain those?

The conviction with which he confronts the questions might surprise his accusers. When asked about specific cases involving breaches of the privacy of blameless people he doesn't recall, he cites a ready answer. 'If something bad happened, it would have been for one of three reasons,' he says now. 'Either I was given an untrue pretext, in that I was told to go after someone and lied to as to why.' He then named various commissioning people on the paper's news desk. 'Generally, if it was something bad, Greg Miskiw would say nothing rather than lie. He tended to be straighter than the others,' he said. 'Or sometimes they would simply pile the work on me, and slip in something they thought otherwise I wouldn't want to do. Often there would be a VoC (victim of crime) in there. It's called packaging, when you get a pile of work and you just have to plough through it because it has to be done. They don't say what it's about, you just get the number, or whatever it is.' In other words, he argues, his work had become just a 'commodity'. The fact that it might be providing access to someone's intimate, painful secret was overshadowed by the need to keep the beast fed. The job in question would often be 'reversing' a number, that is, finding a name and address from a mobile phone number, or acquiring the PIN number that accompanied a mobile number.

The third category of story on which Mulcaire would sometimes be working unaware would be a 'Special Projects' story. The facts of such a story would be made known only to those who needed to know, such was the requirement of complete discretion. Mulcaire's ability to keep a secret was not, it seems, ever in doubt, but occasionally voices in the office would require a secret to be kept as tight as possible. It was sometimes claimed in the office that for all the secret squirrel work, Mulcaire wasn't that good at his job, and that, as an example, he would not be able to hack the phones of Rebekah Brooks and Andy Coulson, then editors of the *Sun* and the *News of the World*, and of Rav Singh, editor of Bizarre. All three were considered prone to the attentions of story-hungry rivals and had taken special precautions to ensure their phones were interception-proof.

Perhaps to goad Mulcaire, a news executive mentioned these precautions to him in a phone conversation. Whatever the intention, it had the effect of spurring Mulcaire to prove he could get access to their voicemails. 'Within four minutes I had done it,' he remembers with satisfaction. He also recalls providing himself with something of an insurance policy by confirming in an email to the office that he had in effect been commissioned to hack his editors' phones. The email, saying something like 'as requested, here is Andy's PIN number', elicited a prompt and panicky call back from the office, chastising him for making explicit this lawlessness in writing. The email in question has never surfaced. Mulcaire doesn't remember how many times he listened to the voicemails of his editor and deputy editor. He says it is possible, as has been claimed, that it was quite a lot, but he doubts it. 'If that is the case, I will gladly admit it, but as far as I remember, there was no call to do it more than once. I was only working under instruction.' Sean Hoare said there were frequent attempts (by senior executives) to hack one another's phones.

Mulcaire is less certain as to whether the reason he was given was the real reason for his being asked to get into the voicemail box of his and the *Sun*'s editor. 'I always suspected they wanted to know what was going on between them,' says Mulcaire. 'We know they were having an affair, although I admit I didn't know that at the time. It may be that they just wanted to know the gossip, or it may be that they wanted to be in on what stories they were working on, in order to be better prepared professionally.'

It may be difficult to believe that Mulcaire was unaware of the upset he was causing in the carrying out of his duties for the paper. How could he not know? Did he not read the paper?

Well, no, actually, he says, frequently he didn't. Even if 'all human life is here', in the *News of the World*, he had little interest in it, or in the telling of stories. His curiosity was that of a technician, focussed on how best to acquire information, on the establishing of fact. What journalists chose to do with it, how they presented it, was of not the faintest concern. This may be a surprise, but whereas he had begun his spell with the paper doing what he regarded as serious, worthwhile and remunerative digging, by the middle of the decade much of it was just a job. A job he was well paid for and, with a wife and five children, a large mortgage and an ultra-demanding boss, he could not easily walk away from.

That period, at its worst in 2005 and 2006, was, for Mulcaire, the grimmest of his career. Greg Miskiw, the closest thing he had to a protector in Wapping, had gone, although they were still in touch and doing bits of work together. Mulcaire felt trapped.

In hindsight he wishes he had made more effort to cultivate possible employers on other papers. Clive Goodman arranged for him to meet Charlie Rae, a veteran on the *Sun*, then under Rebekah Brooks's editorship, but nothing came of the proposed meeting. His workload piled up as he sought to keep his bosses happy. He was uncomfortable with his brief, but having signed up to it, he felt he had little option. And it wasn't just a matter of 'stay or go'. The costs of jumping ship were incalculable, he believes. 'If I'd not done what I was asked,' he says, 'I would have been blacklisted and unemployable. I would have become a bad name in the trade, so I was perfectly placed to be betrayed. It was damned if you do, damned if you don't. How do you explain to the kids that we can't go on living in this house any more? I couldn't have done that. The carrot got shorter and the stick got longer, and I should have cultivated other outlets.'

Anyone appalled by the extent of lawlessness commissioned and carried out by those working for the *News of the World* may see more mitigation than justification here. Mulcaire, however, knows he broke the law, acknowledges it and doesn't seek to defend it. He pleaded guilty after all to all charges, except one (which was dropped). He does, though, speak with the self-acknowledged frustration of someone who was part of a criminal enterprise for which, for over 7 years, only he and Clive Goodman paid a price. He affects little bitterness at that fact alone, and became indifferent as to whether others came to suffer the same fate. What does rile him is how the whole story has been hung on him and prevented him getting back to a normal life. The refusal of his former bosses to come clean has hampered his prospects of finding respectable employment. Having pleaded guilty and served his sentence, he hoped to return to what he does best – investigative work. Yet the slow dawning on the public consciousness of the fact that phone hacking was not so much the work of a rogue investigator but a veritable flourishing industry has held up that rehabilitation, he feels.

He admits, too, to frustration that he has had to (or felt he had to) keep his counsel for so long. Partly this was down to the confidentiality agreement he had signed, and partly to the many ongoing civil cases being brought against News International (and often against him personally). But, notwithstanding what his lawyers have told him about incriminating himself, his silence may not have been a legal necessity. Looking back, his evidence could have been of great use to the House of Commons Committee for Culture Media and Sport, during their investigations into phone hacking. The same goes for the IPCC's investigation into the Dowler affair, and the Leveson inquiry, but it didn't happen.

After Miskiw left, Mulcaire's place at the paper was under constant threat, and there was regular talk of his contract being terminated. But Mulcaire's record, for one reason or another, made him effectively unsackable, or so it seems. At one point, when it looked as if chief reporter Neville Thurlbeck was seemingly endorsing a plan to get rid of Mulcaire, Mulcaire's sense of natural justice was offended. Mulcaire recalls arranging to meet Thurlbeck to discuss the situation. 'I asked my friend Steve Mills [a football contact] to come along to a pub on Fleet Street and stay out of sight but simply to listen to the conversation,' Mulcaire recalls. 'I told Thurlbeck that was fine – if he really wanted me pushed out, Ok, but he should know that I planned to make public the fact that the Beckham story, for which he won the 2005 British Press

Awards prize for Scoop of the Year, was stood up by me…. After that I think it was pretty much agreed I was unsackable.'

A former *News of the World* stalwart says: 'Mulcaire was too good at his job. He just brought in too much good stuff.' But in his chat with Thurlbeck Mulcaire had touched on another reason why he had become unsackable. 'They couldn't get rid of Mulcaire because he had done the Beckham story,' says a *News of the World* source. 'It has never been confirmed that they did his phone. If he had left the company and let it be known how they stood up the Beckham story, Beckham could have sued Murdoch['s empire] for millions.'

At the 2005 Press Awards in March, which looked back on the previous year in journalism, The *News of the World* won both National Newspaper of the Year award for the second consecutive year and the Scoop of the Year award, for the story of Beckham's Secret Affair. One of Andy Coulson's assets as a manager was a willingness to put professionalism ahead of personal popularity, a huge plus in an industry where affability goes a long way. He always wanted more, so there was to be no complacency as a result of the awards. The usual pressure applied to senior executives and reporters was to be ratcheted up ever further. The following month, Coulson sent a memo to his senior staff, proposing some minor changes to the working week. More importantly, they were being put on notice:

> 2005 has been a great year for *News of the World* awards… and an average one for *News of the World* stories. The truth is we have not fulfilled our brief

this year. Few very good stories, plenty of good stories and far, far too many stories that fall into the 'fine' category.... I've no doubt you are all as aware and concerned about this as I am and I'm not for a moment doubting your efforts. But we need a hit. Badly.

No limits on this in terms of cash or other resources. We should all be coming into the office on Tuesday with two or three potential splash ideas –preferably with a couple of calls already made....

We had an unprecedented year of success in 2004 and your brilliant work has been rightly recognised and celebrated.

On the upside last year we broke Beckham in April, Sven in July and Blunkett in August. Time we got started this year I think...

The pattern in the news machine was for pressure to be passed downwards. Someone who worked on features recalls how the *News of the World* features department was 'put under horrible pressure' by Andy Coulson and his executives, who 'would come and just scream at us – they always wanted more. It had been a fun and exciting place to work but that changed entirely.' The introduction of Dan Evans was a direct response to that pressure, the employee believes. 'We knew they were hacking phones on news, and features had to get into that. Dan Evans's news list used to be unbelievable, he had some amazing stories on it, and compared to that we were failures. We couldn't compete. So they hired this guy who we knew had been doing that dark arts stuff at. There was no secret about it. We talked about it in the pub.'

One of Glenn Mulcaire's targets during this period was troubled Atomic Kitten singer Kerry Katona, whose personal life could fill the *News of the World* for a year. Mulcaire had been in and out of her phones since she split from Westlife singer Brian McFadden in September 2004. This brought the paper up against Max Clifford, who was representing her. In June 2005, he and editor Andy Coulson fell out badly over the paper's handling of Katona. They felt she was too rich a source of stories to ignore, and in December 2005 ran a story headed 'Kerry in New Coke Shocker'. When asked later why he had run the story, Coulson replied crisply: 'Because it was true.'

In redtop land, the Clifford-Coulson split was a big event. Clifford was the king of buy-ups, the man to whom those mistreated by celebrities would go in search of financial consolation. He, indeed, had brokered the deal with Rebecca Loos that exposed David Beckham's infidelity, and the judges who gave the story the Scoop of the Year award were torn as to whether 'a Clifford buy-up' was a fitting winner of such a prize. (In the end, they gave it the award largely because of the level of detail it contained, most of it supplied by Mulcaire.)

Whatever the immediate cause of the argument, the effect was that Clifford's close relationship with News International had been damaged. He decided to withdraw co-operation with its papers. A major source of stories had dried up.

As we will see, Clive Goodman came under mounting pressure during this period, but this was part of a continuing cranking up of demands. At around the same time, Coulson's falling out with reporter Sean Hoare, his erstwhile drinking buddy, became complete, and Hoare left the paper. Hoare had his own demons, and complained that the paper had not shown the duty of care he was owed. His behaviour had certainly become unprofessional, but he maintained in part that the pressure had driven him to it. He said later: 'There is so much intimidation. In the newsroom, you have people being fired, breaking down in tears, hitting the bottle…. I was paid to go out and take drugs with rock stars – get drunk with them, take pills with them, take cocaine with them. It was so competitive. You are going to go beyond the call of duty. You are going to do things that no sane man would do. You're in a machine.'

In January 2006, not long after the falling out with Max Clifford, Coulson was doubling his exhortations to greater productivity at the *News of the World*. In another memo to senior staff he wrote: 'This is going to be an incredibly tough year…. I'm going to be more and more reliant on home grown material…. But the agenda is simple: How will the *News of the World* break more bigger, agenda setting exclusives?… I'm not looking for decent spread ideas – I want splashes, two-/three parters, long term investigations etc.' Many of these types of features had previously come from PRs like Clifford.

In May 2006, at long last, the Information Commissioner's report, 'What Price Privacy' was published. Quite why data that had been in existence for many months surfaced only then is unclear. It was suggested by the ICO's former investigator Alec Owens that the Commission had been afraid to upset the press, and only published in 2006 when it got wind of the coming storm over Mulcaire's work. In any event the report's impact (if that is the word) was slight. Certainly it did little to impair celebrations on the *News of the World* table at the 2006 press awards (by then in the hands of the London Press Club) when – yet again – it won the Paper of the Year award. Jokes on the table about the paper's debt of thanks to Vodafone and other mobile phone companies were by this time old hat.

The fact that that summer a sport reporter, Matt Driscoll, was cutting up and making allegations of bullying, or that Tommy Sheridan, a Scottish politician, had won a libel case against the paper, were probably of little concern in that context. The man they had been unsure would ever make an editor was riding high.

7

What £330,000 Will Buy You

The paper was winning awards, but the climate had changed from the paper Mulcaire had joined. The interest in celebrity-driven stories was greater than ever, and some of the older guard were feeling less and less welcome. Clive Goodman, a long-time servant, was demoted from the post of assistant editor on the news desk – effectively the control room – reporting directly to the editor Andy Coulson, to a post as a mere news-getter, reporting to the news editor. The pressure to bring in stories or be replaced was insistent, and not what a senior reporter approaching his sixth decade might reasonably have expected.

The pressure was mounting on Mulcaire, too. If another paper broke a big story, there was always – as on any successful paper – an inquest into 'why we didn't have the story'. The fact that, in April 2006, the *Mirror* broke the story of cabinet minister John Prescott's affair with Tracey Temple had a huge effect. It was absolutely a *News of the World* story, but had appeared elsewhere. It was an outrage!

The news desk was coming under pressure for other reasons – to cut budgets. The casual resort to intercepting voicemails was widespread, as *News of the World* reporter Dan Evans testified in court, and if money was to be saved, some thought Mulcaire was expendable. After all, it was argued, there was no mystique to hacking a phone, and some reporters spent much of their time doing precisely that, unassisted by Mulcaire. Of course Mulcaire actually offered a great deal more than that, and those who couldn't get access to voicemails would report back to the desk, which would then have to fall back on Mulcaire's talent for blagging or otherwise identifying PIN numbers.

Mulcaire became concerned that having helped the paper in its mastery of the dark arts, he had become the author of his own obsolescence. Having shown many the way, he might then not be needed, or so he feared. So on occasions, having cracked a particularly difficult number that he knew would be of value to the news desk, he would make a note of the information and change the PIN number again to a number that only he knew, to secure his own role as gatekeeper to that celebrity.

That said, there were other blaggers in the field, and some of the bosses thought they could find another one, and probably cheaper than Mulcaire. Besides, there was no harm done by reminding Mulcaire that nobody was indispensable. The paper's ethos required that everyone be kept on their toes, after all.

So in February 2005, the news desk told the accounts department to stop Mulcaire's weekly payment of £2019. This was the most explicit sign that even Mulcaire, access to whom was one of the paper's Holy of Holies, was not beyond threat. As we have seen, chief reporter Neville Thurlbeck was deputed to speak to the investigator about whether there might be scope for some sort of revised deal, or whether this might be the end of the road.

As we have seen, Max Clifford had just fallen out with Andy Coulson. So, if Clifford was no longer to come to the paper with his stories, the paper would go to him, although without feeling the need to tell him. Clifford's client list would be invaluable, no doubt, so he came under the full scrutiny of Glenn Mulcaire, who confirms that both Clifford and his PA Nicola Phillips had all their calls monitored by him. Mulcaire set about itemising all the calls, doing pattern analysis (evaluating the time of call, the frequency and so on), identifying those who called, listening in to voicemails and so on. 'They wanted a full comm[unication]s profile,' he remembers.

At around the same time, royalty reporter Clive Goodman was deputed to see if he couldn't come to some arrangement with Mulcaire. The pair had something in common – both were at odds with the *News of the World* incumbent hierarchy, but, when working at their best, were considered too valuable to lose. Goodman asked Mulcaire how he was getting on with the news desk. He complained that he was being overloaded, being made to work Saturdays and they were trying to get him to do Mondays too. 'I'm out of the loop,' Clive saidm mentioning one executive in particular who he regarded as 'a nob.'

At around this time, as a sort of insurance policy for himself, Mulcaire asked Goodman to arrange for him to become a member of the National Union of Journalists. Although he had had no desire to become a journalist, and continues to hold most of them in contempt, he felt his chances of continued employment would be improved by having a press card. He also sought to offer 'oven-ready' stories to the newsdesk, and pushed a story about Professional Footballers' Association boss Gordon Taylor, which a freelance friend from Wimbledon was to write up on his behalf. Mulcaire had been increasingly unhappy at how he was being treated by the news desk and by the sort of stories he was being asked to pursue. He also felt out on a limb, his most trusted contact in the office, Greg Miskiw, having left the paper. He began to look around for other outlets. But when Goodman, who he knew of old, got in touch, he was happy to listen.

Goodman suggested a scheme whereby he and Mulcaire would work in tandem on specifically royal stories. Goodman was well-liked and respected by his fellow reporters, and held the record for the number of front-page stories in succession (three), but the demand for royal stories had declined, and they needed to be stronger than ever to get in the paper. More generally, among the upper echelons there was a demand for constant improvement. Goodman had joined the paper in 1995 and risen to become royal editor in 2000, but his stock had fallen. One senior executive in particular did not rate his work and, Goodman later told the Old Bailey, a 'massive chunk of [his] work was taken away'. Having initially got on Ok with Andy Coulson – the pair had gone to one another's weddings – Goodman found he changed after becoming editor. 'He became more aggressive and bullying, I was forever being berated for the lack of quality of my stories; he meant to degrade you'. Goodman found he was attending conference but not even being asked to say what stories he had to offer. 'It was humiliating, and intended to be humiliating,' he said.

In Mulcaire he saw an entrée to all sorts of royal

goodies. 'He floated a trial balloon,' remembers Mulcaire, although Goodman's memory was that it was Mulcaire who proposed the idea. 'I would collaborate with him, maybe with payments being made in cash. I wasn't certain at that stage if they were going to renew my contract, or if I wanted them to, so I thought "hang on, this might work",' says Mulcaire. 'I could see what Clive's personal agenda was, and actually I felt a bit sorry for the way he had been edged out, but I could see how it might work for me as well.' Most importantly for Mulcaire, he hoped Goodman would be his 'ears' in the office, someone to tell him the gossip and who was up, who was down. The 'need to know' rule was all very well, but Mulcaire wanted more reassurance from head office than he had been getting. As Mulcaire was to learn, Goodman was not that well placed to oblige.

A plan was drawn up to ring-fence royal stories, on which Mulcaire and Goodman would collaborate, separate from news desk. Goodman sent Coulson an email that said the following: 'A few weeks ago you asked me to find new ways of getting into the [royal] family, especially William and Harry and I came up with this. "It's safe, productive and cost effective and I'm confident it will become a big story goldmine for us."' For this Mulcaire, known in the office as 'Matey', would receive a fixed rate of £500 a week (a fourth of his previous weekly fee), an arrangement agreed with Andy Coulson, says Goodman. The deal began on a trial basis. Goodman would supply Mulcaire with phone numbers, Mulcaire would acquire the PIN numbers and the reporter would do the rest. 'He didn't come back to me and say I got such and such a story from what you gave me,' says

Mulcaire. 'I just opened the gateways and left him to get on with it.'

Goodman recalled later in court: 'Glenn's skill was to lie and he had access to every type of airtime company you can think of to get information. He would get them to reset the number to default, and anyone who has the default number can access the voice message. Sometimes Mulcaire would do it, sometimes I would do it.... It was a day to day practice and approved by my editor'.

A number of stories with a decent ring of truth began to appear in the paper. They included a tale about Prince William getting lost while out on an exercise, how Prince William had called his brother, pretending to be Chelsy Davy and another about him having had too much to drink the night before. In October, Goodman sent Coulson an email, gleefully reporting 'new project starting to get results, William's office in meltdown'.

In November the story about the Prince having a knee injury, of which only a tiny handful of people knew, appeared in the *News of the World*. The story went down well in the office and, for Goodman, this was a vindication of the arrangement with 'Matey'. 'Our new project is yielding results,' Goodman wrote to Coulson in an email. Such was the flow of detailed information about the princes (what pictures they had in their bedrooms, what their essays were about, who they were inviting to their parties and so on) that they reached that happy state for a journalist whereby they have sufficient information that they need to self-censor in order not to reveal their source. It emerged in court that on a transcript, William is reported saying to Kate Middleton: 'I was pissed but I wasn't that bad.' Clive Goodman, ever under pressure for more and better, was asked by a senior journalist if that line could be used in a story, to which Goodman replied: 'Too much information, would be incredibly dangerous to the source.'

That same month, the trial period was extended. The following week, a second article claimed that Tom Bradby, ITV's political editor, had lent the Prince some broadcasting equipment. This was a domestic detail too far. When Bradby and the Prince met a week later, they concluded this was not just somebody being indiscreet. There was something very wrong going on.

Mulcaire remembers Goodman losing sight of the seriousness of what he was doing. 'This wasn't a normal interception story,' he recalls. 'This had immense security issues attached.' The actual accessing of the royal household's voicemail had been comparatively easy, but there were warnings along the way that concerned him. 'There were security flags left on the voicemails. We were talking about a higher level of clearance. I knew a threshold had been crossed.' He sensed the security services would have become alert to what was happening and would be looking out for eavesdroppers.

'I remember saying to Goodman that we need to cool off. There's a security warning flag on the account, and they don't get any higher than that. If you're not going to stop at those warning signs, you're going to be in trouble. Why he kept crashing in like a bull in a china shop, I just don't know, but he just didn't grasp the gravity of the warning. I told him we need to calm down, go off the grid some time, and I wasn't even sure we'd get back on. It was that serious.' He says that in its haste to publish, the *News of the World* was drawing attention to its eavesdropping. Journalists know that often a story must not be printed too quickly, to avoid making the source identifiable. Once a few days have passed, the possibility that it has seeped out through run-of-the-mill gossip gains weight. But by publishing stories 'before they had even left the room', as Mulcaire puts it, huge risks were being taken. This may have been a symptom of Goodman's anxiety to impress.

Mulcaire's feeling was that any further incursions into what he called royal 'airspace' would be closely monitored henceforth. 'They'll be all over this, I thought. With the Lord Stevens investigation into the death of Diana going on, everyone was at a heightened state of alert. And once you're in that airspace it's hard to turn round and say you have legitimate reasons.'

'If I was on the other side – although actually I regard myself and the security people as basically being on the same side – but if I was them, I'd want to know everything about who was getting into royal airspace, even if they went in and out. Who they were, what were they up to? There are definitely national security issues there. On a professional level, I am immensely proud of having got past their protocols. I don't know how many other people could do that then, and I don't want to claim retrospectively that I was doing it to flag up breaches in security, but I realise now that I, or rather the paper, could have done that at the time.'

Asked if he feels guilty about compromising the security of the royals in order not to reveal some great item of public concern but a piece of the flimsiest tittle tattle, Mulcaire's answer is 'if I had come across anything serious, of course I would have done something about it…. But I would rather it was me than anyone else.' And did it do any harm? 'It's not for me to judge,' he says. 'What I do know is that if things had carried on at the crazy rate the *News of the World* was demanding, everyone across the globe would have been on the grid. It would have made the US's echelon system revealed by Edward Snowden look like Lego. They were relentless.'

Looking back, Mulcaire wonders why it took the Anti Terror squad nine months, from November to August, to get together enough information to arrest him. He strongly suspected he was being watched closely, and that the BT engineers who came to visit his house a couple of months after the Prince's knee story to attend to a 'fault' were bogus and were actually putting a listening device in place.

On 7th August 2006, the Mulcaires drove back from a family holiday in Newquay, Cornwall. They were tired from the journey, and the children went to bed early. It was to be an abruptly interrupted sleep. Early the next morning, as Mulcaire was lying in bed, he heard the steady, throaty roar of a helicopter engine. Soon after came a loud banging on the door. It was 6.00am. Mulcaire jumped out of bed and ran downstairs. The police had come not just to arrest him, but to search the family's house and two cars.

When the police arrest someone at their home, they give them a specified amount of time to answer the door before they break it down. Mulcaire, typically, knew how long that period is, and that he needed to move quickly if he was to minimise his wife and family's terror. (In preparing this book, we discussed whether to specify the allowed length of time. Mulcaire said not to, to prevent the wrong people knowing things they shouldn't know.)

Looking back, he cites a near-cliché: 'The greatest feeling I had as I walked down stairs was relief. It was the first time for God knows how long that I'd come down and there was no cloud. My head felt clear. 'This is closure now', I thought. Those months and years of being overworked, overstressed, training too hard to compensate, medication, panic attacks, not enough sleep, even drinking a little too much. I was real heart attack material, but I felt then all that was coming to an end.'

Within moments the house was swarming with police officers, uniformed and plain clothed. The children, having heard the noise and seen the police vehicles outside, rushed to the top of the stairs. Surely their Dad, who had always taught them to stand up for themselves but always to respect authority, could not be in any trouble?

Alison had no idea what was going on, other than that they had 'come for Glenn'. 'Are you aware that your husband has been intercepting voicemail messages?' asked one officer. She – a less likely gangster's moll could hardly be imagined – looked at him in bemusement. She had no idea what the term meant, let alone that her husband might be guilty of it. 'What are you talking about?', she said. Another mentioned that he was being arrested under the Regulation of Investigatory Powers Act of 2000, which he referred to by its colloquial name of 'RIPA'. She imagined some connection with the Yorkshire Ripper.

As the police led Mulcaire out, she came to the bottom of the stair to give him a kiss. There was no 'I can explain everything', which must have been tempting, given that she seems to have been totally bemused by so alarming an experience, or 'Look after the children'. He said, simply, 'Keep cool', echoing the motto on a necklace she wears, given her by him. He seems to have had faith in her faith in him. And for himself, rather more familiar with both dealing with the law and the protocols of the intelligence world, he slipped into 'say nothing' mode. He says the Bono line just about fits the bill: 'Talk without speaking, cry without weeping , scream without raising your voice.'

'Do you know what he does?' Alison was asked, to which she gave her stock answer: 'I know he works for the *News of the World*.' Seemingly the truth is that, pretty much, that is all she did know. 'All that day I just kept thinking "What is all this about? Why are they keeping Glenn?"' 'The whole day I didn't have a clue,' she remembers. 'I took the children round to a friend's house because I didn't want them being upset staying there. Then I got home, and I still didn't have a clue what was going on. I put the TV news on a 7.00 o'clock, and there it was. We just looked at each other… it was all over the news.'

The shock must have been immense, but at no time did she doubt or the children doubt her husband. If he had done something wrong, she remained unshakeable in the belief that it was for the greater good. 'Glenn's always been very private with his work, and my job was to be at home with the children, do the school run and so on. I had noticed that on holidays he had been a bit bogged down, and looking back I can see that they waited till we came back to arrest him. But they said if he hadn't been there they would have broken down the door.

That same day, the police also raided Mulcaire's parents' home in Fulham. His mother, who lives with the memory of when the police arrived to tell her her first son had been killed in a car crash, was terrified by the appearance of police at her door. She asked if Glenn was alive. Initially, no one answered, a brief silence which, even if inadvertent, still upsets the family.

Mulcaire was detained – as if he was a terrorist – at Belgravia police station, not far from where he was brought up. In his own mind he was detached. This was the end of that particular chapter he thought, one which had seen him get into areas of work that weren't him at all. He rested when he could. He asked for a copy of the *Evening Standard*. Initially this was denied him, but then allowed, only with the front page story – the one about him – cut out. The police didn't want him knowing too much, it seems. He was examined by a doctor, who found him in good condition (despite a lack of morning toast, he still grumbles) and a duty sergeant took pity on him and allowed him a chance to stretch his legs. Outside, photographers waited.

Back at home, his fretful children lay down on cushions in front of the television, turned on Sky News and stayed there all night, perhaps subconsciously hoping the news would change. Mulcaire called home during the evening to say goodnight and tell his wife and children: 'Don't worry, we'll be fine.'

That same day, 8th August, 2006, police arrived – together with Clive Goodman – with a search warrant at *News of the World*. The *New York Times* later reported that 'as word of the detectives' arrival ricocheted around the office, two veteran reporters stuffed reams of documents into trash bags', but were relieved when the police went no further than Clive Goodman's desk. 'We only had authority to do that desk,' said the police, who had a concern that police barging into the affairs of a free press would look repressive. Indeed, there was a stand-off, with senior staff claiming the police were there unlawfully, and there was even a fear that violence might ensue. The police wanted to seize more material from Goodman's desk, but were prevented from doing so, and agreed not to force the issue. It is fair to assume, though, their attitude might have been different had the paper belonged to a less powerful proprietor.

Mulcaire was kept in until late the following evening. Knowing that an answer leads to another question, he said nothing for 36 hours. At one point, after countless 'No comments', he said 'well actually… no comment.'

The day after their arrest, Mulcaire and Goodman were charged with various counts of unlawful interception of communications contrary to s.1(1) RIPA 2000 and conspiracy to intercept communications. The day after the arrest of Mulcaire and Goodman, another SO13 Operation 'Overt' had arrested 25 people for a conspiracy to blow up 9 transatlantic airliners which was at the time the largest Counter Terrorism investigation undertaken. As detective chief superintendent Keith Surtees later told the Leveson inquiry, 'it was against this backdrop that I organised for the material seized from Mulcaire's home address to be examined. There were no available officers within the SO13 Counter terrorism command to carry out this exercise. Following briefings with detective chief superintendent Tim White it was established that 8-10 security cleared officers from SO12 were to systematically examine all the documents and create a spreadsheet of the names and numbers of all people mentioned'.

When he eventually got home, Mulcaire and Alison had a big heart-to-heart. He told her what he had been doing and why. What had started as an acceptable compromise while he was working with Greg Miskiw had turned nightmarish.

'I knew at work he was always doing something for the good,' says Alison. 'He did loads of good work… he would sometimes look at the paper and say: 'I caught that person… I helped them catch him'. To be honest I was never that interested. The kids were so young and I was so busy I never really asked.' At the end he was having to do pretty well anything, regardless of its justification, to keep his bosses happy. Although obviously I didn't think it at the time, but in a way at the end it was almost a relief when he was arrested,' says Alison.

It was clear the police were not going to let the matter drop. These raids were too public, and the people involved too high-profile, for that. The royal princes had had personal information compromised in the process. Working under (then) detective chief inspector Surtees, Special branch officers had found 11,000 pages of scrawled notes, many with mobile phone and PIN numbers on them. The officers inputted the names of 418 potential victims, including a large number of high-profile figures.

In July the police had asked for guidance from the Crown Prosecution Service, given how some of what they were discovering was highly personal, and might involve 'extraneous matters' getting dragged into the prosecution area. On 25th July they were advised that the case against Mulcaire should be deliberately limited to 'less sensitive' witnesses.

At a case conference a few days later [21st August], detective sergeant Phil Williams reported there were potentially around 180 victims. The crown prosecution said later that it had asked if there was any reason to think Mulcaire was in touch with other journalists at the *News of the World*, and they were told not.

The view on the arrests from Wapping was not appetising. This was not one of those instances where a discreetly delivered warning from a bewigged courtier to a grateful subject was going to be sufficient. That meant court, and in all likelihood prison for the pair. And, for the bosses at *News of the World*, whose 'news drug habit' had been glimpsed for the first time by the wider public, that meant making sure that that was the worst of it. The police were bound to want to know more. At the very least, Goodman and Mulcaire needed to be squared. In short, there was a cover-up to be arranged. The loyalty, if that is the word, of most of the *News of the World* staff could be relied upon, partly because most knew little of what had gone on, and partly because they wanted to go on working there.

The problem might come with the two people likely to be punished for what they had done in the company's name. Why should they go quietly when they had been doing what was required of them? Certainly Clive Goodman was disinclined to go along with the idea that he should 'take one for the company'. To his mind, it was the company's responsibility for placing him under so much pressure as to make him cut corners. As a respected royal correspondent, at least as far as his counterparts on other papers were concerned, his loyalty to the company had already been waning. He was regarded by rank-and-file reporters as 'one of the good guys', yet he had been demoted the year before his and showed little sign of enjoying the pressure under which he was expected to perform.

If Goodman blew the whistle on just how extensive the lawbreaking at the paper was, he would expose some of his bosses to unimaginable damage. The Murdoch empire was highly professional and ultra-efficient. If it cut corners, it did so with extreme discretion and always in the public interest, or so it claimed. Yet Goodman was in a position to expose extensive quantities of lawlessness. He had to be neutralised.

Goodman had been arrested at his home in a quiet crescent in Putney at 6.00am on the same day as Mulcaire, Tuesday 8th August. The danger the pair posed was obvious. These were two people a long way down the food chain, doing what their bosses wanted, often under pressure. Why should they stay silent? The day after his arrest, Goodman had been advised by Henri Brandman, the solicitor provided by News International, who passed on information to the company (in defiance of Goodman's wishes, the reporter claimed in court), that he should admit guilt. But, said the lawyer, he should say he was a 'lone wolf', a suggestion Brandman was to repeat six days later, and one Goodman said he felt uncomfortable with. The plan was endorsed by Coulson, who followed up the lawyer's call by ringing Goodman. He told him: 'We're mates, but we'll have to suspend you.'

On the afternoon of Andy Coulson's next day off, the following Monday, he made the short journey to South West London to meet Goodman at Café Rouge in Wimbledon Village. The meeting lasted little more than half an hour.

Coulson had a proposal. The police had raided Glenn Mulcaire's premises but the offices of the *News of the World* too. They had secured a mountain of evidence. Coulson knew how reliant the paper had become on the dark arts, and he knew that some parts of the paper were more dependent on them than others. Each would have their own mitigation, no doubt, but they had broken a law which recognised no public interest defence. In short, there was no excuse and Coulson knew resistance was futile. The matter needed not to be challenged but to be buried – as quickly as possible.

Coulson hoped that if Goodman and Mulcaire were to plead guilty and take their punishments on the chin, there would be no need for the details to come out, in court or anywhere else. That way, surely, the paper could just move on. Coulson knew that industrial amounts of phone hacking had been going on, but he knew too that little of it had been established, and that there was nothing to link the strands together. Goodman and Mulcaire could do so, but, with judicious use of sticks and carrots, why would they?

It would require a hefty inducement, though, for Goodman to agree to keep quiet. In a way that few employees ever manage in dealings with their seniors, Goodman had his bosses over a barrel. But, outwardly at least, the streetfighter in Coulson would not acknowledge the hole he was in.

Summoning as much authority as he could from a weak hand, he explained there was no need for Goodman to lose his job. 'He asked me to plead guilty and if I did so I would be one of the people asked back,' Goodman recalled. Coulson explained that 'through his papers' influence' he had learned that there was no wish for Goodman to go to prison. Goodman later told the court: 'Mr Coulson gave the impression that he had been having some kind of discussions with people who were making decisions about the case… the impression was it was the police and the Home Office. The clear inference was that he had arranged for me not to go to prison.'

Coulson offered him an employment deal as a writer or subeditor. The condition was that Goodman should say his actions were entirely of his own volition, and that he had gone 'off the reservation'. Goodman was not happy at being the only staff member to carry the can, but could see no alternative to pleading guilty. As was the custom among many on the *News of the World*, Goodman took the precaution of covertly recording the meeting, giving himself an insurance policy for use should things turn against him.

He had been suspended by the paper. He later revealed that Coulson had told him he had to do so, but that the editor would feel free to use Goodman's services nonetheless. It was simply a PR exercise, he said. So below the radar Goodman continued to be involved, helping with newspaper serialisations and some re-writing and subediting tasks.

News International had sent the necessary signals to Goodman to say he would be looked after, but executives on the paper couldn't be sure that he and Mulcaire were the police's only target. On 7 September the police wrote to News International to ask for its files on the investigator and details of calls made to him. A week later, its lawyers Burton Copeland replied, having found only one such document, and saying that under protection of sources legislation they would not be handing over their phone records.

Among those whose name appeared as one of Mulcaire's victims – fortuitously, it seemed at the time – was the editor of the *Sun* Rebekah Brooks. She was informed of this (as many of Mulcaire's victims weren't) and on 15th September she attended a meeting with detective chief inspector Keith Surtees, receiving from him an extensive breakdown on what the police knew and what they suspected. With hindsight, this was trusting in the extreme, but then the Met's relations with senior News International executives had been such as to assume they were on the same side. Not only did the police assume good faith on her part, as protocol required, but it went far further than necessary in revealing police thinking. She was told the police were confident of nailing Goodman and Mulcaire for intercepting royal voicemails, that there were 100 to 110 other victims, that they wanted to bring charges against Mulcaire that demonstrated the full extent of his activities.

With hindsight – given how big an affair the phone hacking saga later became – the period soon after Mulcaire and Goodman were arrested takes on a particular weight.

Its significance lies in how little salience it was given by the police, notwithstanding the desire to protect the privacy of the Princes. They had other fish to fry. The commissioner of the Met, Sir Paul Stephenson, later told the Leveson inquiry: 'I do not recall having any substantive or detailed discussions about phone hacking with anyone else during this period. Indeed, it is fair to say that set against the other issues facing the MPS (including counterterrorism issues, the investigation into the 'night-stalker', the reinvestigation of the murder of Stephen Lawrence, very real budgetary challenges, the Olympic security preparations, Government proposals for significant changes to the governance arangements for the police and national structures for dealing with serious and organised crime), phone hacking was not a matter which I prioritised. I was satisfied that it was being overseen by a highly experienced and very senior officer. I was reassured by the fact that to my knowledge the case had been reviewed by the CPS and by counsel.'

The court was later told how in eight months, Goodman and Mulcaire made 609 calls to the voicemail boxes of three identified members of the royal household. One of them, Helen Asprey, personal secretary to the princes, became concerned when she found that messages she had yet to hear were identified as old calls (as if they had been listened to). In one 17-month period her phone was rung 102 times. As we shall see, this was not all, but further evidence was not to become publicly apparent until later.

On 29th November 2006, at the Old Bailey, Goodman and Mulcaire pleaded guilty of conspiracy to intercept communications, just as their paymasters had hoped they would. Goodman's barrister John Kelsey-Fry QC announced: 'Mr Goodman wishes through me to take the first opportunity to apologise publicly to those affected by his actions. It was a gross invasion of privacy and Mr Goodman accepts that is accurate. He wishes to apologise to the three members of the royal household staff and, moreover, to their principals – the Royal Highnesses Prince William, Prince Harry and the Prince of Wales.' A lower bow than the royal correspondent's could hardly be imagined.

It was matched by Mulcaire, whose barrister Neil Saunders, told the court that he also apologised to the royal family, and extended his apology to include Max Clifford, Elle Macpherson, Liberal Democrat MP Simon Hughes, Professional Footballers Association boss Gordon Taylor and Sky Andrew, a sports agent'.

Andy Coulson was anxious to show due humility, and added his own apology, taking 'ultimate responsibility' for the conduct of his reporters. 'Clive Goodman's actions were entirely wrong,' he said, 'and I have put in place measures to ensure that they will not be repeated by any member of my staff. I have also written today to Sir Michael Peat, the Prince of Wales's private secretary, to this effect. The *News of the World* will also be making a substantial donation to charities of the Princes' choice.' There was no mention of Goodman's future on the paper, or indeed Coulson's own. If he had his way, neither would be in any danger. Sir Christopher Meyer, the chairman of the Press Complaints Commission, chipped in, describing 'phone message tapping' as 'a totally unacceptable practice unless there is a compelling public interest reason for carrying it out.' That sweeping remark highlights a remarkable shortcoming. The PCC code said that there was a public interest defence (and was later cited in mitigation in court), yet the law of the land says there is not, a discrepancy nobody, including the PCC's £150,000 a year head, seems to have been aware of. Given the confusion, it is little wonder journalists came to be accused of taking the law into their own hands.

The judge, Mr Justice Gross, was clear, however, and warned: 'I am not ruling out any options. It's a very serious matter', and told the court he would consider their punishments and the court would reconvene in January. But there was still work to be done.

Elsewhere, the lawyers were getting busy. On 30th November 2005, the day after Mulcaire pleaded guilty, his solicitor Moray Laing, recommended by a friend of Mulcaire, contacted Fiona Spink at News International's legal team, mentioning that he understood senior management were 'keen to discuss the matter with a view to coming to an amicable resolution of any claims [Mulcaire] may have'. The tone was more courtly than menacing, which may have been a relief at Wapping. Nothing happened for over three weeks, whereupon Laing sent the email again, this time to News International's legal affairs manager Tom Crone.

On December 12, Goodman, with his solicitor Henri Brandman and John Kelsey Fry, his barrister, met a News International executive. It was spelt out once again, at least according to Goodman's recollection, that if Goodman didn't implicate others, he would retain his job. If he did, he wouldn't. This was the opposite of a cleaning out of the stables. But Goodman was clearly angry, and reiterated several times that he was not happy with the role he had been handed. He spelt out how the editor had complete control of everything that happened, that phone hacking was a day-to-day practice and approved by the editor, how Glenn Mulcaire's work was 'key to the organisation', that he felt he had been lied to, manipulated and felt very aggrieved, having performed with the full knowledge of some senior people. Addressing such matters lay in the future.

At News International, everything was on hold until punishment for the two 'rogues' was decided. Coulson believed the pair would not go to prison, in which case, it was believed, the affair would probably blow over, amid pious expressions about 'lessons having been learned' and so on. But, just in case, the press office was refusing to answer questions as to whether Andy Coulson had known about the hacking.

Goodman, according to his barrister John Kelsey Fry, was in 'utter terror' at the prospect of going to prison, and was having to sell his house.

Mulcaire was pretty sure he would be given a custodial sentence, but he didn't want to alarm his family in case he was wrong. His protectiveness of his family is striking. He was particularly concerned about the possible effect on his wife, whose uncomplicated sweetness of nature makes her a non-starter as the controlling evil genius that some tried to portray her as. 'We'd say "You're going to prison Glenn, aren't you," and he'd say "I don't know, maybe not,"' says Alison. ('But he did know,' says his daughter Georgia confidently). The night before sentencing, Mulcaire packed a small bag with clothes and books – 'just in case', he said – which he handed to his solicitor. It was at that point that Alison's uncertainty dissolved. There was also some wild talk about how long he would get. An apparently well-informed soul, attempting to soften the eventual blow, and overlooking the fact that the maximum allowed for the crime was two years, mentioned between three and five years.

Nonetheless, on January 26th Clive Goodman was given four months in prison. Glenn Mulcaire was sentenced to four months for conspiracy plus two months for the other offences relating to the five celebrities. (In the event, Mulcaire served 13 weeks with three weeks on a tag. Goodman served just four weeks.)

The judge didn't stint in his criticism. Their behaviour, he said, was 'low conduct, reprehensible in the extreme'. 'This case was not about press freedom; it was about a grave, inexcusable and illegal invasion of privacy. 'It was not pushing at the limits, or at the cusp: it was plainly on the wrong side of the line. It is essential for the decency of our public life that conduct of this kind is clearly marked as unacceptable. 'This was serious criminal conduct to which we must not become numbed. It is to my mind [of] the very first importance to the fabric of our public life that such intrusive, sustained criminal conduct should be marked by immediate loss of liberty,' the judge said. Goodman was motivated by 'career advancement and protection', but his thirst for inside information led him to break the law.

There was not necessarily as much contrition in the air as the judge might have hoped. Mulcaire will still tell friends that it was a journalist who got him into this mess. 'Clive was in way above his head, and he made a grave error by not being careful enough,' he says. 'Clive was worried about his job. He wasn't privy to enough of the real stuff in conference, and wasn't being asked to do enough. He was worried he wasn't getting the stories and was pushing the boundaries as a result.' In other words, the feeling was less: we deeply regret what we did because it is wrong, and more a) we were only doing what everyone else was doing and b) it was only because of a mistake that we got caught.

But the stigma of prison wasn't the end of the damage. Andy Coulson, who had promised to bring Goodman back into the fold after a decent interval, resigned. His carefully assembled statement said: 'I have decided that the time has come for me to take ultimate responsibility for the events around the Clive Goodman case. As I've said before, his actions were entirely wrong and I deeply regret that they happened on my watch.' His hope of Goodman being given a no-custodial sentence had vanished. If there was to be damage-limitation, Coulson was to play no further part in it.

Max Clifford wrote at the time that he couldn't understand why Andy Coulson hadn't resigned when Goodman was convicted. 'We are told they decided a fortnight ago,' he wrote, 'but my suspicion is that the decision was dependent on what punishment Goodman received. If he had been ordered to do community service, I believe Andy Coulson would still be the *News of the World*'s editor.'

Versions vary as to why Coulson resigned. It has been said that the decision was his and his alone, and that he had decided to go a fortnight earlier, but others say he didn't want to go and only agreed to do so after a conversation with Rupert Murdoch's most trusted confidant Les Hinton, on the understanding that he would be back in the fold once the fuss had died down.

Certainly one senior colleague who saw him that day said he seemed in surprisingly good spirits, the blow softened by a substantial payoff. A figure of £600,000 was mentioned in court, but a well-placed Wapping insider points out that while the norm for deposed News International editors is to receive two years' money on leaving the company, Coulson got three (which would take the figure beyond £600,000).

Goodman was in limbo, and now had little or no guarantee that he could make the agreement stick. And there was more. Just a couple of weeks into his sentence, Clive Goodman received a call from his wife to say that he was being dismissed, with one year's money. Goodman was astounded. He had been promised that if he pleaded guilty, his job was safe. Now the company had ratted on the deal.

In other circumstances, the sack would have been no surprise, given that Goodman had not merely broken the law, but intruded on the personal privacy of the heirs to the throne. Given that the press had had a major hand in the death of their mother less than a decade earlier, the black mark this cast on the newspaper can hardly be exaggerated.

But Goodman had every right to feel aggrieved. He was carrying the can for something half the office, seemingly, had been up to. Hinton, gamely but lamely, sought to sugar the pill by saying that in the light of his distinguished years of service to the *News of the World* and in recognition of the pressures on his family, he would receive one year's salary. Asked later, Hinton told MPs he had had discussions with others about the decision – he didn't recall who, unsurprisingly – but that the decision was his.

Goodman had had enough. The payment of a year's money didn't begin to satisfy him. On 2nd March he wrote to Daniel Cloke, Human Resources Director of News International, saying that he planned to appeal against the termination of his employment. This was bad news for his former employers, and had to be kept under wraps. Things were to get worse. Goodman, who had previously told Wapping bigwigs about the complicity of senior staff, went to town with the detail. In an angry denunciation of attempts to stifle the issue, he appealed against his sacking following his release from prison. He called the decision to sack him 'perverse' and 'inconsistent' in that the actions leading to this criminal charge were carried out with the full knowledge of senior staff at News International. 'Other members of staff were carrying out the same illegal procedures…. This practice was widely discussed in the daily editorial conference, until explicit reference to it was banned by the Editor. As far as I am aware, no other member of staff has faced disciplinary action, much less dismissal.'

What had escaped the media at the time Goodmand and Mulcaire were sentenced was the judge's telling remark towards Mulcaire. He said: 'As to Counts 16 to 20 [the phone-hacking of Max Clifford, Simon Hughes MP, Sky Andrew, Elle Macpherson and Gordon Taylor], you had not dealt with Goodman but with others at News International.' In other words, the judge supported what Goodman was claiming. This is worth remembering when looking at subsequent claims by News International to have got to the bottom of the matter. The police erroneously took this assertion by the judge to relate only to lawful research work.

Goodman demanded to be shown emails sent to him by six of his colleagues in the 16 months up to his imprisonment. News International refused the request, but asked a firm of lawyers, Harbottle & Lewis, to review the emails. They asserted that the messages did not provide evidence that the six other employees had knowledge of phone hacking. It was a decidedly partial use of their findings, Harbottle & Lewis later complained in court.

And over in Cheam, the Mulcaire family were having to get by without Glenn. Alison admits she didn't cope well. They would visit him in Belmarsh every Sunday, where he was torn between putting on a brave face for his beloved family and despairing in rage at how his employers had so spectacularly abandoned him. In his absence, Greg Miskiw, under whose news editorship Mulcaire's association with the *News of the World* had started, was in regular contact, an expression of support that the family took as genuine and heartfelt. Certainly it was received better than the earlier suggestion from reporter Neville Thurlbeck that Mulcaire and his family should 'move to a small village in Wales'. They felt they had no more reason to feel ashamed than, say, Neville Thurlbeck.

Ostensibly solicitous phone calls came from another executive, but this one still on the paper. One executive called – according to Alison's memory – every day during the first week that Mulcaire was in prison. 'He used to ring up and say "hello, how are you? How's Glenn getting on? How's the family coping", all that,' she recalls. 'I used to just stonewall… I always said yeah, yeah he's fine. And then towards the end of the call, you could tell what he was up to, he'd always say "Do you still have any of Glenn's emails… are there any emails in the house?" You knew he was worrying about anything that would incriminate other people.'

One day, soon after Mulcaire had learned – in a roundabout way, shall we say – of his release date, he was summoned to the prison governor of Belmarsh's office. He was asked if he was planning to write a book. Evidently, Lord Archer having shed a certain amount of light on his time at Her Majesty's Pleasure, the governor was hoping to be spared. 'Ask a journalist, they do the writing,' Mulcaire told him. But that didn't seem to be the governor's chief concern, and indeed, he had a second question. How had Mulcaire known before even the governor when he was going to be released?

The prison listens in to inmates' conversations, and Alison had been heard telling her husband that a well-connected friend had told her when Glenn was to be released. Glenn, knowing the call to Alison was monitored, had tried to laugh off the information as unreliable, but she, understandably anxious to raise his morale with some good news, had doggedly insisted on the reliability of her information. 'I'm hopeless at all that stuff,' she says. It is only and plentifully to her credit that that is easily believed.

The below the radar fretting of the guilty men was in striking contrast to their public lack of concern. It is a mark of how successful News International had been in sailing serenely on and closing down the hacking story that, within weeks of Andy Coulson resigning, George Osborne was meeting the former editor at a London hotel to talk to him about his working alongside David

Cameron. According to George Osborne's biographer, Coulson joked that on the day he had resigned, both Tony Blair and Gordon Brown had been touch to commiserate, and the fact that the Tories had taken much longer was a mark of how much they needed to up their media game. Anyone who knew the truth of how dirty Coulson's hands were would have been astonished at the affirmation of his unsinkability, as they would have been by his appointment. But few outside News International did.

Coulson and Steve Hilton, David Cameron's loyal friend and proprietorial conveyor of the Cameron message as campaign manager, had already been sizing one another up to see if they could work together. Hilton had given his blessing, and Osborne's benediction (though never in doubt as he had been one of the idea's midwives) was the next stage in his recruitment. If the waves were closing over the affair, publicly at least, that surely suited all concerned.

As the Coulson-Cameron courtship was getting under way, Mulcaire's solicitor Moray Laing emailed News International's lawyers again on 23rd February, this time in rather more urgent terms. He told the company that for legal purposes Mulcaire was effectively an employee of the *News of the World*, and was entitled to compensation. This was based on the paper's degree of control over Mulcaire's activities, the exclusivity of his services and the 'mutuality of obligation' that existed in showing he was treated the same as other employees. He also cited discussions with an News International individualwho on at least one occasion told Mulcaire that if he did not do the work he was instructed to do he would not be paid.

As an employee, therefore, he was claiming unfair dismissal, since the usual procedure had not been gone through. Laing said, further, that Mulcaire had been dismissed in part because of the possibility of his whistle blowing a) on the company and b) specifically on executives who had instructed him to access the voicemails of a number of individuals, including former Met boss Lord Stevens. ('He was the next on my list,' remembers Mulcaire now.) Laing said he had emails and audio evidence to support this claim. Mulcaire would be willing to come to a 'constructive conclusion... in a confidential fashion', he said. He favoured meeting in a constructive fashion, and that if that was not possible, proceedings would be issued.

If News International was worried about what tales Mulcaire could tell, it was doing a good job of pretending otherwise. Once again, Laing was made to wait. The email from the south London employment solicitor to the global conglomerate was ignored for some weeks. This may be a measure of the continuing high-handedness of News International management at the time, plus the fact that the relevant legal affairs person was on holiday for ten days after the email was sent. Even after his return, though, the email went unanswered for three weeks. He was prompted for a reply, and on 26th March he asked for the original to be sent again.

Goodman, too, was still seething. He had a meeting on 20th March with News International human resources, which he covertly recorded. Three weeks later, he met Rebekah Brooks, then editing the *Sun*, at the RAC club for lunch. Brooks suggested he work for her. When

Goodman expressed a doubt that she might be in a position to employ a sacked senior reporter such as himself, she said dismissively: 'I can employ who I like.' But the offer was temporary, not well-paid and – he told the Old Bailey – would undermine any thought of blowing the whistle on wrongdoing, so he turned it down. Asked in court about the job offer, Brooks said she 'wanted to stop him making unfounded allegations against the paper', having been assured by Coulson and others that there was no truth to what Goodman was claiming. (To her answer, her questioner replied: 'to shut him up'.)

Goodman wrote to News International on May 5th 2007, alleging that News International notes taken at a meeting he had attended some months earlier were grossly flawed and misrepresented much of his evidence. He identified 47 inaccuracies, which to those of a conspiratorial cast of mind was more than enough to suggest a shepherding of the evidence towards the narrative that subsequently emerged – namely that the blame was confined to as small a number of people as was credible. Equally, the note taker was evidently not well versed in the saga and can be excused some errors. In any event, Goodman listed a number of inaccuracies. While it was becoming evident that Goodman would probably stay silent about what he knew had been going on at the *News of the World*, it was equally clear that one year's salary was not going to be enough, and negotiations continued for some months. Nonetheless, his former bosses were not admitting to any concerns about the strength of his position.

By this time, the Tories had decided they wanted Andy

Coulson on board. He was in many respects just what they needed, but by any standards Coulson's copybook was shop-soiled. Two people had gone to prison on his watch, and another *News of the World* employee, recently sacked while being treated for depression, was bringing a legal case against him for bullying. The Tories needed to give at least a nod to due diligence and, according to a very senior Tory, wanted to reassure themselves that there were no further legal cases that would compromise Coulson's appointment.

By late April, News International were at last addressing Mulcaire's claim seriously. They met Moray Laing on 10th May, and on the following day Jon Chapman, the director of legal affairs at News International, made an offer for a full and final settlement. It was £80,000, which was £52,600 as half a year's salary, plus £10,000 in compensation. There was also, at Mulcaire's suggestion, a clause stipulating that Mulcaire 'assist/co-operate… in any investigation' into the events that led to the conviction' of Goodman and Mulcaire.

With hindsight, £80,000 looks a good deal less than what Mulcaire might have got. Certainly Mulcaire regrets not pushing for more, although Greg Miskiw at the *News of the World* Manchester office, who Mulcaire believed had his interests at heart, warned him 'if you don't take it, you'll get nothing'. 'It is one of the very few things Alison and I have disagreed about,' he says. 'I knew that a whole lot of people knew what I was doing on behalf of the company, and I didn't want to just roll up and concede, but Alison was worried about where our next meal and mortgage payment was coming from. Now of course she wishes we'd turned it down.'

As May came to an end, Mulcaire came to believe that this was as good an offer as they were going to get, and that he should accept. Now both Goodman and Mulcaire, far from exposing the fact that they were not 'rogues', were coming into line. Relief all round.

It may or may not be a coincidence that Andy Coulson was appointed as the Tory party's head of communications on 31st May. Only the Daily Mail expressed any surprise at the timing of the appointment, although even that may have had more to do with professional rivalry and the prospect of the Murdoch papers being closer to the prospective PM than Associated Newspapers.

Elsewhere, the legal skirmishing over the two 'rogues' was petering out. Mulcaire signed his agreement in the first week of June, but Goodman and News International were still being obdurate. On 10th May, at a meeting in Wapping, he had been told the company was 'minded to reject his appeal' over being sacked. A week later Rebekah Brooks emailed him, offering to send him on a sub-editing course, which a reporter of Goodman's experience could reasonably have regarded as a sideways step at best and which he ignored. On 30th May he was told his appeal had been formally rejected, upon which he announced he said he planned to appeal to a tribunal, which effectively meant going public.

Goodman got his reward for holding his nerve. Three days later, he recalls, he was called by the head of corporate and legal at News International Jon Chapman and offered another £50,000 to settle the employment claim. That was more like it. A few weeks later, after further negotiations, the company agreed a payment of a further £153,000, comprising £40,000 in compensation, £13,000 in legal expenses and a further £90,000 in notice. The company later struggled to explain how the supposedly disgraced reporter, to whom the company had threatened to pay nothing, was now receiving a second notice payment, totalling nearly two and a half times what he had been offered.

To most people, Goodman's threat to expose the extent of lawlessness had been seen off with the help of nearly £250,000. If so, he was not the last to apply such pressure. But executives at the company sought to explain everything. 'There was an issue of a long process,' they protested, 'which... was going to hamper the company's, or the newspaper's, opportunity to get back on track, and I decided at the time that the right thing to do was to settle this and get it behind us....' Jon Chapman agreed that this was not hush money, but was to 'allow the *News of the World* under its new editor to move on' and allow the paper 'to recover as a brand'. The company later said the size of the payment was in part down to its failure to follow statutory procedures. In any event, both Goodman and Mulcaire had been silenced.

Andy Coulson started work for the Conservatives on 9th July 2007. The phone hacking saga seemed to have died a very silent death.

8

'We Don't Need F**king Murdoch.'

The aspect of the phone hacking affair that most impinged on Westminster was the appointment of Andy Coulson to be David Cameron's communications chief on 31st May of 2007. Of all the decisions Cameron had to make as leader, it was the one to cause him the most unshakeable embarrassment. Cameron admitted within months of Coulson's resignation from Downing Street (accepted against Cameron's will) in January 2011 that, with hindsight, he would not have appointed him. And 29th June 2014 he apologised to the British people for having employed Coulson. Yet at the time it had barely caused a ripple in the media.

The first 18 months after David Cameron's December 2005 accession to the Tory leadership were characterised by an engaging lack of preparedness and a charming learn-on-the-job feel from the mostly youthful, tieless cohorts around him. Their eccentric and brilliant guiding light was Cameron's professional blue-skies thinker Steve Hilton, his former colleague and friend from Central Office.

The Cameron project owed a great deal to the blueprint of the man Cameron had been seeking to unseat, Tony Blair. The new leader and his prospective chancellor referred to Blair as 'the master', such was their admiration for a man who had helped turn Labour from the loser of four successive elections into a formidable election-winning machine. Having comprehensively lost three elections, the Tories, led by a new breed of careerist politicians, were not above learning some difficult lessons. And if that meant conveying some uncomfortable truths to their party – and possibly advertising their hard-headedness in doing so, as Blair had done – that was fine too.

One of the axioms of Hilton's thinking was that the old print media was continuing to lose its grip on the national conversation, and that voters were making their choices on the basis of what they had seen on television and in the new media.

So on that issue at least, the Tony Blair playbook was to be flung out of the window. The presumed need to secure the support of the Murdoch papers (the endorsement of the *Mail* and *Telegraph* groups was all but taken for granted) was to be defied. For these young men (mostly) on the make, that particular magnate had lost his power of attraction. In 2006 one of Cameron's closest lieutenants exclaimed off the record, to a journalist: 'We don't need fucking Murdoch.'

Such thinking was understandably the source of some frustration at News International, which had marched in step with Tony Blair for most of his time as Labour leader and which enjoyed the fact that for better or worse, politicians were forever on the phone trying to woo them. Murdoch and election-winners tended to go together. Psephologically they were as inseparable as the chicken and the egg.

But in early 2007, the Hilton media strategy thinking

wasn't cutting the mustard. Notting Hill's clever young media types were delighted when Cameron advocated hugging hoodies on housing estates and huskies in the Arctic, and the newness of it all certainly caught the eye, but the polls didn't suggest it was going down well, and the old-fashioned press worried that the whipper-snapper had gone too far. Further, why was someone as self-evidently traditional as Cameron adopting these outlandish positions? Was there nothing he wouldn't say to win office? With Gordon Brown by contrast – seemingly bristling with conviction and serious intent – about to take over as prime minister and with a snap election a clear possibility, Cameron risked looking rootless and lightweight. He told friends it was conceivable he would have to quit the leadership by the end of the year.

At about the same time, an answer to a nagging problem presented itself. Cameron's lead press adviser, the low-key, ultra-loyal George Eustice, was looking for a parliamentary seat. If successful, he would be unavailable to David Cameron after the election, whenever that came. Besides, Cameron had been feeling the need of a 'heavy-hitter', someone with presence and comment-page experience who would command respect among senior journalists. Many people were approached, but those who wanted the job were not quite right. Those best qualified didn't want it.

The solution was Andy Coulson, recently deposed as editor of the *News of the World*. For him and his predecessor, Rebekah Brooks, the dismissing Goodman and Mulcaire's exploits as a rogue operation seemed to have avoided what could have been an almighty scandal.

(To the bemusement of those who knew how the *News of the World* operated, this close call had done nothing to trim/curtail the rise and rise of Rebekah Brooks. She continued as editor of the *Sun* and to enjoy the support and indulgence of her boss Rupert Murdoch.)

Given Murdoch's penchant for backing winners, his endorsement would add enormous credibility to any politician's ambitions. So just as Cameron's jejune experiment in defying the press barons was coming to an end, the availability of Coulson was perfectly timed. Indeed, there may have been a degree of cause and effect.

The problem, though, was that Murdoch needed convincing about Cameron and Rebekah Brooks was to be the architect of winning him over. With James Murdoch in tow, she set about persuading the media baron. David Cameron, of course, lapped this up. He showed a puppyish and uncharacteristically light-headed willingness to please her and her bosses. Although she has denied it, Rebekah Brooks has been mooted as the person who suggested initially to George Osborne that Coulson, with whom she was effectively still in a relationship, albeit a complicated one, was the person for the job.

Though not renowned as a political player, Coulson promised the sort of knowledge of the real world that the Cameron entourage notably lacked. His modest Essex background ticked the social mobility box, and he was known as highly competent and professional. Who better to help change Rupert Murdoch's privately stated view that there would never be another Etonian in No 10? Murdoch, after all, had agreed to give him a substantial payoff, presumably believing – to a degree at least – that he had been hard done by. Other lieutenants of the Tory leader knew and liked Coulson, including Michael Gove and William Hague, whose goodwill towards the Murdoch papers had been cemented four years earlier by being given a £200,000-a-year column for the *News of the World*. (Hague may not have known – may still not – that in 1998 it had been Coulson's idea to portray the Tory party as a dead parrot, with Hague's head superimposed, on the *Sun*'s front page, or that Coulson had voted Labour the year before.)

Coulson had many attributes, and it would be a mistake to say he was chosen solely because of his News International pedigree. One close Cameron associate said: 'We should talk to this guy, and when he came in, I thought this is the guy, and he did a brilliant job for us. We'd been saying "where's our Alastair Campbell?", and this seemed to be it.' But his News International connections cannot have done his prospects any harm. One account says that Rebekah Brooks edged another candidate, Guto Harri, aside because he was not 'acceptable' to News International. According to a story in the *Mail on Sunday*, 'Rebekah indicated the job should go to Andy. Cameron was told it should be someone acceptable to News International. The company was also desperate to find something for Andy after he took the rap when the phone hacking first became an issue. The approach was along the lines of, "If you find something for Andy we will return the favour."' The story has the ring of truth, but the fact that such a possibility could even be entertained says much about Cameron's new-found desperation to win Murdoch's approval.

When the shadow cabinet was told of the decision to hire Coulson, it was presented as a *fait accompli*, with barely the faintest discussion. Cameron and Osborne were delighted. There was no sense that the appointment needed explaining or excusing, an attitude the press coverage seemed to endorse, perhaps revealing a concern about journalists' need to work closely with Coulson. The editor of the right-wing *Spectator*, Matthew d'Ancona, might have been speaking for Downing Street when he wrote: 'That's a real coup for them because Andy's a very good journalist and highly respected.'

It is hard to credit that more hurdles were not put in the way of Coulson's appointment. With hindsight we can see that Coulson, fresh from presiding over illegality and with several hundred thousand pounds in his hip pocket, was being given a top job, presumably to the delight of his then lover Rebekah Brooks. Certainly, considering what is now known about his immediate past, it is extraordinary that anything other than disaster was expected to come from it.

Moderately well-informed journalists at the time could have told the Tories that Coulson had been reluctant to resign, but it was agreed that a senior head had to roll if the impression of a clean-up was to be convincingly conveyed. Coulson would not have been human had he not thought 'Why me?' when so many others who knew about red-top methods were spared. But as captain of the ship, he acknowledged the symbolic importance of a price being paid. The Fleet Street consensus was that Andy would be 'looked after' once the affair had blown over. For sure, financially he was looked after, whether his resignation was voluntary or not. In News

International, it looked as if he was the sacrificial lamb.

How would Cameron explain the hiring of someone with a questionable recent record? The line he decided to take, a colleague recalls, was that he had been reassured that Coulson's past was nothing to worry about, and later on, if that didn't wash, he would say that, Coulson having lost his job, there was no reason why he should be punished twice. In the event, Cameron didn't have to answer questions about Coulson's past for a couple of years, something which seemed to vindicate the decidedly lax appointment process.

So what had Coulson been asked, when he took the job, and what had he said? This remains a thorny issue.

Osborne had a drink with Coulson at a London hotel. He told the Leveson inquiry that he asked Coulson, 'in a general sense, as you might do in a social encounter, whether there was more in the phone-hacking story that was going to come out, that was not already public, that we needed to know about – and he said "no". According to George Osborne's biographer, Janan Ganesh, on the way back from the hotel, Osborne called Cameron to say Coulson was open to an offer of employment.

A number of people asked David Cameron privately if he was sure he was doing the right thing in appointing Coulson, but his mind was made up. One senior former Fleet Street editor told Cameron the very fact of having edited the *News of the World* meant an editor would have done things that would disqualify him from holding such high office. But Cameron's biggest concern was quite different. He was fixated on the idea that there would be a repeat of what had happened to William Hague, whose media adviser Amanda Platell had written a video diary while in the job and which hugely embarrassed Hague subsequently. If that could be resolved (which it was), Cameron was sold on the idea, and as a tidy-minded politician, he hates going back on decisions. Coulson was to be his media magus, the man to help steer him to Downing Street.

As far as Coulson's own pronouncements are concerned, a certain amount of mythology has built up. The phrase Andy Coulson 'has always denied knowing' (about the phone hacking) became something of a mantra in the media. In fact, it is quite inaccurate. The press bought the most spectacular dummy. When he resigned from the *News of the World*, Coulson issued no such denial, nor did he do so for more than two years afterwards. As former prime minister James Callaghan once said, a lie can be half way round the world before the truth has got its boots on. In the digital age, that should read 'several times' round the world.

Coulson, well-rewarded and heading for David Cameron's office had to walk a tightrope. On the one hand Murdoch had to be convinced that Coulson knew nothing in order to secure his payoff. Murdoch would surely not have compensated a guilty man so generously. On the other, Coulson couldn't publicly deny it in case any concrete evidence came out, because in that case he would have been showed to have lied, which would cause him to lose that job and jeopardise the great News International switch from Labour to the Conservatives.

And so, on 26th January 2007, an enduring untruth was born, when journalists, possibly briefed by people who knew no better, were given the impression that Coulson had known nothing of what royal correspondent Clive Goodman and private investigator Glenn Mulcaire had been up to. It became the accepted truth even though, in Coulson's own statement, there was no such denial. He said merely 'I deeply regret that [these actions] happened on my watch'. The closest anyone came to an on the record denial was when Les Hinton, News International executive chairman, told the Commons Committee on Culture Media and Sport in March that the editor 'told me he had no knowledge of this activity but … [felt he had to resign]'. There was to be no explicit denial for more than two years.

Did this glaring omission not raise concerns when the Tories came to do the due diligence on Coulson? Seemingly not. Indeed, there is no sign of anyone having even noticed. 'Our biggest concern was to check whether all the court cases had concluded, whether there were outstanding tribunals,' said one leading Conservative, perhaps aware that Clive Goodman had launched a case against the paper for unfair dismissal (although surely in normal circumstances a cabinet minister would not normally know that). Coulson's appointment was announced on 31st May. The settling of Glenn Mulcaire's case for unfair dismissal was imminent, but the case brought by sacked sports reporter Matt Driscoll, who eventually won a huge payout for bullying against the *News of the World*, had barely got off the ground.

But who had made sure that there was nothing in Coulson's past that might embarrass the Tories? The answers here are inadequate, and there is no sign it even struck anyone as odd that he had issued no public denial.

Early on in the saga, in one of Cameron's few statements on the matter, he was strikingly vague as to who had reassured him Coulson was in the clear: 'I am satisfied that Andy Coulson was not aware that a journalist at the News of the World was engaged in this practice.'

A version of events has been proposed by journalist Matthew d'Ancona, a defender of Coulson. In his book *In It Together*, d'Ancona claims that Cameron's conversation with Coulson was the subject of wilfull blindness. When Cameron had raised the issue, Coulson had chosen a form of words which suggested he knew nothing of the detail of what the pair were doing on that particular occasion, but didn't deny knowing about the widespread practice of phone hacking. Cameron, we are invited to believe, takes Coulson to mean he knew nothing at all. 'Coulson had said one thing and Cameron had heard – or remembered – quite another.'

D'Ancona's offer of a lifeboat wins points for generosity and novelty, but is still damning for Cameron. Coulson's version – that he said something like 'no, I didn't know what Goodman and Mulcaire were up to' and that that was effectively the end of the conversation – leaves the Prime Minister looking either a fool or a knave. If he is a fool, it is for failing not to spot the evasiveness of his reply, which seems unlikely. Or a knave, because Cameron is perfectly aware of the inadequacy of the denial, but cynically turns a blind eye, knowing that one day, in extremis, he'd be able to accuse Coulson of misleading him. The second option suited them both, but if true, suggests Cameron, by nature trusting and generous-spirited, had no interest in knowing the truth about Coulson's past, only in his ability to help get him into Downing Street. What d'Ancona calls Cameron's wilful blindness in his context is not that of an indulgent parent benignly pretending not to see a child taking the last biscuit. It is taking a gamble, knowing a course of action is highly risky and still pursuing it in the hope that no one will notice.

And for a while, no one did, or seemed to. In the absence of further evidence of phone hacking, the issue seemed to have gone for good. The politics of the affair returned below the public's radar. But it was no less vigorous for that.

Rebekah Brooks and David Cameron had decided they had shared interests. Cameron knew he needed her support if he was to persuade the Murdoch papers to endorse the Tories, and she knew that getting on with prime ministers (potential and actual) never did her any harm. Happily at about this time she was beginning a relationship with Charlie Brooks, a school contemporary of Cameron's brother Alex, whose family lived in Sarsden near Cameron's constituency home of Dean, in Oxfordshire. As we have seen, Brooks has few rivals in her capacity to love-bomb people she wants to get on with, and Cameron, not reluctant, came under sustained assault. Rebekah was constantly popping round at the weekend and bumping into Cameron at one or other home of the illustrious Cotswolds circle that became known as the Chipping Norton set. 'They do see an awful lot of Rebekah,' said a surprised friend of Cameron, struggling to see what the pair had in common.

The ingratiation reached a new level when Rebekah, at the early stages of her relationship with Brooks, a raffish horseman of the old school who had given her a pair of Hermès riding boots, decided she would like to acquire a retired police horse. David Cameron had been brought up in the countryside, had tried and enjoyed hunting comparatively recently and had expressed an interest in taking up riding again. It was a further opportunity to ingratiate herself with Cameron, a prospect Cameron showed little inclination to resist.

The horse story, which oddly given his brief, Lord Justice Leveson regarded as a trivial issue, was one of those microcosms that reveals a far bigger truth, both in itself and as a result of its revelation. In late February 2012, Tom Harper reported in the London *Evening Standard* that Rebekah Brooks had been loaned a retired horse by the Metropolitan Police. This gave rise to a good deal of merriment, and a twitter account @Rebekah'sHorse quickly attracted followers.

Christopher Hope, a journalist on the *Telegraph*, asked if David Cameron had ever ridden the horse, named Raisa. Initially Cameron's spokesman sought to portray the inquiry as not even deserving of a response. Two days later, Cameron sought to clear things up with a denial. 'Since becoming PM I may have got on a horse once, but not that one,' he said, ducking the issue of whether he had ridden the horse beforehand. Eventually he came clean, confirming that he had indeed ridden Raisa and had known that she had been loaned her by the Met. The intriguing lack of candour chimed with Downing Street's denial a year earlier of a claim that he and Charlie Brooks had ever been riding together, which they had.

So why so evasive? The reason, it can now be revealed, is that the horse was acquired from the police by Brooks *partly for David Cameron's use.* It is a story which speaks volumes about both her and Cameron.

In the summer of 2007, over lunch with Ian Blair, head of the Metropolitan Police, Rebekah Brooks and the Met's head of media, Dick Fedorcio agreed that a horse should be provided for Brooks. In September 2007, she and Dick Fedorcio went to the Met's horse training centre at Imber Court to find a suitable beast. Alan Hiscox, the Met's longest serving boss at Imber Court, remembers: 'I got a call a day or two after Ian Blair and Rebekah [Brooks] had seen one another. It was from his staff officer, I think. I was asked if I knew who [she] was. I said I did and was told Ian Blair had just had a meal with her and that she would like a retired police horse. I was told that this would, "definitely be a good idea for the Met Police."'

Hiscox remembers that it was clear 'people in authority' were interested in the issue. 'I had calls from both Dick Fedorcio and Rebekah Brooks's PA asking when a horse would be ready.' In about October, Hiscox went to the Cotswolds to meet Rebekah and Charlie Brooks to check on the riding and stabling facilities near their house where a horse would be kept. He declared himself satisfied with the conditions, and impressed by the stable manager – 'clearly knowledgeable about horses' – who would be giving Mrs Brooks lessons.

What happened next took Hiscox by surprise. He remembers: 'As we were being shown round the stables she told me that David Cameron would also be riding the retired police horse. At the time I did not think much of it, other than to wonder why she told me that. She may have been trying to show off, but it was a curious thing to say.'

Hiscox returned to his office and told his boss that the stables were satisfactory and passed on the information that Cameron would be riding the horse. 'This information would have been passed up the chain and I feel sure Dick Fedorcio and Ian Blair would have known', says Hiscox. The horse arrived in July 2008, but when it was clear it was hardly being ridden it was returned to Imber Court. Hiscox defends Charlie Brooks against the charge that he had not cared for the horse. 'When it was returned the horse looked as if it had been put to grass for some time. Clearly it had not been ridden or groomed much, but there was no suggestion by me that it had been mistreated, as was claimed in the press. Quite rightly, Charlie Brooks was cross at this suggestion.'

'It struck me as quite odd that everyone was so evasive about the retired police horse,' said Hiscox. 'Why did David Cameron's office not say he had ridden the horse in the first instance? I have nothing to hide about this episode and it wasn't clear to me why they were so embarrassed about it. It is possible, I suppose, that Rebekah Brooks was trying to ingratiate herself with Mr Cameron and that she had told him she was going to get it for him, but in normal circumstances it should not have been a big deal.'

As the Brooks-Cameron equestrian bonding proceeded, at about the same time, late 2008, Andy Coulson was asked by a journalist, this book's author, to clear up what at the time might have been a misapprehension. Coulson had claimed, in a private conversation, that in his resignation statement he had denied knowledge of phone hacking. He was subsequently asked, on the record, to clarify where this denial was to be found, which of course he was unable to do (having done no such thing). Having not demurred when confronted with his non-denial, he was also asked, simply: did he know about the phone hacking? The answer he gave begged more questions about other versions of events. He asked to go off the record, giving an inconsequential reply. He was then asked: 'Now, on the record, are you saying you knew nothing about the phone hacking at the *News of the World*?' There was a long pause, and he said: 'I really have nothing to add to what I've said before.' He was given another opportunity to answer the question, but he didn't take it. In other words, he was choosing to continue with his non-denial stance.

This was curious. If he didn't know about the phone hacking, why not say so? If he did know, he had either come clean to anyone who asked him about it, which presumably would have made him unfit for the job, or he had lied. If the latter, why did he not repeat the same lie to me? Or, with hindsight (the d'Ancona version had not been published at that point), maybe he had only been willing to deny knowing about the fine detail of what Mulcaire and Goodman were up to? In which case, what an interesting conversation that must have been.

It was not until July 2009, by which time his ducking of the issue could no longer be ignored, that Coulson made his first public denial. The *Guardian* had just revealed that PFA chairman Gordon Taylor had been paid £700,000 by News International to drop his breach of privacy complaint. The obvious question was why was News International so keen to keep him quiet if they had so little to hide? Rebekah, having just married Charlie

Brooks and been made chief executive of News International, should have been asked the question then, but wasn't. And fortunately for Coulson, he was able to say that he had nothing to do with the settlement, having left the paper some time earlier. Privately he was more worried. He spoke to Cameron's private advisor Ed Llewellyn and told him he understood that the time might have come for him to go.

But Coulson told the House of Commons Media Select Committee 'my instructions to the staff were clear – we did not use subterfuge of any kind unless there was a clear public interest in doing so. They were to work within the PCC code at all times'.

Matthew d'Ancona has reported how, in preparation for a trip to Afghanistan, Cameron and Coulson had undergone training together to learn what to do in the event of being kidnapped. One lesson they had learnt was that if one of their group was raped, the others should embrace him, by way of showing solidarity. When Coulson returned from his Select Committee grilling, in a gesture that shows more decency than judgment, Cameron interrupted a meeting to embrace Coulson.

But privately he was advised that no good would come of Coulson's continuing presence by his side, and the drip-drip of news was not encouraging. Nor was Coulson's confessional assertion that 'I wasn't running sweet shop, Dave.' So Cameron invited Guy Black, his predecessor at Conservative Central Office in the late 1980s and much more recently a fulcrum first of the Press Complaints Commission and then of Press Standards Board of Finance, which oversaw and funded the PCC, to a quiet supper at his home in Notting Hill.

Assuming Black would be familiar with the ways of the press, Cameron, understandably concerned by the continuing revelations, asked Black if he thought he should be concerned. Black reassured him, saying no, apparently believing, as many did, that since the police long had the evidence and nothing new and substantial had emerged, that was that. When surprise was expressed that the worldly Black should believe that to be the case, it was pointed out that Rebekah Brooks was one of the witnesses at his civil partnership ceremony. 'He does believe it, but even if he doesn't, he's not likely to dump on his best man, is he?' said a friend of Black's.

Following the 2010 election, when Mr Cameron became prime minister at the head of a coalition government, he insisted on Coulson staying on board. He wanted and needed him, he felt, and took a gamble on the whole thing going away, a hope that infected his whole office.

Coulson had made himself a key member of the team by now. Cameron respected his opinion and knew he stood for a part of the electorate poorly represented among the rest of his circle. And of course he was well known to the press, particularly his former colleagues at News International, where he was not bashful about using his standing as a former editor when suggesting ideas for his former paper, the *Sun*. While it would be an exaggeration to say that News International editors 'took dictation' from No 10, Coulson's word carried a lot of weight. The headline 'Bottler Brown', for example, accompanied by a mocked up picture of a bottle of beer with Gordon Brown's face on it, after he failed to call a snap election in 2007, was widely assumed in

Westminster to have been Coulson's idea, as was the portrayal of Brown as a tenant who wouldn't budge from No 10 two days after the 2010 election. Dominic Mohan, the *Sun*'s editor from 2009 to 2013, who succeeded Rebekah Brooks, was regarded by Coulson as always receptive to good ideas.

The issue of Coulson's security vetting once he reached Downing Street is often raised, and still there are no satisfactory answers. A minimal check had been done on him in 2007, but to work in Downing Street required a higher level of clearance. However, he was not subjected to 'Developed Vetting', as his predecessor Alastair Campbell had been, which has given rise to a good deal of speculation.

Due probably to an oversight, Coulson is believed to have been privy to files that should only have been seen by those who have been 'DV-ed', because colleagues assumed he had been. But the question of why Sir Jeremy Heywood did not insist on Coulson facing such scrutiny remains unanswered. One serving police officer with extensive high-level experience in counter-subversion reports: 'You can imagine what happened. If the boss wants someone, that's that. So if he says: 'Get him in', all the protocols go out of the window. They jump to it.' Cameron, though, says it was entirely a matter for the civil service.

After Cameron became Prime Minister – thanks in part to the endorsement of the *Sun* – an idea that had been mooted by the Murdoch clan became a concrete goal. News Corporation decided to try to acquire the 61% of broadcaster BSkyB that it did not already own. The decision as to whether this should be allowed to go ahead, or whether it was in breach of competition law, was likely to be a political one. On the government side the decision was put into the hands of a Liberal Democrat, Vince Cable, the Business secretary, but the closeness of Cameron to the bigwigs at Wapping gave rise to suspicion that News Corporation was angling for, and possibly getting, preferential treatment. This concern did not abate with the revelation that in the fifteen months after the election, Cameron had 26 meetings with its executives. The Prime Minister's office had been called upon to compile a list of these meetings, but it forgot several of them, including the fact that Rebekah Brooks (to the surprise of his oldest friends) had been invited to Cameron's exclusive 44th birthday party at Chequers. Small wonder that Cameron was so shifty about the extent to which they socialised, or that, for example, at a point-to-point they texted one another to agree to meet in a marquee, to avoid being seen arriving together.

Some months after the 2010 election, Cameron's director of strategy Steve Hilton was given confidential and legally sensitive information about Coulson's acquaintance with certain aspects of the dark arts. Hilton passed it on to Ed Llewellyn, Cameron's chief of staff, but for reasons still unclear, the information was not passed on to the PM. Cameron did not like going back on his decisions. Besides, why should he, he thought. When under pressure to sack Coulson, he told an aide: 'You can't just sack people on hearsay.' Not that he wanted to get rid of Coulson in any case. On the contrary. Coulson had given Cameron's media operation a notably tougher edge, and the pair had become friends. In their three and a half years together, Cameron was warned that, as further investigations continued, Coulson's past would come back to haunt him, but it was news Cameron just did not want to hear.

Only when the mood music from News International changed did Cameron reluctantly accept Coulson's recognition that he had to go. It was not a moment too soon. In July of the same year it was revealed that Milly Dowler, a kidnapped (and murdered, it later emerged) Surrey schoolgirl had had her voicemails listened to. The story became politically unignorable. The *News of the World* was closed down by News International, Andy Coulson was arrested, the News Corporation bid for BskyB was withdrawn and Rebekah Brooks resigned from her position at News International. The deluge of scandal was threatening to engulf the PM himself. Cameron's closeness to Brooks and Coulson was laying him open to charges of impropriety. He set up the far-reaching Leveson inquiry, to look into the practices of the press. Its scope went far further than many in the press felt necessary, but Cameron was in charge when some fairly major law-breaking became evident. If he was to show he was personally beyond reproach, he had little choice, but it was a move that many in the newspaper world resented.

Cameron's performance in front of Leveson was notable for his nervousness. He said he had agreed with his Cabinet Office Minister Francis Maude MP and his chief of staff Ed Llewellyn about the importance of obtaining assurances from Coulson, and Cameron said the pair had asked Coulson, but Coulson himself had no recollection of any such questioning. Cameron told Leveson he had sought assurances himself from Coulson about phone hacking, in a meeting in the Norman Shaw building in Westminster. 'I remember it was very important that I ask him that question,' he added.

Coulson recalled speaking to Cameron in a phone call in which Cameron said security checks had been done on him. That call effectively confirmed he had got the job. Coulson said Mr Cameron had called while on holiday in Cornwall (seemingly it was the same call). 'Mr Cameron sought assurances about his knowledge of the hacking at the *News of the World*. I was able to repeat what I said publicly, that I knew nothing about the Clive Goodman and Glenn Mulcaire case *in terms of what they did*,' he said. Here was the fogginess that formed the basis of the account published by Matthew d'Ancona. 'In terms of what they did' could mean anything. Asked whether any further assurances were sought by Mr Cameron in relation to the matter, Mr Coulson replied: 'Not that I recall.'

Cameron had told the House of Commons he had hired Coulson 'on the basis of assurances he gave me that he did not know about the phone hacking and was not involved in criminality'.

The reality was that Coulson had been hired on the basis of an assurance he would give only in private. Two years later he did finally give a public denial, but still neither man spelt out what he had said when he was hired. As time went on and the issue refused to go away, Cameron's concern grew. He sought to spread the blame when he said: 'I think on all sides of the House there's a bit of a need for a hand on heart. We all did too much cosying up to Rupert Murdoch.' Finally, in June 2014, after Coulson's conviction for phone hacking, he apologised for his decision to hire Coulson, and strongly implied he had been lied to.

During Coulson's time at his side, Cameron had asked many people, including Rupert Murdoch, who said there was nothing new in the story, and that the police had all the evidence. This, of course, was true. Everybody had been too trusting, nobody really knew how redtop newspapers worked, including the press regulatory body, and the police dropped the catch.

So, it was all the Met's fault apparently.

9

Milly Dowler

The story that transformed the allegations of phone hacking from a tale of marginal interest with little traction beyond the media village was that of Milly Dowler. On Thursday 21st March 2002, the 13 year old schoolgirl took a train at the end of the schoolday at Heathside Comprehensive from Weybridge, but she never reached her home in Walton-on-Thames, Surrey. Normally she got off at Hersham, but this day she got off at the first stop, Walton. There she stopped briefly to go to a coffee bar with a friend. At just past 4.00pm, she said goodbye and began on the ten-minute walk home. She was never heard from again.

At 7.12pm, her father, whom she had called shortly before 4.00pm to say she'd be home soon, called the police. It was a call that was to spark searches of more than 350 locations and countless news stories. If ever there was a story made for the *News of the World*, it was this one. The paper had been campaigning for 2 years for greater public scrutiny of sex offenders, and here was a story that seemed to vindicate that demand. A blameless schoolgirl disappears unaccountably within yards of her home. As the media cliché has it, it was every parent's nightmare, an eventuality most parents find too horrifying to contemplate in reasoned terms.

Stories at the time speculated as to who would want to kidnap a lively young teenager. There seemed to be no reason why she might go missing of her own volition, although police did attend a school disco on the Friday night, for which she had bought a ticket, in the hope that she might turn up there. More than 50 extra police officers were brought in to search empty buildings, allotments and wasteland, and a helicopter with a thermal imaging camera deployed. Local people rallied round with help and expressions of support. A thousand posters showing the girl's face were put up around the area. Milly's father Bob said he and his wife Sally had been 'absolutely overwhelmed' by the extent of people's kindness.

In cold-blooded media terms, it was by any standards a big story. Everyone wanted to read about the Dowler family, whose everyday lives, comparable to those millions newspaper readers in the UK, had been so shatteringly disrupted. Papers vied with one another to solve the case. The chase was on, and the sparring of stablemates, under normal circumstances unseen by the public, came out more than ever. The *Sun*, then edited by David Yelland, had reason to claim the story as its own, a feeling amplified by his personal antipathy for Rebekah Brooks then editor of the *News of the World*. The greatest prize for any paper, of course, would be to restore Milly, as the media proprietorially referred to her, alive and well to her parents. Reporters set about their duties with such a 'trophy' in mind.

As far as what was evident to the public at the time was concerned, the nation was united in its desire to find Milly. The problem was, there were precious few leads. It was apparent that police were checking on Milly's close family, but 6 days after her disappearance, they were admitting they were baffled. 'We are obviously looking into abduction but if she had been forced into a vehicle against her will it is astonishing that not a single person on a busy main road on a bright sunny afternoon saw anything at all,' he said. 'I would have expected someone to register something. A 13-year-old is not going to go with someone against her will without a struggle.'

The idea that she might have planned her own disappearance, for reasons unknown, began to be floated. There was vague talk of a possible 'secret boyfriend', but there was not the faintest sign of one, so this was more about official desperation than anything. The area around the Dowlers' house was the focus of the search, with police checking the allotments, gardens and streams between Walton railway station, her home and Hersham station.

Curiously, Sarah Payne had grown up in Hersham, within miles of the Dowlers. Her killer, Roy Whiting, had been jailed for life the previous year. Police officers from that inquiry had been brought in to advise, but were able to shed little light. A police spokesman said the Dowlers' home 'remains the most fertile ground for possible clues as to where Amanda [Milly] may be or why she has disappeared. The search is with the full and free consent of Mr and Mrs Dowler and none of the family are suspects in this investigation.'

There was a flurry of activity when, two weeks later, the *News of the World* claimed she had applied for a job with an employment agency. On 14th April, the first edition of the *News of the World* ran a story headlined

'Milly "hoax' riddle", which suggested that messages had been left on her phone after she vanished. Specifically, it reported that at 10.13am, on 27th March, just six days after Milly had disappeared, a woman left a voicemail message saying: 'Hello Mandy. We're ringing because we have some interviews starting. Can you call me back? Thank you. Bye bye.' It also mentioned two other calls. The second edition, which went to press at around 9.30, contained a similar story, but talked in more veiled terms about voicemail messages and omitted the verbatim quote from the agency. In the last edition, the story was changed again. It referred to a '"hoax" outrage', and reported that 'a deranged woman has been posing as the missing youngster'.

Similarly, interest peaked when, separately, a body was found nearby, word getting round quickly, but erroneously, that Milly had been found dead.

The police's obvious struggle to make any progress was causing concern. Mark Williams-Thomas, a former a detective constable in Surrey's child-protection squad, acknowledging the difficulties the force faced, expressed a commonly held concern. Two and a half weeks after Milly's disappearance, he was quoted as saying: 'They don't seem to have a clue what has happened to her.' He added, 'I heard recently that they had taken away a computer from her home, but they seem to have done that only recently, while it should have been one of the first things they did.'

Seven weeks after Milly's disappearance, the *News of the World* managed to have a photographer at the scene when her parents conducted a re-enactment, intended to be in secret, of her walk home from the station. It was not until that September that a shocking revelation was made. Police found the decomposing body in woodland in Yateley Heath, Hampshire, on September 18 2002. Levi Bellfield, by then convicted of two other murders, was found guilty of her murder on 23 June 2011.

The story had exercised a lot of journalists and alarmed the reading public. Its monstrous cumulation was extensively covered, but then it faded from the news pages. There was little new to write, and even the papers that had championed her cause could see little to be gained from stories that would merely amplify the silence. The story exploded again late on Monday 4th July 2011 when the *Guardian*'s Nick Davies reported that Milly Dowler's voicemails had been unlawfully intercepted. It was among a large number of cases revealed by the paper, including many victims of crime, and caused such widespread outrage that it catalysed the closing down of the *News of the World* and the resignation of chief executive Rebekah Brooks, News International's Legal manager Tom Crone, Les Hinton of Dow Jones and one of Rupert Murdoch's closest lieutenants.

Included in the story came a comparably calamitous claim, with an even more obvious human angle – that whoever had hacked into her voicemail had deleted messages on her voicemail. Sally Dowler later told the Leveson inquiry how she had rung her daughter's phone many times before the message box filled up. 'It clicked through on her voicemail, so I heard her voice, and it was just like, "She's picked up her voicemail, Bob. She's alive."' This cruel 'false hope' allegation was the most explosive story of all, with its suggestion that there were no lengths to which newspapers would not go to beat their rivals. Mulcaire's name appeared in the article together with that of the *News of the World*, and the inference as to the culprit was an obvious one.

A storm erupted, the story having become unignorable, even for News International's most loyal outlets. The *Sun* carried a prominent story reporting that Rebekah Brooks found the allegations 'almost too horrific to believe'. The Chief Executive wrote: 'I am sickened that these events are alleged to have happened. Not just because I was editor of the *News of the World* at the time, but if the accusations are true, the devastating effect on Milly Dowler's family is unforgivable.'

David Cameron, called upon to respond during a visit to Afghanistan, said the allegation that Milly Dowler's phone messages had been intercepted were 'quite quite shocking… a truly dreadful act'. The Dowlers' lawyer Mark Lewis said: 'It is distress heaped upon tragedy to learn that the *News of the World* had no humanity at such a terrible time.'

In the public airing of the story about Milly Dowler's disappearance, Mulcaire's name had barely been mentioned. Now he was centre stage. The next day, on 5 July, the *Guardian* published a statement by Mulcaire through his lawyer: 'I want to apologise to anybody who was hurt or upset by what I have done. I've been to court. I've pleaded guilty. And I've gone to prison and been punished. I still face the possibility of further criminal prosecution. Working for the *News of the World* was never easy. There was relentless pressure. There was a constant demand for results.'

This was pretty much the first thing Mulcaire had

uttered in public for four years. Dr Evil, as he perceived the public to regard him, had been lured from his lair to answer charges of being even more shameless and uncaring than he had hitherto appeared. But he said no more, and slunk back into the shadows. That was the story as the newspapers reported it, for better or worse. So far, so public.

The story was not as it seemed, however. Mulcaire, it emerged in court in 2014, had indeed hacked into Milly Dowler's voicemails, and for many, there need be no further discussion. But his claim for mitigation is striking and worthy of every bit as much scrutiny as those journalists who claim they were 'just trying to find Milly'.

As for the 'false hope moment', Mulcaire, looking back 9 years, was confused. He had not confirmed he had been responsible for any such thing. The *Guardian* article of 4 July had not directly accused him, but nor had it cleared him. It seemed that he probably was responsible, but he could not understand how. Beyond the human considerations, the suggestion that he might have deleted a voicemail was an affront to his humanity and his professional sense of self. He had built a lucrative career on treading stealthily. The inept deletion of voicemails suggested a crassness, an artlessness, that undermined the professionalism upon which he prided himself. Only someone lacking his knowhow could have done such a thing, he thought, and yet, from his outcast's vantage point in 2011, cut off from most of those in the know, the newspapers were reporting that he had blundered spectacularly. Was it possible they were right? After the *Guardian*'s allegation, he was distraught. It was a dose of his own medicine, some might say, but he was adamant that his motivation and competence had not been at fault.

In fact, the *Guardian*'s story turned out to be wrong in a key respect. Voicemails had indeed been deleted from Milly Dowler's phone, but they were nothing like as easily explained as the paper had claimed (and, it seems, as the police also believed). Indeed, to this day, there is dispute as to how they came to be wiped. And in inviting the inference that Glenn Mulcaire had been culpable, the *Guardian*'s article sent the investigator into an unprecedented emotional turmoil.

Mulcaire, with his 'Special Projects' role and track record in such cases at *News of the World*, had been straining at the leash to look into the case after Dowler disappeared on that Thursday afternoon in March 2002. When he was tasked, finally, he started a file called Project Dowler, as if to emphasise that this wasn't 'any old job'. Yet, contrary to common belief, he wasn't asked until others had failed. The public narrative which suited many of the others involved in the whole saga has placed Mulcaire firmly in the role of baddie, the man in the black hat at whom the audience boos ritually. And as long as the 'rogue' who had 'gone off the reservation' remained silent, gagged by expensive lawyers, he would retain that role, rightly or wrongly.

So a key fact in the story is the following. The police log revealed that in fact the 'false hope' moment happened on Sunday 24th March. Mulcaire was not tasked to look for Milly Dowler until Wednesday 10th April, nearly three weeks after she had disappeared, almost three weeks after the cruellest privacy invasion of all. It was in few people's interest to point this out, but the *Guardian*, the leader in the field of phone-hacking studies, had let itself down, a fact some of its rivals – never keen on the phone hacking story – were not slow to advertise. In her initial recollection of the matter, Sally Dowler said she thought the 'false hope' moment had happened in April or May, which was indeed after Mulcaire had been tasked.

If someone had deleted her messages on or before 24th March (as seems highly likely), it was almost certainly not Mulcaire. A human story as touching and engrossing as this one had a great many journalists seeking answers. Given how widespread phone hacking was in certain sections of the market, it would not be surprising if someone's zeal had not got the better of them.

Mulcaire couldn't understand what had happened, but the fact that so many people believed he was responsible for the false hope moment was mortifying. His family, too, was devastated. Within three days of the allegation being made, 2 of his daughters, distraught at the claim (that neither for a moment believed), had passed out through worry for their father, by then tarred as beyond the pale. He had journalists outside his front door for days, including CNN with a satellite dish, but he wouldn't speak to anyone. His name was as black as anyone's could be. He worried that even his solicitor believed the claim was true.

'Alison was a total rock,' Mulcaire remembers. He was shocked that something so wrong could be laid at his door by a newspaper. 'She kept me going. She never doubted me... even when I had really dark moments and I thought "I must have done something wrong", she was the one who said "no, you never". You remember what happened....'

Mulcaire, in a depressed state after the Dowler story appeared, met Nick Davies the following morning with his solicitor Sarah Webb. At that meeting, Davies put a number of suggestions to Mulcaire, and asked him about who had tasked him in his activities. Davies had had it confirmed that Dowler's phone had been hacked. Mulcaire did not confirm it, but nor did he deny it. At that stage, of course, while he knew he had intercepted her voicemails, he didn't know that the false hope moment had happened before he got involved. So he was tormented by not understanding how he could have deleted them (when in fact he hadn't done so).

With a large number of civil legal claims against him and facing the possibility of further criminal charges, Mulcaire said very little to Davies. He refused to answer questions that might prejudice those cases, and was unable to recall (as he is to this day) many details of the jobs he did. 'He was trying to get an admission and add to the story,' says Mulcaire, 'but I confirmed nothing'. Davies agrees with this, but says the informal nature of a long meeting (which also gave rise to an abortive attempt for Mulcaire to turn Queen's evidence) gave Mulcaire every chance to steer him away from the inference that he had been responsible, but Mulcaire did not take it. Mulcaire had not been explicitly accused in the article, but as the convicted hacker nearest the scene of the crime, as it were, the juxtaposition was clearly suggestive, and at that stage – not knowing about the date in the police log either – he had no choice but to make the same assumption.

Mulcaire's version of events remains considerably at

odds with the one that, by design or by default, has established itself in the public mind. As we have seen, he believed he was on the side if not strictly of the law, then certainly of humanity. The Dowler case shocked the nation, and the *News of the World*, with its special interest in bringing child abductors to justice, was bound to be at the fore in the hunt for her.

So what had happened? After Milly disappeared on that Thursday afternoon, newspapers readied themselves for a big denouement. Possibly she would be triumphantly reunited with her family, or the polar opposite would emerge, or maybe a waiting game would begin. In any event, the public would be interested, and want to read more.

The *News of the World*, never bashful about its authority in this field, was desperate to 'own' the story. When Rebekah Brooks sets her mind to getting something, she tends to get it. Her news executives were left in no doubt what was wanted – the securing of Milly's release. And if she couldn't have that, the paper was to lead the field. The idea of the paper being embarrassed by another having a better tale – least of all the *Sun*, edited by David Yelland, who had pipped her to the editorship – was too humiliating to contemplate.

As news editor, Neville Thurlbeck was central to cracking it. Experience of such cases suggested that the kidnapper might be someone close to home, possibly a family member. Initial suspicions turned towards Bob Dowler, in whose house were found items suggesting an interest in bondage. To heighten suspicion, investigators discovered that his wife Sally had been unaware of his interest in such paraphernalia until Milly herself had recently come across it inadvertently and brought it to her mother's attention. The easiest assumption – 'the father did it' – must have been a tempting one indeed, for both police and press. But where was the evidence?

It was a day short of three weeks after Dowler's disappearance that Mulcaire was put on the case. The call came from Neville Thurlbeck (it was later agreed in court), although knowing the pair's previous work on what Mulcaire calls the 'greater good' projects, it is probably fair to assume that Miskiw, who had been away the week Milly had disappeared, had been wanting to deploy Mulcaire on the case for some time. To this day, Mulcaire is at a loss to explain why his services were not called upon sooner.

He remembers rushing into his house, having got the call, just as his wife was about to serve their evening meal. 'I've got the lead eye,' he told his wife Alison excitedly. 'I can't eat my dinner, I've got to get onto it.' He went straight back out to his office. Alison remembers his enthusiasm at being tasked. 'He just wanted to find that girl, that's all he wanted. That's what he's like,' she recalls.

As part of his tasking, Mulcaire recalls, he was given Milly's phone number by Neville Thurlbeck, which – according to Mulcaire – he said the police had given him (which Thurlbeck disputes). The fact that the number had come from the police – assuming it had – didn't strike him as unusual. Thurlbeck and Miskiw were forever cooking up deals with the police, trading information and swapping tips. It's what they did.

Mulcaire was preparing to put his standard procedures in such cases into operation, but at this stage, three weeks after Dowler's disappearance, he assumed many of them had already been performed. He checked with Miskiw. He was horrified by the response. Precious little.

'When I asked him what had been done, he was just sheepish and embarrassed on the police's behalf. I couldn't believe the stuff they hadn't done. On a case like that, process goes out of the window. You get what you need. A girl's life was in the balance. You get the info in as quick as possible. Greg was a coordinator, rather than the investigator, so he would listen to me on the best techniques to use on a case like this. I would not be dictated to… I would either do it or not. It was a relationship that worked well, and we both respected the other's patch.'

At an early stage, Miskiw asked Mulcaire to do an FP (full profile) on 'X', a known sex offender who had come under suspicion. Again, Mulcaire did as requested, assuming Miskiw had his own reasons for wanting to know about this character, possibly inspired by his chats with the police. 'That didn't go in the paper. There was no story saying "there's a suspect by the name of X being held"… why did Greg ask for it? That time I think I did ask, but they didn't want to discuss that.' Mulcaire is confident that Miskiw was passing information on to the police that Mulcaire could obtain more easily than they could. This a) helped the police and b) helped oil the wheels of Miskiw's relationship with them, with the promise of a quid pro quo implicit. Again, there was no necessary reason to tell Mulcaire why it was wanted.

Years later, at Sutton Police station, Mulcaire was gratified to have his suspicions confirmed when police told him that they had indeed questioned the man that

Miskiw had asked him to profile. Clearly, Mulcaire believes, someone in the police had given Miskiw the name – or at any rate, Miskiw had acquired it – and Miskiw was asking Mulcaire to find out what he could. Mulcaire was duly tasked to do a quick turnaround job. 'I could do the comms stuff the police couldn't do,' says Mulcaire. 'They knew Greg could get that sort of stuff, and it would have taken them ages with court orders and so on to get the same sort of detail. So what I did was helping both Greg and the police. I may have helped them ask the right questions.'

Mulcaire, nothing if not a passionate man, affects reluctance to point fingers over an extremely raw episode, although ultimately he fails to suppress the human impulses of a father of five. Initially he will only talk about what he would have done. 'Certainly I would take all the family's computers away, and their phones, and make sure I was on top of all the communications everyone in the family had had in the previous weeks.' This is not just completeness for the sake of complete-ness. As Mulcaire says: 'There are always little giveaways – switches in data patterns and so on – that wouldn't occur to most people. These can be much more revealing than you might think, and I would have expected the police to have been on top of this. There is no reason why the family wouldn't have been happy to go along with that.'

He reflects on what he regards as something of a specialist subject, 'In that first golden hour, you do an FP. You're on an egg timer. Every second counts. You've got to save that girl…. There are a lot of rumours, but you should only work on the intelligence you have gleaned, on the hard facts, as far as possible. Leave out the commonly held 'root causes'. You can go back to that later if you need to and haven't made progress otherwise. Unless you've done an FP, you risk making a big leap into other areas, whereas in fact what you're looking for is on your doorstep. The data mining needs to be done in the first hour, not the first 3 weeks,' he laments. 'When you're brought in between stage 2 and 3 you're just picking up the pieces'

'I would have made sure everybody was profiled. You build a grid, and identify who has phoned her, and get everyone's call history in the last six months… even as that's going along, and it's quite time consuming getting that data in, I'd be working on the MICE format [a recognised acronym designed to whittle down possible motives] Money? No. Ideology? No. Compromise? Ego? No. 'It is more clinical, more surgical more decisive… high direction, high support.'

The central part of his technique in an abduction involves locating individuals via their mobile phones. This is done either by working out the distance of each phone from three given phone masts. As any geometry student knows, if you know the distance of an object from three set points, and draw a circle around each point, you can identify a triangle showing where it is. There is another technique called 'pinging', which is used with digital mobile phones, and is an even more accurate way of locating a phone. So if Milly Dowler had been taken by someone who had been in phone contact with her or members of her family (and they had their phone on them when she was taken), that person should be evident on the grid. 'I would put every cell section on the grid,' he says. 'I'd identify them, turn the numbers around... so you identify everyone who was near her... it's geolocating.... We call it the Bermuda triangle, we don't let anyone out of that triangle... we get them flashed up, turn the numbers round and give them a visit.... With a bit of luck, within an hour you have a great position. Maybe you can say 'these are the three people'... knock on that door, that door and that door... these are the people who were within 2, 3, 5, 10, 20 yards... we're not calling them suspects necessarily, they're people of interest, they might have seen something... let's give them a visit... if you know the number is on the phone... if you ask them, "Why have you got that number on your mobile phone?", their reaction tells you a hell of a lot.... These are not mobile phones floating around on their own, they are with human beings who were in the area at the time.... But it's critical to get to them in the first hour.' Mulcaire insists that such technology, though not as effective as it is now, was available (and invaluable) at the time. 'You have to do immediate data mining as forensic analysis. It makes all the difference in the world.'

But on the available evidence it seems none of this had been done, to Mulcaire's horror. He set about doing it, but a good many horses had bolted. 'It was spectacularly unbe-f***ing-lievable, catastrophic and embarrassing. Given what's been missed, I just thought 'in this sort of case, we're heading for a really bad outcome here. There's only a 5 per cent chance we'll be lucky, and when you get a call that late... but so much stuff just hadn't been done.'

And what of the Dowler family being ambushed by a

photographer in their distress as they conducted a secret reconstruction of Milly's last walk? This is news to Mulcaire. 'I knew nothing about that at all,' he says. 'It's not just that I don't remember that. I know I would remember that if I had been involved. I would not have been involved in something on that scale. It looks very much to me as if the paper was getting drip fed intel from the inside.'

Mulcaire is not the sort of person to sit around saying 'isn't it awful, that poor girl, her poor family' and so on, but his human empathy for the victim and her family is implicit – powerful, even – in what he says. Maybe this shouldn't need saying. After all, what sort of person, let alone a parent, would not be moved by an innocent young daughter being abducted? Yet it is an assertion that needs to be made. His family know what the allegations of callousness towards Milly Dowler and her family did to Mulcaire. If he did wrong (and he denies this, believing he was acting effectively with the state's authority in trying to save a girl's life), he knows a great many people who did much worse, he says. 'My conscience is absolutely clear. I do not have a dark heart, and those who know me know that. In the same situation again, with the same facts in my possession, I would do exactly the same thing again. Given the conversations I had had with my superiors, and knowing they had been talking to the police, I don't see what further authorisation I could have had.'

And yet… his account is so eloquent of his keenness to save a young life that issues like whether his methods were legal are in danger of being overlooked. When he talks matter-of-factly about finding out who had phoned

Milly's parents' phone number in the previous few weeks (as he did, according to detective sergeant Greg Smith's evidence in court), that is of course illegal without a court order. When he mentions 'turning numbers round' – the devining of a person's identity and address from their mobile phone number – that, too, is illegal. It generally requires an employee of a phone provider to break the terms of their contract, presumably for money, to hand over the details. It is something the police can do with the help of a production order, but that can be time-consuming, or so the argument goes. In fact, experienced police officers say that if needs be the person providing the authorisation will often be willing to backdate permission if the perceived need at the time is great enough. Yet one imagines that, had one of these unlawful ruses uncovered Milly's assailant, we would be leaping to applaud the person in question, and any suggestion of a prosecution of the offender would be an outrage. There is, surely, some sort of lesson here.

And, as admitted, he did intercept Milly's voicemails. Transcripts shown to the jury revealed anxious friends asking: 'Please come home. I miss you so much… Hey, Milly, if you get this, call me…. Hallo, Milly. It's just that we want you home.'

He also did a voice analysis on the Dowler voicemails. 'I had the whole download on tape. Alison heard it as well. There was a very distinctive American voice on there. I wondered if she had been taken abroad. That would have been good news, I thought… at least she had more chance of being alive.

Recalling that period, he says now he regards that call as being potentially more significant than the one which later attracted the greatest attention, from a recruitment agency in Telford, West Midlands, apparently using Milly's real name, Amanda, left on Wednesday March 27. As mentioned above, the *News of the World* initially published a version of the message and also has an internal record of the message (worded slightly differently from the one that appeared in the paper, presumably to avoid alerting rivals) saying: 'Hallo, Amanda. This is Jo from Mondays Recruitment Agency. We are ringing because we have some interviews starting today at Epson. Please ring.' The message was actually for a woman called Nana who had a similar phone number, although of course nobody had any clue of that at the time. Mulcaire remembers being concerned that the message didn't ring true.

He recalls now dismissing the call as a hoax, and says he wrote as much on his notes. That, as far as he was concerned, was that. He reported his view back to the office (he thinks to Neville Thurlbeck, but is not sure), and continued with his researches. But at the *News of the World*, this was gold dust. Clearly Milly must be alive. She must have had an argument with her family, it was assumed.

Rather than inform the police, the next day, Thursday 11 April, Neville Thurlbeck sent a team of 6 journalists to an Epson factory near Telford. Thurlbeck told the court later that the decision to hold the information back from the police for 24 hours was made by Stuart Kuttner and Andy Coulson, although the judge asserted that Thurlbeck must have also had a hand in it. Mulcaire had passed the information to his taskers as soon as it reached him, and neither he nor the police knew of the sending of the journalists to Telford. Seemingly, though, The *News of the World* was convinced it was on the verge of getting a world-beating story.

Mulcaire's scepticism was shared by Vanessa Altin, who in a statement to the Leveson inquiry said: 'I, and other colleagues, dispatched by Neville thought the idea far fetched in the extreme. Milly had been missing for several weeks and we were certain she would not have been able to slip in unnoticed and hold down a job at Epson when she was just a child.'

News of the World reporters on at least three occasions called the recruitment agency claiming to be Milly Dowler's mother, asking if they had given work to her daughter. The owner, Valerie Hancox, told police that a 'well-mannered' *News of the World* reporter had come to her house and said he was helping police with their inquiries. 'He asked if I wanted to help Milly Dowler,' she said (in a statement). 'He informed me he was working with the police investigation team.'

But the team in the midlands failed to unearth anything. In fact they were on a wild goose chase. So, although reluctant to reveal to the police that they had been listening to Milly Dowler's voicemails, the paper sought to apply pressure with increasingly explicit references to the intercepted message, hoping the police would 'come clean' about something they might have expected the police to have known about already. In fact, the police, having acquired a production order from Guildford Crown Court, had done a download from Milly's voicemail box on 25th March, the day before the message from the agency was left, and were not to repeat the task for several days. (Curiously, and still unexplained, on that day, the PIN number was reset twice by the phone provider.)

This download, one might think, was surely overdue, and tells more of the story of the police being a little behind the curve. In any event, when confronted with the excited scribe from the *News of the World*, the police knew nothing about the message from the agency and, besides, had their own reason not to respond as urgently as the *News of the World* wanted. For one thing, the force heard that day from their colleagues in the West Mercia police about the reporters claiming to be Sally Dowler, Milly's mother. And as we shall see, they had another reason.

In any event, on the afternoon of Friday April 13, growing increasingly conscious of the looming deadline for Sunday, the *News of the World*'s managing editor, Stuart Kuttner, called the police. This was a new front, a more formal one, in Surrey/Wapping relations. He told them: 'The purpose of this call from the *News of the World* is to alert the Surrey Police to what may be, and I can put it no higher than may be, significant information in connection with Milly Dowler.' This was clearly not something to be ignored. Sarah McGregor, the force's head of communications, put Mr Kuttner in touch with a senior officer. Kuttner went for broke. In his note, Det Sgt Kevin McEntee noted Kuttner saying 'The *News of the World* are in possession of a recording of the message.' The same detective then spoke to the news editor, Neville Thurlbeck, noting: 'Thurlbeck told me he had accessed Milly's voicemail with PIN no 1210.' A little later, Thurlbeck told Sarah McGregor the paper had spoken to the recruitment agency, which, he said, had confirmed that Dowler was registered with them. (The police found later that there was no evidence to support this claim: 'the contrary is the case'.) McGregor told the trial that Thurlbeck had said he had obtained Milly's phone number and PIN code 'from schoolchildren'. In a police report prepared by Deputy Chief Constable Jerry Kirkby, it was concluded that the paper 'had *confirmed* with Milly's school friend that this was her mobile number [my italics]', as if the number had been obtained elsewhere beforehand. This may be a crucial difference.

At the end of the trial in 2014, Thurlbeck said, rather curiously, that he had claimed he had acquired the number through schoolchildren to protect Mulcaire's police sources. Mulcaire is at best mystified by this, citing the fact that Thurlbeck, a registered police informant, was the one with the police contacts. "It just makes no sense at all," he says.

Meanwhile, the *News of the World*'s enthusiasm about its supposed scoop was unabated. This was despite the fact that Milly Dowler was not registered with the agency, and, the mysterious voicemail aside, the idea that she might have did not survive the faintest scrutiny. We also know that the police had not known of the message left, supposedly, for Milly, and that when they heard of it, they were disinclined to credit it with much weight, to the *News of the World*'s undisguised disappointment. In fact, as the paper may not have known, a hoaxer was strongly suspected by the police to have been impersonating Milly closer to home. Over time, the evidence mounted and their belief strengthened, and a year later the hoaxer, a man called Paul Hughes, was imprisoned for 5 months.

It remains in some doubt that the paper had obtained Milly's PIN number from schoolchildren. Glenn Mulcaire is certain not only that he was given the PIN number by Thurlbeck, but that he was told the number had come from the police, a notion that raises all sorts of questions. If Mulcaire is correct, one of Thurlbeck's accounts must be wrong.

Those who doubt Mulcaire might say that he must have blagged the number himself. This is almost certainly wrong, even should one be disinclined to believe his assertion that Thurlbeck gave him the number. For one thing, it is known that the *News of the World* had the number before Mulcaire was on the case. But what is equally important is that once someone had that particular number, it would not be difficult to hack her phone. Milly's was the type of phone that used an unregistered SIM card, which means there was no provider in a position to pass on the key details that would have given access. In fact that wouldn't be necessary. It would take no great expert to identify the provider from the phone number (phone companies are given a range of numbers to give out, so the provider could be easily inferred by anyone with a knowledge of the industry). Once the provider is known, the default PIN code would be easily identified, and it is known that Milly had not changed her PIN number.

In other words, in the first five days after Milly's disappearance (before the PIN number was changed), it was comparatively easy to listen to her messages. Perhaps this was why it was felt Mulcaire's services would not be required. In any event, the answer as to who deleted the voicemails has its source, perhaps self-evidently, with who had the number, and how it was acquired.

Here, there are some clues, even if still no settled

answers. We see in the 'blue book', private investigator Steve Whittamore's record of inquiries from News International, the names of Ada, Robert, Sally and Lucy Dowler, and the family's ex-directory telephone landline (but no mobile), requested by the *News of the World*'s crime reporter Sarah Arnold. The number was seemingly not found by Steve Whittamore, but was subcontracted to another private investigator, John Gunning.

The possible significance of this is great, given what is known about the search for Milly Dowler's number. For having the Dowlers' landline number would have more than the obvious use: it would, with enough guile and indifference to the law, enable a blagger to find, say, the names of those who were called most frequently from that number. And that number would, almost certainly, include their daughter's. We are speculating here, and there is no evidence to say that Gunning did blag the Dowlers' phone numbers. Simply that somebody who knew how to do so could well have done so, but Gunning had that knowledge and is named as having provided the Dowler's ex-directory number. 'Once a blagger had the land line, getting the 'Friends and Family' numbers is the easiest thing in the world', says Mulcaire. As we have seen in chapter 2, it was not difficult to acquire, and that is indeed what Mulcaire believes someone on the paper did.

So, late on Friday 13th, the *News of the World* executives were in a quandary. They believed with great conviction that they had some sort of Dowler story for the paper for Sunday – they just weren't sure what. It was clear that somebody had indeed left a message on Milly's voicemail. The question was why. What did they think they were doing? Had she really applied for work? Or had a hoaxer applied, pretending to be her? In which case, how on earth had the hoaxer got her number? Nothing made complete sense.

Rebekah Brooks, who had been the moving spirit behind the Sarah's Law campaign, was desperate to crack the Dowler case. From her holiday in Dubai with her husband Ross Kemp. She and her deputy, lover and eventual successor, Andy Coulson were in frequent contact by text, voicemail and phone. Nonetheless, a jury conceded that Rebekah Brooks knew nothing about the voicemail messages, so we must conclude that the decisions were left to Coulson, and they went down to the wire.

The paper drew up two versions of its story, one saying the call had been a hoax, and the other reporting that the police were taking it seriously and treating it as a new line of inquiry. After much deliberation, The *News of the World* decided its information was too good to go to waste, although it ended up running a story that they didn't believe, or so subsequent conversations suggested. The account, headlined 'Milly hoax riddle', quoted directly from the voicemail from the recruitment agency. The word 'riddle' is a bit of an old newspaper favourite, a savoury enticement to readers which seeks to disguise the fact that the newspaper has failed to crack the big story. It said, 'It is thought the hoaxer even gave the agency Milly's real mobile number… the agency used the number to contact Milly when a job vacancy arose and left a message on her voicemail… it was on March 27, 6 days after Milly went missing, that the employment agency appears to have phoned her mobile.'

As late as 8.10pm, a *News of the World* journalist called

the Surrey force to say the next day's paper would carry a story quoting the police as saying: 'We are intrigued, but believe the message may have been left by a deranged woman hoaxer thought to have hampered other police inquiries.' The journalist was told the quote was too strong, and asked for time to amend it. The journalist said it was too late, that the first edition had already gone and that the quote would be used in all 5 subsequent editions.' In later versions, the verbatim quote from the voicemail message was removed.

The following morning, the police agreed the following line for media inquiries: 'We are evaluating the claim that Amanda may have registered with a recruitment agency. At this stage there is the possibility that a hoaxer may have been involved in generating this story.' And the following off the record guidance was also adopted: 'At this stage we are confident that this woman attending the recruitment agency is a hoaxer and not Milly. The woman is older than Milly and hence would be able to register at a recruitment agency (would question how a 13-year-old would be able to register for a job)'. On the Monday (15th), West Mercia police, which had been asked by the Surrey force to look into the call to the recruitment agency, came back and said that an employee of the agency had said they had no one on their books called Amanda Dowler, nor had they ever interviewed anyone of that name.

Certainly 'Milly hoax riddle' was a story, but it wasn't *the* story, the one that would thrust the *News of the World* unassailably out in front of its competitors. The paper's top brass were getting agitated. During that week, managing editor Stuart Kuttner got in touch again with the police, challenging their assertions about the hoaxer story and reminding the police they had 'passed on information about messages left on Amanda Dowler's phone... We offered a copy of a tape-recording of the messages.' (In the context, for good or ill, this admission to having broken the law was secondary to the search for Milly which may have played a role in the jury's decision to acquit Kuttner in June 2014). But the police stuck to their guns, reasserting their faith in the story. Crime reporter Ricky Sutton replied: 'This is not true. It's inconceivable... Milly has been up there in person. She has registered and applied for a job at the factory. We know this for 100 per cent.' Of course, he knew no such thing.

On Wednesday 17th, police performed a second download of Milly's messages, and this time picked up the call relating to the employment agency. Two days later, a Surrey officer listening closely to the message concluded that the name sounded more like 'Nana' than Mandy. The officer called the agency and was told they had a lot of ladies from Ghana on their books and that this was a popular Ghanaian name. Further, the agency had indeed spoken to a 'Nana' on 26th March, when she called to say she had changed her mobile number. The following day, the agency had called her about job interviews. How the wrong number had come to be written down wasn't clear.

So when on Saturday 20th April, when the paper went into battle again to say the hoaxer line was inaccurate, the police were ready for them. Mrs McGregor confirmed their belief, but relayed what the officer had concluded the previous day – that the name on the message was 'Nana' and not Mandy, and that the number was simply wrong. (The police later told the House of Commons Culture Media and Sports Select Committee that 'contrary to Surrey police's initial suspicions', the message did not come from a hoaxer but was 'a pure coincidence' and 'of no evidential value'.)

But, she was to tell the court in 2013, she said Ricky Sutton, the paper's crime correspondent, still refused to accept the explanation and had told her the paper was '100 per cent absolutely certain' of its source on the information. He also said the paper was switching its investigation to the north of England, where they believed Milly had applied for a job in a factory. The paper's excitement of the previous 10 days had dissipated.

About 2 weeks later, the *News of the World* had to accept a major humiliation, as it will have seen it. Plans for a reward for information leading to the return of Milly Dowler had been in the air for some time. The problem was that the *Sun*, their stablemates, had had the same idea. Stuart Kuttner was deputed to spell out to the police that this was not what was wanted at all. He sent an email on 1 May saying he was unhappy about the *Sun* being involved, pointing out that his paper had 'better circulation and more resources'. 'Rebekah Wade [Brooks]' he explained, 'has stated that she couldn't do this on a joint basis.' That was supposed to be that, evidently.

The police had the temerity to ignore Brooks's edict. It adopted Solomon's judgment, thanked both papers and said they would gratefully accept £50,000 each in reward money. This prompted a furious call from Ricky Sutton, who said 'You have killed us stone dead in the water' before putting the phone down.

The big question that remains unanswered over the Milly Dowler affair is how the cruel 'false hope moment' that led Milly Dowler's parents to think their daughter might have listened to her voicemails came about. The narrative that has a certain currency, is that the voicemails were deleted not by a human being but by technology. This might have been the result of them dropping off the system, as they are programmed to do, 72 hours after they were left. Or some say the introduction of new 'platforms' over that weekend would have done for the messages.

Neither explanation is satisfactory. The 72-hour explanation won't wash, because other message left in the previous day or two were also deleted. And, all being well, the switching of a 'platform' should have no bearing on whether messages are retained or not.

Detective chief inspector John Macdonald of the Metropolitan Police was tasked with getting to the bottom of the matter. He concluded that we may never know how the voicemails came to be deleted, and he may well be right. He also said there was no evidence to suggest Milly's phone had been hacked before 26th March 2002. This is to suggest that at even though the *News of the World* had paid to get Milly Dowler's family's phone numbers, that nobody had tried to intercept her voicemails during that time, this despite hacking now being common practice on more than one of the redtop papers. Certainly it is a suggestion Mulcaire has trouble believing. MacDonald did confirm that there was evidence hacking had taken place after that, and there was evidence that two voicemail messages may have been manually deleted. Equally they may have been automatically deleted.

There was further consternation at the fact that the police, having been alerted to the fact that the *News of the World* had a recording of a phone message, took no steps later to pursue the matter. According to the Independent Police Complaints Commission report on the matter, 'officers and former officers from Surrey Police... expressed surprise and dismay that it wasn't investigated'. It continued: 'We have not been able to uncover any evidence, in documentation or witness statements, of why and by whom that decision was made: former senior officers, in particular, appear to have been afflicted by a form of collective amnesia in relation to the events of 2002'. It concluded that it was 'scarcely credible' that no one connected to the investigation 'recognised the relevance and importance of the information Surrey Police held in 2002 before this was disclosed by Operation Weeting'.

Mulcaire's continuing sense of anger at the assertion that he was responsible for the 'false hope' moment is palpable. For one thing, as is now generally accepted, he almost certainly could not have been. But there is a boiling sense of indignation that stems from his own personality that continues to frustrate him. Mulcaire sees himself as being on the side of the angels in the whole story. He admits he intruded on the Dowler family's privacy, but for noble reasons. At the time he was tasked, there were precious few clues about what had happened to Milly, and there remained suspicions about the role of Bob Dowler. Further, executives on his newspaper were desperate to appease their editor by solving the crime.

For those inclined to dismiss Mulcaire as a low-life hoodlum, the idea that he believed he was acting on the police's behalf may be incredible (though by this stage of the story, I hope marginally less so). His claim should be heard. He was given Milly Dowler's number by Neville Thurlbeck who said it had come from the police.

This, of course, is a key moment. There may appear to be an irony in an information-getter of Glenn Mulcaire's background needing to be given such a number. It is an idea that in this context positively riles Mulcaire. 'At that stage, when a girl had been missing all that time, you would have to have any relevant details there and then. This wasn't some grubby hole-in-the-wall job. It was a serious investigation, and the fact of being given the number was confirmation that this was sanctioned job.'

It seems clear that Mulcaire's modus operandi was more sophisticated than the police's. In his own words, he was 'pinging and triangulating for breakfast', while the police – for reasons either of technological knowhow or legal obligation (or so Mulcaire believed) – were cumbersome and slow on their feet. As we will see, there are many examples of the police/Fleet Street nexus working together and exchanging information, supposedly for the common good. Individual police officers, confronted by headlines demanding progress on the disappearance of a missing child, might fall back on their friends in the press if they think it might produce results. And even if the number reached the *News of the World* from people close to the Dowler family (as Neville Thurlbeck maintains), that too is plausible, even if, in the case of children, strictly speaking a breach of Press

Complaints Commission rules. As one senior figure in the Met puts it: 'Friends and family in that situation will do anything, they will tell anyone anything if they think it will get the child back.' Few journalists would spurn such an offer. It is what they might do with the number that is more questionable.

Could the false-hope moment have been the result of messages automatically 'falling off' Milly's voicemail box? Possibly, although the number of people with an interest in this being so inclines the sceptic against it, as does the fact that other messages, left less than 72 hours before, were also deleted. Was it a bungled attempt to hack into Milly's messages? More sinisterly, could it have been a successful attempt to hack her voicemails (by a journalist from who knows where?), followed by an intentional deletion to prevent rivals getting a message? For what it is worth, a police investigation has said there was no evidence of anyone accessing the voicemails.

The *News of the World*'s deputy features editor Paul McMullan, who has plenty of experience in the ways of redtop papers, says 'a reporter would do all they could to protect their story... you want to protect your story, esp[ecially] on a Sunday paper.... If you get scooped on a Saturday, it's gutting... you do anything; you fly people out of the country, anything, to keep the competition away from the source. In the Dowler case you would almost certainly record it and then delete it.... But everyone was trying to find her... police were shit, absolutely hopeless. They were so shit they let a murderer wander round for seven years hitting people with hammers.... People abroad have said how lucky we are to have vigorous investigative journalists and we're not tied to just using a useless police force. Bunch of incompetents.'

In July 2012, Mulcaire was again charged under RIPA: this time with both the interception of Dowler's voicemail messages and conspiracy to do so. He admitted the first charge, but resisted the conspiracy charge with some vigour. He was interviewed by the police three times in 2011, having not been invited to speak about the Dowler affair when he was charged in 2006. He told them he believed he was acting not only in the public interest, but also with an 'empowering authority', i.e. with the knowledge of the police. The word 'conspire' has connotations of planning premeditatedly and cold-bloodedly with others to perform a crime, whereas his own interpretation of it was that it was the purposeful deployment of a technique in the hope of saving life.

When he turned up at Sutton police station, he was ready for an argument. He wanted his day in court to explain his position.

> I told them 'I did not conspire…. I had an empowering belief to hack phones…. I believe I was doing it legitimately…. I was prepared to go all the way down the line and plead not guilty on conspiracy. I would call key witnesses and paperwork to explain why I believed I was doing it on behalf of the law… it was not like the three other charges [of 2006], which were celebrity-based bits of nonsense. But I was not going to plead guilty to conspiracy.' He says he has the impression the police had wised up to who he was and what and why he had done it. Their tone, by

the end, showed more respect than would be due a 'rogue'. 'By that time,' he said, 'they'd got the picture as to why I did what I did. Not before time.

In fact, a lawyer would say that Mulcaire's claim to have lawful authority or an empowering belief is not sufficient to get him off the hook. To have lawful authority, it has to be formally bestowed by an arm of the state. A nod from, say, Greg Miskiw is not sufficient, although Mulcaire's vehemence on the matter shows the strength of his belief. His anger over the case is evident. Soon after that, the conspiracy charge against Mulcaire was dropped. Conveniently, he says. 'do they really want me there, in Leveson etc… police had a lot to lose if they left him in conspiracy charge… they knew full well I was determined to stick with this in a court of law. I would have liked Neville to go "not guilty". I would have welcomed the chance to thrash it out in court. Ok, let's talk about all this.'

Mulcaire maintains a faith in the legal system to get to the bottom of an issue, as long as the evidence is presented in court. He insists he has told no lies throughout his legal odyssey, but as a result of pleading guilty on all charges apart from the (dropped) Dowler conspiracy charge, has deprived himself of the opportunity to appear in court to explain himself.

For those unfamiliar with how the paper worked, this idea of his wanting the whole issue exposed to public transparency may seem extraordinary. But Mulcaire was essentially uninterested in most of the stories he worked on. He wanted to find the nugget, to crack the secret. The finding of it was its own reward, while the parading of it was for others. He often didn't even buy the paper in which they appeared, and he prided himself on not being a 'trophy hunter', as he dismissively referred to some of the journalists with whom he worked. And few of those who were in charge of him discouraged him in that attitude. It suited them to keep things on a 'need to know' basis, not least because once he started asking questions he might never stop. We will see that Mulcaire was something of an expert in the twilight world where official public bodies meet the dark arts, and he knew when it was inappropriate to ask too many questions. And with a young girl missing, it would surely be no surprise if the police were throwing every trick in the book into solving the problem. The police team working on the case, too, were under enormous pressure from their bosses to come up with leads.

And the fact that he might be doing work for the police by the back door was neither discreditable nor surprising. In a different context, his wife Alison recalls one holiday in Great Yarmouth in particular, when she was at her busiest with their young children, in a caravan. She was giving Mulcaire a hard time, because he kept going outside to speak to someone on the paper when she needed help. 'I'm sorry, but we've got to do this, we're doing it for the police.' She says that was a fairly frequent occurrence, and in the Milly Dowler case, he was seeking to free a young girl from her kidnapper.

Neville Thurlbeck had had a remarkable past as the breaker of big stories. His exposure of criminals made dealing with the police a pretty much daily experience. In 2000 he had come close to going to prison for bribing police officers. Thurlbeck was registered as a police informer (No. 281), bearing the codename 'George' and gave a 'substantial volume of information that was 'extremely useful' to Scotland Yard and the security services. In return, Thurlbeck received confidential information from the Police National Computer that enabled him to write about a Labour MP with a conviction for committing obscene behaviour and, separately, a supposed 'stalker' threat to the Queen.

It later emerged that Thurlbeck was actually an unpaid employee of the National Criminal Intelligence Service (NCIS), a liaison body between Scotland Yard's Special Branch and MI5. 'Sources close to' Thurlbeck said that 'people right at the top of News International were aware of his role'.

Following his release, Thurlbeck displayed plenty of insouciant candour when he told the *UK Press Gazette*: 'The police were very impressed about the type of intelligence I was coming up with and that was revealed in court. The judge said it was a substantial volume of information that was extremely useful to police.' Mr Justice McKinnon said the relationship between Thurlbeck and his source was a 'symbiotic one – a two-way relationship with information passed both ways'. The case was thrown out, with the judge accepting Thurlbeck's assertion that no money had changed hands, so no law had been broken. Thurlbeck said at the time: 'When you deal with police officers in the year 2000, the currency is information not money…. The *News of the World* crime desk receives a huge amount of information about criminal activity – and the police have always been eager to tap into that resource. In return policemen give information to us. That is our most valuable currency.'

Mulcaire's self-image is as 'one of the good guys', and it's a belief that has bolstered him through several years of vilification. A weaker man would certainly have crumbled, given the reputational and financial strain he has come under. 'Reputation is one thing, character is something quite different,' he is inclined to say, the latter, of course, being the one that matters. But such faith cannot be self-sustaining forever, and he needs his side of the story to be better understood. Hence his cooperation with this book presumably.

For one thing, he remains enraged that, having put up with being dismissed as a 'rogue' when he was first convicted, it later became convenient to saddle him with numerous other heinous offences. A scapegoat was needed, and he, gagged by lawyers, was ready made. Now, though, he wants a full inquiry into the Dowler case. He persists in disbelieving much of the evidence that has been given in court, and wants all his files returned to him.

There have been claims that the police's own voicemails were listened to. He doesn't know if he did so, but says it is possible and, given his low regard for the police's record on child abductions, quite understandable. For one thing this might have helped find the child, and for another, it was known that in one such case, an officer was having an inappropriate relationship. Again, if that was the case, there was no reason it shouldn't be known about. If it was true, he says, his files would reveal the reason. He estimated a great many (possibly as much as 25 per cent, he says) are still missing, despite attempts to get them back. Those, he says, would tell much of the story, but he says they remain unattainable in the police's safe keeping. 'God alone will flush out those people (who listened to her voicemail early on and made such a mess). It may take a long time, but I can't do to them what they have done to me.'

10

Arms of the State

In a book about life on a redtop paper, the author Graham Johnson talks about the closeness of the police to parts of the press, and how lawlessness can thrive as a result. He ends by saying: 'The police looked upon us as the good guys, or so we believed.' This throw-away remark resonates for anyone looking at the police's performance over the phone hacking affair. The police's faith that essentially that their 'friends in the press' had virtually identical interests to the cops was largely responsible for one of the biggest messes in the recent history of the Metropolitan Police. A relationship of co-dependency became one of exploitation. But it took the police a tragically long time to realise it.

Those who recall a supposed golden age of policing were horrified, and with good reason. In the 1950 and 1960s, the cry 'Send for the Yard' meant the calling in of what might now be called a 'celebrity copper' to investigate. This might be '(Robert) Fabian of the Yard', or '(Jack) Slipper of the Yard', whose name would be known across the land and in whose judgment and inde-fatigability an expectant public would place enormous faith. This aura of rectitude was generally reinforced by an obliging pack of crime reporters which would follow them round the country, waiting to be fed snippets over an innocuous whisky in the hotel bar. The relationship was largely controlled by the police, with the press grateful for what it could get.

There was police corruption, of course, and there was some well reported tales of porn barons and gang bosses bribing police. On a smaller scale, one reporter (now deceased) admitted he kept a 10 pound note in the breast pocket of his jacket in case he thought it would loosen the tongue of a police officer, and buff envelopes were not unknown. There might be a habitual Christmas delivery of a crate of brown ale or a bottle of whisky, just to oil the wheels, but the assumption, drummed into the police from early in their training, was to distrust the press.

Stewart Tendler, crime correspondent for the *Times* from 1978 to 2007, recalls: 'They were told that journalists were always after something, and that one could never be sure how and when something you had told them could cause problems for the officer and his force. But in London the proximity of one of the biggest forces in the world and the headquarters of the national media was bound to wear that hostility down, especially as the Yard was involved for decades in the cases that made the biggest headlines.' Some officers simply didn't take the risk, but, says Tendler:

... others saw the media as a useful source of intelligence, part of the armoury of detection or a useful tool for their own advancement by attracting publicity for their work. There have also been others operating from venal motives: for many years police pay was poor.

But as newsgathering became more intense and crime fighting part of the political agenda many other officers lost their reticence and were prepared to meet for a drink or lunch. The more cautious ones either paid for themselves or picked up the bill. Others would simply never meet in that sort of social milieu. They were more likely to suggest a coffee in their office. Others might reciprocate at a later stage.

The details of the wining and dining between journalists and police that Lord Leveson found show how things had changed. Was this corruption? It certainly looked dreadful in hindsight. It looked still worse when an HMIC report found there had been 298 cases of 'inappropriate' hospitality, even if it found that most officers had shown common sense in this area.

The fact that that the police swallowed a pack of lies about a 'rogue reporter' at the *News of the World* in 2006, that as a result the Prime Minister hired one of the leading wrongdoers as one of his closest confidants in 2010, that hundreds of victims of crime had to resort to the civil courts, and that it took nearly 7 years to bring the *News of the World*'s main malefactors to justice, and even longer to identify their counterparts on papers other than the *News of the World*, is a pretty open and shut case of a bungled investigation, at best. Coming after the force's failure to identify the killers of Stephen Lawrence, this would have been bad enough. And given that in the course of the investigation into the *News of the World* it emerged that police officers were being paid for stories by the paper, there was plenty for those inclined to find dark forces at work to get their teeth into. After all, they had plenty of ammunition already. There had long been allegations of undue masonic influence inside the Met. On top of this were ever-present allegations of racism, political bias and suspicions of corruption, compounding a more general loss of deference towards authority. Seemingly the police were not earning the public's trust.

And for those who smelt a rat, there was a more specific cause for concern. In 1987, a private investigator, Daniel Morgan, was murdered in a pub cark park in Sydenham, south London. It was believed that Morgan was on the verge of blowing the whistle on widespread police corruption. Morgan had set up Southern Investigations, a private investigations company, and it was after having a drink with his business partner Jonathan Rees that he was found with an axe embedded in his head. The officer charged with interviewing Rees was also moonlighting for him, which undermined the investigation's credibility from the start. Arrests were made, but all those charged were acquitted, leaving the murder unsolved. Given what emerged subsequently about drugs and police corruption, the idea that Morgan knew too much would not go away.

What made it all the more potent, and did all the more to undermine the police's efforts to get to the bottom of *News of the World*'s misbehaviour, centred on Rees. The *News of the World*'s former crime reporter and later news executive Alex Marunchak was an associate of Rees, and Rees used to sell him stories for the *News of the World* (for up to £150,000 a year, it later emerged). It was claimed many of Rees's stories came ultimately from corrupt police officers, so, regardless of who had committed the murder, too deep an examination of *News of the World* news-gathering might expose some uncomfortable truths about the Met at the same time.

Another was that that in December 2000, Rees was jailed for 6 years, extended to 7 years on appeal, for conspiring with a corrupt police officer to plant cocaine in the car of a woman so that she would lose custody of her children. Any association with a man capable of such a thing was going to need some explaining.

The third surrounded detective chief superintendent Dave Cook, a talented and assiduous detective who, in 2002, became the latest officer to investigate the murder of Daniel Morgan. Because of the sensitivities of the case, Cook and fellow officer Jacquie Hames, a presenter of the BBC's Crimewatch programme, were placed under a witness protection scheme. Nonetheless, they suspected they were being put under surveillance by the driver of a white van, who seemed to be waiting for them at the end of their drive. When police stopped the van, they discovered it was leased by News International through its *News of the World* executive Alex Marunchak. It was later claimed by Rebekah Brooks that they were being watched because of a tip that Cook and Hames were having an affair. In fact, this was no secret. They had been living together for 12 years, had 2 children and had married 4 years earlier. Some months later Cook was able to confront Brooks in person at Scotland Yard. Nonetheless, even though there seemed to be evidence of a possible interference with Cook's investigation, it was decided no further action should be taken. The impression created was that of a bad smell, at best.

Alex Marunchak later pointed out to the *Press Gazette*

that at that time he was the editor of the Irish edition of the *News of the World*, and was based in Dublin, professionally at least. He confirmed that he had been given a tip, that Hames and Cook were having an affair, and merely passed it on, unchecked, to the desk in London. Apart from a 30-second conversation with the newsdesk, he said, he had no involvement in the story. Marunchak also said that he had never even heard of Daniel Morgan, or of his PI company Southern Investigations, at the time of Morgan's death.

While most of the dark allegations were yet to register on the broader public's radar (let alone their denials), those who had looked into it were unimpressed. It is fair to infer that the feelings ventilated in a newspaper article by former assistant commissioner at the Met John Yates in 2013 reflected the feelings of campaigners 10 or so years earlier: 'For many years, [the Morgan family] were lied to, fobbed off, patronised and dismissed as crackpots by the very people who should have been helping them – the police.... It is one of the most, if not the most, shameful episodes in Scotland Yard's history.'

As the phone hacking story developed, further grounds for suspicion about the police's role emerged. The head of the counter-terrorist unit, the body running the phone hacking investigation, was Andy Hayman. He had been brought in as assistant commissioner for specialist operations (ACSO) by the new commissioner of the Met Ian Blair, in February 2005, and just months later, in July 2005, he was in charge of the biggest criminal investigation Britain had ever seen, the search for the 7/7 bombers. He was also in the thick of the action when Jean Charles de Menezes, a Brazilian electrician, was shot at Stockwell underground station in the mistaken belief that he was a terrorist. In 2006, he was appointed Commander of the Order of the British Empire.

Andy Hayman was gregarious by nature, and positively encouraged the mixing of business with pleasure in the company of journalists, frequently holding meetings with journalists and press officers at The Sanctuary hotel or some similarly convivial location round the corner from Scotland Yard. He was as aware as anyone of the influence of the Murdoch papers, and made sure as far as possible that they were kept abreast of developments in the fight against terrorism. The *News of the World* was often a beneficiary of this, its reach to a wide public being used, for example, to publicise an FBI film showing how much damage the so-called 'shoe bomber' Richard Reid might have caused had he not been stopped in time.

But there were questions about Hayman's use of his expense account, of his mobile phone and the extent of his fraternising with colleagues. The fact that 2 months after he decided to resign, in December 2007, he took up the offer to write a column for the *Times*, another Murdoch-owned newspaper, did not look good, as he admitted later. In the 10 months before he stood down, he had met representatives of the Murdoch media 5 times for meals, which also did not help make him look like an ideal Caesar's wife either.

Assuming good faith on the part of senior Met officers, though, the investigation in to the *News of the World* was a humiliation. To understand why, it is necessary to go back to the year 2000. 'Over the years, the

Met had become more and more secretive and cautious: officers had not been allowed to talk to the press without the authority of an inspector or someone of more senior rank, and this attitude had tended to attract suspicion and contempt. The Stephen Lawrence case had put our reputation on the floor, and it seemed to me that we needed to make strenuous efforts to rehabilitate ourselves and restore our own confidence. Perhaps because we ourselves had gone into our shell, the press, for their part, had withdrawn and distanced themselves.' Those words were written in 2005, so still the balmy days of Police/press cross-fertilisation, come from Sir John Stevens, reflecting on his arrival in the Met commissioner's chair 5 years earlier.

Hindsight is unkinder still. 'I myself worked hard to foster good relations with national newspapers,' continued Stevens, 'mainly by being open and making myself available to the editor... Piers Morgan at the *Daily Mirror*, Rebekah Brooks at the *Sun*, Andy Coulson on the *News of the World*, Dominic Lawson on the *Sunday Telegraph*, Alan Rusbridger of the *Guardian* and Paul Dacre at the *Daily Mail*.... Sometimes this policy alarmed my own public relations staff... but on the whole it paid off handsomely.' Stephens was also notably friendly with Paul Dacre, Max Hastings at the Standard and the Barclay brothers, owners of the *Telegraph*.

One journalist Stevens didn't mention in that context was Neil Wallis, then deputy editor of the *News of the World* and an assiduous cultivator of senior police officers. In 1995 Wallis had set up the *Sun*'s Police Bravery Awards, which have been attended by every Prime Minister since. Wallis has said in an interview, 'I was used to dining with senior police officers. There was an understanding we could work together. Paul Condon [Now Lord Condon, Met commissioner 1993-9], [Now Lord] John Stevens, [Now Sir] Paul Stephenson (Stevens's successor). All became Metropolitan Police Commissioners. I was able to talk to them all. Journalists, particularly in the tabloid press, discover things the police can't. Co-operation with the Met can help catch criminals.' The police looked on us as the good guys.

The relationships that Wallis had built up would have been the envy of any senior journalist, and as long as due proprieties are observed, there is nothing wrong – on either side – with journalists and police officers having mutually beneficial relations. So it will have been a shock when Neil Wallis was questioned by police at Hammersmith Police station about his knowledge of phone hacking. In the event, the matter was dropped, but at a time when the police's relationship with News International was undergoing exceptional scrutiny, it gave rise to a great deal of innuendo.

Wallis is by all accounts good company, with those who are his equals and above at least. He was well placed to help John Stevens improve the Met's relations with the press, having written the then deputy commissioner's strategy plan when he applied to be given the top job. Lord Condon, Stevens's predecessor as boss of the Met, had been a reserved presence, not someone naturally comfortable in the company of prying journalists. Stevens's natural gregariousness by contrast must have played well by comparison.

In the new collaborative climate, Wallis's friendliness with Stevens would have been seen as a plus by both his newspaper colleagues and senior people in the Met. The pair would meet over dinner, sometimes in the company of deputy commissioner John Yates, Stevens's right hand man, who was seemingly also destined for the top, and Dick Fedorcio, Scotland Yard's head of press. All being on the same side had convivial advantages, with the assumption that they were all seeking to put bad people behind bars a given. As one senior former colleague puts it, 'John Stevens wrote the book on how to schmooze the press.'

Wallis's friendship with Stevens spawned a friendship between Wallis and Yates, and it was this that was to cause the end of Yates's 30-year career in the Met. Rightly or wrongly, their association was held up as the benchmark of an unhealthily close relationship between press and police. During the Leveson inquiry, the name of Wallis acquired a toxicity it had never previously had, yet all other things being equal, both legitimately claim to have been doing their job – having constructive relationships with people who knew useful things.

Wallis, a keen Man United fan, arranged to watch football with the sociable, upstanding Yates, who supports Liverpool. The pair used to exchange larky emails, texts and blokey jokes, perhaps going beyond what their opponents would have thought appropriate. But there is no evidence of the sort of impropriety that would have attracted attention in other circumstances. . Yates told the Home Affairs Committee when he resigned in 2012 that his integrity was intact and his conscience clear. He had gone to some lengths to ensure that was the case, informing his boss about the end of his marriage, for example, lest, say, anunscrupulous journalist seek to take advantage of the fact.

The Yates-Wallis friendship was well known at the Met. And higher up it was felt important to maintain the best of relationships with Metropolitan Police Commissioners. 'The strategy was, get them on side and everything else will fall into place,' according to one News International insider. 'They'll keep you well stocked with stories. The one who didn't conform in that respect was [commissioner] Ian Blair.'

They did indeed keep them well stocked. One of the *News of the World*'s better known reporters was Mazher Mahmood, famous for being faceless. Mahmood's picture has never appeared in the paper because his stories often involve impersonating someone rich, foreign and mysterious, persuading his victims to team up with him in unsuitable schemes. As a 'Fake Sheikh', he has gulled former England football manager Sven-Goran Eriksson into suggesting that together they buy a football club, and as a bogus Indian businessman he exposed a spot-fixing scam among Pakistani cricketers.

Mahmood is something of a redtop legend, though a highly controversial one, and claims to have helped put 94 people behind bars. (Previous claims to a figure nearly 3 times that size have been scaled down.) His stories involve a high degree of subterfuge and the sort of contact with his victims that in some countries might be regarded as entrapment, so of necessity they sail close to the wind legally. Nonetheless he is an outstanding example of how an ingenious journalist can entertainingly expose the greed and delusions of the rich and powerful.

One senior police officer recalls the sort of collaboration that went on with News International in the early 2000s. 'There was a time when they were all over us, he says. 'Mazher Mahmood was for ever giving us jobs, and us coming in on the back of it. It was always a *fait accompli*, there was no question of us saying: "Hang on, is this one a sensible use of our time and resources?" We just had to get on with it. The commander at the time was quite aware of it. It was generally their management talking to our management, but it always came through a chain of command down to us on the shop floor.' Another senior Met figure echoes this, suggesting that the Met did not appreciate every aspect of the arrangement: 'The deal was always that the paper had to be able to print the story first, then they'd hand the stuff over to us. The stories always used to come in on a Thursday or Friday, just when we were starting to think about packing up, so it generally meant a ruined weekend.'

In a more general sense, the *News of the World* identified itself as being on the side of law and order. Deputy features editor Paul McMullan remembers that subeditors used to write at the bottom of his stories the words 'our dossier is available to the authorities', almost as if that bestowed respectability. He says they also used to encourage him to pass on information to the police, whereas for many journalists there is a squeamishnesss about getting in to bed with an arm of the state. 'I did a story about some swingers up to no good which they wanted to know all about, and [managing editor] Kuttner wanted the paper's reputation defended by helping the police', but McMullan was reluctant and felt this was more about a desire for respectability (undeserved, he felt, given the type of advertisements the paper was carrying and the sort of work he was doing) than anything else.

The mood of friendliness was well established at the top of News International and the Met, and was cemented when Sir John Stevens, as he had become, agreed to write a column for the *Sun*. Handily enough, this was ghost-written by... Neil Wallis. According to Hacked Off, which lobbies against press intrusion, Stevens was paid £5,000 for seven articles in the first year, and £7,000 each for the second. Lower down the chain, staff on both organisations knew the power of the other. Making waves was not encouraged.

So the arrest in 2006 of two people working for the *News of the World* was a shock. Clive Goodman and Glenn Mulcaire had been the subject of complaints from the royal family, no less, so the matter could not be managed away with assurances of lessons learned and so on. It was not to be ignored, although those involved remember a higher degree of discretion than usual was deemed appropriate.

Yet it wasn't a big story, surely. The case – having been treated initially as a serious security issue – was being handled by the anti-terrorist branch, which had responsibility for the royal family's safety. Detective chief inspector Keith Surtees, senior investigating officer on the case, said later that he 'fully understood the rationale as to why SO13 had been tasked to deal with this given the national security implications and the potential consequences of a person having access to such sensitive information'. Surtees was also flying to and from Iraq, attempting to secure the release of a British hostage, and had several other cases on the go. The anti-terrorist branch, too, had other fish to fry. A year earlier, Islamist terrorism had come to mainland Britain when 52 innocent people were killed on the streets of London in the 7/7 attacks. And, as if the emphasise the point, the very day after Goodman and Mulcaire were arrested, police seized terrorists plotting to blow up at least 10 planes travelling crossing the Atlantic from the United Kingdom. It is as a result of that vast plot that the restrictions on carrying liquid on flights remains so stringent.

Nevertheless, the case had to be examined, and in some secrecy. When they started, the police had no idea what had been going on, simply that the royal princes suspected they were being subjected to even closer scrutiny than usual. The police soon found that the voicemails were the issue, but not much more than that. Clearly they were going to have to rely on the phone companies for the relevant data, but, senior investigating officer on the case Surtees reported later, they were not well placed to do so. 'From the outset, the phone companies had not appreciated that this illegal access was possible, nor had they a means by which they could assist us to ascertain how often and how widespread this was.'

Given that several bags full of evidence from Mulcaire's notebooks had been seized, the police had plenty of evidence that if the phones of the royals and their staff had been hacked, so had hundreds, maybe thousands of others. Mark Lewis later claimed he'd been told there were 6,000 victims, a figure that became the subject of some vigorous legal exchanges later on. In any event, other journalists also seemed to be involved. Surtees later testified that in meetings, in discussing widening the investigation to other journalists' hacking, it was 'highly unlikely in our view to be restricted only to Goodman and was probably quite widespread'.

Detective inspector Mark Maberly endorsed this, telling Lord Justice Leveson: 'There were still lines of enquiry that I would have been keen to follow. In particular, I'd identified three names who, if I had sufficient evidence, I would have liked to have spoken to. I accepted the decision that, you know, the resources were not there to widen the enquiry, and I myself was deployed on other anti-terrorist branch enquiries at the time.'

Yet there were further difficulties, aside from the phone companies' professed ignorance. Legally, the crown prosecution was in uncharted waters, for RIPA, the new law on phone hacking, had not been tested in court. The legal advice they had received was that inter-ception of phone messages was only a criminal offence if it could be proven that the message was listened to before its intended recipient did so, rather than after. This narrow interpretation of an untested law became the widely accepted doctrine of the 'unopened letter'. To add to the police's problems, they had learned enough from the aborted trial of butler Paul Burrell in 2002 to know that the princes would almost certainly refuse to appear in court, and would want to prevent further exposure of the contents of their calls.

In early May of 2006, the police embarked on a test period, during which members of the royal household would only check their voicemails at agreed times. This would help the police monitor who else was picking up messages. As before, Clive Goodman was a regular, but also a 'Paul Williams' was doing so, Williams being one of

Mulcaire's pseudonyms. The two candidates for prosecution had thereby unwittingly presented themselves.

Another Williams, detective chief superintendent Philip Williams, and his colleague Keith Surtees, were getting somewhere, while being very conscious of other, real terrorist demands on their time. The plod-like recitation of Surtees's duties is typical, yet revealing.

> Given the sheer volume of operations within SO13 that we were dealing with at the time, it was not always possible to maintain the operational structure. It was often a case of reacting and dealing with matters as and when I could. There were a number of operations I was working on as were all the other members of SO13. There were not infinite resources available and in order to fulfil our primary objective of ensuring public security was not compromised, we had to prioritise each operation according to the risk. An operation where there was the real possibility of a threat to life on a mass scale would always take priority. The advantage of focussing the investigation on the current two suspects was that it would mean the investigation would quickly get to the point where a prosecution could be brought against them and thereby provide protection to the individuals who had been targeted and swiftly prosecute the appropriate offenders.

When people ask why only Mulcaire and Goodman were prosecuted in 2006, one contributing answer lies here, for better or worse.

The decision to narrow the scope of the prosecution meant omitting potentially promising evidence such as the now famous 'For Neville' email. This was a message in which a junior *News of the World* reporter copied a transcript of more than 30 messages hacked from the phones of the Professional Footballers' Association chief executive, Gordon Taylor, and his legal adviser Jo Armstrong. 'Neville', now known to be news editor Neville Thurlbeck, was never interviewed by the police, nor was the message in question included in the police's submission to the Crown Prosecution Service, the source of some complaint and point-scoring later. The police's failure to use that email added to a sense among some journalists that police were involved in covering up the extent of the illegality. Met deputy commissioner John Yates later told the House of Commons Media Select Committee, 'I would say it is 99.9 per cent certain that, if we were to question Neville Thurlbeck on this matter, he would make no comment.' He said that had been the case with Goodman and Mulcaire. 'I have no evidence to put before him other than the fact that this is a Neville, that he has not read it and we know he has not read it because it has not been transmitted by Mulcaire to Neville Thurlbeck.' In other words, expending time on this would be unlikely to take the case any closer to court.

If the police kept the focus narrow for defensible reasons, how is one to explain the fact that David Perry, the crown prosecution lawyer who provided the advice, specifically asked the police if other journalists were involved, at a case conference on 21st August 2006. No, he was told, there was no such evidence, but he couldn't remember which officer told him that. That case conference, held less than a fortnight after the raid on Mulcaire's premises, was not made aware of the 'for Neville' email, possibly because, as Perry acknowledged, it may not have been found at that point.

It was later pointed out that the crown prosecution had had access to the famous bin bags holding what had been found during the Mulcaire raid, so the evidence had been there for them to inspect. They were not alone in failing to appreciate the significance of the bin bags' contents. Head of the Met counter terrorism command Peter Clarke told the Home Affairs select committee in 2011 that even the Met had decided against doing an 'exhaustive analysis' of their content. 'I could not justify the huge expenditure of resources this would entail over an inevitably protracted period', he said.

Many were inclined to believe, whatever the police doing the investigation may have said, that the mood was set higher up. As we have seen, making waves was discouraged, in the interests of the News International-Met relationship. To the sceptics, the investigation looked half-hearted, an obligation imposed less by a desire to expose unscrupulous journalists and more by a deference to royal sensibilities.

Perhaps surprisingly, John Whittingdale MP, the chairman of the House of Commons Culture, Media and Sport select Committee, found himself in this camp. Not a notable hothead as a critic of News International and occasional dining partner of Les Hinton, he said later: 'There was simply no enthusiasm among Scotland Yard to go beyond the cases involving Mulcaire and Goodman. To start exposing widespread tawdry practices in that newsroom was a heavy stone that they didn't want to try to lift.' It was claimed later by the *New York Times* that police had failed to show the crown prosecution much of the evidence against other victims of hacking, and that press officers at Scotland Yard were urging their own investigators not to upset vested interests. The first, it seems, was explicable, given the police's focussed strategy, and the second, if true, appears to have been robustly ignored by the newspaper's source.

Certainly there were hundreds of names of hacking targets on Mulcaire's files in the bin bags, but many fewer that proved criminality, as opposed to general 'research'. Executives whose names appeared as 'top lefts' on Mulcaire's research sheets also escaped on the same grounds: who was to say, let alone prove to a jury's satisfaction, that they had asked for anything unlawful to be done? The police may have thought intercepting voicemails was just a handy trick. They showed no signs of realising it was an industry. As one very senior officer admitted simply in Freudian terms: 'We just didn't think it was a story.' And in one sense, nor did a great many redtop reporters.

What would have been a story, surely, and arguably endorsed the call for stiffer charges against Mulcaire, was the evidence that he had breached the witness protection programme by looking into child killers Robert Thompson and Mary Bell. The police had evidence that, 8 years later, was sufficiently serious to be raised with the Attorney General, that there had been an apparent breach of High Court injunctions that protected their new identities (and that of two others). Yet no action was taken, and it seems 2 senior officers, in 2006 the then

Commissioner Ian Blair, and John Yates in 2009, were not made aware of the evidence, even though, with hindsight at least, some felt the apparent offences were sufficient to warrant alerting the top brass.

Here is further food for conspiracy theorists. Yet even those not well disposed to the police admit that had they taken action, it might well have been necessary to re-settle them yet again, which would have incurred further enormous expense, and there was no certainty of securing a conviction. In other word, the wider public interest was not best served by pursuing the matter. And Mulcaire, after all, insists he did nothing to make them any easier to trace by possible vigilantes, and that any encounter between either of them and a third party was conducted away from their new homes. He says he never let a journalist have their home addresses.

Confidence within the Met that the correct decision had been taken was stiffened by the fact that ultimately the call had been made by deputy assistant commission-er and the head of counter terrorism command Peter Clarke, a highly respected figure among his peers, and a man to whom the cliché 'unimpeachable integrity' is frequently attached. Whereas his boss assistant commis-sioner Andy Hayman was, as we have seen, a colourful character (and as such has attracted a lot of fire), Clarke was more low-key. Hayman was happy to leave the inves-tigation to Clarke, and had fewer than 5 substantive con-versations with him over the minutiae of the case. He said later that he was shown a list of possible victims of phone hacking. 'As I recall, the list... ran to several hundred names. Of these, there were a small number – perhaps a handful – where there was evidence that the phones had actually been tampered with.'

While Hayman's view of the ongoing case was almost certainly of interest to the *News of the World*, there is no reason to think that he behaved other than correctly. Indeed, he was seemingly in no position to mark their card in any event. He told Lord Leveson that he didn't even know when the search warrants were to be made or the search warrants issued. And the suggestion of unhealthy Met complicity with the paper – whatever else it might be – is not sustained by evidence from the day police arrived at Wapping. One officer recalled in a newspaper interview later: 'There was a Mexican stand-off, a lock down, and they wouldn't let us in. Most newspaper desks would do the same if a cop turned up with a dodgy looking warrant.'

It is a mark of the Met's faith in the senior people at News International that when Rebekah Brooks was called in by the Met to be told that, seemingly, she had been a victim of phone hacking, she was given a thorough briefing as to the state of the investigation. Had she been treated with the suspicion that she warranted (given that she was later put on trial, though acquitted), the police would have played their cards close to their chest. Instead, when she returned to her office she was able to give News International legal affairs manager Tom Crone a full briefing on the state of play. She reported that police had a list of 100-110 victims, that they were visiting those who had been targeted most, that the police wanted to show that Mulcaire's crimes were not restricted to Palace people and that at that stage they had no evidence of other *News of the World* staff hacking phones. Tom Crone passed the news on to Andy

Coulson at the *News of the World*. Four days later, Coulson had dinner with Met commissioner Paul Stephenson. Did they discuss phone hacking? Who knows, but Coulson barely needed to. The police looked on us as the good guys.

Deputy assistant commissioner Clarke later described breaches of privacy as 'odious' and 'distressing', but 'to put it bluntly, they don't kill you', a fact of life doubtless amplified by his colleagues in the anti-terrorism force. By including five non-royal household victims of phone hacking in the charges, the crown prosecution felt a shot had been fired and a message sent.

The decision to confine the charges was a get-out-of-jail-free card for News International executives. Although, as we have seen, the heads of its employees Coulson, Goodman and Mulcaire, had to roll, the edifice of lawless phone interception had survived. Through its lawyers Burton Copeland, the paper had given the impression of being helpful to the enquiry but, as one officer involved said later, they 'employed every legal means possible to avoid allowing the police to delve further than Goodman'.

In fact, contrary to what one might imagine, at News International there was a degree of resentment at the police investigation. Ian Blair had followed John Stevens in the top job at the Met, and he was a different proposition. Blair and Stevens did not get on at all, 'and that is an understatement', says a former colleague of both, although both are insistent in denying any ill feeling. Emotionally, politically (one imagines) and intellectually, they were chalk and cheese. Blair was less inclined to accede to the News International way of doing things, and some in Wapping detected his hand in what they saw as the police's unnecessary diligence in prosecuting Goodman and Mulcaire. As Andy Coulson put it in court in 2014, when it was suggested that he had tried to use his influence to ensure the pair were not sent to prison, the paper 'had a difficult relationship with Ian Blair and I did not feel very influential at that time,' adding 'no other newspaper was investigated in the way we were.'

Whatever the niggles about not being above the law, there had to be some ostentatious mutterings about the learning of lessons and the rigorous upholding of high standards. Those who worked at the *News of the World* – though surprised at a prosecution having been brought – knew the paper had had the narrowest of escapes. The police, too, were anxious to move on. They had secured 2 convictions through guilty pleas, 'sent a message' to other journalists tempted to stray and were now able to get back to catching 'proper' criminals.

For some, the decision to charge just Goodman and Mulcaire was a little too convenient. Was there a deal between the police and the *News of the World*? Much later, in 2013-14, it became publicly apparent that not only had the voicemails of members of the royal household staff been intercepted, but those of the royal princes and Kate Middleton too – although this was not something it was felt needed to be made public. One senior figure denies there was any such explicit deal, but the fact that Goodman and Mulcaire were going to plead guilty must have been a mighty relief all round. He says 'There was no agreement, it just became a self-fulfilling prophecy which suited all sides at the time – a sort of passive gentleman's agreement. The police were rushed off their feet with the airlines plot and not wanting to upset the royals, and the *News of the World* more than happy to air only a fraction of their dirty linen.' Mulcaire's view, as someone directly concerned but outside the process, is as follows: 'If I we hadn't pleaded guilty, the princes would have had to go into the box. Minimising royal embarrassment was part of the deal. Everyone apart from me was a winner, although they could have done us on national security grounds, which would have meant a much longer stretch.' So, remarkably, the royal princes and the bosses at the *News of the World* had identical interests, and the police, with much else on their plate, did not rock the boat.

The matter did live on, but beneath the public's radar. The police agreed after the convictions they needed a strategy for telling those who appeared to have been hacked. Should they tell all of them? Anyone whose name appeared in Mulcaire's notebooks? Just those about whom stories had been written? It was agreed that just a handful of people in sensitive positions should be told. Those who complained later about the cost of Operation Weeting can surely not criticise this earlier, presumably cost-based decision.

But News International had some 'afters' to address. Mark Lewis, a Manchester-based solicitor with an interest in privacy, had represented the Professional Footballers' Association and its chairman Gordon Taylor. Previously he had had dealings with legal affairs manager Tom Crone at the *News of the World* over pictures taken of Taylor with Joanne Armstrong, the PFA's in-house solicitor. The paper believed the pair were having an affair. Lewis applied for an injunction on the grounds of both privacy and the story being untrue. Crone refused, saying the story had been obtained by 'proper journalistic enquiries'.

Lewis remembers it as a curiously defensive response to a run-of-the-mill legal inquiry. His sense of being onto something was hardened both by Tom Crone's willingness, unprecedented in Lewis's cases against News International, to meet Lewis at his Manchester office, and by his opening remark 'we thought this had all gone away.' After that meeting, on 3rd May 2007, Lewis set the legal wheels in motion, launching a case against the paper and against Glenn Mulcaire, and demanding to see relevant documents from Mulcaire's files.

This was getting dangerous for News International. But on the surface, all was calm. After the flurry of activity that followed the jailing of Mulcaire and Goodman, and the departure of Andy Coulson, Colin Myler had become the paper's new editor. He was considered a safe pair of hands, one well versed in the ways of the redtops. In February 2007 Myler asked the Press Complaints Commission to give a seminar on privacy issues and undercover journalism and emailed every member of staff individually, and written to them at home, with the PCC code of practice. *News of the World* staff were told of a new clause in their contracts that meant a failure to comply could result in summary dismissal. In March Les Hinton reassured the House of Commons's Culture Media and Sport Select Committee that the stables did not need further cleaning out. He said 'I believe absolutely that Andy did not have knowledge of what was going on'. He was asked if a rigorous internal inquiry had been conducted. He replied: 'We went, I promise you, to extraordinary lengths within the *News of the World* to find further evidence, and was 'absolutely convinced that Clive Goodman was the only person who knew what was going on'.

Hinton was not alone in asserting that the paper's methods were spotless. Managing editor Stuart Kuttner was similarly confident. He told the Today programme that February that only one *News of the World* journalist had been involved in illegal phone hacking: 'It happened once at the *News of the World*. The reporter was fired; he went to prison. The editor resigned.'

In late May, the Press Complaints Commission obligingly published an exculpatory report, declaring it had no reason to doubt the claim that Goodman's hacking was 'aberrational' and that there was no evidence of systematic phone hacking at the paper. Two days later, just to put the most public of seals on things, Andy Coulson was confirmed as David Cameron's head of communications.

At around this time, Clive Goodman was making a number of extremely serious allegations about widespread unlawful behaviour authorised by senior executives, but only those senior executives were privy to his claims. As we have seen, he settled his case that summer for around £250,000. By November of that year (2007), though, the *News of the World*'s last editor Colin Myler felt free to tell his colleagues at the Society of Editors: 'In the Goodman case, his activities were inde-fensible, but were isolated to a single journalist…. The editor resigned. He wasn't personally culpable for what

Goodman did but he did the honourable thing and took responsibility – a principle we rarely see in public life these days.... There are lots of bad and uncaring people out there. We are on the side of good not evil. Right not wrong. Justice not injustice.'

The world knows now that Goodman did not act alone. So what had happened to the 'rigorous' internal investigation that had been supposed to root out the wrongdoers? Whatever they discovered produced no radical action, at least as far as exposing what had happened in the past was concerned, even if safeguards were amended for the future. So how had they failed to find the source of the stench? Someone close to those looking into it said: 'They have always told friends they knew nothing about what went on – that everyone had read the code, been told to obey the rules.' Yet the investigation was laughably incomplete. Why wasn't there a proper inquiry? 'Don't ask me,' says a friend. 'But the fact that they didn't shows you the level of confidence that it didn't need to be shut off.' In other words, the penny hadn't dropped. The story was not going to go away but – in their attitudes at least – Murdoch's people were behaving with as great a sense of unshakeable entitlement as ever. And why not? Politicians were falling over themselves to be in Rupert Murdoch's good books, and surely *nobody* was interested in phone hacking?

That summer, the game was to change again. In August, Rupert Murdoch won control of Dow Jones, giving him one of the prizes he had long sought, the *Wall Street Journal*. He insisted that he bring his great confidant Les Hinton over to New York to help him oversee it, and so at the end of that year, Hinton crossed the Atlantic.

According to journalist Michael Wolff, Rebekah Brooks hoped she might move up to fill Hinton's shoes. Murdoch, though, wanted to promote his son James, but was unsure how far he should do so. Previously he had promoted his son Lachlan to be News Corporation's deputy operations chief, but it had not worked well. Knowing he was the boss's son, as opposed to someone who had unambiguously earned the title, many members of staff had all but ignored him. Roger Ailes, boss of Fox News, called Lachlan 'callow' and 'unsubstantial'.

'Rupert didn't want that happening to James,' recalls one close associate, 'so he made sure he was quite the biggest fish in the pond.' Rupert made James chief executive of News Corporation Europe and Asia, which meant he was in charge of News International in the UK, as well as many other things. 'Running News International was the rounding off of his education,' says the source. 'Rupert backed off for two years in order to let James run things. Rebekah was the go-between between James and Rupert. She was the one who told Rupert what was going on. James hated it at News International, being a guy with a background in TV. It wasn't his thing at all. He didn't want control of News International, whereas Rebekah was desperate to have it.'

The evidence James Murdoch was to give to the Commons media select committee endorses that impression. He had arrived at a smoothly running ship (with the obvious exception of the ongoing legal concerns), and to a degree had to go with flow. He also knew that his father had enormous faith in the ability of Rebekah Brooks, so it would be understandable for him to be guided by her. James Murdoch inherited the phone hacking mess, but his attempts to clean it up or even were undistinguished, at best. There was an opportunity for the company to start afresh, but it was shunned, presumably because somebody concluded that opening the Pandora's box of Mulcaire's files would be a disaster. It was decided, probably by default, to fight fires as they flared up.

One such was the continuing Gordon Taylor case. On May 24 2008 Tom Crone told Colin Myler that PFA chief executive Gordon Taylor's legal team have 'fatal' evidence and pointed to the so-called 'for Neville' email proving 'we actively made use of a large number of extremely private voicemails'. They sought outside counsel's advice, calling in Michael Silverleaf QC. His verdict was predictably bad. On June 3, 2008 Silverleaf told Crone that News International had a 'culture of illegal information access.' He also warned it would be extremely damaging to the publisher's reputation if that info became public' as a result of the Gordon Taylor case. There was, he declared, 'overwhelming evidence of the involvement of a number of senior journalists' in relation to accessing information about Gordon Taylor.

A week latera meeting was held at which, allegedly, it was made clear to James Murdoch that hacking was not restricted to a single journalist. It later emerged that Murdoch had been sent an email mentioning the 'nightmare scenario' of Taylor having discovered the involvement of another journalist in phone hacking. Murdoch said he failed to read the email properly.

Things went from bad to worse at the end of June (on June 27, 2008), when a judge in the case ordered Mulcaire to identify the journalist in question. This had to be prevented at almost any cost. Gordon Taylor was promptly offered a £425,000 settlement, to include his legal costs, which brought the figure to around £700,000. Two associates of Taylor also received awards, raising the total for what would otherwise have been a run-of-the-mill privacy issue to around £1 million.

The Taylor settlement was astonishing. It was a vast sum, and spoke volumes for News International's nervousness. Executives later claimed unconvincingly that the alternative, to fight the case, would have ended up costing a comparable amount. The problem for those who were confident of there being many similar victims was that the settlement was a secret. Until, that was, on 8th July 2009, Nick Davies revealed the details in the *Guardian*. The paper reported that journalists for whom the Prime Minister's communications spokesman was responsible 'were engaged in hundreds of apparently illegal acts', that police knew 'two or three thousand' mobile phones had been targeted, that executives 'albeit in good faith', misled a parliamentary select committee and that police had failed to inform many of the victims. To those who had been following the case, it seemed like a great leap forward.

To the police, though, it was underwhelming. The Met's new commissioner Paul Stephenson asked John Yates for his view. Should the police re-open the investigation? After just eight hours he decided no, it shouldn't. This surely, was a major stitch-up, or so it seemed to many. The *Guardian* had not only revealed the extent of the wrongdoing, but also police knowledge of it. Why was no further action to be taken?

But for Scotland Yard, there was nothing new. Met

deputy commissioner Yates said later: 'The *Guardian* had raised a lot of issues. It was a bloody great story but the question was: was there anything new in it for us? The answer was no there wasn't.' Yates was concerned that the claims in the *Guardian* had come from unnamed sources, and that the payment to Taylor, while strikingly large, was in itself proof of nothing. 'I held a series of meetings with the senior investigating officer. We looked at what the CPS had said. It was a landmark case and we still don't have case law on it. To have given the go-ahead for a full review of a case of that nature would have involved 4 or 5 people and 5 or 6 months work and a lot of resources and in July 2009 why would I do that?' At the same time, the director of public prosecutions Keir Starmer, who had 'ordered an urgent examination of the material supplied to the CPS', also concluded on the basis of his department's researches that there was no new material that could be fruitfully examined. The fact that Starmer had lunch with Rebekah Brooks the following month aroused a degree of interest. It took place in the company of his then director of comunications and the *Sun*'s political greybeard Trevor Kavanagh at their offices, and covered the role of the Director of Public Prosecutions, the Crown Prosecution Service and the Human Rights Act. Strikingly, for reasons unknown, one issue was not on the agenda. 'Phone hacking was never discussed,' says Starmer. This non-discussion was perhaps down to it remaining an issue for a few obsessives and still didn't loom large on the national radar.

The Met also knew that Murdoch's power was undi-minished, and reopening the case would cause a lot of trouble. One officer well acquainted with the Met's thought processes recalls: 'It was certainly part of our thinking – perhaps the single most important part in deciding whether to investigate further – knowing that the *News of the World* would stonewall and claim they had cooperated fully, which would mean that it was most, most unlikely that any requests for additional (and incriminating) information would have been met.'

In hindsight, it was a calamitously bad decision. Yates admitted later to a journalist it was it was 'pretty crap'. He was to tell the Home Affairs Select Committee that at that time the *News of the World* 'appears to have failed to co-operate in the way that we know they should have… we didn't have the information we should have done'.

There is no reason to doubt the reasons he gave for it, but other considerations should be added. One is the feeling that if so saintly a figure as deputy assistant commissioner Peter Clarke had concluded three years earlier that further resources expended on phone hacking rather than counter-terrorism were likely to be wasted, why would anyone argue? 'We did tend to say: "Why doubt Peter Clarke's view?"' said another very senior Met figure. 'It wasn't a concern about corruption or cover-ups or anything, it was the opposite. We had so much faith in Peter Clarke's judgment that we didn't review things afresh as we should have done. That was definitely part of the problem.'

Another is that pressure to have the case re-opened had been led by the left-of-centre *Guardian*. Executives at News International attributed its keenness on the story to the paper's generally anti-Murdoch stance. In short, it was all 'political', they said. The fact that the likely next Prime

Minister had a former *News of the World* editor at his side added to journalists' appetite for the story. One very senior officer involved in the case said he thought the perception of the story being a groundless anti-Tory smear did infect the police. 'I just thought…. "What is this? What *is* the *Guardian* on about?" It was a minor issue… were we naïve? Yes, in hindsight we certainly were.' Another officer involved in the case said: 'We thought it was political, but should have known journalists don't go on like that unless they have good reason.'

The decision could not have done more to feed the conspiracy theorists. In a PR sense, it was certainly the wrong decision, as it stoked a belief that the police were complicit in a cover-up. Yet, remarkably, there are still those attached to the Met who believe that even if the case had been reopened in 2009, it is doubtful how much would have been uncovered. They would certainly have had to go through the bin liners rather more assiduously than they had. But who would have talked to them? News International had shown no inclination to come clean, and its journalists were all back in harness and unlikely to make trouble.

To compound the police's evident lack of enthusiasm for the case, a mounting number of instances were identified where victims of Mulcaire's hacking were not informed of the fact, despite police promises. This was partly because it was unclear whether they had actually had their voicemails intercepted, partly because some were simply unidentifiable, and partly for reasons unaccountable. It is fair to assume that the police simply decided in 2006 that it was too much of a distraction and too expensive to catalogue all the victims and inform them. Various criteria were adopted at various times, but these were not rigidly adhered to, with the result that some illustrious targets were left in the dark. Among these was former deputy prime minister John Prescott, whose name was found in Mulcaire's files but whose phone may not have been hacked. Prescott was furious that he was not informed until years later. It has been claimed by Peter Clarke that John Reid, as Home Secretary, was given a briefing about the phone hacking affair. Reid denied this, saying: 'I can categorically say that I did not receive any briefing from the Met suggesting that there was widespread hacking including MPs and the deputy PM.'

Campaigners and the growing number of lawyers pursuing civil cases against News International were stupefied by the decision not to re-open the case. In November of that year, as if to add to the mounting incredulity and with timing worthy of Gilbert and Sullivan, the Press Complaints Commission published a second report, once again failing to find evidence of further wrongdoing. Three months later, as the general election loomed, the House of Commons Media Select Committee, after a marathon tussle over the correct wording, concluded that it was 'inconceivable' that Clive Goodman had acted alone, and soon after, another victim, Max Clifford, announced he had been paid £1million to drop a legal action that would have named the others involved.

The police did sit up and take notice when in September 2010, the *New York Times* published a 6,000-word inquiry of its own. It quoted former *News of the*

World reporter Sean Hoare, saying that Andy Coulson had actively encouraged the hacking of phones, and contained a number of witnesses, by now willing to speak on the record. John Prescott announced he was seeking judicial review over the police's handling of the case, having learned that his name was in Mulcaire's files but nobody had informed him, allegedly because it was feared he would leak it to the press. And, wonder of wonders, the police announced they were to re-open the enquiry, though looking only at new evidence. The director of public prosecutions Keir Starmer announced (though few noticed) that the interpretation of the law on phone hacking was to be widened, to include messages already listened to by the intended recipient. With the ending of the doctrine of the 'unopened letter', surely now the police's job would be easier? In early November, at last, the police interviewed Andy Coulson, by this time working in Downing Street, but afforded him the courtesy of being a witnesss, rather than interviewing him under caution. Was the New York *Times* article, at last, to be the turning point? No. In December, police said they had found no new evidence.

Given how much the black bin bags could have revealed about Mulcaire's taskers, this was getting silly.

The straw that broke the camel's back came from one of the lawyers representing the celebrity victims. Solicitor Mark Thomson had been beavering away in his small office in the Strand, bringing his legal expertise to bear to make the police let Mulcaire's victims see the files relevant to them. Fourteen months earlier it had been confirmed that his client Sienna Miller's name was in Mulcaire's files, and 5 months earlier he had asked for an order to make the police hand over Mulcaire's notes that related to her. Eventually, on 15th December, the 'top left' name of the person who tasked Mulcaire was revealed as being that of someone until then claimed to be blameless.

Who knows if the development was even mentioned when David Cameron and James Murdoch sat down to a cheery Christmas dinner at Rebekah Brooks's Cotswolds farmhouse a week later, but it cannot have been a very happy festive period for News International's lawyers. If ever the 'rogue reporter' defence took a body blow, this was it. The news meant the police had to change its position – this was unignorable, a point not missed by Keir Starmer, who could not allow the Met to ignore the mounting accusations. And News International now needed a new version of events. The previous one, involving a rogue reporter, had become laughable.

January 2011 brought another torrent of developments. The crown prosecution announced a comprehensive review of all the phone hacking material, following the Sienna Miller development. Andy Coulson resigned as David Cameron's director of communications, saying it was difficult to give his job its full attention. Operation Weeting was set up by the Met, under deputy assistant commissioner Sue Akers. It emerged that Gordon Brown and Tony Blair and their families were concerned that they had been victims of phone hacking and had asked police to investigate.

And News International came up with what the police had been waiting 4 years for. 'Significant new evidence', in the form of emails about Tessa Jowell and David Mills, Lord Frederick Windsor and an adviser to John Prescott, was handed over. This was a game-changer. Where previously the police had believed News International bosses, and later had had mounting scepticism, here at last was concrete proof that all the talk of rigorous investigations had been nonsense. News editor Ian Edmondson, suspended before Christmas, was sacked.

The steam train was now rolling, the police were desperate to make amends, and the handing over of the emails marked the unavoidable change in News International's position. The company had appointed new executives to handle the case, and a great many civil cases were settled in recognition of past wrongs. Quite where the blame lay remained a moot point, one the police were going to look into. In April, three executives were arrested under suspicion of unlawfully accessing voicemail messages, but that was just the start of the carnage.

For the police, though, there was a problem. News International had an automatic archiving system for email installed in 2005, but some executives had opted out of using it. So as it happened, very few of, for example, Rebekah Brooks's emails survived her time in some of the company's most senior chairs. Hardly any emails remained from the years 1999 to 2005. Nearly 4.5m emails from 2005 to 2010 were purged by News International as part of a routine clean-out in September 2010, but 1.49m had subsequently been recovered from other sources. Jurors also heard that Brooks' old hard drive from her office in Wapping had been removed before the computer was thrown away after an office move.

Further evidence had been emerging casting doubt on

the police's impartiality. John Yates, as we have seen, was a known friend of Neil Wallis. The *News of the World*'s former executive editor's name had not been mentioned in the context of the phone hacking scandal, and Yates saw little problem in their association. In early 2009 Wallis's daughter Amy had applied for a job working with the Met, and Yates forwarded her email of application to the head of the Met's human resources, saying Wallis had been a 'great friend' to the force. The boss of HR reportedly said she was keen to accommodate Ms Wallis 'particularly in the light of her father's position/relationship', although she later said she had no memory of having said that. Amy Wallis was given a 6 month contract and a more secure position subsequently. Though she was clearly talented, the proper procedures had not been followed. Again, this didn't look good. (Wallis was later to point out in mitigation that deputy commissioner Tim Godwin and Catherine Crawford chief executive of the Metropolitan Police Authority had requested work experience at News International for their children, which just compounded the sense of cosiness. He forgot to mention head of communications Dick Fedorcio's son doing work experience on the *Sun* in 2003 and 2004, and former Met commissioner Ian Blair's son doing the same in 2007).

Further inappropriateness came to light when it was revealed that Met commissioner Paul Stephenson, head of the Met, had an operation on a growth on his femur, and accepted an offer from a friend, Stephen Purdew, to stay at Champneys, a health farm in Hertfordshire, of which he was the managing director. The stay, which included considerable amounts of physiotherapy, was worth around £12,000. Stephenson reported that he had accepted it because he felt guilty at the amount of time he had taken off work, and wanted to speed up his recovery. The problem for Stephenson was that Neil Wallis was responsible for the spa's PR. By this time, Wallis had come to great prominence for his work at the *News of the World* and the police investigation was continuing. There was a clear conflict of interest.

The press made merry with the story, which was moving into the realms of hysteria. If as blameless and decent a figure as Paul Stephenson was seemingly 'on the take', was there no senior police officer who was not compromised in some way? Inside the Met, there was sympathy for Stephenson. A close family member had suffered a major bereavement, a former colleague points out, and there had never previously been any suspicion of impropriety against him. Indeed, he may be open to the charge of excessive honesty and even naivety. Courtesy of the *News of the World*, his Met colleague John Yates had enjoyed expensive meals at Scalini, Scotts and the Mandarin Oriental Hotel in London, which had helped enhance a developing caricature of high living at the Met. Other officers had also laid their work habits open to misinterpretation, so, knowing that there was increasing suspicion of the motives of some on his staff, Stephenson had brought in measures requiring them to declare anything that could look as if it created a conflict of interest. Thus by declaring his own recuperation at Champneys to the Metropolitan Police Authority, he sealed his own fate. Had he not declared it, he might still be in the job today. The fact that his declaration was publicly available, and that it took a while for the press to notice it, suggests somebody may have tipped a journalist off that it was there, but there is no evidence as to who, if anyone, that was.

On July 4th, The *Guardian* reported that Milly Dowler's voicemail had been hacked. This caused, as we have seen, the stratospheric development of the story. Previously the issue could be dismissed as being only of concern to whingeing celebrities and navel-gazing media types. Now it was about gross intrusion into a ghastly human tragedy. In the following fortnight David Cameron launched what became the Leveson enquiry, the *News of the World* closed down, Andy Coulson and Neil Wallis were arrested, the Murdochs dropped their bid to buy BSkyB, and Rebekah Brooks, Les Hinton, Met chief Paul Stephenson and Assistant Commissioner John Yates resigned.

Yet more mud was thrown at the Met when it was revealed after he left the *News of the World* in 2009, Neil Wallis was asked to submit a tender to Scotland Yard to offer PR advice for two days a week. One of the reasons the Met chose Wallis was that he would offer the Met access to Andy Coulson, and thus to his boss David Cameron, then regarded as likely to be in Downing Street after the election. At that point, as everyone was very quick to point out, Wallis appeared to be a spotless figure. Such doubts as there were were linked only to the fact of his being questioned by police, and those faded again once the matter was dropped.

When Paul Stephenson resigned, he spoke, seemingly, for many in the police, when he pointed out the curiosity of Cameron having appointed Andy Coulson to be his communications chief. The message was, if the PM, with all the back-up of the state at his disposal, had Ok'd Coulson, it was no surprise if others did so too.

Though Stephenson later denied having had a swipe at the Prime Minister, it was not an attack Cameron appreciated, later raising it with Stephenson in person, according to police sources. Cameron's remarks to the Leveson inquiry in 2012 were a reflection of a continuing frustration, one senses: 'Yes, I accepted [Coulson's] undertakings but so did a number of other organisations,' he said, citing the Culture Media Sports Select Committee, the police, the Press Complaints Commission and the jury in a perjury trial.' Even the Prime Minister was playing the blame game.

While some of the cases of unhealthily close links between police and press could be explained as arising from forgetfulness as to how it would look from outside, much less ambiguous instances were coming to light. As part of the supposed clean-up, cases of police officers (and other public servants) being paid for stories were emerging. A large network of 'coppers-on-the-take' had been built up, and News International, now desperate to be seen to be cleaning up its act, was throwing its sources, and some of its journalists, to the wolves. It was as different from the situation in 2008-9 as could be imagined. One Met officer, April Casburn, was sent to prison for offering information to a journalist on how the phone hacking investigation was proceeding. It could not have done more to blacken the police's name. The sense of an inept, complicit force was irresistible to many. Many careers have been ended by this story, some through the bad faith of certain individuals, some through incompetence, some through sheer naivety.

Among those accused of turning a blind eye was Craig Denholm. He was a detective chief superintendent in 2002 and was in charge of the search for missing schoolgirl Milly Dowler. As we have seen, Stewart Kuttner contacted the Surrey force and played them he had a recording of the message from the employment agency. The Independent Police Complaints Commission later said the Surrey force had been afflicted by 'collective amnesia' over the case. The search for Dowler had been led by Denholm, and the IPCC concluded that the *News of the World*'s accessing of the voicemails had been known about 'at all levels' and that it was 'hard to understand' how Denholm could have been unaware of it. While the search for Dowler would have been his main preoccupation at the time, Denholm did nothing subsequently to draw attention to the paper's interception of voicemails, let alone blow the whistle on it. 'Denholm had a chance to lift the lid on the whole thing, but didn't', says one former colleague of the Surrey man. If his silence in 2002 was understandable, his continued holding of his tongue as the investigations continued and while the police were known to be looking for evidence was remarkable for an upholder of the law. 'Denholm could and should have acted in 2002, 2006 and 2009. Heaven knows why he didn't', said a former colleague.

There is the key issue. It's fair to assume that most police were unaware about the possibility of listening in to voicemails. Those who did know probably concluded it wasn't a hanging offence, that they had a great many more important things to attend to and would never have imagined how widespread it was. So when they were reassured by News International people that nothing was amiss, they were relieved. People on whose side they thought they were said there was nothing in the story, and they were trusting enough to believe them. If, as Labour former minister Alan Johnson asserted, they were either 'evasive, dishonest or lethargic', the last of these seems most appropriate. There was dishonesty, in that clearly there were individual officers who were on the take from reporters, but the police is no monolith. That does not mean there was an institutional cover-up across the board by senior officers. In their case, the crime was being too busy and too trusting, a naivety that complemented the belief that 'it wasn't a story'. The case of Daniel Morgan's murder is appalling, but this case teaches us that before looking for a conspiracy, eliminate the cock-ups first, and there are plenty to choose from.

If there was a conspiracy, it was of a curiously British type, and a most almighty cock-up resulted. Having been alerted by the Palace to a possible national security issue, the police satisfied themselves that it was no such thing, more like an issue they regarded as being the responsibility of the press's regulatory authority ('we are not a trade regulator,' said a senior officer very early in the process.) As such, it was a serious one, but not sufficiently grave to require anything as alarmingly democratic as the Royal princes going into the witness box. In a spirit of deference, the issue needed to be both addressed and put to bed, and with minimal royal embarrassment, so when it became clear that Goodman and Mulcaire were willing to plead guilty, pretty well everyone was happy. Had more searching questions been asked, the taxpayer would have been spared having to fork out millions on Operations Weeting, Elvedon and Tuleta years later, and the Met would have been spared quite reasonable complaints, from within its own ranks and beyond, about the diversion of nearly 200 officers from the job of fighting 'real' crime.

11

Spooks

If the news gods wanted to ruin Glenn Mulcaire's children's school summer holidays, they could scarcely have planned anything more devastating than what happened on 4th July 2011. More than four years after he had been released from prison, and just as he felt he was re-emerging in the world of work, things had started to go wrong again, and often in inexplicable ways. A few days earlier, as the legal wheels continued to turn and more and more victims, often at the urging of a burgeoning group of lawyers, came forward to claim compensation, his former *News of the World* boss Greg Miskiw telephoned Mulcaire out of the blue. The pair had not been in touch for a year or so.

The *News of the World* was by now fighting an increasingly desperate battle to prevent the truth about the extent of the paper's lawlessness coming out. There was a huge amount at stake, so lawyers were being followed, witnesses watched, threats issued. Three executives had been arrested in recent weeks, and the picture looked bleak. Rebekah Brooks had been confronted with something pretty serious, too. On 23rd June 2011, she contacted her ex-husband Ross Kemp to say she needed to talk to him about phone hacking. She also asked her PA Cheryl Carter to find her notebooks from 2002 and 2003.

A few days after the 23rd came the call from Miskiw to Mulcaire. He was saying goodbye. He told Mulcaire that he had decided to go abroad, to Florida. Mulcaire didn't really know why he was going, but it was hardly a surprise. Whatever was coming next was not going to be good news. 'We will always be close. You're one of my top 6 best friends,' said Miskiw, who seemed to realise that clouds were gathering, but did not spell out in what form. Mulcaire says: 'It was a very odd phone call. I have replayed it in my mind a hundred times.' It was what Miskiw didn't say that made its mark on Mulcaire.

Within days, the *Guardian* had run the story saying that the *News of the World* had hacked and deleted Milly Dowler's phone messages, thereby encouraging her parents to believe she had picked up the messages and therefore was still alive. As the article effectively invited the reader to infer that Glenn Mulcaire was responsible, thus began the worst period of Mulcaire's adult life. The opprobrium he attracted as a result came in a deluge. He was as disreputable as it is possible to be. For a person whose self-image is of someone who tries to 'do the right thing', it was shattering.

We have seen how the story exploded from there. But looking back, Mulcaire wonders about that phone call from Miskiw. Had Miskiw known what was coming? He may have done, as he was presumably still in touch with people at News International. Mulcaire suspects Miskiw did know. 'If he did, to ring up and say "I'm one of your best friends" and not give me a heads up… I find that extraordinary,' says Mulcaire. 'Maybe he thought it would get out that he had told me, or that the conversation was being listened to, which I assumed. But if he had something to say, but couldn't spell it out, so we had to use some sort of code or subliminal message, he knew me well enough to know that I would be able to draw an inference. But he didn't.' That was the last time the pair spoke until a fruitless approach was made in the preparation of this book.

The Dowler claim, as we have seen, inflated and infected coverage of the phone hacking story for years, but the legal process ground on unrelentingly. More and more legal letters arrived at Mulcaire's house, telling him that another celebrity was demanding that he reveal who had tasked him to intercept their voicemails. Lawyers had long been including him in their claims, in the hope of putting pressure on him to give evidence against his former bosses. Though under enormous pressure of a different sort, he showed no signs of buckling. He had been advised to say nothing by his lawyers and, after a hiccup when Rupert Murdoch publicly expressed surprise that Mulcaire's fees were being paid by his company, his legal costs were covered (although he had to take legal action to ensure that). So indifferent did he become to the writs that he failed even to open most of the letters, throwing them on the floor and allowing them to pile up in the corner of the family's kitchen.

The Weeting Inquiry had been set up in January 2011, and the police – humiliated and uncomfortably conscious of the need to get it right this time – were trying to leave nothing to chance. A total of 185 officers were employed on the 3 operations (into phone hacking, illegal payments to public officials and computer hacking), at an expected cost of £40 million. Whereas previously the process of informing victims of phone hacking had been performed unenthusiastically and incompletely, this time no hostages were to be left. Eighteen months after its inception, deputy assistant commissioner Sue Akers, who ran the three Met investigations, said just over 1,000 likely victims of phone hacking had been identified, from an estimated 4,700 names in Mulcaire's files, rather fewer than initial estimates had suggested.

Many of the files were little more than hand-written scrawls of uncertain intent. The originals of those files were formally confiscated, so Mulcaire had no legal claim to them beyond that of any defendant in a criminal case. The vast majority of the entries contained personal details, the dissemination of which would breach the data protection laws. But lawyers representing victims were allowed access to digital images of the relevant pages, though often in redacted form. The court demanded Mulcaire only see them on a computer in his solicitor's office, but he persisted in calling them 'my files'. This, he insisted, was not out of a particular proprietorial feeling towards them, but because he said they would show his motivation and, in particular, who he was working for. Yet in many cases, he says, the 'top lefts' (the names of his tasker, usually written on the corner of the page) were absent, seemingly torn off, and some pages were missing entirely. He couldn't understand why.

When in December 2011 Mulcaire was arrested for the second time, it followed the awful claim that he had deleted a key voicemail message on Milly Dowler's phone. Having carried the can, with Clive Goodman, for the voicemail interceptions in 2007, he was horrified to have the issue brought up again. Yet since the story had exploded, the police had had an obligation to do the job properly this time, so, though he was annoyed, he was not entirely surprised. Once again, his house was raided. This time the police's arrival was even more invasive. They came back and took away the rest of his files, as if acknowledging that they should have taken them the first time.

Alison Mulcaire remembers the second raid being worse than the first. 'They wrecked Georgia's bedroom, and broke lots of glass. They picked up the bed and bashed it on the ground and were pulling stuff off the radiator. I was terrified, the girls were screaming. I thought it was some kind of a setup. The paperwork they had had a chance to take the first time had never been touched, so they looked at all the same stuff again. They were just nasty.'

A day or two later, she, who even at that late stage knew very little about her husband's work, was asked to come into the local police station on the following Monday. 'I remember crying from Friday till the Monday, worrying about what they are going to ask me. On the Sunday we had Sam's first communion, so it hung over that horribly.' She was asked, she says, 'the most ridiculous questions, like "were you the one in control of the phone hacking?", "Who was working under you?", "When did you first meet Rebekah Brooks?"'

This time, several more people at the *News of the World* had been arrested. The true story was to be given a chance to emerge, Mulcaire trusted. He had always said that he had acted for the greater good, but felt he had had little opportunity to explain himself. In the context of the Dowler claim, this time, at least, he believed he would get a chance to spell out his position.

Conversely, though, a different legal tack was being pursued. Nicola Phillips, former assistant to Max Clifford, was pursuing her case against Mulcaire and News International, and was demanding to know who had commissioned Mulcaire's work. Although he wanted to spell out his position, he was being advised by his lawyers not to do so, on the grounds that he was not obliged to self-incriminate. It was a finely balanced decision, but in the end he followed his lawyers' advice and fought the case as far as the Supreme Court, opting not to reveal the names. He did this partly in the belief that that way, at least, he would avoid being charged a second time.

But in July 2012 the Supreme Court came to its decision, and Mulcaire lost. He was to be forced to reveal who had ordered him to intercept voice messages. This was the decision that Mark Lewis and a string of other lawyers had been hoping for. And only a few days later, on 24th July, the Crown Prosecution Service announced that he would have to return to court, to face charges relating to Charles Clarke, Andy Gilchrist, Delia Smith and, crucially, Milly Dowler.

During his three interviews with the police in May 2013, he had spelt out his 'belief system'. He told them how he believed the *News of the World* was working hand-in-glove with the police. While this does not reach the statute's narrow definition of explicitly stated 'lawful authority' through an 'empowering belief', it illustrates Mulcaire's fierce conviction of his motives that were internationally trashed when the Dowler allegation was first made in 2011. If there was an explicit authorisation on the part of the police, it has still not been uncovered.

His critics might doubt his motives where snooping on celebrities is concerned. But nobody could doubt the force, the self-belief and the humanity with which he speaks of crime against the young and innocent.

In one statement to the police, Mulcaire speaks of having been given information about a possible suspect: 'I was given information, led to believe he was in custody, to find out information about him, between the eyes…. To make sure that he could be clear on certain dates and my information on my notes will confirm that. So that's where we're at regarding lawful authority and it was more than evident in my corner work, it was more than evident on my Project Dowler in the notes saying 'Tell the Police' you know, you can't, there can't be any other key points that I can put on that piece of paper in regards to what I believed at the time. My mission statement at the time was to find that little girl as quickly as possible.'

By the third interview, he felt he was getting somewhere, that the police were coming to understand his point of view. A detective inspector, previously absent, joined the interviewers. One officer, Emma King of the Weeting investigation, in particular, seemed to 'get it', he felt. He was also treated rather more accommodatingly than before, with a 'where would you like to sit, Glenn?'

But for his lawyers, his stated motives were not enough to provide a defence in the eyes of the law. When it came to confronting the legal hazards ahead of him, he was advised to plead guilty on all counts. He admitted he had hacked the celebrities' phones but insisted unshakeably that his work on the Dowler case was done with good intentions. When it came to pleading on this charge, he played his cards close to his chest.

> I wasn't sure who I could trust during that court
> process and didn't even tell my lawyers how I was
> going to plead. I wanted to have my say in court,
> and was prepared to go all the way down the line
> and plead not guilty on conspiracy. I wanted to call
> key witnesses and paperwork to explain why I
> believed I was doing it on behalf of the law. It was
> not like the three other charges, which were
> celebrity-based and I felt fell into a different
> category. I wanted to explain in court why I
> thought I was acting with police agreement.

He pleaded guilty to the interception of celebrities'
phones, and that of Dowler, but he refused to admit guilt
to 'conspiracy' on the Dowler charge, as mentioned
earlier. In his mind, the connotation of a conspiracy was
sinister and based on bad faith. By pleading 'not guilty' he
hoped he would have his day in court. That way, he
believed, he would be able to explain to the judge why he
had done what he did, and how he had always told the
truth during legal proceedings.

But he never got his chance to explain himself in
court. Others against whom the charge was laid pleaded
guilty, but when he refused to do so, the charge against
him was dropped. His fox was shot. So instead of
throwing himself on the mercy of the court, he is now
reliant on his own efforts, supported by the documents
taken from his home in the 2 raids.

To someone who is not familiar with Mulcaire's notes,
there is no way of knowing what documents are missing.

There is no index, and the sheets of paper were only ever written *ad hoc* and for his own use. There was no filing system that would identify any gaps. But Mulcaire is certain that files are missing and wants to know why. In some cases he thinks he knows, but he does not want to speculate or point fingers without hard evidence. In one case in particular his wife Alison confirms his account, having seen the originals herself.

The police have acknowledged that some individuals' files – around 20 according to one estimate – were held back for 'operational reasons'. This term relates to files on people still of interest to the police, and, to speculate, may include taskings on terrorists or paedophiles, the largest two categories that fell within his early 'Special Investigations' work for *News of the World*.

But among the most startling absences are files relating to the Milly Dowler case. In his remarks at the end of the trial, Mr Justice Saunders rejected the idea that Mulcaire had been working on behalf of the police. He said: "Mulcaire knew perfectly well that he was hacking Milly's phone to assist the News of the World to obtain a story by finding her." He went on to say he did not intend to hear evidence on the issue of whether Mulcaire was assisting the police because he was "quite satisfied that it is incapable of belief". Some on Mulcaire's team took these remarks, made on the day of sentencing, to signal the fact that he was to receive a suspended sentence, as if to offset any criticism that Mulcaire was being let off lightly. In any event, he was indeed given a suspended sentence.

As the judge suggested, he had not seen all the evidence on this, but it seems very few people have. Mulcaire insists, and is supported by his wife Alison, that a handful of sheets, with a 'top left' name on it, are missing, and that one or more of those sheets bear the name of a third tasker, whose role in the affair he believes to be crucial. That person cannot be named for legal reasons, but Mulcaire insists a whole new chapter to the story will emanate from that document, if it is ever made public. He has given that name to the police, and he sees no reason why it should not be made public once any necessary legal processes have been exhausted. The fact that Neville Thurlbeck, through his barrister, called Mulcaire's claim 'intrinsically ridiculous' seemed merely to strengthen Mulcaire's belief. More significant, he says, was the silence of Greg Miskiw on the matter.

There are other files that are equally perplexing. The deployment of Mulcaire to look into the royal princes' relationship with Guy Pelly, a gregarious student at Cirencester agricultural college, is one. The Queen is said to have told former butler Paul Burrell that 'there are forces at work in this country about which we have no knowledge'. For those, like Her Majesty, who detect a sinister hand, and who heard references at the Old Bailey to mysterious representatives of the secret state, Pelly's story has plenty to offer.

It is well known that what started the phone hacking scandal was a complaint by Prince William that he suspected unlawful means were being used to acquire stories about him. A blunder by the *News of the World* made it obvious to the Prince that they had written about an event 'before the story had even left the room'. What is more easily forgotten is how the *News of the World* had been targeting him and his friends for some years. The young princes had every reason to loathe the press after the high-speed chase and death of their mother in Paris in 1997, and in subsequent years they appear to have indulged themselves extensively. In February 2000 the *Sunday Times* reported that royal bodyguards were becoming increasingly concerned about drug use by people who hang around the Prince. Elsewhere there was a story about Tom Parker Bowles, son of Camilla, having been caught taking cocaine. Helpfully 'a family friend' was reported as saying: '[Prince Charles] is happy that his son is wise enough to know how to keep away from such things.' 'Family friends' tend to pop up when potentially damaging stories are being sanitised with the help of expert press handling.

But the extensive bacchanalia at the Rattlebone pub in Sherston, Gloucestershire, just 5 miles from Highgrove, was enough to set tongues wagging, whatever else may have been going on in Wapping. The story wouldn't go away, and kept getting that bit closer to the throne itself. A story by Mazher Mahmood and Clive Goodman said that Prince Harry was using cannabis, and that his father was shocked at how often he did so. Guy Pelly, a friend of Prince Harry since prep school, was singled out as being a bad influence, and was named as being the person 'who introduced Harry to cannabis in June [2001]', reported a well-placed source. The same family friend explained how seriously Prince Charles took the matter, and how his sons were 'on their guard against such a thing ever being allowed to happen again.'

Further drugs exposés were run in January and February 2002. Attempts were made in senior circles to isolate Pelly. Mark Bolland, Prince Charles's deputy private secretary, managed to defuse the worst aspects of the story while painting the Prince in a benign and sagacious light. The Press Complaints Commission obligingly agreed that the matter was 'an exceptional matter of public interest', so there was no unpleasant talk about anybody's privacy being invaded.

Just the engineering of the story and its impact said plenty about powerful forces. Mark Bolland was the partner of Guy Black, head of the Press Complaints Commission. The pair took occasional holidays with Rebekah Brooks, then at the helm of the *News of the World*, and in 2006 she was to be a witness at the couple's civil partnership ceremony.

The fly in this agreeable ointment was that the Princes were quite happy jogging along as before. Indeed, Pelly was lodged at Highgrove the weekend the *News of the World*'s story appeared, and the princes were photographed 'shoulder to shoulder with shamed pal Pelly in a brave show of support at Twickenham'. The pictures enabled the princes to talk of the importance of loyalty to friends, and once again for Prince Charles to emerge as a beacon of regal magnanimity. It also became apparent that Pelly had in fact been in Australia when much of the naughtiness took place, and his supporters are proud to point out that his lawyers had all the allegations against him withdrawn.

The sense remained – and remains – that somebody had been trying to put some distance between the princes and Pelly. Pelly was regarded as bad news, rightly or wrongly, and Palace insiders, far from being scandalised by the intrusiveness of the press (on this occasion at least), show few signs of regretting the matter having been brought to a head. If he was targeted, was it by somebody at the Palace (or thereabouts, though not Bolland, it should be emphasised) feeding dirt to the press for them to 'stumble on'? There is some evidence, as we shall see below, to encourage that view. Or, less sinisterly, was it simply a matter of the Princes' media handlers making the best of a difficult news story that had emerged after a great many local rumours and some assiduous sleuthing (which included voicemail interceptions)?

Mulcaire worked extensively on the story of the princes' supposedly wild friend, and when Pelly took legal action against the *News of the World* some years later, Mulcaire's records had to be handed over. On the files it became apparent that Mulcaire had targeted Pelly and many of those close to him. The legal papers on Pelly's behalf claimed Mulcaire 'recorded in his notes that [Pelly] had an MI5 profile', concluding that 'this information was obtained unlawfully by the Defendants'. Those familiar with royal protocol express surprise at this: if there was a concern about those in the princes' circle, surely it would appear on a police (royal protection) file, rather than an MI5 file? But someone familiar with the episode (neither Mulcaire nor anyone in Pelly's camp) insists that it was indeed an MI5 file.

News International's response to this is revealing. Its press officer said there was no reason to think that 'Mulcaire or *News of the World* had access to MI5 files'. She also said the company's interpretation of the evidence was that Mr Mulcaire found out about the MI5 profile from a hacked phone message, a version of events consistent with the prevailing narrative.

Though News International's response seems to

encourage this view, it would surely be highly surprising, bizarre, even, for MI5 to be so casual as to leave a mention of Pelly's file on a voicemail message, ripe for any techno-savvy snooper to pick up.

This leaves a third option, that there was someone supplying information, presumably either for money or because they believed the public ought to be told.

Mulcaire says that the top page of the relevant Pelly file is missing from those he has seen, but he is pretty sure he was tasked on that project by one of his regular taskers. His memory of the case is not good, but he says it doesn't surprise him that there was a reference to such a file in the *New York Times*'s story that revealed it in October 2011. It was not his job to filter out which jobs he was to do, and which not. He was under contract and trusted his employers to act responsibly. If information had come in from the security services or the police for him to work on, that was a matter for them.

Does he agree that his work might, wittingly or unwittingly, have been prompted by MI5? Given what he calls his 'belief structure' as to what he was doing, he remains confident of his ground, without feeling able to go into details. If the security services had some involvement, was it official or unofficial? In other words, was it the work of a 'rogue', to coin an unfortunate phrase in the context, or did the revelations about Pelly have some sanction from above? Mulcaire, whose own attitudes have little truck with drug-taking, will not be drawn. Speaking more generally, he says simply: 'It wasn't unusual for MI5 to initiate an exercise on people… there were times when a bad press was needed to move things on. It was known as a black project.' So did he know, or have suspicions, at the time that he might have been helping blacken someone's name in the interests of the royal family? He would not comment.

Some believed that the story which exposed Max Mosley's sado-masochistic tastes was delivered with an MI5 postcode, as it were. Mosley, when President of the body that runs Formula 1, used to pay for sex parties, and the husband of one of the participants alerted Neville Thurlbeck to the story possibilities. It was arranged that she would film their next encounter, complete with German overtones, and on 30th March 2008 a story headlined 'F1 Boss has Sick Nazi Orgy with Five Hookers – Son of Hitler-loving fascist in sex shame'. What followed has been well documented, and Mosley said the orgies lacked the Nazi theme that the *News of the World* had claimed. He was expected to slink off, humiliated and embarrassed at the intimate details that were revealed of his preferences. But he took his breach of privacy claim way beyond what had been expected by lawyers, who had hoped a sense of dignity would get the better of his indignation.

Was this brought about by MI5? Probably not, although there are many in motor racing circles who believe Mosley was targeted. Mosley is thought to believe that the motive was money, having identified the individual concerned, although he does not rule out one of Thurlbeck's MI5 contacts having told him of Mosley's tastes. Mulcaire later did some work for Mosley under the umbrella of Quest, a large security company for whom Lord Stevens now works, too.

For a journalist, the world of the private investigator is a nightmare to get involved in. Mulcaire counters that the world of journalism is a snake pit and that nobody can be trusted. Mulcaire's world is one of tradecraft, suspicion and constant security checks. He's inclined to launch into a lighthearted riff on what deviousness those he is in conversation with might be up to. Unprompted, he will make jocular accusations about secret cameras and listening devices. The tone is always jokey, but it suggests a man who finds relaxing difficult outside the company of family and close friends.

Having been blocked in his attempt to make it into 14th Inc Duke of York, as related earlier, he immersed himself in a number of courses, while getting a toehold in the world of tracing and surveillance. There is no corroboration for the following story, but it is very much part of the Mulcaire narrative. Nonetheless, it is very much part of the Mulcaire narrative. When he went for an interview at Worldwide Investigations in the early 1990s, he was told it was due was to start imminently, requiring him to take a cab to get there on time. The cab driver struck up a probing conversation, which Mulcaire believes was a test of his discretion. Having reached the chambers, he realised there had been no tearing rush after all, but felt he was being closely observed. He met a series of people, before meeting the boss, a distinguished-looking and evidently well-travelled former police and military figure called Steve Rowlands, who asked him to start the following Monday.

Is this the delusion of a hyper-wary wannabe James Bond, or was this the first time he came on the eager and public-spirited young security services' radar? If so, did it lead to anything?

Mulcaire's reluctance to be drawn invites speculation, but he will not provide answers. By the 1990s, as we have seen, he had done a good deal of work for Argen and Worldwide Investigations. These companies were useful to the security services, being quick, discreet and cheaper than maintaining investigators on staff when there was insufficient work to justify their salaries. So occasional checks, tracing and background profile work would be parcelled out.

Once Mulcaire joined the *News of the World*, he expected to be helping fill its pages with the paper's traditional fare. He did that, but frequently, while doing work for the investigations unit, he was also asked to provide 'profiling' information on a number of people under suspicion of having terrorist sympathies, seemingly which the police needed doing. Very often, no story would appear in the paper, but Mulcaire would be confident that his handler, usually Greg Miskiw, would have found a mutually beneficial home for whatever nuggets he had been able to find. Mulcaire did not see it as his place to ask what the information was wanted for.

There appear to be just under a hundred names of people on whom he was asked to perform some sort of search and about whom no story appeared in the *News of the World*. Many of the names in the files are Arab-sounding, and include men who have since gone to prison for terrorist offences. Some, it is clear to those who see the entries, were tasked by his customary handlers at the *News of the World*, or the tasking corner is missing. There are other files, says Mulcaire, that have been retained by the police and which, Mulcaire says, also relate to serious crime. When asked about the tasking on those files, he is not forthcoming but says simply that he wants to see the originals.

Mulcaire's belief is that his bosses on the paper were often using the information he provided to 'grease the wheels', to help provide the police with information they could not easily acquire otherwise, which could be swapped or bartered for information about stories for the paper. It is not hard to imagine how such a relationship might build up. If an investigator can tell the police that Suspect A, previously on their radar but now missing, was now living at such and such an address, that information is invaluable. If the police believe the source is credible, he or she is unlikely to doubt its reliability, nor be needlessly officious about how the information was acquired. If noble ends ever call for questionable or unorthodox means, surely this was a harmless enough. And, best of all, it was free from the scrutiny of pesky journalists. In any case, rightly or wrongly, it could probably be denied without any comeback. If a terrorist was thus more likely to be put behind bars, so be it. All parties could happily consign themselves to the side of the angels.

Thus was Mulcaire happy to feel he was doing his bit to help confront antisocial elements. He didn't ask where his information was going, but the known links between the police and News International suggested they were on the same side. On that score, if he felt he was working for the security services, albeit at one remove and deniably, that may be correct.

One case possibly in this category is what he calls the Etch-a-Sketch story. He was in the car, near their home in Cheam, with his wife, and received a call from Greg

Miskiw. He wanted him to drop everything as he had an urgent job. Mulcaire explained that he was driving and couldn't stop, but he asked Alison to write down the details of what needed doing on the nearest thing to hand, an Etch-a-Sketch board. The details, Alison remembers, were of someone with an Arab-sounding name, which she dutifully wrote down. The pair returned home and Mulcaire got down to work, transferring onto note pads and logging the details, later calling Miskiw with the details of the man's whereabouts. The man's arrest was on the television news that evening.

It was suggested during the 2014 trial that there might be some significance to the fact that Andy Coulson had been reassured that Goodman and Mulcaire would not be sent to prison. According to Goodman, Coulson had understood from 'the police or the Home Office' less than a week after the arrests that there was no desire to press for a prison sentence as long as Goodman pleaded guilty'.

Coulson wanted Goodman to plead guilty, so this may have coloured his reporting of what he had been told, but those of a conspiratorial cast of mind may be delighted by the thought of Mulcaire and Goodman being given preferential treatment. Rather more disappointing to them will be the fact that they didn't get it, and went to prison.

Mulcaire's claim to exceptional levels of access to people's phones is the subject of much fascination among those in the investigators' profession. One former *News of the World* employee said that when he was said to be able to divine someone's PIN number, in fact he couldn't. (And of the few people would could, they did not generally include those who answer calls for phone providers.) They claimed that, some years ago, what he did was call the phone provider (posing as an employee of the company) and get them to reset the PIN number to the factory setting. This would then allow him to get into the phone and reset the PIN number to a setting of his own choice, which he would then pass off as the one the target had been using all along. It requires a degree of skill and deviousness, but is not the awe-inspiring trick of great repute in some circles.

However, more recently it has been said that Mulcaire did acquire the ability to obtain PIN numbers. These numbers are 'double encrypted', and, by repute at least, the only people who have that capability are the security services. Again, this is an aspect of tradecraft he prefers not to discuss.

Mulcaire's ability to obtain what was previously thought unobtainable made him ripe for exploitation in a cash-rich environment like the *News of the World*. The need to both pay and protect sources offered cover for all sorts of abuse (and a great deal of conspiratorial nose-tapping), much of which may never be accounted for. It was precisely the sort of thing that the management had been trying to clamp down on, though of course not at the cost of alienating a genuine source. One such case, possibly, was the occasion referred to in court during the evidence of Stuart Kuttner, the *News of the World*'s managing editor, when he wrote a memo to himself about a meeting he had at the home of Clive Goodman, the royal reporter, two days after Goodman's 2006 arrest. The note says 'Glen [*sic*] approached CG & intro CG to senior "spook".... sd [?] leftovers from SIS bugging.'

The note continues: 'Told Andy this from the start.' Kuttner was questioned about this, and asked: 'Obviously this "spook" would be committing crime by handing over intercepts?' Kuttner agreed, 'assuming there is some validity to this'. He went to on to say that in his experience Goodman, with whom he was said not to have good relations for some years, was inclined to embellish, a line used on several occasions by some of those on trial. Andy Coulson was asked in court about the matter. On a day when his memory was evidently below par, he said he was sure he would have remembered such a development, and that he would have told Goodman 'that is the best story you have ever had'.

Goodman told the court that Mulcaire had said some of the royal phone information he had acquired 'was a by-product of information gained by the security services but I have no way of knowing if this was true.' Goodman said Mulcaire had introduced him to someone he said was a 'serving spook' but as far as he knew 'it could have been his next door neighbour'.

Mulcaire refuses to give the name of this mystery person, but a smile comes to his face at the mention of it. When challenged about his identity, and told that it was fundamental to the relationship on which the book is written, Mulcaire agreed to talk about that person's identity on condition that he was not named here. There is a need for natural discretion here, but this journalist can confirm he has little reason to believe there has been a breach of the Official Secrets Act.

So what was the point of the meeting? Was it to convince Goodman of the brilliant quality of Mulcaire's contacts, in order to get yet more cash out of the office?No, says Mulcaire, who repeats that he signed for all his cash payments. On the 'senior spook', he says, as he has said many times, that he was worried Clive Goodman did not appreciate the seriousness of listening in on royal household voicemails, and that the meeting was intended to remind Goodman that he should be aware of the risks they were taking. He hoped it would also help Goodman 'regain his place at the top table', which would enable both of them – fearful for their jobs – to know better what the bosses were thinking.

Another such example came from Sean Hoare, who spoke to the indefatigable Jo Becker of the *New York Times*, who wrote many stories about the affair. In one, when he was trying to locate someone for a story, he told of how he came across 'pinging'. He approached Greg Miskiw, gave him the cellphone number of the person in question and was amazed when Miskiw returned later with the person's precise location, in Scotland. The cost of this service was about £500 a time. Hoare asked how he got the answer, to which Miskiw replied 'It's the old bill, isn't it?' 'At that point you don't asked questions,' said Hoare.

Mulcaire laughs at the idea that it was the police. 'I'm not saying who it was, but I can tell you it wasn't the police!' Somewhere along the line, somebody was doing well financially out of pinging. Mulcaire insists he was not a beneficiary, because he always signed a chit for every payment he received. So, if there were ghosts in the machine, at least some of them must have had bulging wallets.

12

Postcript

As was mentioned at the beginning, this book has sought to shed a little light on 'how we got here'. There remain a great many unanswered questions, to do with Milly Dowler and the 'false hope' moment, the extent of the missing Mulcaire files, the precise chain of command at the *News of the World*, the degree of official complicity with the paper's unlawful means, and doubtless more will emerge that relates to other forms of information-gathering (computer hacking, bank fraud, payment to public officials and so on) that this book has not been able to examine.

To be continued....

Author's Note

Writing about phone hacking and press regulation has become absurdly polarised, and given the customary pieties about the importance of a vigorous, rumbustious free press, it is surprising how little interest there seems to be in finding common ground in the middle. This book was not meant to throw stones at anyone, but it is clear something went badly wrong, and I write as someone who can't imagine not being a journalist. Justice John Saunders put the legal side in the Coulson sentencing on 4 July 2014: 'There is a certain irony in seeing journalists, who have shed light in dark corners and forced others to reveal the truth, being unprepared to do the same for their own profession.'

From the time when I was first scandalised and fascinated by some news methods, many have patiently indulged me on the subject and I owe them a great deal. There are countless people involved in the story who (if not named may recognise themselves in the text) are owed huge thanks. Lack of space, a vague stab at discretion and a fear of forgetting someone gives me a lame excuse for not naming them here, but Francis Elliott, John Mullin, Lisa Markwell, Heather Holden-Brown, Matthew Norman and Mary-Ellen Field have all given generously and paid heavily. The degree to which they inwardly rolled their eyes at my latest rant varied, but all were unfailingly polite and constructive. Thanks are also due to Martin Rynja of Gibson Square for believing in what this project was trying to do. Most thanks of all are due to my family, who have suffered considerably during the writing of this book and whose generous and entertaining support I do not begin to deserve.

I have always been keen to write a book on phone hacking, even if only for cathartic reasons. But, where were the publishers, hammering on Glenn Mulcaire's door? There were precious few. There are limits to how much a passing public interest can be exploited in a book, and in the eyes of most in the book trade, Mulcaire was beyond it. 'Good subject,' one eminent publisher told me, 'not sure there's a book in it.' And when told such a book would contain the testimony of the man at the centre of the storm, the disdain grew greater still. Mulcaire, after all, was the person accused of deleting the voicemails of a kidnapped schoolgirl, giving her unimaginably distressed parents a cruel moment of false hope. He had not just done it once or twice. His job had been invading the privacy of thousands of people, all for private gain. This was inexcusable. He may be telling the truth, but who says he deserves to be listened to?

I have had plenty of moments of thinking the same thing myself. How could I team up with someone so monstrous, someone for whom law-breaking was casual?

Graham Johnson, a former *News of the World* reporter, wrote about his relationship with the law in his book *Hack*: 'I never stopped to think if any of this was illegal. To tell you the truth, I didn't care. There was a definite feeling that we, the *News of the World*, were above the law, and that we could do anything we wanted. Who was going to turn us over? No one. Why? Because that was our job. We turned people over, not the other way round.' What is to be gained by allowing a criminal to recount the whys and wherefores of his inexcusable behaviour?

Quite a lot, I concluded. To seek to explain is not to justify. He was the man charged with these tasks. Having served his time, he is in a better position than most to understand the motivation of many of those involved. How could so many experienced journalists lose all sense of judgment and publish stories that with hindsight seem bound to have brought them discredit. Johnson also wrote that 'reporters and editors began to build personal fiefdoms based on their access to inquiry agents. The types of personality that the *News of the World* attracted were greedy for power and status; once they realised PIs were an instant fix the phenomenon created a kind of arms race to see who could get the ones that would break the law further and faster.' If one such person was prepared to talk to me, great.

And there were so many other questions. How (or perhaps why) did the police come to ignore so many clues? Who knew what was going on? Mulcaire was also in a position to offer a corrective to a version of events that, still, after eight years, offers little that is definitive. His version would be partial, of course, but of all the participants bar Clive Goodman, it was less likely than anyone's to be coloured by the threat of a spell at Her Majesty's Pleasure.

And besides, Mulcaire is an interesting personality. My profession is surely about more than writing people off as cardboard low-lifers, toffs, fat cats, six-times-a-night lotharios, killer bimbos and love rats. There might just be some light and shade. In a story as big as this, shouldn't that be brought out? He is a private investigator, not a journalist. While part of him is the dutiful professional who does what his patron pays for ('at heart, I'm a loyal dog', he has said), another part of him sees his exceptional sharp-wittedness being used for the public good. He is not short of self-belief and can be impetuous. His early years are characterised by schoolboy mischief, but also consistent acts of humanity and public-spiritedness. His mother's greatest upset was on hearing the judge denounce him in 2007 for telling lies. Even aiming off for a mother's blind loyalty, surely there was at very least an interesting human study here and more than likely a great deal more. As someone famously said in a very different context, where did it all go wrong?

But most importantly, I believed in his anger. If this was a con, the grandest blag of all, it was an astonishing performance. It did not look bogus to me, and although he had clearly done a great many things he shouldn't have done, his sense of justice had been affronted. Even if he was a cold-blooded, dark-hearted crook (which didn't seem to me the case), he had been dumped upon mightily by his bosses. He and Goodman had carried the can, and nobody believed they were solely responsible.

On one occasion, in front of his wife Alison, I put to him a suggestion that I had heard, that he had been offered an enormous bonus for finding an abducted child. He exploded. He turned to his wife and said 'Have I ever mentioned that? Has it ever occurred to you that might be true? I can't believe that… I can't believe it. How low will they go? I want to know who put that about! I want to know! That is disgusting.' It all but ruined the evening. He was visibly upset for about half an hour, constantly returning to the claim. I could not tell him who had passed this on, but when I went back to my source I had no sense there was any substance to it. Libelling Glenn Mulcaire was a free-for-all. I quite fancied kicking the tyres on some of those tales about him.

This was complicated. Two wrongs do not make a right and criminals are forever falling out, arguing and getting into an escalating whirl of complaint and counter-complaint. But this wasn't like that. Glenn held certain individuals responsible for what had happened, but even though he has been on the financial breadline for years, he didn't seem to have it in for them personally. There was no talk of retribution in dark car parks, settling scores and so on. Of course he was furious about what had been done to him and, strikingly, to his family, his anger was more with the corruption of abstract ideas, like loyalty, the truth, the greater good, a notion he constantly returned to. The morally irretrievable criminal mastermind that News International had wanted us to believe him to be had a confoundingly well-developed sense of right and wrong. This was no Ronnie Biggs indifferently flicking v-signs to the world. A crook, a cynic, simply wouldn't bother with being angry. He would have moved on to become a burglar, a computer fraudster or an identity thief, and Mulcaire, with his capacity for dissimulation, would be in a position to do that with some success. But he insisted he wanted his own position explained and the world put to rights.

There were plenty of people who wanted to write him

off as a fantasist, a wannabe Johnny English and an out of control hoodlum. But few fantasists (etc) are paid over £100,000 a year. So who is he?

This not a book for the insider particularly, or for techies wanting to understand the finer points of how cellular phone masts work. Because there are so many sensitivities at stake, there are more unattributed quotes than I would like, and many participants in the story were unavailable to corroborate parts of it, having failed to answer calls, letters or emails. Nothing should be inferred from the non-naming of some of those who worked with Mulcaire, even if they have already been convicted. This is done to avoid creating legal problems of identification in case others are charged in the future.

The last resort of the scoundrel is to say 'trust me', but I will just have to ask the reader to trust me that the quotes are used honestly and because, I hope, they represent a view of the truth. The mistakes, of course are mine, and if I have been unfair or credulous towards anyone, that too is my fault. But this book is an attempt, aimed at anyone who might be interested, to explain how we got here. There will be plenty of unanswered questions, and those without a degree in psychology may be left as baffled as I am by the performance of some of the participants. It is in part a study in deniability, a look at how one person's work, the consequence of which was read by millions, was supposedly not known about by anyone. When Mulcaire was caught an entire corporation just shrugged and said 'Not me, guv'. It was a ludicrous denying of responsibility.

The writing of this book has been an education. I have learned things about my trade that I didn't know, and which its regulators certainly didn't know. I have also learned that Glenn Mulcaire is a proud man. Once or twice I tried to remember what he had said about something, and checked with him the next day to be sure I hadn't mis-remembered. On one occasion I put the words 'I wince at some of the things I did' into his mouth. He did not 'wince' at all, he told me. No, no, no. He did what he did, and most of the things he did were a source of great pride. If a journalist misused information that he had provided, that was a matter for the journalist's conscience. I suggested that he needed to earn the right to be listened to, such were the crimes of which he was accused, and that surely his only defensible position would be to express contrition. As this book seeks to show, sometimes he did, sometimes he didn't. But most evident of all, to my disappointment, is his mistrust of many journalists. How can they live with themselves, he would ask? How could they endanger a child's life for the sake of getting the story before a competitor? And how could a journalist be so driven as to be the cause of him going to prison?

'If journalists got me into this mess, maybe it needs a journalist to get me out,' he has said more than once. This book does not seek to get anyone out of any mess, nor does it seek to excuse. All it can do is offer the man a fair hearing. This is his platform.

Neither Glenn Mulcaire nor his family has received any financial benefit for their cooperation with this book.
Where surnames changed over time, the current name is used throughout: Rebekah Brooks (rather than Wade) Kimberly Fortier (rather than Quinn).

Appendix

'In a way I don't care what is in this book,' Mulcaire has said several times. 'What I want most of all is that people know I do not have a dark heart, that people know why I did what I did over Milly Dowler. What I was accused of would have finished off many people. I can't stand the idea that people think I could have done what I was accused of.'

So long has Mulcaire remained silent that it is tempting to expect that when he does express himself, it will be about how he had to carry the can while others got off scot-free. That situation has now changed, of course, because others have been called to account. But while frustration remains at previous claims that no one knew what he was up to, the wound he feels over the Dowler accusation, that he caused the notorious 'false hope' moment, is deep. He returns to it constantly. It caused illness in his family, endless heartache at home and resulted in his name, hardly spotless, being blackened yet further.

His lawyer Sarah Webb drafted a statement on his behalf, which he authorised, apologising to the Dowler parents, but he wishes he had used different words. He would have liked to have explained what he believed at the time, and above all wants to do so now. His words are those of a proud man injured.

'It is the elephant in the room,' he says. 'I know a lot of people have moved on and want to talk about other things, but I want people to know what was really going on there. When the Dowler thing happened, people who hardly knew me but knew about me and what sort of family I have came up to me and asked if I was ok… some people said "this isn't right, doesn't sound right". I went and played football alone with my son when I was being called every name under the sun… it's very hard to forgive that and what was done to me.'

The truth is that Mulcaire *did* intercept Milly Dowler's voicemails. He pleaded guilty to doing so, but his plea was that, to use the legal term, he had an 'empowering belief' that, having been given the number, he was doing so on behalf of the police. And by general agreement, confirmed by the judge in the 2013/14 trial, he first listened to the voicemails over a fortnight after the false hope moment, having not been tasked till then. His frustration lies in the idea that he could have been so inept as to delete a message and thus cause such distress, and that his motives in intercepting the voicemail was motivated by the kind of 'trophy hunting' that can afflict journalists.

His fondness for journalism as a profession is minimal. Those who come fresh to journalism are often shocked by the strength of the rivalry between newspapers. Some stories are of interest to the public because of their human component, like, for example, the abduction of a child. For newspapers, that fact is a given. Their job is to provide added value, to cover the story better than their competitors, every day to outdo the other side. Usually this is for the benefit some common purpose, like the finding of a missing child, in good health, akin to members of the public combing a field in parallel, united by a common goal. Such rivalry between media outlets tends to be harmless (or peevish as when the *Sun* and *News of the World* refused to offer a reward together), but not always. In the case of Milly Dowler, in 2014 the judge said this 'unforgivable' decision to withhold that information could have placed Dowler in 'avoidable danger'. 'We are human beings first' is a line journalists could do with bearing in mind.

Mulcaire is scandalised when that line is crossed. 'I don't know how some journalists can live with themselves,' he says. 'What about ringing up an agency pretending to be Bob Dowler, or Sally Dowler? It's outrageous. Impersonating, in hindsight, a dead girl's mother? I hacked Jade Goody's phone in 2001/2, but way before she contracted cancer. They put me and her together, and said I'd done it when she had cancer. Anyone who knows me knows I would never do a thing like that.' He also expresses frustration at the conflating intrusion into the health of Gordon Brown's family – by others – with his own work. 'The only thing I did in the case of Gordon Brown was to get addresses and do background checks. The story about his son and cystic fibrosis appeared in the *Sun* in late 2006 and was nothing to do with me. In any case, I had been arrested by then and wasn't working. In fact, I wasn't in any communication with anyone, apart from the odd one from Greg, with suggestions about legal matters, and from Neville with his "helpful" advice to get out of town. Cheeky bastard.'

Doesn't blagging require a degree of dishonesty, so that in effect you were, to put it crudely, a professional liar? How do you feel about that?

'That's just bread and butter, doing my job. There is a difference between merely telling the truth and actively seeking it out. And there are occasions when lying is the only way to find out the truth. I am not ashamed to say that, and it seems to me a defensible code. But I wouldn't impersonate one of the Dowler family. I'd find a million other ways of doing it rather than that. People have pretended that's all right. When a child goes missing you just drop everything. The law doesn't really come into your thinking, or I'm not sure it should. I assumed the police had done all sorts of checks when I was asked to look into it, but I was told they had not done the most basic checks and searches. I was astonished.'

After the police reopened the phone hacking investigation, Mulcaire was charged with intercepting Milly Dowler's voicemail and conspiring to do so. He strongly resisted the second charge, believing it had connotations of a dark plot, rather than something with nobler aims: 'I did not conspire… I believe I had an empowering belief to intercept phones… I believed I was doing it legitimately.… I was advised I would have my day in court if I did that, but they dropped the conspiracy charge against me. In one way of course I was pleased, but it meant I didn't get the chance to make my case in court. Had I done so, I would have been able to shed a lot of light on the whole affair. My question to them was: "have you got the guts to go 'not guilty' on the Milly Dowler conspiracy charge if your intentions are good?" I would have liked more than one of them to go not guilty. That way we could have had the whole thing out in court, which I would have welcomed. But then they pleaded guilty after years of denying anything to do with this stuff. I just hope they can live with themselves.'

There is still a sense of grievance, a feeling that it suited no one for him to get up in the box and say his piece. 'My hands have been tied. They took me out of conspiracy straightaway. Did they really want me there in court, at Leveson and the IPCC, the select committees and so on? The police had a lot to lose if they'd left me in the conspiracy charge… they knew full well I was determined to stick with this in a court of law. I got a good mark from the judge. He understood what was going on. I remember the judge remarking that it was a brave decision. "We don't need Mr Mulcaire here, let him go." I made the distinction between special projects and other stuff. At the end, at last, they seemed to get the point about the distinction between the lawful authority stuff and the rest.'

The days after Dowler 'false hope' moment allegation have clearly had a huge impact on Mulcaire. His children were intensely concerned about their father. 'We know what Dad's like, we just know he wouldn't be either incompetent like that or so callous,' says Georgia, his 20 year old. I was really touched to receive a very supportive letter from Father Bernard, my local priest at St Christopher's Church. If it had been a News International story, it would never have run. Three million fans of the paper believed in our ability to get the details right. I must have been doing something right.'

In the whole story there is a danger that the Dowler episode, ghastly as it is, crowds out all the other cases. What about Soham, where two girls, Holly Wells and Jessica Chapman, were abducted and killed. Mulcaire was active there too. Some suspects had their phones hacked and, he believes, the police knew about it (or certainly do now). Why is that file also not available, he asks.

'Again, on Soham… I cannot find the file. I would like

to know who the taskers were. I would not have done that without lawful authority. I found a lot of information on various people there. It was probably Greg. He would have given me *carte blanche*. I did a lot of work involving people who went off the grid, but I'm not allowed to see that material. It's a protected file. I want to show what my belief structure was. I wasn't doing it for a story. I wanted to get those children back. I can accumulate information, or give it back.... I would produce the currency which bosses could barter. If I could get any clinical detail on a child abduction, I would. How that was used by the tasker, you know, the journo, is up to him. They were the broker. He would give stuff to the police that the police couldn't get in their timelines. I was that much quicker than them, so of course what I was able to provide was useful to them.'

This is a slightly different argument, surely. Either you say you were doing it with the police's knowledge and authorisation, or, simply, that it was being done (in a way the police may or may not have guessed at) and much of the information was then fed to the police in exchange for other information about the inquiry?

'You give the police bits and pieces… whether you give it all to them is up to the journalist, that wasn't my call. To my mind, there are three sorts of power in this game knowledge power, positioning power and tasking power. As soon as I give you that knowledge power, you've got all three… it's the intelligence triangle. When you're in that position, you're in a better position than the police. You have autonomy, all the cards, which the police don't have, because they have to get production orders and so on.'

The issue of Mulcaire's motivation, both past and present, has returned constantly in the writing of this book. His insistence on having acted for the greater good should be clear by now, but his current spur is harder to PIN down. Is he motivated by anger? The question has become contentious. He says anger is a negative emotion, that he should not be angry and will happily recite that it poisons the soul. But for someone who carried the can for the practice that kept the news machine fed and was scapegoated while the similarly guilty looked on disapprovingly, takes some stomaching. He does not want it thought he is angry, but no other word does the trick. He is more than peeved, but not particularly vengeful towards those who sat on their hands when he went to prison. He just wants his motivation understood. 'I have always believed that you should retain your emotional control, that you should be better, not bitter.' He may not want to be angry, but it strikes me he is.

It is easy to dismiss Mulcaire with a black and white reference to the law. If he broke the law, does that mean he is beyond rescue? To those whose privacy he plundered (or enabled to be plundered by others), maybe he is. But he has some conditions which he says were ingrained from his early professional life, which mitigate law-breaking. These are that better outcomes must be the result, a person's actions mustn't undermine rule-following in general, rule breaking must be the only means to a better outcome, and that the collective obligation is to uphold the rule of law but individual duty is to do what's best, inside or outside the law.

Since the phone hacking scandal exploded, precious few people have defended the run of the mill redtop journalism from which it grew. Politicians and newspaper editors have argued about how the post-Leveson rules are to be enforced while barely mentioning what those rules should be.

In short, is it a legitimate story if, say, a married professional footballer is cheating on his wife? What if he is receiving millions in sponsorship deals from companies which believe him to be a pillar of probity? They greyness of the borders left them virtually imperceptible in the most competitive part of the market. Only Paul McMullan (former deputy features editor at the *News of the World*) has been brave enough to defend the 'anything goes' principle, while many have hidden behind claims of ignorance or spurious claims of defending the public interest. McMullan, with more honesty than many of his fellow practitioners could summon, told the Leveson inquiry: 'I see [journalism] as a noble profession which sometimes requires ignoble acts and believe passionately in freedom of speech which is indeed occasionally safeguarded by those acts.... Just because exposing devious self-interest, ineptitude and corruption which taints many in the public eye requires a devious and illegal route itself does not make it wrong.... The job of the whistle blower and the brave journalist who condones and uses illegal means to bring this corruption, false representation which debases our democracy to the public attention is one to be cherished and protected, long may it continue.' In short, the law ought to allow a public interest defence for law-breaking.

Where is Mulcaire on all this? How does he feel about the case of someone like Sienna Miller, who was tormented by 360-degree intrusions into her private life? In hindsight he says he agrees that such trawling in the hope of picking up a titbit, cannot be excused. But what about her entire existence – her friends and family – coming under extreme scrutiny to prove something of little ultimate importance? And what about intruding into people's bank accounts and so on? How can that ever be defensible, whoever they are?

'I agree that fishing exhibitions are indefensible. If there's a greater good, fine, but otherwise not. The fact that I did it, for a bit of tittle tattle, I agree, is wrong, but I don't feel I'm particularly qualified to make that judgment. I do know that I would not be happy if my own daughter was behaving like that, but maybe that is not the point.'

Those expecting heartfelt outpourings of remorse on this issue from Mulcaire are likely to be disappointed. The cost-free, easy apology is not his style. He does not want to say sorry insincerely, seeming to regard it as dishonourable.

'I don't know how I feel about this. I feel things have moved on for me. If I had been asked about this in 2006, maybe I would feel worse about this. But now, with the Dowler case and others, and being charged a second time, I feel I'm back on the trauma mill and it's hard for me to stop adopting a siege mentality. I was punished the first time round, when others weren't, when I was acting under their instruction, so now my defences have come up again. It's hard for me to feel fully unqualified remorse on some of those privacy issues. They ask me to apologise for a second time, although actually it was the *News of the World* that apologised to her. I know it's not Sienna Miller's fault how badly this has been handled, but how many times can you apologise for something?'

By way of his own mitigation, he says an action can be

wrong but a person can still be blameless. 'People around me made the choices… they were journalists, lawyers and others who were very successful and I trusted them. But after the Dowler allegation there was a club mentality against me, and the whole game changed then. All bets were off.' And he returns to his insistence that his notes show how he was tasked, and that when he was asked to look at a victim of crime, for example, it was not presented as such, but was merely slipped into a batch of jobs to work through.

After the case was reopened, Mulcaire had to decide how the renewed criminal issue related to the continuing civil cases. He had a brief opportunity to turn Queen's evidence and tell all to the police, which would involve a major process of 'cleansing himself' to ensure no skeletons came out of the closet at a later stage to undermine his credibility. Would that jeopardise his position in the civil cases?

'Once you've gone through that trauma once, been arrested at gunpoint, had your house raided, with your kids watching. I didn't feel I owed the police anything. My elderly parents got raided, with my mum housebound and ill and my dad's moveability is pretty much zero…You pay the price, you go through that trauma mill, you spend longer than the average time in prison… then to rehabilitate yourself, get back to doing some investigation work for Lord Stevens's unit in London, get back on your feet a bit, and then the game-changing moment comes with Milly Dowler. To be Public Enemy No 1 is beyond belief. It is gut-wrenching to see the effect it has had on my family. To go through that phase again, two kids collapsing, your wife in a dreadful state. The media goes after you… and then as you are trying to keep your family's morale up… on top of all that, my wife gets arrested… for money laundering! It was the first time she has ever been in a police station, or had had anything like that happen. Imagine the kids seeing that, people at school seeing that, in the community locally. If you had seen all that immense emotional baggage my wife had to carry around. I couldn't face all that again. I was also arrested for perverting the course of justice and money laundering, because they thought all that cash that had gone from the News of the World had gone to me. They just ran the same uniform mentality gunboat diplomacy, raising the anxiety of co-dependents. They should have been a lot more grownup about that. They should have had a serious conversation about what I was doing and why, but they didn't want to do that. So after all that, being arrested for a second time, with my mum (a signatory on one of his company documents) being interviewed by the police for a second time, seven years on – after which I was released without any charge – can you wonder why anyone would want to give Queen's evidence?'

If there is more than a degree of animus there, he also has a more cerebral explanation.

'Certain people have been in this story for five minutes, and for them self preservation is paramount, so they have chosen a cut-throat mitigation. I have held my position for seven years. That degree of self preservation leads to self deception, because it will make you do anything to save yourself and you persuade yourself to believe things that are wrong. And that will lead to self betrayal. Once you are there, you are led into a situation of either trying to correct it, which is a flushout, a cleansing system, or you are wise to it and you try and learn from it and you gain experience from it... I chose the latter, otherwise I would have given Queen's evidence.'

In short, as he told a friend, he's not a grass. Or is it that he did not want to 'cleanse himself'. Surely all those company documents invite suspicion that that might be the case? Why were there so many different names of companies, and why did he keep using different names, as emerged in court? In 2007 you had to pay back £12,500, which was the maximum the judge decided you could have had in cash from the company. And the police initially accused you of money-laundering, and wondered where all the money had gone. Do you have anything to say to that?

'The company name thing all started with John Boyall, when people set up limited companies, and people would just put down relations' names and so on as company directors, and you'd just change the name slightly every year, just to minimise tax, which to my understanding lots of small companies do. I didn't have an accountant, and my mother kept my payment documents, which doesn't seem to me such an extraordinary thing. But I am unhappy with what was said about me and money in court. It was said that I had used lots of different names to try and bamboozle people, which all fitted the Walter Mitty thing they have tried to pin on me, but it's just not true. What is true that I used two names for undercover work, which were Paul Williams and Dr John Jenkins, but on my children's life, the other ones they used for me... I had never heard of them, and I certainly didn't ask to use them. Matey, Mr Lemon, Mr Strawberry, Alexander, all those. Greg used to occasionally call me Alexander, if he wanted to flatter me, as in Alexander the Great, and in the office I heard they talked about an Alexander project or something, but that wasn't my idea. And the other ones – I never even heard of them until they came up in court. They must have been names they used in the office. The police went through all my bank accounts and found nothing wrong. There was nothing to find.'

'I said to them, I signed for every single payment I had from that company. If you can find the Lamborghini and the house in the Bahamas, please show me. You can have them. I thought of doing what Fletcher did in Porridge, when he was accused of money laundering. He needed a new patio, so he told them he'd buried it under his crumbling patio. The police dug it up and found nothing, because there never was anything, but they had to put things back to normal, so the police had to redo it all and he got a new patio out of it. Alison was accused of money laundering. Can you imagine that? She was never actually shown the documents on which they arrested her. We all wanted to see the documents but never did, but it did sound as if someone had cooked them up. It was absolutely ridiculous, outrageous. Someone must have made a decision somewhere down the line to let that information come out in the interview process. I actually wanted Alison to be charged and to get my hands on that, the legal team weren't allowed to get their hands on that. That's not right. That is abuse of process.'

On the subject of abuse of process, two other questions suggest themselves. Why did he go as far as the Supreme Court in order to prevent having to name his taskers, as requested by Nicola Phillips, PA to Max Clifford, who wanted to know who had hacked her phone and why. And why did he not pursue an 'abuse of process' argument? Some lawyers felt that because the police had had his files for several years and then had to return to the fray, he could claim he had been treated unfairly.

On the supreme court argument, he says: 'I was advised by my legal team to take that all the way. We had a very long and heavy session in chambers, and there were a lot of civil claims coming through. At the end of the meeting the chambers made a massive, very powerful case against me incriminating myself, so for me to go against that would have been pretty unusual, and they thought it unlikely that, as I had been charged and sent to prison before, that I would be charged again for some other thing they thought I might have done, so I shouldn't take the risk by incriminating myself. The irony is at the end I still got charged on 4 counts, so following their advice didn't help me… and on the second one, on abuse of process, that is partly why I decided not to take their advice, even though logically maybe I could have brought a stronger case. I chose not to, because if I had come out of that case having won, people would still have gone into a court of law and blamed me, and I wanted to try and clear my name as far as possible.'

Do you wish now you had gone for an abuse of process case? 'I don't like to look back with regrets, all I can do is listen to the advice I was given at the time and the powerful argument they made at the time and take a decision based on it.'

You have made reference to 'the man upstairs'. How important is religion to you?

'I am very wary about talking about that. I don't want people thinking I am some kind of David Icke figure who was driven by religion to do this or that. At the same time I am not going to deny my faith. I was brought up with it, I believe in it, I enjoy it and I think it gives my children a very solid and admirable framework for life. I know I have to live with the consequences of my actions, and I know I can answer for them. I also ask myself how some journalists can live with themselves after what they have done. I don't wish bad on anyone but I do look at some of the things that have happened, at some of the victims of crime, for example, that the paper went after, and, yes, I enabled the paper to get into contact with, and I wonder how they can look themselves in the mirror. I feel bad that work I did made it possible for those things to have happened, of course, but I do not feel they were my responsibility, something I have to answer for. In many, possibly most, of the cases I did not know what use the PIN numbers I was providing were being put to. Had I known, of course I would have done different things.'

The shock of hearing about those innocent, often grieving people he targeted, or enabled to be targeted, will probably never fade. In some cases, though, he would point out that at the time they were put under scrutiny, some may have been under suspicion themselves. The quantities involved will keep others sceptical, but Mulcaire says he would welcome a chance to discuss in public any piece of work with those who tasked him.

How do you feel when the court hears you say 'Go on, say I love you and it's 25 grand'. You may say you were exposing a cabinet minister's affair with a married woman, and that that is something the public has a right to know about, but surely it's not very classy, is it? In fact doesn't it suggest a rapacious indifference to his feelings? Or the jury also heard you saying 'fuck' when you accidentally deleted a message. The bit about the tape proves you are mortal and can make mistakes, but more generally I mention that because in many conversations with you and in the way you bring up your children, it is clear that dignity and good grace are important to you.

'If I said that, that was because that was what they offered. Don't ask me if it ever materialised, because it didn't. They led me on that. As for the idea of being given an incentive…. It's a bonus, just like bankers get bonuses. Don't tell me everyone else works for free? I've never met a poor doctor. If they weren't motivated by money they'd work for free. I don't have to justify an incentive of £25,000. I was just working for need, to feed my family, not greed'

Because a certain amount of NoW cash remains unaccounted for, some continue to speculate as to where it might have gone. There has been a suggestion of one or two executives having an expensive drug habit. Was Mulcaire aware of any such suggestion? He seems shocked when I put it to him.

'Well, if that was the case, I never saw any evidence of it. I would be really surprised. Anyone I dealt with knows how strongly I feel about that sort of thing. I don't even like even being with puffheads, so anyone who wanted to do that knows I wouldn't approve. I like a drink, and my children are old enough to like the odd glass of wine, but anything beyond that just isn't us at all.'

A friend of Mulcaire who is very familiar with police work says of Mulcaire's belief that he did much of his work on the police's behalf: 'There is no way the cops would have asked Glenn themselves. Someone may have told him "the cops need your help." It looks to me as if Miskiw was so out of control he had his own private police force in Glenn and led Glenn to believe that his work was being sanctioned by the police.' Given all that, do you feel you were too trusting? It's not a great mark of friendship that when Mulcaire left a message to ask for Miskiw's help, Miskiw told Alison: "I hope it's not financial."'

'He came to stay at my house when he was in London, he and I did some great work together, he called and visited my wife a lot when I was in prison. I felt we had a good relationship. But in hindsight the people he was working for needed him to be doing that, to keep an eye on me and make sure I wasn't going to rock the boat. He was useful to them and they needed him, so once again someone, in this case Greg, was deriving a use from me. In the later stages, he was upping his own value inside the company because he was the only one I was talking to. And when he called me to tell me he was going to the US but didn't tell me about the huge storm that was coming over Milly Dowler, that really changed my view of him, although I can't be 100 per cent certain that he knew about it. Alison and I always liked him, but he was always distant. Maybe we were just being used all along. Obviously I would find that very disappointing. And I am disappointed that he didn't feel able to help with this book. He knows the truth about me, and about what I have gone through. I could have done with a hand from him.'

Do you think he exploited your desire to do greater good work by telling you the work was for the police when actually it wasn't, and that in that respect, you were a victim? Somebody who has known you a long time said about you: 'Victim is strong word, but he was naïve. He made that decision to get into that position where he could be exploited, and I don't know how much he expected to be doing all that celebrity stuff.' Someone else, who knows Mulcaire and Miskiw well, when asked if Miskiw was a friend to Mulcaire, said: 'No, Glenn was a contact to Greg. They were not close. Greg's quite a detached person emotionally. He's not that kind of person. Glenn came across as quite friendly and warm. Was Greg cold-blooded? He took his job very seriously.' So how does Mulcaire feel about that now?

'Naivety is a strong word. The word Greg used to use a lot is "schmoozing". He would be very keen on schmoozing people. That means, offer incentives to people. It's a ladder game and they help you up the ladder, but then they keep control of the ladder, so you have no control. I've seen that done plenty of times with other people, and I suppose that is what happened with me.'

You have lived with this, and with yourself and with your conscience all this time, and there is plenty of conviction behind what you say. A friend of yours, a former senior figure in the police, has said: 'To his credit, Glenn has always been completely consistent in saying that he believed he was doing it for the greater good. Now whether he was told that or not, I don't know. He likes to think if the cops can't work it out, they would send for Glenn. I am not sure about that and can't be certain that is true, but he may well have been told that. Certainly he has always been very very discreet, to my knowledge.'

Your father-in-law has talked to me about his anger. 'What about all the good work Glenn did, for the good?' And his wife has talked to me about Glenn having to work round the clock and you telling her 'I have to do this for the police'.

But to someone who doesn't know you, who looks at the thousands of files and what they have read about you, is there anything you can say that you aren't retro-fitting your past, you know, re-writing history, to get yourself off the hook? Because a great many people will want to write you off as someone who believed he had superhuman powers, in short, as a fantasist.

'I know I am not a fantasist, or a Walter Mitty or an obsessive or any of those things. I have faith in my ability, and I know what my motives are. It doesn't matter what people think of you, it's what God thinks of you. Let me see all my files , and all the people who tasked me, and find out why so much stuff has been held back, and then we'll see who the fantasist is. Somebody, at some level, has held things back. Conspiring to commit an unlawful act is a bad thing to do, and I know I didn't do that on Milly Dowler. I am the only one who has consistently told the court the truth on that story. I think there should be a proper public inquiry on the Dowler case. Just let me have all my files and leave me there to defend myself. That will make clear who is telling the truth. I challenge all those people involved to see me in a court of law, with all my documents, and then we'll see who is telling the truth. The files on my work with Quest have also been put into quarantine with the police. Again, if people knew about the sort of work I did for them, they wouldn't use names like that.'

It should be said, for legal reasons, that the police themselves insist that only a few files have been held back, and those are for 'operational' reasons. One senior figure close to the Weeting investigation said: 'After what has gone before, we'd be mad to hold back any files. I just can't imagine why people would lay themselves open to that charge. That is the sort of malpractice that could bring a trial to an end.'

The aftermath of the 2006 trial requires you to look back on a version of yourself that is, frankly, unflattering, some would say greedy, even. You have said your head was turned by the money you were earning, but through blagging, you persuaded a lot of innocent people to do things they would not normally have done, yet you say you have no regrets about that?

'My big regret is that I didn't recognise the spike, as I call it, the massive build-up of phone interceptions in 2004-6, due to the huge amounts of pressure in the office and coming from the office. I feel I was still doing good work then, but often it was not the sort of work I wanted to be doing. I had too much faith in what I was being asked to do and the people who were tasking me. Many of the jobs were slipped in front of me in a bundle using quite a different pretext.'

'But on the serious investigations side, on many of those jobs, as far as I was aware, I was working on behalf of the police. I've got nothing to apologise for, and I never will…On many jobs, I was much quicker than the police, and I make no apology for that. Don't tell me about production orders next week or the week after. If it was your daughter, would you stop and say 'hang on, we've got to do this by the book'? You've got to do anything you can to save that girl's life. You don't get given jobs like that, with people who have done great work, immense work, you don't get contracted with someone like that unless you've got outside form, and I was very proud of where I worked, of working for Rupert Murdoch, who, incidentally, I don't believe knew anything about what I was doing. But I wasn't always proud of some of the individuals I worked with'

It seems to me you have a very high level of self belief, and you have had to be strong, for yourself and your family, to get through this. You did some work for Lord Stevens at Quest, but since 2007 you have not had a lot of luck. You studied employment law, and toyed with setting up a couple of companies, one to help individuals with counter surveillance and one, Celebrity Makers, to film people holding parties, but with the resurfacing of the story you have had a struggle, not least financially. You have managed to stay in your house, now with an interest-only mortgage and a couple of years ago you were made bankrupt for non-payment of £187,000 in tax. (The non-payment was traceable to documents found at News international, which seems to confirm that his payments were indeed signed for. As with his tasking files, they were to be his undoing. (Mulcaire says an agreement was in place with the revenue to repay tax but after the Dowler allegation was made the deal was taken off the table, a source of further grief: 'an agreement is an agreement', he insists.)

But do you ever worry that a part of you is in denial? That quantity of work, which you say was slipped in under a different pretext, can't just be brushed aside and its consequences blamed on the journalists you were helping, can it? Maybe you have told yourself certain things because you wanted to be sure you hadn't lost your bearings. It seems to me that people with a lot of self-belief are particularly inclined, more than most of us, to re-jigging the past expediently, and in not following much of the coverage of the trial and so on, you have averted your gaze from your past. You have talked extensively about your belief in what you were doing, but I suppose I am asking more about the extent to which you have questioned that certainty in yourself. Is there something in that?

'I made a distinction between tittle tattle and the serious investigations. I know what the difference was, and I did a deal with myself that one was the price to pay for the other. And I still insist a hundred per cent that we did some great work on the paper early on. What happened was that it all became just a process, just job after job. I was being piled up with work and yes, I was being paid well to do it, and in that situation I don't think many people with five young children would just walk away. Plus, I didn't realise that a lot of what I was doing was illegal. If I had, would I have kept all those files? I have told you I regret not recognising the spike for what it was, but then again, it wasn't like I was enjoying it then. My health was in a terrible state, I was working day and night just to try and keep them happy. I do wish I had walked away, but if I had, I would have been unemployable and could have been bad-mouthed as an investigator in that world.'

The world of private investigators seems unlikely to be clasping Glenn Mulcaire to its bosom. The above-board, respectable side of the profession are likely to say that he should have joined one of the trade's associations and, at the very least, stayed within the law. Others, less scrupulous, will say that he has let the side down. You shouldn't keep records, they say, suggesting that there's something almost comical about keeping all those files believing there was nothing wrong with what you were doing. And you kept them twice, of course, so they were there in your house when the police came the second time.

The effect of all this has been to disrupt much of that world, in which some investigators skated pretty close to the law, but were discreet and the information was used judiciously, so nobody was to know if the law got broken. I suppose you might say that was an arm of the privatisation of justice, a racket in which most newspapers colluded to varying degrees. How do you feel about that, not as it relates to you particularly, but as a general view, and do you ever wish you had signed up to one of the investigation profession's trade bodies? Do you think, one way or the other, they might have helped avoid what has happened?

'I didn't want to join a professional body. I didn't want to put myself on the grid. I had done loads of courses of a variety of sorts, which I would rather not go into, and was keener to do more military style stuff. I think it is a legacy of my grandfather, who lived with us when I was very young. He had been in the war, and he was a great hero to me. I would very much like to be able to live up to him. He was in the Irish Guards in the war, and later worked in the War Office. The way he dealt with some really major family situations was just so impressive. Plus, when his own wife died, the way he dealt with that. That's what leaders are made of, I thought.'

'You have suffered a prolonged period of anxiety attacks and depression, and have been on Cipralex, escitalopram, beta blockers and valium. Your financial position has also been very precarious. After 2007, you got a qualification in neurolinguistic programming, you did a course in employment law, were a senior investigator at Quest and did work for another large company. And then the allegations about Milly Dowler came out, which obviously made things difficult for you, but when the dust has settled a bit, you must be wanting to get back to work?'

'I have managed to keep things together, and I must have something to have done that. I have been called all sorts of things, and I expect I'll be called a great many more, but I know what sort of person I am, and I have had a lot of support from really good people with good families – people like Dickie Guy [a Wimbledon goalkeeping hero from the 1980s], a good character and a very nice man, who makes sure things are done right. People like that wouldn't support me if I was what some people have painted me. And I am confident I am a very competent investigator. All I really want is to get back to the starting line.'

Acknowledgements

I cannot express enough thanks to my personal committee for their continued support and encouragement; Dr Ruse, Father Bernard, Martin Smith, Rod Fletcher QC, Gavin Millar QC, Teus Young and my uncle big T. This also applies to my late brother stephen, Grandma, Grandad (war office) whose wisdom was light years ahead of others.

The support from Gibson Square has been invaluable along with my literary agent Heather Holden Brown whose genuine caring nature is refreshing in todays business climate. Any proceeds due to me have been donated to charity.

Finally, to my caring, loving and supportive wife Alison my deepest gratitude. Her encouragement kept me focused so i did not become a prisoner of woe..the ultimate safety valve.

Glenn Mulcaire, 2 July 2014

Publisher's Note

In view of ongoing trials no index has been provided.

CLIMATES AND WEATHER EXPLAINED

What do we mean by 'weather' and 'climate'? How do we account for them? Why is it necessary to understand meteorological processes to explain the climate? These are some of the questions dealt with in *Climates and Weather Explained*, a comprehensive introduction to the study of the atmosphere, integrating climatology and meteorology.

The book provides an entry to an understanding of the climate system, with clear explanations of basic principles, concepts and processes. It covers matters ranging from the origin of the atmosphere to the future of global climates. It is shown how patterns of evaporation, temperature, clouds, winds etc. arise from the weather and determine climates. The text is supported by a wealth of informative illustrations and a vast array of case studies demonstrating the relevance of the subject matter to everyday life.

There is a focus on the southern hemisphere, to redress a bias in existing literature, which concentrates on northern hemisphere conditions. This allows fresh insight into many topics. However, the universal nature of the basic information makes the book almost equally relevant to northern readers. Considerable attention is given to topics of quite general interest, such as global warming, natural hazards, the sustainable global population, agriculture, heat deaths, drought, windchill, weather forecasting, human comfort, and much else.

The book is supplemented by a novel feature – an attached interactive CD-ROM, which contains an enormous amount of additional material in greater detail and for more advanced study. This unique resource is closely related to each chapter of the book, with extensive cross-referencing and hypertext presentation. The CD-ROM contains valuable information for both student and teacher, as follows:

- over 170 scientific notes, with 40 additional illustrations and more tables
- application to northern climates
- a gallery of meteorological photographs
- an extended glossary, with key-word searching
- multi-choice questions (with answers)
- suggestions of essay topics and instructive experiments
- advice on writing and assessing scientific papers
- ideas on the teaching of topics in each chapter
- WWW addresses, a guide to further reading and a full bibliography.

Information is included for enabling the reader to navigate through the information, for print-out and download options, flexible access and user pathways.

A special *Instructors' Resource Pack* is also available from the publisher, containing an additional *Instructors' CD-ROM*.

Edward Linacre is Visiting Fellow in the Department of Geography at the Australian National University. **Bart Geerts** is Assistant Professor in Meteorology at the Embry-Riddle University, Prescott, Arizona.

CLIMATES AND WEATHER EXPLAINED

Edward Linacre and Bart Geerts

London and New York

First published 1997
by Routledge
11 New Fetter Lane, London EC4P 4EE

Simultaneously published in the USA and Canada
by Routledge
29 West 35th Street, New York, NY 10001

Typeset in Garamond by J&L Composition Ltd, Filey, North Yorkshire

Printed and bound in Great Britain by Clays Ltd, St. Ives PLC

British Library Cataloguing in Publication Data
A catalogue record for this book is available from the British Library

Library of Congress Cataloging in Publication Data
Linacre, Edward
Climates and weather explained: an introduction from a southern
perspective/Edward Linacre and Bart Geerts.
p.   cm.
Includes bibliographical references and index.
1. Atmospheric physics.   2. Climatology.   3. Meteorology.
4. Southern Hemisphere—Climate.   I. Geerts, Bart.
II. Title.
QC861.2.L547   1996
551.5–dc20   96–13601
CIP

ISBN 0–415–12519–7 (hbk)
ISBN 0–415–12520–0 (pbk)

CONTENTS

Part III Water

Part IV Winds

Part V Climates

Part VI Supplements

PREFACE

This book is intended to be useful, interesting and easily understood by means of five features:

1 It deals primarily with *general principles*, applicable anywhere in the world. They are explained in a straightforward text with 267 drawings and 66 tables, suitable for a beginner in this field of study.

2 The book is supplemented by 177 separate notes, 41 more drawings and 22 tables, containing material for the more advanced student, all on a CD-ROM. This includes recommendations for further reading, essay questions, numerical exercises for the student, suggestions for teachers of the subject, descriptions of simple experiments, and a full list of the literature used in writing the book. The contents of the CD-ROM are also available free on the World Wide Web at the following address: http://www.atmos. uah. edu/~geerts/routledge.html/

3 We have tried to *integrate meteorology and climatology* to an extent that is unusual for a textbook, though increasingly common in practice. The integration makes the book interdisciplinary, yet detailed enough to be suitable as an introduction to either discipline alone. This arrangement offers greater depth to geography students, and unusual breadth for students of meterology, helping to bridge the customary gulf between the 'exact' and social sciences.

4 The book contains numerous cases of the *relevance* of weather and climate to ordinary life. These include agriculture, droughts, housing, human comfort and newly important subjects like skin cancer, climate change, and the effects of temperature on mortality.

5 Most examples are taken from the *southern hemisphere*, to complement other textbooks, which almost all concentrate on the northern half of the world. The south has no equal to the huge Eurasian and North American land masses. On the other hand, the greater area of ocean in the south leads to more evaporation and less variable temperatures, and the huge southern Pacific ocean is the scene of El Niño episodes. Also, synoptic weather patterns are smaller and more mobile, and there is less air pollution on the whole than in the northern hemisphere. The Antarctic continent is more extensive and elevated than the Arctic, so the South Pole is far colder, which indirectly explains why the ozone over the Antarctic vanishes each spring. Related to this are the powerful winds blowing from west to east across the southern oceans. Another difference concerns the motions of oceans and winds; they circulate in the opposite direction in the southern hemisphere. This applies to circulations in entire ocean basins, as well as to fronts, tropical cyclones, sea breezes, even thunderstorms. In brief, southern hemisphere weather and climates

are quite distinct, though few textbooks deal with this. Nevertheless, the principles and processes which are explained in this book apply equally to both halves of the world. So the book is useful to students in the northern hemisphere too.

The arrangement of the book is as follows. In Part I we discuss the atmosphere's origin, composition and structure (Chapter 1). In Part II there is a consideration of the energy flows in the atmosphere, from the Sun (Chapter 2), to the air and ground (Chapter 3), and that used in evaporation (Chapter 4). Finally, Chapter 5 deals with the interrelationships between these and other flows of energy.

Part III deals with the movement of water after it has evaporated, chiefly from the oceans. Evaporation (i.e., vapour formation) creates atmospheric humidity (Chapter 6), and temperature patterns in the air control the ascent of water vapour through the atmosphere (Chapter 7). As a result, clouds form (Chapter 8). Thereafter, various processes can occur within the clouds, notably the making of rain (Chapter 9). Then Chapter 10 outlines features of the precipitation. Much of it eventually flows back to the oceans, discussed in Chapter 11. Subsequently, there is evaporation again from the oceans, starting the next cycle of water through the atmosphere.

Part IV is concerned with the winds that govern our weather. The Sun's heating of the Earth's equatorial regions, especially, induces patterns of winds on a global scale (Chapter 12). Within those vast movements are smaller regional-scale circulations, discussed in Chapter 13. Then there are local winds (Chapter 14) on a yet smaller scale. All of these winds combine with radiation (Part II) and water (Part III) to determine the weather. This and the resulting climates are considered in Part V (i.e., in Chapters 15 and 16) to draw everything together. At each stage there is an emphasis on the interaction between the surface and the atmosphere.

Unfortunately, the apparent logic of this or any other order of topics is contrived, imposed on a subject of enormous complexity. In fact, items in Part V do not depend exclusively on those in Part IV, nor those in turn on Part III, for instance. On the contrary, some matters discussed in Part I, for example, depend on what is considered in later chapters, because the atmosphere is a single entity, any individual aspect of which affects all the rest. Indeed, it is one of our aims to help the reader to appreciate the complexity of the interrelationships. This is done by considerable cross-referencing. The first mention of each figure, table or note is shown by printing in bold type; the notes are in the accompanying disk.

Part I

AIR

1

THE ATMOSPHERE

1.1 INTRODUCTION

The title of this book implies two questions – what do we mean by 'weather' and 'climate', and how do we account for them? As regards definitions, 'weather' concerns the conditions prevailing during a particular few hours over a specified area which is perhaps 30 km across, whilst 'climate' is the atmospheric character of such an area, shown by records over thirty years or so. We are especially interested in the weather and climate near the surface, i.e. temperature, radiation, humidity, rainfall and wind. The difference between weather and climate is that the latter is the aggregate or composite of the weather. It involves the extremes and variability of the weather as well as average values: floods and droughts at a place do not create a good climate overall. However, any brief definition of climate needs to be greatly expanded to be satisfactory.

The short answer to the second question is that various atmospheric processes and surface features explain the weather, and that in turn explains the climate. Surface features include the latitude, elevation, landform, orientation

to the Sun and distance from the sea. Whether the surface is ocean, vegetated, ice, desert or densely populated is also important. The meteorological processes are numerous and interrelated, but can be grouped for convenience into four categories – (i) those concerning the air's composition and structure, (ii) those involving the Sun's energy, (iii) processes related to the transformations of water from liquid to vapour, cloud, rain and snow, and (iv) winds. These are dealt with respectively in Parts I to IV of the book.

Processes that affect the weather operate on various scales, from the microscopic scale of the formation of cloud droplets (discussed in Chapter 8) to the size of the Earth, e.g. the winds discussed in Chapter 12. This range of spatial scales applies to climates too (**Table 1.1**). For example, we can talk about changes of the Earth's climate, or the climate of Australia, or differences between the climates of Wellington and Santiago, or those of the front and back gardens of a house. The climate of each these *domains* is influenced by the climate of the next largest, shown in Table 1.1, and also by the conditions actually within the domain. So, for

Table 1.1 Scales of climate

Scale	Domain	Typical extent*	Relevant features of the atmosphere	Typical time†	Relevant chapters
Global	Earth	20,000 km	Solar radiation, ocean gyre, general circulation	1 year	2, 11, 12
Synoptic	Continent	1,000 km	Frontal weather, weather forecasting tropical cyclone	4 days	13, 14, 16
Mesoclimate	Region	50 km	Thunderstorm, sea-breeze, weather	4 hours	9, 14
Topoclimate	Locality	5 km	A thermal, cumulus cloud, rainfall	1 hour	7, 8, 10
Microclimate	Site	10 m	Irradiance, evaporation, humidity, gusts	1 minute	2, 4, 6, 14

* The representative horizontal extent
† A time characteristic of the features in the previous column

instance, a garden's *microclimate* is affected, firstly, by the suburb's *topoclimate* (i.e. the overall climate of the *locality*, determined by its elevation, nearness to the coast, etc.), and, secondly, by the site, e.g. the garden's wetness, shelter and slope towards the Sun.

In what follows, we shall consider examples of various scales of time and distance, with especial attention to the southern hemisphere, which consists largely of water (**Note 1.A**). We begin with the largest space, the atmosphere as a whole, and the span of time since the Earth began.

1.2 ORIGIN OF THE ATMOSPHERE

The Earth's present atmosphere is unique. The Moon and the planet Mercury are airless, whilst Venus and Mars have atmospheres consisting almost entirely of carbon dioxide (**Table 1.2**).

Even our own air was quite different in the earliest part of the Earth's history, as we shall see.

History

Present evidence suggests that the Earth was formed about 4,500 million years ago (i.e. 4.5 giga-years before the present, written as 4.5 GaBP), and a transient *primary atmosphere* formed at the same time, consisting mostly of water vapour. That condensed to form the oceans at about 3.3 GaBP, and then the present *secondary atmosphere* arose, initially from gases released by 'outgassing', as the more volatile materials boiled off from the heavier components of the Earth's molten interior, escaping through fissures in the embryonic crust or, latterly, by way of volcanoes. Volcanic gases may consist of 80 per cent water vapour, 12 per cent

Table 1.2 Comparison of the climates of three planets

Feature	Mars	Earth	Venus
Mean distance from the Sun	228×10^6 km	150×10^6 km	108×10^6 km
Approx. mean surface temperature	$-50°C$	$+12°C$	$+460°C$
Main gas in atmosphere	95% carbon dioxide	78% nitrogen	97% carbon dioxide
Surface pressure	6 hPa	1,013 hPa	90,000 hPa
Gravitational acceleration	3.8 m/s^2	9.8 m/s^2	8.8 m/s^2

carbon dioxide, 6 per cent sulphur dioxide, for instance, with small amounts of other gases but no free oxygen. The original lack of the oxygen which now comprises just over a fifth of today's suface air, and makes our present atmosphere so distinctive amongst planets, is demonstrated by rocks with grey-green *unoxidised* iron sulphide, until 1.9 GaBP. Significant amounts of oxygen subsequently are indicated by abundant rocks coloured brown or red by *oxidized* iron. Thereafter the amount of oxygen increased, as indicated in **Figure 1.1**.

It remains uncertain how free oxygen first came about. There were probably several mechanisms. One involves *photolysis*, the splitting of molecules of the volcanic water vapour by solar radiation, thus forming separate hydrogen and oxygen atoms. Hydrogen is light and relatively mobile, and so escaped from the Earth's gravity into space, whilst the oxygen remained. That oxygen would absorb precisely the radiation responsible for its formation by photolysis, so that less and less could form. Such an automatic limitation of further oxygen creation is sometimes called the *Urey effect*. It would result in an oxygen concentration less than 0.3 per cent of present levels, unless there were other processes creating oxygen.

Further creation depended on *photosynthesis*, which occurs in some bacteria and in the leaves of plants (**Note 1.B**). It is the basic process of plant life and involves the combination of carbon dioxide, water and sunlight energy, to form oxygen and kinds of *carbohydrate*, the building-block of plant tissue. Photosynthesis within blue-green algae may have occurred from 3 GaBP, and green-plant photosynthesis from about 2 GaBP. The outcome was an oxygen concentration of about 1 per cent of that now, by 1.6 GaBP. Until that time, most of the oxygen released by photosynthesis was captured by unoxidised iron and dissolved in the sea.

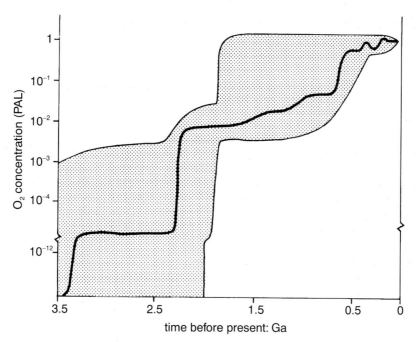

Figure 1.1 Estimates of the maximum and minimum possible concentrations of oxygen at various times, as a fraction of the PAL. PAL stands for 'present atmospheric level'. The bold line is a suggested best estimate.

The creation of oxygen accelerated with the evolution of plant *respiration* (Note 1.B), allowing increasingly complicated vegetation, suited to a wider range of environments. The increased area of plants raised oxygen concentrations rapidly, to about 10 per cent of present levels by 1 GaBP (Figure 1.1).

Initially, the lack of oxygen meant that the Sun's sterilising ultra-violet radiation (see Chapter 2) could reach to ground level, preventing the development of any life in exposed situations. As a consequence, life forms could exist only under at least 10 metres of water. Subsequently, life in ever shallower depths became possible as the concentration of atmospheric oxygen rose and protected the living tissue. The shallowness allowed better access to the air's carbon dioxide, needed for photosynthesis, and so yet more oxygen formed. In fact, the atmosphere appears to have had enough oxygen to allow life on land by 0.4 GaBP. As a result, another rapid acceleration of the evolutionary process took place, with an increase of oxygen to present levels by maybe 0.3 GaBP, i.e. 300 million years ago.

Plant Life

Plants and the atmosphere have greatly affected each other, and still do. For example, fire would destroy most vegetation if the oxygen content of the atmosphere were to increase from the present 20 per cent to be as high as 25 per cent. Then the reduced plant-life would result in decreased oxygen production, restoring the *status quo*. Conversely, if the oxygen concentration went down because of more carbon dioxide, the latter increase would accelerate photosynthesis, increasing the vegetation and hence oxygen creation, so that once again the *status quo* would be re-established. In other words, the oxygen concentration appears to be held steady by the vegetation, automatically.

The interaction of vegetation and climate can be considered in terms of the *Gaia hypothesis*, first advanced by James Lovelock in 1972. He regarded the climate as part of a self-regulating global system, called Gaia, after a Greek Earth-goddess. The system includes living things and the environment, and these evolve in mutual interaction, in a way that appears to optimize conditions for living things. However, any regulatory ability of Gaia is now challenged by human activities such as air pollution, soil erosion, fossil-fuel burning, damming rivers, deforestation, acid rain and damage to the ozone layer. Most of these are discussed later in the book.

1.3 COMPOSITION OF AIR

Air is a mixture of various gases added together. It also contains water vapour, dust and droplets, in quantities which vary with time, location and altitude.

Samples collected by balloon as early as 1784 showed the uniformity of air's composition up to 3 km. Later measurements have confirmed that the air up to 80 km or so consists chiefly of nitrogen and oxygen in almost constant proportions, forming a well-mixed layer called the *homosphere*, within which only the amount of water vapour and ozone vary. But the ratio of oxygen to nitrogen at 300 km is twelve times what it is at sea-level. Beyond about 600 km there is a preponderance of helium and then hydrogen, the lightest gas. Gases at those heights exist mostly as isolated atoms, rather than molecules of linked atoms.

If the components of a litre of surface air were separated, 0.781 litres (i.e. 781 millilitres, 781 mL or 78.1 per cent by volume) would be occupied by nitrogen, a colourless, tasteless, odourless gas. The proportion is slightly lower if masses are considered instead of volumes, because the densities of nitrogen and oxygen differ (**Table 1.3**). Volume proportions are usually of more importance, in practice.

In addition to the gases shown in Table 1.3,

Table 1.3 The proportions of dry air within the homosphere taken up by component gases, apart from traces of other gases such as neon, helium, krypton, hydrogen and xenon, which are mostly inactive chemically

Gas	Proportion by volume (%)	Proportion by mass (%)
Nitrogen	78.1	75.5
Oxygen	21.0	23.1
Argon	0.93	1.28
Carbon dioxide	0.035, approx	0.053, approx

air near the ground holds substantial amounts of water vapour according to location and season. At the equator there may be 2.6 per cent by volume of water vapour, while colder air (e.g. at 70 degrees latitude or on high mountains) might have less than 0.2 per cent. (This is explained in Chapter 4 and discussed further in Chapter 6.) Incidentally, the density of water vapour is less than that of nitrogen, and therefore less than that of air as a whole (**Note 1.C**).

Carbon Dioxide

Only about one molecule out of each 3,000 or so molecules of air consists of carbon dioxide. That is much less than on nearby planets (Table 1.2). Despite its small concentration, it is important because of the effects of carbon dioxide on photosynthesis and on global temperatures (Chapter 2), and the fact that the concentration is increasing. Analysis of bubbles of air trapped in Antarctic ice down to 2 km depth suggests that there were about 200 parts per million by volume (ppmv), 160,000 years ago. This increased to 270 ppm by 130,000 BP, falling to 210 ppm again by 18,000 BP, when the last Ice Age was at its most extreme (Chapter 15). There was a subsequent global warming and around 10,000 BP the concentration had risen to 275 ppm, where it remained until the middle of the nineteenth century, prior to industrialisation. It is now over 350 ppm and increasing at an accelerating rate (**Figure 1.2**), so that 600 ppm may well be exceeded in the next century (Chapter 15). The atmosphere

already holds about 2.7 million million tonnes (i.e. 2,700 gigatonnes, written as 2,700 Gt) of CO_2, containing 740 gigatonnes of carbon, written as 740 GtC. There is almost 60 times as much carbon dioxide in the oceans, which readily dissolve it, especially in the cold water near the poles (**Figure 1.3**).

Even the world's human population adds about 0.4 GtC to the atmosphere annually by exhaling; about 5 per cent of what we breathe out is carbon dioxide. However, the main sources of carbon dioxide in human society are industry, power generation, heating and transport, due to the combustion of the carbon in wood, oil, coal and natural gas. Emissions are chiefly in the northern hemisphere, but concentrations are uniform around the world because the time taken to circulate the gas in global winds (Chapter 12) is much less than the time it remains in the atmosphere (**Note 1.D**).

One way of reducing the amount of CO_2 is repeatedly to grow trees for felling, and then to lock up the carbon by using the wood in permanent structures like housing. A hectare of mature *Pinus radiata* in New South Wales (NSW) takes about 11 tonnes of carbon from the atmosphere annually. That means that continually planting and harvesting 10 million hectares (i.e. 1.3 per cent of Australia's area) would extract 0.11 Gt of carbon annually, which is only about half as much as the country's mining of carbon as coal in 1992–93. Old-growth forests, on the other hand, make little contribution to removing carbon from the air, being in equilibrium, giving off as much

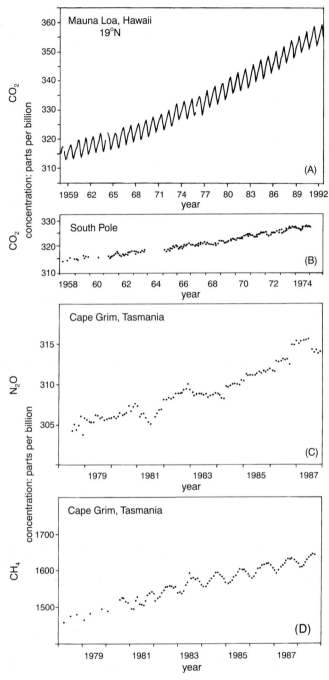

Figure 1.2 Changes of concentrations of (a) carbon dioxide in the atmosphere, measured on a mountain in Hawaii, (b) carbon dioxide measured at the South Pole, (c) nitrous oxide measured in north-west Tasmania and (d) methane in Tasmania.

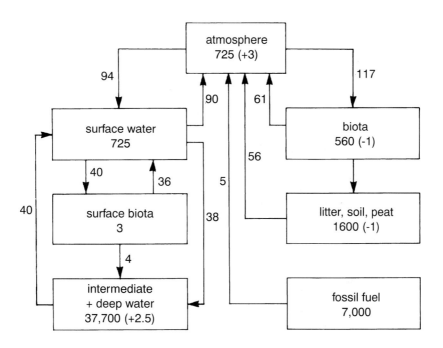

Figure 1.3 Estimates concerning the global carbon cycle. The diagram shows the approximate amounts stored at each stage in the cycle (in gigatonnes of carbon, i.e. GtC), and the annual transfer of carbon in the carbon dioxide moving between stages (GtC/a), and the resulting annual change of storage, in brackets. Inequality in some stages between (a) the change of storage, and (b) the difference between inputs and outputs, is due to the still approximate nature of the data.

carbon dioxide in decay as is absorbed in growth. So the huge forest of the Amazon basin, for instance, does not help, except in a negative sense; its continuation prevents the liberation of considerable carbon dioxide which occurs in *destroying* a forest.

The carbon dioxide concentration in the air varies in time. It may rise during the early morning to 40 ppm above the daily mean at 10 metres height within a forest, and fall to 15 ppm below in the afternoon, because of photosynthesis locally. There is also an annual swing, with a decrease at midlatitudes of about 5 ppm at midyear, due to plant growth in the northern hemisphere summer, and a similar increase at year end due to the decay of foliage from deciduous plants there (Figure 1.2). The seasonal variation is only about 2 ppm at the South Pole (Figure 1.2), on account of much less vegetation in the southern hemisphere, and considerable mixing of the atmosphere across the equator.

Carbon dioxide is one of the 'greenhouse gases' affecting world temperatures, discussed in the next chapter. Other such gases include methane, denoted by CH_4 in Figure 1.2. It comes from rice fields (for the swelling human population), swamps, the flatulence of cows, and leakage from natural-gas pipelines and coalmines, for instance. Present emissions amount to about half a gigatonne of methane annually, of which 6 per cent accumulates in the air. The methane concentration was less than 700 parts per billion until three centuries ago, but has now more than doubled (Figure 1.2). There is much less methane than carbon dioxide, but it is about fifty times as effective in causing global warming, so that the annual augmentation is equivalent to about 0.8 Gt/a (i.e. $0.5 \times 0.06 \times 26$) of CO_2, or 0.2 Gt/a of carbon. Similarly, there are rising concentrations of nitrous oxide (N_2O) and chlorofluorocarbons (CFCs), but reduced ozone (Section 1.4). Emissions of N_2O are increasing by 0.3 per cent annually, partly from the increased use of certain agricultural fertilisers, and the burning of timber. The combined warming potential of these various gases has become comparable with that of the carbon dioxide.

Circulations of Gases

It is important to realise the dynamic character of the atmosphere's composition. The total amount remains more or less unchanged, but only because the quantity entering almost equals what leaves. Individual atoms of carbon in carbon dioxide, for example, continually go through a cycle of change: the gas becomes part of plant tissue, with subsequent respiration by plants or animals, maybe solution in ocean water and then escape back into the atmosphere, as indicated in Figure 1.3. The time that a molecule spends as a gas is described in terms of its *atmospheric residence time*, the average period between a molecule entering and leaving the air (Note 1.D). Figure 1.3 shows how the difference between the annual amounts entering and leaving a stage equals the increment of storage there. (Such an equality is called a 'mass balance', mentioned in Chapter 5.) Similar diagrams of *bio–geo–chemical cycles* can be constructed for other components of air. These cycles are interrelated, e.g. the cycle of carbon meshes with that for oxygen, at the carbon dioxide stage.

A complete cycle of a carbon molecule may take several years, whereas nitrogen takes 10 million years for a cycle of *fixation* and

denitrification. 'Fixation' is the conversion of nitrogen into nitrates (chemicals containing both nitrogen and oxygen) by lightning or industrial processes, and by organisms in the soil or oceans. On the other hand, 'denitrification' is the liberation of nitrogen from decaying organic matter back into the air. The fixation–nitrification loop is supplemented by another involving the simple dissolving of nitrogen in the oceans and its subsequent release back into the atmosphere. It exists there as a stable constituent of the air (Table 1.3).

Similarly, there is a cycle of water (the *hydrologic cycle*), which involves evaporation, the formation of cloud, precipitation, stream flow, absorption into the oceans and then evaporation to form water vapour once more. This is discussed in detail in Chapters 6–11.

1.4 OZONE IN THE UPPER ATMOSPHERE

Another atmospheric gas is *ozone*, a form of oxygen in which each molecule consists of three atoms instead of the usual two. Ozone within the lowest 2 km of the atmosphere results from air pollution and is dangerous to health (Chapter 14). But it occurs also at 15–40 km above sea-level, where it protects us from the Sun's ultra-violet rays (UV), and its current depletion by about 4 per cent per decade is a matter of great concern (Chapter 2).

The upper ozone is formed chiefly in the summer hemisphere and over the equator, where solar radiation is strongest, and then it circulates towards the poles. The highest concentrations are found at latitudes above 50 degrees, but even there they are less than one thousandth of a gram in each cubic metre, representing about one hundred-thousandth part of the air. If all the ozone in the atmosphere were separated out at sea-level, the layer would be only 3 mm thick. Nevertheless, that small amount is important because it shields us from UV, which inhibits photosynthesis and is dangerous to health. In addition, the absorption of the UV leads to warming of the upper stratosphere, discussed in Section 1.8 and Chapter 2.

Processes

The formation of upper-atmosphere ozone involves *photo-dissociation* of normal oxygen. The molecules are split into pairs of separate single atoms by the impact of UV (**Figure 1.4**), as explained by Sydney Chapman in 1930. These single atoms can subsequently collide and combine with other normal oxygen molecules O_2, to create ozone O_3. The interaction of the UV and oxygen happens most around 40 km, because there is too little photo-dissociation at *lower* levels, where the UV has been attenu-

ated by the gases already traversed, whilst the thin air at *higher* levels contains insufficient oxygen for the collisions of single atoms and normal molecules needed to form ozone.

The upper ozone is eventually destroyed, either by photo-dissociation back into normal oxygen and a single atom, or by reactions with either particles and droplets in the air, the ground or various pollutant gases. The gases of special importance nowadays include chlorofluorocarbons (i.e. CFCs) from spraycans, refrigerators and from making some insulation foams of plastic. CFC concentrations are very small (Note 1.D), yet the reactions are *catalytic*, i.e. the same CFC molecule can eventually destroy an infinite number of ozone molecules (**Note 1.E**). The concentration of CFCs in the atmosphere rose rapidly after about 1970, and

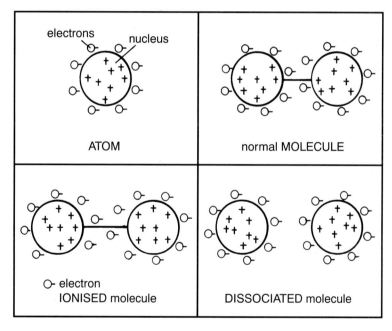

Figure 1.4 Various arrangements of the smallest units of oxygen, for example, showing the processes of *ionisation* (separation of electrical charges) and *dissociation* (separation of atoms). Ionisation requires bombardment by high-energy cosmic radiation (Section 1.7), whereas dissociation is caused by solar-radiation energy of particular wavelengths. In the case of oxygen, each atom includes eight positive *protons* (shown by the positive signs in the nucleus) balanced by eight negative electrons. *Atoms* normally combine to form a *molecule*, e.g. oxygen molecules (O_2) consist of two atoms, whereas ozone is represented by O_3.

the increase has been matched by a decline of October ozone at the South Pole (**Figure 1.5**). The increase is now slowing down as a result of cuts in CFC production since an international agreement in Montreal in 1987, and should reverse at the start of the next century. Unfortunately, the CFCs already existing will take decades to disappear (Note 1.D). Also, they are not the only man-made gases in the atmosphere which can attack the ozone layer. There are increasing amounts of methyl bromide (a fumigant) and various nitrogen oxides (especially nitrous oxide, N_2O) from agricultural activities, from supersonic transports at an altitude of about 20 km, from atom-bomb clouds and from combustion at the ground. The various gases facilitate ozone destruction by acting as catalysts in the presence of clouds of ice crystals formed by winter's cooling of the upper air (Note 1.E). The ozone layer is also damaged by sulphurous dust from major volcanic eruptions, e.g. the great eruption of Pinatubo in the Philippines in June 1991 and the smaller one of Cerro Hudson in Chile in August were followed in September by 10 per cent less than normal ozone above McMurdo at 78°S in Antarctica.

Variations

The amount of Antarctic ozone varies from day to day by as much as 30 per cent, as a result of changing weather, so it is advisable to consider monthly averages. These are found to be least during October–December, the southern spring. The reason is that then there is both sufficient cloud from the previous winter and enough solar radiation (as summer approaches) for the ozone-destruction reaction described in Note 1.E. Later, the ozone layer refills, as increasing summer warmth evaporates the ice-crystal clouds and increasing radiation creates more ozone in the southern hemisphere.

The annual polar depletion of ozone was first appreciated in 1985, and subsequently confirmed by re-examination of disregarded measurements since 1971. Since then, there has been a growing enlargement of the extent and duration of the hole (Figure 1.5) with corresponding alarm about increased UV concentrations at ground level. Observations in Antarctica in October 1993 showed a total absence of ozone at 14–19 km, for the first time.

A similar but less dramatic annual thinning of the ozone layer has been found more recently over the North Pole too, with an accompanying increase of springtime UV in Canada, for instance. The difference between conditions at the two poles is due to the lower temperatures in the south (Chapter 16) and the greater intensity of a vortex of upper winds around the South Pole in winter (Chapter 12). The vortex excludes ozone coming from the equator.

There has been some evidence of a two-year fluctuation of the thinning of the ozone layer, which might be related to the Quasi-Biennial Oscillation (Chapter 12).

1.5 ATMOSPHERIC PRESSURE

The various gases of the air together amount to a layer around the Earth which appears from the Moon to be no thicker than the skin on an apple. But this mass of air is attracted by the Earth's gravity and so has a considerable weight. The weight of air in a room 3 m × 4 m × 6 m at sea-level is approximately the weight of an adult. The result is that the air exerts what is called *barometric pressure*. At sea-level it is approximately 10 tonnes (i.e. 10,000 kg) on each square metre of surface. This means a pressure of about 10^5 kg/m.s^2, i.e. 100,000 Pascals. Such a pressure is more usually referred to as 100 kilopascals, or as 1,000 hectopascals (written as 1,000 hPa) in the units used by meteorologists, equal to the older units of millibars (**Note 1.F**). The pressure due to the weight above is exerted in all directions; an airtight

(a)

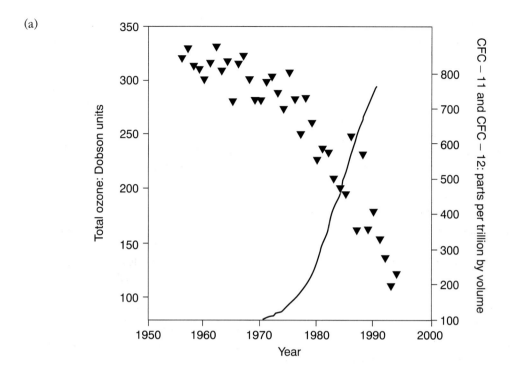

Figure 1.5(a) The simultaneous changes of ozone in Octobers over Halley Station in Antarctica (Chapter 16) and of the CFC content in the global atmosphere. A 'Dobson unit' is the thickness of a layer of ozone, assuming it has all been separated out and lowered to sea-level; one unit is equivalent to a layer 0.01 mm thick. The solid line shows the change of CFC concentration.

(b)

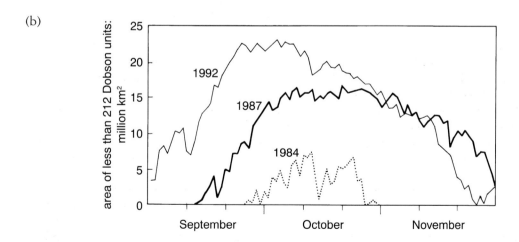

Figure 1.5(b) Changes of the area where there were less than 212 Dobson units of ozone.

(c)

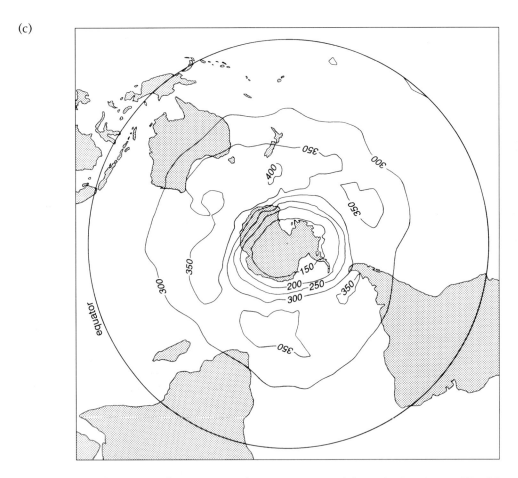

Figure 1.5(c) Dobson units of ozone in October 1993, measured from the Russian satellite Meteor-3.

box that is evacuated is pressed inwards on all sides, not just the top.

It is important to grasp the differences between pressure, mass, density and weight. They are discussed in Note 1.F. Pressure is important in meteorology, because its measurement tells us how much air there is above. A fall of pressure shows a net loss from the entire air column above, indicating a wind outwards. Differences between pressures at various places indicate the direction and strength of the wind (Chapter 12). There are also seasonal variations of surface pressures, and departures from the normal annual cycle imply unusual tempera-

tures aloft, for instance, which are relevant to weather forecasting (Chapter 15).

Measurement

There are several ways of determining the barometric pressure. It used to be measured most commonly with a mercury barometer, with a column of mercury (**Figure** 1.6) replacing a similar device using water, invented by Evangelista Torricelli in 1643. (Mercury is 13.6 times more dense than water and as a result a more convenient column only about 760 mm tall is needed to measure a typical sea-level

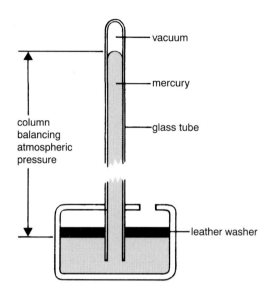

Figure 1.6 A mercury barometer, in which the atmospheric pressure on the leather washer is balanced by that exerted by the column of mercury.

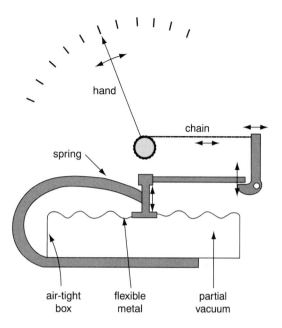

Figure 1.7 The operation of an aneroid barometer. A partially evacuated box with a flexible end is attached to an indicator arm. An increase of external atmospheric pressure compresses the top of the box and moves the arm.

atmospheric pressure, instead of about 10 m of water.) The mercury is surmounted by a vacuum, inside a vertical tube sealed at the top. Thus, only the weight of the mercury presses down and is balanced by the atmospheric pressure, so the height of the column is a measure of that pressure. This kind of barometer should be mounted on a solid wall in a place of constant temperature, with protection from sunlight and damage, but with good light.

The *aneroid barometer* (i.e. one without liquid) is more usual nowadays. It was invented in principle by Gottfried Liebniz around 1700, and constructed by Lucien Vide in 1843. In this instrument, the pressure being measured is opposed by the elasticity of a partially evacuated metal cylinder, and the movement of the ends of the cylinder is amplified by levers to show any pressure change (**Figure 1.7**). Aneroid instruments have the advantages of lightness, portability, fast response to rapid changes of pressure and easy adaptation to the recording

of data. On the other hand, they do need regular calibration. Both types of barometer can measure pressure changes as small as 0.3 hPa, corresponding to an altitude change of about 3 m near sea-level. As a rule-of-thumb, the pressure drops by approximately 1 hPa per 10 metres elevation near sea-level (**Note 1.G**).

Air pressure varies horizontally also (and we shall be concerned with that in Chapters 12 and 13) but there are much greater variations with height. (The distinctions between 'height', 'altitude' and 'elevation' are detailed in **Note 1.H**.) To determine the much smaller horizontal differences of pressure which are important in meteorology, it must be expressed in a standard manner. This is usually done in terms of the pressure at the mean level of the sea, after averaging tidal fluctuations over a few years. That pressure is called the Mean Sea-Level

Pressure (i.e. the MSLP) of the atmosphere. Deriving it necessitates correcting surface measurements of pressure for the effects of height (Note 1.G) and making small adjustments for the latitude, gravity, temperature and the time of day. For instance, a measurement of 850 hPa at Johannesburg (at 1,665 m altitude) implies about 1,017 hPa at sea-level (i.e. 850 + 1,665/10).

Values

As air pressure depends on the amount of air above, pressing down under the influence of gravity, the highest average values occur in sunken valleys like that of the Dead Sea in Israel, which is 395 m below sea-level. In terms of equivalent sea-level pressure, the highest yet recorded (1,084 hPa) occurred during a winter in Siberia. At the other extreme, a value of only 870 hPa was encountered in the middle of a tropical cyclone in the Pacific ocean (Chapter 13). More typical values are around the global average of 1,013 hPa. For instance, half the measurements at Sydney lie within 1,004–1,014 hPa.

The latitudinal variation of *average* pressures (**Figure 1.8**) is connected with the pattern of global winds discussed in Chapter 12, e.g. the

steep change of pressure between 35°S – 65°S is related to the strong westerly winds between those latitudes. More locally, daily or hourly changes of pressure by only a few hectopascals are important in determining the winds and weather (Chapters 13–15).

The pressure at sea-level is normally about 1,013 hPa, but only about 700 hPa at 3 km elevation, where there is less air above. That is why your ears 'pop' when you are driving up or down a big hill. The barometric pressure at the top of Mount Everest (8,848 m), and hence the air density and oxygen concentration (per unit volume) are only about a third of what they are at sea-level (Note 1.G). Other effects of low pressures at high elevations are considered in **Note 1.I**.

1.6 ATMOSPHERIC TEMPERATURE

Measuring Temperatures Aloft

Measurements on mountains, with kites and from manned balloons (since the Montgolfier brothers' ascent in 1783) show that not only does the pressure fall with increasing elevation, but the temperature does too.

The change of air temperature with height, i.e. the *temperature profile* is nowadays measured

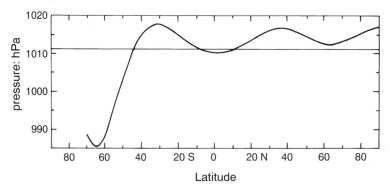

Figure 1.8 Variation with latitude of the annual-average mean-sea-level pressure. The curve shows the *meridional profile* (i.e. variation with latitude) of *zonal means* (i.e. averages of places at the same latitude but different longitudes).

in three principal ways. The most common method since 1930 is by means of a *radiosonde*. This is a balloon-borne instrument package invented by Pavel Molchanov (1893–1941). It rises at about 6 m/s, transmitting a radio signal of the surrounding temperature, humidity and pressure as it goes. (The pressure and temperature values are used to indicate the altitude of the measurements.) Something like a thousand radiosondes are launched once or twice daily around the world. The ascending rubber balloon expands in the low pressures and is made brittle by the low temperatures, so that eventually it bursts at an altitude of perhaps 20 km. The package then descends by parachute. Some meteorological services encourage people to look for sondes which have come down and mail them back for a reward, so that they can be re-used.

A second source of information about temperatures has become available recently. Passengers on long-distance flights are periodically shown the current altitude of the plane and also the temperature outside, so that one could plot an instructive graph of temperature against height as the plane rises to cruising level, and descends from it.

In addition, meteorological satellites are nowadays used to determine the temperature profile. This is done by measurement of the amount of radiation of various wavelengths emitted by molecules of either carbon dioxide or oxygen at each level in the atmosphere, as explained in Chapter 2.

Lapse Rates

The change of temperature with height is called the *lapse rate*. A *positive* lapse rate represents the normal condition with *cooler* air above, the temperature *falling* with increased height. The opposite, a negative lapse rate (ie the temperature increases with height) is called an *inversion* (Chapter 7). Temperature profiles show the *actual lapse rate* (or *environmental lapse rate*) at

each level, i.e. the tangent to the profile at that level.

Typical profiles in **Figure 1.9** show positive lapse rates at most places in the lowest 10 km or so, and we will see in Chapter 7 that positive lapse rates promote convection and turbulence. This churning has led to the layer being called the *troposphere*, from the Greek word 'tropos', meaning to turn or change. The layer contains about 80 per cent of the mass of air and almost all the clouds. It is deeper in the tropics (about 17 km) than in temperate climates, where it is higher in summer (about 12 km) than winter (10 km), though there are also significant changes from day to day, e.g. from 8 km to 14 km. Convection is rare at the poles, where the surface is so cold and consequently the troposphere is relatively shallow at high latitudes, especially during the polar winter.

A surprising consequence of the temperature patterns in Figure 1.9 is that the average temperature of all the air above the pole is *higher*, especially in summer, than that of the column above the equator, where the coldest air occurs, at about 15 km elevation. Therefore, the relative lightness of warm air leads to lower

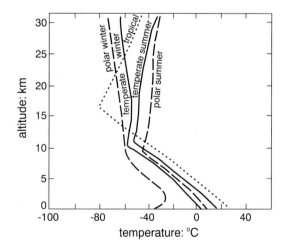

Figure 1.9 The vertical variation of temperature in the lowest 30 km of the atmosphere at different latitudes and seasons.

Plate 1.1 Releasing a balloon carrying a radiosonde to measure temperature and humidity conditions in the troposphere and lower stratosphere. The radiosonde equipment is in a box in the meteorologist's left hand. The box is attached by a cord to the pyramidal radar reflector which hangs beneath the balloon. The reflector enables location of the balloon's position by means of the radar equipment seen behind, and the change of position shows the sideways displacement (i.e. the wind) at each height. Notice that the meteorologist is wearing protective clothing in case the hydrogen in the balloon ignites, which is possible in dry conditions.

sea-level pressures at high latitudes, as seen in Figure 1.8.

Measurements at top and bottom of a kilometre-thick layer of the troposphere might show values of 10°C at the top and 16.5°C at the bottom, for instance. Such a positive lapse rate is written as 6.5 K/km, or 6.5 milliKelvins per metre (written as 6.5 mK/m), in Système Internationale units (**Note 1.J**). Note that temperature *differences* or *changes* are preferably described in degrees Kelvin (**Note 1.K**). Thus, the difference between 5°C and 10°C is written as 5 K, and is equal to the temperature difference between 41°F and 50°F, whereas a *temperature* of 5°C does not equal 9°F.

A *standard atmosphere* is a nominal relationship between altitude and mean temperatures. For instance, that adopted by the International Civil Aviation Organisation (ICAO) is based on measurements over the USA but applied widely in calibrating aneroid barometers for measuring the altitude of light aircraft. (Larger planes use radar to measure their height above the ground.) The ICAO atmosphere has the following features: a mean pressure of 1,013.25 hPa and an air temperature of 15°C at sea-level, a lapse rate of 6.5 mK/m to 11 km, then isothermal conditions at −56.5°C up to 20 km, followed by a negative lapse rate of 1 mK/m to about 32 km (Chapter 7).

So far we have been discussing only lapse rates in the free air. The change of temperature with elevation on the side of a mountain may differ (Chapter 3) on account of the local effect of heat from the ground, which is warmed by the daytime sun and cooled by the radiation of heat to the night sky (Chapter 2).

1.7 ATMOSPHERIC ELECTRICITY

An important feature of the upper atmosphere is its ability to conduct electricity through the movement of *negative ions*, which are whole or part-molecules to which *electrons* have become attached. Electrons are the negatively charged parts of an atom. They are stripped from normal atoms of the air's gases in the course of bombardment by *cosmic radiation,* which consists of high-energy atomic nuclei from outer space, along with the products of their collisions with air molecules. In other words, the electron-stripping process in the upper atmosphere results in *ionisation* (Figure 1.4). The process absorbs cosmic radiation, and thereby protects us from it.

Ionosphere

Ionisation is almost negligible at heights where gas molecules are few, and cannot occur near the ground either because the cosmic radiation has become insignificant by the time it has penetrated that far. Consequently, this kind of ionisation happens mainly at an intermediate elevation of 50–100 km.

The ionized region is called the *ionosphere.* It comprises several layers, including the D layer at around 80 km, the E layer around 110 km, and F layers at 170 and 270 km. The D layer disappears at night, because ionising radiation from the Sun is then absent, and there is sufficient air at 80 km for existing negative and positive ions to collide and neutralise each other. So the E layer becomes the base of the ionosphere. As a result, the space between the ground and the ionosphere becomes deeper at night, facilitating the bouncing of radio signals around the globe and consequently improving reception.

The electrical conductivity of the ionosphere also plays a part in the cycle of atmospheric electricity described in Chapter 9. Most strikingly, the ionosphere is responsible for the beautiful curtains, veils, arcs, rays and bands of greenish or dark-red light above 100 km in the sky at night, seen in the southern hemisphere within about 25 degrees of the south magnetic pole. James Cook named them *Aurora Australis* (or Southern Lights) in 1773. It has been observed from Hobart (43°S), as the south magnetic pole is currently located near the same longitude at 66°S. The light is due to the *solar wind*, atomic particles moving at around 500 km/s from the Sun.

Other Features

Above the ionosphere lies the *magnetosphere,* a region extending thousands of kilometres, containing only separated (negative) electrons and (positive) *protons* (i.e. hydrogen atoms stripped of electrons). These ions are aligned by the magnetic field of the Earth (which orients any magnetic compass similarly), forming two zones of higher concentration called the *van Allen belts.* The inner belt is found only at low latitudes, at a height of about 3,000 km. The outer belt lies at about 10,000 km above the equator, but much lower at high latitudes because of attraction by the Earth's magnetic poles.

1.8 ATMOSPHERIC STRUCTURE

The various features of composition, radiation absorption and emission, ionisation and convection that we have now considered tend to stratify the atmosphere into layers. **Figure 1.10**

shows the average conditions schematically, though there are great variations with season and region. Let us work downwards through the different layers, considering them in terms of temperature especially.

Highest Layers

There is no air beyond 32,000 km because the Earth's gravitational attraction there is

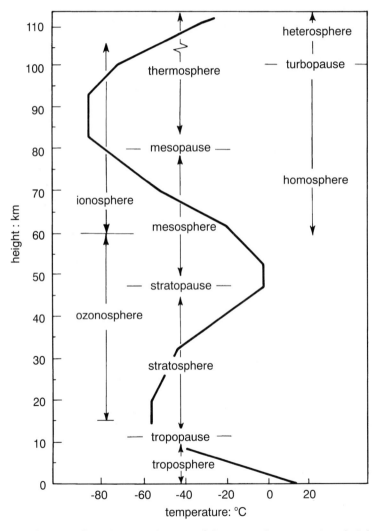

Figure 1.10 Typical features of the layers and zones of the atmosphere at various heights.

exceeded by the centrifugal force away, caused by the Earth's spinning. Then, down to about 200 km from the ground, there is the *thermosphere*, so-called because of high temperatures, nominally around 1,000 K, due to absorbing the energy of ultra-violet radiation (Section 1.4). Such a temperature of what is almost a perfect vacuum merely indicates the high speed of the individual molecules present, energised by solar radiation.

The thermosphere corresponds very approximately to the *heterosphere*, the region above 100 km where the air is stratified, with lighter gases above heavier. At about 100 km is the *turbopause*, bounding the *homosphere* beneath, where the air is mixed enough to have a uniform chemical composition.

Within the homosphere are three layers (or 'spheres'), each capped by a transition zone (or 'pause'). The *mesopause* separates the thermosphere from the *mesosphere* (the 'middle region') beneath, and may lie at about 80 km elevation. Temperatures there are typically as low as −90°C. There is normally very little moisture in the mesosphere, though thin purplish patches of 'nacreous' (i.e. pearl-like) cloud occasionally occur at 60–80 km elevation (Chapter 8). Lapse conditions exist in the mesosphere, but less steeply than in the troposphere (Figure 1.10).

The next dividing zone is the *stratopause* at around 50 km, which separates the mesosphere above from the *stratosphere* below. More than 99.7 per cent of the atmosphere is found below the stratopause. The temperature there is about 0°C on account of heat produced by (i) the absorption of solar UV radiation by ozone, formed after the dissociation of some of the oxygen and then recombination as ozone (Section 1.4), and (ii) absorption by the ozone of longwave radiation from the ground beneath (Chapter 2).

There is normally a negative lapse rate throughout the stratosphere, due to the relatively high temperature at the stratopause. But the stratosphere has a slightly positive lapse rate in the polar winter (Figure 1.9), due to the absence of sunshine for several months. The result is that temperatures are below −100°C at the polar stratopause in winter, and this produces upper winds exceeding 60 m/s at the highest latitudes (Chapter 12). On the other hand, the temperature at the polar stratopause often exceeds 30°C in summer because of the long days then.

Troposphere

Lower down again is the *tropopause*, where there is generally a temperature minimum of around −50°C and a change of the lapse rate. It was first detected by Teisserenc de Bort in 1898. There is no agreed definition of the tropopause, but it does separate the stratosphere's ozone and temperature conditions from the positive lapse rates of the *troposphere*, the lowest layer. This contains all the Earth's mountains, about 80 per cent of the atmosphere and virtually all the water vapour. **Note 1.L** gives characteristic values of the temperature, pressure and density at various levels of the troposphere.

Within the troposphere but close to the ground is the *planetary boundary layer* (PBL), also called the 'Ekman layer' or 'mixed layer', in which the air is well mixed by heating (Chapter 3) and surface roughness (Chapter 14). Typically, the PBL is about 1 km thick, according to wind speed and solar radiation (Chapter 2), but may be less than 100 m on a still, cold, night. It is a feature of the topoclimate (Table 1.1).

Towards the bottom of the PBL is the *surface layer* (or 'friction layer'), where winds vary rapidly in speed and direction with height, in response to the friction of the ground (Chapter 14). In the case of a city, which has an irregular profile, there is a *roughness layer* where turbulence is caused by the buildings, and between them is the *canopy layer* of air (**Figure 1.11**).

The lowest tenth or so of the surface layer is

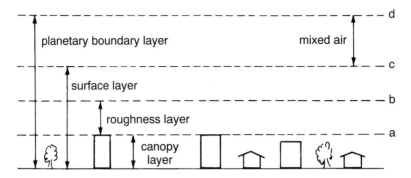

Figure 1.11 Schematic diagram of the layers of air over a city. Level *a* is at roof top height, *b* is the limit of stirring caused by the city's individual buildings, *c* is the extent of the effect of the city as a whole, and *d* is the base of the inversion layer (Chapter 7) which defines the planetary boundary layer.

the *interfacial layer* or 'constant-flux layer', constituting the main barrier to vertical exchanges between the surface and the air, e.g. evaporation from the ocean and the transfer of carbon dioxide to vegetation. It is a feature of the 'microclimate'. There is negligible horizontal advection within this layer, i.e. little carrying of heat or moisture sideways in winds.

Lastly, there is the *laminar (viscous) sub-layer*, which consists of air held almost stationary around all solid and liquid surfaces by molecular forces. This layer is only millimetres thick, depending on the wind speed, but it provides important thermal insulation.

So we have outlined the entire atmosphere. From now on we shall concentrate on the troposphere, because that is the arena of processes which produce weather and determine our climatic environment (Table 1.1).

NOTES

1.A Features of the Earth's surface

1.B Photosynthesis and respiration

1.C The densities of air and water vapour

1.D Ground-level concentrations of gases

1.E The chemistry of the destruction of ozone

1.F Mass, density, weight and pressure

1.G The hydrostatic balance

1.H Height, altitude and elevation

1.I Effects of the rarefied atmosphere at high elevations

1.J SI units

1.K Scales of temperature

1.L Mean properties of the atmosphere

1.M The 'ideal-gas' law

Part II
ENERGY

2

RADIATION

2.1 KINDS OF RADIATION

In this second part of the book we will consider how energy moves in the atmosphere. In particular, we discuss three forms of energy – radiation (discussed in this chapter), 'sensible heat' (Chapter 3), and energy absorbed in evaporating water (Chapter 4). They are connected by what is called the 'energy balance', considered in Chapter 5. We begin by discussing the radiant energy from the Sun.

It is not obvious how solar energy reaches the Earth because the intervening distance of about 150 million kilometres is practically a vacuum. So the Sun's heat is not carried in a wind, nor is conduction possible. Instead, the energy is transferred by *electromagnetic radiation* (**Note 2.A**). Such radiation differs from sound, which requires air to carry the vibrations, but is similar in being characterised by the velocity and wavelengths involved. The radiation travels at a speed close to 3×10^8 m/s (in vacuum) and therefore takes 8.3 minutes to travel from the Sun to the Earth. The wavelengths of this radiation form a segment of the entire range (i.e. *spectrum*) of electromagnetic

radiation, which spans radio to cosmic rays (**Figure 2.1**).

In this chapter, we are concerned especially with visible light and radiant heat. Light has wavelengths of less than a millionth of a metre. (This is called a *micrometre* or *micron,* with the symbol 'μm'. Sometimes the unit used is a *nanometre*, written 'nm', equal to a thousandth of a micron.) On the other hand, radiation from bodies at the much lower Earth temperatures has wavelengths about twenty times as great, the difference reflecting the ratio of the temperatures of the Sun and Earth, effectively 5,770 and nominally 288 degrees Kelvin, respectively.

The radiation from a body involves a range of wavelengths, and the body's temperature determines both the dominant wavelength (given by *Wien's Law,* see **Note 2.B**) and the overall rate of energy emission, given by the *Stefan–Boltzmann equation* (**Note 2.C**). The consequence is that a diagram of the amounts of energy of various wavelengths from each of the Sun and the Earth shows different humps, the one for solar radiation being higher and to the left, since the Sun is hotter (**Figure 2.2**). Its

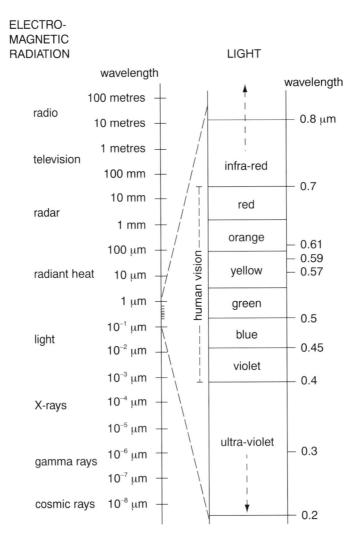

Figure 2.1 The spectrum of electromagnetic radiation.

emission spectrum peaks in the visible range (Figure 2.1), i.e. we can see much of the radiation from the Sun.

Solar radiation has wavelengths mostly within 0.1–3.5 μm and is called *shortwave radiation* (SW) (**Note 2.D**). The part which is visible is a mixture which can be separated into the colours of the rainbow by a prism, from violet to red. Violet light has a wavelength about 0.40 μm, while red light has wavelengths up to 0.76 μm. In addition, about 9 per cent of the Sun's radiated energy is invisible because it has wavelengths less than 0.4 μm, shorter than that of violet light, so it is called *ultra-violet radiation* (UV) (Sections 1.4 and 2.6). At the other extreme, about 50 per cent of the radiation has wavelengths beyond the red end of the visible range (i.e. beyond 0.7 μm) and is there-

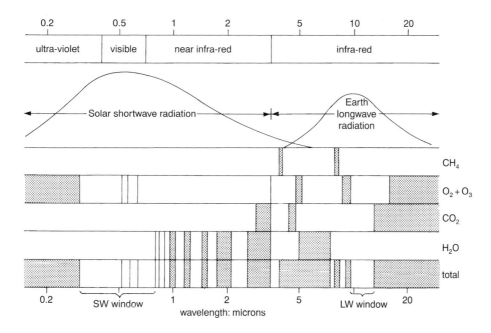

Figure 2.2 Indicative graphs of the energy radiated by the Sun and the Earth at various wavelengths. The spectrum of the radiant energy from unit area of the Sun is scaled down. In reality the area under the Sun's curve should be about 160,000 times the area under the Earth's curve (i.e. approximately $6,000^4/300^4$, from the Stefan–Boltzmann equation, see Note 2.C). Wavelengths absorbed by various gases are shown as dark bands.

fore called *infra-red radiation* (IR). This includes what is called *longwave radiation* (LW), which is the radiation whose wavelengths exceed 3.5 μm (Section 2.7).

The Earth emits only longwave radiation, which can be felt but not seen. A graph of this peaks around 10 μm (Figure 2.2). It is discussed in Section 2.7.

2.2 SOLAR RADIATION REACHING THE EARTH

The amount of radiation received by the Earth from the Sun is governed by the geometry of the Earth's motions (**Figure 2.3**). Its orbit around the Sun is not quite circular and the Sun is offset from the centre. As a result, the Earth is only 147.1 million kilometres distant

from the Sun at the nearest point (the *perihelion*), presently on 3 January, and 152.1 million at the *aphelion* on 4 July, so 6.5 per cent more radiation reaches the Earth in January (**Note 2.E**). This would tend to make global temperatures higher in January than in July, i.e. summer in the southern hemisphere hotter than in the northern. This is not observed in practice, as the tendency is masked by the effects of different amounts of ocean in the two hemispheres (Chapter 11).

The Earth moves around the Sun in the *plane of the ecliptic* and spins on its own axis, which is tilted from a line perpendicular to the plane (Figure 2.3). All of these features are subject to slow, regular changes, described by Milutin Milankovic in 1930, following the ideas of James Croll in 1867. First, the Earth's path around the Sun varies from almost circular to

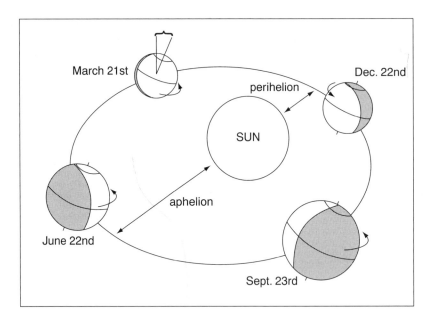

Figure 2.3 The geometry of the Earth's movement about the Sun, in an orbit which forms an ellipse on a flat plane (the *ecliptic*). The Earth spins about an axis which currently points to the North Star, Polaris. Both rotations are clockwise if viewed from the South Pole.

more elliptical and back, each 97 millenia. Second, there is a variation of the tilt (or *obliquity*) of the Earth's axis, between 21° 59′ and 24° 36′ degrees and back, each 40,400 years. The tilt (presently 23° 27′) is now becoming less, tending imperceptibly to reduce the annual range of surface temperatures. Third, the Earth's tilted axis wobbles (or 'precesses'), describing a cone each 21 millenia. Each of these variations alters the difference between summer and winter temperatures (Chapter 3). Occasionally, the three rhythms come briefly into coincidence, working together then to either maximise or minimise the difference between summer and winter. Rare coincidences of minimum difference probably triggered past ice ages, as a result of the increased precipitation of relatively warm winters and the reduced snowmelt of cooler summers (Chapter 15).

Position of the Sun in the Sky

The tilt of the Earth's axis makes the Sun appear either north or south of the equator, and the latitude at which the Sun is overhead (i.e. 'in the *zenith*') at noon is called the Sun's *declination*. The seasonal variation of the declination has been monitored since the times of the ancient Egyptians, 5,000 years ago. The declination is furthest south on about 21 December (a *solstice*) when the Sun is directly overhead at 23° 27′S (the *Tropic of Capricorn*) at noon. The South Pole then tilts most towards the Sun, and the southern hemisphere has its longest day; south of 66° 3′S (the south *Polar Circle*) the Sun is still above the horizon at midnight. (Notice that 66° 33′ is 90 degrees minus the angle of tilt.) Likewise, the Sun lies at the same latitude in the north (at the *Tropic of*

Cancer) in the middle of a southern-hemisphere winter, on about 21 June, the other solstice.

The angle of the Sun above the horizon at any moment is called the *solar elevation*, and its value can be shown by a diagram such as that of **Figure 2.4**, for any place. Its value at noon equals $[90 - f + d]$, where f is the latitude and d the declination of the Sun at that time of year. Both f and d are regarded as positive in the southern hemisphere. The annual extremes of the Sun's elevation allow us to design houses which accept the Sun's warmth in winter but shade the windows in summer (**Figure 2.5**).

The midday Sun is overhead on two dates each year, at latitudes between the two Tropics, which means that there are two seasons of maximum insolation in such places. The midday Sun is overhead at the equator at the *equinoxes*, on about 21 March and 22 September, when day and night are of equal duration, at all latitudes (**Table 2.1**).

Sun's Radiation

The amount of radiant energy received or emitted every second at a surface of one square metre is properly known as the *radiance*, though we lazily refer to it simply as the 'radiation'. The radiance on a surface facing the Sun, just outside the Earth's atmosphere, is called the *solar constant*, equal to 1,367 W/m². This is more than the output of a kilowatt electric heater on each square metre of surface facing the Sun. The 'constant' was 30 per cent less

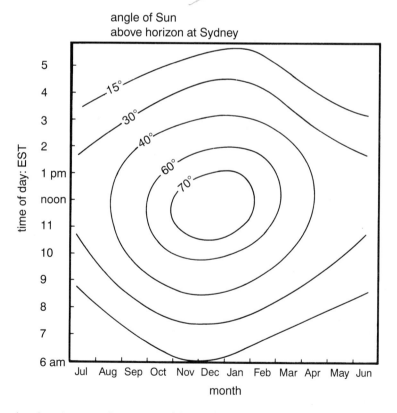

Figure 2.4 The solar elevation at various times of day and in various months, at Sydney (34°S). For instance, the Sun is about 40° above the horizon in September at 10 a.m.

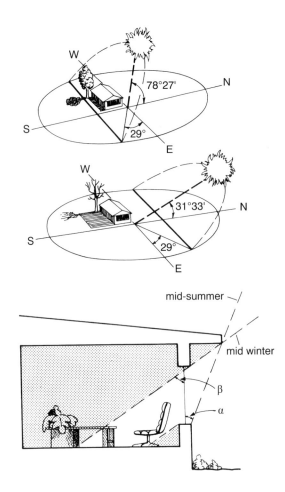

Figure 2.5 Solar elevation and the amount of light entering a window on the equatorward side of a house. The upper diagrams show the Sun's path at 34°S, at mid-summer and at mid-winter, respectively. The Sun's noontime elevation is 78° 27′ (i.e. 90 − 34 + 23° 27′) at mid-summer, and 31° 33′ at mid-winter (i.e. 90 − 34 − 23° 27′).

The consequences are shown in the lowest diagram. The angle α (the departure from vertical of a line from the window-sill to the eaves) needs to be more than $[f - 23°]$, where f is the latitude, to exclude radiation in summer, and β has to be less than $[f + 23°]$, to maximise the intake of sunshine in winter.

when the Earth initially formed 4.5 billion years ago, assuming that the Sun developed like other stars of its size and composition. Also, there are variations due to the elliptical orbit of the Earth each year, to Milankovic changes of orbit over millenia, and (by less than 1 per cent) to sunspots, discussed below.

The energy onto a *horizontal* surface on top

of the atmosphere, *parallel* to the ground, is called the *extra-terrestrial radiance* (**Figure 2.6**). It is necessarily less than the solar constant because it is the radiation onto a surface oblique to the Sun's rays. It depends on the solar constant and the orientation of the ground to the Sun (which are both known for any chosen time of the year), so it can be calculated and

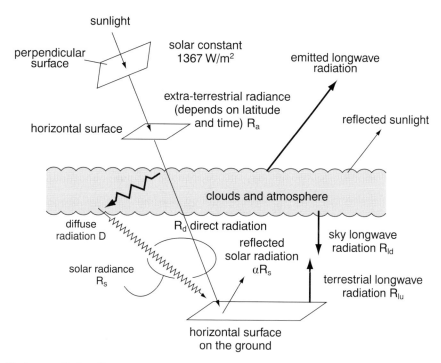

Figure 2.6 Various radiation fluxes.

tabulated for various latitudes and months (**Note 2.F**).

The combination of the tilt and the elliptical orbit of the Earth leads to a minimum of seasonal variation of extra-terrestrial radiation at a latitude of 3.4°N, which may be called the *radiation equator*. It happens to be close to the average latitude of the 'thermal equator' (Chapter 3).

Daylength

The daylength varies greatly with latitude and month, as shown in Table 2.1. Daylength is 24 hours in midsummer within the *south Polar Circle* (i.e. at latitudes above 66° 33′S), with continual sunshine over several days. Conversely, there are 24 hours of darkness each day in midwinter. At a midlatitude city like Dunedin (48°S), daylength is about 16 hours in

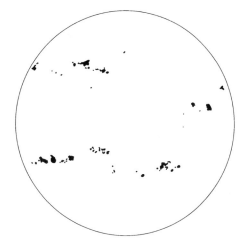

Figure 2.7 Sunspots on the Sun. (Note that it is dangerous to try to observe them directly with the naked eye, doubly so with binoculars, and trebly with a telescope. It is safer to look through *very* dark glass at the Sun's reflection in a pool.)

Table 2.1 Effect of latitude and season on the fortnightly mean daylength

Hours of daylight in the northern hemisphere

Lat	January	February	March	April	May	June	July	August	September	October	November	December
70°	0.5 2.2	4.5 7.0	9.8 12.7	15.5 18.0	20.3 22.4	24.0 24.0	24.0 22.4	20.2 17.8	15.1 12.2	9.5 6.9	4.5 2.3	0.3 0.0
60°	6.3 7.3	8.5 9.9	11.0 12.5	13.8 15.0	16.5 17.7	18.6 18.8	18.5 17.5	16.4 15.0	13.6 12.2	10.9 9.5	8.2 7.0	6.2 5.9
50°	8.3 8.9	9.7 10.6	11.3 12.4	13.3 14.2	15.0 15.8	16.2 16.4	16.2 15.6	14.9 14.1	13.2 12.2	11.3 10.3	9.4 8.7	8.3 8.1
40°	9.5 9.9	10.4 11.0	11.5 12.3	13.0 13.6	14.2 14.6	14.9 15.0	14.9 14.5	14.1 13.5	12.8 12.1	11.5 10.9	10.3 9.8	9.5 9.3
30°	10.3 10.6	10.9 11.4	11.7 12.2	12.7 13.1	13.5 13.8	14.0 14.1	14.0 13.8	13.4 13.0	12.6 12.1	11.7 11.3	10.8 10.5	10.3 10.2
20°	11.0 11.2	11.4 11.7	11.9 12.2	12.5 12.7	13.0 13.2	13.3 13.3	13.3 13.1	12.9 12.7	12.4 12.1	11.9 11.6	11.3 11.1	11.0 10.9
10°	11.6 11.7	11.8 11.9	12.0 12.1	12.3 12.4	12.5 12.6	12.7 12.7	12.7 12.6	12.5 12.4	12.3 12.1	12.0 11.8	11.7 11.6	11.6 11.5
0°	12.1 12.1	12.1 12.1	12.1 12.1	12.1 12.1	12.1 12.1	12.1 12.1	12.1 12.1	12.1 12.1	12.1 12.1	12.1 12.1	12.1 12.1	12.1 12.1
	July	August	September	October	November	December	January	February	March	April	May	June

Hours of daylight in the southern hemisphere

Lat

midsummer, but less than 9 hours in midwinter. In contrast, it fluctuates only between 11.7 to 12.8 hours at Darwin (12°S).

Sunspots

A *sunspot* is a relatively dark area on the Sun, at temperatures of only about 3,000 Kelvin, occupying up to 0.2 per cent of the Sun's visible area (**Figure 2.7**). Each spot appears to drift eastwards (showing that the Sun rotates once

every 27 days) and towards the Sun's equator, before disappearing.

Sunspots alter the solar constant by less than 0.3 per cent, but are associated with very slight increases of ultra-violet radiation and of *solar wind*, which consists of high-speed electrons and nuclear particles. The annual number of sunspots varies (Chapter 10), with a maximum about every eleven years (e.g. in 1906, 1917, 1928, 1938, 1947, 1958, 1969, 1980, 1988), as reported by Samuel Schwabe in 1843. The

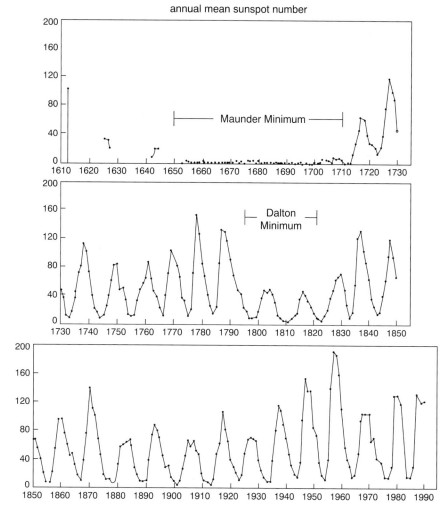

Figure 2.8 Variation of the number of sunspots observed each year.

maxima are especially marked every eighty-five years or so (**Figure 2.8**). When the cycle of sunspot numbers is less than eleven years, there tend to be more sunspots and Earth temperatures show some warming. Also, there were hardly any sunspots between 1650–1710, a period called the *Maunder Minimum*, named after Annie Russell Maunder (1868–1947). It coincided with the Little Ice Age (Chapter 15). Later there was the *Dalton Minimum*, between 1795–1823 (Figure 2.8).

2.3 ATTENUATION WITHIN THE ATMOSPHERE

The radiation reaching the ground is a fraction of that at the top of the atmosphere, because of reflection of some back to space (chiefly from the clouds), and because of the absorption of some by clouds, by the air's gases and by the fine dust particles and tiny droplets which together are called *aerosols*. The diameters of aerosols are mostly less than 1 m and therefore they are so light that they remain airborne indefinitely (**Note 2.G**).

The intensity of the Sun's rays on the ground is less at higher latitudes for two reasons (**Figure 2.9**). First, each ray is spread over a larger area because of increasing obliqueness to the ground. Second, the rays have to traverse a longer path through the atmosphere, so that more radiation is absorbed and scattered by the air.

In the case of the absorption by gases, particular wavelengths are affected especially, as shown in Figure 2.2. Oxygen and ozone absorb radiation with wavelengths below about 0.3 μm, while water vapour and carbon dioxide deplete that with wavelengths above 0.7 μm. Water vapour absorbs radiation in several broad spectral bands with wavelengths up to about 8 μm, and carbon dioxide absorbs almost all the IR radiation above 14 μm. Methane (CH_4) and nitrous oxide (N_2O) absorb longwave radiation between 7.7–8.3 μm.

The combined effect is to create a '*window*' around the visible part of the spectrum; most shortwave radiation penetrates the atmosphere through this window (**Note 2.H**). However, longwave radiation passes through the atmosphere only by means of a window between 8–14 μm, which is split by an ozone absorption band of 9.4–10.0 μm. This window is less transparent, so most longwave radiation from the Earth's surface is absorbed by air molecules and then re-emitted before it reaches outer space.

Scattering

The air's molecules and aerosols scatter the Sun's rays, which increases their paths within the atmosphere and hence their absorption. The scattering of radiation by gas molecules and the smallest aerosols is called *Rayleigh scattering*. This occurs with particles which are between a hundredth and a thousandth the size of the wavelength and scatter incoming radiation according to the inverse of the radiation's wavelength. In other words, blue light (with a relatively short wavelength) is scattered ten times more than red light. That explains the blue sky above (**Figure 2.10**). But on the Moon, where there is no atmosphere, the consequent absence of Rayleigh scattering makes the sky always black, even in sunshine. Back on Earth, blue light in solar radiation is notably scattered away by air pollution or fine dust, which makes the remaining direct sunlight seem red, especially when the Sun is low and the ray's path through the atmosphere is long (Chapter 15). Beautiful red sunsets occur in the desert after a hot day allows dried dust to rise in the air. Bushfires and other air pollution also create red sunsets. Large volcanic eruptions produce a veil of sulphuric-acid aerosols in the stratosphere and these cause red sunsets covering much of the sky (Note 2.G). Sunsets are never so red when viewed from an

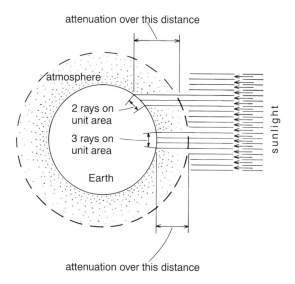

Figure 2.9 The twofold effect of latitude in reducing the amount of solar radiation reaching the ground. Firstly, the distance travelled through the atmosphere is greater at high latitudes because of the oblique angle of the rays; secondly, fewer rays impact on unit area of the ground.

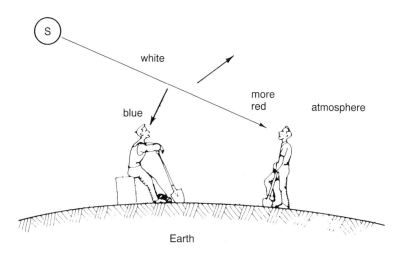

Figure 2.10 Effect of Rayleigh scattering of the Sun's radiation by atmospheric molecules and aerosols. Preferential scattering of blue light makes the sky seen by the person on the left appear blue, whereas the Sun seen by the person on the right appears red.

aircraft flying above the troposphere, which contains most of the air and aerosols.

Larger particles and droplets, of a size like the light's wavelength, cause *Mie scattering*, where light of all wavelengths is *equally* deflected, giving the sky a hazy white appearance. This kind of scattering is in all directions, but primarily forward and backward. Also, it is much more intense than Rayleigh scattering, which explains the bright whiteness of clouds.

The main effects of clouds on solar radiation are twofold – to increase reflection to space and to reduce the transmission of light to the ground. On average, only about a quarter of extra-terrestrial radiation reaches the ground when the sky is overcast, instead of about 75 per cent with a clear sky. Other properties of clouds are discussed in Chapter 8.

Diffuse Radiation

About 6 per cent of the extra-terrestrial radiation is reflected to space by the atmosphere and 20 per cent by clouds, and around 23 per cent is scattered downwards to the surface of the Earth as *diffuse radiation.* This is part of the *global radiation,* the solar radiation reaching a horizontal surface on the ground (Figure 2.6). (The adjective 'global' is used because it consists of solar radiation from all directions.) The other part comes straight from the Sun, without scattering, and is called *direct radiation.*

Direct radiation leads to shadows, while diffuse radiation provides what illumination there is in the shadow. So shadows are very black in the rarefied clean air of high mountains or on the Moon, where there is little atmosphere and few aerosols to cause scattering. On the other hand, the scattering within clouds increases diffuse radiation and therefore reduces the intensity of shadows, or even eliminates them.

2.4 RADIATION AT GROUND LEVEL

The distribution of global radiation reaching sea-level (**Figure 2.11**) is the result of the variations of extra-terrestrial radiation, cloudiness and turbidity. Relatively high values are measured near the Tropics at about 23°, because of the clear skies there, especially over land, and intensities are greater in summer than in winter, because of the seasonal variation of the extra-terrestrial radiation (Note 2.F). At Darwin at 12°S in Australia, the global radiation is

higher in July (**Table 2.2**), when skies tend to be clear, than in January, during the rainy season (Chapters 12 and 16). The annual swing is greatest at high latitudes, and there is great similarity of the ranges across Australia in January.

The amount of radiation falling on a particular surface depends on its *aspect*, i.e. its orientation to the Sun. This is governed by the steepness and the direction of slope of the ground surface, e.g. a slope facing north in the southern hemisphere receives more insolation than the opposite side of a valley or mountain. Mountains may cut off direct sunshine into valleys, while insolation on top of high mountains is increased by the lower horizon, the reduced thickness of the atmosphere above, and sometimes by fewer clouds.

Uses

An enormous amount of solar energy is intercepted by the Earth each day – equal to the output from 180 million thousand-megawatt power-stations. No wonder people consider the possibilities of harnessing such abundant and pollution-free power. Unfortunately, the energy is spread thinly and attenuated by air molecules, aerosols and clouds (Section 2.3).

An important use of solar radiation is in photosynthesis within green leaves (Note 1.B, **Note 2.I**). In fact, if the water supply, nutrients and temperatures are suitable, plant growth and hence crop yields are directly related to the amount of *photosynthetically active radiation* (PAR) (Notes 2.D and 2.I) intercepted by the foliage. The PAR determines the *potential net photosynthesis* (PNP), which is the maximum amount of dry plant carbohydrate that can be photosynthesised by absorbed radiant energy. In theory, this is 3.4 grams per megajoule of incident radiation, but less than this is achieved in practice, on account of several factors; these include shortages of water or plant nutrients, incomplete covering of the ground by vegeta-

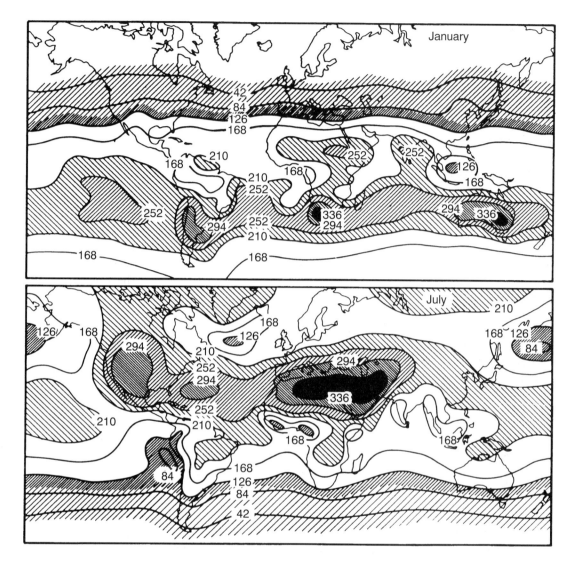

Figure 2.11 The January and July mean global radiation onto a horizontal surface at the ground, in units of W/m².

tion, inappropriate temperatures at critical stages of crop growth, the inability of leaves to cope with the highest radiation intensities, pests, weeds, diseases and the inefficiency of senile leaves. **Figure 2.12** implies values of less than 6 per cent for the ratio of actual to theoretically possible yields.

The important point is that, even when farming problems are overcome, the most food that can be grown is limited by the available solar radiation. That sets an upper bound to the sustainable population of the world (Note 2.I).

Table 2.2 Monthly mean global radiance at various places, mainly in Australia

Location		Mean global radiation (W/m²)			
Name	Latitude (°S)	January	April	July	October
Rabaul	4	203	204	191	222
Darwin*	12	229	251	235	282
Townsville	19	251	216	189	275
Port Hedland	20	319	231	205	310
Longreach	23	333	231	189	302
Alice Springs	23	309	224	185	291
Brisbane*	27	275	161	135	250
Perth	32	316	173	114	261
Sydney	34	271	175	117	236
Adelaide	35	289	154	103	227
Canberra*	35	308	152	109	245
Melbourne	38	286	128	76	211
Hobart*	43	262	117	71	201
Macquarie Island	54	163	–	21	–
Mirny	67	190	–	1	–
South Pole	90	242	–	0	–

* From satellite measurements by Nunez (1990: 345)

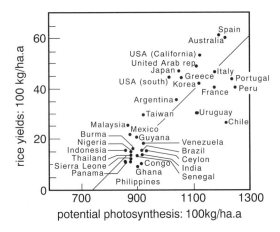

Figure 2.12 The relationship between average annual yields of rice in various countries and the rates of photosynthesis, calculated on the assumption of total use of the photosynthetically active radiation within the available solar radiation during the four summer months when the crop grows. For instance, the actual yield of each year's crop of Australian rice is about 6 tonnes per hectare, which is only 5 per cent of the 120 t/ha that is theoretically possible there.

2.5 ALBEDO

Some of the shortwave radiation reaching the ground is reflected upwards. The ratio of upwards to downwards fluxes is called the *albedo* (or *shortwave reflectivity*), denoted by the symbol α. Note that the albedo is a *ratio*, not a flux.

The higher the albedo of an object, the more light is reflected, making the object appear brighter. Also, a surface with a high albedo (like a white car) does not become as hot as one with a low albedo (like a black car), because more radiation is reflected away (Chapter 5). Aluminium foil facing the Sun may reach 46°C in air at 28°C, whereas black paper reaches 75°C, for instance.

The albedo is the average reflectivity for white light as a whole, but in fact an object's reflectivity usually varies with wavelength, as shown in **Figure 2.13**. This determines the object's colour, which depends on the wavelengths that are particularly reflected. Thus, a leaf appears green in white light because green wavelengths (of about 0.55 μm) tend to be reflected, whilst others are absorbed or trans-

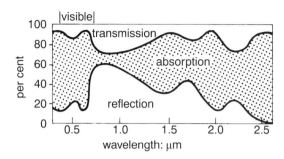

Figure 2.13 The variation with wavelength of the reflected, absorbed and transmitted parts of radiation onto a leaf. It may be seen that most of the visible solar radiation is absorbed for photosynthesis and warming of the leaf. But most near-IR radiation is either transmitted or reflected.

mitted (Figure 2.13). But a leaf illuminated by a beam of red light appears black as red light is not reflected.

Satellite measurements of the radiation in two bands from surface vegetation provide a means of assessing its health. It is flourishing if there is more radiation reflected in the IR range 0.72–0.98 μm, but the ground is dry and the vegetation desiccated if there is more radiation in the visible range 0.57–0.70 μm.

Values

There is a wide range of albedo values, as shown in **Table 2.3**. Surface values inferred from satellite measurements range from 0.08–0.20 for parts of Tasmania (**Figure 2.14**). The albedo of the sea is affected by cloudiness, wave size, and the angle of the Sun above the horizon. It is about 38 per cent when the Sun's angle is 10° in a clear sky, but only 4 per cent when the Sun is overhead. (The exact value depends on the smoothness of the water surface.) For an overcast sky, these figures change to 13 per cent and 6 per cent, respectively. The figures for the case of the Sun overhead are the important ones because insolation is then at its greatest, and so the albedo of water is usually taken as about 6 per cent overall.

Table 2.3 Typical values of the albedo of various surfaces

Surface	Albedo (%)
Aluminium foil	90
Dry concrete	17–35
Black bitumen	10
Red clay tiles	30
New galvanised iron	45
Rusty iron	10
Thatched roof	15–20
Window	negligible
Fresh white paint	75
Red, brown or green paint	30
Clean white car	54
Dirty black car	10
Caucasian human skin	40
Negro skin	18
Snow	80*
Wet soil	10
Dry sand, desert	40
Rainforest	13
Eucalypt forest	18
Pine forest	13
Grassland, green vegetation	22
Water with Sun above	3.5
Water, Sun at 45° elevation	6
Water, Sun at 25°	9
Water, Sun at 10°	38

* See Linacre (1992: 307) for more details

This is far less than the albedo of ice, i.e. about 50 per cent in the case of sea-ice and 80 per cent for fresh snow. So the extent of sea-ice around Antarctica governs how much solar radiation is absorbed and hence global temperatures (**Note 2.J**). The high albedo of fresh snow almost doubles the solar radiation onto the faces of skiers, which can lead to sunburn, even *under* the chin.

The albedo of clouds is less when the density is low or the droplet size large (**Table 2.4**). A typical figure for thin cloud like cirrus (Chapter 8) is 35 per cent and for cumulus 85 per cent. The high figures help explain why so little solar radiation is absorbed by cloud, and therefore why cloud is not readily evaporated away.

The *planetary albedo* is the reflection of solar radiation from the entire globe, as a fraction of

Plate 2.1 The low albedo of the beach at Kusamba in Bali means that almost all the incoming solar radiation is absorbed and can be used to evaporate moisture from the sand, which makes it practicable to extract salt from the sea. The beach's unusual blackness is due to the volcanic eruption of nearby Mt Agung in 1963, showering dark-coloured rock and dust over a wide area. The photograph shows small subdivisions of the beach, each fronting the sea. A man scoops sea water into large buckets and carries it up onto his patch in the morning and then waits for it to dry in the sunshine, leaving a salty surface layer of sand. This is subsequently scraped off and carried into a hut, where the salt is rinsed out as a concentrated solution, which is then completely dried in wooden troughs discernible further inland.

the extra-terrestrial radiation. It is about 30 per cent for the Earth as a whole. This is much more than the albedo of the Moon, which has neither clouds nor polar ice: the value there is only about 7 per cent. So the Earth appears about four times brighter than the Moon when viewed from space.

The variation of the planetary albedo with latitude is shown in **Figure 2.15**. The slight maximum at the equator is due to the cloudiness there. High values at the poles result from cloudiness, the covering of ice and snow, and the dependence of albedo on solar angle.

2.6 ULTRA-VIOLET RADIATION

Solar radiation with wavelengths less than 0.1 μm is absorbed in the ionosphere (Section 1.7) and wavelengths up to about 0.29 μm are absorbed by the dissociation of oxygen in the ozone layer (Section 1.4), so that only around 6

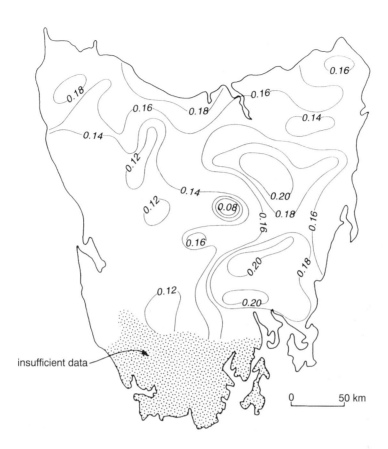

insufficient data

0   50 km

Figure 2.14 Values of albedo in parts of Tasmania, from satellite measurements taken at 10 a.m. or 1 p.m. on eight days in January and February 1985.

Table 2.4 The albedo of clouds

Cloud density (g/m²)	Albedo for different droplet diameters	
	4μm	17μm
60*	75%	50%
270†	90%	70%

* For example, stratus cloud
† For example, cumulonimbus (Chapter 8)

per cent of the Sun's radiation reaching the ground is ultra-violet radiation (UV), instead of 9 per cent at the top of the atmosphere. This includes UV-A (i.e. 0.32–0.40 μm) and the shorter-wavelength UV-B (i.e. 0.28–0.32 μm) and even shorter wavelength UV-C (sometimes called 'vacuum' or 'far' UV). The last penetrates in negligible amount down to sea-level; it is a hazard only on high mountains. UV-B comprises about 1.5 per cent of extra-terrestrial radiation and most is absorbed in the ozone layer. Only around 0.5 per cent of the solar radiation at ground level is UV-B, but this small amount can be very harmful.

The damage caused by UV-B includes sunburn, skin cancer and eye problems such as cataracts, both in people and in cattle. Plants are affected too; a 25 per cent increase of UV-B

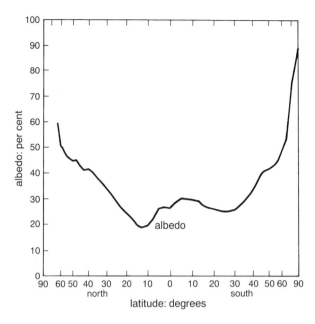

Figure 2.15 The variation of the planetary albedo with latitude.

onto a soyabean crop, for instance, causes a similar decrease of yield.

Controlling Factors

The amount of UV at ground level is slightly reduced by clouds, but visible light is reduced far more. This applies especially to high and thin cloud (Chapter 8). Unfortunately, the reduced illumination makes people feel that it is unnecessary to seek shelter, though UV levels are still dangerous. Even in shade, one does not escape the UV entirely, since much of it is diffuse, coming from all angles, as Rayleigh scattering by air molecules is more intense at the short wavelengths of UV. Typically, half the UV is diffuse when the Sun is high in a cloudless sky.

Air pollution lowers the UV intensity at the ground, especially in the case of the ozone-rich photochemical smog found over large cities like Sydney and Santiago (Chapter 15). As a result, UV-B intensities have decreased by 4–11 per cent in the USA and intensities in industrial Germany are half those at a place free of pollution of similar latitude in New Zealand. So reducing air pollution is likely to *increase* the harm from UV.

The intensity varies also with latitude, season and time of day. The annual UV dosage at Brisbane (27°S) is about 50 per cent higher than at Melbourne (38°S) and four times as much as at Macquarie Island (55°S).

The rarefied atmosphere at high elevations leads to less attenuation of the UV. Compared with the dose at sea-level, it is 20 per cent more at 1,500 m elevation, and almost twice as much at 3,000 m, when the Sun is at 50 degrees. The amount that people receive is further increased if there is snow present, reflecting UV upwards.

Risks to People

Exposure to UV leads to either suntan or sunburn, and to skin cancer. UV-A creates suntan, which dries the skin, leading eventually to a texture like used teabags. UV-B is more dangerous. Without suncream, the outer skin (the epidermis) is penetrated by UV-B, which causes dilation of blood vessels in the underlying tissues, resulting in a redness called *erythema*. Radiation around 0.3 μm wavelength is especially effective. Fair-skinned people absorb more UV-B than those with a naturally dark complexion, and therefore have to be especially careful.

A *dose* is the product of intensity times the exposure duration, and the dose required for erythema is one unit of sunburning tendency, the *equivalent sunburn unit* (ESU). More precisely, an ESU is the minimum dose causing erythema with an overhead Sun, a clear sky and a specified amount of atmospheric ozone. It amounts to 200 joules/m^2 of solar radiation at a wavelength of 0.297 μm. This typically involves only 12 minutes exposure for a Caucasian skin. Exposure to 5 ESU produces painful sunburn, whilst 10 ESU causes blisters and a consequent risk of infection.

The annual variation of dosage at places in Papua New Guinea and Australia is shown in **Figure 2.16**. With typical summertime values around 25 ESU, Cloncurry (at 21°S in Queensland) is clearly a relatively dangerous place. The hazard is reduced at Goroka (6°S) by equatorial cloudiness (Chapter 8).

When the Sun is 50 degrees above the horizon, the UV is only half what it is when the Sun is overhead, and there is little danger from UV if the Sun is below 30 degrees. In general, about two-thirds of a day's dose occurs between 10 a.m. and 2 p.m., so that is the time to seek shade.

The most serious outcome of undue exposure to UV is *skin cancer*, an abnormal, cumulative and irreversible growth of cells of the skin. The incidence of skin cancer is three times as much at Cloncurry as at Brisbane, 7 degrees further south, though the amount of UV is only 30 per cent more. About 1 per cent of Australia's population acquires skin cancers each year,

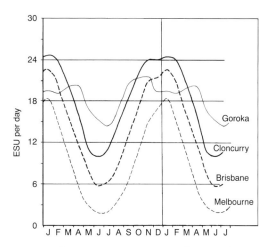

Figure 2.16 The annual variation of the sunburning power of sunlight with normal amounts of cloud. ESU is 'equivalent sunburn unit'. These are figures for a horizontal surface, not for the skin on the body of someone moving about.

including over 7,000 people with *melanomas*, a type which can become lethal.

There has been a worldwide increase of skin cancers, e.g. an 82 per cent increase in Scotland between 1979–1989. The rise is chiefly due to the popularity of suntanning. The problem will worsen if the annual hole in the ozone layer over the poles (Section 1.4) continues to extend towards more inhabited latitudes, and it is unfortunate that the ozone hole occurs in a season of relatively high radiation intensities in the southern hemisphere. Harmful UV is increased by about 1.3 per cent if there is 1 per cent less stratospheric ozone. Measurements at Invercargill (at 46°S in New Zealand) have shown an increase of UV by 6 per cent between 1981 and 1990.

2.7 LONGWAVE RADIATION

The longwave radiation (LW) emitted by any object at Earth temperatures differs in several ways from shortwave radiation *reflected* from it. The LW is invisible, it flows day and night, and both the wavelength and amount of LW from an object depend on the object's own temperature, not on that of the Sun. And whilst the albedo of a surface (i.e. its *shortwave* reflectivity) may be either large or small, the reflectivity of longwave radiation is nearly zero for almost all materials. In other words, LW is almost totally absorbed by the recipient surfaces, e.g. by clouds thicker than about 500 metres, or by the ground. Another difference between shortwave and LW radiations concerns their transmission through the atmosphere, as follows.

Longwave radiation is emitted upwards by the ground and oceans and is called *terrestrial radiation*. Then water and carbon dioxide in the air intercept much of it (Figure 2.2), becoming warmed by the energy absorbed. Subsequently, the same molecules radiate LW in all directions at wavelengths determined by the molecules' temperatures (Note 2.B).

Cloud droplets are particularly efficient absorbers and emitters of LW, and clouds which are thick enough to hide the Sun are completely opaque to LW. The longwave radiation from such clouds is governed by their temperature, not by any source behind them, whereas SW from clouds is unaffected by cloud temperature.

The downwards LW from clouds and air is called *sky radiation* (or atmospheric radiation or counter radiation). This is more than offset by the terrestrial radiation upwards because the ground is warmer than the sky. For example, a ground surface at 20°C radiates about 28 per cent more than a sky which is effectively at 0°C (Note 2.C). The difference accounts for the cooling of the ground at night, when there are only longwave fluxes. Latitudinal averages of the longwave fluxes show that the difference between sky and terrestrial radiation is most at low latitudes, i.e. nocturnal cooling is fastest there (**Note 2.K**).

Effects of Moisture

Sky radiation comes partly from the carbon dioxide in the air, but mostly from the water which is confined to the lower levels of the atmosphere (Chapter 6). The downwards sky radiation received at the ground comes from a layer of the lower atmosphere whose thickness is sufficient to contain enough water to be opaque to longwave radiation. Such a layer of cloudless air is commonly only some hundreds of metres thick, depending on the humidity. Consequently, the effective temperature of the layer radiating to the ground is only a few degrees below that at the surface. Also, the layer responsible for sky radiation is thinner (and therefore lower, warmer and emitting more) if the air is humid, as occurs over low-latitude seas.

A result of the effect of atmospheric moisture on sky radiation is that the surface cools more rapidly at night in winter, as winter air holds less water vapour (Chapter 6). The effect also explains why particularly cold nights are experienced in dry climates, with a consequent large diurnal range of temperature (Chapter 3).

Clouds increase sky radiation, depending on the elevation of cloud base: if the base is low, it is relatively warm, and therefore emits more sky radiation. The increased sky radiation due to cloud offsets more of the upwards terrestrial radiation, so that surface cooling at night is slower with an overcast sky. As an example, measurements at Sydney showed cooling by 6.2 K between 6–9 p.m., when the sky was clear, but only 2.3 K when totally cloudy.

The lowest kind of cloud is a thick fog (Chapter 8), so it is a most efficient blanket, its temperature and hence its longwave radiation being about the same as that of the underlying surface.

Greenhouse Effect

As mentioned in Section 2.3, some terrestrial radiation escapes through the atmosphere by means of a window for radiation with wavelengths around 11 μm, though this is much less effective than the window around 0.5 μm for incoming solar radiation. In other words, the atmosphere is much less transparent to LW than it is to SW. This causes what is called the *'natural* greenhouse effect' on global temperatures. Heat is trapped, so that the Earth's surface is warmed to around +15°C on average, instead of the −18°C that it would be otherwise (**Note 2.L**). Nowadays the additional carbon dioxide emitted by the burning of fossil fuels in recent decades (Section 1.3), together with increases in other gases such as methane, has created an *enhanced greenhouse effect* (EGE), an additional trapping of terrestrial radiation, leading to gradual global warming (Chapter 15).

The name of the effect arose from a mistake in explaining the warmth of a horticultural glasshouse. It used to be thought that the warmth arose from the properties of glass, which readily transmits solar radiation inwards but will not allow the escape of longwave radiation outwards from the surfaces within the greenhouse, as in the atmosphere. However, an experimental greenhouse of a material which *does* transmit longwave radiation proves to be equally warm. In fact, a glasshouse's temperature is mainly due to shelter from the wind. Nevertheless, the explanation which is incorrect for glasshouses does apply to the Earth's atmosphere, and the name has stuck.

The carbon dioxide atmospheres of Mars and Venus (Table 1.2) lead to appreciable greenhouse warming. The surface on Mars is at −47°C, instead of −57°C without the effect, and on Venus +525°C instead of +50°C [*sic*]. The fact that we can calculate the actually observed temperatures is some reassurance that we understand the greenhouse effect.

Greenhouse gases other than carbon dioxide are relatively small in amount but inherently much more potent. The *global warming potential* (GWP) of methane is about 50 (Section 1.3), i.e. its warming effect is 50 times that of a similar amount of carbon dioxide over a period of twenty years. For CFC-12 the GWP is 8,000, making elimination of this gas highly desirable.

The opposite effect results from haze in the sky, notably volcanic dust in the lower stratosphere (Note 2.G). It transmits terrestrial radiation, but absorbs and reflects solar radiation so that less reaches the ground. As a result, haze tends to *cool* the surface.

2.8 NET RADIATION

So far we have discussed separately the downward (i.e. positive) radiation fluxes (comprising global shortwave radiation R_s and longwave sky radiation R_{ld}) and the negative fluxes upward from the ground, consisting of (i) reflected shortwave radiation $\alpha.R_s$ (where α is the surface albedo) and (ii) the emitted terrestrial radiation R_{lu}. If the combined upward fluxes are subtracted from the combined fluxes downward (Figure 2.6), the result is what we call the *net radiation flux R_n* at the surface. (Sometimes it is called the 'radiation balance', but that might be confused with the 'energy balance' dealt with in Chapter 5.) The symbolic definition of the net radiation (flux) at the surface is as follows:

$$R_n = (1 - \alpha) R_s + R_{ld} - R_{lu}$$

It represents the *overall input* of radiation energy absorbed at the ground, and clearly depends on all the factors which govern the four constituent fluxes – the Sun's elevation, the cloudiness, atmospheric turbidity, surface albedo, the temperature and dryness of the air, and the altitude. Net radiation is important because it comprises the energy available for heating the ground and nearby air (Chapters 3 and 7), and for the evaporation of surface water (Chapter 4).

The difficulty of measuring net radiation accurately means that it is rarely done. Instead, it can be estimated approximately from either measurements or estimates of the solar irradiance R_s (**Note 2.M**).

The components of the net radiation at a place can be set out in tables, such as **Tables**

2.5 and 2.6, which show their relative magnitudes. The longwave figures are comparable with those for solar radiation R_s, which may seem surprising, since the Sun is so much hotter than the surfaces which generate the longwave fluxes. But those surfaces of the Earth and its atmosphere are much closer than the Sun. Also, longwave fluxes occur throughout each day, whereas shortwave radiation exists only in the daytime.

Values

Typical radiation conditions are shown in Table 2.5 for a forest and meadow. Even though the solar radiation onto the meadow happened to be more (i.e. 336 instead of 292 W/m^2), the net radiation onto the forest was greater, on account of a lower albedo. The *radiation efficiency* (i.e. the ratio R_n/R_s) was 64 per cent for the forest and 51 per cent for the meadow at the time of the measurements. The ratio is quite different at

the South Pole, where R_n is negative (Table 2.6).

The net radiation at the surface varies primarily according to latitude (**Figure 2.17**), as do the components of the net radiation *at the top of the atmosphere* (**Figure 2.18**). The latter shows the variation with latitude of (i) the longwave-radiation loss to space, and (ii) the net solar-radiation income $R_a.(1 - \alpha)$, where R_a is the extra-terrestrial radiation (Note 2.F) and α is the planetary albedo according to latitude (Figure 2.15). The shortwave income varies greatly with latitude because of latitudinal differences of albedo (due to ice and cloud) and of R_a. But the longwave loss is remarkably unaffected by latitude, despite the variation of surface temperature from equator to pole. This is because much of the loss is from the tops of clouds, which tend to be warmer than the ground at the poles, but *cold* in the tropics because clouds there are so tall, on account of the strong convection. Even in cloud-free parts of the humid

Table 2.5 Typical radiation budgets for a forest and a meadow at 44°N in Oregon, averaged over different entire clear days

Radiation*		Symbol	Forest	Meadow
Shortwave	Incoming	R_s†	100	100
	Reflected	$\alpha\,R_s$†	−10	−24
Longwave	Incoming	R_{ld}	108	86*
	Outgoing	R_{lu}	−135	−112
	net	R_n	63*	50*

* Radiation components are expressed as percentages of the incoming solar radiation, i.e. of 292 W/m^2 for the forest and 336 W/m^2 for the meadow
† Note that the figures for R_s and $\alpha.R_s$ imply an albedo of 10% for the forest (i.e. 10/100), and 24% for the meadow

Table 2.6 Components of radiation fluxes on the ground at the South Pole in units of W/m^2

Direction	Shortwave SW	Longwave LW	All-wave
Downwards	+137	+113	+250
Upwards	−116*	−143†	−259
Net	+21	−30	−9‡

* Note the high albedo, inferred as 85% (i.e. 116/137).
† This was estimated by means of the Stefan–Boltzmann equation (Note 2.C), from the mean temperature of −49°C.
‡ The net radiation is negative at the South Pole even in January (i.e. −1 W/m^2). Different values have been measured at Vostok (78°S, 3,450 m elevation), i.e. an annual mean of −5 W/m^2, ranging from a net income of +11 W/m^2 in January to a net loss of −22 W/m^2 in July.

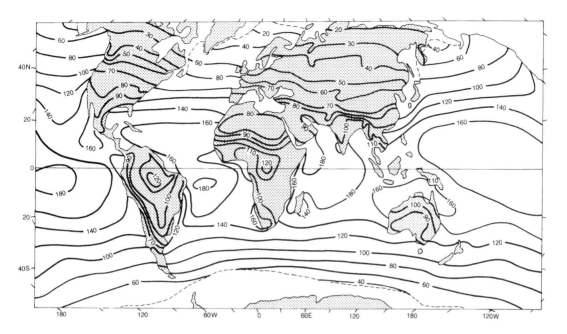

Figure 2.17 The annual mean net radiation at the Earth's surface in W/m². The dashed line is the annual mean boundary of sea-ice; net radiation to the surface can be negative poleward of that line, i.e. upwards.

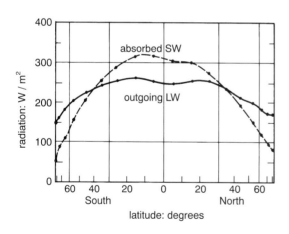

Figure 2.18 Effect of latitude on the extra-terrestrial fluxes of (i) the net shortwave radiation absorbed by the Earth, i.e. $[1 - \alpha] R_a$, where α is the average planetary albedo and R_a is the average extra-terrestrial radiation at the particular latitude, and of (ii) the longwave radiation emitted by the surface and atmosphere of the Earth.

tropics the longwave radiation loss is less than might be expected, since it comes not from the hot surface but from the atmospheric moisture at cooler levels above.

The comparison shows that the global income is exceeded by the loss over the 43 per cent of the Earth's area which is above about 35 degrees latitude, i.e. there is an overall *inflow* of radiation from space (i.e. the Sun) equatorward of 35 degrees latitude, but an *equal outflow* from higher latitudes. That would mean a tendency for the equator to become ever warmer and the poles to cool, except for the flow of energy from the equator to the poles in winds and ocean currents (Chapters 5, 11 and 12).

There is a notable contrast between the net radiation onto oceans near the Tropics, and onto adjacent lands. A high intensity over the oceans (Figure 2.17) arises from the low albedo (Table 2.3) and a reduced upward LW due to a combination of high humidity, cloudiness and a surface cooled by evaporation (Chapter 4).

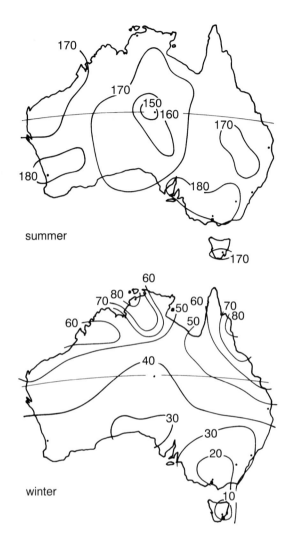

Figure 2.19 Net radiation onto Australia in units of W/m².

However, adjacent land areas near the Tropics tend to be dry, so that net radiation is reduced by a high albedo (Section 2.5) and an extreme LW loss, due to low humidity, an absence of clouds and high daytime surface temperatures.

Cloud alters the net radiation at the surface less than might be expected, despite the reduced solar radiation R_s. That reduction tends to be offset by (i) less upward reflected solar radiation ($\alpha.R_s$), (ii) an extra downward flux due to some reflection of the upwards $\alpha.R_s$ back down by the cloud, (iii) increased sky radiation downwards, and (iv) less terrestrial radiation up on account of the cooling of areas shaded by cloud. A similar compensation applies with an increase of altitude; greater solar radiation (due to less attenuation by the atmosphere) is offset by less longwave radiation from the colder and drier sky.

Surface net radiation in Australia is low in

the south of the continent in winter but fairly uniform in summer (**Figure** 2.19). Part of the reason is that summers in northern Australia are cloudy, offsetting the reduced insolation at higher latitudes. Such values of the net radiation explain the patterns of surface temperature in time and space, which are the topic of the next chapter.

NOTES

2.A Electromagnetic radiation
2.B Shortwave and longwave radiation
2.C The Stefan–Boltzmann equation
2.D Effects of the various components of solar radiation
2.E The inverse-square law of radiation
2.F The monthly mean extra-terrestrial radiation
2.G Aerosols and volcanoes
2.H Effects of the atmospheric windows
2.I Radiation and crop growth
2.J Effect of an albedo change on global warming
2.K Annual mean longwave radiation
2.L The greenhouse effect
2.M Simple estimation of net radiation

3

TEMPERATURE

3.1 TEMPERATURE MEASUREMENT

In the previous chapter, we introduced the concept of surface net radiation, which is absorbed at the Earth's surface. Much of that energy is then used to warm the ground or ocean surface, and thence the adjacent air. The resulting surface air temperature is the topic of the present chapter.

Heat

The *temperature* is a measure of the concentration of one kind of energy, called *sensible heat*. It has this name because it can be *sensed* by touch or by a thermometer. Sensible heat is a measure of the speed of the molecules of the object being observed; the molecules of a hot object move around fast. It does not include the chemical energy involved in photosynthesis (Note 1.B), nor radiation energy (Chapter 2), nor the energy used in evaporation (Chapter 4), because these forms of energy do not register on a thermometer.

In solids such as the ground, sensible heat is transmitted from a hot to a cold part by *conduction*: the heat is transferred by contact from one molecule to the next. The conducting material does not itself move. But heat is mainly transferred by *convection* and *advection*, in fluids like air and water. 'Convection' involves the stirring of heat away by either local turbulence or buoyancy, as in cooling an object by putting it into a bucket of water which is swished around. 'Free convection' in the atmosphere and oceans is due to buoyancy and therefore vertical, as in the case of smoke eddying from a cigarette. 'Forced convection' is due to wind. Convection is the chief means by which the ground heats the air above (Section 1.6), the rate depending on the difference between the surface and air temperatures (**Note 3.A**).

The convection of heat is a kind of 'advection', the transport of something in a moving fluid. The advection of heat, for instance, involves a stream of warmed fluid carrying heat away to a distant cooler place. Advection is generally horizontal, although important cases of vertical advection in the atmosphere and oceans are discussed in Chapters 7, 12 and 13.

Temperature Scales

There are several scales for measuring temperature (Note 1. K). In 1709 the German physicist Gabriel Fahrenheit developed the oldest scale still in common use, taking as zero the lowest temperature he had recorded in the city of Danzig, and fixing the upper limit of the scale at the temperature of the human body, which he (erroneously) took to be 100°F. (It is actually near 96°F.) The boiling point of water at sea level is 212 degrees on such a scale.

However, another scale, based on the properties of water, has now become universal. Zero corresponds to the temperature at which ice forms and 100 degrees is the boiling point of pure water at sea level. It was called the Centigrade scale until 1948, but such a hundred-unit scale may be used for measuring things other than temperature. Also, there is now a convention to relate all units to the names of famous scientists, in this case Anders Celsius (1701–44). The relationship between the Celsius (°C) and the Fahrenheit (°F) scales can be found in Note 1. K.

There is also a third measure of temperature, the Kelvin scale (Note 1. K), commonly used in science. In this book, we use both °C and K. In particular, we use K to designate a temperature difference, so that 8°C and 10°C differ by 2 K, for example.

Thermometers

The first thermometer was invented in 1592 by Galileo, who measured the expansion of *air* and found that its volume increases in proportion to its temperature if the pressure is kept constant (Note 1.M). His air thermometer tube was bent round, and so temperatures were described in 'degrees' around the circle.

In 1714, Fahrenheit used the expansion of mercury instead of air to obtain a less bulky method of temperature measurement. Mercury thermometers are widely used nowadays, though they have defects – markings wear off, bubbles can occur in the liquid, errors of observation arise unless the thermometer is read squarely (at right angles to the mercury), and there is a time-lag in taking up a steady value

after a rapid temperature change. The lag is greatest in still air and, to allow for it, one should ventilate the thermometer and take repeated readings until three consecutive readings are the same. Finally, a broken thermometer releases mercury, whose fumes are dangerous to health.

Alcohol has several advantages over mercury. It expands about six times as much with heat, e.g. 1 per cent for a change of 10 K, and is much cheaper. But it too has disadvantages: the liquid may adhere to the walls of the thermometer's glass tube so that the main column reads too low; the column is easily disrupted during very hot weather or in transport, forming a bubble which falsely raises the apparent reading; the liquid may undergo a gradual chemical change and contract, thus giving a low reading. The tendency for alcohol thermometers to read too low contrasts with that of mercury thermometers, which tend to read too high.

Henry Cavendish invented a form of the mercury thermometer in 1757 which registers the highest temperature reached since the instrument was last reset. This is a *maximum thermometer*. As the temperature increases, mercury in the bulb expands through a constriction into the graduated thermometer stem (**Figure 3.1**). When the temperature falls, the column

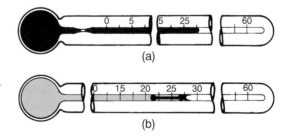

Figure 3.1 (a) A maximum thermometer, showing the constriction near the base and (b) a minimum thermometer, showing the meniscus and index. Both thermometers are shown in the usual horizontal position, to prevent the weight of the liquid affecting the reading.

of mercury breaks at the constriction, where a small vacuum forms. Consequently, the reading remains at the highest value so far. The vacuum at the constriction is refilled only if the temperature later rises beyond the previous maximum. Resetting is done by shaking the mercury back into the bulb. If the thermometer is read and reset at 9 a.m. each day, the value recorded usually corresponds to conditions in the afternoon of the *previous* day.

A lowering of temperature in a *minimum thermometer* (Figure 3.1) leads to withdrawal of the alcohol surface towards the bulb. Surface tension then pulls on a lightweight metal index, which tends to rest against the walls of the almost horizontal thermometer. When temperatures rise, the alcohol expands past the index, which is left at the position of the lowest temperature since it was last reset. It is reset by means of a magnet.

Maximum and minimum mercury thermometers are combined in a design devised by James Six in 1782 (**Figure 3.2**). This is convenient and cheap, but less accurate than separate thermometers.

Other Instruments

Temperatures can also be measured in the following ways:

1 Two sheets of different metals are bonded together by rolling, to form a *bimetal* combination which bends when warmed because the metals expand differently. The bending controls a pointer which indicates the temperature on a suitably calibrated scale. This is the usual basis for an instrument called a *thermograph* which records temperatures on moving graph paper.
2 The electrical resistance of a wire increases with higher temperatures and can be measured by means of a battery and an electric current meter.
3 Thermal expansion of alcohol in a closed,

curved tube of metal causes the tube to straighten and thus to move a pointer along a temperature scale.
4 Heat applied to the junction of a pair of different metals, A and B, makes an electric current flow from one to the other, i.e. there is a voltage difference between the metals which depends on the junction's temperature. So a loop consisting of two different wires, joined at the ends to make two junctions, creates a voltage which depends on the *difference* between the temperatures of the junctions. This arrangement is called a *thermocouple* and many junctions in series (i.e. a zig-zag of ABABAB, etc) comprise a *thermopile* which provides a voltage large enough to be measured easily. Alternate junctions of the thermopile are exposed to the temperature to be measured T ($^{\circ}$C), with the others kept at a known temperature, usually that of melting ice (0°C) so that the voltage is proportional to T.
5 A portable radiation meter carried by an aircraft or satellite permits rapid measurement of the temperatures (Note 2.C) of surface or cloud top beneath, from the amount and dominant wavelength of the radiation emitted (Notes 2.B and 2.C).

In each case, the thermometer measures only the *temperature of the sensing element*. In a mercury-in-glass thermometer, the reading shows the temperature of the *mercury* in the bulb at the end, which is not necessarily the temperature of its surroundings. The reading is increased if the thermometer is exposed to the Sun, even though the air around is unaltered. A wet thermometer underestimates the air temperature because evaporation at the surface of the bulb cools the mercury. Therefore accurate measurements of *air* temperature require shading of a dry thermometer bulb and a brisk airflow past it. Stronger ventilation of the bulb gives a reading nearer to the air temperature, one less affected by radiation.

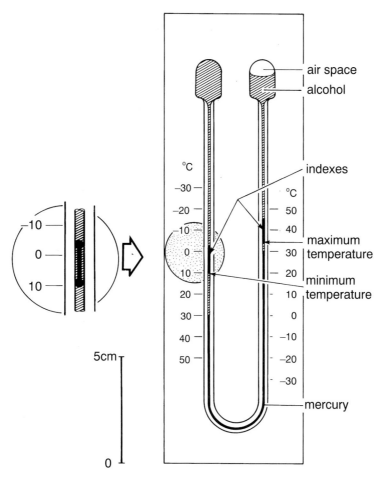

Figure 3.2 Six's thermometer, combining a minimum thermometer (on the left) and a maximum thermometer on the right. In each column there is a metal index pushed up by mercury, which itself is moved by the expansion of alcohol in the upper part of the left column. The bottom of each index shows the respective extreme temperature, whilst the current temperature is shown in each side by the mercury meniscus.

The thermometer must not be held too close to the observer or for too long, or with fingers near the bulb. Thermometers should be read to the nearest tenth of a degree and as rapidly as is consistent with accuracy.

Screen

Weather observers usually take the air temperature by means of mercury-in-glass thermometers housed in a louvred white box, called a *Stevenson screen* (**Figure 3.3**) after its designer Thomas Stevenson (1818–87). The whiteness of the screen reflects away most of the direct heat of the Sun and the louvres provide shading, good ventilation and protection from rain. The screen is oriented with its door facing away from the equator, away from the Sun. The temperature measured in such a box is called the *screen temperature,* often regarded as

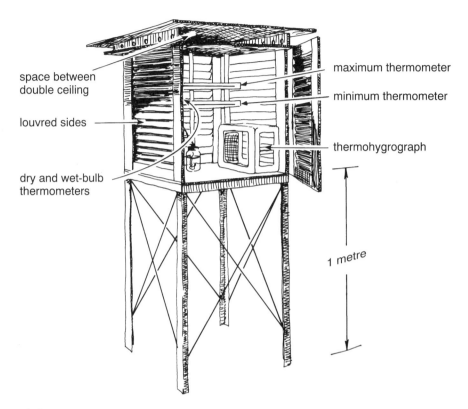

Figure 3.3 A Stevenson screen.

space between double ceiling

louvred sides

dry and wet-bulb thermometers

maximum thermometer

minimum thermometer

thermohygrograph

1 metre

the surface-air temperature, though, strictly speaking, it refers to conditions about 1.5 m above the ground.

3.2 SCREEN TEMPERATURES

Air scatters visible light, but absorbs very little, so that it is not appreciably heated by the Sun directly. Instead, solar radiation heats the ground surface and then *the ground heats the nearby air*. Likewise, surface air is cooled by the ground at night. In both cases, screen temperatures *follow* the ground-surface temperatures. However, the lag is negligible near the times of the daily extremes at dawn and early afternoon, when temperatures change only slowly (Section 3.4).

Heating and cooling of the air by the ground lead to screen temperatures varying with elevation, time and space. To consider spatial variation across the globe, it is convenient to link places which have equal surface temperatures by lines on a map called *isotherms*. The positions of isotherms depend on several factors – (i) latitude, (ii) elevation, (iii) the advection of heat in the wind, (iv) advection in ocean currents, (v) distance from the sea, (vi) orientation of the ground to the Sun, (vii) cloudiness, (viii) urban warmth and (ix) wetness of the ground. Some of these are discussed in what follows, and the rest in other chapters.

Latitude

The latitudinal effect on temperature is dominant and is chiefly a response to the amount of net radiation received (Figure 2.19, **Note 3.B**). **Table 3.1** shows how monthly mean temperatures decrease towards the south, especially in summer; the table indicates a fall by about 1 K for each extra degree of latitude in New South Wales (NSW). Temperatures fall by around 0.7 K for each degree of latitude in Australia as a whole, so that Sydney at 34°S averages about 5 K warmer than Hobart at 42°S. Globally, there is little change between the equator and the Tropics, and a most rapid variation (of about 1.5 K/degree) between 45–55° of latitude. There is sea-ice at latitudes beyond 55°S, which forms at −2°C and cuts off the surface air from the relative warmth of the ocean, so that there is then a dramatic lowering of air temperatures.

The frequency of hot days depends somewhat on the latitude at the coast, but much more on the distance inland (**Table 3.2**).

Distance from the Sea

As one travels inland in Australia the average temperature tends to rise (Table 3.1 and Table 3.2), because summers at the coast are cooled by sea breezes (Chapter 14). This is quite different from the pattern in the huge land mass of Eurasia, where July mean temperatures are about 14°C at both Narvik (at 68°N on Norway's coast) and also at Verkoyansk at the same latitude, far inland in Siberia, whereas the respective January means are −5°C and −50°C, so that the inland place is about 22 K *colder* than the coast over the whole year.

Coastal temperatures are influenced by that

Table 3.1 Effects of the season, latitude, elevation and distance inland (km), on temperatures at places in Australia between 29–37°S.

Factor		Latitude: (°S)		Elevation (m)		Distance inland (km)	
Effect		29–33	34–37	25–400	600–1800	25–200	300–1100
Mean	Jan.	24.4	21.5	24.4	18.2	21.4	25.8
	July	9.9	8.0	10.2	4.9	8.7	9.6
Daily range	Jan.	14.1	13.8	13.9	13.9	12.6	15.7
	July	12.5	10.9	11.9	10.7	11.8	12.1
Annual range		14.5	13.5	14.0	13.2	12.6	16.2

Table 3.2 Effect of latitude and distance from the sea on the temperatures exceeded for 7.5 hours in January and July, respectively.

Place	Latitude	Distance inland (km)	January temp. exceeded (°C)	July temp. exceeded (°C)
Alice Springs	24°S	900	40.7	25.1
Giles	26°S	700	41.0	25.0
Broken Hill	32°S	400	39.4	18.6
Canberra	36°S	100	33.8	13.6
Darwin	12°S	coast	33.4	31.8
Townsville	19°S	coast	33.9	26.2
Port Hedland	21°S	coast	41.2	30.0
Perth	32°S	coast	39.0	20.0
Adelaide	34°S	coast	37.0	16.8
Sydney	34°S	coast	32.4	19.8
Melbourne	38°S	coast	35.8	16.1

of the nearby ocean surface, which in turn is affected by the advection of heat in ocean currents (Chapter 11), either from lower latitudes (bringing warmth) or from higher latitudes, cooling the shore. The directions of the main ocean currents (Chapter 11) tend to make the western coast of a continent cooler than the eastern, as seen in **Figure 3.4**. For instance, the cold current off Lima in Peru limits monthly mean daily maximum temperatures to 28°C, even though it is at 12°S, the same as Darwin, where the equivalent is 34°C. The Gulf Stream from the Gulf of Mexico towards Europe raises the mean temperature of Dublin (at 54°N) about 4 K above that of Tierra del Fuego (at 54°S), at the tip of South America.

As regards Figure 3.4, the obvious similarity between the pattern of temperature and that of incident solar radiation (Figure 2.11) shows the close connection between sunshine and warmth.

Elevation

Average temperatures from many places show that they tend to decrease by about 4.2 K per kilometre extra elevation (**Figure 3.5**). (This average rate for *surface* temperatures is less than the rate of about 6.5 K/km measured during ascent *in free air*, see Note 1.L.) An analysis of data from Australia alone, and therefore over a smaller range of heights, shows a variation between 4.5 K/km in January and 6.5 K/km in November. The coolness at higher elevations is the result of the expansion of ascending air (Section 1.6), which spreads the air's warmth over a larger space, reducing the amount of sensible heat in unit volume, i.e. lowering the temperature. A similar cooling is observed in air escaping from a car tyre, and a corresponding warming results from the compression within a bicycle pump.

The combined effect of latitude and elevation is seen in **Figure 3.6**, which shows the variation with latitude of the summertime *snowline*; snow

persists throughout the year above this line. Consequently, there is snow on the top of Mt Kilimanjaro (5,895 m), even at 3°S, and a glacier at about 5,000 m on Mt Carstenz at 4°S in West Irian Jaya (Plate 3.1). The Quelccaya ice cap is at 5,670 m at 14°S in Peru. Elsewhere in South America, the snowline is at 5,180 m at 17°S in Bolivia, 4,500 m at 33°S in Chile and 1,140 m at Tierra del Fuego (54°S). It is highest around the Tropic, where solar radiation is at its greatest (Figure 2.11).

Wind Direction

Advection of heat in winds may affect surface temperature, especially when the winds flow directly from high latitudes, for instance. Advection is insignificant near the equator where all winds have much the same temperature, but is an important cause of day-to-day changes of temperature at midlatitudes.

Extremely High Temperatures

The highest shade temperature yet recorded is 58°C at Al'Aziziyah in Libya, in 1922. In the southern hemisphere, 48.9°C has been recorded at Rivadavia in Argentina and 53.1°C at Cloncurry in Queensland. The records in Melbourne and Sydney, are 44.7°C and 45.3°C, respectively, and at Adelaide 47°C. A particularly hot place is Marble Bar (Western Australia), with a long-term mean daily maximum of 35.3°C and temperatures above 37.8°C (100°F) on each of 162 consecutive days during a *heatwave* in 1923–24. (Sometimes a 'heat wave' is arbitrarily defined as a series of consecutive days with maximum temperatures above 32.2°C, i.e. 90°F.) Marble Bar is hot because it lies in the north-west of Australia, i.e. towards the equator, and on the downwind edge of the continent (with respect to the prevailing easterly winds), at the greatest distance from the relatively cool Pacific Ocean. Proximity of the sea everywhere in New Zealand

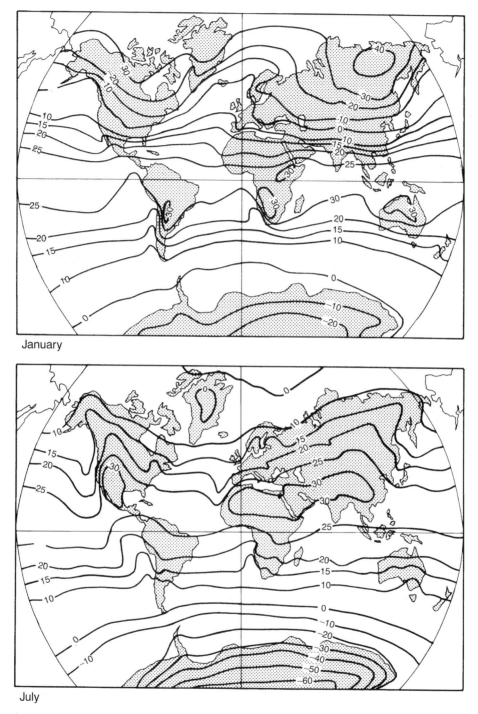

January

July

Figure 3.4 Comparison of the global patterns of isotherms in January and July, respectively.

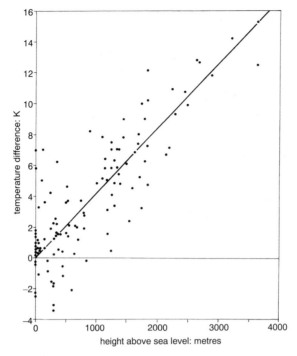

Figure 3.5 The effect of the elevation of a place on the difference there between the latitudinal-mean long-term-average sea-level temperature and the observed mean temperature. The data come chiefly from places in South America and Africa (south of the equator) and North America. The slope of the line is 4.2 K per kilometre.

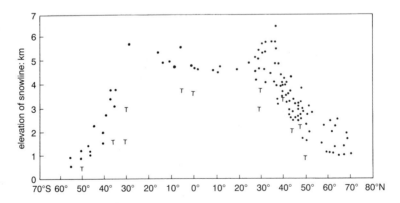

Figure 3.6 Effects of latitude on the elevation of the *snowline*, shown by black dots, and on the average height of the *treeline*, shown by the letter T, above which all monthly mean temperatures are too low for trees to thrive, i.e. below 12°C.

Plate 3.1 The glaciers on Mt Carstenz (5,029 m), above the snowline, near the equator (i.e. at 4°S). The two photographs were taken respectively in 1936 (a) and in 1991 (b), showing the same scene but from opposite ends of the valley. The area of snow decreased appreciably over the half-century in accordance with the global warming discussed in Chapter 15. In other words, this plate suggests that global warming has not been occurring only at high latitudes, as sometimes reckoned.

limits the record maximum there to 35.8°C (at Oxford in the South Island). The record at Auckland (37°S) is only 32.5°C, since it is surrounded by water. New Zealand's highest temperatures occur on the south-east side of the South Island; this happens when north-westerly winds subside from the mountains (Chapter 7).

The hottest places in the world are joined by a curving line called the *thermal equator*. It fluctuates during the year from near the geo-graphical equator in January (with excursions of 20 degrees latitude south within the South American, African and Australian continents) to about 10°N over the oceans in July, but 35°N in North America, 20°N in Africa and 30°N across Asia. The average is about 5°N, so the Earth's surface temperatures are asymmetric about the equator, because of the different amounts of land in the two hemispheres. The asymmetry is like that of solar radiation (Section 2.2).

Highest screen temperatures in the southern hemisphere tend to occur sometime *after* December 22 (Section 2.2). The lag is only two or three weeks inland, but a month or more near the sea. It is greatest for a small island, again because of the sea's slowness to change temperature (Section 3.3). Of course, variations of cloud and weather complicate matters, and so the hottest month is November in the north of Australia, but later in the south.

The pattern of the energy needed for air conditioning in Australia (**Figure 3.7**) reflects the latitude, the distance inland and the distance downwind of the east coast, where the dominant winds impinge in summer (Chapter 12).

One important effect of a heatwave is its impact on human mortality (**Note 3.C** and Table 3.3), even though the effect is partly offset by adaptation and acclimatisation (**Note 3.D**). As a result, increased urban heating (Section 3.7), air pollution and global warming (Chapter 15) will worsen conditions for a population which is ageing and becoming more urban.

Low Temperatures

The counterpart of a heatwave is a *cold spell*, a period of unusually low temperatures. The lowest daily minimum ever observed was −88.3°C at Vostok in Antarctica, due to the high latitude (78°S) and elevation (3,420 m), the relative absence of surface winds from warmer climates, remoteness from the sea's influence (being about 1,400 km inland), and the permanent snow cover, with its high albedo reflecting solar energy away (Table 2.3). Such tempera-

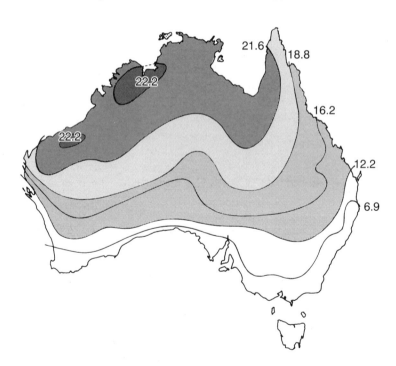

Figure 3.7 Electrical energy needs for domestic space cooling in Australia, in units of gigajoules per person annually, given current building standards and air-conditioning equipment.

Table 3.3 Effect of daily temperatures on mortality from various causes during the 1966 heatwave in the New York metropolitan area

Date	Daily temperatures (°C)			Causes of death*		
	Max.	Mean	Min.	Stroke	Heart attack	Other
June 30	34	29	23	89%	83%	97%
July 1	31	27	23	109%	94%	134%
2	38	30	22	99%	91%	114%
3	39	31	24	214%	162%	147%
4	37	31	25	302%	258%	390%
5	31	27	22	219%	178%	173%
6	33	27	22	156%	129%	107%
7	34	29	23	172%	120%	108%
8	33	26	20	115%	117%	66%
9	33	26	19	94%	106%	103%
Total heat-related deaths†				109	372	548

* The numbers shown are the mortality rates expressed as a percentage of the normal mortality rate at that time of the year, due to the causes listed.
† The number of heat-related deaths was estimated by subtracting the normal death rate from the death rate during the ten-day heat wave.

tures cannot be measured with a thermometer containing mercury, which freezes at −39°C.

Australia is warm by comparison; the record low is −23°C, measured on 29 June 1994 at Charlotte Pass, at 1,759 m near Mt Kosciusko (NSW). The effect of such low temperatures on people is aggravated by wind, and in cold climates one refers to the *windchill temperature*, which combines the effects of temperature and wind (**Note 3.E**).

Long-term Variation

Annual mean temperatures change from one year to the next. In Sydney, for instance, the difference between the annual means of consecutive years has been as much as 1.2 K. The scatter of annual mean values may be expressed in terms of the 'standard deviation' (Chapter 10); it is 0.5 K at Sydney. That is comparable with the apparent climate warming this century (Chapter 15), making it still hard to discern long-term trends with certainty.

Several factors which affect the year-to-year variations are discussed elsewhere. These include the temporary cooling due to the veil of dust from a large volcanic eruption (Note 2.G), changes of ocean temperatures (Chapter 11) and fluctuations of wind patterns (Chapters 12–14). The variations are partly responsible for differences of crop yields. Plant growth tends to vary as shown in **Figure 3.8** for optimal soil, radiation and water-supply conditions, often increasing with temperature up to 30°C or so (**Note 3.F**). At higher temperatures net growth is reduced by increased respiration, the opposite of photosynthesis (Note 1.B).

3.3 SEASONAL CHANGES

There is an annual swing of temperature due to the tilt of the Earth's axis, either toward the Sun (summer) or away (winter), as shown in Figure 2.3. However, there is no single well-defined season of relatively high temperatures between the Tropics, which includes the northern 40 per cent of Australia. At the equator, the midday sun is well above the horizon in every month, so the seasonal changes of temperature

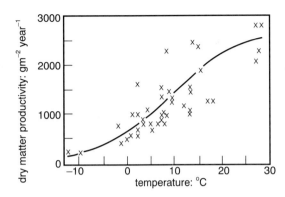

Figure 3.8 The effect of annual mean temperature on the 'net primary productivity', which is the measured total amount of photosynthesised organic material less what is lost in respiration, assuming optimal conditions of soil moisture and nutrients, etc.

are less than 3 K. Consequently, seasons between the Tropics tend to be defined by *rainfall* rather than temperature. For instance, there is 'the Wet' in the 'Top End' of Australia (to use the local terminology) starting around year's end and lasting about three months (Chapter 10). At the opposite extreme, a polar 'night' of several weeks allows long uninterrupted cooling and hence a large annual range of temperatures in Antarctica (**Table 3.4**). Monthly mean temperatures at the South Pole vary from −25°C in January to −60°C in July.

A strong dependence on latitude is evident in South America (**Figure 3.9**), but the annual range is strikingly unaffected by the elevation of the Andes mountains.

Annual ranges in the south are less than in the northern hemisphere, because there is more ocean to cushion changes of temperature. The average range of monthly mean temperatures is about 30 K at 60°N compared with 13 K at 60°S, and 20 K at 40°N compared with 10 K at 40°S. The role of latitude is discussed further in Note 3.G.

Distance from the Sea

The annual range of temperature is increased by remoteness from the sea (Table 3.1, Note 3.G, **Figure 3.10**). **Table 3.5** shows ranges to be 14.8 K inland but only 8.5 K at the coast. The effect is commonly called *continentality*, though that is merely a label not an explanation. The explanation is that water changes temperature only slowly, compared with a land surface, for the following reasons:

(a) the absorption and sharing of radiation heat over a substantial depth;
(b) evaporation cooling, which compensates for any increase of radiation input (Chapter 5);
(c) a comparatively large specific heat (Note 3.A);

Table 3.4 Effect of latitude on the annual range of temperatures; the mean temperatures are averages of values from the same latitudinal band and month

Latitude (°S)	January mean (°C)	July mean (°C)	Range (K)
Equator	26.4	25.6	0.8
10	26.3	23.9	2.4
20	25.4	20.0	5.4
30	21.9	14.7	7.9
40	15.6	9.0	6.6
50	8.1	+3.4	4.7
60	+2.1	−9.1	11.2
70	−3.5	−23.0	19.5
80	−10.8	−39.5	28.7
90	−13.5	−47.8	34.3

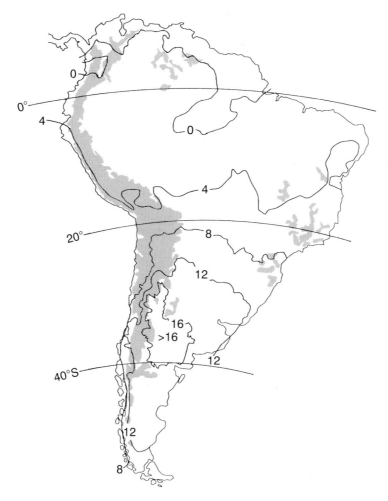

Figure 3.9 The difference between January-mean and July-mean temperatures in South America. The lines labelled zero separate places where January is hotter than July from those in the north where the reverse is true.

(d) the dispersion of heat by oceanic advection between hot and cold regions (Chapter 11); and

(e) the mixing of surface heat into the bulk of the water through the stirring caused by waves.

As a consequence, the annual variation of sea-surface temperatures is below 1 K at the equa-tor and only about 5 K near 30°S in the Pacific and Indian Oceans, and around Australia.

The difference between the hottest and cold-est months is 5 K at the tip of Cape York Peninsula in the north of Queensland, where the measuring site is almost surrounded by sea. By contrast, the annual range of monthly mean temperatures is as much as 18 K over the wes-tern interior of Australia, and even more on the much larger land masses of Eurasia and

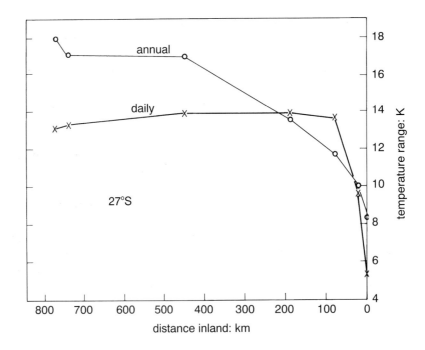

Figure 3.10 The effect of distance inland at 27°S in Queensland on the annual and daily ranges of temperature.

Table 3.5 Effect of distance from the sea on the daily and annual temperature ranges; the comparison is between two places at 35°S on the east coast of Australia, i.e. Jervis Bay at 77 m and Canberra at 571 m

	Jervis Bay, at the coast		
Month	Daily maximum (°C)	Daily minimum (°C)	Average (°C)
January	23.7	17.4	20.5
July	15.1	9.0	12.1
Difference (K)	8.6	8.4	8.5
	Canberra, 100 km inland		
January	27.5	12.8	20.1
July	11.1	−0.5	5.3
Difference (K)	16.4	13.3	14.8

northern America. It exceeds 40 K in parts of Siberia, China and Canada.

Wind Direction

The yearly range is also governed by any variation of the prevailing wind direction, as in monsoonal regions (Chapter 12). Australia has relatively small annual ranges, as the lack of any great north–south corridor in the lee of high mountain ranges like the Rockies or the Andes means that there is no obvious route for large invasions of polar air in winter. Such inflows occasionally lower temperatures in Dallas (east of the Rockies at 33°N) to below −20°C, compared with −2°C as the lowest temperature ever observed at Hobart at 42°S.

Temperatures in Adelaide yield a larger annual range than in other Australian cities (i.e. 11 K, between a monthly mean of 22°C in February and 11°C in August) because summer winds tend to come from the hot interior, whilst the prevailing wind in winter is from the polar south.

3.4 DAILY CHANGES

Screen temperatures do not rise and fall over equal periods of the day; the cooling period lasts longer (**Figure 3.11**). This can be explained as follows. Heating of the ground occurs when the net radiation is positive downward, which is the situation between dawn and mid-afternoon (**Figure 3.12**). Solar radiation declines after noon (Figure 2.4), but the gradual rise of ground temperature leads to a continued increase in the loss of terrestrial radiation (Note 2.C). As a result, the net radiation on a sunny day changes from positive to negative about two hours after solar noon – slightly earlier in winter than in summer – and the surface temperature is then at a maximum. This timing is little affected by cloudiness, which reduces both the shortwave radiation gain and the compensating longwave loss. The moment of daily maximum temperature is followed by a cooling till dawn next day

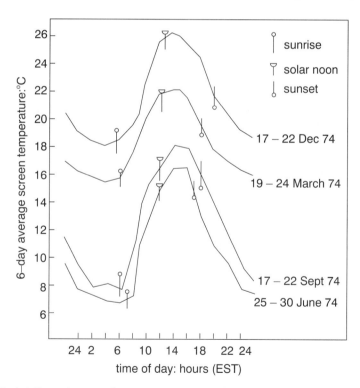

Figure 3.11 Typical daily variations of temperature at Marsfield, Sydney in various seasons. The ranges are higher in winter because the air is drier and the sky less cloudy. (The Eastern Standard Time (EST) is close to the local solar time, i.e the Sun is highest at noon.)

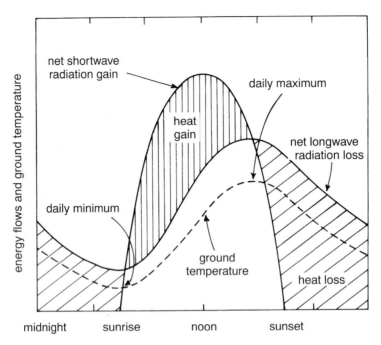

Figure 3.12 Typical daily variations of the radiation input and loss, at the ground. The shortwave input is R_s $(1 - \alpha)$, where R_s is the solar radiation, and α is the ground's albedo. The net longwave loss is the difference between the relatively constant sky radiation and the upwards terrestrial radiation. Part of the net radiation (i.e. the difference between net shortwave gain and net longwave loss) is used to heat the ground.

(**Note 3.H**), i.e. there may be sixteen hours of cooling, for instance, and only eight hours of warming each day.

Daily Maximum

The average daily maximum screen temperature in any month can be identified by a diagram such as that in **Figure 3.13**. The maximum tends to be higher when either the Sun is high in clear skies, when the surface air is damp (which obstructs the loss of terrestrial radiation – Section 2.7), the ground is dry (which reduces both the conduction of heat into the ground and any evaporative cooling – Chapter 4), a warm air mass has settled over the area (Chapter 13), or there is little wind, since wind shares the ground's heat with the atmosphere. Also, warm places tend to be well

inland (away from cooling sea-breezes – Chapter 14) and at a low elevation.

Measurements over oceans, and over land recently wetted by extensive rain, show that daily maximum temperatures there do not exceed 33°C. This is due to cooling by evaporation, which increases as temperatures rise (Chapters 4 and 5).

The time of the daily maximum *screen* temperature typically lags behind the maximum *surface* temperature by 10–30 minutes on a calm day. The time of maximum on a windy day depends on the direction and warmth of the wind. The time is typically closer to noon near the coast, because of the frequent onset of a sea breeze in the afternoon (Chapter 14).

However, changes in the weather may drastically alter the diurnal temperature cycle. For instance, afternoon temperatures may not

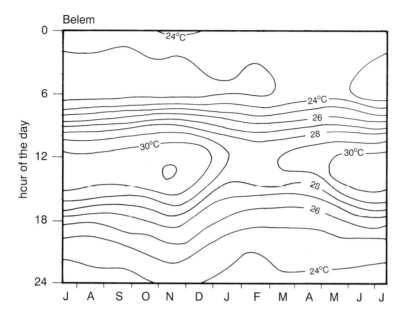

Figure 3.13 An *isogram*, or 'thermo-isopleth diagram', illustrating the times of day and months of the year when particular temperatures are normally to be expected. This one applies to Belem, at 1°S in Brazil.

exceed that at 6 a.m. if a vigorous cold front passes through at 7 a.m. (Chapter 13). Likewise, the daily maximum temperature at Darwin is often reached at 11 a.m. during the Wet, because clouds and thunderstorms occur in the afternoon.

Daily Minimum

Nocturnal cooling is promoted by the same factors, except that latitude is unimportant, and winter 'nights' at places above 67 degrees latitude are days or weeks in duration, so that there is lengthy cooling. A dry atmosphere permits an unobstructed loss of terrestrial radiation, so it accelerates nocturnal cooling. Cloud has a particularly great effect (Section 2.7).

The daily minimum temperature is reached around dawn. It varies across a region much more than the maximum does, since it is lower in hollows, where cold air settles. Table 3.5 shows that minima in Canberra in winter are

9.5 K lower than those 100 km away at the coast. Differences of a few degrees are measured within the city. The minimum is greatly raised by even light winds, which stir in warm air and prevent the cooling which takes place below a 'radiation inversion' (Chapter 7). So a sudden onset of wind during the night is usually accompanied by an abrupt warming.

Daily Range

The difference between the maximum and minimum defines the daily (or 'diurnal') range. It is governed by latitude, elevation, distance from the sea, season, cloud and wind.

The daily range of temperatures is comparatively small near the equator, because of considerable humidity and cloud (Chapters 6 and 8) but it is more than the annual range (Section 3.3) between the Tropics, i.e. at less than 23 degrees latitude. For instance, the *daily* range is 8.6 K in February and 14.5 K in August (in the dry season) at Cuiaba (at 16°S in central Brazil), whilst the *annual* range is only 4.3 K. The daily range is greatest at places inland around latitudes of 30 degrees, where relatively cloudless skies allow considerable warming from the day's strong sunshine and a dry atmosphere permits appreciable cooling at night. At midlatitudes, the range is reduced by cloud and a low Sun. At latitudes above 67 degrees (within the *Polar Circle*) the 'daily range' has little meaning when a 'day' or 'night' may last weeks.

A high elevation tends to increase the daily range, because of less air and moisture above, to attenuate both the daytime input and the nocturnal loss of radiation. **Figure 3.14** shows how ranges at 14–17°S in Peru increase with elevation from about 6 K at sea level to more than 20 K. Likewise, the range is 5.3 K at the coastal town of Antofagasta, at about 23°S in Chile, but 22 K at the equally dry Calama, located 140 km inland, at an altitude of 2,260 m.

The daily fluctuations at the surface of the sea are usually less than 1 K, and less than 3 K at the surface of a lake. This thermal stability has a great effect on coastal climates, creating sea breezes (Chapter 14) and moderating changes of screen temperature locally (Table 3.2).

Figure 3.10 shows that the daily range is roughly independent of the distance inland,

except close to the coast, where sea breezes penetrate (Chapter 14). These may occasionally reach several hundred kilometres inland in arid flat regions bordered by a relatively cold ocean, such as south-west Australia, but arrive after sunset, too late to affect the daily maximum temperature. This late arrival applies also in Canberra, which is 100 km inland and elevated (Table 3.5). In Queensland, the daily range is reduced within 70 km of the sea in winter but 160 km in summer, when sea breezes are stronger.

The diurnal range in Australia tends to be greatest in late December (the summer solstice) and least in late June, i.e. winter. However, there is a lag in the centre of the country; the range at Alice Springs typically changes from a minimum of 14 K in February to a maximum of 18 K in September. Also, the daily range in the north is less in the wet season than in the dry, on account of more cloud. Measurements in Sydney show that the range is about 12 K when there is no cloud, but 3 K when the sky is totally overcast.

Wind reduces the range by stirring the air, moderating the extreme temperatures at the surface.

The range throughout the world appears to be slowly decreasing, chiefly on account of an increase of daily minimum temperatures, i.e. reduced nocturnal cooling. An example is given in **Figure 3.15**. The decrease is consistent with the increased atmospheric concentration of greenhouse gases (Section 2.7), but may also be affected by more nocturnal cloud (Chapter 8) or urbanisation around the weather stations (Section 3.7).

Daily Mean

Daily mean temperature should be calculated by adding hourly measurements and dividing by 24, but is normally taken as the average of the maximum and minimum values. This convenient approximation usually overestimates the average slightly, because the daytime maximum

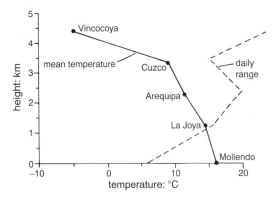

Figure 3.14 Effect of elevation in Peru on the mean temperature and daily range during fifteen days.

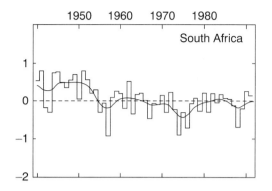

Figure 3.15 Recent changes of the daily range of temperature in South Africa.

is more peaked than the nocturnal minimum. The mean is expressed occasionally in terms of the difference from some reference temperature, selected as important in agriculture (**Note 3.I**) or in assessing human comfort (**Note 3.J**).

3.5 GROUND TEMPERATURES

Temperatures at the surface of the ground are not quite the same as the screen temperatures (at 1.5 m) which are normally recorded. The difference depends on the season, the bareness of the surface, the wind, the amount of cloud and the time of day. At night, the ground surface is colder than air at screen height, and conversely when the net radiation is positive (Figure 3.12). As regards season, the mean difference between ground and screen *minimum* temperatures at Alice Springs is 4.5 K in July and 5.1 K in January, the ground being colder. Likewise, measurements at Cowra (NSW) showed monthly mean differences of 2.1 K in winter but 5.4 K in March, i.e. there is again a greater difference in the warmer months. The surface of bare ground in Pretoria (South Africa) at dawn in summer can be 12 K less than the screen minimum.

The effect of wind is to equalise screen and surface temperatures by linking them convec-

tively. Clouds also reduce the temperature difference, especially precipitating clouds, because net radiation is reduced both at night and during the day (Section 2.8). For instance, the ground minimum in Sydney is typically 6 K cooler on a dry clear calm winter's night, but 2.9 K when daily rainfall is 1–5 mm, and only 1.6 K on wetter days (when there is more cloud).

As to the daily maximum at ground level, it *exceeds* the screen maximum by several degrees if there is little wind or cloud. The surfaces of sand or asphalt can be dangerously hot in strong sunshine; temperatures near 80°C have been recorded in deserts, which is 22 K higher than the world's record screen temperature. Chapter 5 explains such large differences as due to (i) a strong net radiation flux to the surface (i.e. low albedo and no cloud), (ii) little conduction of heat downward from the surface (i.e. a poorly conducting ground material, such as dry sand), (iii) no evaporative cooling from a moist surface (Chapter 4) and (iv) only slight convection between ground and screen, due to an absence of wind. Of these four factors, only the first and last reflect the weather, whilst the second and third depend on the soil and vegetation of the site. To reduce the effects of the site itself at a weather station, we standardise by measuring ground temperatures on a short-clipped, well-watered lawn, unobstructed by surrounding buildings or trees. This is known as the *standard ground temperature*.

The ground maximum can be lowered by increasing its albedo, to reflect solar radiation away. For instance, soil covered with white polythene in Tanzania was observed to be 13 K cooler than soil covered by black polythene. A layer of white chalk on black soil at Pune in India lowered the temperature by 14 K one clear afternoon in summer, whereas black soil on white sand warmed the surface by 10 K. Maori farmers in New Zealand reduce the albedo with charcoal to warm the soil, in order that plant germination be accelerated. Another way of achieving high surface temperatures is to select slopes facing the Sun (Chapter 5).

Ground-surface temperatures, averaged globally and over a long time, *tend* to be around 2 K higher than screen temperatures over land surfaces. For example, a difference of 4 K has been observed at 2,819 m in Ecuador. This positive difference shows that the *ground heats the air,* on the whole. Nevertheless, there are exceptions. For instance, mean screen temperatures are *above* ground-surface averages in Norway, where the oncoming air has been warmed by the Atlantic Gulf Stream.

Subterranean Temperatures

The temperature of the soil near the surface is important in agriculture, e.g. in affecting the germination of tomatoes (Note 3.F). Similarly, maize seeds are planted only when the ground has reached about 10°C.

Regular measurements are usually made at depths of 0.3 m, 1.2 m and, occasionally, at 0.1 m, 0.5 m and 3 m. The results show that the daily pulses of heat from the surface are attenuated with depth, so that there are hardly any daily fluctuations of temperature beyond half a metre or so, depending on the nature of the ground (**Note 3.K**). Annual fluctuations reach almost 20 times further (**Figure 3.16**).

The decrease of daily temperature range with depth makes it possible to live comfortably underground all the year round, where surface extremes are harsh. People at Coober Pedy (South Australia) live in dugouts excavated by the opal miners, where the steady temperature of 20°C is much more agreeable than the January mean maximum of 37°C, or than the frosty mornings in winter.

Diurnal and annual cycles of temperature not only decrease in amplitude with increasing depth within the soil, but also lag behind that at the surface (Figure 3.16). For the annual

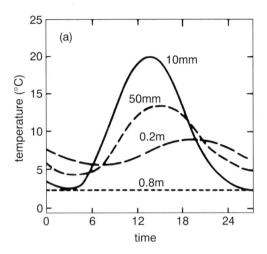

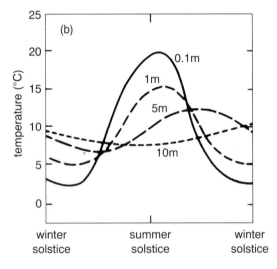

Figure 3.16 Typical variations of ground temperature at various depths (a) during a day, and (b) during a year.

cycle, the lag is about six months at 10 m, which means that the ground is colder at 10 m depth in summer than in winter. Likewise, the inside of a solid wall about 50 cm thick is coolest at around midday and warmest at midnight, promoting a useful stabilisation of indoor temperatures.

On the whole, the annual average temperature increases with depth as the result of radioactive decay in the interior of the Earth. The *geothermal gradient* is higher in regions with volcanoes, such as New Zealand, and is largely unaffected by variations of temperature at the surface. Nevertheless, small irregularities in the subterranean temperatures can be attributed to surface-temperature anomalies a long time ago. For instance, a kink in the temperature profile below 1,000 metres underground in New South Wales is attributed to the last Ice Age 18,000 years ago, when glaciers flowed in the Snowy Mountains. Likewise, temperature irregularities in boreholes a few hundred metres deep in eastern Canada show relative warmth about 1,000 years ago (the Little Climatic Optimum), coldness around AD 1600 (the Little Ice Age) and a warming by up to 3 K during the last century. This is discussed further in Chapter 15.

3.6 FROST

Frost is defined in various ways. *Ground frost* is said to occur when the ground minimum is below 0°C. There is *black frost* (i.e. there is no deposit of ice) if the air is so dry that the frozen ground surface fails to reach the dew-point (a measure of atmospheric humidity, see Chapter 6). A *frosty night* means that the *screen* temperature falls to +2°C or less, which usually implies a ground frost, defined above. A *heavy frost* occurs when the *screen* minimum is 0°C or below, and a *killing frost* (i.e. one that kills plants) may be defined in terms of a screen minimum below −2°C. But it is better to quote the actual temperature and the level at which it is measured than to use such labels.

Hoar frost is a silvery-white deposit of tiny crystals formed by the direct deposition of water vapour onto surfaces colder than 0°C.

Glaze is an ice coating caused by the freezing of 'supercooled' droplets of rain (Chapter 9) when they impact onto surfaces colder than 0°C.

Causes

Occasions of frost are due either to the *advection* of polar air, or to intense *radiation cooling at night*, or, most commonly, to both together. An *advection frost* affects a wide area, such as the whole of southern Brazil, where cold air can drive far north in the lee of the Andes (Chapter 13). Such frosts may cause enormous damage to Brazil's coffee crop. On the other hand, *radiation frosts* are more local, more common and more intense. They result from reduced sky radiation on clear, calm nights in winter. They are less likely in the warm conditions of low latitudes or within a few kilometres of the sea. Further inland, the drier air allows greater nocturnal cooling (Section 2.7), so, for instance, there are about thirty-three frosty nights annually at Alice Springs, in the centre of Australia, despite a latitude of only 23°S.

Occurrence

There is no frost north of 23°S in Brazil. Also, it is hardly known north of 20°S near the east coast of Australia, or 28°S on the west; the asymmetry is due partly to a warm ocean current down the west coast (Chapter 11) and partly to cold southerly winds over eastern Australia and warmer northerly winds over the western area in winter (Chapter 13).

Frosts are less frequent at lower levels. Observations in the Craigieburn Range (in New Zealand at 43°S) show a reduction of the average *frost-free* period by about thirteen days for each 100 m extra elevation. The chance of frost is increased in some low-lying localities by cold air draining from higher (i.e. colder) land into *frost hollows* (**Note 3.L**). These occur in parts of the Snowy Mountains of south-east Australia, so that daily minimum temperatures in a valley bottom may be less than what is needed for tree growth (Note 3.F). As a result, there is a *reversed* tree-line, with trees growing only *above* a certain level.

There has been a gradual reduction in the frequency of severe frosts during the past forty years, in many countries. This is partly due to more urban heating (Section 3.7), but is also evident in rural areas such as outback Queensland. Frosts are fairly common there, on account of the reduced cloudiness when winters are unusually dry.

Crops

Farmers are especially concerned about frosts. A notable frost in Brazil in July of 1975 reduced the country's coffee harvest by 65 per cent, seriously upsetting export trade.

The agricultural *growing season* is often defined in cool areas as the period between the last frost of spring and the first of autumn; crops are suitable there only if they reach maturity within that time (Notes 3.F and 3.I). The date for the start of such a growing season at Walgett (NSW) is within twelve days of 8 September, in half the years of a long record, and the end within twelve of 22 May, so the average frost-free period between is 255 days. It is about five weeks less at Tamworth, which is 270 m higher. Naturally, the periods may be quite different in any particular year. Sometimes the *effective growing season* is referred to instead, the period between (i) the date of all but the last 10% of killing frosts in spring, and (ii) the date of all but the earliest 10 per cent in autumn, in a long series of years.

The best protection against frost is proper site selection (Note 3.L). The risk may also be reduced by either training plants above the ground, covering the soil with black plastic (to absorb more heat during the day), or sheltering the crop within a glasshouse. Frost damage may be reduced by sprinkling water (Chapter 4) or large fans (Chapter 7).

3.7 URBAN TEMPERATURES

Temperatures measured at street level in large cities can be several degrees higher than those in the surrounding countryside (**Figure 3.17**). Isotherms on a map of an isolated city and its environs look like the height contours of an island, which leads to the clumsy notion of an 'urban heat-island effect'; a simpler term is *urban heating*. It is evident in some cities during the day but is particularly apparent at night, being often greatest at about 9 p.m., because city surfaces cool more slowly than those in the suburbs. The consequence is that the daily minimum is raised more than the maximum.

Towns of only 10,000 in the USA show discernible urban heating. It can be considerable in larger places; the centre of Johannesburg may be as much as 11 K warmer than in suburban valleys on a dry winter's night. Measurements in central Sydney have shown temperatures 3 K higher than on the outskirts, and similar urban heating has been measured in Melbourne. The city of Nairobi (1°S) cools about 2 K less than outside during the night, and becomes about 0.3 K hotter in the day (**Table 3.6**).

There have been many studies of urban heating in the USA. Extensive studies in St Louis in Missouri (with a population of 600,000 within 1,150 km^2) have shown urban heating of up to 3 K on summer afternoons. Urban heating in Chicago is most at 9 p.m. in August, least at 1 p.m. in April and October, and averages 1.9 K, or 2.8 K in the absence of wind or cloud. Overall, weather-station temperatures in the USA have an urban bias of +0.1 K for the monthly maximum temperatures and +0.4 K for the minima. The latter is the average of a range of +2.4 K to −1.1 K, for a large city and rural circumstances, respectively. It appears that a tenfold increase of city population raises the

July: minimum

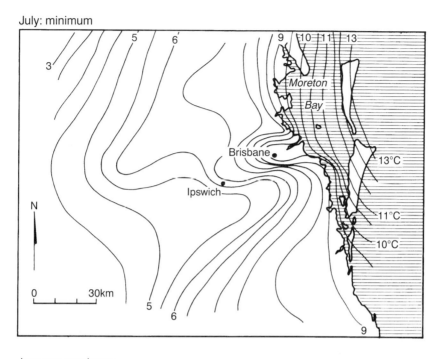

January: maximum

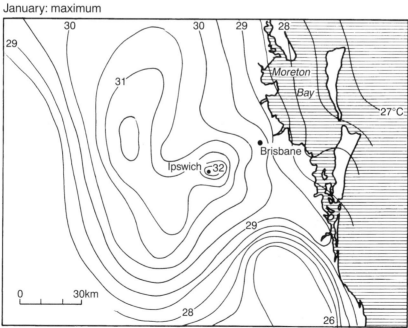

Figure 3.17 The distribution of (a) July minimum and (b) January maximum temperatures, in the vicinity of Brisbane, Australia.

Table 3.6 Urban heating, i.e. differences between temperatures inside Nairobi (1°S and 1,829 m elevation), and outside at the airport, during the dry month of January or the cloudy month of July, at the times of either minimum or maximum temperature, i.e. at about 4 a.m. and between 8 a.m. and noon, respectively

Month	Difference between minima	Difference between maxima
January	+ 2.1 K	−0.2 K
July	+ 1.8 K	−0.3 K

maximum urban heating (relative to the outskirts) by 2 K, on average.

Urban heating is greater on weekdays than at weekends because cities are busiest during the week. This may explain an observation that global temperatures of the lower atmosphere, observed by satellite over fourteen years, are higher during weekdays than at the weekend by a few hundredths of a degree.

The growth of cities has led to an increase of the temperatures measured at weather stations within them. In general, the daily minimum in cities in the USA rose between 1901 and 1984 by about 0.13 K, while the maximum remained steady. This effect in cities has to be borne in mind when examining past records for evidence of global warming.

Causes

Several factors are responsible for urban heating:

1 Artificial heat may be appreciable, especially in the largest industrialised cities. An astonishing 640 W/m^2 has been quoted for Manhattan. Even in Sydney, where the rate of artificial heat generation is only a tenth as much, it is comparable with wintertime net-radiation fluxes (Figure 2.19) and can equal half the incoming solar radiation.

2 The construction materials used in modern cities: concrete, brick, rock and bitumen all readily absorb the daytime heat and release it slowly to the atmosphere at night. The effect of this is to reduce slightly the daytime maximum temperature, which, in combination with the nocturnal urban heating, reduces the daily range.

3 The drainage of water from a city and the lack of evaporation from soil and plants prevent evaporative cooling, so that daytime temperatures are raised.

4 There may be a reduced albedo (Section 2.5) because of the relative absence or removal of snow, the replacement of vegetation by low-albedo material such as roadway bitumen, and because of the canyon structure of built-up areas, which trap radiation. As a result, solar heating of the city is increased.

One side-issue of urban heating may be an aggravation of the incidence of mob violence. Riots are rare in the USA when temperatures are below freezing, but the likelihood at 31°C apears to be twice that at 20°C (**Figure 3.18**). Why this should be so is for sociologists to explain.

Daytime urban heating in temperate climates can be reduced by two or three degrees if there are many trees in the streets and parks, causing evaporative cooling as well as shade. Places in desert areas may be cooled by evaporation from irrigated gardens and crops. However, vegetation has no effect in the evening, when transpiration has stopped.

Thus we end consideration of the manner in which some of the incident radiant energy is used in heating the ground and then the adjacent atmosphere. Much of the remaining net radiation is often used in evaporating water, which is discussed in the next chapter.

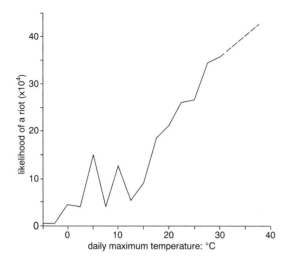

Figure 3.18 The effect of the daily maximum temperature on the likelihood of riots in seventy-nine cities in the USA during the period 1967–71.

NOTES

3.A The transfer of sensible heat
3.B Effects of latitude and elevation on mean temperature
3.C High temperatures and human mortality
3.D Acclimatisation and adaptation
3.E Windchill
3.F Temperature and crops
3.G The annual range of monthly mean temperatures
3.H Cold nights
3.I Growing-degree-days and agriculture
3.J Degree-days and comfort
3.K The conduction of heat
3.L The thermal belt

4

EVAPORATION

4.1 CHANGES OF STATE

A large fraction of the net radiation at the bottom of the atmosphere (Section 2.8) is absorbed by the oceans which cover about 71 per cent of the Earth's surface, and that absorbed energy is mostly used in evaporating water. Some 6×10^{13} tonnes are evaporated from the land each year, but about six times as much from the oceans (Chapter 6). So evaporation is an important part of the movement of energy, the theme of this second part of the book.

Changes of State

Water can exist in any of three 'states' – either as an invisible gas (i.e. water vapour), a liquid (e.g. cloud droplets, raindrops, dew, ground-water, river, lake or sea) or as a solid, such as snow, frost, hail or ice. (Steam which you can see from a kettle is not water vapour but consists of *liquid* droplets formed from the vapour; it is a miniature cloud.) The difference between the three states lies in the tightness of packing the water molecules together; they can be fitted together either stacked closely into a regular

structure as a solid, irregularly packed together as a liquid, or loose as independent vapour molecules.

Water is the only common substance found in all three states. It is unusual in other ways too. It has an exceptionally high specific heat, it expands on freezing, it is most dense at about 4 K above freezing point (which is extraordinary) and the amount of heat needed to vaporise liquid water is large. It takes considerable energy to heat a cupful of water from freezing point to boiling point, but six times as much energy to evaporate that amount of water. These distinctive properties arise from the particular arrangement of the two hydrogen atoms and one oxygen atom in each water molecule (**Note 4.A**).

With three possible states there are six possible transformations of a substance from one form to another (i.e. *changes of state*), shown in **Figure** 4.1. There may be a change from a gas to liquid (called *condensation,* from a liquid to solid (*freezing*), or from a solid to gas (*sublimation*). Also from solid to liquid (*melting*), and gas to solid. The last is also called sublimation (which can be confusing), or *deposition* in the case of clouds. The combination of simulta-

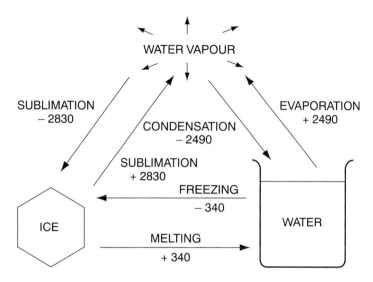

Figure 4.1 Changes of state of water, showing the number of kilojoules per kilogram required for each change, assuming that the air and water are at 10°C and the ice at −10°C. A negative number means that heat is *liberated*.

neous melting and sublimation from ice, such as occurs on a glacier, is sometimes called *ablation*. Finally, the change from liquid to gas is *evaporation*, the topic of the present chapter.

Latent Heat

Any change of state involves the loosening and reforming of bonds between adjacent molecules, as the result of thermal vibrations. The energy involved is described in units of 'kilojoules', defined in Note 1.J. If about 2,830 kilojoules are added to a kilogram of ice at 0°C, the resulting molecular motion disrupts the bonds completely and water vapour is produced, i.e. sublimation occurs (Figure 4.1). Evaporation requires only about 2,460 kJ/kg, because a liquid has weaker bonds to break than a solid has. More precisely, 2,490 kJ/kg are needed for evaporation at 0°C, or 2,430 at 30°C.

Heat added for evaporation makes no difference to the water's temperature, because the energy is used in breaking bonds not in altering molecular velocities (Section 3.1). After evaporation, the vapour contains the energy absorbed during the change of state. It is contained as *latent heat*, meaning hidden heat, as first pointed out by Joseph Black (1728–99). Such heat cannot be felt, or measured with a thermometer.

The rate of latent-heat absorption at an evaporating surface is L.E (W/m^2) where L (kJ/kg) is the latent heat required to evaporate a kilogram of water, and E is the rate of evaporation in units of kilograms per square metre per second. Thus, breaking sufficient bonds to melt ice (at 0°C) requires about 340 kJ/kg (i.e. 2,830 − 2,490), whilst freezing *liberates* an equal amount (**Note 4.B**). Likewise, the amount of heat taken in during evaporation exactly equals the amount *released* when the opposite process of condensation occurs. We shall see that such liberation of heat is important in the atmosphere (Section 4.7 and Chapter 7).

Transport of latent heat occurs when water evaporates in one place and condenses in

another. For instance, consider **Figure 4.2**. Evaporation from the ocean incorporates latent heat into the moistened air, and that same heat is later released downwind if the vapour forms cloud (Chapter 8). This is a major factor in conveying heat toward the poles (Chapter 5).

4.2 VAPOUR PRESSURE AND EVAPORATION

The concept of *vapour pressure* is needed in order to explain why a liquid is sometimes depleted by evaporation and sometimes augmented by condensation. We first consider gas molecules in a box, which move to and fro, continually colliding with each other and with the walls of the box. Everything is at the same temperature. (Such a model of colliding molecules is the basis of the *Kinetic Theory of Gases* outlined by Rudolf Clausius in 1857.) The molecules' impacts press the walls outwards, with a total pressure partly due to the molecules of water vapour. That part is called the 'water-vapour pressure', or, simply, 'vapour pressure'. The rest of the total pressure is exerted by the other molecules of air inside the box, e.g. the molecules of nitrogen and oxygen.

Saturation

If both water vapour and liquid are contained in the same box (**Figure 4.3**), we can show that adjustments occur towards an eventual steady balance, when the amount of evaporation from the liquid equals the condensation back from the vapour. The reasoning is as follows. The temperature governs the rate at which evaporation occurs, because it controls the liveliness of the liquid's molecules and hence their readiness to escape their bonds. Then, as individual molecules enter the space above, they add to the number of vapour molecules, which increases the frequency of bombardment of all the adjacent surfaces, one of which is that of the liquid itself. As a consequence of there being more vapour molecules, more of them hit the liquid's surface and condense, becoming re-imprisoned in the liquid. Eventually, sufficient evaporation into the space has occurred for there to be enough vapour to return molecules to the liquid at an equal rate, i.e. the condensation rate matches the evaporation rate. At that stage, the space above the liquid is said to be *saturated,* and the pressure exerted by the vapour in it is the *saturation vapour pressure,* (svp) represented by e_s. Strictly speaking, this

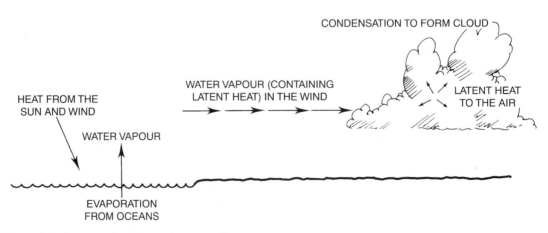

Figure 4.2 An example of latent-heat transfer.

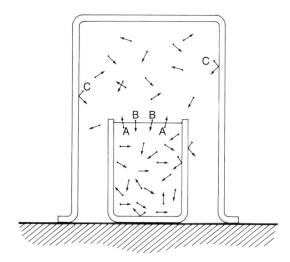

Figure 4.3 The principle of equilibrium between water and vapour in an enclosure. Molecules C impact on each surface with a vigour depending on their temperature, and thus create vapour pressure. Molecules A escape from the liquid, according to the liquid's temperature. On the other hand, molecules B impact on the liquid and are recaptured, according to the number of molecules in the space above the liquid. When steady conditions are reached, the numbers of kinds A and B are equal.

vapour pressure applies only to the water vapour in the saturated space (i.e. to a gas), but since it is in balance with that from the liquid we can regard e_s as applying to the liquid too.

The result is that e_s *depends only on the temperature*, since this alone determines the rate of evaporation, and therefore the amount of vapour needed to provide an equal rate of condensation. This is one of the most basic facts about the atmosphere, and must be grasped to make sense of Chapters 6–8. The increase of e_s with temperature is shown in what is called the *psychrometric table* (**Table 4.1**), determined by laboratory measurements in the context of theoretical work by Clausius. The relationship between e_s and temperature is discussed further in Chapter 6.

In practice, equilibrium between evaporation and condensation is rarely achieved in the real world. Usually one of the processes is dominant since adjacent air and water tend to be at different temperatures, and to have different vapour pressures. So there is a net difference between the flow from the place at higher vapour pressure and the smaller flow from the place at lower pressure. In fact, the (net) evaporation rate from water is proportional to the vapour-pressure *difference* $(e_s - e)$, where e is the local atmosphere's vapour pressure (or *ambient vapour pressure*) and e_s is the *liquid's vapour pressure*, i.e. the saturated vapour pressure (e_s) *at the liquid's surface temperature* (**Note 4.C**).

4.3 FEATURES OF THE EVAPORATION PROCESS

(a) Evaporation rates can be described either in terms of the rate at which the water level falls, or in terms of the rate at which latent heat is consumed in the process (**Note 4.D**).

(b) The rate of evaporation from a water surface is proportional to $(e_s - e)$, and also to the speed of the wind blowing on the water surface. This relationship is named *Dalton's equation* (**Note 4.E**), after John Dalton (1766–1844).

(c) Evaporation is not the same as boiling; boiling always entails rapid evaporation, but evaporation does not necessitate boiling. Evaporation occurs at a liquid's surface at *any* temperature, provided the air is dry enough, whilst the *bubbles* characteristic of boiling form only when the *boiling point* has been reached. This is a temperature which depends on the local atmospheric pressure, for the following reason. Bubble formation requires a temperature high enough to make vapour molecules inside the bubble sufficiently energetic to exert an outwards pressure equal to the squeezing caused by the atmospheric pressure on the liquid. No bubble could survive without such equality. So the saturation vapour pressure at the

Table 4.1 The effect of temperature (°C) on the saturation vapour pressure (svp: hPa) of an atmosphere above a water surface

Temperature (°C)	Saturation vapour pressure (hectopascals)				
	.0°C	.2°C	.4°C	.6°C	.8°C
0	6.1 hPa	6.2 hPa	6.3 hPa	6.4 hPa	6.5 hPa
1	6.6	6.7	6.8	6.9	7.0
2	7.1	7.2	7.3	7.4	7.5
3	7.6	7.7	7.8	7.9	8.0
4	8.1	8.2	8.4	8.5	8.6
5	8.7	8.8	9.0	9.1	9.2
6	9.3	9.5	9.6	9.7	9.9
7	10.0	10.2	10.3	10.4	10.6
8	10.7	10.9	11.0	11.2	11.3
9	11.5	11.6	11.8	11.9	12.1
10	12.3	12.4	12.6	12.8	12.9
11	13.1	13.3	13.5	13.7	13.8
12	14.0	14.2	14.4	14.6	14.8
13	15.0	15.2	15.4	15.6	15.8
14	16.0	16.2	16.4	16.6	16.8
15	17.0	17.3	17.5	17.7	17.9
16	18.2	18.4	18.6	18.9	19.1
17	19.4	19.6	19.9	20.1	20.4
18	20.6	20.9	21.2	21.4	21.7
19	22.0	22.2	22.5	22.8	23.1
20	23.4	23.7	24.0	24.3	24.6
21	24.9	25.2	25.5	25.8	26.1
22	26.4	26.8	27.1	27.4	27.7
23	28.1	28.4	28.8.	29.1	29.5
24	29.8	30.2	30.6	30.9	31.3
25	31.7	32.1	32.4	32.8	33.2
26	33.6	34.0	34.4	34.8	35.2
27	35.6	36.1	36.5	36.9	37.4
28	37.8	38.2	38.7	39.11	39.6
29	40.1	40.5	41.0	41.5	41.9
30	42.4	42.9	43.4	43.9	44.4
31	44.9	45.4	46.0	46.5	47.0
32	47.6	48.1	48.6	49.2	49.7
33	50.3	50.9	51.4	52.0	52.6
34	53.2	53.8	54.4	55.0	55.6
35	56.2	56.9	57.5	58.1	59.8
36	59.4	60.1	60.7	61.4	62.1
37	62.8	63.5	64.1	64.8	65.6
38	66.3	67.0	67.7	68.4	69.2
39	69.9	70.7	71.5	72.2	73.0
40	73.8	74.6	75.4	76.2	77.0

boiling point equals the ambient air pressure. For instance, the atmospheric pressure at sea-level (Section 1.5) is typically 1,013 hPa and that is the saturation vapour pressure at 100°C, which is hence the sea-level boiling point.

One result is that boiling point is lower at a high altitude, where the air pressure is less (Note 1.G). For example, water boils at 93°C on top of Mt Kosciusko (Australia's highest mountain, at 2,228 m above sea-level), and at about 70°C on top of Mt Everest.

(d) There is a reduction in the rate of evaporation from the sea, due to the dissolved salt. Salt attracts water molecules, so they less easily escape from the sea's surface. The result is that sea-water's vapour pressure is about 2 per cent less than that of pure water.

(e) Evaporation from impure water leaves the impurity behind. That is how salt is collected in vast shallow ponds by the sea in South Australia after the water has been evaporated away by exposure to the Sun.

Likewise, polluted water becomes worse. And the salt in water brought to irrigate farmlands gradually poisons the soil by deposition during evaporation unless care is taken to flush the deposit away periodically, using excess irrigation and suitable drainage.

But condensation of the vapour yields pure water. The combination of evaporation followed by condensation is called *distillation*. It occurs naturally when water is evaporated from the oceans and later forms clouds and then rain. It can be done artificially in a 'still', such as that in **Figure** 4.4.

(f) Evaporation from sea-spray leaves an increasingly concentrated solution of salt in each droplet, steadily lowering its vapour

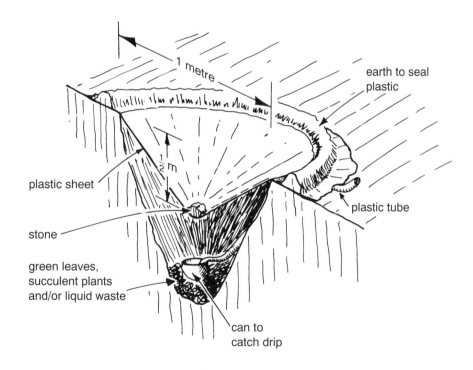

Figure 4.4 An arrangement for distilling drinkable water. A sheet of clear plastic is sealed completely over a hole in the ground, with moist material beneath. The Sun's heat evaporates water from the material, and then condensation occurs on the underside of the relatively cool plastic. A stone on the plastic makes a cone which focuses drips into a can, from which water can be sucked by a tube.

pressure and therefore slackening the rate of evaporation. As a result, droplets survive long enough to be blown well inland.

(g) On the other hand, evaporation from a drop reduces its size, thus increasing the curvature of the surface, which enhances the rate of evaporation (**Note 4.F**).

(h) The evaporation rate from a lake, reservoir or rice-field can be greatly lowered by applying even a thin layer of a material such as an oil or acetyl alcohol, which impedes the escape of water molecules. Unfortunately, the layer is eventually degraded by the Sun and blown away.

(i) If world climates changed and the oceans became, say, 2 K hotter, their vapour pressure would be about 14 per cent more than now. (Compare values in Table 4.1 for 15°C and 17°C, for instance, i.e. 17.0 and 19.4 hPa, respectively.) Dalton's equation (Note 4.E) shows that this increase of e_s would initially promote evaporation. However, it also indicates that there is automatic negative feedback, as the extra evaporation would increase the atmospheric vapour pressure e, thereby *reducing* the difference.

(j) There is a close connection between evaporation from a vegetative crop like sugarcane and its growth, because both processes involve gases diffusing through the small openings in the surfaces of the crop's leaves, called *stomates*. Leaf evaporation involves water vapour diffusing *outwards* through these stomatal openings, from the wet tissue within the leaf, whilst photosynthesis within the leaf requires the diffusion of carbon dioxide from the atmosphere *inwards*. Therefore, any closing of the stomates reduces both water loss and photosynthesis.

  The connection between evaporation and growth is strengthened by the fact that both depend on the prior rainfall, on the temperature and on the radiation input. As a consequence, the amount of evaporation is

an index of crop growth, at least in areas where water availability is the factor mainly limiting crop yield (**Figure 4.5, Note 4.G**).

(k) Extended periods of high evaporation from grass, bark, twigs, etc. create dry tinder and therefore a bushfire hazard. This is important in rural and suburban Australia.

(l) Evaporation from the skin affects human comfort. If the rate of evaporation is less than the rate of perspiration, the skin becomes moist and one feels uncomfortable (**Note 4.H**).

(m) What is called the equivalent temperature remains unchanged even if condensation or evaporation takes place within a given parcel of air. This is the measured temperature plus the heating resulting from condensing all the water vapour within the parcel. If there are x grams of vapour per gram of dry air, the heating is L.x/C degrees, where L is the

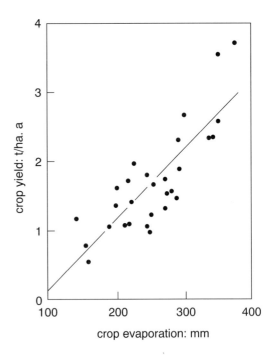

Figure 4.5 The relationship between the yield of wheat in South Australia and the crop's evaporation.

latent heat of evaporation (Section 4.1), and C the specific heat of dry air (Note 3.A).

4.4 DETERMINING THE EVAPORATION RATE

The rate of evaporation from water or land surfaces can be measured in several ways. The following are a few examples.

1 The change of water level is a direct index of evaporation and routinely measured at many weather stations, generally with an American 'Class-A' evaporation pan (or *evaporimeter*) shown in **Figure 4.6** and Plate 4.1. The rate of evaporation from this standard device is known as the *pan evaporation rate*, E_p.

2 For a lake or reservoir, one may construct a *water balance* (Chapter 10). This involves adding all the inputs of water, such as rain (P) or stream flow (I), and subtracting all the losses, such as evaporation (E) and outflow (O), during a month. A rise in water level (R) during that period implies that the inputs exceed the losses, so

$$P + I - (E + O) = R$$
i.e. $$E = P + I - O - R$$

The evaporation rate E can be estimated if the other terms are known. A negative rise (R) implies a fall of water level.

3 The evaporation from a well-watered crop can be measured by means of a *drainage lysimeter* (**Figure 4.7**), set within the crop. A measured amount of water is applied each day to the soil

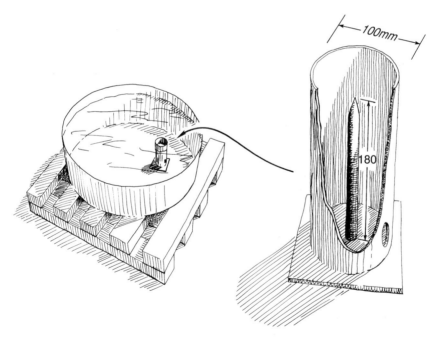

Figure 4.6 A *Class-A pan evaporimeter* for measuring daily evaporation, showing the stilling cylinder for preventing waves affecting the level of the water within. The pan has a diameter of 1.22 m, and a water depth of 180 mm, and stands about 40 mm above the ground on a wooden platform. Sometimes the pan is covered by wire-mesh to prevent birds and animals from drinking the water, though this reduces evaporation by 10 per cent or so. Each day, water is added to the pan until the surface is just level with the tip of the spike in the stilling cylinder. The added water (plus any rain collected since the last refilling) equals the amount evaporated.

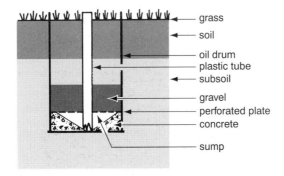

Figure 4.7 A *drainage lysimeter* made from an oil-drum, for measuring the evaporation from a *well-watered* crop. The central tube is made of plastic, for instance, and reaches down to the sump at the base. The soil rests on a perforated plate.

in the oil drum, and then the water which has drained to the sump since the day before is pumped out and measured. The difference between applied water (and rain) and pumped water is the daily evaporation.

4 For crops in a field, the evaporation rate can be measured by the *gravimetric method*. This involves taking a sample of soil from the top 300 mm, or more if the crop's roots go deep. The sample is weighed, dried and reweighed, and the loss of mass gives its water content. The process is repeated with numerous other samples to obtain an average water content for the field. Further samples are taken after a week, for instance, and examined similarly. The decrease of average water content (plus any rainfall meanwhile, and minus any run-off) is a measure of the weekly evaporation. But the procedure is obviously tedious, damages the field and ignores the possibility of seepage of moisture down into the ground.

5 In addition, there are several high-tech methods, more suited to research than routine measurements.

Estimation

An alternative to measuring an evaporation rate is to use some relationship, such as that in

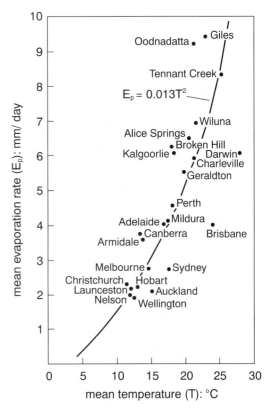

Figure 4.8 The relationship between annual mean evaporation rates from Class-A pans at various places in Australia and New Zealand, and the annual mean temperatures there.

Figure 4.8, for *estimating* the rate instead. In this case, the curve is based on previous measurements of pan evaporation and temperature and allows one to estimate the evaporation corresponding to current thermometer readings, though the scatter of values about the curve shows that such an estimate could only be very rough. The relationship is affected by proximity to the coast, and no account is taken of the local wind speed which Dalton's equation shows can be important (Note 4.E). A more accurate method of estimating evaporation is mentioned in Chapter 5.

Plate 4.1 A US Class-A evaporation pan at a climate station in Melbourne. It is covered by mesh to exclude birds, whose drinking or splashing of the water would affect the daily lowering of water level due to evaporation. The congestion of the equipment and the undue proximity to a busy street are unfortunate but typical consequences of the growth of a city.

4.5 VARIOUS EVAPORATION RATES

Lake Evaporation Rate E_o

So far we have mainly considered the simplest case, that of evaporation from an extensive water surface, i.e. the *lake evaporation rate E_o*. It is useful to consider this as the surface has a more or less standard roughness, albedo and wetness, and reservoirs are important to us. But it is difficult to measure E_o accurately. Also, there is the complication that evaporation from the upwind edge of a large lake moistens the air, so that evaporation downwind is reduced.

Evaporation from a choppy sea is complicated by the effects of dissolved salt and spray-droplet curvature, mentioned in Section 4.3, and the effect of a surface roughened by waves.

Pan Evaporation Rate E_p

The *pan evaporation rate E_p* is what is measured with an evaporimeter, such as the Class-A pan (Figure 4.6). It is simple to measure, but is not the same as E_o. The ratio E_o/E_p is called the *pan coefficient*. It is normally less than unity, i.e. a pan loses more water per unit area than a lake, because a pan gains extra heat through the base and sides during the day, so that the water's vapour pressure is increased. The ratio for a Class-A pan varies widely, according to the weather and season, e.g. measurements at Lake Eucumbene in the Snowy Mountains in Australia gave monthly mean values of 0.6 in summer and 1.8 in winter. Annual mean values for eight reservoirs in Australia ranged from 0.63 to 0.94, so it is not possible to infer E_o accurately from E_p. Despite this, a coefficient of 0.7 is often taken as typical for the Class-A pan.

Potential Evaporation Rate E_t

The *potential evaporation rate* applies to a *well-watered* surface, as measured by a drainage lysimeter, for example (Section 4.4). It combines evaporation from the ground with evaporation from the plants. The latter is *part* of the process of *transpiration*, the flow of liquid water from soil to roots, through the plant ('transpiration' means 'breathing *through*'), and then evaporation from within the leaves into the atmosphere. The combination of soil evaporation and plant evaporation is sometimes called *evapotranspiration,* but this is clumsy, unnecessary and often wrongly taken to imply that evaporation from vegetation is somehow different from other evaporation. To distinguish 'plant evaporation', 'soil evaporation' and 'crop evaporation', it is simpler to label them accordingly.

The ratio between a crop's potential evaporation and adjacent lake evaporation, E_t/E_o, depends on the respective albedo and surface-roughness values of crop and water. For well-watered grass, it is typically about 1.2. Comparing this with the pan coefficient for a Class-A evaporimeter (which implies that E_p/E_o equals 1/0.7, i.e. 1.4), shows that potential evaporation for a crop such as grass is roughly similar to nearby pan evaporation E_p.

Actual Evaporation Rate E_a

In practice, the *rate of actual evaporation* taking place in a field is more important than either E_o, E_p or E_t. But it is the most difficult to measure. So it is often deduced from evaporimeter measurements E_p, using values of the *crop factor, E_a/E_p,* calculated from previous measurements of E_p and E_a with the same crop at that same stage (**Figure 4.9**). Unfortunately, the climate, soil and crop management now are likely to differ from those in the previous measurements, so that the crop factor they yielded is hardly applicable, and therefore the actual evaporation is inferred only very approximately.

One feature of actual evaporation is its dependence on the soil's wetness. There are two stages involved, illustrated in **Figure 4.10**. Initally, drying proceeds at a rate which depends on the climate, and equals the poten-

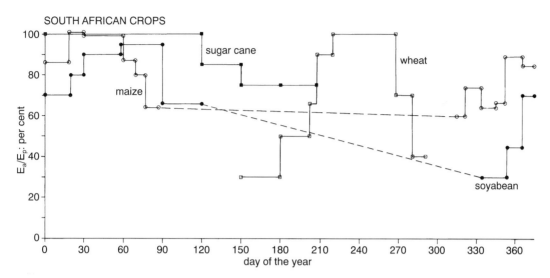

Figure 4.9 Seasonal variations of the crop factors E_a/E_p per cent for four crops in South Africa.

tial rate E_t. After that, E_a equals the rate at which the soil can deliver moisture to the roots, E_m. The latter depends on the relative moisture content M of the soil within the layer containing the roots, where M is expressed as a fraction of unity. A value of zero means that the soil contains no moisture available to the plants, so they wilt. (The soil still contains some moisture, but it is held too tightly between the particles to be available to the roots.) A value of unity for M corresponds to soil at '*field capacity*', which is soil that has been saturated and then allowed to drain for a day. The difference between these extreme conditions defines the '*maximum available moisture*', which amounts to 111 mm depth of water in a metre depth of heavy clay soil, but 155 mm for a sandy loam, for instance.

Figure 4.10 shows E_m as equal to $16\,M^2$ mm/d, determined experimentally. So E_a *equals whichever of E_t and E_m is the less*, given the particular soil wetness M.

The actual evaporation rate from vegetation is affected also by the rainfall and dew (Section 4.7) held by the canopy. This can amount to a layer a millimetre deep on vegetation with a large total leaf area. Such a layer is a significant fraction of a typical day's evaporation. This intercepted water on leaves evaporates rapidly, presumably at the potential rate E_t. On the other hand, evaporation from the soil depends on how much it is shaded by the vegetation. The combined evaporation from intercepted water and soil can sometimes equal that from the crop itself.

In broader terms, the actual evaporation E_a is slightly less than the precipitation P in any region where P is less than the potential evaporation rate E_t. Then the difference $(P - E_a)$ approximates the runoff (Chapter 10). On the other hand, E_a approximates E_t in humid climates.

4.6 VALUES OF THE EVAPORATION RATE

The global average of the evaporation rate must equal the annual mean rainfall of about 1,020 mm (Chapter 10), since the input into the atmosphere must equal its output. This implies an average latent-heat flux from the surface of

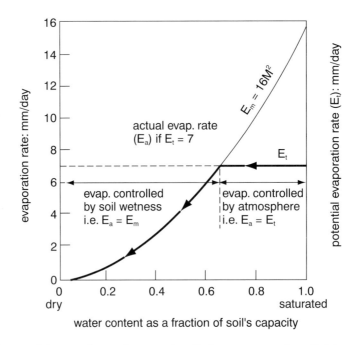

Figure 4.10 The change of the actual rate of evaporation E_a from a crop as the soil dries out, showing it as a two-stage process. When the soil is initially fully wetted, E_a is the potential rate E_t, which depends primarily on atmospheric conditions (i.e. net radiation, temperature, humidity and wind speed), and secondarily on the crop's roughness and albedo. In the first stage of drying, E_t is maintained so long as the soil can provide water to the crop at that rate. The water content of the soil M is eventually insufficient to allow evaporation to continue at that rate, and so E_a declines during the second stage. Various measurements have shown that the rate at which soil can supply water is proportional to M^2, and E_a falls correspondingly. In this second stage, E_a is limited by the soil's ability to *supply* water, whereas the limitation in the first stage was atmospheric *demand*.

80 W/m^2, which is a substantial fraction of the net radiation available at the surface (Figure 2.17).

The evaporation rate varies with latitude for reasons associated with the Dalton evaporation equation (Note 4.E). Firstly, the surface water's vapour pressure is affected by its temperature, which varies with latitude (Chapter 11). **Table 4.2** shows the importance of evaporation from the oceans, and from the lowest latitudes, where global radiation is greatest (Figure 2.11). Secondly, the air's humidity varies between the pole and the equator (Chapter 6), affecting the vapour pressure e in Dalton's equation. Thirdly, there are differences of wind strength

Table 4.2 Effect of latitude on the actual annual evaporation, in millimetres depth per annum

Latitude (°S)	Oceans (mm/a)	Land (mm/a)	Overall (mm/a)
0–10	1,380	1,330	1,370
10–20	1,550	1,050	1,510
20–30	1,390	410	1,310
30–40	1,200	520	1,180
40–50	880	530	860
50–60	560	–	550

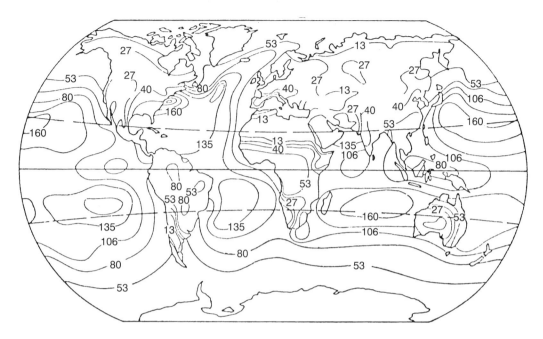

Figure 4.11 Variation over the Earth of the annual mean latent-heat flux (W/m^2). Multiply the numbers by 12.7 to convert from latent heat flux (W/m^2) to annual evaporation (mm/a).

around the globe (Chapter 12). Fourthly, evaporation inland is less because water is scarcer (Section 4.5).

The global pattern of actual evaporation rates is illustrated in more detail in **Figure 4.11**. Values exceed 150 W/m^2 (i.e. 1,920 mm/a or 5.3 mm/day) over subtropical oceans in the southern hemisphere, especially just north of the Tropic of Capricorn where cloudiness is least (Chapter 8). Other high values are seen just east of the continents, locally exceeding the energy available from net radiation – a paradox which is considered in the next chapter. The lowest evaporation values occur at the Poles and over subtropical deserts, such as the interior of Australia, where they are less than 200 mm/a. The average evaporation rate from all the Earth's land is about 420 mm/a, and from the oceans about 1,260 mm/a.

The distribution of *pan* evaporation E_p is almost opposite to that of actual evaporation E_a. Over the oceans the two are similar, but E_p is more in subtropical deserts, whereas E_a is much less. E_a in a desert might be only 5 per cent of E_p, for instance. Over Australia, E_p ranges from less than 800 mm/a in western Tasmania (i.e. 2.2 mm/d) to more than 16 mm/d in January in central Australia (**Figure 4.12**).

Rapid Evaporation

Evaporation is generally limited by the available amount of net radiation (Chapter 5), except that the rate can be substantially enhanced in small and isolated wet areas, like an irrigated field in dry country. This happens in two ways. Firstly, a gradually diminishing *oasis effect* (or edge effect) extends some 50 m into the field from the upwind boundary due to heat and dryness in

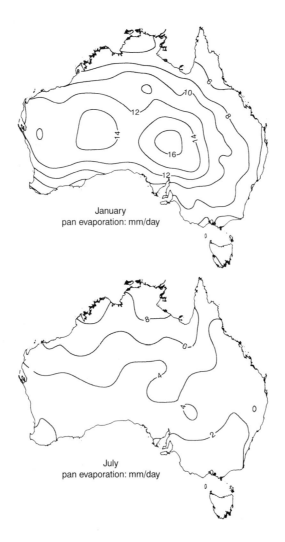

Figure 4.12 Class-A pan evaporation (mm/d) at places in Australia, in January and July.

the wind from relatively arid surroundings. Thus, evaporation of 5.3 mm was measured from a plot of irrigated lucerne in a dry area at Deniliquin in New South Wales during 7.5 daylight hours, which is fast, and a field of irrigated lucerne in Nevada evaporated 14.2 mm in one day. The same oasis effect has been found to lead to pan evaporation of up to 24 mm/d within dry surroundings in California.

Secondly, there can be a *clothes-line effect* in a tall crop or forest due to air flowing *through* the canopy and not just over it. The throughflow creates extra evaporation from within the canopy.

We have seen that evaporation rates can vary considerably, and hence the fraction of the incoming energy that is consumed as latent heat. This governs how much of the incoming radiant heat remains to warm the surroundings. Reconciliation of these aspects of climate is the subject of the 'energy balance' considered in the next chapter.

4.7 DEW

The opposite of evaporation is condensation (Figure 4.1), involving the same amounts of latent heat but *released* as sensible heat, instead of being absorbed (Section 4.1; Chapter 5). Some of the atmosphere's water vapour may condense onto surfaces chilled at night by the net loss of longwave radiation (Section 2.7). This is *dewfall*. It occurs once the air's temperature is such that the corresponding saturation vapour pressure e_s is less than the actual vapour pressure. It is as though a sponge has been shrunk by cooling so that its capacity becomes less than the volume of fluid it contains. We say the air has become 'supersaturated'. The excess spills out, condensed into liquid.

The condensation of that excess forms fog (Chapter 8) if the air is humid and the nocturnal cooling rapid. Otherwise it forms as dew on nearby surfaces, such as the leaves of plants. These tend to be colder than screen temperature at night (Section 3.5), so the adjacent air is first to become supersaturated.

As much as 0.3 mm of dew may be deposited during a twelve-hour night, liberating 17 W/m^2. However, less than that is normally deposited, even though it may seem more when concentrated on the tips of leaves. For instance, the average nightly deposit when dew fell was 0.13 mm during a series of measurements in Sydney There was dewfall only when the air was moist and calm, and the nocturnal sky was clear.

Even the small amount of moisture in dew can be useful in arid areas such as northern Chile. There it is collected by means of piles of stones, where the condensation drips to the inner base of the pile and is then shielded from the following day's sunshine. Dew may also be collected on sloping metal sheets. It makes plants grow at the foot of telegraph poles in the desert.

The latent heat which is released when dew condenses tends to offset the usual cooling at night, so that dewfall governs the subsequent day's minimum temperature (Section 3.4). In fact, the minimum cannot be much below the *dewpoint*, the temperature at which dew first forms (Chapter 6), because cooling below that causes further condensation which releases compensating latent heat.

Dew does not arise only from the cooling and supersaturation of the adjacent air. An additional kind is caused by *distillation* from the ground. The ground at night is warmer than the air and may be wet, so that it evaporates moisture into an atmosphere already almost saturated. Condensation follows onto surfaces like the leaves of plants, which cool more rapidly than the ground because of a smaller heat content and wider exposure to the sky.

A third source of moisture on leaves at daybreak is *guttation*. This is the exudation of moisture from the leaves of some plants, as a carry-over from the transpiration of the previous daytime. Neither guttation nor distillation affect the transfer of heat from the surface to the atmosphere, so they are irrelevant to the flows of energy which are related together in the next chapter.

NOTES

4.A Water molecules

4.B Protection of crops from frost

4.C Saturation vapour pressure and temperature

4.D Rates of evaporation

4.E Dalton's evaporation equation

4.F Effect of drop radius on its evaporation rate

4.G Crop evaporation and yield

4.H The Relative Strain Index of comfort

5

ENERGY BALANCES

5.1 THE ENERGY-BALANCE EQUATION

So far we have given separate consideration to three major determinants of the climatic environment: (i) the net flux of the radiation energy from the Sun to the ground (Section 2.8), (ii) its subsequent use in heating both the air (Sections 1.6 and 3.2) and the ground (Section 3.5), and (iii) the evaporation of water (Section 4.1). In later chapters, we shall elaborate on the ways in which these account for the humidity, cloudiness, rainfall and wind, which – along with temperature – constitute the weather in the short run and the climate in the long term. But at this point it is worth while to tie together what has been said about radiation, heating, and evaporation, as well as the melting of ice, photosynthesis, artificial heating (Section 3.7), wind friction and horizontal advection.

The processes just mentioned are all equivalent to flows of energy which can be combined by means of an *energy balance*, a special case of the general *balance equation*. In brief, this states that change equals the difference between input and output. We have already considered another special case, that of the *water balance* of an area (Section 4.5), which states the obvious truth that the change of water level

over a specified period equals the input minus the output during that time. Here, instead of water, we balance the amounts of *energy* flowing in unit time:

$$\begin{array}{c} \text{inflow} \\ \text{of energy} \end{array} = \begin{array}{c} \text{outflow} \\ \text{of energy} \end{array} + \begin{array}{c} \text{increase of} \\ \text{stored energy} \end{array}$$

or

$$\begin{array}{c} \text{increase of} \\ \text{stored energy} \end{array} = \begin{array}{c} \text{inflow} \\ \text{of energy} \end{array} - \begin{array}{c} \text{outflow} \\ \text{of energy} \end{array}$$

Either of the above is the *energy-balance equation*. An energy balance can be considered for any volume (in terms of joules per second, i.e. watts) or any surface (where the fluxes have units of W/m^2). The volume might be a person's body (Section 5.5), the bulb of a thermometer (Chapter 6), a parcel of air (Chapter 7) or the global atmosphere (Chapter 12). On the other hand, the surface that we consider most is that of the ground.

The energy-balance equation applies either to instantaneous conditions or to fluxes averaged over some period, such as a day or year. The equation is universally true, expressing what is called the 'principle of the conservation of energy' or the 'first law of thermodynamics' (Chapter 7).

Surface Energy Balance

The equivalent to the previous equations is the following, for energy fluxes at the ground surface:

$$R_n = \text{L.E} + \text{H} + \text{G} \qquad \text{W/m}^2$$

where R_n is the input of energy in the form of net-radiation, L the latent heat of evaporation (J/kg, Section 4.1), E the rate of evaporation (kg/m^2.s), H the convective flux of sensible heat away from the surface (Section 3.1), and G the heating of the ground (Section 3.5). The product L.E is the latent-heat flux (Section 4.5), often written as simply LE for short. An equation like that applies to most surfaces. Exceptions include an ocean surface, fast-growing vegetation or melting snow, which would require extra output terms on the right of the equation, for advection, photosynthesis (Section 1.2) or latent-heat-of-melting, respectively.

Notice the difference between the two kinds of equation involving net radiation R_n, here and in Section 2.8, respectively. The expression in Section 2.8 *defines* the net radiation, gives it a label; R_n is the sum of all radiation fluxes onto the surface. On the other hand, the energy-balance equation here is more than word-play, it describes an important quantitative feature of reality, the conversion of R_n into non-radiative forms of energy.

The simple form of the energy-balance equation at the ground's surface is shown in **Figure 5.1**. In that case, a net radiation *towards* the surface is regarded as positive and LE, H and G are positive if they move *away* from it. LE and H are usually positive, but the LE term is negative if dew forms, since the latent-heat transfer is then towards the surface. Likewise, the sensible-heat flow H is negative if the air is warmer than the surface, so that heat moves downwards to the surface. Also, the flux of heat conducted through the ground G is usually negative at night, as it then flows upwards towards the cooling surface.

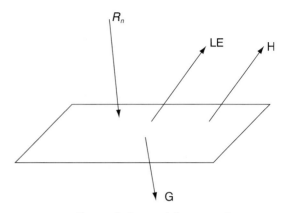

Energy balance at the ground

Figure 5.1 The chief components of the energy balance at the ground. Incoming net radiation R_n is balanced by the fluxes away from the surface, in heating the ground G, heating the air by convection H and in evaporation LE.

The ground-heat flux G in the equation above is typically about 20 per cent of R_n over an hour or so. However, it is negligible over the course of a whole day or more, since the daytime absorption is almost exactly cancelled by the night-time loss. The error in ignoring G is then no more than the uncertainty in measuring R_n. In that case, R_n is balanced by the sensible-heat flux H and the latent-heat flux LE, together. If the surface is also dry (so that LE is zero), R_n equals H, i.e. all the net-radiation input goes into heating the adjacent air. For example, H in central Australia is shown in **Figure 5.2** as $40 - 60$ W/m^2, which accounts for much of the net radiation, shown in Figure 2.17 as 80 W/m^2. On the other hand, H over the subtropical oceans is small compared with R_n, indicating that R_n there is largely balanced by LE, which is large (Figure 4.11).

Applications

A zero heat-storage term G means that temperatures are steady, and the balance equation

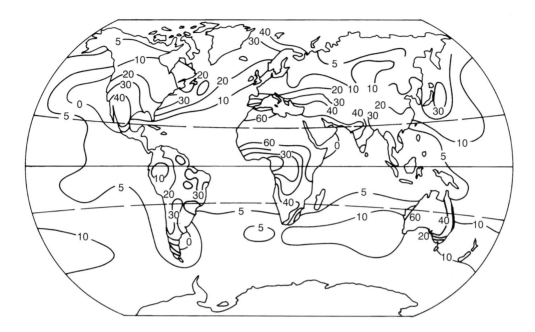

Figure 5.2 Annual mean sensible-heat flux H from the Earth's surface to the atmosphere, in units of W/m^2.

becomes simply the statement that inputs and outputs are equal, as in the case of the entire Earth (**Note 5.A**). Such an equation of equilibrium allows us to calculate the temperature of a white vehicle, in comparison with a black one in a hot climate (**Note 5.B**).

An energy-balance equation permits deducing any one of the terms from a knowledge of the others. For instance, consider the case of an ocean surface over a month. The overall storage term G is negligible over such a period, with daytime heat gains cancelled by nocturnal loss. Also, measurements show that there is little difference between the temperatures of the air and water near their interface, which implies zero sensible-heat flux H (Section 3.2). Moreover, advection is negligible in the case of a large ocean basin, where the affected edge is only a small fraction of the entire volume. Therefore, the energy-balance equation reduces to an equality between R_n and LE. So we can obtain the approximate long-term rate of evaporation from an ocean (which is hard to measure) by the relatively straight-forward determination of the net-radiation flux R_n there (cf. Figure 2.17 and Figure 4.11).

Also, the energy balance helps us to understand the processes causing cooling at night (**Note 5.C**) and to estimate evaporation (**Note 5.D**). In addition, the energy balance explains a *sol-air temperature*, the reading of a thermometer exposed to the Sun's radiation and the ambient wind (**Note 5.E**). It is the temperature reached by any exposed dry surface (Note 5.B) and by people outdoors, so that bright calm days feel acceptably warm even when the air is cold. Further examples of the usefulness of the energy balance are considered in the following sections.

Other Components of the Energy-balance Equation

Relatively small amounts of heat are used in heating of the ground G, in photosynthesis and in frictional heating of the ground by wind. Plants also use merely a small fraction of the incoming solar radiation R_s (Note 2.I). Heating due to the friction of the wind on the ground is trivial compared with net-radiation values (Section 2.8); it is less than 0.2 W/m^2, even with the high winds in Antarctica, for instance (Chapter 16). Wind is more important in causing the advection of sensible and latent heat (Notes 3.A and 4.D) than as a source of energy itself.

Until now we have mainly considered vertical heat fluxes, but there are *horizontal* transfers of energy too. These occur as sensible heat in the wind (especially during storms) and in ocean currents, and as latent heat in moist wind. There is a net advection of heat *towards* an area (i.e. *heat-flux convergence*) when the inflow exceeds the outflow, and this has to be included in the energy-balance equation for the area. Such contributions are important on a global scale (**Note 5.F**, Chapters 11 and 12).

5.2 ENERGY BALANCES OF LARGE SCALE

Figure 5.3 represents the annual average vertical fluxes of energy within the whole world. The three boxes represent different zones and the arrows stand for fluxes of energy between them. The energy-balance equation applies to each zone, with the total input exactly equal to the total output. Let us consider some details.

The top of the Earth's atmosphere receives an average of 342 W/m^2 from the Sun (Note 2.F) and we represent this as 100 units of energy in Figure 5.3. On average, the Earth returns about 30 units of shortwave radiation (i.e. 3 + 27) to space by reflection, which implies that the 'global albedo' is 30 per cent (Section 2.5), as seen from a satellite.

The surface receives about half the incoming extra-terrestrial radiation, with 24 units as direct radiation, and the other 26 units in the

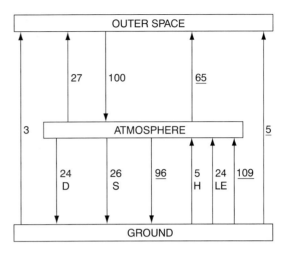

Figure 5.3 Long-term average fluxes of energy in the global atmosphere, with the underlined numbers representing longwave radiation, while D denotes diffuse shortwave radiation, S is direct solar radiation, H is sensible-heat flux and L.E latent-heat transfer. Numbers are percentages of the incoming solar radiation. Slightly different numbers are given for the various fluxes by other authors.

form of scattered radiation. The scattering is due to clouds (77 per cent, Section 2.3), gases in the atmosphere (18 per cent), and either dust particles or aerosols (5 per cent). There is absorption by the atmosphere of 23 units (100 − 50 − 27), due mainly to the gases (58 per cent), such as water vapour (Figure 2.2) and ozone (Section 1.4), and rather less to aerosols (28 per cent) and clouds (14 per cent).

It is evident from the numbers in Figure 5.3 that the atmosphere is a natural greenhouse (Note 2.L), because only 4 per cent of the longwave radiation emitted by the Earth's surface reaches space directly (i.e. 5/[109+5]). The 5 units emitted directly from the ground into space are mostly at a wavelength within the longwave-radiation window (Section 2.3, Note 2.H). The other 65 units of longwave radiation into space come from the atmosphere. The total of 70 units of longwave radiation plus the 30 units of reflected sunshine balance the input of 100 units, so that there is no overall warming or cooling. Likewise for the other zones in Figure 5.3.

We are particularly interested in the global energy balance at the Earth's surface, indicated by the box labelled 'ground'. The global-average *surface* albedo is only 6 per cent {3/(24 + 26)}, which is much less than the planetary albedo discussed above. The chief reason is that oceans cover so much of the Earth (Note 1.A) and have a particularly low albedo (Section 2.5).

Net radiation to the ground (Section 2.8) amounts to 29 units (i.e. 24 + 26 + 96 − 3 − 109 − 5), whilst the shortwave radiation from the sky is (24 + 26) or 50 units, so the radiation efficiency (Section 2.8) is 58 per cent (i.e. 29/50). The net radiation is offset by a latent-heat flux of 24 units (mainly from the oceans) and 5 units of sensible-heat flux.

Figure 5.3 shows that, on the whole, the radiation received by the ground contains almost twice as much longwave sky radiation (96 units) as shortwave solar radiation (50 units), which may seem surprising. Observe also that the terrestrial radiation (109 units) exceeds the sky radiation, since the ground is warmer (Section 2.7).

Latitude

The distribution of vertical energy fluxes in various latitudinal belts of the Earth's surface is shown in **Figure 5.4**. (The evaporation figures reflect the variation shown in Table 4.2.) The greatest inputs are at latitudes around 30°, where there is least cloud (Chapters 8 and 12). Sensible and latent-heat fluxes are about equal from the world's lands, on average, but sensible heat is dominant in the dry subtropics (at 20°–30° latitudes) and evaporative-energy transfer dominant in the humid tropics and at sea. The energy-balance equation for a latitude belt of ocean includes a term for advection,

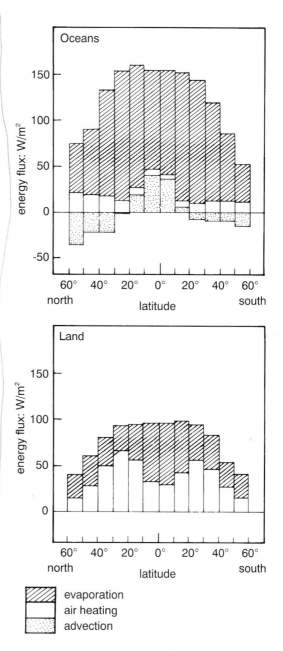

Figure 5.4 Components of the energy balance at the ground in each latitudinal belt. Each bar in total represents the magnitude of the input of net radiation, divided according to the outputs of latent heat L.E and sensible heat H, and advection A in the case of oceans.

which is *negative* if there is a net input of heat from the currents (Note 5.F).

Table 5.1 shows the long-term average net radiation onto several continents and an ocean and its use in evaporation, sensible heat and advection. Net radiation is upwards at the poles (Figure 2.17) and heat convection downwards. Warming of the air by the ground is particularly strong in Australia.

Values in Table 5.1 enable a comparison of the climates of Australia and South America, which receive similar amounts of net radiation. However, the much greater rainfall in South America (Chapter 10) leads to wetter conditions and hence much more evaporation than in Australia, leaving less energy to heat the atmosphere.

5.3 LOCAL ENERGY BALANCES

Let us now consider some examples of local energy balances at the ground-level surface, which change continuously according to the position of the Sun, the weather and the surface

conditions. First we deal with balances at specific sites, and then variations over a day and from one year to another.

Cold Surfaces

At noon on a day in February at 4,400 m on the Meren Glacier (near the equator in New Guinea), there was both (i) incoming net radiation of 398 W/m^2 to the snow and (ii) a 31 W/m^2 flux of sensible heat from the air. The total income of 429 W/m^2 went into sublimation and evaporation from the surface (153 W/m^2) and into warming and melting the snow (276 W/m^2, i.e. 429 − 153). Such a description of the energy flows shows precisely what processes were dominant. It shows, for instance, that 64 per cent (i.e. 276/429) of the incoming energy was used in warming and melting the snow (Chapter 10).

Values from Antarctica in midwinter are shown in **Table 5.2**. The net radiation is opposite and equal to the total of the other three factors, and is negative (i.e. upwards, away from the surface). It is offset partly by a downward

Table 5.1 Average energy fluxes in selected regions. The fluxes are of net radiation R_n, latent heat *LE*, vertical convection of sensible heat into the air *H*, and horizontal advection *A*. The signs of the energy fluxes (W/m^2) are consistent with Figure 5.1

	Average energy fluxes: (W/m^2)			
Region	R_n	L.E	H	A
Antarctica	−15	0	−15	0
Australia	93	38	54	0
South America	93	67	25	0
Indian Ocean	113	102	9	2

Table 5.2 Typical Antarctic energy balances in midwinter; the signs of the energy fluxes (W/m^2) are consistent with Figure 5.1

Place	R_n	L.E	H	G or A*
South Pole	−20	−1	−18	−2
Coast	−43	+6	−39	−10
Ocean	−12	+24	+29	−65

* Ground heat-flux *G* for land surfaces, but advection *A* in ocean currents

flux of sensible heat from the air, which must therefore be warmer than the ground (Figure 1.9, Note 3.A). Also, there is some sublimation of vapour onto the ground at the pole, and considerable advection of heat in ocean currents from lower latitudes.

The circumpolar oceans are generally frozen in winter, except for temporary gaps in the ice. They occupy only a few per cent of the area, but importantly affect evaporation and the sensible-heat flux.

We can compare the fluxes in Antarctica shown in **Figure 5.5** with those in Figure 5.3 for the whole world. There is less attenuation of the incoming solar radiation by cloud and air turbidity, since 78 per cent reaches the ground instead of 56 per cent, and the ice of Antarctica reflects a notable amount of shortwave radiation (65 units instead of 6). The surface flux of sensible heat is downwards towards the surface, and exceeds the upwards latent-heat flux due to the sublimation of snow. The net radiation loss of 27 units (i.e. $100 - [65 + 16] - 46$) shows that Antarctica is an *energy sink,* i.e. it absorbs energy on the whole (Figure 2.18). The absorption of heat is made good by heat-flux convergence in the winds.

Another set of data was obtained over six days in summer, from an ice-free rock valley in Antarctica. The surface at noon was about 10 K warmer than the air 1.6 m above the ground, and simultaneously the upwards flow of heat into the air was 33 W/m^2. This was only a small part of the incoming net radiation, which was 130 W/m^2. The heat consumed in evaporation was measured as 16 W/m^2. So the energy-balance equation shows that the remainder (due to the noontime flux of heat into the ground) was 81 W/m^2 (i.e. $130 - 16 - 33$).

A Lake

Figure 5.6 shows the terms of the energy balance each month at the surface of a reservoir in New South Wales. The highest rate of evapora-

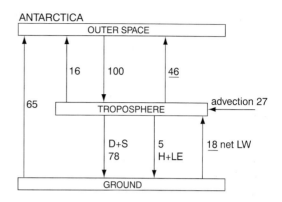

Figure 5.5 Annual mean fluxes of energy over the Antarctic. Underlined numbers refer to longwave radiation. [D + S] is the sum of direct and diffuse shortwave radiation. [H + LE] is the sum of sensible and latent-heat fluxes.

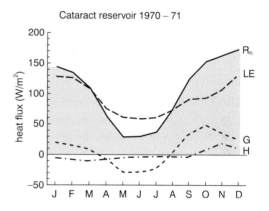

Figure 5.6 Variation of the components of the energy balance at the surface of Cataract reservoir in New South Wales.

tion (equivalent to a latent-heat flux of about 130 W/m^2) represents a lowering of the lake level by 4.6 mm daily (Note 4.D). Incoming net radiation was less than the heat used in evaporation from March–August, but greater in the warmer months. The small values of H indicate that little heat was carried away in the wind, i.e. there was not much difference between lake-surface and surface-air temperatures (Note 3.A).

The term G in the case of a lake is a heat-storage term, and a negative G implies heat flowing upwards towards the surface (Figure 5.1), i.e. the lake is cooling. In the present case, the lake cooled between April and July, allowing the latent-heat flux to exceed the net radiation. The lake was coldest in August and warmest in late March.

Other Examples

(a) The energy balance in Chilton Valley in the South Island of New Zealand shows a strong seasonal variation (**Figure 5.7**). All fluxes are small in winter. November is a dry month so there is less evaporative cooling of the soil, consequently its surface temperature rises, and therefore there is an increase of the sensible-heat flux to the atmosphere. Data on soil heating G show a small absorption of heat from October to February and a corresponding release in the cooler months.

(b) **Figure 5.8** shows the seasonal variations of net radiation, evaporation and convection at four places. There are two net-radiation maxima at the lowest latitudes, when the Sun passes overhead at noon (Section 2.2). Annual fluctuations increase with latitude, in accord with the larger annual range of temperature (Section 3.3). Most of the net radiation is used in evaporation in the cases of the oceans and the moist climate of Manaus in the Amazon basin. The opposite is true of Mocamedes at the northern end of the Namibian desert, where there is practically no water for evaporation.

(c) Apart from average values over a month or more, there can be large changes from day to day, or hour to hour, depending on changes of cloud, rain or wind temperature. **Figure 5.9** illustrates the example of a recently irrigated wheatfield near Canberra in spring. The latent-heat flux exceeded the radiation energy for

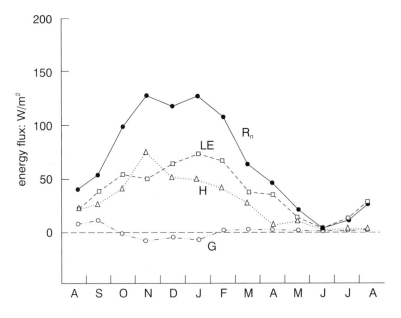

Figure 5.7 Monthly means of the energy-balance components in the Chilton Valley (NZ, 35°S). For each month, R_n equals the sum of H, L.E and G.

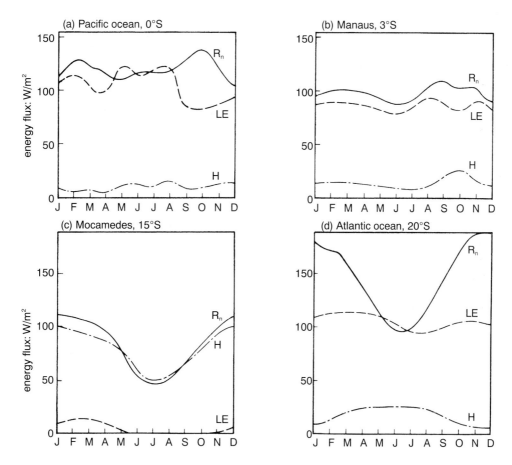

Figure 5.8 Annual variation of net radiation (R_n), evaporative cooling L.E and convection H, at four places. (a) Pacific ocean at 0°S, 150°E, just off New Guinea; (b) Manaus, Brazil, at 3°S; (c) Mocamedes, Angola, at 15°S; (d) Atlantic ocean at 20°S, 10°E.

much of the daytime, and a substantial amount of heat flowed into the ground, so H was negative, indicating air much warmer than the ground, especially from 10 a.m. till noon.

(d) Another example of varying energy balances is in **Figure 5.10**, relating the monthly rainfall to the monthly mean daily-maximum temperature at Alice Springs, in January, in different years. The temperature is lower in wet months because of the cloud and the heat used in evaporating the rain.

5.4 ALTERING THE ENERGY BALANCE

As examples of changing an energy balance, we will consider the effects of preventing evaporation at the surface, altering the ground's albedo, and differences due to the orientation of sloping ground.

A layer of oil on a lake greatly reduces evaporation, and a clear-plastic cover has the same effect on a ground surface (**Table 5.3**). This leaves all the incoming net radiation available to warm the surface and the adjacent air. The

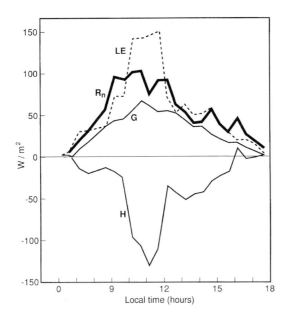

Figure 5.9 Comparisons of the available energy R_n with the amounts used in evaporation L.E, heating of the ground G and heating of the air H from a wheat crop in Canberra, Australia. At any moment, R_n equals the sum [LE + G +H].

warmer surface increases three fluxes: (i) the upwards terrestrial radiation (*reducing* the incoming net radiation R_n, (ii) the sensible-heat flux to the atmosphere H, and (iii) the conduction of heat downwards into the ground or lake G. So a new balance arises automatically, with a reduced R_n matched by an increased (H + G).

Carbon powder spread onto clean snow dramatically increases the absorption of incoming radiation and therefore promotes the clearing of snow. The albedo of snow is thus reduced from about 80 per cent to 5 per cent, so that the

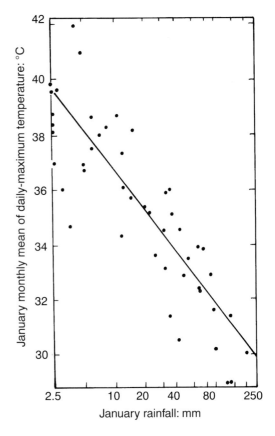

Figure 5.10 Effect of summer rainfall at Alice Springs on the daily-maximum temperature.

surface absorbs almost five times as much short-wave radiation, warming the surface. This promotes sublimation, and melting and runoff occur when temperatures reach 0°C.

Also, a lowering of albedo accelerates evaporation in getting salt from sea water within shallow ponds exposed to the Sun. Adding methylene-blue dye to the brine reduces its

Table 5.3 Example of the effects of a clear impermeable plastic cover on components of the energy balance; the signs of the energy fluxes (W/m²) are consistent with Figure 5.1

Energy flux	R_n	L.E	H	G
Bare soil	154	143	24	−13
Covered	138	0	127	+11

albedo, so that more solar radiation is absorbed, increasing the net radiation (Section 2.8), thereby making more energy available for evaporation.

Coating the leaves of an orange tree with (white) kaolinite to increase the albedo has been found to lower leaf temperatures in the daytime by 3–4 K, and so the rate of evaporation falls, conserving water. Likewise for leaves of a rubber plant, though to a smaller extent.

The direction in which sloping land faces governs the amount of radiation received, and therefore the amounts of energy going into heating the air and perhaps evaporation. **Table 5.4** gives results showing substantially less heating of the air against a slope facing away from the Sun, whereas evaporation differed little. (Of course, there may have been different rainfalls on the two slopes to complicate matters.)

5.5 THE ENERGY BALANCE OF THE HUMAN BODY

The climate affects our feelings of comfort (Notes 3.D, 3.E, 3.J and 4.H) by challenging *homeostasis,* the maintenance of a steady body-core temperature. This depends on balancing the various energy inputs and outputs of the core of the body, the balance being controlled by a part of the brain called the *hypothalamus.* Body temperatures rise as the result of (i) solar radiation, (ii) shivering, (iii) exercise and (iv) *metabolic processes*, i.e. normal body functioning. Cooling occurs either through panting (i.e. evaporation from the lungs) or an increase of blood circulation to the skin (i.e. the skin flushes), to carry more heat away from the core, followed by (i) sensible-heat flux from the skin to the air, (ii) longwave radiation to the surroundings, and (iii) the evaporation of perspiration (Notes 4.D and 4.H). Clothing provides insulation that reduces all these three processes. Also the body reduces them automatically when we feel cold by constricting the blood vessels near the skin, thus reducing the transport of heat from the body's core (**Figure 5.11**).

Sweat

Humans are outstanding amongst animals in their ability to sweat profusely from the skin, because of hairlessness. An adult can sweat up to 3 litres an hour or so, representing a loss of almost 4 per cent of body weight hourly. A loss of 2 per cent of body weight causes great thirst, and 8 per cent makes the tongue swell so that speech and then breathing become difficult. Hard work in the open at 30°C may take 10 litres a day. However, a typical figure for someone at rest is only 0.8 l/d, about half of which evaporates in the lungs and then is exhaled.

Sweating starts when the skin temperature exceeds about 30°C. This can occur, for instance, when the air temperature is only 3°C, if the body is being heated by 640 watts of exercise. On the other hand, the sweating mechanism collapses if the body temperature reaches 41°C, and then further heating is unchecked. Difficulty in sweating is why the elderly are more vulnerable to high temperatures (Note 3.C).

One's survival in a hot climate depends on

Table 5.4 Example of the effect of a slope's orientation to the Sun on the energy balance of a hillside's bare soil; the signs of the energy fluxes (W/m^2) are consistent with Figure 5.1

Slope	R_n	L.E	H	G
Facing away from the Sun	69	20	41	8
Flat	157	24	109	24
Facing towards the Sun	204	36	146	22

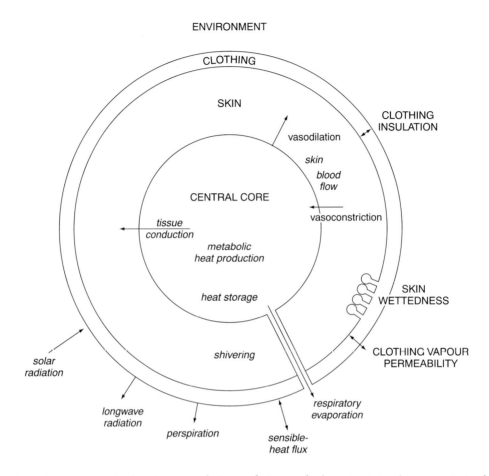

Figure 5.11 Processes involved in the energy balance of a human body maintaining homeostasis, i.e. keeping the body-core temperature steady. There are four different layers – the central core, the skin, the clothing and the ambient environment – and heat fluxes between them are indicated in italics.

the availability of water to replenish what is lost as sweat. With daily maxima above 37°C in a desert, one can survive without water for only about four days by resting still, or two days by travelling at night and resting in the daytime. A night traveller who drank four litres daily could survive for five days.

Loss of a litre hourly by sweating represents 400 W/m² from a nominal skin area of 1.7 m², so the cooling by sweating is considerable. We can compare it with metabolic heating of 44 W/m² when sleeping, 120 W/m² if strolling, 460 W/m² when running at 10 km/h and 520 W/m² during heavy manual labour. At the other extreme, shivering can generate up to 250 W/m².

That example of the human body concludes our consideration of energy balances. It demonstrates again how universally applicable and how illuminating the concept is.

NOTES

5.A Why doesn't the world get hotter?

5.B Does a car's colour influence its temperature?

5.C Factors governing the daily minimum temperature

5.D Estimation of evaporation

5.E Sol-air temperatures

5.F Energy balances of the southern hemisphere

Part III
WATER

6

HUMIDITY

6.1 THE HYDROLOGIC CYCLE

Now we turn from the flows of energy about the Earth to deal with the resulting movements of water. These include the process of evaporation discussed in Chapter 4, resulting in water vapour in the atmosphere. Water vapour is an important greenhouse gas (Section 2.7) and a key component of the *hydrologic cycle* symbolised in **Figure 6.1**.

The hydrologic cycle consists of the circulation of water from land and ocean to atmosphere, then condensation, normally into cloud, followed by precipitation back either to the oceans, or to the land, where the water either evaporates or flows back to sea and evaporates there. The continual movement between the parts in **Figure 6.2** is like the cycles of carbon dioxide illustrated in Figure 1.3. Such a pattern of related processes is called a *system*. Within this system, the atmosphere holds very little of the world's water, and the time any molecule spends as atmospheric humidity is only a few days, on average (**Note 6.A**).

The world contains huge amounts of each kind of water, together constituting the *hydrosphere*. The mass of vapour in the air is about thirteen million million tonnes (i.e. 13×10^{12} tonnes, or 13 teratonnes), which could provide a rainfall of 25 mm over the entire Earth. Lakes, rivers and underground water together make up a thousand times this amount. The Antarctic and Arctic ice-caps hold nearly three times as much again and the oceans a further thirty times as much (i.e. 1.4×10^{18} tonnes). Such quantities imply an important role in atmospheric processes.

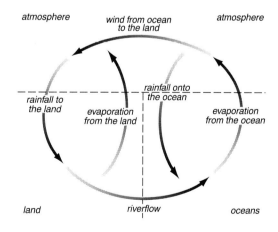

Figure 6.1 Symbolic pattern of flows of water in the hydrologic cycle.

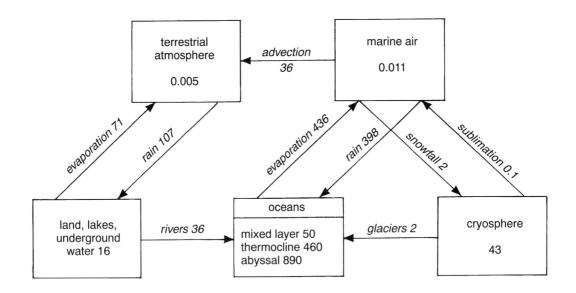

Figure 6.2 Quantities involved in the hydrologic cycle. A box represents a storage, whose capacity is expressed in petatonnes (i.e. 10^{15} tonnes). The italicised numbers represent annual flows in teratonnes (i.e. 10^{12} tonnes). Slightly different numbers are given by various authors.

On the way from atmosphere to ocean, some of the water spends appreciable time in the *cryosphere*, the regions of snow and ice on high mountains and at the Poles. Ninety per cent of the ice now is in Antarctica; there was twice as much there during the Ice Ages of the 'Pleistocene epoch' ending 10,000 years ago (Chapter 15).

A consequence of a greater rainfall and smaller evaporation in the northern hemisphere, compared with the southern (see Preface), is that, on average, winds must carry moisture northwards across the equator, and oceans flow southwards across it, to maintain the continuity of the hydrologic cycle.

6.2 DESCRIBING THE AIR'S HUMIDITY

The quantity of water in a given amount of air can be stated in several ways (**Note 6.B**). The most common are as follows:

Vapour Pressure (hPa)

This index of atmospheric water is indirect, in terms of the consequent vapour pressure e (in hectopascal units) discussed in Section 4.2. It is proportional to the water-vapour content of the air. The variation of the *saturation* (i.e. maximum) vapour pressure with temperature was given in Table 4.1, and is illustrated in **Figure 6.3**, using the right-hand vertical scale. However, the vapour pressure of air in the real world is normally less than the saturation value; air's condition is generally represented by a point to the *right* of the curve in Figure 6.3, like G. Bodies of air with the characteristics shown by A, B, C, D and F in Figure 6.3 are *saturated* (or moist), while air indicated by E (to the *left* of the curve) is *super-saturated*.

When the air's temperature increases from 0°C to 5°C, the extra water vapour that can be held is shown by the distance between the horizontal lines through D and C for instance, equivalent to about 2.5 g/m^3 in this case. The

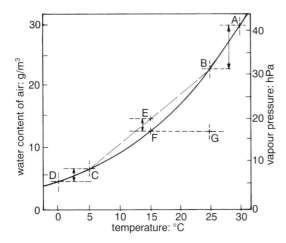

Figure 6.3 The water-vapour content and vapour pressure of saturated air at various temperatures, from Table 4.1. (The values of absolute humidity shown on the left vertical axis apply only at sea-level.)

rapid increase of saturation water-vapour pressure with temperature is known as the Clausius Clapeyron effect. A consequence is that a much larger additional amount BA (i.e. 7 g/m^3) can be accommodated in heating from 25°C to 30°C. These amounts condense back out of the air as cloud or dew when saturated air is cooled back to the lower temperature. Comparison of what can be held at different temperatures explains why rainfalls are much heavier in warm climates (Chapter 10).

Dewpoint (°C)

Another measure of atmospheric water is the dewpoint temperature, already mentioned in Section 4.7 and Note 5.C. The term is often shortened to *dewpoint*. It is a point on a temperature scale, not a point in space, being the temperature to which the air must be cooled for the moisture present to represent saturation. Alternatively, it is the temperature of a can of drink from the refrigerator when the dew just disappears from the surface. In other words, it is

the temperature of water with a vapour pressure equal to that of the ambient atmosphere. Air cooled below the dewpoint deposits dew on available surfaces, or else forms cloud droplets (Note 6.B).

An analogy is with water in a sponge, whose capacity represents the maximum amount of moisture that can be held as vapour, at the temperature around. So a full sponge represents saturated air. The more common situation of unsaturated air is like the sponge when only part full. Then cooling of the air resembles squeezing the sponge smaller, since cool air can hold less vapour (Section 4.2). Eventually the sponge's capacity is reduced to the volume of the water within it, i.e. the sponge is small enough to be full. This corresponds to the dewpoint. Further squeezing of the sponge makes excess water leak out, representing dew or cloud (Section 4.7).

Advantages of the dewpoint as a way of describing air's water content include the obvious physical meaning, the ease of measurement (just cool the air until dew forms, and then note the temperature), simple units (i.e. degrees Celsius) and direct comparability with the current air temperature to ascertain nearness to saturation. Another point in favour is that it can be compared with the measured daily-minimum temperature to check them both: it is unlikely that the minimum can be much below the dewpoint, since condensation occurs below dewpoint, releasing heat which prevents further cooling.

A disadvantage is that the dewpoint changes when the air rises to levels of lower pressure, even when no condensation takes place (Note 6.B).

Frostpoint (°C)

The counterpart of dewpoint is the *frostpoint* when temperatures are below freezing. It is the temperature at which *ice* has the same vapour pressure as that of water vapour in the air. At that temperature, the rate of water molecules escaping from ice matches the rate of those from the air impacting on the ice surface, i.e. their vapour pressures are equal. The rate is less than in evaporation from *supercooled water* at the same temperature, i.e. from water that remains unfrozen despite being colder than 0°C – as can occur in clouds (Chapters 8 and 9). The reason for the lower rate of escape from ice (i.e. its lower vapour pressure) is that water molecules are bound more strongly within the solid than within the liquid. In fact, the extra binding force is why the solid is more rigid and why latent heat is needed for melting (Section 4.1). It follows that the frostpoint is higher than the dewpoint; ice has to be warmer than water to match the air's vapour pressure. For instance, an atmosphere with a vapour pressure of 5 hPa is in balance with water at -2.7°C and ice at -2.4°C. Similarly, the vapour pressure of water at -10°C is 2.86 hPa, whilst that of ice at the same temperature is only 2.60 hPa. These small differences are important in the 'Bergeron process' within clouds which contain both supercooled droplets and ice crystals together (Chapter 9).

Relative Humidity (%)

A measure of atmospheric moisture more widely known than either vapour pressure or dewpoint is *relative humidity*, or simply RH. This is the ratio of the air's vapour pressure (e) to the saturated vapour pressure at the air's temperature e_s, expressed as a percentage, i.e. RH equals 100 e/e_s %. In other words, it is the ratio of the water *actually* present in the air to the maximum amount that *could* be present at the air's temperature.

It is a feature of RH that it determines the absorption of moisture by natural fibres, such as hair or timber. Conversely, the absorption of moisture (causing a string to twist, for example) gives a direct indication of the relative humidity, so it is easy to measure. On the other hand,

it is a poor index of the amount of moisture in the atmosphere, because RH depends on the temperature as well as on the moisture. If the temperature varies, so does the RH, even though the air's moisture (shown by the dewpoint, say) hardly alters (**Figure 6.4**).

The connection between RH and natural fibres is sometimes important. An RH above 85 per cent causes deterioration of stored cotton lint, promotes diseases on the leaves of crops (e.g. potato blight) and makes ironwork rust. Such high RH values occur for about 2,300 hours annually in Sydney, but only 1,700 in Adelaide, for instance.

The RH should be within 50–65 per cent (and the temperature range below 10 K) for the storage of documents; there is fungal damage at higher humidities and embrittlement of the paper at lower. Paintings are best stored at 45–55 per cent RH and 18–22°C. Sudden *changes* of humidity are particularly undesirable.

Saturation Deficit (hPa)

A better index of atmospheric moisture is the *saturation deficit* (D). This is the *difference* between the possible (i.e. the saturation vapour pressure e_s) and the actual vapour pressures ($e_s - e$), whereas the relative humidity is the *ratio* of the two. It differs from the term ($e_s - e$) in Dalton's equation (Note 4.E), where e_s refers to saturation at the *temperature of the water surface*. The saturation deficit D refers to conditions within the air alone, where e_s is the svp at the *air's temperature*. Fortunately, the two temperatures are often similar in the case of evaporation from an open water surface (Section 5.3). So the deficit can be related to evaporation in climates where it depends more on advection than on radiation (Notes 5.D and 6.B). Also, the deficit is related to crop growth (**Note 6.C**).

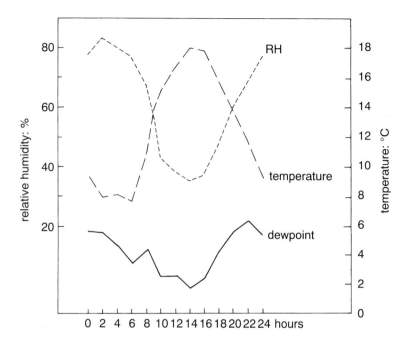

Figure 6.4 Variations during the day of the screen temperature, relative humidity (RH) and dewpoint, averaged over 17–22 September 1974 at Marsfield, Sydney. The large variation in RH is mostly due to the temperature cycle. The small variation in dewpoint is related to the local air flow, especially a sea-breeze in the afternoon.

Mixing Ratio *r* (g/kg)

This is the ratio of the mass of water vapour in a unit mass of air (excluding the vapour). Obviously, the ratio is very small, since air consists mostly of nitrogen and oxygen (Table 1.3). So the figure is multiplied by a thousand and expressed in units of grams of water per *kilogram* of dry air. For instance, air at sea-level at 10°C can hold up to 7.6 g/kg.

Unlike the dewpoint, the mixing ratio has the advantage of remaining unaltered when a parcel of air rises or falls in the atmosphere, so long as there is no evaporation or condensation. Such an unchanging characteristic is easier to consider than those which fluctuate, so the mixing ratio is the preferred measure of humidity in considering cloud (Chapter 8) and rain formation (Chapter 9).

6.3 MEASURING THE AIR'S HUMIDITY

The humidity may be measured by a *psychrometer* (**Figure 6.5**), which comprises two thermometers, one of which has a sleeve of wet fabric around the bulb, cooling the bulb by evaporation. This *wet-bulb thermometer* shows a reading T_w, lower than that of the *dry-bulb thermometer* which reads the ambient air temperature T. The difference $[T - T_w]$ is called the *wet-bulb depression* and is proportional to the rate of cooling of the wet bulb, due to the evaporation from its moist surface. Consideration of the energy balance of the wet bulb (**Note 6.D**) yields the equation of Henri Regnault (1810–78) for deriving the ambient vapour pressure *e*:

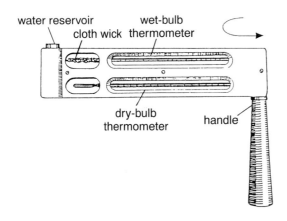

water reservoir   wet-bulb
    cloth wick   thermometer

dry-bulb
thermometer   handle

Figure 6.5 A sling psychrometer. Grasping the handle, one swings the thermometers around by a rapid wrist action to ventilate the bulbs through the air. After a minute or two the motion is stopped and readings are taken immediately.

$$e = e_{sw} - 0.67 \, (T - T_w) \qquad \text{hPa}$$

where e_{sw} is the saturation vapour pressure (Table 4.1) at the *wet-bulb* temperature T_w, *not the air temperature* T.

The equation indicates the practical requirements for reliable measurements. The two thermometers must be matched (showing the same value when both are dry), the wick must be saturated with water at about room temperature, and both thermometers must be adequately ventilated, e.g. by swinging them around (Figure 6.5).

One may obtain the vapour pressure without using Regnault's equation, by inserting the psychrometer readings into a *psychrometric chart* (**Figure 6.6**). This illustrates that all the moisture variables T, T_w, e, RH, T_d and r can be determined when any two are known.

Hygrograph

The current RH is shown directly by a *hygrometer*, whilst a *hygrograph* records the value on a chart. An example is a *hair hygrograph*, which depends on the extension of fibres resulting from their increased absorption of moisture in high humidities; Horace de Saussure (1740–99) found that human hair extends by about 2.5 per cent between extremes of dryness and wetness. But the length changes are not quite proportional to moisture variations, so the RH scale is irregular on the recording paper.

By the way, a *hygrometer* is quite different from a *hydrometer*, which measures the density of liquids and is used to check the battery fluid or radiator fluid in a car, for instance.

There are several sources of error in taking readings with a hygrograph. Dust can cause errors of up to 15 per cent, so the hairs should be washed frequently. The hairs should not be touched by hand, in case they become greasy. Even in perfect condition, a hygrograph may still have errors of 5 per cent, and yet more when cold or in a very dry region. There is also a lag on sudden changes of humidity; a good hygrograph normally adjusts to 90 per cent of any abrupt alteration within about three minutes, but it takes much longer at low temperatures. The instrument should be tapped lightly prior to taking a reading, to overcome friction of the pen on the paper.

Other Instruments

A different device for measuring humidity is used in radiosonde equipment (Section 1.6). It involves materials which are *hygroscopic* (or water-absorbing), such as lithium chloride, deposited in a thin layer on a slip of glass. Its electrical resistance is lowered when it absorbs water in a damp atmosphere, and this alters the transmitted radio signal, indicating the relative humidity of the air around the balloon up to several kilometres aloft. The water-absorption process is reversible, but sluggish above about 6 km, where temperatures are below $-20°C$. So water-vapour concentrations in the upper troposphere are measured nowadays by means of satellites.

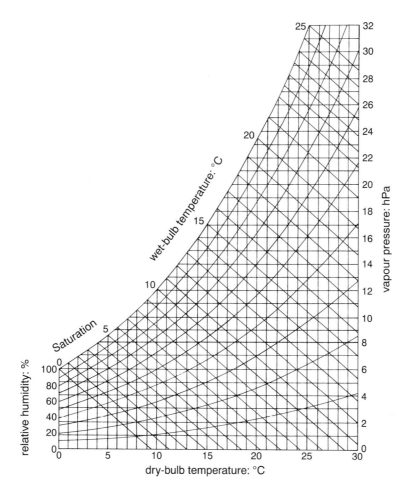

Figure 6.6 A psychrometric chart, to determine humidity variables (plus temperature) from any set of two known variables at a pressure of 1,000 hPa. Temperature is on the horizontal axis, vapour pressure on the vertical. The slanted, curved lines indicate relative humidity, and the diagonal straight lines show wet-bulb temperature.

Dewpoint hygrometers are used for accurate automated measurement of humidity. They determine the temperature of a tiny metal mirror, which is cooled electrically until the reflection of a laser beam is scattered by the formation of dew on the mirror.

An alternative to measuring atmospheric moisture is estimation, which can be done approximately by means of **Table 6.1.** This was derived empirically from measurements of daily extreme temperatures and dewpoints at many places, on the basis that nocturnal cooling (to the minimum) depends chiefly on the previous daily maximum and on the air's moisture (Section 3.4). The notion can then be turned into the proposition that the air's moisture content is roughly indicated by the daily extremes.

Table 6.1 Approximate estimation of the dewpoint from the daily extreme temperatures, based on monthly mean data from 127 places worldwide; values in italics at the bottom right have been extrapolated

Daily max. temperature (°C)	Daily minimum temperature (°C)										
	6	8	10	12	14	16	18	20	22	24	26
16	–	–	–	–	–	–	–	–	–	–	–
18	–	7	10	–	–	–	–	–	–	–	–
20	5	7	9	12	–	–	–	–	–	–	–
22	–	6	9	11	14	16	–	–	–	–	–
24	–	5*	8	10	13	15	18	–	–	–	–
26	–	–	7	9	12	14	17	20	–	–	–
28	–	–	5	8	11	13	16	19	22	24	–
30	–	–	–	7	9	12	14	18	20	23	26
32	–	–	–	5	8	11	13	16	19	22	25
34	–	–	–	–	6	9	12	15	18	21	24
36	–	–	–	–	5	7	10	13	16	19	22
38	–	–	–	–	–	5	7	10	13	17	20
40	–	–	–	–	–	–	5	8	11	*14*	*17*

* That is, the dewpoint is approximately 5°C when the daily maximum is 24°C and the minimum 8°C

6.4 HUMIDITY AT THE SURFACE

Values of vapour pressure at screen height depend on the latitude, proximity to the sea, elevation, the season, time of day and urbanisation. We will consider these in turn.

Latitude

Increasing latitude is associated with lower vapour pressures (**Figure 6.7**), because of lower temperatures. For instance, the average is only 0.07 hPa at Vostok, at 78°S in Antarctica. Figure 6.7 also shows that air is relatively dry over continents, especially in the winter, when particularly low temperatures reduce the saturation vapour pressure. Australia and the Sahara stand out as arid areas, whereas the Amazon basin is notably humid.

Mixing ratios decrease with latitude similarly (**Table 6.2**), and **Figure 6.8** shows how surface dewpoints too vary regularly with latitude at places in South America.

Distance from the Ocean

Vapour pressures are increased by evaporation from nearby warm oceans. Values from coastal places in Table 6.2 are notably higher than those from Alice Springs, in central Australia. Particularly low *relative humidities* occur inland; values at 3 p.m. in January east of Carnarvon on the coast of Western Australia are only about 15 per cent, on account of high temperatures and winds from the dry interior. Dewpoints may be only 2°C in winter in the interior of Queensland (**Figure 6.9**) and in Alice Springs (Table 6.2).

Elevation

Elevation is associated with less atmospheric moisture because of the colder temperatures and greater distance from the sea. Figure 6.8 shows that an increase of elevation by 1 km around 30–40°S in South America has the same effect on dewpoint as an increase of latitude by about 8 degrees, i.e. a reduction by

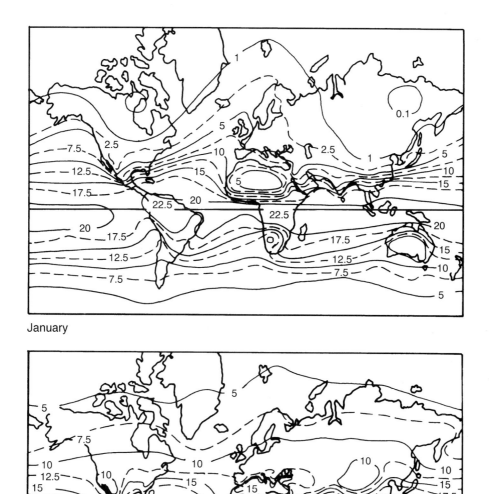

January

July

Figure 6.7 Global distribution of monthly mean vapour pressure (hPa) near the surface in January and July.

Table 6.2 Monthly mean vapour pressure (hPa) measured at 9 a.m. at various places in Australia; all places are coastal, except Alice Springs (546 m elevation), Canberra (570 m) and Kiandra (1,395 m)

Place	Latitude (°S)	January	April	July	October
Darwin	12	31.1	27.0	17.6	27.7
Townsville	19	26.1	22.1	14.1	19.7
Alice Springs	24	11.9	10.1	6.5	6.8
Perth	32	14.8	13.4	10.9	11.7
Sydney	34	18.8	15.0	9.6	13.0
Adelaide	35	11.9	11.3	9.4	10.1
Canberra	35	13.1	10.3	6.6	9.7
Kiandra	36	11.1	7.6	4.7	7.3
Hobart	43	11.0	10.0	7.6	9.1

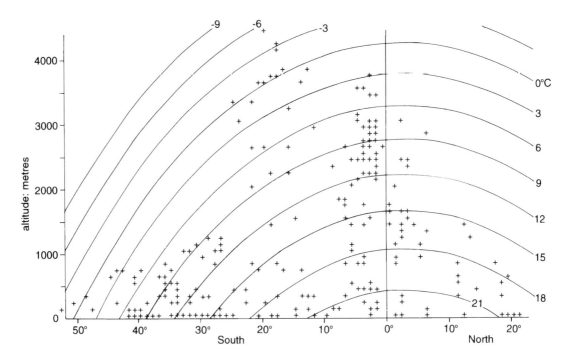

Figure 6.8 The variation of the annual mean dewpoint with latitude and elevation in South America. The crosses indicate surface stations.

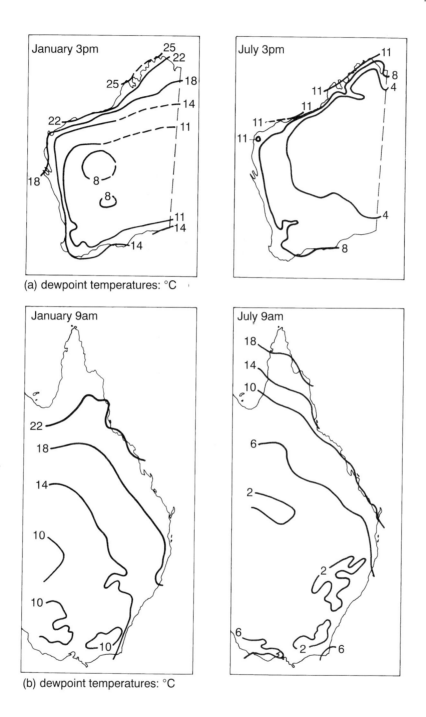

Figure 6.9 Lines joining places with equal dewpoints (a) in Western Australia, and (b) eastern Australia in summer (left) and winter (right).

about 5 K, though the variation is less nearer the equator.

Values from places at various elevations in Australia also illustrate the fall in vapour pressure. It is only 4.7 hPa (at 9 a.m. in July) at Kiandra (New South Wales) at 1,395 m, and 6.6 hPa on average at Canberra (at 570 m), compared with about 9 hPa in Melbourne and Sydney, beside the sea (Table 6.2). Likewise for the surface mixing-ratio at Pretoria in South Africa (**Table 6.3**). An analysis of data from places over the whole of Australia shows that the average rate of fall of dewpoint with elevation is between 3 K/km in July and almost 6 K/km in May, which resemble the annual-mean value of 5 K/km from Figure 6.8 for similar latitudes in South America. Figure 6.8 also indicates that an increase of elevation by 1 km around 30–40°S lowers the average dewpoint as much as an increase of latitude by about 8 degrees.

Season

Surface air generally contains more moisture in summer (Table 6.2, Table 6.3, Figure 6.7 and Figure 6.9). This is shown more dramatically by changes of the dewpoint temperature or saturation deficit than by figures for the relative humidity (**Table 6.4**). Dewpoints in eastern Australia are below 2°C in winter along the Dividing Range in south-east Australia, but above 22°C in northern Queensland in summer (Figure 6.9). Mixing ratios in South Africa also demonstrate great changes seasonally, as well as the effects of latitude, elevation and remoteness from the sea (**Figure 6.10**). Comparison with Figure 6.9 shows a similar decline of humidity with latitude, the equivalent dewpoints in Figure 6.10 ranging from around 27°C to 4°C, like the 25°C to 2°C in Australia. In both continents, the decrease of moisture is less rapid from the east coast, where low-latitude easterly winds (Chapter 12) extend the sea's humidity inland. Particularly dry conditions obtain in winter, because of the air's coldness, especially inland (Chapter 3).

Daily Variation

Several factors alter the water content of the surface atmosphere during the day. Weather

Table 6.3 Effects of latitude, season and height above sea-level on monthly mean mixing ratios

Place	Lat. (°S)	Month	Mixing ratio (g/kg)			
			Sea level	1,500 m	3,000 m	5,500 m
Lima	12	Jan	13.7	9.8	5.0	2.6
		July	10.0	3.2	2.5	1.6
Nandi	18	Jan	18.2	11.9	6.1	2.4
		July	13.4	8.3	3.9	1.5
Pretoria*	26	Jan	–	12.6	7.3	1.9
		July	–	4.7	1.6	0.3
Invercargill	46	Jan	7.5	4.6	2.5	0.9
		July	4.6	2.7	1.2	0.4
Argentine Island	65	Jan	3.3	2.3	1.4	0.4
		July	1.4	1.3	0.7	0.2
Halley Bay	76	Jan	2.0	1.4	0.7	0.3
		July	0.8	0.5	0.3	–
South Pole†	90	Jan	–	–	0.2	–

* Pretoria is at 1,368 m above sea-level
† The South Pole is at 2,992 m above sea-level

Table 6.4 Monthly variations of the daily mean temperature and 9 a.m. values of the dewpoint, vapour pressure, saturation deficit and relative humidity, at Sydney airport in 1969

Month	Temperature (°C)	Dewpoint (°C)	Vapour pressure (hPa)	Saturation deficit (hPa)	Relative humidity (%)	Mixing ratio (g/kg)
January	23.7	17.2	19.6	9.7	67	12.0
February	22.3	17.2	19.6	7.3	73	12.0
March	21.7	17.2	19.6	6.4	75	12.0
April	18.7	11.7	13.7	7.9	63	8.4
May	14.9	9.4	11.8	5.1	70	7.2
June	12.7	7.8	10.6	4.1	72	6.5
July	12.2	6.7	9.8	4.4	69	6.0
August	13.2	8.9	11.4	3.8	75	6.9
September	13.6	6.1	9.4	6.2	60	5.8
October	16.9	11.7	13.7	5.5	71	8.3
November	19.7	13.3	15.3	6.3	71	9.4
December	21.2	12.8	14.8	10.4	59	9.1

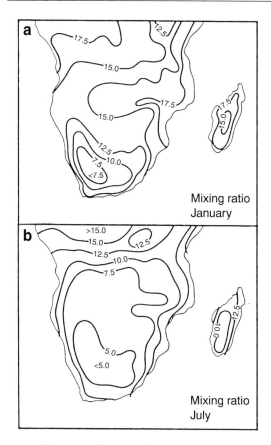

Figure 6.10 Distribution of monthly mean mixing ratio (g/kg) near the surface in January and July in southern Africa.

changes alter the import of moisture in winds, and there are nocturnal dew formation (which subtracts moisture from the surface air), evaporation of the dew in the morning (which raises the air's humidity again), daytime convection (which stirs dry air from aloft into the surface air), and sea breezes (which bring marine air inland in the afternoon). The outcome is that the dewpoint decreases in summer between 9 a.m. and 3 p.m. anywhere in Australia, but in winter there tends to be an *increase* in coastal south-east Australia.

Cities

Cities may reduce the surface humidity, because rainfall is drained away and not re-evaporated into the air. Thus measurements at St Louis (Missouri) showed reductions of 1.5 g/kg compared with the suburbs, and the difference was 3.5 g/kg at Mexico City at 2 p.m. in July. This leads to a lower RH, aggravated by urban heating (Section 3.7).

On the other hand, there can be a locally increased humidity within oasis-like cities such as Alice Springs, because of water brought to the city or pumped from underground. The mixing ratio averages 0.8 g/kg higher in Alice

Springs than at Ayers Rock, in similar country but remote from any city. Likewise, it is about 0.3 g/kg higher in the centre of Johannesburg than in the countryside around.

Effects

The humidity of surface air has an important effect on human comfort, which is considered in the next section. It also governs the drying out of forest kindling and grassland, and therefore controls the possibility of bushfires. A relative humidity maintained below 25 per cent makes timber and grass easy to ignite, whereas bush-fires will not spread when the RH has long been above 60 per cent.

6.5 HUMIDITY AND HUMAN COMFORT

We have already seen how the surrounding temperature can affect mortality (Note 3.C). It also affects our perception of comfort. People prefer a *neutral temperature* (i.e. neither too cool nor too warm) which depends partly on what they are currently used to. This preferred temperature is typically 21–22°C in air-conditioned buildings in the USA and Australia if the outdoor monthly mean temperature is below 10°C, but 24–25°C when the outdoor mean is above 20°C. The difference is chiefly due to clothing. However, the neutral temperature depends also on external factors such as the wind, sunshine and atmospheric humidity, and personal factors such as the amount of exercise being undertaken. The various components in the human-energy balance are shown in Figure 5.11. Clothing, wind, radiation and humidity control the loss of heat from the skin, and comfort generally arises from maintaining the skin at about 33°C. In that way, the core of the body can be kept close to the optimal 37°C, even when heavy exercise generates much heat.

The effect of the wind is generally to remove heat from the skin, cooling the body. But heat is transferred *to* the body by the wind when the air is hotter than the skin, worsening conditions. In that case, an energy balance can be maintained only by profuse perspiration (Section 5.5).

The air's humidity affects comfort by influencing the rate of evaporation of sweat, and hence the amount of evaporative cooling of the skin (Note 4.H). In fact, the sweating person is like a wet-bulb thermometer, so that the wet-bulb temperature has been suggested as a criterion of comfort. Unfortunately, that ignores the effects of radiation (Note 5.E), exercise (**Table 6.5**) and clothing (**Table 6.6**).

Many indices of climatic comfort have been proposed to allow for those other factors, apart from the wet-bulb temperature and the Relative Strain Index (Note 4.H). One of these involves a *weather-stress index*, discussed in **Note 6.E**, and another is a *thermal sensation scale* described in **Note 6.F**. More recently, extensive experimentation has led to the general adoption of the *standard effective temperature* (SET), as the basic index of comfort (**Note 6.G**). This is the temperature of air at 50 per cent RH (when the wind is 0.5 km/h and radiation *to* the body is equalled by that *from* it) which yields the same skin temperature and fraction of the skin which is wet as occurs in reality, in the *actual* temperature, humidity, radiation, activity and clothing conditions. It is assumed that the person is seated, with the corresponding metabolic rate (Table 6.5), and normal clothing (Table 6.6). This index of comfort is theoretically superior, but it depends on so many factors and is so complicated to derive that a simplified version is often used instead. This is the *new Effective Temperature* (ET*), the temperature of air at 50 per cent RH that creates the same heat loss from the body, assuming that standard radiation, wind, clothing and exercise conditions prevail. In other words, ET* takes only temperature and humidity into account (**Figure**

Table 6.5 Typical metabolic rates of adults (W/m^2); a rate of 60 W/m^2 is considered standard but this varies widely with the individual

Sleeping	40	Lifting, packing	120
Sitting	60	Sawing	105–235
Relaxed standing	70	Handling 50 kg bags	235
Walking on level		Pick-and-shovel work	235–280
at 3.2 km/h	115	Dancing	140–255
at 6.4 km/h	220	Tennis	210–270
Running at over 8 km/h	290	Basketball	290–440
Driving car	60–115	Competitive wrestling	410–505
House cleaning	115–200		

Table 6.6 Components of the total clothing insulation of a person, in clo units (a *clo* equals 0.155 m^2.K/ W). For instance, someone wearing only underpants, T-shirt and shorts would have insulation *I* equal to 0.18 clo (i.e. 0.04 + 0.08 + 0.06); total insulation of 0.6 clo is reckoned as standard

Hat	0.06	Thin skirt	0.14
Underpants	0.04	Thick skirt	0.23
Thick long socks	0.06	Thin short-sleeve dress	0.29
Boots	0.10	Thick long-sleeve dress	0.47
T-shirt	0.08	Thin long-sleeve sweater	0.25
Long-sleeve thin shirt	0.25	Thick long-sleeve sweater	0.36
Long-sleeve flannel shirt	0.34	Thin single-breasted jacket	0.36
Shorts	0.06	Thick double-breasted jacket	0.48
Thick trousers	0.24	Thick overcoat	0.73
Overalls	0.30		

6.11). The effect of humidity is trivial when ET* is below 23.6°C, but it becomes important at high temperatures. A drop of relative humidity by 10 per cent at 40°C improves conditions by lowering ET* by about 2 K.

An instance of humidity affecting human comfort is the annual 'Build-up' in Australia's Top End (i.e. northern part), in October and November, just prior to the onset of the monsoonal Wet in December to March (Chapter 12). Daily maxima remain about 33°C, but there is a gradual increase of afternoon dewpoint during the Build-up from about 19°C to 27°C, so the RH increases from 38 per cent to 69 per cent, and ET* rises from 32°C to an uncomfortable 35°C (Figure 6.11).

An indoor environment can be made more comfortable in climates as hot and dry as those of inland Australia by means of an *evaporative cooler,* discussed in **Note 6.H.** These are much cheaper than air conditioners, but need water.

6.6 HUMIDITY ALOFT

The water content of the atmosphere decreases greatly as one ascends in the free air into cooler layers (**Figure 6.12**). Most of the air's water is within 3 km of the ground. Mixing ratios at 1,500 m, 3,000 m and 5,500 m are typically only two-thirds, one-third, and one-eighth, respectively, of the value at sea-level (Table

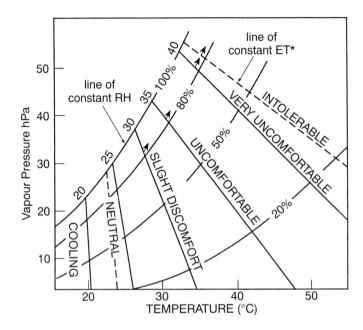

Figure 6.11 The variation of comfort in terms of the new Effective Temperature (ET*). The curved diagonal lines are relative humidity isopleths, just as on a psychrometric chart (Figure 6.6). The straight diagonal lines fanning out from the 100 per cent RH line are ET* isopleths with the value shown on top. Various human comfort zones are shown also. For instance, there is neutral comfort when ET* is 24°C, and conditions are intolerable when ET* exceeds 41°C.

6.3). This implies that cloud and rain form chiefly in the lowest layers of the troposphere (Chapters 8 and 9).

The relative humidity of subsiding air becomes low for two reasons. Firstly, it starts from levels where the vapour pressure is less, as just mentioned, and, secondly, the air is warmed by compression as it comes down (Chapter 7).

The pattern of the vertical distribution of moisture (i.e. the *humidity profile*) can be shown most conveniently by a special graph of the dewpoint or the mixing ratio, called an *aerological diagram*. This includes a temperature profile also. There are several versions, but the one used in Australia is the *skew T − log p diagram* (**Note 6.I**).

It is possible to total the amount in the column of air above a unit area of ground from a knowledge of the moisture content of the air at various levels, shown by an aerological diagram. The sum is the *precipitable water* (Note 6.B). This is all the atmospheric water vapour, omitting any moisture in the form of cloud droplets or ice crystals. It amounts to about 97 per cent of the atmospheric water mentioned in Figure 6.2. It is the depth of liquid water on the ground that would result from precipitating all the vapour in the air column.

It varies with latitude, as shown by **Figure 6.13**. There is around 38 mm at the equator, 27 mm at 20°S, 16 mm at 40°S, 8 mm at 60°S, and 2 mm at 80°S. The pattern is more like that of

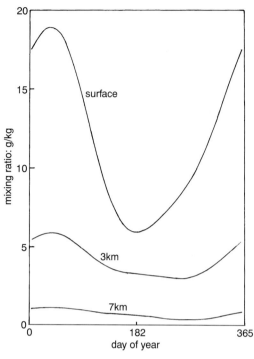

temperature (Figure 3.4) than of evaporation (Figure 4.11).

It also depends on the season, being most in summer, e.g. the average at 30°S is 27 mm in January, but only 18 mm in July. The mean precipitable amount for the whole southern hemisphere is 26 mm in January and 20 mm in July. That seasonal variation is smaller than the range from 19 to 34 mm in the northern hemisphere. The reason is that the north has a greater land area and therefore experiences a wider annual range of temperature (Section 3.3). Higher temperatures in summer lead to more precipitable water, and this increase of water vapour leads to higher temperatures, as water vapour is a greenhouse gas (Section 2.7). So the effect is amplified by a 'positive feedback process', of the kind discussed in the next chapter.

Figure 6.12 Variation of the mixing ratio at Port Hedland (Western Australia) with height and day of the year.

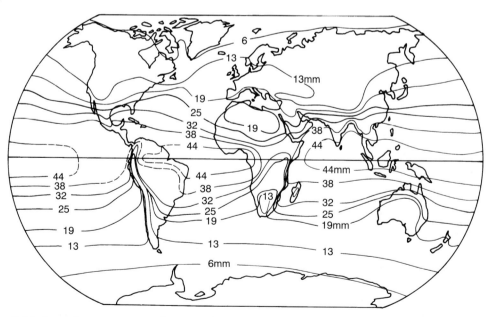

Figure 6.13 Annual mean pattern of precipitable water in units of a millimetre.

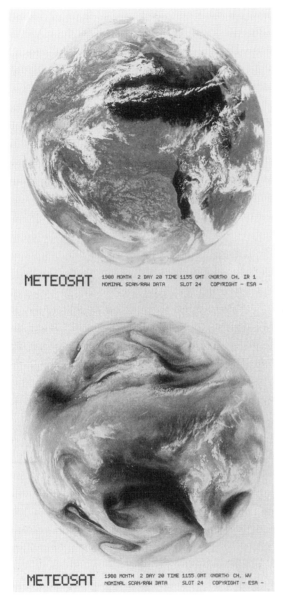

METEOSAT   1988 MONTH 2 DAY 20 TIME 1155 GMT (NORTH) CH. IR 1
            NOMINAL SCAN/RAW DATA   SLOT 24   COPYRIGHT - ESA -

METEOSAT   1988 MONTH 2 DAY 20 TIME 1155 GMT (NORTH) CH. WV
            NOMINAL SCAN/RAW DATA   SLOT 24   COPYRIGHT - ESA -

Plate 6.1 Moisture in the atmosphere (especially in the upper troposphere) can be detected by means of satellite photographs such as these. They came from the geostationary satellite Meteosat over the equator near Africa, at 1155 GMT in February 1988. The upper image shows radiation in the infra-red band, i.e. indicating the temperatures of the radiating surfaces, with the cold tops of high clouds being whitest and the warm land of Africa black. Notice the band of cloud at the ITCZ over the Indian ocean at about 20°S. Also, there was intense convection over much of southern Africa, except on the west where skies are shown clear as a result of the anticyclone over the South Atlantic ocean. Heavy cloud obscures Brazil, far to the west.

The lower image was obtained at the same time for the same area, but shows the amount of water vapour in the atmosphere, in terms of radiation of other wavelengths. Whiteness here means moisture. There is a clear resemblance to the upper image, with dry (i.e. subsiding) air over the South Atlantic ocean, but there is a more clearly defined trough line.

NOTES

6.A Aspects of the hydrologic cycle

6.B Alternative ways of stating the air's humidity

6.C Saturation deficit and crop growth

6.D Psychrometer measurements

6.E The weather-stress index (WSI)

6.F A thermal sensation scale

6.G The Standard Effective Temperature

6.H Evaporative coolers

6.I The skew $T - \log p$ diagram, part 1

7

ATMOSPHERIC INSTABILITY

7.1 INSTABILITY AND FEEDBACK

In the previous chapter we considered the humidity of air near the surface, and in the next we shall deal with cloud formation, often at levels far above the ground. The connection between the two is usually the uplift of low-level air. In the present chapter we will examine how the uplift results from features of the temperature profile (Section 1.6) and the humidity profile (Section 6.6).

There are several ways of creating uplift:

(a) wind may be forced to rise by hills (*orographic uplift*),
(b) or there is a wedging action of heavier, cooler air sliding under a warm, moist air mass (*frontal uplift*, discussed in Chapter 13),
(c) converging low-level winds squeeze air upwards,
(d) diverging upper-level winds suck air from below, or
(e) turbulence within strong winds over rough terrain stirs some air down and some up.

In all those cases, the uplift is forced. Alternatively, there may be uplift caused by thermal convection due to the spontaneous buoyancy of warmed air; it is this process in particular which is considered in the present chapter. More than one process may operate in practice. For instance, a cold front (Chapter 13) might initiate uplift, which is then continued by convection.

Stability and Instability

The tendency towards thermal convection depends on the vertical profile of temperatures and the consequent *vertical static instability* of the layer, To understand this, it is helpful first to consider the concept of 'instability' in general.

A situation is said to be 'unstable' if a small disturbance automatically becomes amplified. The traditional example is a marble on an upturned saucer: a slight displacement of the marble to one side leads to an accelerating movement in the same direction. Conversely, a 'stable' situation resembles a marble on a saucer placed normally, where a slight temporary displacement, or even a large one, is followed by the marble rolling *back* to its initial position, the *status quo* is restored. So the saucer's shape *aggravates* any disturbance in the unstable case, whereas the shape *hinders* change in the stable case. Between the stable case and the unstable, there is the situation of *neutral stability*. An example is a marble on a level table, where a disturbance leads to displacement but then there is neither acceleration onwards nor restoration to the original position.

The atmosphere is stable in the first five types of uplift mentioned above and therefore resists uplift. But it is statically unstable in the case of uplift due to thermal convection.

Other examples of stable, unstable or neutral conditions are found in nature, in human society, in the oceans (Chapter 11) – in fact, everywhere. Some cases of *instability* have been mentioned already. For instance, there is the effect of any extra melting at the edge of Arctic ice, which reduces the albedo there (Table 2.3), causing greater absorption of solar energy and hence an increase of local heating and therefore even more melting. Hence, melting leads to *more* melting. Or there is the case of global warming, leading to increased oceanic evaporation (Section 4.3), hence more rainfall, more vegetation and therefore a reduction of the albedo of land surfaces, greater absorption of sunshine and consequently *more* warming. Other cases are considered in **Note 7.A** and in Section 7.4. In every instance, there is a circular chain of events, with each cycle *augmenting* the earlier change.

Stable situations have been mentioned previously too, where the tendency is towards restoring the original state. The Urey effect (Section 1.2) concerns the way in which ultraviolet light forms oxygen from water, but then the oxygen that is created itself obscures the UV and thus inhibits further formation of the gas. Secondly, any global cooling would increase the wavelength of the ground's long-wave radiation (Note 2.B), which would therefore pass less readily through the atmospheric window (Note 2.H), so that the world would warm up again. Stable situations lead to *curtailment* of the initial fluctuation, not reinforcement.

Feedback

Ideas of stability and instability are linked to the notion of *feedback* (Note 7.A). Stability arises from *negative feedback*, where an initial impulse results in an opposite effect, offsetting the original perturbation. In contrast, instability is the result of *positive feedback*, where the effect aggravates the impulse. In general, instability leads to change, which persists until some negative-feedback process becomes dominant.

Feedback processes occur throughout the natural world. Notably, the enhanced greenhouse effect (Note 2.L) becomes more serious if it is indeed dominated by positive feedbacks in the atmosphere, exaggerating any fluctuation of global temperature. Also, the interaction of positive and negative feedbacks produces the ceaseless changes of atmospheric conditions we call weather, notwithstanding the steady input of solar radiation. Our incomplete understanding of all the feedbacks involved, and their interactions, partly accounts for the uncertainties in weather forecasting and climate-change predictions (Chapter 15).

The feedback processes most relevant to weather forecasting are those acting rapidly, especially processes connected with two particular kinds of instability (i) (vertical) *static instability* and (ii) *baroclinic instability*. We will discuss the first of these in the present chapter, and the second in Chapter 13. In general, static instability depends on the temperature and humidity profiles, and is important at low latitudes. It governs the occurrence of thunderstorms. On the other hand, baroclinic (or dynamic) instability depends on the wind profile, and concerns the development of frontal disturbances which determine the weather in mid-latitudes (Chapter 13).

7.2 LAPSE RATES

A *lapse rate* is the change of temperature with unit rise of elevation, and the rate at any particular level is given by the *temperature profile* (or 'sounding'), measured by radiosonde (Section 1.6). Typical profiles near the ground in the valley of the Parramatta River near Sydney are shown in **Figure 7.1**. At about 8.40 a.m., for instance, there is a *fall* of temperature with increased elevation within the lowest 100 metres (i.e. a *positive* lapse rate), then an inversion layer up to about 180 metres, surmounted by a roughly *isothermal* layer, i.e. one of equal temperature. The slope of the measured profile at any level in Figure 7.1 is the *environmental lapse rate* (ELR) of temperature. A corresponding *dewpoint lapse rate* (DLR) at that level can be derived from the measured profile of dewpoint temperatures (Note 6.I).

We use the ELR value for comparison with two theoretical lapse rates, in order to assess the stability of an atmospheric layer. The first of these is the *dry adiabatic lapse rate* (DALR), the rate of cooling of a parcel of air lifted *adiabati-*

cally, i.e. fast enough for there to be no time for heat to flow in or out of the parcel. (By a *'parcel'* of air, we mean an amount like that inside a limp balloon, it being assumed that no air enters or leaves the parcel.) The DALR depends solely on the physical properties of air, as it expands on rising to levels of lower pressure. It is nearly 10 K/km (**Note 7.B**). This figure is used in designing conditions inside large aircraft.

The DALR allows one to calculate the *potential temperature* of air at any elevation z (km). This is the temperature dry air would have if it were lowered adiabatically to the level at which the atmospheric pressure is 1,000 hPa, i.e. to about sea-level. The potential temperature is calculated by adding $10\,z$ degrees to the air temperature measured at the height z.

It can be inferred that the DALR line joins points representing the same potential temperature, and the potential temperature of dry air

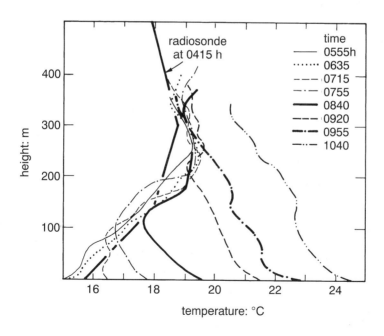

Figure 7.1 Typical temperature profiles measured during a clear morning in the Parramatta River valley, just upwind of Sydney.

does not change when it rises or falls adiabatically. In other words, this property of air is *conservative*, i.e. it is one of those unchanging features which simplify what otherwise is a complicated subject. Other such features include the mixing ratio (Section 6.2), provided there is no evaporation or condensation. The potential temperature is a measure of the inherent heat content of dry air, with the height factor removed.

The following example illustrates how we use the concept of potential temperature. Imagine dry air at a temperature of 10°C at 1 km height on the upwind side of a mountain range, and air with a temperature of 20°C at sea-level in the lee. One might think that the air on the windward side is becoming colder, so that people at the coast should brace themselves for chilly weather. But both air masses have the same potential temperature (20°C), so the difference of temperature is not due to a change of weather, but simply to the different elevations.

An even more conservative property is the *equivalent potential temperature*, which is the equivalent temperature (Section 4.3) of air brought down to sea level adiabatically (Note 7.C).

Saturated Air

So far we have assumed that the rising parcel does not become saturated as it cools. If it does become saturated, then any further adiabatic cooling is partly offset by the resulting condensation, which releases latent heat (**Note 7.C**). The consequent lapse rate of the *saturated* parcel is referred to as the *saturated adiabatic lapse rate* (SALR). This is the second of the two theoretical lapse rates mentioned above for comparison with the measured lapse rate, the ELR.

Clearly, offsetting some of the cooling makes the SALR *less* than the dry adiabatic lapse rate DALR. The SALR also differs from the DALR in being variable, not fixed, since the amount of latent heat released depends on how much condensation occurs, which in turn is governed by

the air's temperature. In practice, values are usually around 6 K/km, which is not far from the lapse rate of the standard atmosphere (Section 1.6), though the SALR is less in warm climates than in cold (Note 7.C). In view of the importance of the DALR and the SALR, they are both represented by appropriate lines on aerological diagrams (**Note 7.D**).

The difference between the DALR and SALR can be used to explain the *foehn effect* (**Note 7.E**). (The German word is pronounced 'fern', and comes from the Latin name of a wind in Rome coming from the warm south.) The effect is the drying and warming observed downwind of mountains, after moist air has been lifted by the mountains to the extent that temperatures fall to dewpoint, cloud forms and there is precipitation (**Figure 7.2**). The downwind air is relatively dry because rain has been removed from it, and it is warmer because of the latent heat from the condensation of the water which became the rain. The resulting warm dry wind is known as a 'foehn wind' in the European alps, a 'chinook' (i.e. 'snow-eater') east of the Rockies in North America, and a 'zonda' downwind of the Andes, in Argentina. They have also been observed near the Ballany Islands at 67°S in Antarctica. The foehn effect partly explains why temperatures at Bega (on the New South Wales south coast) can be 10 K higher in winter than upwind at Albury, on the other side of the Dividing Range.

7.3 INSTABILITY OF THE ATMOSPHERE

Having considered various lapse rates, we can now examine how these affect the vertical static instability.

Dry Air

Figure 7.3 shows two hypothetical conditions of a dry atmosphere. On the left, the lapse rate

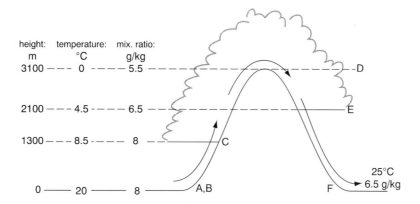

Figure 7.2 Illustration of the foehn effect. There is cooling at 10K/km until cloud base is reached, then cooling at the SALR within the cloud. Once the mountain is surmounted, the descending air first warms at the SALR, using the heat to evaporate cloud droplets. Cloud base is reached when all the droplets have gone, and thereafter there is warming at the DALR. It is assumed that rain falls from the cloud on the windward side of the mountain, so that the cloud on the lee side has less moisture absorbing heat in evaporation than was condensed on the windward side, liberating latent heat. So less heat is absorbed than was previously released. As a result, there is warmer, drier air downwind (Note 7.E).

is 6 K (i.e. 20 − 14) in 900 metres (i.e. 6.7 K/m), whereas it is 13.6 K/km on the right, twice as much. In each case, a parcel of air is shown lifted by 300 m by some means, and the question is, what happens next? In both cases, the parcel has cooled by the dry adiabatic lapse rate of 10 K/km, so that it now has a temperature of 17°C. The parcel on the left finds itself amongst air at 18°C, which is warmer and therefore lighter. As a result, the relatively heavy parcel sinks back to where it was before the temporary nudge upwards. So the situation is stable. However, the uplifted air on the right finds itself within air at only 16°C (i.e. 20 − 0.3 × 13.3), which is cooler than the parcel, i.e. the parcel is less dense. So the lifted parcel on the right now has positive buoyancy and rises spontaneously, without further nudging. When it has risen another 300 m, the parcel has become 2 K warmer than the surroundings (i.e. [17 − 3] − 12), so that the buoyancy has actually increased, and ascent consequently accelerates; the initial perturbation has become

runaway ascent. This is instability, as described earlier.

The difference between local static stability and instability is seen to be due simply to *different environmental lapse rates*. The ELR is less than the DALR (or *sub-adiabatic*, i.e. less than 10 K/km) in a *stable* environment, shown on the left in Figure 7.3. Or, put differently, the line representing the ELR of a stable atmosphere is oriented *clockwise* of the DALR line. In some conditions the ELR line is so far clockwise that it implies that the temperature actually increases with height, i.e. there is an inversion. Clearly, inversions are extremely stable.

As regards instability, we have deduced that conditions are locally *unstable when the ELR exceeds the DALR*, as in the part ab in **Figure 7.4**, where the ELR line is seen to be relatively anticlockwise, approaching the horizontal. Such a lapse rate is known as *super-adiabatic*. It is uncommon (except close to the ground when it is heated by sunshine), because the resulting instability leads to a vertical circulation which carries hot air aloft and brings cool air down,

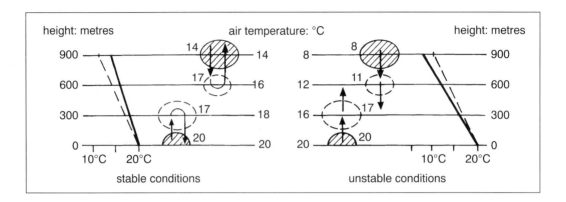

Figure 7.3 An illustration of how static stability arises. The vertical axis is height, the horizontal is temperature and the dashed slanted lines represent the DALR (10K/km). The bold sloping lines are different hypothetical soundings, determining the ELR. On the left, the ELR is more vertical than the DALR, since the measured temperature change is only 6K (i.e. 20 − 14) in 900 m. On the right, the ELR is more horizontal, representing 12K in 900 m. In both cases, two parcels of air are shown (shaded), one on top and one at the bottom of the layer. These parcels are disturbed to the positions of the unshaded ellipses, and their new temperatures are shown, along with their further displacements, according to the difference between each parcel's temperature and that of its new environment.

automatically changing the temperature profile towards that of neutrality, where the ELR equals the DALR.

Another way of expressing the condition for instability is in terms of the potential temperature. A layer of the atmosphere is locally *unstable* if there is a *decrease* of potential temperature with elevation. Again, this may be deduced from Figure 7.3; the potential temperature at 600 m is 18°C (i.e. 12 + 10 × 0.6) at 600 m on the unstable right, compared with 20°C at sea-level (i.e. there is a *positive* lapse rate of potential temperature), whereas the potential temperature *rises* to 22°C (i.e. 16 + 10 × 0.6) on the (stable) left.

Moist Air

Now we turn to the case of the *saturated* air within a cloud. Here the test of stability or instability is a comparison of slopes of the observed temperature profile with the SALR, not the DALR. Both are included in **Figure**

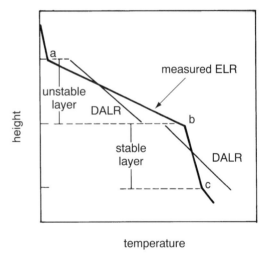

Figure 7.4 A comparison of the dry adiabatic lapse rate (DALR) with the environmental lapse rate (ELR) in each of two layers, showing, for example, that atmospheric local static stability corresponds to an ELR (in section bc) more clockwise than the DALR.

7.5, where the SALR is different for hot and cold climates, respectively (Section 7.2). The lines for both extremes of SALR are more vertical than the line for the DALR.

Figure 7.5 also shows a pair of lapse rates labelled *'conditionally unstable'*; this needs explaining. They are environmental lapse rates of a layer which is either stable, if the air is unsaturated (i.e. the line is more vertical than the DALR line), or unstable if there is saturation. In other words, instability depends on the *condition* of the atmosphere, whether or not it is saturated, when the ELR is like those indicated by the lines labelled 'conditionally unstable'. The lapse rate for a conditionally unstable layer lies between the DALR and the SALR. The lower of the two labelled lines in Figure 7.5 implies conditional instability at all latitudes, whilst conditional instability applies only near the equator for the upper one. Therefore, conditional instability is more likely at low latitudes. To distinguish conditional instability from instability in dry air, the latter is sometimes called *absolute instability*.

Non-local Instability

So far we have assumed constant values of the environmental lapse rate ELR (i.e. straight lines in Figs 7.3 and 7.5), to be compared with the SALR or DALR, according to whether the air is saturated or not. Such a comparison indicates the *local static stability*. However, the ELR is rarely constant in practice, so measurements do not yield a straight line but a curving line as in Figure 7.1 and **Figure 7.6**. The practical consequence of this is that the occurrence of convection does not depend on the local static instability of individual layers of the atmosphere, but on the entire profile over an appreciable depth. This can be shown by considering Figure 7.6, taking various layers in turn (**Note 7.F**). Such a consideration reveals that a parcel of air at the level of J and K in Figure 7.6 will rise as far as the *level of neutral buoyancy* (LNB) or 'cloud top', despite some static *stability*. Static stability of the layer between J K and the LNB would be inferred from the difference between the slopes of the ELR and SALR lines up from J and K, respectively. The reason for the actual

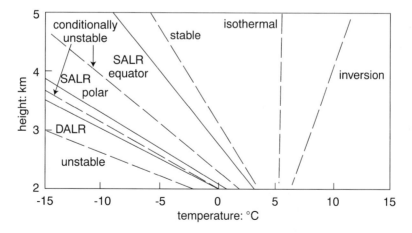

Figure 7.5 Temperature profiles of atmospheres with various degrees of moisture and static stability. The three bold lines show the DALR and two SALRs.

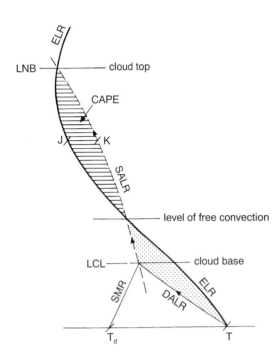

Figure 7.6 The track of an air parcel lifted from the surface, plotted on a skew $T - \log p$ diagram. The bold line is a hypothetical sounding (ELR). The dew-point sounding is not shown, though the dewpoint (T_d) at the surface is plotted. SMR is a saturation-mixing-ratio line, CAPE is the 'convective available potential energy', LCL is the lifting condensation level, and LNB is the level of neutral buoyancy.

instability is that an air parcel at what is labelled the *level of free convection* rises spontaneously along the SALR curve all the way to the LNB, because the parcel (at temperatures along the SALR curve) is always warmer than the environment, shown by the ELR curve.

As temperature comparison (rather than relative slope) is really the basis of assessing overall atmospheric instability, we use this in describing the instability of the part that is chiefly the arena of weather, from the ground to about 5 km elevation (**Note 7.G**).

7.4 EXAMPLES OF INSTABILITY

There are several ways in which a layer becomes unstable (**Note 7.H**). They are described in the following:

Uplift

The instability of a deep layer of air is automatically enhanced when the layer as a whole is raised by hills or a front, for instance. This is because the layer expands in thickness as it moves to lower pressures, and so the top of the layer rises more than the base. Therefore the top cools more, which implies destabilisation of the layer.

An additional factor arises if the layer is dry but *conditionally* unstable, because cooling by uplift will make it saturated and therefore actually unstable. Destabilisation by uplift is further enhanced if the top part of the layer is dry whilst the bottom is saturated. This condition is known as *potential instability* (or convective instability). The top cools at 10 K/km during ascent whilst the bottom cools less rapidly, at the appropriate SALR. So the layer becomes less and less stable. It can be shown that a layer is potentially unstable if the equivalent potential temperature (Section 7.2) decreases with height, just as absolute instability occurs when the potential temperature decreases with height. Potential instability occurs on the Australian east coast or the coastal plains of Uruguay and Argentina, for instance, when warm moist air from the tropics flows under a dry westerly airstream aloft.

Surface Turbulence

The flow of wind past surface obstacles, and daytime heating of the ground, both induce a random stirring we call *turbulence*. It is important in transferring sensible and latent heat between the Earth's surface and the free atmosphere, and in the dispersion of air pollution (Chapter 14).

Turbulence depends on both the wind speed and the atmosphere's lapse rate, so it is categorised as in **Table 7.1**. Note that the first three lapse rates mentioned (A, B, C) are all superadiabatic. The last column shows how instability means a great variability of wind *direction*, and the same applies to wind speed, creating gustiness (Chapter 14). The reason is that parcels of the stronger winds at the top of the planetary boundary layer are stirred to the surface by strong instability. The circumstances in which each category of Table 7.1 occurs are shown in **Table 7.2**. As an example, the ELR near the surface is close to neutral on windy days because of the constant vertical stirring, whereas the lapse rate is superadiabatic during a calm day, changing to an inversion at night.

Cumulus Cloud

Cumulus clouds are one manifestation of the release of static instability. Cloud base is usually flat, at the height of the Lifting Condensation Level (LCL) (Note 7.F, Figure 7.6), whilst the top is initially cauliflower-shaped because of internal convection extending the cloud upwards. It eventually reaches a stable layer, and then the cloud top spreads out as a broad anvil (Chapters 8 and 9).

Tropical Rainfall

Tropical rainfall often comes from the release of static instability by thunderstorms – what is called 'convective rainfall' (Chapter 9). This is true especially over land and over archipelagos like Indonesia, where rainfall is more

Table 7.1 Pasquill's classification of the stability of the surface atmosphere, according to the degree of insolation and wind speed

Pasquill class	Condition of the air	Lapse rate (K/km)	Standard deviation* of wind direction (degrees)
A	Very unstable	−17	25
B	Unstable	−15	20
C	Slightly unstable	−13	15
D	Neutral	−10†	10
E	Stable	+5	5
F	Very stable	+25	2.5

* A measure of the scatter, discussed in Chapter 10
† That is, the dry adiabatic lapse rate

Table 7.2 The circumstances of various degrees of surface-air stability

Wind speed (m/s)	Strong Sun*, R_s over 580 W/m²	Moderate Sun, R_s of 290–580 W/m²	Slight Sun†, R_s of 145–290 W/m²	Cloudy, day or night	Clear night
0–2	A	A–B	B	–	–
2–3	A–B	B	C	E	F
3–4	B	B–C	C	D	E
4–6	C	C–D	D	D	D
6 +	C	D	D	D	D

* A clear sky, with the Sun higher than 60° above the horizon; R_s is the incoming solar radiation in W/m²
† A clear sky, with the Sun only 15–35° above the horizon

common during the afternoon because of destabilisation of the lower atmosphere by surface heating.

The role of atmospheric instability in causing rainfall over tropical oceans remains uncertain. One theory suggests that rainfall there happens chiefly in the early morning, because of particularly deep convection at that time when the water surface is warmer than the adjacent air. The convection is promoted by cooling of the upper air by longwave radiation lost to space during the night, making the troposphere unstable.

Thermals

A *thermal* is a column of warm-air bubbles, expanding as they rise, each with a central updraught and peripheral subsidence. Thermals commonly occur on warm, calm afternoons above relatively hot patches of the ground (such as a dry field of low albedo amongst irrigated fields, or a slope facing the Sun), forming huge bubbles of warm air, lighter than the air around. They eventually lift off, entrain more air and join other bubbles. Within a couple of hundred metres they form a continuous column, the diameter of which is then around a quarter of its height (**Figure 7.7**). The thermal extends upwards to the top of the PBL at 1,000 m or beyond, usually slanting in the wind and moving slowly along if the ground is uniform. Their upwards growth is usually limited by the stable layer at the top of the PBL but thermals in a hot desert may extend to 4 km, and may reach the Lifting Condensation Level, so that a cumulus cloud forms. The distance to the next thermal is about twice its height.

Locusts may be drawn together into the base of a thermal and lifted up. Then they drift down over a great distance, extending the damage they cause.

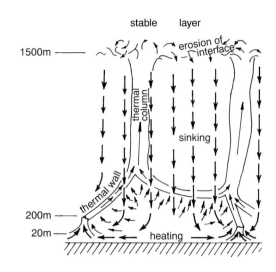

Figure 7.7 Typical conditions associated with a thermal. The dimensions are only indicative; the vertical dimension is exaggerated.

Gliding

Soaring birds, like pelicans or eagles, are too heavy to fly easily by flapping but can attain great height by circling within the updraught of a thermal once they have surmounted the turbulence of the lowest one or two hundred metres. Then they peel off and glide towards the next thermal for another lift. Vultures in East Africa have been observed to climb at 2–4 m/s to 3,500 m, for instance. But they are readily caught on the ground in the morning, before convection has started. Close to the surface of the sea, birds such as herring gulls either flap or glide according to the atmosphere's instability (**Figure 7.8**). The gulls flap when the water is cooler than the air, causing stability, but glide in circles within thermals when the sea surface is warmer.

Glider pilots and hang gliders imitate the soaring birds in using thermals. Particularly good lift is found up to tall clouds, and climb rates are typically 1–3 m/s in Australian thermals. Weak thermals may be 2–5 km apart, while strong thermals are typically 15 km

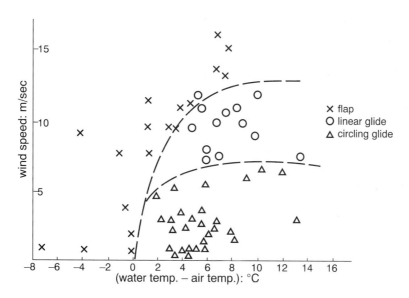

Figure 7.8 Effect of instability on the way in which seagulls fly.

away from each other. Hang gliders may be lifted 400 m or so by a thermal, but the world-record altitude for glider pilots is 14 km, at the top of the troposphere.

Inexperienced pilots may mistake *wave-lift* for a thermal. Wave-lift is due to air deflected upwards by hills, offering limited ascent.

Polar Winds

Cold surface winds from the poles tend to become increasingly unstable as they move equatorward, since the lower part of the air is warmed by the oceans. As a result, there are cumulus clouds which often grow tall enough for precipitation. This explains why exposed coastal areas receive significant rain in the southerly winds which follow the passage of a cold front, even though the air is cold, with little precipitable water (Section 6.6), and despite the subsiding of air behind cold fronts (Chapter 13).

Mirage Shimmer

Dry bare ground can become extremely hot in the tropical afternoon when the sky is clear (Section 3.5), creating a superadiabatic layer of air against the ground. The turbulence of the rising air within that layer causes a shimmer in the view of a 'mirage', a false impression of a lake just below the horizon, some distance ahead on a straight roadway. The apparent lake is really a view of the near-horizon sky, turned by the higher speed of light through the hot air at the surface in the same way that sound waves are turned by a vertical temperature gradient (Section 7.6).

Instability within Water

The phenomenon of instability applies to all fluids. Measurements of surface temperatures of turbid water in a ricefield in New South Wales showed stable conditions from 8 a.m. to 2 p.m. in late spring (i.e. the surface film was then warmer than the water a centimetre below), but thereafter there was instability as the surface film cooled as much as 5 K lower. The water layers would then mix turbulently, and the entire water column cool off uniformly.

Similarly, lake water is warmest on top in summer but cools uniformly in autumn, when cooling at the surface makes the density profile lead to instability. The water density in oceans is complicated by the dissolved salt (Chapter 11), yet the same concepts of static stability apply. The effect of salt on water's density, and hence its pattern of stability, enables the capture of solar energy (**Note 7.I**).

7.5 TORNADOES, DUST-DEVILS AND WATER SPOUTS

A tornado is the result of extreme instability. It consists of a violent whirlwind, a tapering funnel of twisting cloud, dangling like an elephant's trunk from the base of a thunderstorm cloud, with winds stronger than 20 m/s at 10 m from the centre of the vortex. The word 'tornado' comes from the Spanish for 'thunder'. Its passage is accompanied by a peculiar whistling, and then a roar as the funnel approaches, and finally a screech of winds, obscuring the noise of crashing trees and buildings. The aftermath is an intermittent swath of destruction where the whirlwind's tip moves across the ground.

The funnel of a tornado extends waving from a low thick cloud, with a radius of a few hundred metres. It has a suction of possibly 200 hPa, sufficient to lift bricks. Also there are howling winds nearby, estimated as over 90 m/s in some cases, enough to propel timber through 15 mm steel or a spade 15 cm into a tree, and to demolish houses (**Note 7.J**). The funnel moves unsteadily along at 8–33 m/s.

Cause

Tornadoes depend on three preconditions:

1 at least 2000 J/kg of convective available potential energy CAPE (Figure 7.6), which is possible when the planetary boundary layer (PBL) is warm and humid, and the air aloft is dry and cool,
2 a thin stable layer above the PBL (**Figure 7.9**), sufficient to prevent the instability being already released by small thunderstorms, and
3 a great increase of wind strength with height.

This combination arises in the American Midwest when warm, moist, low-level winds blow northwards from the Gulf of Mexico and undercut a strong westerly flow which has lost most of its moisture over the Rockies. Once the stable layer between is breached, there is a sudden updraught of the buoyant lower air, creating a massive thunderstorm which can spawn a tornado.

Some tornadoes occur in association with small thunderstorms ahead of a cold front or within a tropical cyclone (Chapter 13). Many tornadoes in Australia are triggered by convection due to vigorous cold fronts.

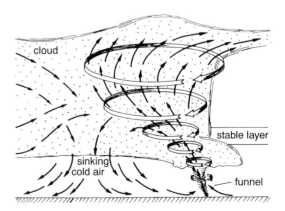

Figure 7.9 A schematic diagram of the circulations associated with a tornado within its parent thunderstorm.

Occurrence

Tornadoes in Australia resemble those of the American Midwest, which have been most studied, but are probably smaller, weaker and less common. There are about 700 reports each year in the USA, against ten or so reported annually in Australia. There were about eight per 10^5 km^2 each year in Sydney between 1950 and 1989, which is roughly a fifth of the rate in *tornado alley* centred in Oklahoma, USA. However, it is notable that a map of the frequency of *reported* tornadoes in Australia resembles that of population density, so there may be further tornadoes in unpopulated areas.

Tornadoes in Perth and Adelaide occur mostly in winter, whereas they are more common in summer along the east coast of Australia, e.g. November–January in New South Wales. Late afternoon is the most common time, when surface heating is greatest. They also occur on the west coast of New Zealand and in South Africa, and in South America east of the Andes, around 25–35°S.

It seems that the centre of a huge city like Chicago or Tokyo is relatively immune to tornadoes, perhaps because of the roughness of the urban landscape. Tornadoes tend to avoid hills and follow valleys, and intensify on downslopes.

Dust-Devils

Dust-devils are silent, miniature tornadoes, due to extreme instability near hot ground. They differ from tornadoes in being less powerful, and in developing up from the ground instead of down from a cloud. Also, dust-devils usually occur under clear skies. They are triggered by wind gusts, which may be very strong when the lapse rate is superadiabatic. The intensity is enough to pick up dust, so they become visible, though there is a strong wind only close to the column. The column may be 1–50 m in diameter and reach several hundred metres high. A small dust-devil lasts only a few seconds, whilst a large one endures for half an hour.

They are common in arid parts of Australia (where they are called 'willy-willies'), as well as in Arizona and Egypt. They occur especially when dry, cleared ground is heated by strong sunshine in summer, typically between 11.30 a.m. and 2.30 p.m.

Water Spouts

A water spout is a tight vortex made visible by cloud and spray within it, extending dozens or hundreds of metres from a water surface. Sailboats and small motorboats have been capsized by water spouts. They are of two kinds, one of which is the marine analogue of a dust-devil, growing up from a warm sea-surface under a clear sky. Such water spouts occur when the cold air behind a cold front passes over a warm sea, for instance.

The second type of water spout is the maritime counterpart of a tornado. It forms under a convective cloud in the same way as a tornado, but it is less intense and shorter lived. One observed in Port Phillip Bay near Melbourne on 11 April 1994 grew down from a thundercloud when the water surface was at about 19°C and the air at 8°C, so that there was considerable instability. The waterspout reached 300 m high and 30 m in diameter, and lasted for 10 minutes or so.

7.6 STABLE LAYERS

Having considered instability, we turn to the subject of stable layers of the atmosphere, in which either (i) temperatures *decrease* with height but less rapidly than the relevant adiabatic lapse rate (i.e. the environmental lapse rate is *sub-adiabatic*), (ii) the layer is isothermal (with a uniform temperature throughout), or (iii) there is an *inversion*, with an *increase* of temperature with height (Figure 7.5). If an inversion has a

Plate 7.1 A tornado in South Australia on 20 August 1971.

strength of 5 K/km, then a parcel of air lifted over 1 km finds itself within an environment that is 15 K warmer (since the parcel cools at the DALR, 10 K/km), so that there is a particularly strong tendency for the parcel to sink back again. Likewise, a parcel pushed down in the layer finds itself in particularly cold air, and consequently has great buoyancy back up towards the *status quo*. The result is that any stable layer, but especially an inversion, resists vertical movement of any kind and therefore separates the air above from that beneath. The layer creates a *stratification* of the atmosphere into distinct layers.

A temperature profile of the troposphere usually has several kinks indicating various stable layers, which in the extreme are inversions, described in **Table 7.3**. These will now be discussed, regarding all stable layers as inversions, for brevity.

Stratospheric Inversion

This was considered in Section 1.8. It suppresses the vertical motions within turbulent air, creating the calmness desirable in air travel, for instance, since long-distance aircraft fly at about 10 km. Also, thunderstorms (Chapter 9) and weather systems (Chapter 13) are confined to the troposphere by the inversion, and its impermeability allows quite different chemical concentrations above and below. For instance, ozone is much more abundant above the tropopause at the bottom of the inversion.

Cloud-top Inversion

A stable layer arises above the top of any layer cloud, as the cloud surface cools by losing long-wave radiation to space.

Subsidence Inversion

A subsiding layer becomes compressed as it sinks to levels at higher pressures, so the top descends further than the bottom of the layer does (i.e. warms more), and consequently the lapse rate within the layer changes in a way that results in greater stability. This is the converse of the instability created within a rising layer (Section 7.4). More importantly, the inversion that commonly occurs above the lowest few hundred metres is due to the air against the ground being unable to descend further, whilst higher levels continue to warm by subsidence.

Subsidence inversions are associated with the air descending within a high-pressure system (Chapter 13). The ground-level high pressure causes surface air to spread out to low-pressure areas around, and that draws air down from above. The subsiding air's warming and the low water content of the original upper-level air (Section 6.6) lead to it having a characteristically low relative humidity at the surface.

One example of a subsidence inversion is the *Trade wind inversion*, common over much of the subtropical oceans (**Figure 7.10**). It lies about

Table 7.3 Types of inversion discussed in the text

	Kind	Base	Depth	Time	Cause
			Typical features		
1	Stratospheric	10 km	40 km	Always	UV radiation absorption
2	Cloud-top	–	10–100 m	Anytime	Radiation cooling of top of stratus
3	Subsidence	~1,000 m	~100 m	Always	Descent of air in anticyclone
4	Orographic	Few km	Various	Always	Orographic lifting towards tropopause
5	Frontal	Various	100–500 m	Anytime	Cold air intruding beneath warm
6	Planetary-boundary layer	~750 m	~100 m	Anytime	Adiabatic mixing
7	Sea breeze	600 m	~100 m	Daytime	Cool ocean
8	Advection	Surface	various	Anytime	Cool ocean
9	Cold-air drainage	Surface	150 m	Night and early morning	Katabatic flow into valley
10	Ground (or radiation)	Surface	50–500 m	Night and early morning	Radiation cooling of ground, to clear sky

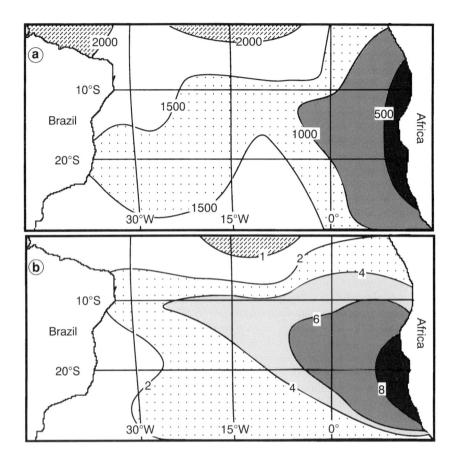

Figure 7.10 Characteristics of the Trade wind inversion in the South Atlantic: (a) height (m) of the base of the inversion, and (b) temperature increase (K) within the inversion.

500 m above sea-level in regions where the surface is relatively cool, e.g. off northern Chile and Peru, and also off the south-west coast of Africa (Chapter 11). The top of the inversion there is about 8 K warmer than the base. Nearer the equator, there is more convection from the warmer surface so that the inversion there occurs at 1,500 to 2,000 m. The inversion there is weaker and thinner because warmer seas imply less subsidence. Overall, the pattern of inversion strength is reflected in the patterns of fog (Chapter 8) and rainfall (Chapter 10).

Even where subsidence is insufficient to create an inversion, it still enhances atmospheric stability. Thus, easterly winds in coastal Peru and northern Chile are stabilised by the descent from the Andes, making uplift less likely and so reducing rainfall (Chapter 10).

Orographic Stability

Paradoxically, it is possible for stability to be created within rising air, as well as by subsidence. The reason is that a subsidence inversion occurs within the free atmosphere, far from the ground, whereas orographic stability is caused when dry air is forced to rise over a high mountain range and squeezed against the stratospheric inversion. As a result, the air at the lowest levels is raised (i.e. cooled) more than the upper air of the layer, so that stability increases.

Frontal Inversion

Where adjacent air masses of different temperature intrude on each other there is a 'frontal zone', discussed in Chapter 13. A 'cold front' occurs when a cold air mass wedges underneath a warmer one. So a temperature sounding through the wedge shows a slanting boundary between colder air below and warmer air above, i.e. there is an inversion at the boundary. In this case, the inversion indicates the inclement weather associated with a front, whereas a subsidence inversion implies calm and clear weather (Chapter 13). Frontal inversions exist from the surface to about 3 km elevation, and typically are only a few hundred metres deep.

Planetary-boundary-layer Inversion

The PBL inversion (or 'turbulence inversion') is due to the stirring of air caused by surface roughness and moderate wind. The stirring leads to good mixing, and hence a lapse rate equal to the dry adiabatic rate. This adiabatic profile connects at the top of the PBL (Figure 1.11) with conditions determined by the wider region (Table 1.1), and there is an inversion at the discontinuity. It is typically 500–1,000 m high, depending on the degree of roughness which stirs the PBL. There is often a subsidence inversion coinciding with a PBL inversion, though the formation process is quite different.

Sea-breeze Inversion

This occurs at the coast, especially in summer, between the daytime cool air drawn inland in a surface sea breeze (Chapter 14), and the compensating return flow of warmed air above, completing the loop of air circulation. The inversion layer is usually a few hundred metres above the surface, becoming lower towards evening.

Advection Inversion

Sometimes called a 'contact inversion'. Such an inversion arises wherever the surface cools the lowest air, as where warm air blows over a cold ocean, or an onshore wind in Antarctica passes over ice colder than the sea.

Cold-air Drainage (or Katabatic) Inversion

A cold airflow down an open valley in the morning creates an inversion at the interface with the environment above. In the case of a closed valley, cold air ponds at the bottom during the night, having rolled from higher land. This gives rise to frost hollows when the ponded air is below freezing (Section 3.6).

Ground (or Radiation) Inversion

The ground begins to cool from about the mid-afternoon (Figure 3.12), increasingly lowering the temperature of the air above and producing a shallow inversion. For instance, one set of soundings in Sydney showed a surface inversion 10 m deep at 5.30 p.m., but 100 m by 8.45 p.m. and 150 m by dawn. Thereafter the ground is warmed by the Sun, and air rising from it establishes a dry adiabatic lapse rate from the surface. Figure 7.1 shows such lifting of the base of the inversion to 100 m by 8.40 a.m., and a total erasing of it by 9.55 a.m.

Ground inversions create problems. They may lead to radiation frosts (Section 3.6) on winter nights, and fans may be required to protect crops (**Note 7.K**). An inversion prevents the dispersion upwards of air pollutants, which is why fire bans are often imposed on calm, clear winter days in large cities such as Sydney. (On the other hand, air pollution from

Table 7.4 The characteristics of layers of air with various lapse rates

Condition	Cause	Lapse rate	Height range	Location	Effects
Environmental	Past events	Various	Any	Measured anywhere	Governs stability
Superadiabatic	Solar heating of ground	Over 10K/km	Lowest few tens of metres	Close to the ground	Absolute instability
Dry adiabatic	Theoretical vertical motion of parcel	10K/km	Not applicable	Not applicable	Not applicable
Dry neutral	Turbulence	10K/km	Lowest km (i.e. the PBL)	The PBL (and other well-mixed layers)	Uninhibited vertical motion
Saturated adiabatic* (i.e. moist neutral)	Condensation plus cooling of parcel	About 6K/km†	Cloud depth	Within convective clouds	Increased instability
Isothermal	Uncertain	Same temp. at all levels	Small	Rare	Stability
Inversion	See Section 7.6	Warmer above cool air	Various	Various	Great stability

* Or 'moist adiabatic lapse rate'
† Values may be between 4–9K/km, depending on the water vapour content of the air, i.e. on the amount of condensation occurring with cooling (Note 7.C)

a high chimney is prevented by a ground inversion from affecting people beneath, see **Note 7.L.**) Also, any sound radiating upwards from the ground is bent back down by the higher speed through the warmer air in the upper part of a ground inversion, which augments the sound at the surface (**Note 7.M**). Therefore, aircraft noise during take-off or landing is more troublesome on calm nights.

Radiation inversions are prevented by even moderate winds, which stir the air together, producing an adiabatic lapse rate. But an established inversion is difficult to erode by wind, because stable air is reluctant to mix. As a result, weak wind occurs below the inversion and stronger wind above (**Figure 7.11**). In other words, a ground inversion disconnects the surface air from the energy of the upper winds, so that calm conditions prevail at the surface at night. This has several consequences. For instance: (i) the intensity of bush-fires is reduced at night; (ii) the surface calmness due to a ground inversion makes sounds more clear by removing the background noise of wind and turbulence and by focusing the sound (Note 7.M); and (iii) an onshore wind encountering a nocturnal ground inversion inland is forced to rise over it, and the uplift may induce rain (Chapter 9), which explains why 14 per cent more rain falls in Perth at night (midnight to 6 a.m.) than between midday and 6 p.m. (Chapters 10 and 16).

The inversions are weak when the sky at night is cloudy because of the reduced cooling caused by increased sky radiation (Section 2.7). Also, the warmth of cities (Section 3.7) and the stirring of surface winds induced by a city's roughness (Chapter 14) inhibit urban ground inversions.

Several of these kinds of inversion may occur simultaneously or leave traces for days after their original formation. This explains the irregularity of temperature profiles within the

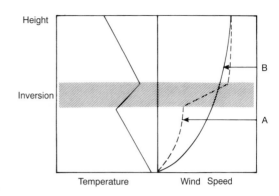

Figure 7.11 Effect of an inversion layer on the wind profile, shown either with an inversion present A (dashed line), or without B (solid line). The upper wind is decoupled from the surface air by the inversion, so speeds become higher above the layer, free of the restraint of surface friction. Speeds are reduced *below* the layer, for lack of momentum from the upper winds.

atmosphere. The variety of conditions is summarised in **Table 7.4**.

Thus we have considered the properties of a stable atmosphere, as well as an unstable one. Stable layers cause the thin flat shape of stratus clouds, whilst instability leads to tall clouds, which are all discussed in the next chapter.

NOTES

7.A Feedback
7.B The dry adiabatic lapse rate
7.C The saturated adiabatic lapse rate
7.D The skew $T - \log p$ diagram, part 2
7.E Calculation of the foehn effect
7.F Non-local instability
7.G Indices of instability
7.H How an atmosphere becomes unstable
7.I Solar ponds
7.J Tornado damage
7.K Dispersion of ground inversions by fans
7.L Atmospheric instability and air pollution
7.M Temperature profiles and sound

8

CLOUDS

8.1 THE FORMATION OF CLOUDS

In this chapter we examine the next stage of the hydrologic cycle (Section 6.1). Evaporation was considered in Chapter 4, and the consequent atmospheric humidity in Chapter 6. Then Chapter 7 dealt with atmospheric instability, which is a major cause of uplift, often cooling air to its dewpoint temperature so that it is saturated and cloud forms. Now we will explain how this occurs, and some of the consequences.

Clouds consist of tiny ice particles or water droplets, so small and light in weight that impacts from the air's randomly moving molecules are sufficient to keep the particles and droplets from falling. They control climates in several ways. Clouds are the source of rain, and they obscure and reflect radiation (Chapter 2),

so they govern the net radiation which energises photosynthesis (Note 1.B), heating of the ground (Section 3.5) and evaporation (Chapter 4). An increase in low-level cloudiness by just a few per cent would offset any global warming due to more carbon dioxide in the atmosphere.

The ice particles and water droplets of clouds derive from the condensation of water vapour in cooled air (Section 6.2). The cooling may be caused (i) by mixing with colder air, (ii) by local cooling due to either (a) nocturnal radiation loss (Section 2.7), or (b) flow over a cold surface (creating *advective cloud*), or (iii) by uplift (Section 7.1). Uplift is the most common cause, and the only way to produce rainfall (Chapter 10). The form of uplift cooling determines the kind of cloud (**Table 8.1**). In more detail, the forms of cooling are as follows.

Table 8.1 Typical cloud dimensions

Cloud type	Horizontal size (km)	Thickness (km)	Updraught speeds (m/s): Typical	Maximum
Convective	1–10	3–15	3	15
Orographic	1–500	1	1	10
Stratiform	100–3,000	1–5	0.03	0.5

Cooling Due to Mixing with a Cold Air Mass

The mixing of two volumes of almost-saturated air at different temperatures results in condensation (see Note 4.C, Figure 6.3 and **Note 8.A**). In other words, cloud can result from the mixing of two cloud-free layers of air, if they have widely different temperatures. This ocurs, for example, when cold air from surrounding hills rolls down over the moist air lying on a lake of water warmed by the previous day's sunshine. The result is 'steam fog' (Section 8.4).

Radiation Cooling

Radiation cooling of the ground at night lowers the temperature of the lowest air (Section 7.6), perhaps below dewpoint, in which case fog arises (Section 8.4).

Advective Cooling

This forms fog at any time of the day, wherever wind brings air into contact with a surface which is below the air's dewpoint temperature. Such fog is encountered in coastal regions, particularly.

Cooling Due to Uplift

Different kinds of cloud are generated by the cooling caused by uplift, according to the cause of the rising (Section 7.1): (a) hills, (b) low-level cold currents, (c) large-scale uplift, (d) convection, or (e) a convergence of winds. Convective uplift is the most rapid, generating *cumuliform* (or convective) cloud, which is vertical and cauliflower-like (Section 8.6). In the other cases, slow uplift leads to *stratiform* cloud (Table 8.1), which is shallow and spread out (Section 8.5). However, any kind of uplift destabilizes the atmosphere (Section 7.4), especially in the presence of potential instability, and may eventually result in convection. This explains why thunderstorms are more common near mountains.

Let us now consider the different kinds of cloud, according to the manner of uplift.

Orographic Cloud

Hills deflect winds upwards, so that the air cools, possibly to dewpoint. In that case, clouds form at the Lifting Condensation Level (LCL) (**Note 8.B**), shown in **Figure 8.1**. For example, the west coast of the South Island of New Zealand is more cloudy and wet than the east coast (Chapter 10) because of the orographic uplift of the mainly westerly winds.

A *cap cloud*, shaped like a contact lens, forms at the crest of an isolated mountain, if winds rise over it sufficiently high to attain the Lifting Condensation Level (LCL). Wind blows through the clouds, condensing on the upwind side and evaporating in the lee. The first reported unidentified flying objects (UFOs) were actually cap clouds, seen above an isolated 4 km-high volcano, Mt. Rainier in Washington State, USA. The likelihood of cap clouds depends on the atmosphere's stability and the wind speed: a stable weak wind tends to flow around rather than over a mountain.

The height of the LCL ranges from below 300 m in winter in wet regions of high latitude, to more than 3 km over northern Chile or inland Australia, which are dry. It is governed by the difference between dry-bulb and dew-point temperatures at the surface (Note 8.B), so cloud base is usually lower at night than during the day, in winter than in summer, and at the coast than inland. A city's relative dryness (Section 6.4) raises the LCL there by a few hundred metres.

Apart from cap clouds on the mountain-tops, a range of mountains can also create *wave clouds*, which are long and lens-shaped (*lenticular*), parallel to the range and downwind of it (**Figure

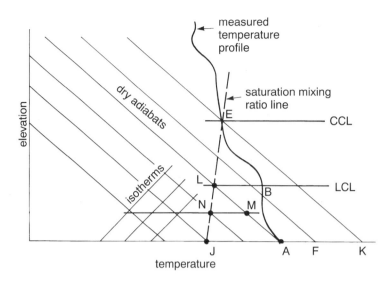

Figure 8.1 Derivation of the Lifting Condensation Level (LCL) and the Convection Condensation Level (CCL) for a measured temperature profile and surface dewpoint T_d (at J) plotted on a skew $T - \log p$ diagram.

Plate 8.1 Orographic clouds on the peaks at the south end of Lord Howe Island at 32°S.

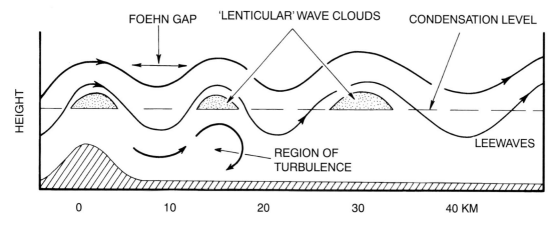

Figure 8.2 The formation of mountain waves. Wind crossing a mountain range experiences a wave motion, which creates the possibility of lenticular clouds in the crests of the waves.

8.2). They are due to waves in the atmosphere of several kilometres amplitude, caused by the range when there is a stable layer near the ridge-top level, against which the air bounces down again. The wind has to be at least 7–15 m/s across the ridge of the range, and faster at higher levels. Uplift towards the wave crests creates the cloud, if the wind is close to saturation.

Wave clouds are stationary; the air moves through them, condensing on the uphill side of the crest and evaporating on the downward side. The space between adjacent rows, called the *foehn gap*, can be used to estimate the wavelength of the waves, typically 10–20 km. Five or more rows may sometimes be seen in satellite pictures of eastern New Zealand, when westerlies blow over the north/south ranges. Also they often occur over Sydney when strong westerly winds blow over the Blue Mountains just inland. The waves have their highest amplitude well above the height of the mountain ridge, e.g. the effect of a range 1 km high can be felt at 10 km. But the uplift in wave clouds is insufficient to create rain.

Cloud Due to Shallow Currents of Cold Air

'Cold currents' (or *density currents*) are cold winds, perhaps a kilometre deep or so, which wedge under a warmer air mass simply because the cold air is more dense, i.e. heavier. The uplift provided to the warm air ahead causes cloud if it is moist. Some examples are given in Note 8.C.

Cloud Due to Large-scale Uplift

Most mid-latitude cloud and rain are due to ascent on a synoptic scale (Table 1.1), caused either by upper-level 'divergence' near a jet stream (Chapter 12) or low-level 'convergence' in low-pressure regions (Chapter 13) or both. The rate of such large-scale ascent is typically small, e.g. 10 mm/s or about 1 km/day, which is too small to measure amongst the turbulence of the horizontal winds. Nevertheless, the small vertical movements are important in forming cloud. Unsaturated air ascending at 10 mm/s cools at almost 10 K per day, and such a rate of

Plate 8.2 Wave clouds downwind of Macquarie Island (at 55°S), which is near the top left of the picture. The ribs of cloud are about 8 km apart. The photograph was taken from an orbiting satellite at 0512 GMT on 17 October 1985.

cooling soon lowers the air's temperature to dewpoint, with consequent cloud formation. So one of the least measurable variables in meteorology – large-scale vertical motion – is one of the most important. This makes weather forecasting more difficult.

Cloud Due to Frontal Uplift

The low-pressure region and the uplift just mentioned are associated with a well-defined boundary between (polar) cold air and (subtropical) warmer air, called a 'front', discussed in Chapter 13. A *cold front* involves cold air underrunning warmer air, just as with a small-scale density current, and results in the uplift of the warmer air. This creates long bands of cloud over the front and behind it. But sometimes the warm air advances over the cooler air, creating a *warm front* and then the cloud tends to be more widespread and uniform. Frontal ascent is generally about 10 km/day.

Convergence Clouds

Air is forced upwards when winds converge at low levels. This happens at the Intertropical Convergence Zone (ITCZ) near the equator (Chapter 12), which explains why most equatorial regions are cloudy. It also occurs at a collision of sea breezes (Chapter 14) from opposite sides of an island, or a meeting of land breezes from opposite sides of a waterway.

Convective Cloud

This is the most common kind of cloud inland and near the equator, and results from thermal convection which is either shallow or deep. Shallow convection results from daytime heating of the ground's surface and produces non-precipitating 'fair-weather cumulus' clouds (Section 8.6). Cloud base is at the *convective condensation level* (CCL), shown in Figure 8.1. Cloud forms at this height when the surface is at the *convection temperature* T_c, represented by K in Figure 8.1 (Note 8.B).

'Deep convection' reaches through most of the troposphere and results in thunderstorms (Chapter 9). It is *initiated* by several factors, including local surface heating. But the trigger might be daytime 'anabatic flow' up mountains, or uplift caused by sea breezes near the coast (Chapter 14), both of which lead to most thunderstorms in the afternoon. As an example, the sky is normally clear at night on Mt Wilhelm (which reaches 3,480 m in Papua New Guinea), but clouds begin to form at about 2,000 m around 8 a.m., and then they grow until there are intermittent showers from 11 a.m. until sunset. However, thunderstorms are more common during the night over the waters of tropical archipelagos like Indonesia, because of uplift started by low-level convergence of nocturnal land breezes (Chapter 14) from nearby islands.

Whatever cloud is formed, an immense amount of latent energy is released as the water vapour condenses. The condensation that provides a modest shower of 6 mm over an area of 10 km² releases 150 million megajoules, which is as much as is produced in a whole day by Australia's 2,000-megawatt Snowy Mountain hydro-electric scheme, and about equal to the energy in the two atom-bomb explosions at Hiroshima and Nagasaki together.

8.2 CLOUD DROPLETS

Cloud is created almost immediately an atmosphere is cooled to its dewpoint temperature (**Note 8.D**). The droplets form by condensation on motes in the air, called *cloud condensation nuclei* (CCN). Without these, the air's relative humidity would need to be 110 per cent or more before droplets could form by the spontaneous collisions of water-vapour molecules (Section 4.3). But there are generally ample CCN in each cubic metre, even in clean air.

They are classified according to size – *Aitken nuclei* are less than 0.2 μm in diameter, so-called *large nuclei* are 0.2–2 μm, and *giant nuclei* are larger still. A cubic metre of maritime air reaching Cape Grim in northern Tasmania in summer typically contains 300 million particles larger than 0.01 μm, 100 million over 0.1 μm, and just 2 million giant nuclei. Such air contains many fewer CCN than continental air, so the droplets in marine clouds are fewer and larger.

The relatively clean air from off the ocean contains nuclei consisting mostly of sulphate crystals formed from *dimethyl sulphide*, a gas evolved by *phytoplankton*, which are minute organisms in the sea. (Extra sulphide is produced in a warmer ocean, resulting in more, smaller cloud droplets. This would increase cloud albedo and thereby perhaps reduce the initial warming – another possible negative feedback process, see Note 7.A). CCN above cities are mostly ammonium-sulphate particles, produced by sulphur dioxide and ammonia from air pollution reacting within cloud droplets. Other CCN are formed biologically.

Large nuclei are the most effective in creating cloud droplets (Note 8.D). Droplets form exclusively on the large nuclei if cooling of the humid air is gradual, so that there are bigger but relatively few droplets. Sea-salt particles are notably suitable. Even small nuclei are adequate if moist air is cooled rapidly, as in the strong updraughts of convective clouds (Table 8.1). This produces a dense white cloud of numerous, tiny droplets, with consequent poor visibility.

Cloud droplets are typically around 10 µm in diameter, so tiny that they float in the air, the fall speed being less than 1 mm/s. The space between them is likely to be about 200 times their diameter, so they amount to much less than the water vapour within the cloud's volume (Note 8.E). Nevertheless, the huge volume of a large cloud means that it may contain thousands of tonnes of liquid water.

The droplets are no more than a millionth of the mass of typical raindrops and the change from one to the other is not straightforward. The formation of raindrops usually requires particles called *ice nuclei*, which are *quite different* from cloud-condensation nuclei. Such raindrop nuclei are not always adequately available, unlike CCN. As a result, even slightly supersaturated air always produces clouds, but most clouds do not yield rain (Chapter 9).

8.3 CATEGORIES AND CHANGES

There are various kinds of cloud, and they were originally classified according to shape (Note 8.F). Luke Howard was the first to do this, in 1803, recognising three main groups – streaks, sheets and heaps. Streak clouds were called *cirrus* (which is Latin for 'hair'), sheet clouds were designated *stratus* ('layer') and a heap cloud is called *cumulus* ('pile'). Layered clouds are called stratiform, whereas billowing clouds are cumuliform.

The modern International System of cloud classification adopted by the World Meteorological Organisation (WMO) in 1956, refers first to the cloud's altitude, and then to the descriptive terminology of Howard (**Table 8.2**). There is a separate class for clouds of great vertical extent. All the various kinds are illustrated in **Figure 8.4** and typical values of water content, thickness and equivalent water depth are summarized in **Table 8.3**.

Changes of Cloud Form

Figure 8.3 shows how a change in surface conditions across a coastline can induce certain clouds, depending on whether the wind is onshore or offshore, and whether the land is warmer (in summer) or colder (in winter) than the sea. Convective clouds may form if the lower troposphere is unstable, e.g. when humid air from a warm ocean flows over even warmer land in summer (upper left of Figure 8.3) or when offshore cold air blows over a warmer sea (upper right), especially as the sea increases the dewpoint (Section 7.4). If the sea is cooler than the offshore wind (lower left), a shallow stably stratified cloud may form offshore, i.e. stratus or fog. In winter, relatively warm, moist onshore winds (lower right) become more stable over the coast, and form advective fog (Section 8.4) or light rainfall on rising ground. However, Figure 8.3 is a simplification; most clouds and rain form well above the planetary boundary layer and the coastline itself induces winds (Chapter 14). For instance, a sea breeze in summer may advect offshore fog (lower left) onto the land.

Clouds may change in character after they are formed, for several reasons. Here are three:

1 Destabilisation of the atmosphere by uplift may cause cumulus to grow out of stratus.

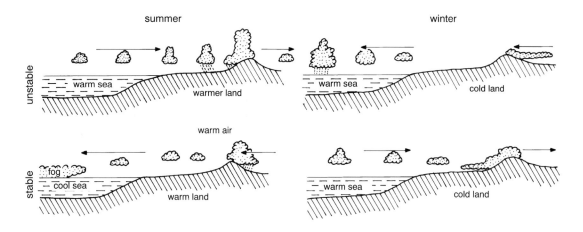

summer

winter

unstable

warm sea

warmer land

warm sea

cold land

warm air

stable

fog

cool sea

warm land

warm sea

cold land

Figure 8.3 Cloud development near the coast in various circumstances.

2 Stabilisation causes afternoon cumulus clouds to flatten out as stratocumulus. This occurs when solar heating of the surface is reduced at sunset, or as a consequence of cloud shadow reducing surface temperatures.

3 A thin layer of stratus often changes to a ribbed or dappled form (**Figure 8.5**) because of cellular stirring due to internal instability, caused by cooling of the top through the loss of longwave radiation to space, and warming of the layer's base by radiation from the ground.

Clouds disappear when the droplets evaporate, because of either the *entrainment* of dry air from the environment, or warming due to subsidence, or the absorption of longwave radiation from the ground (especially with shallow stratus on summer mornings). Small fair-weather cumulus (Section 8.6) often dissipates by entrainment after only a few minutes, whilst large cumulus may last several hours. Cirrus cloud is usually long-lived because it consists of ice, which sublimes only with difficulty at the temperatures of around −40°C.

8.4 FOG

Cloud at ground level is *fog,* if visibility is less than one kilometre; otherwise it is *mist.* The better visibility in mist is due to the larger size of the droplets, i.e. about 100 μm: the larger the mean drop size, the better the visibility (**Note 8.G**). 'Thick' fogs have a visibility below 200 m and 'dense' fogs less than 40 m. We will consider seven kinds.

1 *Hill mist* or *upslope fog* arises from orographic lifting of stable air when the Lifting Condensation Level is lower than the mountain top.

2 Rain is usually cooled by evaporation, so the immediately adjacent air becomes cool as well as moist. Mixing of this air with that around may lead to supersaturation (Note 8.A), in which case separate patches of cloud called *scud* or *stratus fractus* form below the cloud which is yielding rain. The scud may hug a hillside or even level ground, in which case it is known as *rain fog.*

3 *Radiation fog* or *ground fog* is formed at night if the surface air is moist and the ground is

Table 8.2 Classes of clouds

Cloud type	Abbreviation	Description	Typical height (km)	Vertical motion involved	Atmospheric stability in formation
High cloud:					
1 Cirrus	Ci	Separate white filaments, in streaks or bands	6–10	Widespread, prolonged and regular ascent at around 70 mm/s	Strong wind shear
2 Cirrocumulus	Cc	Dappled layer like beach sand ripples	As above	As above	
3 Cirrostratus	Cs	Fused veil of cirrus, forming halo round Sun or Moon	As above	As above	
Medium-level cloud:					
4 Altostratus	As	Grey, uniform fibrous sheet	3–6	As above	
5 Altocumulus	Ac	Dappled, flattened globules in billows	As above	As above	Elevated unstable layer
Low-level cloud:					
6 Stratocumulus	Sc	Soft, grey layer of flakes or globules in groups, lines or waves*	Below 3	Widespread irregular stirring with below 10 cm/s vertically	Turbulence within stable air
7 Stratus	St	Featureless elevated fog	1–2	Widespread lifting of cool damp surface air	Stable
Cumuliform cloud:					
8 Cumulus	Cu	Flat base, cabbage-shaped top piled high	0.6–6	Thermal convection with large bubbles rising at 1–5 m/s	Unstable, spreading out to Sc in evening due to stability
9 Cumulonimbus	Cb	Huge, heavy, dense, with fibrous top, often spread into anvil shape, producing rain	To the tropopause	Internal convection of 3–30 m/s upwards	Deep instability

* Due to spreading out of the tops of earlier cumulus clouds

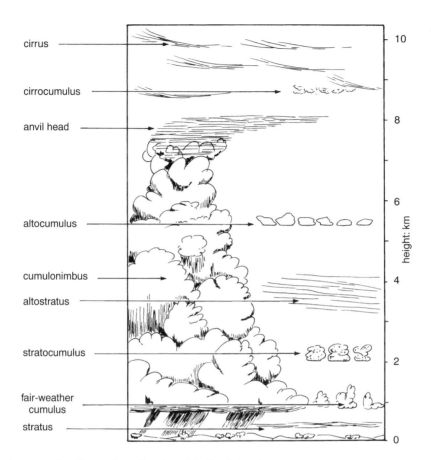

Figure 8.4 A composite illustration of various kinds of cloud.

Table 8.3 Typical values of the water contents of clouds in the southern hemisphere

| Feature | Type of cloud | | | | | |
	Ci	Ac/As	Cu	St	Cb	Ns
Thickness (km)	3.6	0.6	1	0.5	6	2
Water content (g/m³)	0.01	0.1	1.0	0.25	1.5	0.5
Equivalent depth of water (mm)*	0.04	0.06	1	0.13	9	1

* The equivalent water depth is the depth of rain if all the *liquid* water in the cloud were to fall; it is the product of the cloud thickness (km) and the average water content (g/m³)

cooled by longwave radiation to a clear sky (Section 7.6). It is more likely when the ground has been wetted by earlier rain, and at high latitudes where long winter nights allow prolonged cooling. Also, the ponding of cold air and moisture in hollows promotes ground fog there. It is often less than 10 m thick, but may become 250 m thick in valleys. **Figure 8.6** shows that fog in Canberra is most likely around 7 a.m.,

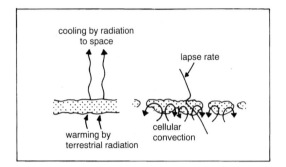

Figure 8.5 Formation of a ribbed type of cloud as a result of convection within a stratus cloud, induced by radiation cooling of the top.

and in winter, when temperatures are lowest.

4 *Advection fog* or *sea fog* occurs where relatively warm, moist and stable air moves over water whose temperature is slightly below the dew-point of the air (lower left in Figure 8.3, and **Note 8.H**), e.g. off the coast of northern Chile, and over Antarctic sea-ice, especially near a 'lead' (a line of clear water between ice floes) or the open sea in winter. Advection fogs tend to be more extensive and deeper than radiation fogs. The depth depends on the wind strength; less air is stirred down to be cooled if the speed is much below 7 m/s, whilst a stronger wind dissipates the fog by stirring it with warmer air above (Note 8.A).

5 *Steam fog* or *sea smoke* forms when cold air flows over a relatively warm wet surface (Section 4.3). Evaporation from the latter into the unstable lower atmosphere leads to convection of the moisture upwards, and then the vapour condenses to drifting filaments of wispy mist, a few metres high (**Note 8.I**). You can see it after a shower onto a hot roadway and it occurs at sea around Antarctica, where the air may be much cooler than the water. The likelihood of steam fog is increased by thermal pollution of waterways, and by radiation cooling on cloudless nights chilling the ground and hence the air around a shallow lake (**Table 8.4**).

Note the paradox that fog may be formed either by cold air over warm water (steam fog) or by warm air over cold water (advection fog).

6 *Ice fog* occurs when temperatures drop below −20°C or so. For instance, a person breathing out in Antarctica may become

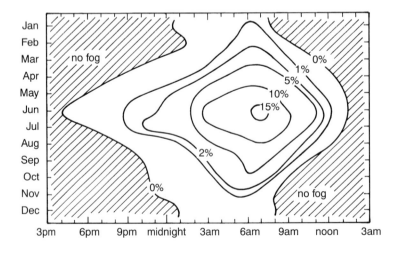

Figure 8.6 The chance of fog at Canberra at various times of the day and year.

Table 8.4 Dependence of the frequency of wintertime fogs at dawn, on the wind, cloudiness and the difference between the temperatures of the air and a river in Sydney

Condition	Number of occasions	Wind speed (km/h)	Cloudiness	Temperature difference (K)
With fog	9	Less than 5	Almost cloudless	7–10
Without fog	5	About 5	Over half overcast	1.5–4

surrounded by a personal cloud of ice fog, and idling airplane engines there can quickly cause the plane to be enveloped in ice fog. Ice fog may deposit on the upwind side of solid surfaces as *hoar frost*, a layer of ice crystals in the form of needles, scales, plates, etc.

7 *Smoke fog* or *smog* is characteristic of polluted cities in damp climates. It occurs when a low-level inversion traps surface air pollution, along with considerable water vapour. The droplets are so tiny that the fog may appear thick even though its water content

is small (Note 8.G). The fog may be highly acidic.

The annual number of days with fog varies around the globe (**Figure 8.7**). In general, there are fewer in the southern hemisphere than the northern, though over eighty each year at spots on the south-west coasts of Africa and South America, where sea-surface temperatures are low (Chapter 11). Fogs occur on more than forty days each year, between 20–30°S along the coasts of Chile and western South Africa,

Figure 8.7 The average number of days each year that fog reduces visibility below a kilometre, some time during the day.

but not on the west of Australia or New Zealand.

Fogs are uncommon in Australian cities. Canberra is the foggiest capital city, with around forty-six annually, followed by Brisbane (22), Melbourne (20), Sydney (17) and Perth (8). There has been a striking reduction in the number of fogs near Sydney, from thirty-one annually during 1931–5, to only five in the period 1976–80.

The dispersal of fog is either by stirring by the wind, or the arrival of drier air or the Sun heating the ground. It can endure if shielded from the Sun by cloud.

Having thus considered cloud near the ground, we proceed to discuss the kinds of stratiform and cumuliform clouds.

8.5 STRATIFORM CLOUDS

A *stratus* cloud (St) may extend horizontally for hundreds of kilometres, but be only 50–500 m thick, with little tendency for vertical growth because the cloud forms by slow uplift within *stable* air (Table 8.2). The top of the cloud is typically surmounted by an inversion due to radiation cooling of the top of the cloud. Such cloud prevents sunshine reaching the ground in winter at high latitudes, when the Sun is low (and therefore the cloud's albedo particularly high – see Section 2.5), and we describe the sky as 'leaden'.

Stratus sometimes results from mixing in the planetary boundary layer (PBL). This cools the top of the layer to about 10 K below screen temperature if it is 1,000 m thick, for instance. If the cooling reaches dewpoint, a thin layer of stratus forms just below the PBL inversion (Section 7.6). Such stratus forms over the cold water of the Humboldt current (Chapter 11) on the west of South America, where the subsidence/PBL inversion is only 300–500 m high, and then it may be blown about 50 km inland to the edge of the Andes. The stability of the onshore wind means that the coastal strip receives almost no rain (Chapter 16), yet plants at around 400 m altitude thrive on water they intercept from the cloud.

Altostratus (As) appears as a grey-bluish, striated or fibrous veil, blurring the Sun. It is stratus of the middle troposphere (Table 8.2, Figure 8.4, **Figure 8.8**). Another reason for altostratus is the spreading and decaying of the anvil from a medium-size cumulonimbus (Section 8.6).

Nimbostratus (Ns) is a large layer of low-level cloud, but precipitating rain, unlike stratus. The rain is usually continuous but light, because the atmosphere is stably stratified and the cloud arises from only gradual lifting. Such cloud can result from orographic uplift; Figure 8.8 shows a stable moist airstream forming a cap of nimbostratus with higher layers of the atmosphere raised to make altostratus.

8.6 CUMULIFORM CLOUDS

Cumulus cloud is the opposite of stratus in several ways, being isolated and vertical rather than horizontal and extensive, and it forms more rapidly. The flat base of cumulus at the condensation level differs completely from its cauliflower-like sides, where turrets thrust upwards and then unfold to spill sideways and down. Buoyant parcels of air within the cloud bulge outward, then entrain air from the environment so that the surface of each parcel expands and becomes cooler by mixing with the enveloped air and by evaporation of cloud droplets into it. This leads to *negative buoyancy* (i.e. air *heavier* than the surroundings) and consequently a downdraught within the cloud, maybe continuing to the surface.

There is a range of size, from small fair-weather cumulus to cumulo-nimbus clouds. Cumuliform clouds can grow to a height of 17 km near the equator. All cumulus has a well-defined appearance, with plenty of surface

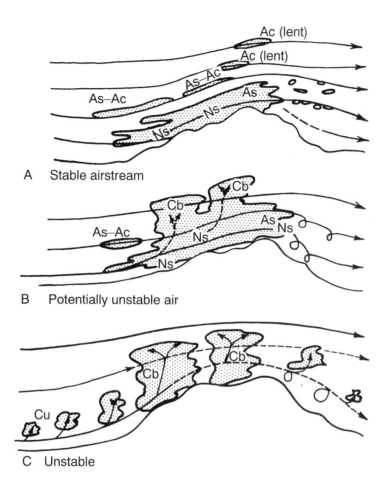

A Stable airstream

B Potentially unstable air

C Unstable

Figure 8.8 The effect of atmospheric stability on the kinds of cloud forming over rising land.

detail where they are composed of water droplets. But the highest parts of tall cumulus seem diffuse and fibrous, because the cloud there is *glaciated*, consisting of ice crystals. The common, essential feature of all cumulus clouds is brisk internal convection, due to instability within a considerable depth of the atmosphere.

Fair-weather Cumulus (Cu)

These are 'cotton-wool' clouds occurring in a clear sky in the daytime, each fluffy cloud sit-

ting on top of an invisible thermal. Such cumulus is formed at the convection condensation level (Figure 8.1), generally between 500 m (over the sea) and 4 km (over dry land). A fair-weather cumulus cloud appears more substantial than altocumulus or altostratus, because it is lower and therefore warmer, so that saturated air contains more water (Table 8.3).

Fair-weather cumulus clouds usually arise in calm conditions, and then are temporarily anchored to the warm spots generating their thermals. The number and size of the clouds increase in the course of two or three hours, until further solar heating of the ground is prevented by the clouds themselves – another case of negative feedback. Individual clouds generally last 10–30 minutes, persisting only if continually nourished by strong daytime thermals. They disappear by subsidence and evaporation, by mixing with the surrounding dry air, or by spreading out to form stratocumulus.

Sometimes the thermal needed to create a fair-weather cumulus cloud is generated by a surface fire. A large fire in a timber yard in Melbourne in 1976 resulted in a cumulus with cloud base at 1.6 km and cloud top at 3.5 km. Heat from a power-station can work the same way.

Stratocumulus (Sc)

This is an extensive kind of *low-level* cloud illustrated in Figure 8.4. It is a common cloud, arising in several ways, including the disruption of stratus by either internal convection due to cooling of the top (Figure 8.5), or by turbulence due to irregularity of the land surface. Alternatively, Sc may form from the spreading out of cumulus either beneath an inversion, or at the end of the day when convection has stopped (i.e. Sc *vesperalis*).

Altocumulus (Ac)

Altocumulus is extensive cloud at *mid-level* in the troposphere, whose lumpy appearance shows the convection within it (Table 8.2). It can take many forms, but is usually a layer of flattened globules of cloud, in groups, waves or lines, often less than 100 metres thick.

One type of altocumulus consists of the wave clouds discussed in Section 8.1. There are also *billow clouds*, which form a ribbed pattern and occur where the air at different altitudes is moving at different speeds. A layer of air becomes rucked up into a wave-like shape and the ridges of the waves are high enough to reach dewpoint, so that they fill with billow clouds. The exact form of the billows is influenced by convection and the overall pattern of wind. The billows move with the wind, unlike wave clouds, which are anchored to the hills that cause them.

Other ways of forming altocumulus are as follows:

1 The release of any potential instability within altostratus by slow uplift breaks the layer into a series of turrets. Afternoon thunderstorms are possible if this kind (called Ac *castellanus*) occurs in the morning, though rain from Ac usually evaporates before reaching the ground.
2 Radiative cooling of the top of a thick stratus cloud in the tropics may break up the flat top into a series of turrets. This tends to happen during the late afternoon.
3 Some ice crystals may form in altostratus (As) which consists of supercooled water (Section 6.2), triggering widespread glaciation throughout the cloud (Chapter 9). The consequent release of latent heat of freezing (Section 4.1) causes convection, which extends the As vertically into altocumulus.

Cumulonimbus (Cb)

This is the largest kind of cloud, like an ice-cream castle or a vast cauliflower, capped by a sideways extension, the *anvil*. The usual great extent of the cloud's growth is caused by deep convective instability within most of the troposphere (Section 7.4). A cumulonimbus cloud is typically higher than 5 km, and often reaches the tropopause, helping define it. The depth of the cloud increases its albedo, so that it has a blinding whiteness from above and appears very dark from below.

There are vigorous *updraughts* within each cloud, with a speed which is typically around

5 m/s but can be over 15 m/s, implying travel from cloud base to cloud top in less than 15 minutes. In the extreme, there have been updraughts of 60 m/s, surrounded by downdraughts of 35 m/s. The commotion leads to thunderstorms, lightning and rain (Chapters 9 and 10).

Patterns of Cumulus Clouds

Distinct patterns of shallow cumulus clouds can sometimes be seen from the distance of a satellite. The clouds may form rows called *cloud streets* when winds are much the same at various heights and there is an unstable layer under a stable layer, e.g. when polar air blows over a warm ocean (Section 7.4). The rows of cloud are parallel to the wind and perhaps hundreds of kilometres long, with a distance between adjacent rows equal to about five times the depth of the convective layer. A glider pilot can fly a long way in the updraughts just below a cloud street.

Other patterns resemble a honeycomb, with numerous *open cells* or *closed cells*, each with a diameter of 50–1,600 km. An open cell involves subsidence in the middle surrounded by gently ascending air, whereas it is the other way round in a closed cell.

8.7 HIGH CLOUDS

The highest clouds of all are rare and occur in the mesosphere at about 70–80 km elevation (Section 1.8). They are mainly seen in summer at latitudes above 50°, and are called *noctilucent* because they can be briefly observed with the naked eye only in the evening, when the Sun has just set at ground level but still shines on these high thin veils. They consist of extraterrestrial dust coated with ice.

Almost equally unusual and tenuous are the *nacreous* (or mother-of-pearl) clouds which form in the lower stratosphere, up to 30 km from the ground. The clouds are due to occasional insertions of ice crystals and aerosols from the troposphere below, which can happen through either volcanic eruptions or extraordinarily strong thunderstorms overshooting the tropopause.

Cirrus (Ci)

This is the main type of high cloud, occurring in the upper troposphere, mainly in the tropics and the mid-latitudes. The water content of cirrus clouds is small and the layers of long, fibrous filaments, streaks, plumes or tufts (Figure 8.4) consist entirely of ice crystals because of the low temperatures at the top of the troposphere. For instance, temperatures at 12 km in midlatitudes are typically about −55°C, which is well below the −40°C to which water can sometimes be supercooled. Growth of the crystals makes them settle out as *fall streaks*, long curved wisps of cloud. Large differences of wind speed or direction in adjacent air (i.e. strong *wind shear*) cause *hooked cirrus*, or 'mares' tails'.

Artificial cirrus is produced by the condensation trails (i.e. *contrails*) of high-flying aircraft, as ice crystals form from the exhaust water-vapour.

Cirrostratus (Cs)

Cirrostratus is a high, uniform *layer* of cloud, so thin as to be no obstacle to sunlight. It can form when cirrus spreads and fuses, and the layer may thicken to 2–3 km in depth. More often it is produced by gradual ascent, maybe due to divergence at the tropopause, in the vicinity of a jet stream (Chapter 12). Or it may result from frontal uplift (Chapter 13).

Cirrocumulus (Cc)

This is a thin dappled layer of small cumulus clouds, higher and more translucent than altocumulus.

8.8 OBSERVING CLOUDINESS

Clouds are observed regularly at weather stations. The extent to which the sky appears covered at the time of observation is expressed in terms of *oktas,* representing eighths of the sky seen by the observer. Thus 8 oktas of cloud represents a totally overcast sky (**Figure 8.9**). A cross is drawn through the cloud circle under foggy conditions. The inexperienced often underestimate cloudiness by ignoring the cirrus, or else they overestimate the amount of cumulus because it tends to cover much of the sky near the horizon. Preferably, separate estimates are made of the amounts of cloud in each of the three main layers of the troposphere – low, middle and high (Table 8.2).

Cloudiness above a weather station can be determined indirectly by measuring the duration of bright sunshine. As an example, if eight hours of sunshine were registered in a daytime of twelve hours, there would have been four hours of cloud. The instrument used is often a

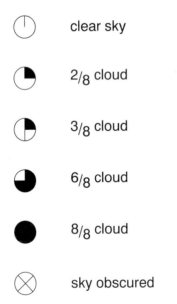

clear sky

2/8 cloud

3/8 cloud

6/8 cloud

8/8 cloud

sky obscured

Figure 8.9 Symbols used to record the amount of cloud, in terms of the number of oktas.

Campbell–Stokes bright-sunshine recorder (**Figure 8.10**), which gives the fraction of time that cloud obscures one *place*. (A visual observation of cloud in terms of oktas gives the fraction of the sky's area obscured at one *time*.)

Observations of cloud are plotted on maps with the symbols shown in **Figure 8.11**.

Satellite Observations

The wide separation of weather stations where clouds are observed, and their relative absence at sea (apart from ship observers), have been major problems, especially in the southern hemisphere where 81 per cent of the area is ocean. Fortunately, total coverage of the world is now provided by satellite observations, developed since the 1960s, notably from satellites described as *geostationary* (**Note 8.J**). These rotate above the equator at the same rate as the Earth, so they appear fixed. Currently there are five of them for meteorological observations, at longitudes 135°W, 75°W, zero, 60°E and 140°E, respectively. Pictures are taken each half-hour (**Figure 8.12**), recording differences over distances down to about 2.5 km – that distance is the *resolution* of the technique. Both visible radiation (0.5 μm) and infra-red (10 μm) pictures are taken. The former show clouds as particularly bright, and the latter detect longwave radiation from the Earth, i.e. the pattern of temperatures of the surfaces seen from space, notably cloud-top temperatures (Note 2.C). As a result, examinaton of the features of cloud pictures (or *nephanalysis*) yields the following information:

(a) the shape and size of cloudy areas;
(b) the spatial organisation of clouds (e.g. cloud streets or cell structures);
(c) cloud height, indicated partly by the shadows cast by high clouds and partly by the cloud-top temperature;

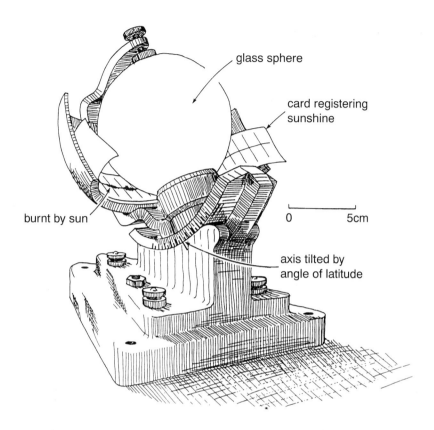

Figure 8.10 A Campbell–Stokes recorder of the duration of a day's bright sunshine. The glass sphere has a diameter of about 100 mm and focuses sunlight onto a card. The focused light is intense enough to burn a hole in the card when there is no cloud in front of the Sun. The Sun moves across the sky, so the point of focus moves along the card, and the length of the resulting burnt slot shows the duration of bright sunshine.

(d) the cloud type from albedo and cloud-top temperature information (**Figure 8.13**);

(e) the movement and evolution of clouds from pictures at 30-minute intervals.

Changes of the position of identifiable clouds show wind speeds at cloud height.

Meteorologists have also used a succession of *orbiting* satellites, which pass over the Poles and encircle the Earth fourteen times a day at a slightly different longitude each time on account of the Earth's rotation. The first such satellite, TIROS 1 (i.e. Television and Infra-Red Observing Satellite), went into orbit in 1960. Orbiting satellites have a finer resolution than geostationary satellites (typically 1 km, but sometimes 30 m), because they pass only 850 km above the ground. They also measure radiation in several parts of the electromagnetic spectrum (Figure 2.1), e.g. at wavelengths between visible (0.5 μm) and infra-red (10 μm), and in the microwave or radar region (with wavelengths of about 1 cm). These measurements together reveal more details about clouds, such as cloud density, liquid-water content, whether liquid or frozen, cloud-top texture (i.e. smoothness) and even precipitation.

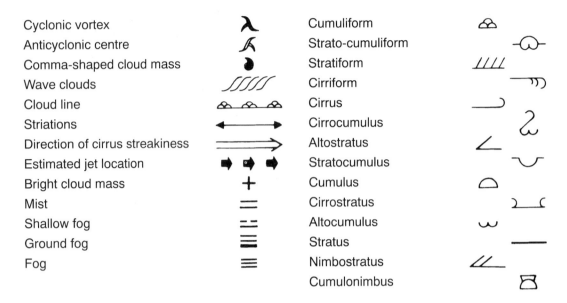

Figure 8.11 Symbols representing various kinds of clouds or cloud patterns, as identified from surface and satellite observations.

8.9 AMOUNTS OF CLOUD

About 52 per cent of the globe is covered by cloud at any time, with a slightly higher fraction in the southern hemisphere where there is more ocean (**Figure 8.14**). On the whole, there is least cloud over North Africa, northern Australia and Antarctica, and most north of 60°N, over high-latitude oceans (especially at 60°S) and south-east Asia. There are persistent decks of stratocumulus over the cool oceans (Chapter 11) off the coasts of Namibia, northern Chile and Peru, especially in summer. On the other hand, high clouds are particularly common on the equator north and north-west of Australia. The South Pole is much less cloudy than the North, because the South Pole is higher, colder and further from the sea, so there is less atmo-

spheric moisture. In general, proximity to the sea and mountains increases cloudiness, though there is a decrease in some places right at the coast on account of reduced convection from a cool ocean surface.

Cloudiness varies with season. There is more (convective) cloud in summer than winter in most parts of the Americas and in southern Africa, but more (frontal) cloud in winter in much of Europe, for instance. The cloudiest regions in the southern hemisphere in *July* are near the equator, and there is a band of cloud around Antarctica at about 60°S, with least cloud at 15°S and the South Pole. In *January*, there is least cloud at 30°S.

The chain of mountains along the west coast of the south island of New Zealand gives rise to the so-called 'long white cloud' that notably

---

Figure 8.12 Comparison of (a) the GMS cloud photograph at noon Greenwich Meridian Time (GMT) on 8 November 1995, and (b) the synoptic chart from ground measurements at the same time (from the Australian Bureau of Meteorology). The cold front across south-west Australia on the chart corresponds to the band of cloud in the photograph. Isolated convective cloud can be seen at low latitudes.

(a)

(b)

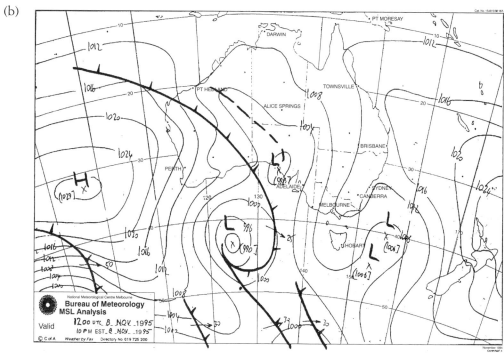

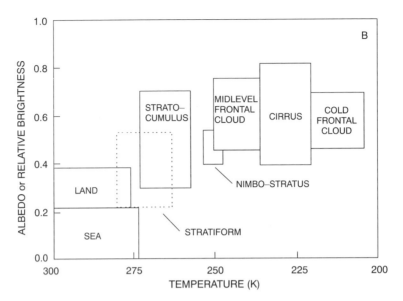

Figure 8.13 The ranges of cloud-top temperature and albedo of various kinds of cloud in the New Zealand region.

reduces the amount of bright sunshine there (**Figure 8.15**). However, central Australia is usually free of cloud. For instance, there are usually five months each year with over 10 hours of bright sunshine each day in Alice Springs and the annual average is 9.6 hours of bright sunshine daily, i.e. 80 per cent of the daylength of 12 hours. Even in west Tasmania (with less than 5 hours daily on average) the figure is more than the 4.2 for London, for example. **Figure 8.16** shows that there is a notable seasonal variation of sunshine in Canberra and Adelaide, due to both the variation of the length of day (Table 2.1) and a difference between amounts of frontal cloud in winter. The different curve for Darwin results from the monsoonal climate (Chapter 12).

It is now generally agreed that there has been a global increase of cloud since about 1950, possibly because of more chimney emissions of sulphates to nucleate cloud droplets (Section 8.2). There was 2.3 per cent more cloud in the northern hemisphere in 1981 than in 1952, and a 1.2 per cent increase in the south-

ern hemisphere, where there is less industrial pollution. The increase was mainly of altocumulus and altostratus.

8.10 EFFECTS OF CLOUDS

Clouds affect flows of radiation by reflecting some, absorbing part and transmitting the remainder (**Table 8.5**). The consequence of obscuring the Sun is that cloudiness is closely correlated with the solar irradiance of the ground (Section 2.3). **Figure 8.17** shows an example from Brazil, illustrating how a fairly simple determination of sunshine duration (Figure 8.10) yields estimates of the radiation, which is much more difficult to measure.

Clouds tend to warm the Earth by radiating sky radiation to the ground, and by preventing the loss of terrestrial radiation to space. Nevertheless, clouds cause cooling on the whole by reflecting solar radiation away (**Note 8.K**). In the absence of clouds, the current concentration of greenhouse gases (Section 1.3) would make

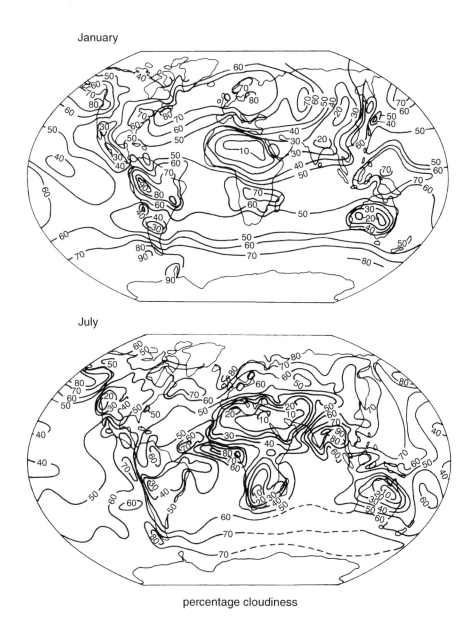

January

July

percentage cloudiness

Figure 8.14 Effect of season on cloudiness over the globe. The units are percentages, e.g. 40 means 4 tenths of cloud (i.e. 40 per cent of the sky is covered with cloud), or 3 oktas.

Table 8.5 Typical fractions of incident solar radiation either reflected, absorbed or transmitted by various kinds of cloud

Cloud	Reflected	Absorbed	Transmitted
Ns, Cb	85	–	–
fair-weather Cu, 450 m thick	50	7	43
St, 100 m thick	40	3	57
St, 600 m thick	50	11	39
Ci	20	1	79

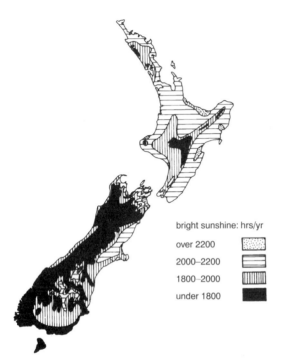

bright sunshine: hrs/yr

over 2200

2000–2200

1800–2000

under 1800

Figure 8.15 The annual mean number of hours of bright sunshine in New Zealand.

the Earth's surface temperature about 30°C on average, well above the observed average of about 15°C (Section 2.7).

In addition, the moisture which yields cloud tends to imply moist air at screen height also, i.e. a high surface dewpoint T_d, which approximates the daily minimum temperature (Section 6.2). Cloud also reduces the daily maximum temperature T_x. As a result, it is associated with a low value of $\{T_x - T_d\}$ as shown in **Figure 8.18**, and with a reduced daily range of temperature (Section 3.4).

The connection between cloud and rainfall is discussed in the next chapter.

NOTES

8.A The formation of cloud by mixing
8.B The Lifting Condensation Level and the Convective Condensation Level
8.C Atmospheric density currents which create uplift
8.D Formation of cloud droplets
8.E The water content of clouds
8.F The evolution of cloud classification
8.G Motoring in fog
8.H Formation of advection fog
8.I Formation of steam fog
8.J Weather satellites
8.K Effect of clouds on global climate
8.L The Morning Glory

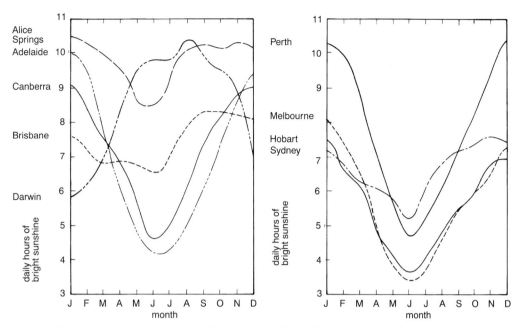

Figure 8.16 Seasonal variation in the daily duration of cloudlessness at several places in Australia.

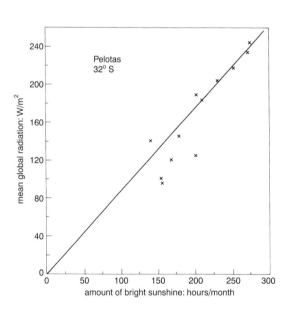

Figure 8.17. Effect of cloudiness (or, rather, its converse, the time when there is no cloud between the Sun and the observer) on the solar insolation of the ground at Pelotas, at 32°S in Brazil.

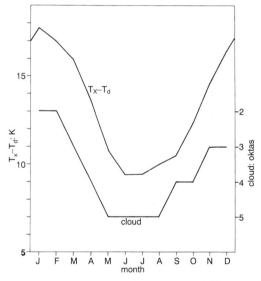

Figure 8.18. Association between the difference of the daily maximum dry-bulb temperature T_x from the dewpoint temperature T_d, and the cloudiness at Perth. The dewpoint values were measured at 9 a.m., before sea breezes bring marine air to the weather station. The cloudiness refers to 3 p.m. conditions, when convection is greatest. The data are monthly mean values averaged over 1947–92.

9

CLOUD PROCESSES

9.1 CLOUDS AND RAIN

This chapter links cloud, discussed in the previous chapter, with rainfall, considered in the next. Some correlation between cloud and rainfall is shown by **Figure 9.1**, with a weaker association in southern latitudes than northern. One reason is that areas between 15–30°S are frequently covered by stratus clouds which produce no rain. But there is a fair connection between cloud and rain in Australia (**Figure 9.2, Note 9.A**).

The various kinds of rainfall can be classified in various ways. For instance, according to either (i) the intensity of precipitation, (ii) the intensity of uplift, or (iii) the mechanism of cloud formation. As regards the first, we distinguish rain showers (which come from cumulus clouds) from drizzle (which involves rain droplets as small as 0.1 mm (**Table 9.1**) and comes from nimbostratus low in the sky). Drizzle occurs when surface relative humidities are high, i.e. the difference between air and dewpoint temperatures is 2 K or less. This is most likely at night, in the early morning or in winter. Usually there is a good breeze during drizzle, creating the turbulence which lifts surface air to dewpoint temperature, to replenish the cloud. Also there may be gentle uplift by hills or a weak front in the vicinity.

As regards classification in terms of the intensity of uplift, there are 'convective' and 'stratiform' rainfalls. *Convective rainfall* involves a vertical velocity maintained at 1 m/s or more, unlike *stratiform rainfall*, which is lighter because updraughts within stratus clouds are much weaker (Table 8.1, **Note 9.B**). Convective rain occurs when the atmosphere becomes unstable (Section 7.3) and is predominant in low latitudes, and in midlatitudes during the summer. It includes rain from thunderstorms, caused by the isolated convection of huge volumes of moist air over ground heated by the Sun (Section 9.5). In addition, convective rainfall may be caused by the passage of cold moist air over a warm surface, which happens off the coast of New South Wales when cold air from high latitudes flows over the warm East Australian Current (Section 7.4; Chapter 11). Convective rain is almost always accompanied by stratiform rain in the final stage of a thunderstorm (Section 9.5).

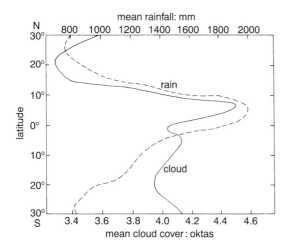

Figure 9.1 The association between annual mean cloudiness and rainfall between 30°N and 30°S.

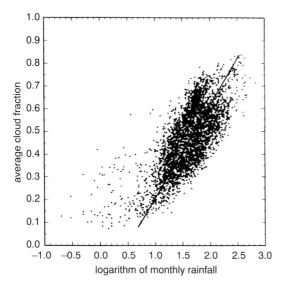

Figure 9.2 The association of monthly mean cloudiness (as a fraction of unity) and the logarithm of the monthly total rainfall at 263 places in Australia from more than twenty years of data.

Alternatively, rainfalls can be classified in terms of the mechanism of uplift. Thus there is orographic, frontal and convergence rainfall. *Orographic rain* comes from stratus or stratocumulus created by hills, as when onshore winds rise over high ground at the coast (Figure 8.8). Rainfall from the consequent stratiform clouds occurs at about the rate of condensation, and so there is drizzle. This can continue for days on end, as long as the onshore wind persists (Note 9.B).

The term *frontal rain* is applied to midlatitude precipitation associated with the uplift occurring when a mass of cold air wedges under a warmer air mass (Chapter 13). It is sometimes called *cyclonic rainfall*, though it has no connection with low-latitude *tropical* cyclones discussed in Chapter 13. This rainfall is usually stratiform.

Convergence rainfall occurs, for instance, when wind is funnelled into a narrowing valley, or land breezes (Chapter 14) converge onto a large lake at night, e.g. Lake Victoria in East Africa. Convergence rainfall is usually convective. It takes place on a large scale near the equator, due to the confluence of air from the two hemispheres (Chapter 12). This happens near Darwin in the summer, producing copious rain (Chapter 10). A further kind of convergence rainfall results from tropical cyclones (Chapter 13) and is of particularly high intensity, often responsible for record measurements. For instance, a tropical cyclone near Broome in Western Australia caused a 24-hour rainfall of 351 mm on 18–19 January 1974, with an intensity reaching 122 mm/h.

A last type of rain is *virga*. This is the name of visible fallstreaks of rain from cloud, failing to reach ground level because the cloud base is too high and the atmosphere beneath so dry that all the rain evaporates before reaching the surface. Usually, less than 10 per cent of the rain from an isolated thunderstorm in the desert reaches the ground, about 30 per cent with large areas of convective cloud in hot and humid climes, but over 70 per cent in the case of stratiform rainfall at middle and high latitudes. The percentage is more on high land, which is nearer the cloud base.

Table 9.1 Typical properties of cloud droplets, raindrops, rainfall and hail

	Diameter (mm) d*	Number of drops/m³ N†	Terminal velocity (m/s) V*	Mass of drops (g/m³) M*	Deposition rate (mm/h) P‡
Cloud/fog	0.01	10⁷§	0.003	0.006	0.00006
Drizzle‖	0.2	2 × 10§	0.75	0.09	0.24
Typical rain	1¶	600	4	0.3	4
Downpour	3	300	8	4	115
Small hail	5	–	5	–	–
Large hail	20	–	16	–	–

* This is from Parker (1980: 373), Zachar (1982: 215) and McIlveen (1992: 149). However, a wide range of cloud-droplet concentrations occurs. For instance, 1 g/m³ has been measured in cumulus cloud (Table 8.3).
† That is, $2{,}000 \cdot M/d^3$, where $d^3/2{,}000$ is the weight (grams) of each drop.
‡ That is, $3.6 \cdot M \cdot V$.
§ Hence the separation of adjacent droplets is about 5 mm, i.e. the cube root of $\{10^9/10^7\}$, there being 10^9 cubic millimetres in a cubic metre. This is about 500 times their own diameter, so spontaneous collisions between cloud droplets are rare.
‖ There is a convention that a cloud droplet has a diameter below 0.1 mm; drizzle between 0.1 – 0.5 mm; and a rain drop over 0.5 mm.
¶ This implies that about a million (i.e. $(1/0.01)^3$) cloud droplets need to collide with each other before they become a typical raindrop.

Surface Conditions

It is notable that surface conditions are almost irrelevant to forming rain locally. For instance, increased evaporation from Lake Eyre (in South Australia) when it was full during the period 1950–2 did not increase the rainfall there in those years; in fact, precipitation was unusually low. Likewise, deforestation is likely to affect the local rainfall only near the equator where evaporation and rainfall rates are high and winds light (Chapter 10).

9.2 FORMING RAINDROPS

Precipitation starts when there are drops heavy enough to have a *terminal velocity* downwards which is greater than the cloud's updraught. The 'terminal velocity' is the speed a body falling under gravity eventually attains in still air, and it depends on the size of a drop, being faster for a larger one (Table 9.1). Therefore larger drops are needed for rainfall to occur where the updraught is greater, as in a convective cloud (Table 8.1). In the case of normal cloud droplets, the terminal velocity is practically zero because of their size, and rainfall depends on their amalgamation into raindrops perhaps a million times as big.

The amalgamation is not easy; it is much harder to form raindrops than to create cloud droplets. The latter arise as soon as the Relative Humidity reaches 100 per cent (i.e. when the air is cooled to the dewpoint temperature – Section 6.2), the droplets growing on cloud condensation nuclei (CCN) which are amply available in even the cleanest air (Note 8.D). On the other hand, amalgamation to form raindrops does not occur spontaneously, because collisions between droplets are infrequent as the spacing between them is typically 500 times their diameter (Section 8.2 and Table 9.1). An alternative to collision as a way of forming raindrops is condensation from the atmosphere onto individual cloud droplets, but this takes hours. The time needed means that such precipitation comes only from clouds that contain sustained (not turbulent) uplift (Section 8.1).

Different processes of droplet amalgamation

occur within *warm clouds* (whose tops are at temperatures above freezing), and *cold clouds*, which extend higher than the freezing level. That level depends on the season and weather, but is typically 2 km at midlatitudes and 4 km between the Tropics (Section 1.8).

Raindrop Growth in Warm Clouds

Raindrops develop in warm clouds through collisions of larger with smaller cloud droplets. The process is sometimes called *accretion* or *collection*. It works best when some droplets are much larger than the others, as in marine clouds. Then the larger droplets or drops fall onto the smaller and collect them, whereas drops of equal size have the same terminal velocity as they fall, so that few overtake and collide with others, and, if they do collide, they bounce off rather than coalesce. In any case, very small droplets cannot be collected easily because they tend to dodge away.

The slow agglomeration of droplets by collection in warm clouds means that they usually yield only light rainfall, despite there being more liquid in warm clouds than in clouds at higher levels (Table 8.3). Warm clouds yield heavy rainfalls only when there is a sustained strong updraught, as on coastal hills in the tropics facing prevailing onshore winds (e.g. north-eastern Queensland).

Raindrop Growth in Cold Clouds

Cold clouds have tops which are colder than freezing, but often consist of liquid water drops, not ice, even though temperatures are between 0°C and −38°C. In that case, the droplets are described as *supercooled*, remaining liquid for want of suitable solid particles on which ice can start. Such particles are called *ice nuclei*, and have a crystal structure like that of ice. They may consist of dust particles, typically between 0.1 μm and several microns in size. Certain clay minerals are particularly effec-

tive. Or the ice nuclei may be bacteria or fungi released by plants, soil and the open sea. (Such biological nucleation is also involved in forming frost − Section 3.6). Few ice nuclei are active in creating crystals above −4°C, but at lower temperatures the supercooled droplets become increasingly indifferent to the kind of nuclei on which they will freeze, so the number acceptable increases tenfold for each 4 K of cooling. Various kinds of ice nuclei require cooling to different *activation temperatures* to become effective, e.g. −3°C for bacteria from leaf mould but around −10°C for many clay particles. At temperatures below −38°C, crystals form automatically without the need of any nuclei at all. This is called *spontaneous nucleation*, where the natural tendency towards freezing is so great that it overcomes the need of preliminary infection by a foreign body.

The best nuclei are ice crystals themselves, so freezing of a few supercooled droplets leads to rapid freezing of those nearby. This process is known as *glaciation*. It occurs in three ways − either because of some larger droplets (which have more chance of containing an ice nucleus), or through *natural seeding*, whereby ice crystals from a high cloud fall into a lower supercooled cloud, as is common near warm fronts (Chapter 13). Or, thirdly, glaciation may occur by *ice multiplication*, often by the splintering of ice crystals. For instance, a freezing supercooled droplet may eject tiny droplets which solidify instantaneously. This occurs less in continental air, where cloud droplets are small on account of numerous cloud condensation nuclei.

The fact that supercooled cloud droplets often occur in nature shows that ice nuclei are scarce, unlike cloud condensation nuclei (Section 8.2). The availability of useful ice nuclei varies greatly with time and location. Air subsiding from the clean upper troposphere has very few nuclei, which may explain the regular occurrence of supercooled droplets near the top of stratiform clouds, whereas ice crystals are found lower down.

Raindrops are created relatively quickly in a cold cloud, because ice crystals develop rapidly amongst supercooled droplets by means of the *Bergeron–Findeisen process* (**Note 9.C**). The crystals grow as snowflakes, whose large surface facilitates collecting more ice crystals and droplets. In addition, the snowflakes become sticky as they descend near the freezing level, so they aggregate into large flakes, which melt into large raindrops, creating heavy rain. A study of a storm in Victoria showed a linear relationship between cloud-top temperature and the rainfall rate, e.g. no rain at 10°C but 0.45 mm/h at −15°C.

Cloud Depth

Not only are suitable nuclei needed for raindrops to form, there must also be enough depth of cloud to ensure that falling drops collide with sufficient cloud droplets to grow to raindrop size. The necessary depth depends on the strength of the updraught; a speed of 1 m/s necessitates a cloud 1,500 m deep to allow time for drops to become heavy enough to descend against the rising air, but 5 m/s needs two or three times the depth. So a strong updraught postpones precipitation from a cloud, but means larger drops once rain starts.

Drop Sizes

Raindrops at the ground are surprisingly uniform in size, i.e. within 0.5–4 mm in diameter. The reason is that smaller drops fall slowly and evaporate before they reach the ground, whilst drops larger than about 4 mm or so tend to distort into an unsteady umbrella-like shape and then break up as they fall.

However, drops differ in heavy downpours from those in light falls. They are around 3 mm in diameter when the rate is 100 mm/h, but only 2 mm in 13 mm/h and 0.5 mm in drizzle. The relation between average drop size and rain rate is discussed further in **Note 9.D**.

9.3 CLOUD SEEDING

There have been several attempts to force clouds to unload their moisture onto parched lands. But these were unsuccessful until 1946, when Vincent Schaefer in the United States first demonstrated that artificially introducing nuclei into a cloud could stimulate rainfall. Initial experiments were encouraging and prompted research in several countries, including Australia (**Note 9.E**).

In the case of warm clouds, raindrop formation can be stimulated by introducing water-absorbing particles of sea-salt or ammonium nitrate with urea. The material is first ground to particles of about 3 μm. The resultant large droplets promote the accretion of raindrops.

Most success in cloud seeding has been achieved with convective cold clouds. Glaciation of the supercooled droplets can be achieved with particles of either 'dry ice' or silver iodide (Note 9.E). The most common method nowadays (in Australia, the USA and Israel) involves releasing silver iodide from burners on an airplane, flying either in the updraught below cumulus clouds or within stratus near the −10°C level. Ice crystals form in a suitable cloud within a few minutes, and rain may fall about twenty minutes later. The effect on convective clouds appears short-lived, but additional stratiform precipitation may continue for over an hour after seeding.

Results

Experiments in Victoria indicated that frontal clouds are unsuitable. The dry north-west winds from inland, ahead of a cold front (Chapter 13), already contain too many nuclei in the form of dust particles, whilst the maritime winds behind the front carry cool clouds whose ice crystals splinter, again leaving no shortage of nuclei. The only clouds there worth seeding are stratus (Section 8.5) associated with 'closed lows' (Chapter 13). Such stratiform clouds were found to occur on twenty-five days during a three-year study in the northern wheatbelt of Western Australia, enough to make the difference between a farmer's ruin and prosperity. Unfortunately, the occurrence of usable clouds is variable; there were fifty-eight days with cold clouds containing adequate water near Melbourne during May–October in 1991 and 1992, but merely fifteen in the previous two years.

It can be seen that there are several problems with cloud seeding, as follows:

1 Suitable clouds may be rare.
2 Seeding of unsuitable clouds actually *reduces* the rainfall (Note 9.E). If the number of active nuclei in a cloud is already high, adding more simply increases the number of drops that are formed, reducing their average size perhaps to the extent that they become too small to fall to the ground as raindrops.
3 It is hard to determine the benefit with absolute certainty; sophisticated statistics, with many repetitions of the experiment, are needed to discern any enhancement of rainfall (**Note 9.F**).
4 Seeding at the wrong stage of the growth of a raincloud may thwart its development. Latent heat is released suddenly when super-cooled droplets are frozen by seeding, which intensifies the updraught. As a result, the cloud extends upwards to levels where the air is cold and therefore dry, causing the ice crystals to sublime away.
5 There is the complication of inadvertent cloud seeding by air pollution or the extra convection caused by urban heating; there are claims of a 40 per cent increase in summer rainfall at La Porte, downwind of Chicago, and an increase of 10–17 per cent is measured 5–25 km downwind of St Louis in Missouri (Chapter 10).
6 It appears that seeding is most effective where natural rainfall is high already, at least

in Australia. There, it is carried out routinely only in Tasmania, already the wettest state.
7 A farmer downwind of cloud-seeding operations might claim damages if he lacks rain or is flooded by excess. Then the cloud-seeder has either to plead ineffectiveness or accept the blame.
8 Cloud seeding can yield only marginal results because it does not affect the factors basic to rainfall – atmospheric instability (Section 7.1), moisture content and low-level convergence.

Benefits

Nevertheless, seeding can be worth while. The benefit–cost ratio of appropriate seeding in wheat areas may be 3–4, in terms of extra crop yield, and the financial benefit of the extra rainfall onto catchments of hydroelectric-power schemes in Tasmania is several times the cost of seeding. **Figure 9.3** shows an extra 20–40 per cent of rainfall in the targeted area.

Cloud seeding has been carried out for drought relief in New South Wales and for inducing rain to lower the bushfire hazard in Victoria. Also, cloud seeding has been tried in Russia for hail reduction (Section 9.8). In addition, it has been tried off Florida in experiments on defusing hurricanes; the hope is to induce precipitation and thus create stirring which can remove the atmospheric instability energising the hurricane. Unfortunately, the hail-reduction experiments proved unimpressive, and practical difficulties of experiments within the violence of hurricanes make it hard to demonstrate success there.

9.4 KINDS OF PRECIPITATION

Precipitation may occur in other ways, apart from rain. For instance, there are snow flakes with their prism-like or plate-like forms in beautiful tree-like (i.e. 'dendritic') patterns of

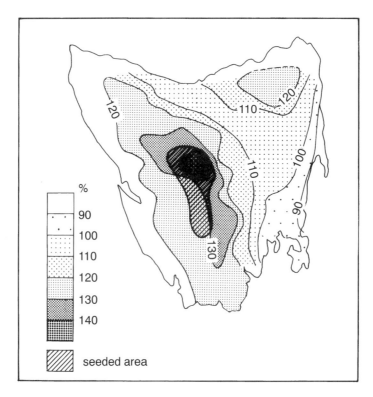

Figure 9.3 Rainfall in Tasmania during 103 months of seeding the shaded area, as a percentage of the long-term average rainfall at each point. The increase of rain in the north-east is attributed to silver iodide carried to the mountainous country there by south-west winds.

hollow columns, needles and hexagonal plates, according to the temperature at which they grow. The flakes fall at a speed of about 1 m/s, irrespective of their size or shape. A consequence of so low a terminal velocity, within horizontal winds which are much faster, is that snow is blown sideways as it descends, and then drifts in the wind, accumulating only in places of relative calm.

Descending snowflakes lose their crystalline appearance when they collect supercooled droplets, as the latter freeze immediately upon contact. This process is known as *riming*. Eventually the original flake structure may become invisible, and such heavily rimed snowflakes are known as *graupel*. Graupel falls at 1–10 m/s, depending on the amount of riming. A hail-

stone is an extreme case of graupel (Section 9.8; Table 9.1).

Rain from cold clouds results from the melting of snow, but the raindrops may later become supercooled once more if there is an intense ground inversion, so that surface temperatures are below 0°C. Such rain freezes on contact with the ground, accumulating as ice on powerlines, trees, etc. The eventual weight of this ice may cause extensive damage. Fortunately, the problem of freezing rain occurs chiefly over land between 40 and 60 degreees of latitude in winter, and there is not much land at these latitudes in the southern hemisphere.

If a ground inversion is very strong and deep, then the falling rain may freeze in the air before reaching the ground, and the resulting precipitation is called *sleet*. Sleet consists of balls of clear ice up to 4 mm in diameter (the maximum size of rain) and is distinct from true hail (Section 9.8).

The various kinds of precipitation are shown on weather charts by the symbols in **Figure 9.4**.

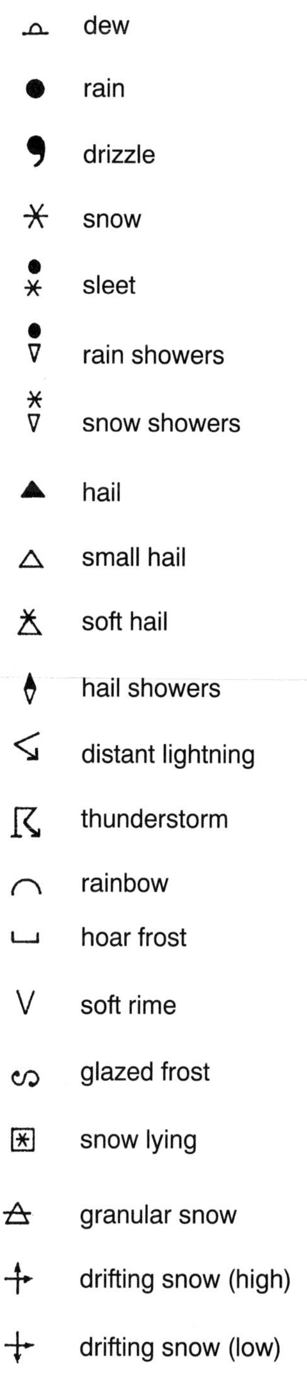

9.5 THUNDERSTORMS

These are events of convective rainfall and, of course, thunder. Aristophanes (450–385 BC), in his comedy *The Clouds*, said thunderstorms are caused by the banging together of clouds impregnated with rain, like vast sodden fleeces. Nowadays we know that thunderstorms are due to deep convection within cumulonimbus clouds, releasing static instability within at least 3 km depth of the atmosphere.

The likelihood of a thunderstorm depends on three factors:

(a) moist air near the surface, e.g. a mixing ratio above 7 g/kg;
(b) an unstable mid-troposphere, e.g. conditional instability created by hills, and
(c) a triggering by surface heating or by confluence due to hills or a front, for instance.

Lifecycle of a Thunderstorm Cell

Once started, there is a sequence of events within each *cell* of the storm, each circulation of updraught and downdraught. For instance, the updraught might be started by daytime heating of the ground in summer, to yield fair-weather cumulus (Section 8.6). This grows upwards if the atmosphere is unstable. If it reaches the tropopause, the cell has an area of several square kilometres. This initial growth is called the 'cumulus' stage and lasts 10–15 minutes (**Figure 9.5**). The top of the cloud then glaciates and spreads out to form an anvil

⌓	dew
●	rain
❥	drizzle
✳	snow
✳	sleet
▽	rain showers
▽	snow showers
▲	hail
△	small hail
⬡	soft hail
⬧	hail showers
⦉	distant lightning
⯗	thunderstorm
⌒	rainbow
⊔	hoar frost
V	soft rime
ꙮ	glazed frost
⊞	snow lying
⊿	granular snow
⥁	drifting snow (high)
⥁	drifting snow (low)

Figure 9.4 Weather-map symbols for various kinds of precipitation.

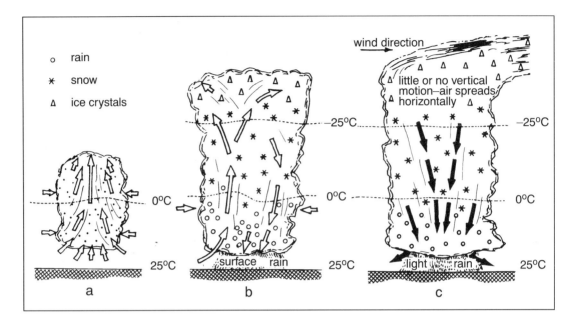

Figure 9.5 The evolution of a thunderstorm: (a) is the early cumulus stage, (b) the mature stage and (c) the dissipating stage.

(Figure 8.4), which heralds the 'mature' stage, lasting about 15–30 minutes. At that point, downdraughts develop under the weight of the water in the cloud, and there is heavy precipitation. Then comes the 'dissipation' stage, when downdraughts are dominant and the rainfall peters out. So the cell's static instability has been discharged, and all that is left is the cirrus cloud of the ice crstals in the anvil, which may take days to vanish. The energy released in an average summer thunderstorm is similar to that of a Nagasaki-size atomic bomb (Section 8.1).

Grouping of Cells

Thunderstorm cells group themselves in four ways:

1 Some are randomly distributed, isolated cells called *air-mass thunderstorms* (or *heat thunderstorms*),which each cover only a few square kilometres and last about an hour (Figure 9.5).

2 There are also clusters of cells, forming *multicell thunderstorms*, which result from downbursts. The airflow from the downburst in a cell often hits the ground as a *squall* of cold wind, whose forward boundary is called a *gust front* (Chapter 14). This pushes adjacent surface air upwards, triggering an updraught which initiates another cell, to discharge instability there. So there is a domino effect leading to a sequence of heavy showers across a region (**Figure 9.6**). Most multicell thunderstorms are loosely organised in a line. The youngest cells are usually at the north (equatorward) end of the line and involve vigorous convection, while stratiform precipitation from decaying cells predominates at the southern (i.e. poleward) end.

3 Cells triggered by their neighbours may be aligned in a *squall line*, a string of thunderstorms with a common, connected gust front.

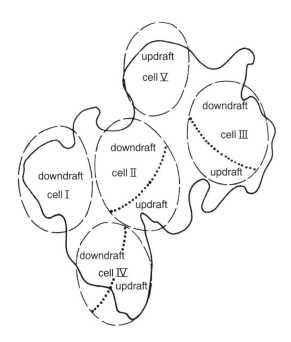

Figure 9.6 A multi-cell thunderstorm with five cells at this moment. The cells discharged their instability and provided rain in the order shown, the downdraught in one cell triggering an updraught in the next.

The line may be several hundreds of kilometres long. Squall lines in SE Australia are usually oriented either north to south or north-west to south-east, and move ahead of a cold front (Chapter 13) with speeds up to 30 m/s, causing strong wind gusts near the surface. Or squall lines may be caused by small boundary-layer disturbances. They can endure for more than a day if the troposphere is sufficiently unstable (i.e. a CAPE exceeding 2 kJ/kg – see Section 7.3 and Figure 7.6) and if also there is a difference of at least 20 m/s between winds at the surface and at 5 km altitude, respectively. Such storms can be sufficiently intense to induce tornadoes (Section 7.5), hail and gusts of strong wind. The squall line is often followed by a broad belt of stratiform clouds (**Figure 9.7**) which may yield as much rain as the squall line itself.

4 Finally, there are *mesoscale convective complexes* (MCCs), which, unlike squall lines, are almost round masses of thunderstorms,

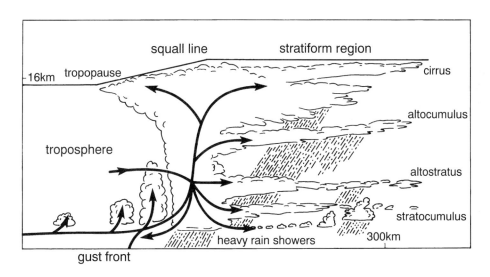

Figure 9.7 A storm in the Amazon valley. It is shown moving from right to left, with new cells forming at the leading edge. Heavy rain falls from the central 'convective line' and ice crystals are carried towards the rear, where they grow in stratiform clouds.

with a common anvil cloud near the tropopause. By definition, the anvil of a MCC is at
least 50,000 km² in area, has a temperature
below −52°C and lasts for over six hours.
However, a MCC may last for several days,
producing heavy rain over 12–16 hours.
They are uncommon: only about twenty
MCC's occur each year over Australia and
the surrounding waters. They appear downwind of mountain ranges such as the Andes,
i.e. to the east at midlatitudes but to the west
at low (**Figure 9.8**), where dry easterly air
coming over the mountains finds itself above
warm moist air from the equator.

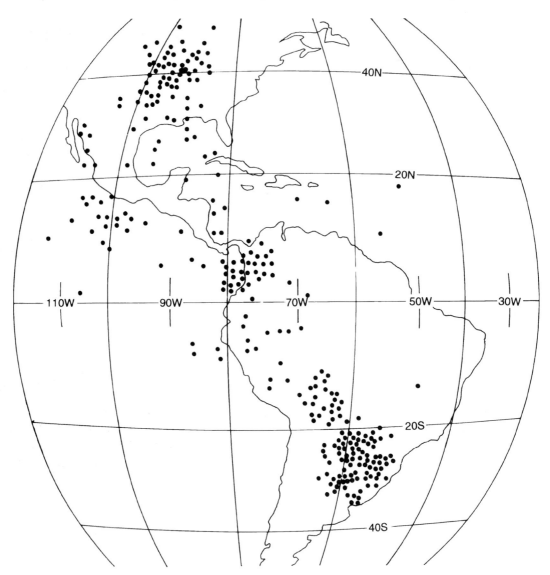

Figure 9.8 Distribution of some 'mesoscale convective complexes' about the Americas between 1983 and
1985.

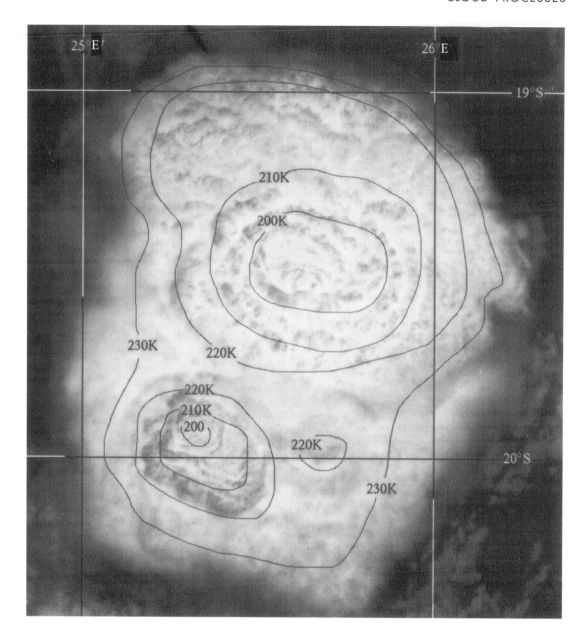

Plate 9.1 A developing mesoscale convective complex (MCC) over Botswana on 8 January 1984, seen from a satellite at 830 km. Isotherms of cloud-top temperature have been superimposed, derived from infra-red measurements taken at about the same time by the geostationary satellite Meteosat. Notice that the lowest temperature was about 193k (i.e. −80°C), showing that the cloud top was about 16 km high at the tropopause.

Distribution

The location of thunderstorms can be determined in at least four ways – by direct observation, from radar echoes, in satellite images, or by lightning detection. Human observations are biased by the population density and are limited in range: thunder can be heard only within 16 km or so (Note 7.M) and lightning seen only at night within about 80 km, depending on the cloudiness (Section 9.6). The difference between these distances might explain why some forty-four days of lightning are recorded annually at Sydney but only twenty-nine of thunder. A similar difference is found at Brisbane (**Figure 9.9**).

The intensity of the echoes seen by radar is a measure of the rate of rainfall, so thunderstorms cause strong echoes within a range of about 300 km. **Figure 9.10** shows a wide area of rainfall, with a rapid movement of the centre of a storm over Sydney, comparable with Figure 9.6.

Geostationary satellites (Section 8.8) can view a whole hemisphere at once and show the progress of entire storm systems. Infra-red photographs show the tops of thunder clouds as particularly cold spots because of their elevation.

Finally, networks of radio receivers for detecting lightning can produce detailed maps of lighting flashes over a large area.

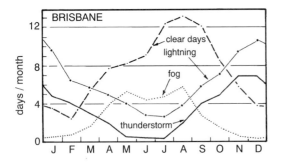

Figure 9.9 The connection between the frequencies of thunder and lightning at Brisbane at various times of the year.

Each receiver can detect radio 'noise' from a thunderstorm up to about 1,000 km away. This noise, called *atmospherics* (or 'spherics'), is due to radio waves (Figure 2.1) generated by the lightning.

The global distribution is shown in **Figure 9.11**. They are most common within 30 degrees of the equator. For instance, there are 225 thunderdays annually at some places on Java. Also, there are regions with 100–180 thunderstorms each year in the high land of northern South America, and many places in central Africa, e.g. 240/a at Kampala on the equator. There are few in arid areas, e.g. less than 10/a in the south-west corner of Africa (**Figure 9.12**), though these few supply most of what rainfall there is. There are between 5–20 annually at places in New Zealand (**Figure 9.13**), mostly among the mountains on the west coast of the South Island.

Mountains increase the chance of thunderstorms by enhancing atmospheric instability (Section 7.3). So most storms in South Africa occur over the mountains of Lesotho in the south-east. On the other hand, thunderstorms are less common over the Andes between 10–30°S than over the adjacent Amazonian lowlands, because the chain of high mountains blocks the flow of low-level moisture from the east.

Thunderstorms are generally less common over the sea, though more than forty occur each year over the Atlantic east of Uruguay. Shipboard records show that thunderstorms at sea occur mostly at 1,000–3,000 km from the tropical and subtropical land masses.

Their frequency in Australia is shown in Figure 9.11. There are relatively few in the south and away from the coast. In Sydney, on the east coast, they occur on about thirty days each year, and the coastal area of New South Wales regularly experiences squall-line thunderstorms ahead of southerly changes in spring and summer. These thunderstorms tend to form over the coastal mountains of the Dividing Range when

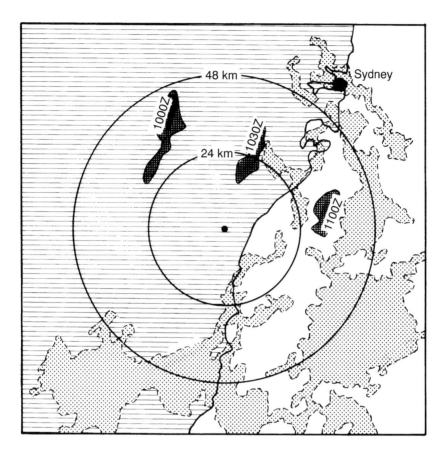

Figure 9.10 The development of a storm on 5 November 1995, indicated by radar reflections from the rain, to a measuring station south-west of Sydney. The diagram shows the respective areas at 1100Z over which rainfall exceeded 2 mm/h (light shading) and 40 mm/h (dark), and also the areas with over 40 mm/h at half-hour intervals beforehand. The storm can be seen to travel to the south-east at a speed of about 60 km/h.

the lower air has been made unstable by surface heating inland, and then they move offshore. Most thunderstorms along the Queensland coast are overgrown cumulus clouds carried onshore by the prevailing south-easterly winds over the Pacific, whereas the storms at the northern edge of Australia are mostly air-mass thunderstorms. Thunderstorms in Perth, Adelaide and Melbourne tend to develop ahead of cold fronts.

Variations in Time

Midlatitude thunderstorms mostly occur in the warmer months, e.g. October to January in Australia. Between the tropics, the region of most storms follows the Sun's movements across the equator (Figs 9.9 and 9.14), for reasons considered in Chapter 12.

The shorter-lived air-mass storms (the first of the four kinds mentioned earlier) tend to

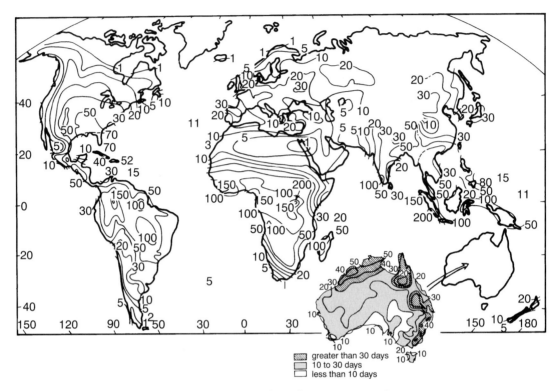

Figure 9.11 Global distribution of the annual number of days with thunderstorms.

happen during the afternoon. For instance, 34 of 93 storms in Brisbane occurred between 3–6 p.m. The longer-lived squall-line storms may occur at any time of the day or night. Mesoscale convective systems typically form near midnight and dissipate around 10 a.m., both in South America and Australia.

There is a pronounced maximum of mountain and coastal thunderstorms in the afternoon, due respectively to 'anabatic flow' up hillsides and uplift caused by sea breezes (Chapter 14). For example, the sky is normally clear at night on Mt Wilhelm (which reaches 3,480 m in Papua New Guinea) but clouds begin to form at about 2,000 m around 8 a.m., and then they grow until there are intermittent showers from 11 a.m. until sunset.

In contrast, thunderstorms are more common during the late night over the waters of tropical archipelagos like Indonesia, because of uplift initiated by low-level convergence of nocturnal land breezes (Chapter 14) from nearby islands. Even over open tropical oceans there is a slight preference for thunderstorms around midnight, on account of instability induced in the lower atmosphere by nocturnal radiative cooling from the top of the moist marine air.

9.6 CLOUD ELECTRICITY

The precipitation from cumulonimbus cloud is often accompanied by lightning and thunder, which will now be considered.

Lucretius, a Roman poet of the first century BC, thought that lightning consists of sparks from the collision of large clouds. But it is usually explained nowadays as due to *charge*

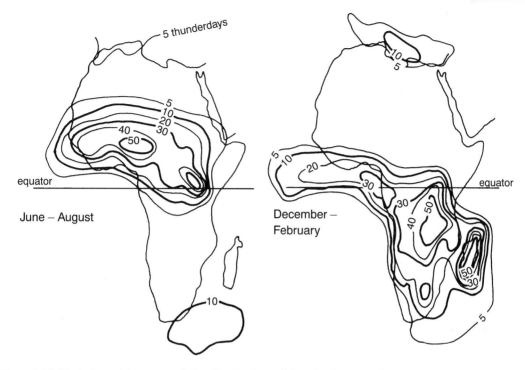

Figure 9.12 Variation with season of the distribution of thunderdays in Africa.

separation within the updraught of a tall convective cloud. This process consists of the detachment of electrons from some drops and crystals within the cloud, and their attachment to others, creating equal numbers of negative and positive ions out of material that was initially electrically neutral (Figure 1.4 and **Note 9.G**). The result is that enormous differences of voltage are created between the top and bottom of a cloud, between adjacent clouds, between cloud tops and the stratosphere, and between clouds and the ground. The consequent occasional flashovers are lightning. Similar lightning occurs in volcano clouds, dust storms and snow storms.

Less than 20 per cent of lightning flashes strike the ground: most occur at 3–10 km above the surface, between parts of the same cloud or across to other clouds. This is especially true in low latitudes, where the tropo-

pause is higher (Section 1.8, Chapter 12) and clouds can grow further upwards. Inter-cloud flashes are known as 'sheet lightning', whilst those from cloud to the ground are 'forked lightning'.

Lightning strikes are pulsatory and take place in stages. In the first stage of a cloud-to-ground strike, the negative base of the cloud attracts positive charge to the ground beneath. As a consequence, electrons flow from the cloud base towards the ground, blazing a trail through the air at a speed of 100 m/s or so. The trail consists of steps between changes of direction, hence the strike's name of *step-leader* or *dart-leader*. An extremely high temperature is generated by the current, which ionises the air in its path, creating a much better conductor of electricity. As a consequence, there is a clear channel for a bright flash of *positive* ions up from the ground, once the leader reaches the surface.

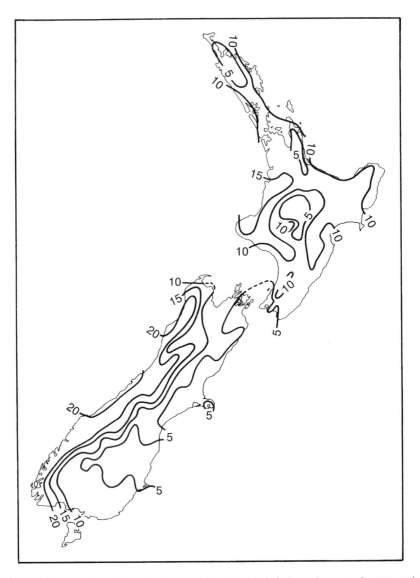

Figure 9.13 Annual frequencies of thunderdays in New Zealand during the period 1955–74.

That main stroke typically peaks at 80,000 amperes, which may be compared with the 0.4 amperes to a 100W light-bulb. The amount of electricity transferred in a flash of 10 microseconds about equals that consumed by the bulb in a day, and generates a momentary temperature above 15,000°C. Next, the cloud unloads the largely negative charge from its base, down the same path. There follows a series of alternate strokes downwards and return strokes up.

Lightning results from every thunderstorm containing cold clouds (as defined in Section 9.2). The amount of lightning is proportional to the speed of the updraughts and downdraughts. Consequently, electrically active

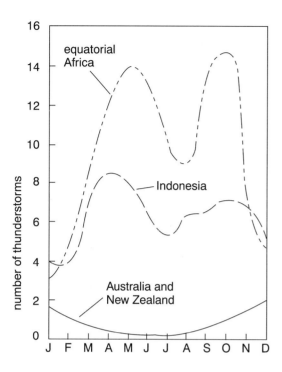

Figure 9.14 The annual variation of thunderstorm frequency at three places. The maximum in Australia and New Zealand coincides with the month when the noon Sun is highest in the sky, whereas the maximum lags one to two months behind at places closer to the equator.

storms tend to be severe in terms of hail, downpours and strong wind gusts too.

There are over a hundred occurrences of lightning annually per square kilometre in equatorial Africa. The number of days a year when lightning is visible in Australia decreases southwards, because the atmosphere is less unstable than in the hot and damp conditions of low latitudes. Lightning is seen on about ninety-six days each year at Darwin (12°S), with almost daily displays during the summertime period called 'The Wet' (Chapter 10). There are about seventy-four days of lightning at Brisbane (at 27°S), forty-four at Sydney (34°S) and eight at Hobart (43°S).

Two-thirds of all lightning flashes occur between the Tropics. There seem to be more lightning strikes above and downwind of a major city than just upwind, presumably because of the plume of warm polluted air.

Hazards

Lightning is dangerous. Hollow trees filled with damp termite nests act as lightning conductors, and explode when struck, as the moisture is instantaneously evaporated by the current. Many bushfires are ignited by lightning; over half those in the Australian state of Victoria are attributed to lightning. Fortunately, some of these fires are put out by the accompanying rain. A different hazard is an electric-power failure, due to lightning striking overhead cables. Radio communication is interrupted by the 'spherics'.

In addition, lightning can stun or kill people. A party of bushwalkers on a track in the Blue Mountains near Sydney were affected by a flash behind them; those at the rear suffered immediate painful leg cramps, whilst those 15 m ahead were unaffected except by the noise. More seriously, there were 1.5 deaths annually per million of the population in South Africa during the period 1950–70, 0.6 in the USA (more than were killed by tornadoes or other weather events), 0.4 in Australia (80 per cent of them men, because more work outdoors) and 0.2 in Britain. The rate for Queensland is ten times what it is for South Australia, whose population is overall less rural. Globally, 5,000 people are estimated killed every year by lightning, most in developing countries. About equal numbers were killed in the USA, (a) on foot in the open, (b) sheltering under trees, or (c) riding on horseback or open vehicle. Fortunately, lightning fatalities are becoming fewer, e.g. 21 per million in Australia in 1825, 4 in 1880, 2 at the turn of the century, half that in 1950, and only about 0.3 since 1970.

It is unwise to be in an open high area, by a wire fence, using electrical equipment like a telephone or electric razor, to be swimming, in a small boat or on horseback. One should avoid isolated trees or the edge of a forest, but you are well protected whilst indoors or in a car. There is no safety in places struck already; lightning *can* strike twice.

Low-flying aircraft are often struck, but harmlessly. Tall buildings are also hit, roughly in proportion to the square of the height, i.e. four times as often if twice as high. Protection is given by a projecting conductor rod leading to the ground, shielding an area with a radius equal to the rod's height.

A beneficial consequence of lightning is the chemical combination of some of the air's oxygen with nitrogen, called 'fixation'. The compounds formed eventually reach the soil and improve its fertility. But lightning also produces ozone at low levels, which is harmful to people.

Thunder

Lightning is often accompanied by thunder (Figure 9.9), caused by shaking of the air when there is first an explosion of air along the lightning trail, due to immediate heating by the electric current, and then, secondly, an equally rapid implosion back into the track after the extremely rapid cooling due to the radiation of light energy from the stroke. High frequencies in the sound of thunder are quickly attentuated, so one hears only a rumble from any distant storm.

The million-times difference between the speeds of light (about 3×10^8 m/s) and sound (about 330 m/s) means that lightning at a distance of D kilometres is heard 3D seconds after it has been seen. (As a result, you can find D by counting the number of seconds between flash and thunder, and dividing by three.) But lightning is often hidden by cloud, or the thunder made inaudible by distance (Note 7.M).

9.7 GLOBAL ELECTRICITY

There are 1,000–2,000 thunderstorms occurring at any moment around the world, and about a hundred main flashes of lightning from the ground every second. The flashes conduct positive charge to the mainly negative base of each cumulonimbus cloud. Then the charge is carried to the cloud top in the internal updraught, where it leaks upwards to the ionosphere above 60 km (Figure 1.10). This layer is highly ionised by cosmic rays (Section 1.7), so that it easily conducts electricity from one part of the world to another, and collects charge from storms everywhere. For this reason it is called the *equalisation layer*, maintaining a voltage around 500 kV above that of the ground. Lower levels of the atmosphere are at correspondingly lower voltages, the gradient near the ground being of the order of 100 V/m in fair weather (**Note 9.H**).

The voltage gradient pulls a steady stream of negative ions from the ground to the equalisation layer, flowing in all the clear sky between storms. Therefore, there is a sort of electrical circuit, shown in **Figure 9.15**. The clear-sky current density is modest (e.g. only about 3×10^{-12} amperes from each square metre of the ground), but is sufficient to cancel the voltage of the equalisation layer in about ten minutes if it were not for continual replenishment by the world's thunderstorms.

Leakage of electricity between the ground and the equalisation layer is carried by two sizes of ions. Small ions each consist of a few molecules of water vapour, nitrogen or oxygen, with an excess electron. Large ions consist of aerosols, which are much larger and thus less mobile, so that they carry electricity less rapidly. The larger ones absorb the smaller when both kinds of ion are present, and reduce the leakage, so that there is an increase of the voltage gradient. Thus air pollution in Samoa resulting from fires on Sundays raises the gradient from the weekday values of 240 to 315 V/m.

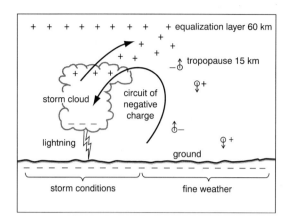

Figure 9.15 The circuit of electricity within the atmosphere. The ground is negatively charged and the equalisation layer is positive, so there is a small but steady flow of negative ions upwards and positive ions down. Flows are in the opposite directions during thunderstorms, i.e. there is a net flux of negative charge in cloud-to-ground lightning strikes, whilst positive ions from the top of storm clouds maintain the positive charge in the equalisation layer.

9.8 HAIL

Hail is ice, in any of three forms. There may be (i) pellets of frozen rain up to 6 mm in diameter, essentially large sleet, (ii) *soft hail*, i.e. graupel, consisting of small, slushy, frozen cloud droplets, found in parts of coastal cloud which are just below 0°C, and (iii) true hail, which is larger, opaque and hard. True hail arises from thunderstorms, and we will focus on this.

One mechanism for the formation of hail involves ice crystals being carried to cloud top, as their gravitational fallspeed is less than the speed of the updraught. At the top they fall outside the main updraught, to be re-entrained near cloud base and carried up once more, completing a cycle which is repeated many times. Each time round, the embryonic hailstone is heavier and therefore falls faster (i.e. is carried aloft more slowly), so that it spends more time accreting other crystals. Such a cycle is suggested by the onion-like structure of concentric layers of hard and soft ice in a hailstone's cross-section, probably due to alternations of the wet conditions (inside the cloud) and dry (outside), within which the hailstone has grown. Air spaces between the accretions make the hailstone opaque.

Occurrence

Temperatures tend to be too high for hail at low latitudes, except on high ground. But thirty-two haildays occur annually near sea-level at Invercargill (NZ, 46°S). At the even higher latitude of Campbell Island (53°S), there are about sixty-nine haildays each year. But there are fewer at the highest latitudes because of insufficient atmospheric moisture or heating of the ground for convection to create the tall clouds that produce hail.

The chance of hail is greater in high country; the number of haildays in New South Wales ranges from about 0.7 annually between 50–200 m above sea-level, to about 2.2 between 500–1,000 m. This is partly because thunderstorms are more common over hills (compare Figure 9.13 with a contour map), but also because the freezing level over elevated terrain is closer to the ground, so that there is insufficient time for precipitation to melt before reaching the ground. That is particularly important at lower latitudes. For instance, the area of most hail in southern Africa is Lesotho, which is over 2 km above sea-level (**Figure 9.16**), with more than eight haildays annually at any point. Similarly, there are more than five in central Madagascar at over 1.5 km. However, the ground's elevation is of little importance for very large hailstones, given their high speed of falling: a hailstone of 50 mm diameter drops from 2 km to the ground within a minute, for example.

Observations in Kansas indicate that hail is

hail: days/year

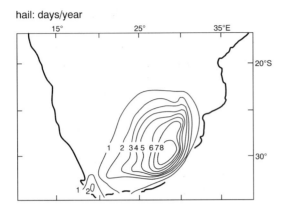

Figure 9.16 Map of the annual frequency of haildays in South Africa. This matches Figure 9.12, since thunderstorms are prerequisite for hail.

most likely downwind of terrain which rises smoothly for several kilometres, with a light-coloured soil, and downwind of cities. There appear to be fewer hailstorms over forests.

Most hail in Sydney is triggered by convection, and therefore occurs during spring afternoons. In other places, such as Adelaide (Australia) and parts of New Zealand, there is most hail in winter when cold fronts are more frequent (Chapter 13). In these cases, hail is due to showers or shallow thunderstorms in the cold air behind mobile cold fronts, and the frequency varies with the temperature (**Note 9.I**).

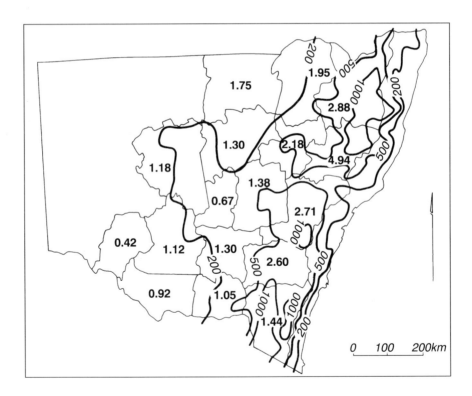

Figure 9.17 Map of the risk from hail in eastern New South Wales, in terms of the approximate number of tonnes of grain lost through hail as a percentage of the number insured. Contours at 200 m, 500 m and 1,000 m indicate the Dividing Range.

Hazards

Hailstones can be dangerous, especially in combination with strong winds. Deaths due to hail are mentioned in the Old Testament (Joshua 10:11). The largest hailstones are the most lethal: a stone the size of a tennis ball weighs about 150 grams and falls at a speed of 40 m/s. The biggest hailstones recorded weighed over a kilogram, killing 92 people in Bangladesh in 1986. Earlier, in 1888, there was a storm in India where 246 people were knocked down by hail and then frozen to death beneath drifts of hailstones. Even in Sydney there have been hailstones as big as 45 mm, enough to damage cars outdoors for instance. Fortunately, such cases are rare and any particular storm usually affects an area only a few kilometres across. The average area of hail in American storms is 20 km^2.

Damage to crops depends on the stage the plants have reached. For instance, most hail forms in Iowa in May when maize is still emerging from the ground and so is hardly affected, whilst most *harm* results from hail in July when the crop is more vulnerable. Hail does millions of dollars worth of harm to fruit crops in New Zealand each year, but much more in North America. A farmer in Alberta may expect to lose his entire crop about three times in the course of his working life.

The frequency of damaging hail can be gauged by the history of insurance claims by farmers. The regional variation of the fraction of grains (oats, barley, and mainly wheat) lost annually to hail damage in New South Wales is shown in **Figure 9.17**. This reveals more risk at lower latitudes and higher elevation.

Efforts have been made to prevent hail damage. One unsuccessful idea was to create a bang to shatter the hailstones (**Note 9.J**). More recently, rockets or ground-based burners have been used in Russia and elsewhere to inject active nuclei into clouds in order to create many small crystals rather than a few large ones (Section 9.3). As a result, the crystals would melt *en route* to the ground, yielding beneficial rain instead of harmful hail. In fact, hail was reduced in this way by about 42 per cent in sixteen studies in various countries during the period 1956–85.

So we have considered hail formation and several other aspects of clouds. The most important is the creating of rain, the subject of Chapter 10.

NOTES

9.A Monthly mean cloudiness and rainfall in Australia
9.B The rainfall rate from stratiform cloud
9.C The Bergeron–Findeisen process
9.D Rainfall intensity and raindrop size
9.E The early history of rain-making
9.F The effectiveness of cloud seeding
9.G Electrification within cumulonimbus cloud
9.H The gradient of electrical potential in the lower atmosphere
9.I Temperature and the frequency of hail
9.J Hail cannon

10

PRECIPITATION

10.1 GENERAL

The importance of rain is obvious in the natural world, and as regards our water supplies, crop growth and so on (**Note 10.A**). The pattern of rainfall and the temperature are often taken as a concise description of the climate of a place.

Kinds of precipitation include drizzle (Table 9.1), snow (Section 10.8) and hail (Section 9.8). Dew was considered in Section 4.7. Symbols for them were shown in Figure 9.4.

Rain may be either continuous or showery. Showers result from convective activity and therefore are more common in spring and summer over land. They may be described as 'isolated' (affecting less than 10 per cent of the area), 'scattered' if they occur over 10–50 per cent of the area, or 'widespread'.

Measuring rainfall is easy to do (but hard to do properly) by means of either rain gauges (**Note 10.B**) or some indirect technique, perhaps involving satellites or radar (**Note 10.C**). One indirect record of seasonal rainfall in times past is given by the width of tree rings in dry climates (**Note 10.D**).

Acid Rain

A particular aspect of rainfall is its acidity, arising from gases dissolved in the drops. The acidity is described in terms of the 'pH', which can range from unity (i.e. extreme acidity – lemon juice has a pH of 2.2) to 14 (i.e. extreme alkalinity) (**Note 10.E**). Droplets in clouds over remote oceans have a pH of about 6.2, not far short of 'neutrality' (which would mean neither acid nor alkaline) represented by a pH of 7. Rain at Cape Grim at the north-east tip of Tasmania in the path of the clean oceanic westerlies, has a pH of 6. 'Pure' rainwater has a value of about 5.6 on account of dissolved carbon dioxide (Note 10.E). Values of 5 have been obtained outside Newcastle, an industrial city in New South Wales, and 4.7 at Katherine, a rural site at $14°S$ in northern Australia. The pH of summer rain in Sydney is commonly around 4.4, chiefly because of sulphuric acid formed by the dissolving of sulphur dioxide and nitrogen oxides from the air pollution of vehicles and the burning of coal. However, the problem of acid rain is more serious at some places in the northern hemisphere.

Plate 10.1 The various kinds of cloud responsible for rainfall. This image from the Japanese geostationary satellite GMS on 4 February 1995 shows a line of frontal cloud (yielding frontal rainfall) over South Australia and Western Australia, with isolated convective clouds (producing heavy showers) near the equator, and orographic cloud over New Zealand.

Heavy rain has less acidity, presumably because of dilution by more water. But fog in industrial areas can be extremely acid.

A different contamination of rainwater is found near the coast, where rain is made corrosive by aerosols of salt, mainly sodium chloride from the sea. The concentration of chlorides in rain at the coast at Perth or in Victoria is reduced by a factor of about 13 at places 100 km inland.

10.2 RAINFALL INTENSITY

Amounts of rainfall are measured in terms of the depth of the layer created by spreading the water on a horizontal surface. It is now expressed in millimetres depth, and the *rate* (or *intensity*) of precipitation during a given period is the total collected divided by the duration, usually expressed in millimetres per hour. It can be measured for periods longer than a few minutes by means of a pluviograph, an instrument for recording the times between refillings of a small cup into which the collected rain flows.

Rainfall intensities fluctuate during a storm. For example, the amounts in six successive five-minute periods in a shower might be 0.5 mm, 2.5 mm, 1.0 mm, 1.0 mm, 0.8 mm and 0.2 mm, implying a maximum intensity on a five-minute basis of 30 mm/h (i.e. $2.5 \times 60/5$), but only 21 mm/h over ten minutes, and 12 mm/h over thirty minutes. So the maximum intensity of rainfall is less for greater periods of averaging. Amounts of rain collected in the course of a year, for instance, are commonly plotted on maps, where places with equal amounts are linked by lines called *isohyets*.

'Light rain' means less than 1 mm/h and 'heavy' rain means more. A rate of over 60 mm/h for at least five minutes is called a *cloudburst*. The intensity may peak at 120 mm/h for a minute or two in a normal storm, though over 500 mm/h was measured at one spot in Sydney during five minutes on 2 April 1992.

Extreme Rainfalls

The world-record rainfall by 1986 during one minute (at Barot, Guadeloupe) was equivalent to 2,300 mm/h; over twenty minutes the highest rainfall rate had been 1,200 mm/h (Curtea-de-Arges in Argentina); over an hour 430 mm/h (Holt, Missouri); a day 76 mm/h (Foc Foc at Reunion, a volcanic island at 21°S in the western part of the Indian Ocean); a week 26 mm/h (Commerson, Reunion); a month 12 mm/h (Cherrapunji, Assam); and over a year 3 mm/h (Cherrapunji). Such figures suggest that a four-fold increase of duration halves the record aver-

age intensity. The same has been found for Sydney record rainfalls, though they are only about a seventh of global record values.

The record daily rainfall in Australia was at Bellenden Ker Top Station near Cairns in Queensland on 4 January 1979, when 1,150 mm fell, equivalent to 48 mm/h. A world record was set there in the same month – 3,847 mm during eight days.

The intensity is related to the drop size (Note 9.D) and soil erosion (**Note 10.F**). **Figure 10.1** indicates that the highest intensities occur especially at low latitudes. The diagram compares rainfalls at Darwin and Hobart, in terms of the average time (or *'recurrence interval'* or *return period*) between rainfalls of a particular intensity and duration. The Hobart curves are lower, so, for instance, 13 mm/h over one hour is likely to be exceeded once a year, compared with 50 mm/h at Darwin. Darwin rates are especially high for recurrence intervals of only an hour or

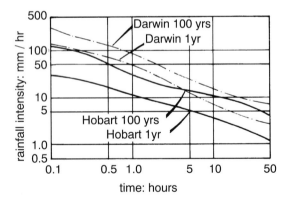

Figure 10.1 Rainfall intensity, duration and frequency diagrams for Darwin (dashed pair of curves) and Hobart (solid pair). The lower of a pair displays the one-year recurrence interval, the upper one gives the 100-year interval. For instance, the wettest hour each year yields 10 mm at Hobart but 50 mm at Darwin, on average. Also, the rainfall on average exceeds 100 mm/h for 45 minutes once each hundred years at Darwin, and 5 mm/h for 5 hours once a year at Hobart.

so, because of the sporadic intensity of the convective rainfall there, whereas rain at Hobart is chiefly frontal, i.e. prolonged but gentle.

The average annual intensity derived from many years of records at Alice Springs is about 250 mm/a, falling within about forty days, i.e. about 6 mm per rainday. Such a figure is a useful index of what a wet day is like. It is about 20 mm/rainday at the equator, but less at higher latitudes (**Figure 10.2**).

Runoff

Urban drainage channels are commonly designed to cope with the maximum rainfall to be expected over an hour, whereas extreme river flows are more related to the 'maximum rainfall' over a day. This 'maximum rainfall' is typically chosen as that with a twenty years' recurrence interval, but if overflowing would have particularly serious consequences the drain or river is designed to cope with rains exceeded only once a century, on average. The design is a compromise between (i) the greater expense of building a larger channel to cope with heavier rainfalls, and (ii) greater costs from flood damage due to more frequent over-

Figure 10.2 Rainfall per rainday in Australia.

flowing of a smaller channel. Unfortunately, such a procedure for optimising the benefit–cost ratio of a channel ignores changes of climate and runoff ratio over periods as long as a century, so any estimate of the best design is only approximate and must have a margin added for safety.

The daily rainfall at a place, likely to be exceeded only once in some specified period, such as a century, can be estimated roughly from measurements over a shorter time (**Note 10.G**).

10.3 SPATIAL DIFFERENCES

We will now describe patterns of rainfall in terms of the annual or monthly average values, as we did for temperature (Section 3.2). Of course, average rainfall may not be typical – the mean of nine drought years and one flood year does not resemble the rainfall in any year. So alternatives to the arithmetic mean are sometimes more useful (**Note 10.H**). For instance, there are the 'modal' and 'median' rates of rainfall. The *mode* is derived after data have been grouped into sequential ranges; it is the mid-value of the range with the most values. But it is possible to obtain the mode only when many values are available. The *median* annual rainfall is exceeded in half the years, and is less affected than the average by outlying values.

Large-scale maps of average rainfalls (**Figure 10.3**) show great differences between seasons and spatially, affected mainly by the latitude (Figure 6.13). Notably, rainfall at sea (1,140 mm/a) is more than that over the land (730 mm/a). This means that the southern hemisphere with its greater area of ocean (Note 1.A) is slightly wetter than the northern half of the world, with 1,080 mm/a instead of 960 mm/a. It also means that a major factor governing the rainfall at places on land is proximity to the sea. Other factors are topography, elevation,

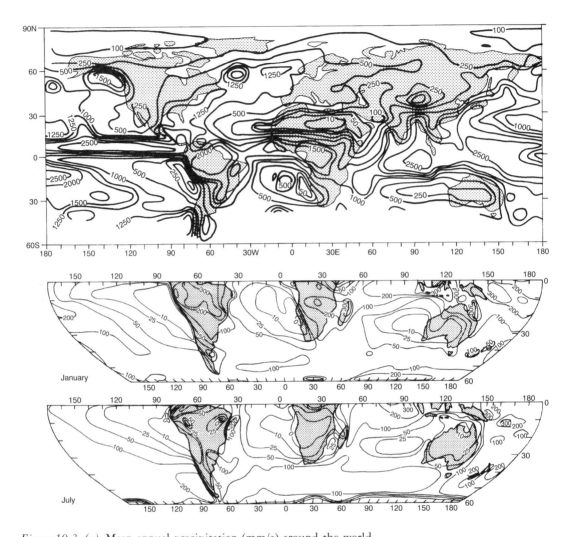

Figure 10.3 (*a*) Mean annual precipitation (mm/a) around the world.

(*b*) Mean monthly precipitation (mm) in January and July in the southern hemisphere.

latitude and the coastal sea-surface temperature, which will now be considered.

Distance from the Sea

Remoteness from the sea tends to lead to low rainfalls, especially in the 'rainshadow' of mountain ranges, where the air's descent and consequent warming (Note 7.E) lead to the evaporation of any cloud, as in Patagonia east of the Andes. Rainfalls on the westerly windward side of New Zealand's Alps in the South Island are up to 10,000 mm/a, but only 500 mm/a on the leeward side (**Figure 10.4**). (This corresponds to the pattern of cloudiness in Figure 8.15.) Similarly, a transect at about 30°S from Australia's east coast, across the Dividing Range, into the interior desert, shows

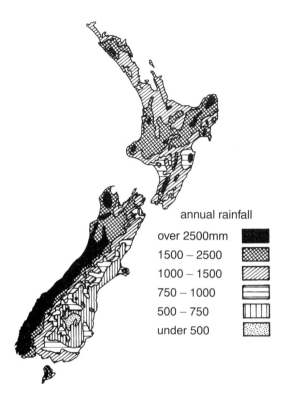

Figure 10.4 Annual mean rainfall in New Zealand.

annual rainfall

over 2500mm
1500 – 2500
1000 – 1500
750 – 1000
500 – 750
under 500

the coast is the situation around 20°S in south-west Africa, for instance. Precipitation is less than 100 mm/a at the coast, but over 400 mm/a at about 150 km inland. This is due partly to the low sea-surface temperature along the coast (Chapter 11), making onshore air masses too stable for the uplift needed to create rain, and partly to the winds being often easterly, i.e. offshore, making the coastal fringe downwind of high land. The same applies at similar latitudes on the west coast of South America; the world's driest place is Arica (at 18°S, on the coast of Chile), where only 1 mm of rain was measured over forty-two years. Several places near the coast of northern Chile have recorded no rain for one or two decades. These dry coastal regions extend thousands of kilometres offshore of south-west Africa, northern Chile and also western Australia (Figure 10.3).

Other exceptions are found at tropical islands, many of which receive more rainfall inland than at the coast on account of uplift in the centre of fairly flat islands (such as Bathurst and Melville islands just north of Darwin in Australia), due to the convergence of sea breezes (Chapter 14). On larger, mountainous islands, such as Papua New Guinea, the increase of rainfall inland (**Figure 10.5**) is due to orographic uplift behind the coastal plain. Moreover, when the wind blows from one prevailing direction, the downwind coast may be

an annual rainfall of 1,658 mm at Coffs Harbour on the coast, 796 mm/a at 130 km inland, 473 mm/a at 416 km and 210 mm/a at about 1,000 km.

An exception to the rule about most rain at

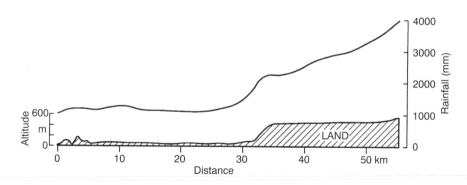

Figure 10.5 Effect of elevation near Port Moresby (9°S) on the annual rainfall.

relatively dry. For instance, Suva on the south-east coast of Viti Levu (Fiji, 18°S) receives 3,024 mm/a, while Nadi on the north-west coast receives less than half that amount, most of it in summer when the prevailing south-easterly winds weaken or vanish.

The driest parts of Australia are well inland. The most arid region is around the ephemeral Lake Eyre, at 28°S in South Australia, where the median annual rainfall is less than 100 mm. It has been suggested that the aridity could be remedied by flooding Lake Eyre, in the hope of thereby increasing local rainfall. The idea is nonsense (**Note 10.I**).

Latitude

Rainfall amounts are heavy at low latitudes (**Table 10.1**), while Antarctica is the driest continent on Earth (Chapter 16). This is explained at least partly by the Clausius–Clapeyron effect (Note 4.C): the troposphere at high, colder latitudes contains less precipitable water than at low, warm latitudes (Figure 6.13).

The poleward decrease of rainfall is not as uniform as the poleward decrease of temperature (Figure 3.4). There is a minimum about the Tropics (i.e. around 23° latitude) and a second maximum around 50° (**Figure 10.6**), due to the 'general circulation', discussed in Chapter 12. Large-scale convective uplift occurs near the equator, whereas the troposphere slowly subsides about the Tropics, producing clear skies without rain. That explains the dryness of Australia, where 37 per cent of the area receives less than 250 mm/a and 68 per cent below 500 mm/a. The second maximum at

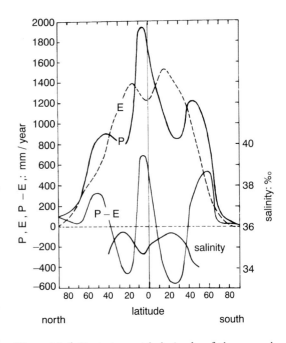

Figure 10.6 Variation with latitude of the annual-mean, zonal-average precipitation (P), evaporation (E), the difference between the two (P − E), and the ocean's surface salinity. The salinity curve is discussed in Chapter 11.

midlatitudes is due to large-scale frontal uplift (Chapter 13). Finally, the air over Antarctica is generally subsiding and therefore free of clouds or rain.

Elevation

Mountains force winds to rise, creating orographic cloud and rain (Figure 10.4 and Figure 10.5) in a complicated way. First, any moist and stable airstream is forced by the wind to rise over a mountain chain, and will lose some

Table 10.1 Effect of latitude and season on rainfall

	Rainfall (mm) during three months, averaged over ten degrees						
Latitudes	5°N–5°S	5°S–15°S	15°S–25°S	25°S–35°S	35°S–45°S	45°S–55°S	55°S–65°S
Dec–Feb	783	783	608	279	357	493	358
Jun–Aug	554	330	248	346	576	651	323

of its moisture upon ascent to the crest (Figure 7.2). This mechanism is important at high latitudes. Second, orographic uplift may destabilise any nearly-unstable airstream (Section 7.4), causing deep convection and additional rainfall. Third, the heating of the sides of an isolated mountain draws winds from the surrounding plains (Chapter 14), creating a convergence which causes uplift. This happens in summer when there is no prevailing wind. Any or all of the three processes may occur.

Even quite modest elevation can enhance rainfall greatly. The most rainfall on St Helena (16°S) is near the central peak of only 600 m, where it is 1,300 mm/a, compared with 250 mm/a on the north-west shore. More striking is the close connection between elevation and rainfall across New Zealand (**Figure 10.7**).

Rainfall tends to decrease at places above a kilometre or two up a mountain, after the air has lost water lower down and temperatures of the ascending air have fallen to the extent that little water can be held as vapour. The maximum rainfall on Kenya's Mt Kilimanjaro (5,895 m high) is at 2,800 m or thereabouts, and rainfalls in central Java are at a maximum between 1–3 km elevation. Near Mt Wilhelm in Papua New Guinea, rainfalls are around

3,200 mm/a below 500 m, but only 2,300 mm/a above 2 km.

In general, orographic rainfall is promoted by strong winds of moist air impacting a mountain chain at right angles, without inversion layers to impede uplift. For instance, 3,500 mm/a is measured where steady winds from the warm Indian ocean strike Tamatave at 18°S on the east coast of Madagascar (Chapter 16). Similar amounts are recorded along the coastal hills of northern Queensland, especially in areas where the coast is oriented north–south, across the moist easterly winds.

Land Use

Cities may increase summertime convective rainfall by around 25 per cent, for instance, at distances of 0–60 km downwind (Section 9.3). An extreme example is Mexico City which experienced rapid growth between the early 1950s and the late 1970s, and the ratio of city to nearby rural rainfalls increased from 1.13 to 1.75, i.e. by 55 per cent. The rise could be caused by additional convection due to urban heating (Section 3.7) or by extra aerosols due to air pollution. A consequence is a slight augmentation of rainfall on weekdays, compared with weekends.

Sometimes it is claimed that a forested surface increases the rainfall. Computer simulation of the atmosphere over Europe (Chapter 15) indicates that a forested surface might induce 30 per cent more frontal rain in some circumstances. But the effect may be small since rainfall depends on atmospheric conditions well above the surface (Section 9.1, **Note 10.J**).

10.4 VARIATIONS OF RAINFALL

Average figures for rainfall fail to indicate the great differences from one period to the next, which occur in many places. The *variability* is important; a farmer would much prefer a

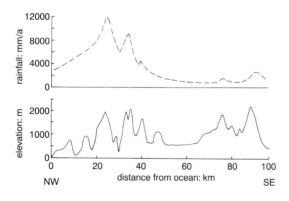

Figure 10.7 Elevation and annual rainfall across New Zealand. The transect is oriented north-west to south-east through Sentinel Peak and Mt Hutt at about 43°S; winds come mostly from the west.

reliable though modest rainfall to an irregular sequence of drought and flood with the same average, and most of the fluctuation of crop yields is due to rainfall variability.

Measures of Variability

Different ways of showing the considerable variability observed in practice are illustrated in **Figure 10.8**. In Sydney, for instance, the annual rainfall can be as low as 700 mm/a, or over 2,000 mm/a, so that the average of about 1,200 mm/a is only vaguely representative.

The variability of a series of values is often considered in terms of the *deciles*. These are values obtained after the set has been rearranged in order from smallest to largest. The first decile is the value lying 10 per cent of the way along this rearranged series, i.e. 10 per cent of the values in the set are smaller than the first decile. The fifth decile is the *median* value. The presentation of data from Santiago in Figure 10.8c gives the decile values directly.

The farmer is most interested in the *dependable rainfall*, often regarded as the amount exceeded in three years out of four (**Note 10.K**). This is called the '25th *per centile*', halfway between the second and third decile. Figure 10.8 shows that it is about 230 mm/a at Santiago, reading from 25 on the vertical axis.

Several ways of quantifying the variability of rainfall are discussed in **Note 10.L**. A good way is to divide the average *departure* from the mean by the mean itself, i.e. the *relative variability*. In general, a map of relative variability (**Figure 10.9**) is the inverse of a map of annual rainfall (Figure 10.3), being higher in drier regions. It exceeds 80 per cent on the west coast of South Africa, where the mean rainfall is low. Values in Australia are typically in the range 10–40 per cent, being highest in the deserts and least in the south-western corner and Tasmania. Relative variability in South America is lowest in the Amazon basin and highest in the Atacama desert. It can be seen that variability adds to the

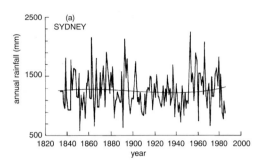

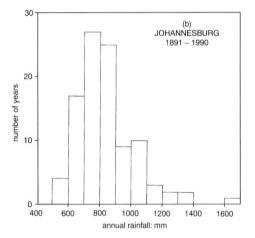

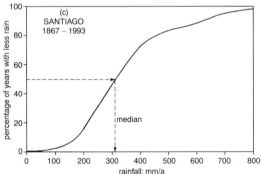

Figure 10.8 Examples of the scatter of annual rainfalls, shown in various ways: (a) a 'time series' of falls at Sydney during the period 1836–1985; (b) a 'histogram' of those at Johannesburg during the period 1891–1990, and (c) a 'cumulative probability chart' of rainfalls at Santiago during the period 1867–1993.

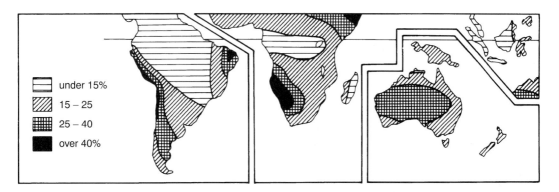

Figure 10.9 The relative variability of the annual rainfall in the southern hemisphere.

problem of water shortage for farmers in dry areas.

Particularly high relative variabilities at the latitudes of eastern Australia and South Africa (Chapter 16) appear to be related to the 'El Niño' phenomenon discussed in **Note 10.M** and the next two chapters.

Aspects of Variability

The variation noted in Darwin indicates a tendency towards alternating periods of almost equally high or low annual rainfalls, as though switching to and from two distinct regimes every few years (**Figure 10.10**). The same has been observed in records from Sydney. Annual rainfalls during a relatively dry time are almost uniformly below normal, so that the 'cumulative sum' curve declines as a roughly straight line, in a fashion that is remarkably consistent. And conversely during the wetter times. The alternation of dry and wet regimes suggests cycles of events created by feedback processes, and the constant conditions between switchings is a feature we call *'persistence'*, a tendency for periods of the same kind of weather to cluster, for a dry time to be followed by another (**Note 10.N**). Persistence is the opposite of variability.

Day-to-day persistence occurs because it takes several days for a given weather pattern to change. In the case of Melbourne, **Table 10.2** shows that the nature of the previous day markedly affects the chance of rain on a particular day; a dry day yesterday in summer, tends to mean the same today, and likewise for a wet day in July. The chance of a dry day today is not increased by two dry days beforehand, in this example, so the so-called *'memory'* of the process involved here is only one day. The degree of persistence depends strongly on the season in Pretoria (**Figure 10.11**), as elsewhere. In this case, there is a very strong persistence of dry days during June–August.

A different kind of persistence is implied in the steadiness of abnormal rainfall at Darwin between 1965 and 1982 (Figure 10.10). An abnormality lasting so long suggests an explanation in terms of ocean circulations. These change only sluggishly because of the huge masses involved (Chapter 11), whereas the 'memory' of atmospheric processes is only a few weeks at most.

Rhythms of Rainfall

There have been many suggestions of rhythms in the amount of rainfall, perhaps linked to the frequency of sunspots (Sections 2.2 and 10.7, Chapter 15) or phase of the moon. For instance,

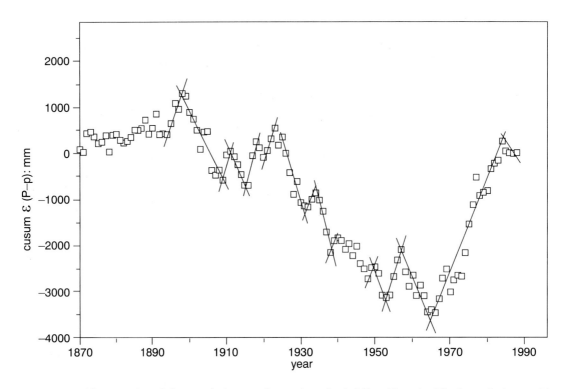

Figure 10.10 The variation of the *cumulative sum* of annual total rainfalls at Darwin. The 'cumulative sum' in any year is the sum of the departures of the annual rainfalls so far from the long-term mean. (So the first and last values of the sum are automatically zero.)

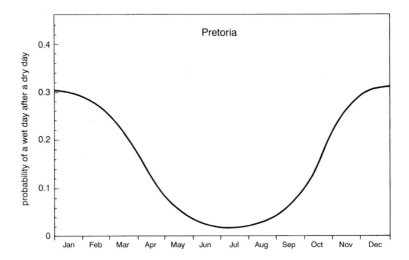

Figure 10.11 The variation from month to month of the chance of a dry day being followed by a wet day in Pretoria, South Africa.

Table 10.2 Probabilities of a dry day at Melbourne after either a wet day or one or two dry days in various months

	Dry-day probability (%)	
	January	July
After one wet day	53	38
After one dry day	81	54
After two dry days	80	58

Francis Bacon suggested in 1625 that annual weather varies in a cycle of thirty-five years, named in 1887 after Eduard Bruckner, though no such variation appears significant. The only reliable rhythms are daily, seasonal and perhaps biennial, discussed below.

Daily Variations

Rainfall is more likely at certain times of the day in some regions (Sections 7.4 and 9.5). Convective rainfall often has a pronounced diurnal rhythm, especially on tropical islands. On land, it is most common in the afternoon after the surface has been heated by the Sun. Over the oceans, the diurnal cycle is much weaker, except over waters surrounded by land, as in the Indonesian Archipelago where convective rainfall peaks around dawn because of uplift due to the convergence of land breezes from the surrounding islands.

Stratiform rainfall occurs at any time of the day, although light rain or drizzle is slightly more common around dawn along the coast, when an onshore moist airflow is lifted slightly over the stable nocturnal boundary layer that formed at night over land (Section 7.6). Also, there may be less drizzle in the afternoon, when the surface relative humidity is low (Figure 6.4), because some of the small raindrops (Table 9.1) evaporate before reaching the ground.

Seasonal Variations

Seasonal variations reflect changes of solar radiation and wind direction (Chapter 12). Figure 10.3 indicated the variation in the southern hemisphere, and **Figure** 10.12 shows the great difference between the summer and winter patterns of rainfall in Australia, i.e. most rain at year's end in the north, and most in winter at higher latitudes. Places on the north coast, like Darwin, receive wet equatorial winds (Chapter 12) at year-end, during the period called 'The Wet', and dry winds from the interior in mid-year. In contrast, wet winds from the Indian Ocean prevail in winter at Perth in the west of Australia, bringing rain, whilst summer winds are mostly easterly, coming from inland (Chapters 12 and 16) and therefore dry. Such a pattern of a dry summer and wet winter is called 'Mediterranean'. The pattern is not so evident on the east coast (**Table 10.3**), where the same prevailing easterly winds are *onshore* in summer, i.e. moist.

More generally, a slanting line across Australia, from 25°S on the west coast to 35°S on the east (Chapter 16), separates regions with a wet summer to the north from those with wet winters to the south, i.e. regions of chiefly convective and chiefly frontal rainfall, respectively. The same happens in southern Africa from 28°S on the west coast to 33°S on the south coast, and in South America, from 10°S on the Peruvian coast to 40°S in Argentina (Chapter 16). The slant is due to the difference between sea-surface temperatures to the west and east of a continent (Chapter 11).

The wettest month near the equator tends to occur a few weeks after the noonday Sun has passed overhead, i.e. once the ground has been most heated to promote convective rainfall. So there may be two rainy seasons if the Sun passes overhead twice in the year (Section 2.2). For example, the Sun passes over in March and September at Quito (0.2°S, in Ecuador) and the wettest months there are

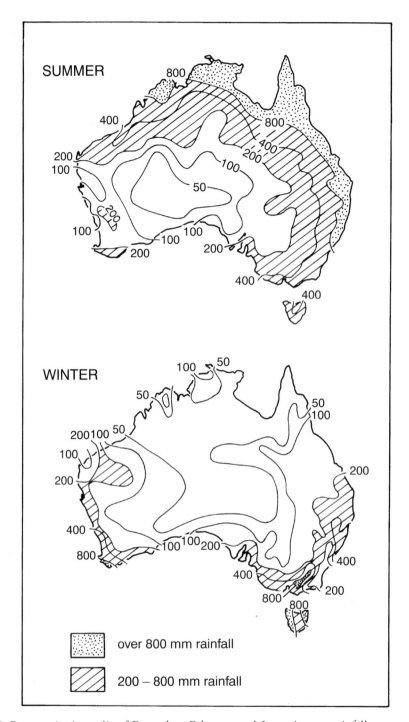

Figure 10.12 Patterns in Australia of December–February and June–August rainfalls, respectively.

Table 10.3 The variation of the monthly median rainfall along the east coast of Australia

Place	Latitude (°S)	Monthly median rainfall (mm)											
		Jan	Feb	Mar	Apl	May	Jun	July	Aug	Sept	Oct	Nov	Dec
Thursday Island	11	399	393	321	168	20	11	8	4	2	1	12	163
Cooktown	15	290	334	340	169	55	40	22	18	11	15	33	14
Townsville	19	249	245	169	42	15	14	5	3	5	11	21	82
Rockhampton	23	121	109	83	39	28	32	21	13	17	34	58	92
Brisbane	27	127	123	115	58	43	41	36	28	41	61	75	107
Port Macquarie	31	115	150	154	135	112	98	80	63	65	74	79	100
Nowra	35	71	57	73	77	50	53	71	36	41	50	42	67
Flinders Island	40	38	47	40	62	79	56	80	73	59	49	54	48
Cape Bruny	43	54	49	60	74	80	79	91	77	70	76	72	67

April and October. The two wet periods merge into a single period at the Tropic of Capricorn, and even near the equator the tendency towards a double maximum is often overridden by other processes.

Wet summers in the north of Australia mean that bushfires there occur naturally in winter (mid-year), whereas they are summertime hazards in the south. Also, variations of rainfall determine the growing season for crops in areas where temperatures are adequate (Note 3.I). There, growth occurs while the soil is at least half full of available moisture (Note 4.G).

There is relatively little seasonal variation of the frequency of precipitation over the southern oceans, but a steady increase with latitude. There is a sharp maximum of convective rainfall around 38 degrees in winter.

Biennial Variation

One feature of rainfall variability is the evidence from many places, including south-east Australia, that years tend to be alternately wet and dry, especially in the tropics. For instance, rainfalls in Victoria during the period 1913–76 tended to be about 10 per cent less than average each 2.1 years or so. More than two-thirds of Australia had subnormal rain in 1957, 1959, 1961, 1964, 1965, 1970 and 1972, for instance. Similar slight 2–3-year

rhythms have been found at Fortaleza in Brazil, in New Zealand and South Africa, and in the date by which a quarter of Adelaide's annual rain has fallen. An almost biennial rhythm occurs in the flooding of the Nile, monsoonal rains in India, rainfall in New Zealand, snowfall in Australia (Section 10.8), and in sugar-cane harvests in Queensland, for instance. These may reflect the 'Quasi-Biennial Oscillation' of winds in the equatorial stratosphere (Chapter 12).

10.5 WATER BALANCES

The change of moisture in an area equals the difference between (i) the gain (as precipitation and inflow) and (ii) the loss by evaporation and outflow. This equality is the 'water balance' (Section 4.4). It may be considered on any scale of space or time. The 'change of moisture' might involve an alteration of level in a reservoir, or wetter soil, for instance. Runoff occurs once the storage is full (**Figure 10.13**).

Water-balance estimates are often made in agriculture to check the need for irrigation. For instance, measurements in a ricefield near Griffith (NSW) showed that the rainfall during a week in February was 13 mm, 86 mm of irrigation water was applied, 10 mm infiltrated into the soil, the water level fell by 23 mm and

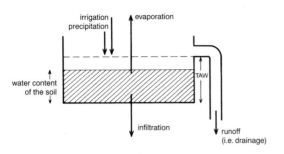

Figure 10.13 The bucket model for the water balance in the soil beneath an irrigated crop. The amount of water stored in the soil increases if the inputs (from rain and irrigation) exceed the losses from evaporation into the air and infiltration into the subsoil. There is overflow in the form of surface runoff, in the bucket model, only when the soil from rootbase to the surface is saturated, i.e. its Total Available Water capacity is filled.

the flow away of drainage water was equivalent to 1 mm. So the evaporation inferred from the water balance was 65 mm (i.e. $86 + 13 - 1 - 23 - 10$), or 9.3 mm/day, which is relatively high (Section 4.6).

Water Balances on a Large Scale

The average rainfall over all the oceans is estimated to be about 1,140 mm/a, whereas the evaporation rate is about 1,260 mm/a; the difference is made up by riverflow into the sea. For the Indian ocean, the rainfall has been estimated as 1,170 mm/a and evaporation 1,320 mm/a, with one inflow from rivers equivalent to 80 mm/a, and another in currents from other oceans of 70 mm/a. In the case of the world's land surface, the average rainfall is reckoned to be about 730 mm/a, 420 mm/a (i.e. 57 per cent) of which evaporates, the difference being carried away in the rivers.

The precipitation and evaporation rates at various latitudes are shown in Figure 10.6. The climate is wet and there is runoff wherever rainfall exceeds evaporation, at the equator and

at latitudes around 55 degrees. On the other hand, most deserts are found at 20–30 degrees latitude (Chapter 16), where the potential evaporation rate exceeds the rainfall (**Note 10.O**).

Rainfall averages 1,630 mm/a in South America and evaporation 700 mm/a, and the difference, equivalent to 930 mm/a, is carried away in huge rivers. The Australian figures are 470 mm/a rainfall and 420 mm/a evaporation, so that the rivers here carry merely 50 mm/a equivalent. More specifically, evaporation amounts to 94 per cent of the rainfall in the arid Murray-Darling watershed of Australia. The mean precipitation is only about 160 mm/a in Antarctica, almost all of which is lost in glaciers flowing slowly to the sea (Chapter 16).

Water Balances on a Local Scale

It is instructive to compare a map of rainfall in Australia (Figure 10.3 and Chapter 16) with the pan evaporation E_p (Section 4.5), from which one can infer approximate rates of lake evaporation E_o, i.e. 0.7 E_p. The comparison shows that annual rainfalls tend to be less than E_o at most places in Australia, e.g. the rainfall and E_o at Alice Springs are 250 mm/a and 2,200 mm/a, respectively. Equivalent figures for Hobart are about 600 and 700 mm/a, approximately. But places like Darwin (where the annual rainfall is 1,490 mm and E_o about 1,680 mm/a) should be compared on a monthly basis because of the highly seasonal climate: E_o greatly exceeds precipitation in the dry season but is less than the rainfall from November to April.

Not all the rain from clouds reaches the ground. Some evaporates below cloud base (Section 9.1). There is also interception of some rain by the leaves of vegetation, though most of that is subsequently evaporated. The fraction intercepted is typically 10 per cent in the Amazon basin, 15–40 per cent for conifers, 10–25 per cent for deciduous hardwoods and 14–22 per cent for prairie grass. Measurements in a mature

Australian wheat crop showed that about a third of the rain was held on the leaves. The amount held can be 2 mm or so in the case of grass, and 8 mm for a cotton crop. Around 5 mm was intercepted during each storm above a rainforest in north Queensland, depending on the leafiness of the foliage. It follows that deforestation increases runoff, e.g. by 5–10 per cent in northern Queensland.

When rain reaches the ground it tends to pond on the surface, and then either evaporates, flows away as runoff or is absorbed into the ground. All the rain is absorbed if the intensity is less than the maximum rate at which the soil can accept it, which depends on the type of soil and its prior wetness. For unsaturated soils it may be around 50 mm/h in the case of sand, but 4 mm/h for clay, for example. So there is a wide range of infiltration rates within a single drainage basin.

The ratio of the runoff (R) to the precipitation is called the *runoff coefficient*. It is greater with high rainfall intensities. It is also affected by surface roughness, vegetation, soil type, soil wetness and the slope of the land (**Figure 10.14**). Values vary widely (**Table 10.4**).

What is called the *effective rainfall* (or *influential rainfall*) is that part which is neither evaporated, intercepted by vegetation nor carried away as runoff. It penetrates into the ground and is mostly taken up by roots, later evaporating from the vegetation's leaves. It is the part of the rainfall involved in growing plants, roughly estimated in various ways. One procedure is to ignore daily rainfalls of less than 5 mm, for instance (which are assumed to evaporate without wetting the ground to root level), and disregard all rainfall falling after 75 mm has fallen on the same day; this is supposed to run off. However, such threshold values are arbitrary, and different in various countries. Another way, used for agriculture in southern Australia, has been to take the *ineffective* part of each month's rainfall

as about equal to a third of the lake evaporation (Section 4.5).

Water Budgeting

An important application of the water-balance concept is in *water budgeting*. This is a procedure for keeping track of changes of soil-moisture content, using data on the rainfall P and actual evaporation E_a, during each successive period of ten days, for instance. P raises the moisture content from a known value at the start of a

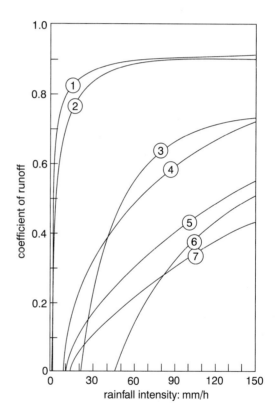

Figure 10.14 Effect of rainfall intensity and kind of surface on the runoff coefficient. Curve 1 refers to impervious roofs, concrete and urban areas generally, 2 to steep rocky slopes, 3 to medium soil on open slopes, 4 to residential suburbs with gardens, 5 to parks, lawns and meadows, 6 to forests and sandy soils, 7 to cultivated fields with good growth.

Table 10.4 Values of the run-off coefficient

Place	Runoff coefficient (%)
Basins:	
Murray-Darling rivers	6
Mississippi river	22
Zaire river	23
Clarence river, NSW	27
Amazon river	42
Various surfaces:	
Parkland	10–25
25% urbanised suburb	13
Well-engineered catchment in South Australia	16
50% urbanisation	26
Totally suburban	52
Downtown	70–90

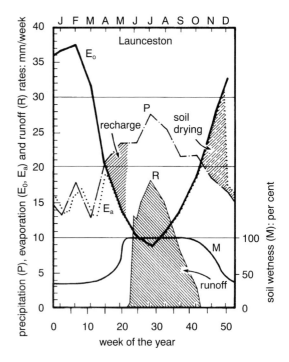

Figure 10.15 Measured values at Launceston, Tasmania, of the precipitation rate P, and values of the lake evaporation E_o (representing the potential evaporation rate E_t), calculated from temperature values. The actual evaporation rate E_a is estimated as whichever is the less of E_o and 112 M^2 mm/wk (Figure 4.10), where M is the soil's actual water content as a proportion of the soil's available-water capacity, assumed to be 100 mm of water. The soil dries out when E_a is greater than P, until M equals $\{E_o/112\}^{0.5}$ (Linacre 1973: 451). Recharge occurs when P is greater than E_o, until the soil is saturated. Thereafter, there is runoff R, as long as P exceeds E_o. The shaded areas of recharge and soil drying in the diagram must be equal because there is a long-term balance of drying and rewetting of the soil.

period, and E_a lowers it, so that the moisture content at the end of that period (and the start of the next) can be calculated by simple book-keeping. Details are given in **Note 10.P**. The procedure shows when and how much irrigation is needed.

Another reason for keeping a soil's water budget is that the *soil-moisture content* (M) indicates the eventual crop yield (Note 4.G). Yield correlates more strongly with *M* than with climatic features such as evaporation, rainfall or temperature. Calculations with climate data for several years show how often a crop's yield would be satisfactory on new land.

Water budgeting also shows the amount of runoff and therefore the expected river flow. For instance, the curves in **Figure 10.15** indicate that runoff at Launceston in Tasmania can be expected from June–October, i.e. that is when flooding is most likely.

10.6 FLOODS

Floods are rivers which overflow their banks. This happens when there is an abnormal runoff from a wide catchment area into the river – from heavy rains or the rapid melting of snow upstream. Abrupt, brief risings of the river are called 'flash floods'. Altogether, floods cause many deaths worldwide (**Table 10.5**), and the

Table 10.5 Numbers of people killed in natural disasters from 1967–91

Natural disaster	Number of deaths
Droughts (Section 10.7)	1,334,000
Tropical cyclones and storm surge (Chapter 13)	896,000
Storms and floods (Section 10.6)	358,000
High winds (Chapter 14)	14,000
Extreme temperatures (Chapter 3)	5,000

number increases with the growing population in flood-prone areas.

Floods are more likely where the ground is too impervious or already too wet to absorb more moisture. Thus the possibility of heavy rains causing flooding is estimated by monitoring or calculating the wetness of the ground of the various areas draining into the river (Section 10.5).

Flooding in a section of a river implies that the inflow upstream exceeds the outflow from the place of flooding, and both flows depend on the shape of the land. Flat areas which are notably vulnerable to flooding are called *floodplains*, which may be well downstream of the region where the rain falls.

The hazard is greater where there is a high variability of rainfall. So Australia is especially prone, particularly in the north (Section 10.4). The heaviest precipitation is often the consequence of depressions or tropical cyclones (Chapter 13), and causes floods if the falls are widespread. That occurred in some famous floods in Brisbane in the last century (**Note 10.Q**). Even earlier, seven major floods in the Hawkesbury Valley behind Sydney in the period 1795–1810 seriously threatened the food supply of the infant colony. The likelihood of such floods now is lessened by dams across the headwaters.

Years of particularly high floods in northern New South Wales are listed in **Table 10.6**.

Flood years at Grafton coincided with those at Lismore, some 100 km away and in a quite separate valley. Almost all the forty-four floods occurred in the first half of the year when tropical cyclones are most prevalent (Chapter 13). Otherwise, there is no evidence of any regularity, and no clear correspondence with El Niño episodes (Chapter 11). The table shows that the frequency of major floods in that region has risen this century from about one to about ten each twenty years.

Extensive flooding occurs occasionally in Lake Eyre, the largest ephemeral lake in the world, draining an area of central Australia roughly 700 km across. It happened in 1916–17, 1920–21, 1949–50 and 1974–77, with minor floodings in 1907, 1940–41, 1953, 1955–59, 1984 and 1989, due to heavy rains in Queensland far away. Again, these dates do not correspond to those of El Niño or La Niña events (Note 10.M).

10.7 DROUGHTS

Wheat yields averaged only 0.67 tonnes per hectare during six Australian droughts between 1940 and 1968, instead of the 1.17 t/ha in the years immediately before and after. In the USA, 41 per cent of crop insurance payouts to farmers are for losses due to drought. Even more importantly, droughts are responsible for more human deaths than other natural disasters (Table 10.5).

They differ strikingly from floods. A drought can be as damaging as a flood, but affects a whole region and not just the low-lying parts. Also, droughts begin imperceptibly but usually end sharply with soaking rains, whereas floods start abruptly and have a lingering aftermath.

Droughts can be defined in several ways. What is called a *meteorological drought* occurs when there is little rain, compared with normal, *in terms of the degree of variability at the place*. For instance, drought may be defined as three

Table 10.6 Times of floods at Grafton and Lismore (NSW)

Grafton: years when river over 2.2 m above reference*							Lismore†
March 1890	**April 1892**	**Feb. 1893**	**June 1893**				1893
May 1921	**July 1921**	**Feb. 1928**					1921, 1931
							1945, 1948, 1950,
June 1945	**March 1946**	**June 1948**	**June 1950**	July 1950	**Feb. 1954**	July 1954	1954
March 1955	May 1955	Jan. 1956	**Feb. 1956**	**Jan. 1959**	**Feb. 1959**	Nov. 1959	1956
April 1962	July 1962	Jan. 1963	April 1963	**May 1963**	March 1964	July 1965	1962, 1963, 1965
Jan. 1967	March 1967	**June 1967**	**Jan. 1968**	Feb. 1971	Nov. 1972		1967, 1972
Jan. 1974	**March 1974**	April 1974	**Feb. 1976**				1974, 1975, 1976
May 1980	**April 1988**	July 1988	**April 1989**	Feb. 1990	April 1990		‡

* The dates shown are of years when the Clarence River at Grafton rose more than 2.2 m above the reference level; on dates shown in bold the river rose beyond 6 m

† The dates shown are of years when the Richmond River at Lismore (100 km north of Grafton) rose more than 10 m above the reference level

‡ No data available

consecutive months with rainfalls each within the lowest decile. This means that even a high rainfall leads to drought if it is much less than usual at that time of year, at that place; drought is not the same as aridity. However, even a modest reduction from normal leads to drought if there is usually little variation from the average. Thus a reduction of annual rainfall to 66 per cent of the average at Perth (where the variability is low) would constitute a severe drought, whereas such a reduction would be hardly noticed at Alice Springs because of the customary high variability of rainfall.

Other rainfall definitions of drought in terms of less than some certain amount within some specified period differ between countries. An *agricultural drought* is determined by soil-moisture conditions during critical stages in the growth of a crop. So it depends on previous runoff and evaporation (i.e. on radiation, temperature, humidity and wind) as well as rainfall. Hence parts of north-east Brazil suffered extreme meteorological drought, but not agricultural drought, during 1983. *Hydrological drought* reflects the drying up of streams, and therefore is governed by all the factors affecting runoff, considered in Section 10.5. This kind of drought, like agricultural drought, is revealed by water budgeting. *Socio-economic drought* is a

time of a water shortage affected by management decisions. For instance, the water stored behind a dam may be reduced in anticipation of predicted heavy rains, giving rise to a drought if rains turn out to be merely normal. Or consider the official decision to 'declare' a drought in a region of New South Wales whenever half the sheep or cattle must be hand-fed or moved away for pasture; this depends on previous management decisions about stocking rates and kind of stock, and human judgement of the need to move it. Such drought may be induced by over-grazing, or by over-commitment of the water supply. We will focus on meteorological drought in what follows.

The best-known indication of the intensity of a drought is the American *Palmer Drought Severity Index* (PDSI), derived from complicated comparisons of (i) measured rainfall and estimated evaporation, with (ii) normal values, and summations of the monthly differences. The usefulness of the PDSI is limited by poor estimation of evaporation, the use of monthly averages, several arbitrary values, and the need for considerable information. It can be improved by more explicit water budgeting (Section 10.5), e.g. for estimating catchment runoff or the dryness of forests. In this case, drought intensity is described in terms of the millimetres of water needed to refill the soil (Note 10.P). There is a serious risk of a forest fire if the deficit exceeds say, 64 mm.

The occurrence and extent of droughts seem at first sight to be hopelessly irregular. For instance, Australian records show that over 20 per cent of the continent had annual rainfalls within the lowest decile on thirteen occasions between 1902 and 1982, spaced 3–14 years apart, with a median value of 5.5 years. Unfortunately, this is neither so rare as to be unimportant nor so frequent as to be accommodated within the normal routine of farming. The irregularity of occurrence is due to a combination of factors: (i) 'natural' variation, (ii) unexplained processes, (iii) weather rhythms, (iv) sea-surface temperatures nearby and (v) teleconnections, all of which operate together and are variously unpredictable. Let us consider them.

Random Element

There is a large random element in all atmospheric processes, reflected in the variability of rainfall considered earlier (Section 10.4). This inherent property of climates inevitably produces a long series of subnormal rainfalls from time to time, just as tossing a coin leads to a long run of heads occasionally. Convective rainfall especially is associated with unpredictable randomness, as thunderstorms occur only in some parts of a region of unstable air but not in others (Note 7.G). When this effect is dominant it causes isolated patches of *natural drought*, mainly in semi-arid areas on the edges of deserts where the variability is greatest. It is quite normal in Australia.

Unexplained Associations

Several occurrences of drought have been linked with preceding atmospheric conditions, indicating causative processes at work which are not yet understood. For instance, two consecutive wet years at Beer-Sheva in Israel are usually followed by drought. Similarly, fifteen drought years out of twenty-two in north-east Brazil were preceded by months of unusual wind patterns in the upper atmosphere of the northern hemisphere.

Persistence (Section 10.4) is a related feature of drought, perhaps due to positive feedbacks in the atmosphere prolonging a random dry period into a drought. Thus, the probability of a relatively dry summer at Alice Springs is 14.4 per cent, so that the chance of two dry summers together would be 2.1 per cent (i.e. 0.144×0.144) if the events were independent (Note 10.N). But, in fact, the chance proves to be 3.9 per cent – almost twice as much – so a dry summer this year somehow enhances the likelihood of one next year. Likewise, records of rainfalls in Africa during the period 1911–74 show more long runs of dry years than would be expected by chance.

Rhythms

Occasionally there seems to be a rhythm of a decade or two in the occurrence of drought (**Note 10.R**). Tree-ring data (Note 10.D) from the American Midwest indicate gaps of about nineteen years between droughts, and a similar time has elapsed between some major droughts in New South Wales in 1809, 1828, 1857, 1866, 1885, 1895, etc. Also, there were extended dry periods in South Africa during the periods 1905–16, 1925–33, 1944–53, 1962–71 and 1981 onwards. Droughts occurred in the Transvaal each eighteen years or so, with about 10 per cent less rain than average. Similarly, the fluctuation of annual rainfall in Argentina shows minima about each 18.8 years, with around 20 per cent less than the mean. Also, droughts in north-east USA since 1840 indicate a periodicity of about nineteen years, like those in north-east China since AD 1500, whilst rings in the cross-section of a cypress tree in North Carolina show a rhythm of 17.9 years.

All this might be due to the Moon, which moves in an ellipse about the Earth, with the axes of that ellipse themselves rotating each 18.6 years, the rotation being called the *lunar nodal precession*. This has the effect of varying the distance between Moon and Earth, and therefore the Moon's tidal pull on our atmosphere. Presumably this changes the pattern of winds and therefore of rainfalls. Alternatively, or in addition, the apparent rhythm of droughts might possibly be related to the time between sunspot maxima, i.e. to a cycle of roughly eleven or twenty-two years, though the relationship is complex and ambiguous (**Note 10.S**). Sadly, alleged links to the sunspot cycle or lunar precession may be based on poor analysis of selected data and in practice are too subtle to be of much help in forecasting rainfall.

Sea-surface Temperatures

A factor which does certainly increase the chance of drought is an unusually low sea-surface temperature (SST) nearby. For instance, the dry years 1957, 1961 and 1965 in Australia were associated with sea-surface temperatures around the coast which were cooler than in the wet years 1950, 1955 and 1968. Similarly, some correlation has been found between the occurrence of drought in north-east Brazil and the adjacent Atlantic SST (Chapter 16), and between droughts in eastern Australia and the nearby Pacific SST off Queensland. Also, the rainfall between November and March along the eastern edge of South Africa depends notably on the temperature of the warm Agulhas Current and on the proximity of the Current to the coast (Chapter 11); drought is more likely when the Current is weak or absent. The top and bottom rows in **Figure 10.16** show some connection between warm seas off South America and rainfalls at Santiago nearby.

This evidence that an abnormal coastal SST increases rainfall onshore is not surprising. The extra warmth means that the onshore winds can hold more water vapour (Note 4.C), and higher surface temperatures enhance convective uplift; both are factors which increase rainfall. The effect of SST on rainfall is one reason for considering the oceans in the next chapter.

Teleconnections

Sometimes rainfall at a place increases in accord with warmer seas *far away*, either at the same time or months previously. For example, **Figure 10.17** shows rainfall anomalies (i.e. differences from normal) in Papua New Guinea occurring about a month after anomalies of SST at the other end of the Pacific ocean, over 10,000 km away. Such a relationship is called a *teleconnection* between the weather at one place and the weather somewhere remote. Other examples of teleconnections involving rainfall are as follows:

1 Warm seas more than 2,000 km east of Brazil are associated with high rainfalls in December at 4°S on the Brazilian coast.
2 Relatively high SST and more westerly winds in the equatorial Atlantic are associated with above-average precipitation over coastal regions of Angola in Africa (**Figure 10.18**).
3 Each of the twenty-two periods of high sea-surface temperature off Peru between 1871 and 1978 (with temperatures 2–4 K above normal) was associated with about 9 per cent less monsoonal rain than usual over most of India.

There are also teleconnections between droughts in separated land areas. H.C. Russell noted in 1896 that droughts in India and Australia tended to occur in the same years. Likewise, Figure 10.16 shows a *tendency* towards a coincidence of droughts in Australia, New Zealand, Brazil and Midwest USA, near the times of the sea-surface warming episodes off Peru, the El Niño (Note 10.M), and of low

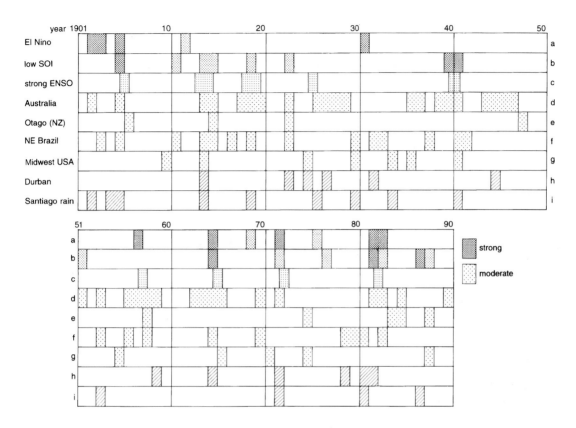

Figure 10.16 The approximate occurrences of El Niño, droughts in various places, and rainfall in Santiago (33°S). The dates of warm sea surfaces off Peru are shown in row (a), and years with a low Southern Oscillation Index (see Chapter 12) in row (b). Row (c) shows years when there were either 'strong' or 'very strong' ENSO warm episodes (Chapter 12), with considerable repercussions economically etc. Droughts in Australia are indicated in row (d), in Otago (NZ) (e), northeast Brazil (f), Midwest USA (g) and South Africa (h). Row (i) shows years when the rainfall at Santiago exceeded 500 mm, i.e. unusually *wet* years. (For more details, see Section 17.3 concerning this diagram.)

atmospheric pressures at Tahiti, shown by a low 'Southern Oscillation Index' (Chapter 12). (The fact of only a 'tendency' towards coincidence shows the influence of other factors which lead to droughts, as well as the difficulty of specifying the year of a drought which extends from spring in one year to autumn in the next.) On the other hand, droughts do not occur simultaneously in both East Africa and South Africa, while droughts in Chile tend to coincide with unusual flooding of the Nile. Also, droughts occur in different years in the east and west of Australia (**Figure 10.19**), presumably because the global pattern of winds affects the two halves of the continent differently (Chapter 12).

The causes of these various teleconnections are not well understood, though their scale implies a dependence on global patterns of winds (Chapter 12).

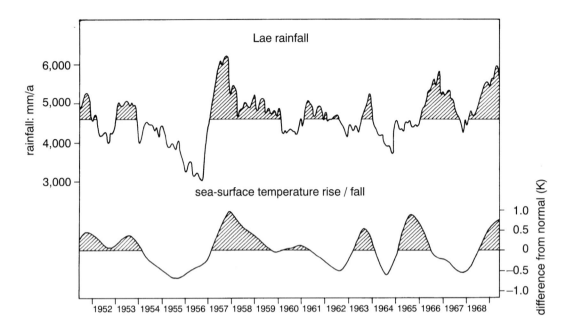

Figure 10.17 Parallelism of changes of rainfalls at Lae (in Papua New Guinea) and of sea-surface temperatures between 5°N–5°S and 80–180°W, in the east equatorial Pacific. The rainfalls and the temperatures shown are twelve-month 'running means' (Note 10.H).

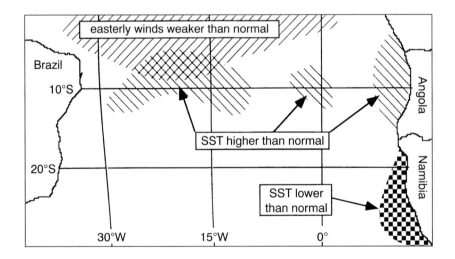

Figure 10.18 Sea-surface temperatures SST and winds in the Atlantic at low latitudes associated with unusually wet weather on the Angolan coast.

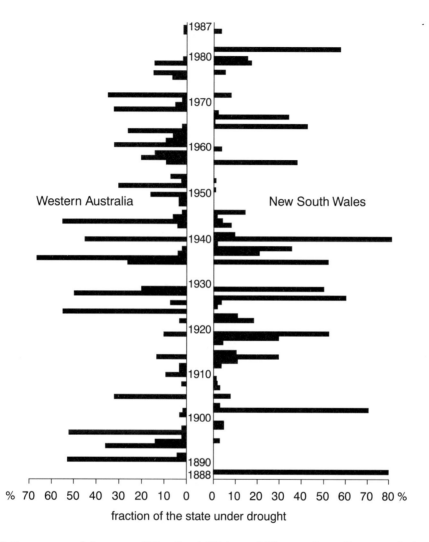

Figure 10.19 Percentages of the areas of New South Wales and Western Australia, respectively, affected by drought, between 1888 and 1987.

10.8 SNOW

Snow falls instead of rain at places of high elevation and high latitude (Figure 3.6). For instance, there is snow every year above about 1,500 m in south-east Australia, and there were nine brief occasions between 1900 and 1979 of snow on the inland edge of Sydney, which is beside the sea at 34°S. But there is no perma-

nent snow even on Australia's highest mountain (Mt Kosciusko at 2,228 m, 37°S) because it is too low (Figure 3.6). Likewise, there is no permanent snow even on the several peaks over 3,000 m in Lesotho, because of a latitude of only 30°S.

Rates of snowfall are low because (i) snow-flakes descend at only about 1 m/s, no matter what size, about a quarter the rate for typical raindrops or a tenth the rate of the large drops in heavy rainfall (Table 9.1), and (ii) almost all snow comes from non-convective clouds (Section 8.1).

The depth of settled snow is initially about 5–16 times that of an equal weight of rain, becoming about 2.5 times the depth by the end of winter, i.e. the density becomes 40 per cent that of water. Where there is permanent snow it solidifies after some months as *firn*, which is granular and has a density which is 40–80 per cent that of water, and then eventually it may become glacier ice with a density of about 90 per cent.

The greatest depth of snow likely on a roof in the Snowy Mountains (which straddle New South Wales and Victoria) increases linearly with elevation (**Figure 10.20**). Years of deepest snow in a valley in the Snowy Mountains were 1956, 1958, 1960, (1962), 1964, (1966), 1968, (1970), (1972), 1974, (1977), 1981, (1984), (1986), 1990, 1994. (The bracketed years were less notable.) These dates are consistent with the idea of a quasi-biennial variation (Section 10.4), i.e. a tendency for a good year for skiers to be followed by a poor one. In fact, records from 1954–87 show that any year of abnormal snowfall is followed by another above-average year on only 20 per cent of occasions. This is an example of *anti-persistence*.

Most years with above-average snowfall in the Snowy Mountains coincide with *below-average* rainfall on the eastern slopes because that rain is due to onshore east winds which are too warm to produce snow, whereas snow comes from outbreaks of polar air from the south-west.

Trends this century indicate a rise in snowfalls during the period 1930–60, and since then a decline (**Figure 10.21**). Figure 10.21 describes the amount of snowfall in a year in terms of the *integrated snow depth* in metres, i.e. the sum of all the daily depths during a year, so that the figure combines depth and duration, and the maximum value is reached with the last

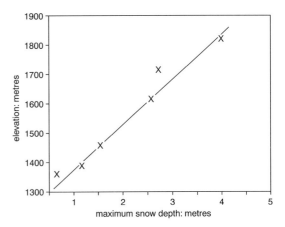

Figure 10.20 Variation with elevation in the Australian Alps of the average maximum depth of snow each year.

snow of the season. The fluctuations shown in Figure 10.21 happen to correspond approximately to opposite trends in rainfalls at Darwin at the other end of Australia (Figure 10.10).

The duration of the snow season is about sixteen days more for each 100 m elevation in Britain, Switzerland and Australia, though this varies from year to year. The ski season in the Snowy Mountains was almost six months in 1968 but only one month in 1979. Global warming will reduce the period, and preliminary calculations for New Zealand suggest that the snowline will rise 100 m for each 1 K of warming.

Large accumulations of snow can lead to avalanches on slopes of 35–45 degrees, in early spring. Avalanches are most likely when there is a fall of at least 50 mm one day, then a week or two of daily maximum temperatures below −5°C, followed by two or three days with maxima over +2°C.

The melting of snow depends on the net radiation, heat from the wind, and latent heat released when water vapour deposits onto the snow. Which is most important depends on the circumstances. Heat from the wind is the major cause of melting in the case of a New Zealand

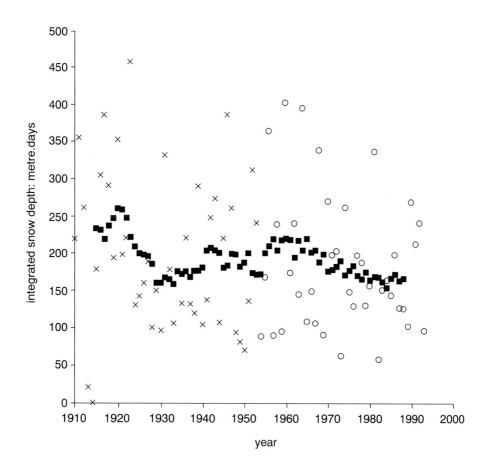

Figure 10.21 The variation of the integrated snow depth in the Australian Alps. The values shown by circles were measured at Spencer's Creek (at 1,475 m), about 5 km from Mt Kosciusko. Measurements at Kiandra (at 1,395 m, some 40 km to the north) were used prior to 1954 until 1968, as measurements at Spencer's Creek started only in 1954; crosses show the measurements at Kiandra, multiplied by the ratio of the mean snowfall at Spencer's Creek to that at Kiandra between 1954 and 1968. Solid squares show 11-year running means, e.g. the value for 1958 is the average of cross or circle values during the period 1953–68, inclusive.

glacier. Cloud accelerates melting when temperatures are above freezing, since snow accepts the longwave radiation from clouds but reflects away shortwave radiation from the Sun (Table 2.3).

The melted snow contributes to rivers, com-

bining with the runoff of rain from the land and with groundwater to flow down to the sea. So the next stage of the hydrologic cycle which is the topic of Part III of the book involves the oceans. These are discussed in the following chapter.

NOTES

10.A Typical effects of rainfall in agriculture
10.B Rain gauges
10.C Remote rainfall measurement
10.D Indication of seasonal rainfall by tree rings
10.E Acidity and alkalinity
10.F Soil erosion
10.G Estimation of rainfalls for long recurrence intervals
10.H Defining the 'typical' rainfall

10.I The Bradfield Scheme
10.J The possible effect of forests on rainfall
10.K Dependable rainfall
10.L Indices of rainfall variability
10.M El Niño, part 1
10.N The chance of a second dry day after a first
10.O Desert runoff
10.P Water budgets of soil moisture
10.Q Flooding of the Brisbane River in 1893
10.R Droughts in New South Wales
10.S Droughts and sunspots

11

OCEANS

11.1 OCEANS AND CLIMATES

The remaining stage of the hydrologic cycle (Section 6.1) consists of the circulation of water in the oceans. This has considerable impact on onshore climates (**Note 11.A**); the oceans affect the atmosphere's temperature (Note 3.G), moisture content (Note 4.D), stability (Section 7.6), rainfall (Section 10.4) and winds (Chapter 14). These effects are felt especially at the coast, and thus are important, for instance, to the 80 per cent of Australia's population who live within 30 km of the sea.

The amount of water in the oceans is huge. The average depth is 3,730 m (Note 1.A), which is over four times the mean elevation of the world's land above sea-level. It takes a 0.4 kg steel ball over an hour to drop 11 km to the bottom of the Mariana Trench in the north-west Pacific. Also, the area of the oceans is vast, covering 70.9 per cent of the Earth's surface (Note 1.A).

The predominance of ocean surface is a special feature of the southern hemisphere. Just over 80 per cent of the hemisphere is covered by sea and about a quarter of the rest is permanently covered by ice. The percentage of ocean is especially high at the latitudes of Australia, and around Antarctica (**Figure 11.1**).

Comparison

The oceans resemble the atmosphere in consisting of a fluid, containing heat, being subject to convection (**Note 11.B**) and horizontal circulation, flowing under the influence of slope and pressure difference, and carrying contaminants. Much of the theory of atmospheric movement applies also to ocean flows.

The fluids also differ greatly. Water is substantially incompressible and over a thousand times more dense than air, so that even slow ocean currents contain much greater momentum – enough to affect the rotation of the Earth. The density of air ranges widely with altitude, whereas there are relatively slight variations of the density of the sea, due chiefly to differences in temperature or salt concentration. In addition, oceans are contained within large connected basins while the atmosphere is almost unbounded. Furthermore, the oceans hold much more heat; the total heat capacity of the whole atmosphere is equal to that of merely 3 m depth of the oceans. Also, the Sun's radiation heats the sea at the *top*, creating a lighter upper layer and hence extreme stability, which helps preserve the layered structure of the oceans, discussed in Section 11.2. All the Sun's infra-red radiation is absorbed within a millimetre of the ocean's surface, while 90 per

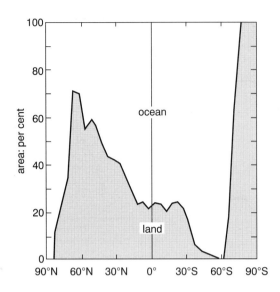

Figure 11.1 The shaded area is below a curve showing the fractions of the area at each latitude taken up by land and ocean, respectively. For instance, about 20 per cent of points at 30°S are on land, and about 80 per cent at sea.

cent of the visible radiation is absorbed in the top 75 m. Overall, half the solar radiation is absorbed within 6 cm. This heating at the top contrasts with the situation in the atmosphere, which is heated by the ground *below*, creating instability and convection, already discussed in Chapter 7.

Interactions

The oceans affect climates in several ways, on both a large and a small scale. They play a part in the transfer of latent heat (Figure 4.2), carry sensible heat to other latitudes (Note 5.F), and sea-surface temperatures affect convective rainfalls.

More immediately, the surface of the ocean influences the planetary boundary layer (PBL) of the atmosphere, the well-mixed layer against the surface (Figure 1.11), whose condition largely defines our climate. It is this lowest tur-

bulent layer of a few hundred metres depth which exchanges heat and moisture, and whose wind contributes momentum to the ocean. Conversely, it is the top few dozen metres of the sea which are chiefly influenced by rainfall, air temperature and the flows of radiation at the surface. This sluggish layer is as well mixed as the PBL as a result of surface waves and downwards convection from any cooled surface. The two adjacent layers, of the ocean and the atmosphere, influence each other so greatly that we say they are 'tightly coupled', interacting substantially and automatically. They are what we shall mainly consider in this chapter.

11.2 OCEAN TEMPERATURES

The sea-surface temperature (SST) was first mapped by Alexander von Humboldt in 1817. Modern maps show long-term values of the SST varying from the sea's freezing point of −1.9°C near polar ice, to over 30°C in the Persian Gulf and the Red Sea in July (**Figure 11.2**). Temperatures offshore tend to be cooler than inland in January (summer) but warmer in July, around South Africa for instance (**Figure 11.3**). These differences of temperature cause coastal breezes (Chapter 14).

Generally, the isotherms depend chiefly on latitude (**Table 11.1**), though there is a variation near the coasts of continents where isotherms bend polewards on the east coasts (especially at 20–30°S, implying extra warmth) and vice versa on the west (**Table 11.2**); ocean currents are the main reason, as explained in Section 11.5. The effect is most against South America, and least around Australia. East-coast places in Australia are hardly warmer than those at the same latitude on the west, because the west coast of Australia lacks a cold current of the kind found off Chile and south-west Africa (Section 11.5). Yet all three continents are similar in having remarkably

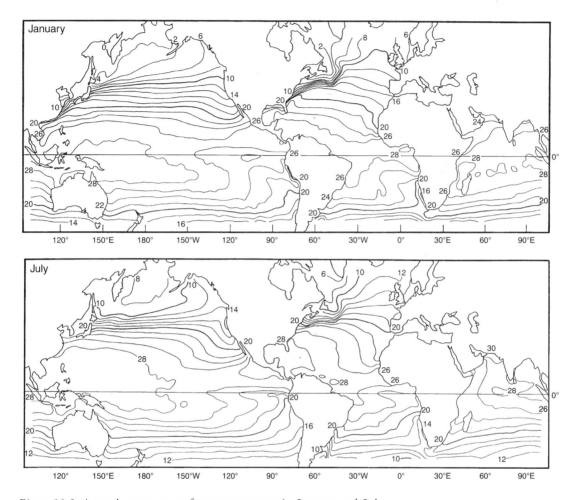

Figure 11.2 Annual mean sea-surface temperatures in January and July.

dry west coasts (Table 11.2), as would be expected with a cold SST there.

Temperatures are below freezing near the poles, so there is sea-ice. It is only a few metres thick and extends from Antarctica to 63–70°S in March and 55–65°S in September, the area increasing from about 4 million square kilometres to 20 million in winter. Even if temperatures are not quite so cold, they can be lethal: a person can last no longer than about two hours in water at 5°C, or four hours at 13°C.

At the other extreme, there is the world's largest *'warm pool'* whose annual mean surface temperature exceeds 28°C. It is larger than Australia and centred in the western Pacific ocean just north of the equator, near Papua New Guinea (Figure 11.2). The pool extends eastward as far as 170°E into the Pacific during a La Niña but almost 6,000 km further to 140°W in an El Niño year. The high temperature and vast area make it the most active breeding ground for tropical cyclones (Chapter 13) and the engine for the 'Walker circulation'

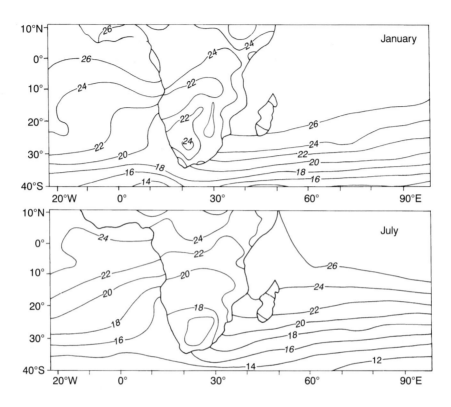

Figure 11.3 Monthly mean SST and screen temperatures around and over southern Africa, in January and July.

Table 11.1 The effect of latitude and season on the monthly mean sea-surface temperature and annual rainfall of South Pacific islands

Place	Latitude (°S)	Elevation (metres)	Maximum monthly mean temperature (°C)	Minimum monthly mean temperature (°C)	Rainfall (mm/a)
Cook Island	9	1	28 (April)	27 (August)	3,655
Pitcairn Island	25	264	24 (Feb)	19 (August)	2,630
Easter Island	27	20	24 (Feb)	18 (August)	1,134
Lord Howe Is.	32	0	23 (Feb)	16 (August)	1,685
Waitangi	44	44	15 (Feb)	8 (July)	851
Macquarie Island	55	6	7 (Jan)	3 (July)	863

Table 11.2 A comparison of monthly mean temperatures (°C) and rainfall (mm) at coastal cities on the west and east sides of three continents

Continent	Coast	Place	Temperature (°C)		Daily range (K)		Precipitation (mm)	
			Jan	July	Jan	July	Jan	July
Around 23°S								
S. America	West	Antofagasta	21	14	7	6	0	5
	East	Rio de Janeiro	26	21	6	7	125	41
S. Africa	West	Walvis Bay	19	15	8	13	0	0
	East	Maputo	25	18	8	11	130	13
Australia	West	Carnarvon	27	17	8	11	20	46
	East	Brisbane	25	15	6	11	163	56
Around 34°S								
S. America	West	Santiago	21	9	17	12	3	76
	East	Buenos Aires	23	10	12	8	79	56
S. Africa	West	Cape Town	21	12	10	10	15	89
	East	Durban	24	17	6	11	127	85
Australia	West	Perth	23	13	12	8	8	170
	East	Sydney	22	12	8	8	89	117

across the Pacific ocean (Chapter 12). The high SST leads to rapid evaporation (Figure 4.11), and rainfalls there average about 3 m/a, and exceed 5 m/a in some parts of the warm pool (Figure 10.3).

There are considerable week-to-week fluctuations in the pattern of sea-surface temperatures. **Figure 11.4** shows the short-term irregularity of SST off the east Australian coast. The small-scale structure, such as the two isolated loops below the 24°C isotherm, is due to ocean eddies which evolve over the course of a few days. In addition, there are seasonal and interannual variations.

Seasonal Variation

Sea-surface temperatures vary over the year (**Figure 11.5** and **Figure 11.6**). The average difference between the extremes (the annual range) is usually only a degree or two at the poles and at the equator, and most (i.e. 5–6K) at 30–40°S (Figure 3.4; Table 11.1). For instance, the range offshore at Sydney (at 34°S) is from about 22.6°C in March to

17.2°C in August, i.e. 5.4 K. Larger ranges are found in seas that are surrounded by large land masses and in coastal waters where there is a wide continental shelf, e.g. 10.5 K offshore from Cabo Corrientes in Patagonia. Even this is less than the range inland, because of the ground's relatively small thermal inertia (Section 3.3).

A large annual range may occur at sea when the ocean currents (Section 11.5) change seasonally. For instance, the south equatorial eastern Pacific and Atlantic are about 5K cooler in winter than in summer (Figure 11.5), because the cold currents affecting these regions are stronger in winter. In this exceptional case, the annual temperature range offshore can be higher than on the coast.

The annual extremes of sea-surface temperature occur about 2–3 months after the extremes of radiation (Table 11.1) because of the ocean's thermal inertia, due to the large volume affected as a result of stirring within the ocean's mixing layer. Temperature variations are less at greater depth, as in the case of temperatures below ground (Figure 3.16). There is no annual

Plate 11.1 The oceanographic research vessel *Franklin* of the CSIRO Division of Oceanography, Hobart. This photograph was taken during experiments in the warm pool of the western Pacific, when a boom forward of the bows carried instruments for measuring the fluxes of heat and moisture from the water surface upwards, and of momentum downwards. The boom also carried an instrument to be lowered into the water for measuring the profiles of temperature and salinity within the upper 3 metres. Other instruments on the foremast repeated the flux measurements, and measured rainfall. Shortwave and longwave radiation were determined by instruments above the wheelhouse. Other instruments were towed from the afterdeck to determine the temperature and salinity profiled to 300 m depth.

variation beyond two or three hundred metres under the surface (Figure 11.6).

El Niño Episodes

There is a variation of SST from year to year, especially in the tropical Pacific ocean. This was mentioned in Note 10.M, in conection with the SST off Peru, which is usually much lower than anywhere else so close to the equator (Section 11.2). However, the temperature there rises by several degrees for twelve months or so every few years, on account of a shifting of the easterly winds and ocean currents along the equator of the Pacific ocean (**Note 11.C**). For example, the temperature was 24°C, instead of the usual 16°C, at one point off Peru between September 1982 and January 1983. Such El Niño episodes are discussed further in Chapter 12.

Icebergs

Some 5,000 icebergs break off from Antarctic glaciers and ice shelves each year, and the total

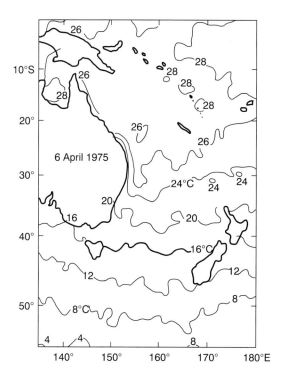

Figure 11.4 Sea-surface temperatures off the eastern Australian coast on 6 April 1975.

volume of this salt-free ice is about a thousand cubic kilometres. Some icebergs are huge, 20–40 m high and ten times that below the water-line. A berg seen in 1956 was 200 x 60 km in area. Another was 150 km long, which broke off the Ross ice shelf (at 77°S, south of New Zealand) in 1987. It was tracked by satellite for twenty-two months, until it became three pieces. One iceberg was initially about 30 km across and then was observed drifting some 10,000 km, nearly round Antarctica. Some bergs drift slowly north, especially in the Atlantic Ocean, where they have been seen at 28°S (**Figure 11.7**).

Relationship to Rainfall

The relatively cloudless skies over the cool eastern half of a southern tropical ocean (Figure 8.14) lead to little rainfall P (Figure 10.3) but a high evaporation rate E_o, so that many islands in these areas have a 'marine desert' climate. The evaporation rate exceeds 2 m/a in some places (Figure 4.11) and the difference $(P - E_o)$ is negative, so that there is a continuous loss of pure water (**Figure 11.8**), leaving the sea surface with a high salt concentration. This in turn helps maintain the currents which lowered the SST in the first place (Sections 11.3 and 11.5), so there is positive feedback, providing another illustration of the tight coupling between atmosphere and ocean.

Climate Change

The oceans' temperature is a major factor in climate change (Chapter 15). Firstly, the water's enormous thermal capacity slows up any sudden alteration of temperature. Secondly, the oceans dissolve much of the atmosphere's carbon dioxide, which governs the greenhouse effect (Note 2.L) and hence global temperatures. In this connection, there is a positive feedback: warm water dissolves less of the gas than cold water, so an increase of SST causes a release of carbon dioxide, thereby increasing greenhouse heating and hence accelerating global warming. Thirdly, the deep waters of the oceans already store about fifty times as much carbon dioxide as the global atmosphere (Figure 1.3), and can hold much more. Fourthly, there appears to be an interaction between global temperatures and the largest oceanic circulations. The pattern of temperatures drives the ocean currents, and they carry heat which alters the temperatures – again an example of atmosphere–ocean coupling.

Warming of the oceans in the course of climate change causes expansion of surface water. For instance, heating just the top 500 m by 3K would increase the volume by 0.06 per cent, so that the level would rise by perhaps 0.3 m (i.e. 0.0006×500). Current indications are of a rise

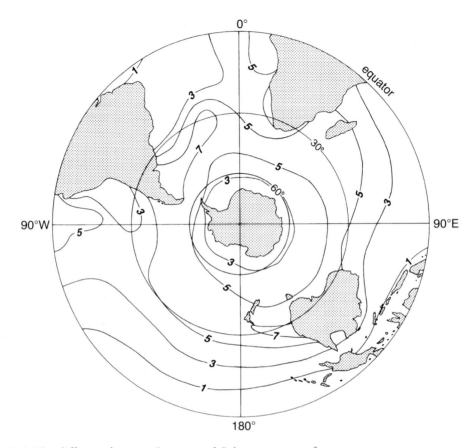

Figure 11.5 The difference between January and July mean sea-surface temperatures.

by around 0.2 m per century, though that may be due partly to the melting of glaciers.

Temperature Profile

Ocean temperatures also vary in a vertical direction, forming layers like those of the atmosphere (Figure 1.10), but upside-down. The main difference is the stability of the ocean below the surface mixed layer. That mixed layer has a depth of only 20 m or so off Peru near the equator, but sometimes 1,000 m west of Vancouver (49°N). Deep convection of (relatively dense) cold surface water to cause stirring within the layer occurs especially at high latitudes and in winter.

The mixed layer comprises the *warm-water sphere* of the ocean. Lower down is a zone with a notable drop in temperature (Figure 11.6), the *'thermocline'*, corresponding to the inversion at the top of the PBL (Section 7.6). It is a few hundred metres thick, with the same stability as an atmospheric inversion, so that fluctuations of surface temperature or oxygen concentration, for instance, do not penetrate below. The thermocline is most pronounced during the summer (Figure 11.6) and in the tropics (**Figure 11.9**). It is especially evident at about 20°S in the Indian ocean, just north-west of Australia,

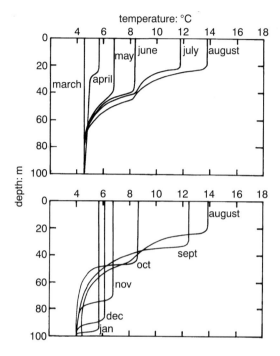

Figure 11.6 The seasonal effect on temperature profiles in the Pacific ocean at 50°N, 145°W.

where there is a difference of 18 K within 400 m. On the other hand, the thermocline hardly exists near the poles.

Remarkably cold *'deep water'* lies beneath the thermocline, and beyond that there is the *abyssal* (or *bottom*) layer, a few hundred metres deep on the sea-bed. It has a temperature of about 0°C, even in the Tropics. These layers are discussed further in Section 11.5.

11.3 SALINITY

There are normally about 34.5 grams of salts dissolved in each kilogram of sea water, written as 34.5‰. The salts consist mainly of chloride (55 per cent) and sodium (31 per cent) ions, which form sodium chloride (i.e. common salt) if the water is evaporated away in evaporation ponds. The amount of sodium chloride in the

sea represents about 12 per cent of saturation, beyond which the water can dissolve no more. Other salts include sulphate (8 per cent), magnesium (3.7 per cent), calcium (1.2 per cent) and potassium (1.1 per cent). The total salt concentration (or *salinity*) affects climates by altering the density of the sea, thus changing the pattern of pressures which govern the ocean currents and hence the transport of heat around the world.

Figure 11.9 shows that the salt concentration varies across the thermocline and around the world. Seas near estuaries or melting icebergs may be covered by a layer of lighter fresh water, and a low salinity is found anywhere that precipitation greatly exceeds evaporation, e.g. at high latitudes (Figure 10.6). Values are only 33.5‰ south of 60°S, around Antarctica.

The salinity of the surface is greater at 37°S off south-west Australia, where evaporation is more than precipitation. The highest salinity in the south Pacific ocean (36.5‰) occurs east of Tahiti (20°S), where rainfalls are less than 250 mm/a (Figure 10.3) but the evaporation rate is high (Figure 4.11). Likewise, salinity in the Atlantic approaches 37‰ off the north-east coast of Brazil.

Effects of Salinity

High salinity increases the water's density (Note 11.B) and lowers the freezing point. In addition, the salt in sea water removes a curious feature of pure water – that it is most dense at 4°C, not at freezing point. The consequence is that sea water is less likely than fresh water to become ice, for the following reason. Cooling of the surface induces convection (Note 11.B and Section 11.5), i.e. vertical mixing with warmer layers below. This ceases in pure fresh water when the surface reaches 4°C because further cooling makes the water relatively light so that it remains on top, to freeze. The ice then insulates the water below from further cooling, and so a thin layer forms

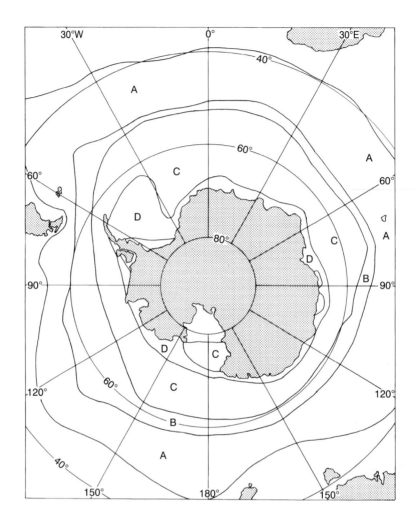

Figure 11.7 Limits of ice around Antarctica. The zones signify, respectively, (A) occasional iceberg sightings, (B) occasional sea-ice in winter and spring, (C) occasional sea-ice in summer and autumn, and (D) permanently frozen.

over water still at 4°C. On the other hand, cooling the surface of *sea* water induces convection which continues until the whole depth has cooled to its freezing point at about −2°C. The resulting convection to the bottom of the ocean creates global circulations within the oceans (Section 11.5).

The dissolved salt also reduces the water's vapour pressure, e.g. a saturated solution has a vapour pressure of only 75 per cent of that of pure water, and therefore the figure for the sea is 97 per cent (i.e. 100 − 0.12 × [100 − 75]). This means a slight reduction in the evaporation rate (Note 4.E).

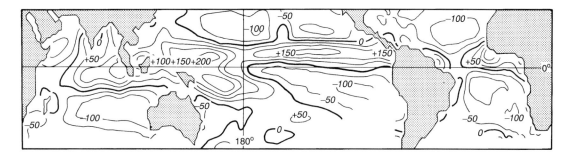

Figure 11.8 The difference between the annual mean *monthly* rainfall and evaporation (in millimetres) over the oceans of the globe. Positive values (mm/mo) indicate rainfall greater than evaporation, and vice versa.

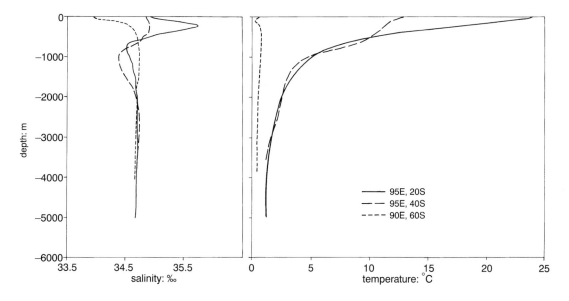

Figure 11.9 Profiles of temperature and salinity at various latitudes in the Indian ocean.

11.4 THE CORIOLIS EFFECT AND THE OCEANS

So far we have considered ocean temperature and salinity, two of the factors controlling currents in the sea, which in turn govern coastal climates. A third factor is the '*Coriolis effect*', the 'apparent deflection of moving objects, due to the observer being on a rotating Earth', named after Gaspard de Coriolis (1792–1843). Unfor-

tunately, it is not easy to understand immediately, being different from commonsense observation, and so various explanations are offered in what follows.

As a preliminary, think of the Earth rotating once each day, and an observer looking at the Sun. There is a paradox, since we know that it is the Earth (and observer) which actually turn, yet the observer sees the *Sun* as moving. Reality differs from appearance. Likewise, if you sit on a

roundabout, it is the rest of the world which seems to spin. In brief, the 'rotation of the observer is perceived as the rotation of the observed'.

In the same way, a rotating observer, looking at an object which is really moving in a straight line, sees the object as turning. This is illustrated in **Figure 11.10**. Drawing along a straight ruler creates a curved line on a rotating disc. Laying the ruler in any direction over a disc turning clockwise, and moving the pencil in either direction along the ruler, always causes the trace to bend to the *left*, whereas turning the disc counter-clockwise instead always causes sidling to the *right*. These different directions of rotation correspond to conditions in the two hemispheres of the globe, where an observer at the South Pole sees the Earth turning clockwise (i.e. the *left* hand advances towards the Sun), whereas an observer's *right* hand moves forward at the North Pole (**Figure 11.11**). In between, at the equator, there is no turning round by the observer, i.e. neither the left hand moves to take the place of the right nor vice versa.

The Coriolis effect can also be understood in terms of a projectile from a cannon at A fixed facing a target B (**Figure 11.12**), all on a disc representing the Earth. The cannon and the target turn a little while the shell is in the air, and during that time the target moves from B to B′, so that when the shell lands at B it is *behind* the target. As a result, the actually straight-line trajectory AB (as seen from space) seems to curve (A′B), deflected to the left when observed where the Earth rotates clockwise. Figure 11.12 and **Note 11.D** show that this is true whichever way the cannon is pointing, whether zonally (i.e. east–west) or meridionally (i.e. north–south).

Theory shows that the effect depends solely on latitude and the object's velocity (Note 11.D). The outcome is that any straight-line motion (as observed from a fixed point in space, such as the Sun) appears circular to a person on Earth, as though the moving object is continu-

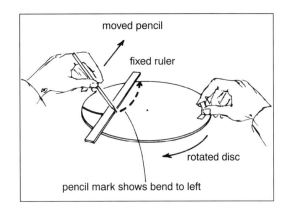

Figure 11.10 Demonstration of the Coriolis effect. A line drawn along the straight ruler registers a curve on the rotating disc, i.e. straight-line motion appears curved when viewed from a rotating platform.

ally pushed to one side by a force. This *hypothetical* force is called the *Coriolis force* and is most important in understanding oceanic and atmospheric motions. It is summarised in *Ferrel's Law*, that 'all motion suffers a bias towards the *left* in the southern hemisphere (and right in the northern)'.

The Coriolis force is negligible near the equator and on the scale of water going down a plug-hole, for instance (Note 11.D). It is significant only on a scale of many kilometres, affecting global winds and large-scale currents in the oceans, particularly at high latitudes.

Upwelling

One important consequence of the Coriolis effect is the way in which winds over the ocean move the surface water. Friction at the surface drags the uppermost water along with the wind, but simultaneously the Coriolis effect operates, deflecting the moving water to the left (in the southern hemisphere). As a result, that top layer of the ocean slowly moves at an angle approaching 45 degrees to the wind. The

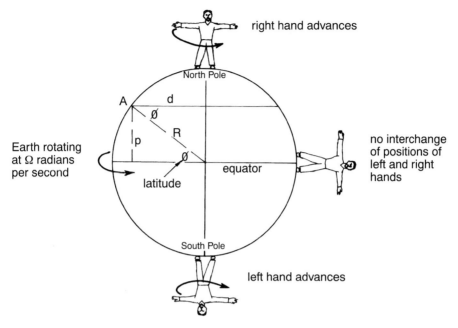

Figure 11.11 Explanation of the opposite directions of rotation in the two hemispheres of the Earth. The left hand advancing in the southern hemisphere means a clockwise rotation there. At the equator, there is no rotation about an axis perpendicular to the surface, and therefore no Coriolis effect. (A radian is an angle of 57.3°.)

top layer in turn drags the layer beneath, which again is affected by the Coriolis force, so that the second layer moves at a greater angle to the wind. Similarly for lower layers, each moving more slowly and more at an angle than the layer above. With each layer's movement represented by an arrow of appropriate direction and a length proportional to the speed, we have the arrangement shown in **Figure 11.13**. The tips of the arrows trace an *'Ekman spiral'*, named after the Swedish oceanographer Vagn Ekman (1874–1954). He proposed this spiral in 1902 to explain Fridtjof Nansen's observation that icebergs move at an angle of around 30° to the right of the wind in the northern hemisphere. The outcome of a complete spiral is an average movement, called *Ekman transport*, which for the whole spiral amounts to motion at right angles to the wind, and the top layer of the ocean (i.e. the *Ekman layer*) is driven towards that direction. This is a surprising result, that the Coriolis effect causes the ocean to move perpendicular to the wind – towards the left in the southern hemisphere. But a complete spiral develops only in deep water. Often a shallow thermocline, or the sea-bed in shallow waters, limits downwards transfer of momentum, and then surface ocean currents are more closely aligned with the wind.

The result of Ekman transport is upwelling of deeper, cold water to the surface near some coasts, as illustrated in **Figure 11.14**. The upwelling happens wherever there is either a polewards wind parallel to an east coast, or an equatorwards wind parallel to a west coast, as in north Chile or Namibia. The wind creates Ekman transport of the warm surface water away from the land, and cold deep water rises to takes its place at a rate of a metre per day or so. This is one explanation for the low temperature

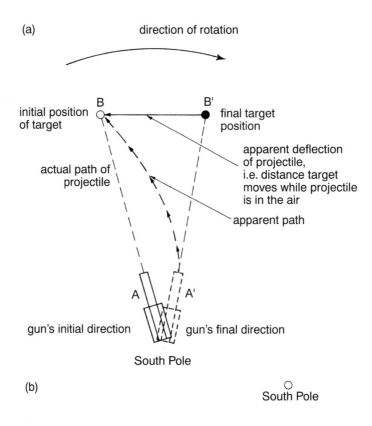

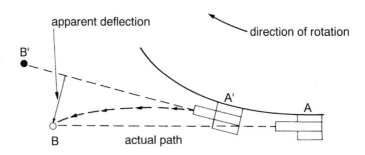

Figure 11.12 Demonstrations of the *apparent* deflections of actually straight-line motions (relative to the Sun, for instance) which are either (a) radial (corresponding to movement along a line of longitude), or (b) circumferential (along a line of latitude). In both cases, the rotation is shown as clockwise (as in the *southern* hemisphere – see Figure 11.11), and in both cases the apparent deflection is to the *left*.

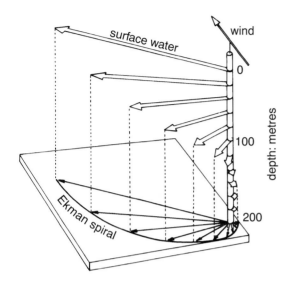

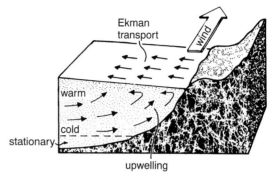

Figure 11.14 Wind-induced ocean currents and upwelling at a coast in the southern hemisphere.

Figure 11.13 The Ekman spiral in the southern hemisphere. The wind is towards the top left (parallel to the right-hand long side of the base), and Ekman transport is towards the bottom left, parallel to the nearest short side of the base.

of waters within 20 km of the Peruvian coast, and for the climate of Lima at 12°S (**Note 11.E, Table 11.3**). The upwelling off Lima results in an SST which is 3 K *less* than that 2,400 km nearer the South Pole at Antafagasta in Chile. Similarly, pleasantly cool conditions near Rio de Janeiro are induced by the upwelling caused by occasional north winds, even though they come from the equator. Coastal upwelling off south-west Africa, south of 15°S, leads to SSTs

near the shore which are as much as 5 K lower than at 320 km out to sea, particularly in summer and at 26°S. This leads to low temperatures in the atmospheric PBL, under a strong inversion (Figure 7.10).

Upwelling also occurs along the equator in the eastern Pacific, because winds from the east deflect the water southward (to the left) just south of the equator, and northward (to the right) just north of the equator, where the Coriolis force though weak acts in the opposite direction. This creates a furrow in the equatorial surface water, which in turn causes upwelling there, and consequently surface temperatures of only about 19°C off the Galapagos Islands, on the equator in the Pacific ocean. Decline of the easterly winds prior to an El Niño (Note 11.C) leads to a rapid end to

Table 11.3 Comparison of the average climates of Darwin and Lima, both at 12°S

	Darwin		Lima	
	July	January	July	January
Daily mean temp. (°C)	25	28	15	21
Sunshine (hours/day)	9.8	6.1	3.4	5.1
Raindays/month	<1	19	1	<1
Rainfall (mm/mo)	1	391	2	1.2
Wind direction at 3 p.m.	E	NW	S	S
Wind speed (m/s)	2.5	2.6	2.5	3.5

upwelling and consequently a dramatic rise of sea-surface temperature.

There are plenty of fish where there is upwelling, partly because the deep water which is brought up contains the deposited nutritious debris of previous generations of fish. Another reason is that cold waters contain more oxygen, e.g. water at 0°C can hold twice as much as water at 25°C. Ninety per cent of the world's fish are caught in the 15 per cent of the oceans where upwelling takes place.

11.5 OCEAN CURRENTS

The winds affect the oceans mostly by influencing surface currents. Let us now consider the pattern of these currents, then an explanation of the pattern and finally the effects on flows beneath the surface.

Gyres and Eddies

The first maps of the main ocean currents were compiled by Matthew Maury in 1855, using data from the ships' logs of ten countries. A modern map (**Figure 11.15**) shows the huge swirls called '*gyres*', which turn anti-clockwise in the southern hemisphere. A complete rotation within each ocean basin takes years. Along the north and south edges of the gyres there are currents about 150 m deep with a speed of 3–5 km/day, though '*boundary currents*' on the east and (especially) the west edges of the oceans are appreciably faster and deeper. For instance, the part of the South Pacific gyre against Australia (called the East Australian Current) flows south and constantly impeded the northward progress of James Cook on his voyage of discovery in 1770.

Embedded within the boundary currents are transient eddies, especially at the western edge of an ocean. These can be discerned on a snapshot map of sea-surface heights over a short period (**Figure 11.16**). The eddies form when

a boundary current meanders so widely that a loop becomes short-circuited, and they are about 30–300 km in diameter, drifting polewards. They stir a warm current into the surrounding colder water, and so contribute to the transport of heat (and momentum) towards the pole in the same way that midlatitude frontal systems in the atmosphere mix warm and cold air masses (Chapter 13). Clockwise eddies in the southern hemisphere have a cold centre and a slightly depressed ocean surface, while the anti-clockwise eddies have a warm core and a slightly elevated ocean surface, as explained later.

If we follow the South Pacific gyre onwards, we see that the East Australian Current eventually mixes into the eastwards flow of cold water through Bass Strait, between Tasmania and the mainland, to become part of the relatively slow *West-Wind Drift* (or Antarctic Circumpolar Current). This takes months to cross the Pacific ocean at about 50°S, becoming colder to match the latitude. (There is a weak *westwards* flow further south, close to Antarctica, driven by east winds there – Figure 11.15.) Having reached South America, most of the Circumpolar Current turns north along the coast of Chile, where it is called the Humboldt Current. This and its extension as the 'Peru current' further north are more shallow than western boundary currents, and the thermocline is nearer the surface. The current turns westward at low latitudes, flowing near the equator towards northern Australia, becoming warmer all the time. A substantial part of the equatorial flow continues westward between the southern islands of Indonesia (the *Indonesian Throughflow*), especially just after mid-year, and some of that forms the Leeuwin Current about 30 km wide down the west coast of Australia in autumn and winter. (This current is unusual in flowing *towards* the pole on the eastern side of an ocean, opposing the much larger anti-clockwise South Indian gyre.) Part of the low-latitude current across the Pacific that does

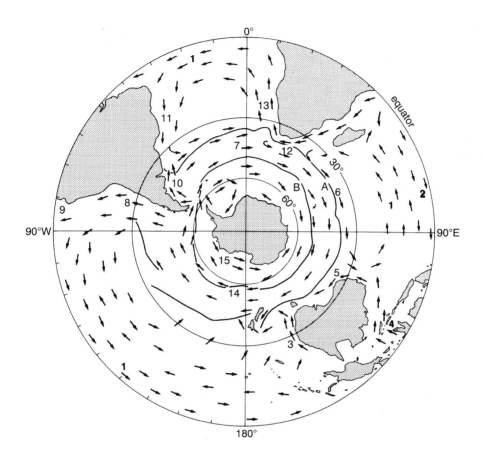

Figure 11.15 Surface currents in the world's southern oceans. The names of the currents indicated by numbers on the map are as follows: 1. South equatorial current. 2. Equatorial counter-current. 3. East Australian current. 4. Indonesian throughflow. 5. Leeuwin current. 6. South Indian ocean current. 7. West wind drift. 8. Humboldt current. 9. Peru current. 10. Falkland current. 11. Brazil current. 12. Agulhas current. 13. Benguela current. 14. Antarctic circumpolar current. 15. Antarctic counter-current. The circumpolar line labelled A denotes the Subtropical Convergence Zone, and that labelled B is the Antarctic Convergence Zone.

not provide the Indonesian Throughflow turns south down the *eastern* side of Australia.

A fraction of the Circumpolar Current passes south of Cape Horn at the tip of South America and then northwards as the Falkland Current up the Atlantic coast. This cold water from the direction of the Pole stabilises onshore easterly winds, which, in conjunction with shelter from the westerlies provided by the Andes, leads to little rain and thus the aridity in Patagonia in southern Argentina (Figure 10.3). Also the Falkland Current carries icebergs to lower latitudes (Figure 11.7).

The gyre in the south Atlantic is complicated by the bulge of north-eastern Brazil, which planes off some of the current, diverting it into the north Atlantic. This promotes the Gulf Stream, which is responsible for the relative warmth of Europe.

The pattern of currents alters during the year.

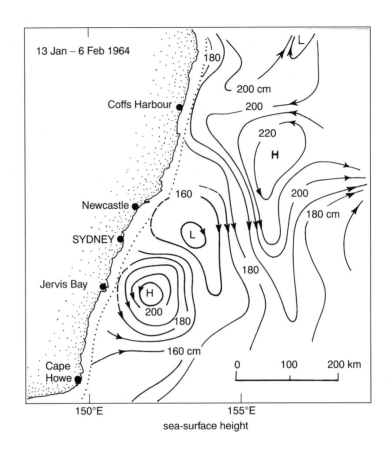

Figure 11.16 Contours of the sea surface (i.e. the direction of surface-slope currents) off New South Wales measured during a 24-day voyage in summer 1964. The arrows indicate the direction of surface-slope currents. A typical eddy of warm water (with anticyclonic flow) can be seen off Jervis Bay, where the surface is more than 0.6 m higher than the cold pool off Sydney.

For instance, the Peru current reaches almost to the equator in winter, while the occasional El Niño in summer deflects it westwards at about 15°S instead (Note 11.C). Also, westerly winds along the coast of New South Wales in winter (Chapter 12) cause a narrow ocean current northward, against the prevailing East Australian current. Similarly, strong westerly winds in winter enhance the Falkland current, bringing cool waters as far north as Buenos Aires. In addition, ocean currents near the equator are influenced by the annual reversal of low-latitude winds called the 'monsoons' (Chapter 12).

Effects

The oceanic gyres explain why east coasts (where the gyres come from the equator) are usually warm and wet (Figure 10.3b), while west coasts are cool and dry because of (i) the advection of coldness from the poles, and (ii) upwelling (Section 11.2). For instance, places in subtropical latitudes (i.e. 20–35°S) along the east coast of South Africa are 3–8 K warmer than those on the west coast. An exception is Australia's west coast, where the southwards Leeuwin current along the coast (Figure

11.15) brings warmth towards Perth and suppresses any upwelling. However, there is no exception to the rule that continental east coasts in the subtropics are humid, and west coasts arid (Figure 10.3, Table 11.2). This rule is due mainly to the predominant easterly winds around the Tropic (Chapter 12).

Gyres transport heat polewards (Figure 5.4), in amounts comparable to those in warm winds, though oceanic advection is less notable in the southern hemisphere than in the northern, which contains the Gulf Stream in the Atlantic and the Kuroshio current past Japan.

Explanation

All these surface currents are governed by four factors: (i) wind drag, (ii) the slope of the ocean surface, (iii) differences of water density, and then (iv) the Coriolis force. The 'absolute current' (with respect to the land) is the outcome of all these factors together, which we will consider in turn.

Ocean currents dragged by the prevailing winds (Chapter 12) are called 'drifts', and some are named in Figure 11.15. These currents are usually less than 50 m deep, or 100 m if winds are strong. They are deflected by the Coriolis force, though this is often weakened by an opposing slope of the ocean surface, discussed below. A drift typically moves at less than 1 km/h, carrying buoys and icebergs at about 2 per cent of the speed of the local wind.

Currents induced by tilting of the ocean surface are called 'slope currents'. The slope is imperceptible, e.g. a metre in 500 km (Figure 11.16), but it is important. Ways in which it arises include these: (i) tides, (ii) differences of mean sea-level pressure, (iii) Ekman transport, (iv) the convergence of currents, (v) drifts piling against a coast, and (vi) ocean-density differences. The first of these, tides, cause changes of level twice daily, by up to 8 m in the inlets of north-west Australia, for instance, but only a metre around most of the continent and less

than a metre in the open sea. Such temporary variations of level do not affect large-scale currents. The second factor, surface pressure, explains why the sea is elevated in the centre of tropical cyclones (Chapter 13).

The third cause of ocean-surface slope, Ekman transport, occurs near coasts with parallel winds (Section 11.4) and within a gyre. The winds which drive a gyre also lead to flows towards the centre, heaping the water there (**Figure 11.17**). The heap consists of surface water and it is relatively warm, i.e. less dense, so that a greater depth of it is needed to create a sea-bed pressure equal to (or very slightly higher than) that created by the cooler water around. Therefore the gyre's centre is elevated, perhaps by a metre or so. The resulting slope makes surface water flow downhill away from the centre, and then this flow is deflected by the Coriolis effect to become an anti-clockwise turning in the southern hemisphere. Such a flow is called a 'geostrophic current', as with 'geostrophic winds' (Chapter 12). In both cases, the direction and speed of the flow results in a Coriolis force which just offsets the slope, and the flow is parallel to contours of the surface's elevation, as in the case of much smaller eddies (Figure 11.16). For example, the warm Coral Sea (east of Queensland) is around 0.5 m higher than the Tasman Sea to the south, causing a geostrophic flow eastwards, away from the Australian coast. Geostrophic currents occur at any depth, wherever horizontally adjacent masses of water differ in density. The only exception occurs near the equator, where the Coriolis effect is too weak (Note 11.D).

A convergence of currents (the fourth factor affecting the surface slope) also causes heaping and then subsidence. It happens, for instance, at the *Antarctic Convergence* (**Figure 11.18**), where the Antarctic Circumpolar Current (which is towards the south-east) flows next and opposite to the northwestward current around the Antarctic coast. The latitudes of such convergences fluctuate considerably. Sea-surface temperatures

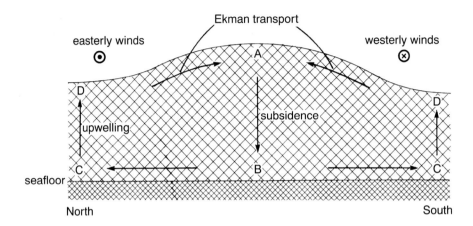

Figure 11.17 Vertical circulations induced in a south-hemisphere ocean gyre. The low-latitude easterly winds and midlatitude westerlies, and the associated Ekman transport cause a heaping of water at A, which maintains the anti-clockwise slope currents. The heaping at A leads to a pressure at B higher than that at C, so there is a flow from B to C and subsidence from A to B. Upwelling from C to D completes the circuit. The entire circulation may take several hundreds of years.

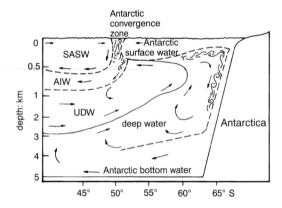

Figure 11.18 Layers and conditions within the Antarctic ocean and the longitude of the Atlantic; SASW is subAntarctic surface water, AIW is Antarctic intermediate water, UDW is upper deep water.

divergence between the Antarctic and the Subtropical Convergence Zones (Figure 11.15) leads to upwelling there and therefore nutrient-rich surface waters, which attract whales and other marine life.

The barriers between different bodies of water created by continents, by convergence zones, by the self-contained nature of gyres, and by the stratification of the oceans (Section 11.2) all inhibit the mixing together of seas with different temperatures and degrees of saltiness. Consequently there are distinct bodies of water (or *water masses*) in various parts of the oceans, each with its own characteristic temperature and salinity. The boundary between adjacent water masses is called a '*front*', and may be discernible for weeks.

on opposite sides of the boundary may differ in temperature by about 4 K, as cold water from the south meets warmer water from lower latitudes.

There is a compensating divergence of surface waters between regions of convergence. The

Thermohaline Circulations

These are circulations in a vertical plane due to differences of density caused by horizontal variations of temperature and salinity. The reason for the circulations is that any parcel of water in the ocean rises when it is less dense than the surroundings, and subsides when it is more dense, like parcels of air in the atmosphere (Section 7.3). For instance, sea-ice consists of water alone, so that the previously dissolved salt is rejected into the water beneath, making it heavy and thus subside. This water from just beneath the ice is near freezing point (at −2°C) and therefore more dense than any other water, so that it sinks to the bottom of the ocean. This is called *deep-water formation*, and is most common in the Weddell Sea in Antarctica (Chapter 16). It occurs only occasionally and briefly, usually triggered by an outbreak of strong, cold winds off Antarctica. The process creates *Antarctic Bottom Water*, which spreads out along the ocean floor of the entire globe (Figure 11.18), and may resurface in some area of upwelling, several thousands of years later.

A similar subsidence occurs off south-east Greenland, creating a layer called the 'Circumpolar Deep Water', which lies just above the Bottom Water, because it is slightly less dense. The subsidence carries carbon dioxide in surface water down, to be sequestered in the much larger volume of the ocean depths (Figure 1.3). So it is an important factor in determining how much carbon dioxide remains in the atmosphere, which governs future climate change (Note 2.L).

Deep-water formation is an example of a thermohaline circulation, a circulation driven by density differences caused by temperature and/or salinity differences (Note 11.B). Such currents are often discontinuous and fairly small. An example is the occasional flow of water from the Red Sea, with a salinity as high as 40‰ (due to little precipitation but evaporation at about 10 mm/day), into the Indian Ocean, where it forms a density current just like an atmospheric density current (Note 8.C).

Flows Beneath the Surface

Deep ocean currents are too slow to be measured directly but can be inferred from measurements of density and salt concentrations; similarity at two places suggests that water flows from one to the other. In this way, we deduce that Bottom Water, even at the equator and off Alaska, all comes from the Antarctic.

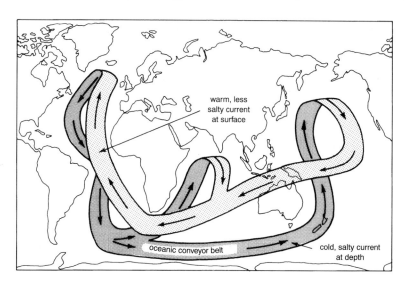

Figure 11.19 The oceanic conveyor belt which carries cold deep ocean water to lower latitudes.

A consequence of the deep-sea currents is the global circulation shown in **Figure 11.19**, a huge 'conveyor belt' driven largely by convection in the north Atlantic, caused by an increase of surface-water density due to evaporation and to chilling on contact with Arctic winds and waters. The circuit includes the Indonesian Throughflow to the north of Australia, and a sub-surface westwards flow to the south. It seems possible that shutting down or reversal of this massive circulation was responsible for past Ice Ages, and might affect future climate change. In other words, even the deep ocean affects the atmosphere.

Thus we conclude our consideration of the hydrologic cycle, which repeats itself endlessly with evaporation from the oceans, cloud, rain and then runoff back to the ocean. The cycle is linked intimately with energy balances (Chapters 2–5) which determine rates of evaporation and the atmospheric heating which creates instability and hence clouds. It is also closely connected with the patterns of winds over the Earth which distribute the water vapour and its associated latent-heat energy. These patterns comprise the 'general circulation' of the atmosphere, to be considered in the next chapter.

NOTES

11.A Effects of the oceans on climates
11.B Buoyancy in the oceans
11.C El Niño, part 2
11.D The Coriolis effect
11.E The climate near Lima
11.F Traverse measurements

Part IV

WINDS

12

GLOBAL WINDS

12.1 SURFACE WINDS OF THE GLOBE

Any climate depends on, firstly, local factors and, secondly, advection. The former include radiation, rainfall and evaporation, and the latter the heat and moisture brought by oceans and winds. We have dealt with each of these by now, except the winds, which are the topic of this fourth part of the book.

We can distinguish various scales of air movement, just as distinctions were made in Table 1.1 between different scales of climate. There are 'local winds' (which will be discussed in Chapter 14), within the context of a larger pattern of winds on the scale of an area like Australia or New Zealand (Chapter 13), and they in turn form part of the long-term average pattern of global winds, the *general circulation*. This last is the background to weather, the explanation of global patterns of rainfall, a means of sharing heat between the equator and the poles, and the arena of climate change. It is the subject of the present chapter.

Surface Winds

Winds within 30° of the equator in the Atlantic and Indian oceans were first mapped by Edmund Halley in 1686, and his maps were not superseded till 1855, when Mathew Maury issued charts, based on a recent international exchange of ships' logs, at a conference in Brussels. These charts proved invaluable. For instance, they showed the advantage of sailing from England to Australia by way of the east coast of South America and then passing well south of South Africa (**Figure 12.1**), whereas on the return journey it is best to hug the African coast.

Intertropical Convergence Zone (ITCZ)

Figure 12.1 shows that winds between the tropics converge on a line which we call the *Intertropical Convergence Zone* (i.e. ITCZ) or *equatorial trough*. This line of convergence near the equator is also discernible in a map of *streamlines* (**Figure 12.2; Note 12.A**). It is actually a band a few hundred kilometres wide, enclosing places where winds flow inwards (are 'confluent') and subsequently rise convectively. It is the latitude of the highest air temperature and vapour pressure near the surface, and the coldest and driest air at the tropopause. As a result,

January

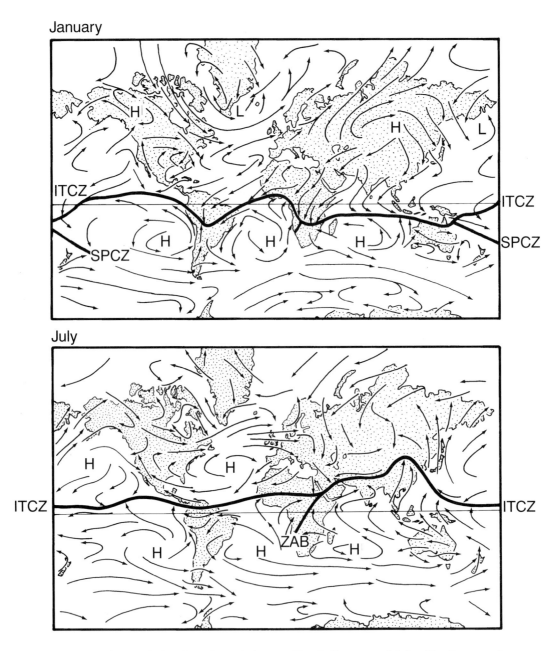

July

Figure 12.1 Maps of the global-scale surface winds prevailing in January and July. The line near the equator shows the Intertropical Convergence Zone (ITCZ), where Trade winds from the two hemispheres meet. A spur from this line over southern Africa is called the Zaïre Air Boundary (ZAB), where air converges from the Indian and Atlantic oceans, respectively, and another spur over the western South Pacific is known as the South Pacific Convergence Zone (SPCZ). The letter H indicates a centre of high pressure (i.e. a 'high'), and an L stands for a 'low'.

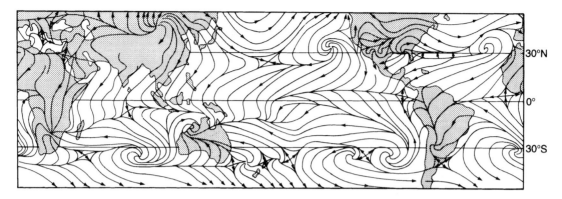

Figure 12.2 Mean streamlines of surface winds in January. Note the convergence of winds at the ITCZ, as in Figure 12.1. The whorls correspond to highs.

convective uplift yields copious condensation well above the ground, which releases notable amounts of latent heat, and that in turn stimulates convection.

The ITCZ lies at about 5°N on average. This is known as the *meteorological equator*, matching the equators of radiation (Section 2.2) and temperature (Section 3.2). It wanders seasonally (**Figure 12.3**), lagging about two months behind the change of the Sun's declination (Section 2.2), this being the time taken for the surface to respond to the Sun's heating. The latitudinal variation is most pronounced over the Indian Ocean because of the large Asian continent to the north. The ITCZ does not move with the seasons over the eastern Pacific and Atlantic oceans, being permanently confined to the northern hemisphere by the cold Peru and Benguela currents (Figure 11.15) in the south. (There is no surface convergence of winds where the surface is cool.) This explains why the meteorological equator is slightly north of the geographic equator.

The movement of the ITCZ across South Africa (Figure 12.1) is complicated by the land's shape, elevation and location, and there is a southerly spur called the *Zaïre Air Boundary* (ZAB). Similarly, there is a spur over South America east of the Andes as far south as Paraguay in February. But the largest and most

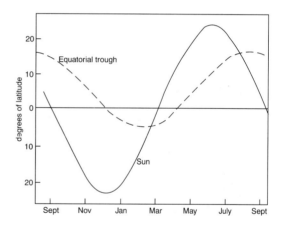

Figure 12.3 The annual march of the latitude of the noon Sun (i.e. the declination) and of the 'equatorial trough', i.e. the mean latitude of the ITCZ.

persistent spur to the ITCZ is over the south-west Pacific, known as the *South Pacific Convergence Zone* (SPCZ). It is related to the 'warm pool' near Papua (Section 11.2) and is most prominent in summer, contracting towards Fiji in winter. Unlike other spurs, it lies mostly over water (Figure 12.1). There is a convergence of (i) moist northeasterlies from the semi-permanent high in the south-east Pacific (Figure 12.1) and (ii) southeasterlies from mobile highs moving across the south-west Pacific in summer. The zone is unique in spawning both tropical cyclones and 'frontal depressions' (which are both discussed in Chapter 13).

Winds at the ITCZ are commonly light or non-existent, creating maritime calms called the *doldrums*. But there is occasionally a week or two of strong westerlies, called a *westerly wind burst*, especially during November to March. The disturbances seem to occur each 40–50 days or so, and this loose rhythm is known as the *Madden–Julian Oscillation*, first noted in 1971. It is associated with a zone of active convection within the ITCZ, moving eastwards from Sumatra into the western Pacific. Meanwhile, cloud clusters move west within the zone, affecting the amounts and distribution of rainfall, including the timing of the Wet in northern Australia. Then the disturbance weakens.

Low-latitude Winds

Winds are mainly *easterly* at latitudes between 10–30°, i.e. *towards the west*. The winds are reliable and therefore known as *Trade winds* or simply the *Trades* (**Figure 12.4; Note 12.B**). The Trades are especially strong around mid-year in the eastern half of the oceans of the southern hemisphere. They occur about 10 degrees further south at year's end, in the southern summer. In Australia they blow all year across almost the entire Queensland coast, and penetrate almost across the continent, especially around the Tropic of Capricorn (at 23°S). The Trades in Brazil are most evident between 3–15°S.

Midlatitude Winds

Westerly winds prevail between 35–60° latitude, dominating southern Australia and New Zealand, for instance (Figure 12.1). The winds are powerful across the southern oceans at all longitudes. They show none of the steadiness of the Trades, since they contain rapidly moving and evolving *low-pressure systems* (or *lows* – see Chapter 13), around which winds circulate.

Midlatitude westerlies blow over 24 per cent of each hemisphere, whereas the low-latitude (easterly) Trades affect about 31 per cent. These contrary winds impose frictional forces on the ground, which are opposite in direction and more or less equal after allowing for the winds' strengths and also the areas involved. The result is that the atmosphere as a whole is neither slowed down by the Earth's rotation nor accelerated by it, but turns with it.

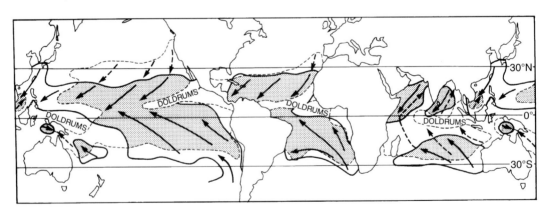

Figure 12.4 The Trade wind belts, showing the areas where at least half the winds come from the east in January (solid lines) or July (dashed) or both (shown shaded).

High-latitude Winds

There are *polar easterlies* at latitudes above about 60°S (i.e. over Antarctica), which are explained later.

Summary

Any of these prevailing surface winds may be considered as partly east–west (i.e. zonal), and partly north–south (i.e. meridional). The zonal components of winds at a certain latitude can be averaged over all longitudes and over a whole year, to obtain **Figure 12.5**. This shows that there are specially strong westerlies at the latitude of Cape Horn (56°S) at the tip of South America. They are far stronger than those in the northern hemisphere, partly because of the virtual absence of land between 45–60°S (Figure 11.1); the other reason is the notable coldness of Antarctica (Chapter 16).

Monsoonal Winds

A feature of winds near the equator is their annual reversal. This was pointed out by George Hadley in 1735, who explained the reversal as due to the movements of the ITCZ. For instance, the south-east Trades

from the southern hemisphere cross the equator when the ITCZ is in the north in July, and thereafter the Coriolis effect influences them to the right (Section 11.4). So southeasterly winds from the south of the equator become southwesterlies. And conversely for north winds in January, again producing a narrow band of westerlies near the equator within the limits of the seasonal fluctuations of the ITCZ. The resultant winds can be seen in **Figure 12.6**. Air movements across northern Australia, for example, are from the south-east in July (i.e. from the arid inland), but from the warm oceans to the north-west in January. So they are alternately dry and wet winds. Similarly, the Trades in Papua and New Guinea prevail from the south-east in May to October, and then there are winds from the north-west during December to April.

This seasonal switching of direction we call *monsoonal*. (The term 'monsoon' comes from a word meaning 'season'.) Nowadays, it signifies either a wind or the rainy season of the summer monsoon. To qualify as a monsoon wind, the seasonal change of direction has to be at least 120 degrees. South of the equator they are found only on the east coast of Africa, down to northern Madagascar, and over south-east Asia, including Papua New Guinea and the

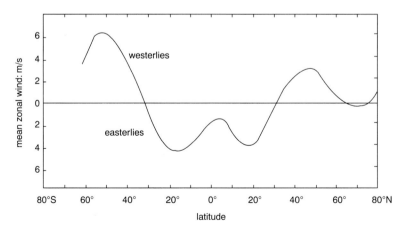

Figure 12.5 Annual and zonal average winds at various latitudes.

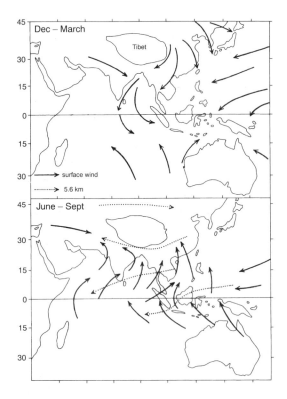

Figure 12.6 Upper and surface winds near the monsoonal equator.

erating an offshore land breeze at the surface (Figure 12.6 and Chapter 14). Another factor affecting the monsoons is the Plateau's obstruction of the strong winds in the upper atmosphere, so that they flow round, either to the north or the south, with a consequent deflection of surface winds.

The monsoons are ill-defined or non-existent in the Americas because north–south mountain ranges obstruct the Trade winds, and because sea-surface temperatures to the west of South America stay permanently lower than land temperatures. Monsoons do affect northern Australia, but more modestly and briefly than in India, for instance, for lack of mountains or of a land mass as big as Asia to generate the equivalent of a vast sea breeze. Also, there is some removal of moisture by prior rainfall over Indonesia. Nevertheless, north-west winds from the equatorial Indian ocean bring heavy rains to Australia north of 25°S, during the Wet at year's end. The Wet is sometimes interrupted by a dry spell lasting a few days or weeks, when surface winds are mostly easterly and the upper-level winds more westerly. But particularly wet spells can arise from surges of cold air into south-east Asia from Siberia, where it is winter.

12.2 FACTORS GOVERNING GLOBAL WINDS

The surface winds just described are explained in several ways, which will now be considered. There are obvious parallels between these and the factors discussed in Section 11.5, controlling ocean currents.

Pressure Gradient

The driving force of any wind is the local *pressure gradient*, expressed as $\Delta p/\Delta n$, where Δp is the difference between the pressures at points separated horizontally by a distance Δn. It is like the slope of a hillside (i.e. the gradient of

northern coast of Australia. They are induced by Asia, the Earth's largest continent, which drives strong Trades south across the equator in the northern hemisphere winter and pulls in the southern Trades during its summer.

The explanation of monsoons given above is incomplete, as the Coriolis force is only slight near the equator – especially with the light winds that prevail there. At least two more factors are involved in the case of the main (Indian) monsoon. One is the reversal of temperature difference between the Indian ocean and Asia. The continent becomes much hotter than the ocean in mid-year, drawing air inland as a great sea breeze (Chapter 14). Conversely, the Tibetan Plateau at about 4,500 m becomes much colder than the ocean at year's end, gen-

elevation) that governs the speed of water flowing downhill. Similarly, the speed of surface winds depends on the gradient of mean sea-level pressures (MSLP) (Section 1.5)

Mean sea-level pressures around the world can be averaged in time and corrected for elevation to obtain a map like **Figure 12.7**, after joining places with the same pressure by lines called *isobars*. An isobar is like a contour line on a map which connects places of equal height. Places of maximum pressure are generally marked H, for 'high pressure', and likewise L for 'low-pressure'. It is important to emphasise that places marked H in Figure 12.1 and Figure 12.7 do not have high pressures at every moment. High-pressure systems are mobile (Chapter 13), but *linger* in the places marked H so that the *annual average* pressure there becomes high. Likewise for the low-pressure regions, marked L in Figure 12.7.

Particularly high pressures occur over Asia in winter (Figure 12.1) because of the low temperatures there (Figure 3.4). The cold air contracts, leaving room above for adjacent air to converge, adding to the weight of the column which causes the pressure (Note 1.G). For the same reason, relatively low sea-surface temperatures lead to high pressures over the subtropical oceans, especially in summer. Conversely, the MSLP is then generally low over the continents, on account of high surface temperatures there, leading to atmospheric expansion and so a spilling away of upper air, i.e. a reduction of the amount of air in the column above the continent. However, a different process operates at about 55° around Antarctica, where a ring of lows constitute the *circumpolar low*. The remarkably low pressures there (much lower than in the northern hemisphere) result from the shallowness of the troposphere at high latitudes, and the consequent warmth of the tropopause (Figure 1.9).

High pressures dominate at around 30° latitudes. The highs are centred over the oceans in summer (Figure 12.1), and adjacent continents in winter (Figure 12.7), whichever is the cooler. The belt of these *subtropical highs* expands equatorward in winter (Section 12.3). For instance, the South Pacific high-pressure zone is centred at 23°S in July but 32°S in January (Figure 12.1). The shift drives the Trades into the other hemisphere and contributes to the monsoon there (Figure 12.6).

Overall, the variation of zonal-mean MSLP with latitude is shown in Figure 1.8, which also indicates the Equatorial Trough. There are steep gradients between 30–60°S (where zonal winds happen to be strong – Figure 12.5) but the curve is flat at 30°S and the equator, where winds are light. The relationship between the north–south gradient of pressure, and the strength and direction of the zonal winds, is due to the Coriolis effect, which has now to be discussed.

Coriolis Effect

Large-scale winds (such as the monsoons – Section 12.1) are deflected by the Coriolis effect, just as ocean currents are (Section 11.4). Therefore, air flowing from a high-pressure region to one of low pressure is turned to the left in the southern hemisphere, until the pressure-gradient force to the right exactly matches the Coriolis force (**Figure 12.8**). This balance of forces is known as the *geostrophic balance*, and the resulting wind is the *geostrophic wind* (**Note 12.C**). The adjective 'geostrophic' means 'Earth turning', the cause of the Coriolis effect.

The geostrophic wind blows along an isobar, not directly from a place of high pressure to one of low, but at right-angles to the pressure gradient. This fact, that winds blow *along* isobars, may seem surprising, as if water flowed along a contour line *round* a hill, instead of down it. The important point is that *the geostrophic wind in the southern hemisphere blows clockwise around a low and counterclockwise around a high, at a speed which is proportional to the spacing between the isobars* (Note 12.C). The situation was summed up

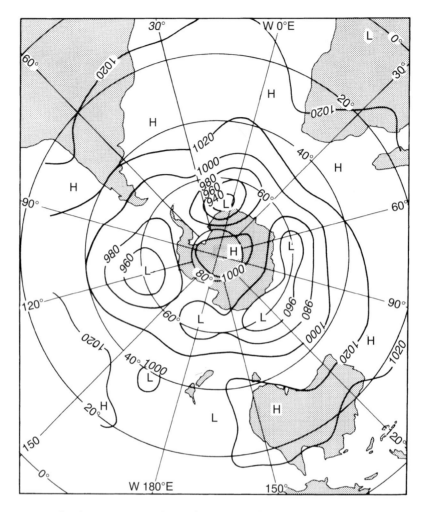

Figure 12.7 Mean sea-level pressures in July in the southern hemisphere.

by Christoph Buys-Ballot (1817–90) in his 'Rule' (1857) – pressure is *Low on your Left* when you *face the wind in the southern hemisphere.*

Wind measured about 1,000 m above the ground is close to geostrophic. In fact, the similarity between (i) arrows or streamlines showing the wind's direction, and (ii) tangents to the isobars, is so good that forecasters customarily plot the isobars alone, for places away from the equator. Near the equator, the Coriolis force is too weak to balance any pressure-

gradient force (i.e. the winds are non-geostrophic), so air there does flow directly down the pressure gradient, tending to equalise adjacent highs and lows. The consequently flattened pressure gradients are the reason for the weak winds around the ITCZ (Figure 12.5). Forecasters use streamlines to show such winds.

Circulation of the Wind

Another factor affects any global wind that takes a circular path. There is then a *centrifugal*

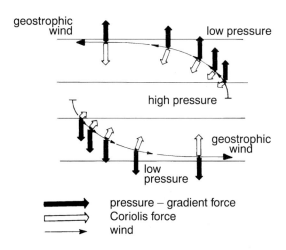

Figure 12.8 The apparent deflection of a parcel of air moving from a belt of high pressure in the southern hemisphere, e.g. from the band of subtropical high pressures. The parcel is assumed stationary initially. As soon as it starts to move, it suffers a sideways Coriolis force, increasing in proportion to its acceleration. The force deflects the parcel until it is travelling along an isobar, with a constant speed such that the Coriolis force balances the pressure-gradient force.

force outwards, the force you experience when driving a car rapidly round a corner. When this also is taken into account, the resultant wind is called the *gradient wind* (**Note 12.D**).

The inward and outward forces are shown in **Figure 12.9** for the cases of winds circling a high-pressure region (i.e. a 'high' or 'anticyclone') and a low-pressure region (i.e. a 'low' or 'cyclone'). The Coriolis force on air which is moving around a high is matched by the pressure-gradient force *plus* the centrifugal force. This necessitates a larger Coriolis force than in the case of a geostrophic wind (where the centrifugal force is zero). Such a larger force requires a faster wind speed, since the Coriolis force is proportional to the speed (Note 11.D). In other words, the wind around a high is *supergeostrophic*. Similar reasoning

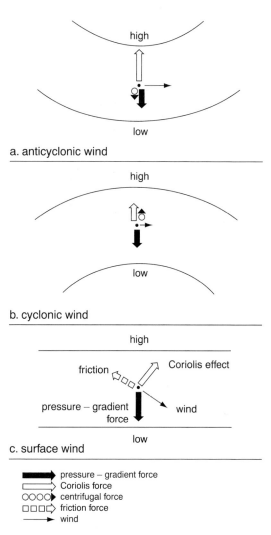

Figure 12.9 The forces involved in winds around (a) a high, and (b) a low. Also, (c) the forces acting on winds near the surface when the isobars are straight and friction retards the flow.

shows that the wind around a low is *subgeostrophic*. In every case, winds go faster around a high than around a low for a particular pressure gradient (Note 12.D).

Friction of the Ground

The drag exerted by the Earth's roughness is a fourth factor affecting winds within the lowest kilometre of the atmosphere. Friction reduces the wind's speed, so lessening the Coriolis effect, causing the pressure-gradient force to exceed the Coriolis force and therefore the air to flow slightly towards the lower pressure. This explains why surface winds do not precisely circle high-pressure regions but spiral out to the right of them instead, while winds around lows spiral inwards, again to the right of the isobars in the southern hemisphere.

This deflection to the right and the reduction of speed due to friction are most at levels closest to the ground, and so winds at various levels may be represented by an Ekman spiral like that near the surface of an ocean (Section 11.4). In a fully developed Ekman spiral, the surface wind blows from a direction 45° clockwise from the isobars. (We say that the surface wind is made to 'veer' by the friction in the southern hemisphere, whereas an anticlockwise change of direction is called 'backing'.) However, a full spiral rarely develops in reality, certainly not on warm days, when the planetary boundary layer becomes unstable and there is vertical mixing to disturb the distinct layers implicit in the Ekman effect. Variations of wind speed and direction in the lowest kilometre are greatest when the atmosphere is stable, and then the depth occupied by the spiral (called the 'Ekman layer') is the same as the PBL.

Friction is less over the oceans because they are flat, so winds at sea tend to be stronger than inland and blow at only 10–20 degrees from the direction of the gradient wind. The angle is larger over a rough surface like a forest or city. In the Australian desert, sand-dunes tend to be blown to lie 20–30° clockwise of the prevailing gradient wind.

Summary

The combination of all four factors is illustrated in Figure 12.9. The diagram illustrates the following features:

(a) the pressure-gradient force always acts from high to low pressure regions,
(b) the Coriolis force is always at right-angles to the wind's direction, pulling to the left in the southern hemisphere,
(c) the centrifugal force is also always at right-angles to the wind, pulling outwards,
(d) surface friction involves a complex dissipation of energy in generating turbulent eddies, and the resulting drag normally acts in a direction opposite to that of the wind, and generally increases with wind speed.

Note that Figure 12.9 applies only in steady conditions. In practice, forces fluctuate in space and time. For instance, the pressure gradient along a coast may be reversed by daytime heating of the land. In fact, the surface wind near coastlines and mountains is usually very different from the geostrophic or gradient winds, especially when the latter are weak. Large differences also occur near thunderstorms and jet streaks (Section 12.5).

12.3 CIRCULATIONS WITHIN THE TROPOSPHERE

So far we have been considering winds near the suface, but they are only half the story. There is another but related pattern of winds aloft in the troposphere. Different winds at various levels are shown by movements of cirrus cloud in directions quite distinct from those of low-level clouds.

We shall consider winds at two levels especially, where the pressures are around 850 hPa (at about 1,500 m) and about 300 hPa (at about 9 km), respectively. The first represents conditions in the lower troposphere, but well

Plate 12.1 The patterns of cloud over Africa associated with the global circulation of winds, seen from *Apollo 17* on its way to the Moon on 9 December 1972. Antarctica was surrounded by cloud, with several frontal disturbances shaped like inverted commas. There was a band of cloud along the ITCZ over the Indian ocean, and orographic cloud along the east coast of Madagascar, fronting the Trade winds.

clear of the PBL, while the second represents winds not far below the tropopause (Figures 1.9–1.11). The region above the tropopause is separate because of the stability of the stratosphere and the consequent absence of vertical motion (Section 7.6).

There are several ways of observing winds aloft. For instance, a high cloud is identified from satellites by the coldness of the cloud top (deduced from the wavelength of the infra-red radiation detected by radiometers on the satellite), and the winds carrying such a cloud can be inferred from its shift in position over time. Other information on winds at high levels is obtained from the sideways movements of ascending radiosondes (Section 1.6) and from aircraft reports. In addition, winds aloft can be inferred from surface winds combined with theory based on measured temperature profiles (**Notes 12.E** and **12.F**).

But why consider winds away from the surface, whose climates are the main concern of this book? The reason is that the troposphere's circulation consists of both upper and lower winds, interacting with each other, and therefore upper winds considerably influence the lower winds which largely determine the advection of heat and moisture and thus affect climates. In particular, winds aloft help moderate the difference between equatorial and polar climates. Second, differences between higher and lower winds imply circulations with compensating regions of ascent and subsidence. These vertical motions are important because they are responsible for cloud and rain. They cannot be measured, as they move at only a few millimetres per second within the turbulence of horizontal winds which are hundreds or thousands of times bigger, but they can be inferred from a comparison of upper and lower winds.

An understanding of the vertical circulations of which high-level winds form part explains why some parts of the world have mostly subsiding air and are consequently arid, for example.

Zonal Winds

Figure 12.10 shows the average zonal winds at all levels. The bottom of the diagram indicates surface equatorial easterlies, then a belt of westerlies in each hemisphere, with easterlies again at higher latitudes. There are westerlies of over 30 m/s (i.e. above 108 km/h) in the subtropics at a height of about 12 km, just below the temperature minimum of the tropopause (Figure 1.9). These strong winds result from steep north–south gradients of temperature at that level. Note 12.E explains why there are steep gradients, and Note 12.F accounts for their effect on wind speed.

The tropopause is shown in Figure 12.10 as having discontinuities at midlatitudes. These

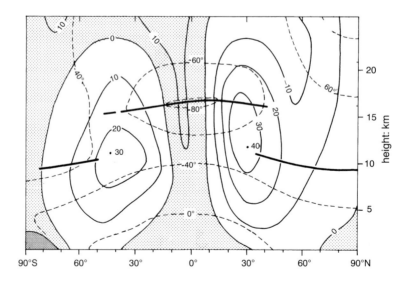

Figure 12.10 The average distribution of zonal-mean winds and atmospheric temperature in January. Shaded areas show east winds. The dark area at the bottom left indicates Antarctica. The most solid bold lines show the tropopause, while the numbered solid lines joining places of equal wind speed (i.e. '*isotachs*') show the speed in metres per second. The dashed lines show the temperature (°C).

are due to the differences between the temperatures of air masses meeting at the 'polar front', which is discussed below. The warmer surface air of low latitudes raises the tropopause there by promoting convection, and the development of waves in the front involves subsiding air on the poleward side of the front, depressing the tropopause there (Chapter 13).

The asymmetry in Figure 12.10 is partly due to the time of year, i.e. summer in the southern hemisphere, so there is more cooling in the northern hemisphere, increasing the difference from equatorial temperatures. As a result, the high-level westerlies in the winter hemisphere are stronger than in the summer hemisphere (Note 12.F). Over the year as a whole, the westerlies aloft are slightly stronger in the southern hemisphere on account of the low temperatures above Antarctica.

Particularly strong winds occur in winter at heights of 10–25 km near 60°S because of the extremely cold conditions in the polar stratosphere in winter (Figure 1.9). The vortex of these strong winds around the pole is known as the *polar night jet*. It tends to fend off warmer (ozone-rich) air from lower latitudes, allowing the stratosphere to become cold enough to condense the small amount of moisture present into wispy clouds. These facilitate the destruction of polar ozone by chlorine and bromine compounds arising from human activity (Section 1.4).

Hadley Cells

There are great differences between surface and upper winds at the tropical latitudes (Figure 12.10), with easterly Trade winds surmounted by westerlies, notably in winter. The explanation is as follows. The Trades tend towards the ITCZ (Figure 12.1), where there is a chain of centres of convergence associated with convective storms and these lift air into the upper atmosphere. The raised air increases the upper-level pressure locally, which creates

winds poleward as irregular *'anti-Trades'*. These vary considerably with season and longitude. For instance, the upper-level winds diverge in all directions over the west equatorial Pacific warm pool (Section 11.2). The anti-Trades are deflected by the Coriolis force to become patchy upper westerlies much interrupted by other winds, especially over the continents.

The Coriolis deflection prevents the anti-Trades reaching further towards the pole than about 30° latitude, so they bank up there, and the extra air creates the belt of *subtropical highs* at sea-level seen in Figure 12.1 and Figure 12.7. The accumulated air aloft gradually cools by radiation loss to space, and therefore contracts, leaving room for more air, whose extra weight leads to the relatively high pressures at surface level. The consequent subsidence in areas where surface pressures are high (**Note 12.G**) replaces air that spirals out near the surface to create the Trades once more. Thus a cycle is completed, defining what is called a *Hadley cell*, named after George Hadley (1685–1768). It involves ascent at the ITCZ and subsidence in the belt of highs which lies (in the southern hemisphere) at about 35°S in summer and 30°S in winter. There is a similar low-latitude meridional circulation *north* of the equator, and the two Hadley cells extend and contract with the annual swing of the Sun's path (**Figure 12.11**). The cell extends over the equator in winter, towards the ITCZ in the summer hemisphere, and the circulation is several times stronger than in the other (summertime) cell.

The north–south parts of a Hadley cell's circulation occur at the same time and latitudes as the east–west flows shown in Figure 12.10. The Hadley cell involves simply the average of the *meridional components* of the real winds. The cells are *secondary circulations*, so-called because they are weaker than the primary zonal circulation around the Earth, shown in Figure 12.10. On the other hand, they are important in carrying warm moist air to the ITCZ, leading to conden-

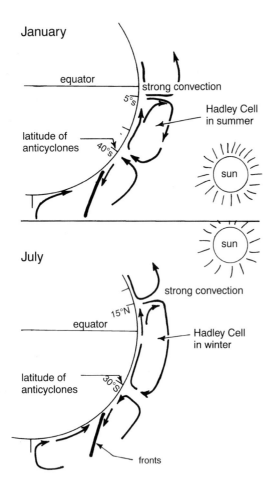

Figure 12.11 Schematic diagram of the meridional flows at about the longitude of Australia, showing the contraction of the southern Hadley cell in summer and extension in winter. The depth of the troposphere is exaggerated about 140 times, in order to make the global circulation pattern visible.

Further energy comes from the reduced loss of longwave radiation to space (Note 2.C), due to the coldness of the high tops of equatorial cumulonimbus.

The Polar Front and the Ferrel Cell

Not all the air subsiding around 30° latitude spirals out from the surface highs to become the Trades. The winds on the *poleward* side of each high in the southern hemisphere tend to emerge as midlatitude northwesterlies (Figure 12.1), carrying relatively warm air towards the pole. These winds encounter cold southwesterlies at around 45°S, and the convergence brings together air masses of different temperatures. The highly irregular interface is called a 'front', in this case the *polar front* (**Figure 12.12**). It is like the fronts between different water masses (Section 11.5). Fronts are discussed in the next chapter; here it is enough to know that the cold air at a front slides under the warmer air, wedging the latter upwards. William Ferrel suggested in 1856 that such ascent combines with the previous subsidence in the subtropical highs, and the polewards surface winds from them, to form part of a midlatitude circulation. This would be something like a weak Hadley

sation in the convective updraughts there, accompanied by the release of latent heat, which is then carried polewards by the upper limb of the Hadley cell. This lessens the difference between polar and equatorial temperatures.

Hadley circulations are driven chiefly by the solar energy absorbed in the high rate of evaporation from tropical oceans (Figure 4.11).

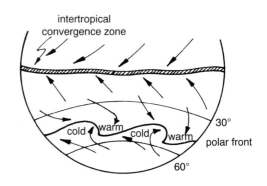

Figure 12.12 Tropical surface winds converge on the ITCZ, whilst cold and warm winds meet at the irregular midlatitude polar front, which is continually distorted.

cell, but rotating in the opposite direction (Figure 12.11) and therefore intermeshing with the lower-latitude Hadley cells.

For a more sophisticated account of midlatitude winds it is necessary to consider differences between temperatures of the lower troposphere at various latitudes. There is little variation of temperature with latitude near the equator for any particular level of pressure, but there is an abrupt cooling in midlatitudes. In the first case, we say the atmosphere is *barotropic*. In the second case, the atmosphere is called *baroclinic*, i.e. imaginary surfaces of constant temperature in the atmosphere are *inclined* to isobaric surfaces, those of equal pressure (**Note 12.H**). Baroclinic conditions exist at the polar front mentioned earlier, where warm and cold air masses are adjacent. The front is usually well defined, but its location and the temperature gradient across it fluctuate daily, and it readily breaks up into *frontal disturbances*, consisting of tongues of cold air towards the equator behind others of warm air penetrating towards the pole. These disturbances cause the variability of winds and weather at midlatitudes (Chapter 13).

The Polar Cell

Winds at the highest latitudes tend to be easterly (Figure 12.1, Figure 12.5 and Figure 12.10), which can be explained by a circulation like that of the Hadley cell. Air over the pole continually cools, becoming more dense and therefore subsides, eventually sliding down the dome of Antarctic ice. This flow is deflected westward by the powerful Coriolis effect of high latitudes, forming the south-easterlies which help form the *Antarctic front* between 60–65°S, where the MSLP is lower than anywhere else (Figure 1.8). Then the air is raised by frontal disturbances which break up the front, as at the polar front. (However, the disturbances and the Antarctic front are limited to low levels only, whereas the polar front affects the entire troposphere.) Air above the Antarctic front flows back towards the pole, completing a meridional circulation called the *polar cell*. It is the weakest and most shallow of all three cells in each hemisphere, and covers the smallest area.

There are strong westerly winds between the Antarctic and polar fronts, with uplift at the disturbances on each side. Sometimes the two fronts temporarily combine into one.

Quasi-Biennial Oscillation

A remarkable feature of winds near the equator at about 25 km elevation (where pressures are about 25 hPa) is their reversal between comparatively fast easterlies and slow westerlies and then back again, taking about two years in all. So it is called the *Quasi-Biennial Oscillation* (QBO). For instance, the easterly winds over Singapore reached a maximum of around 15 m/s in 1982, 1985, 1987 and 1990, i.e. there is a cycle of variation lasting about twenty-six months. It was first discovered in 1952 over Canton Island at 3°S in the Pacific and later traced as far as 30 degrees from the equator. The QBO is the only clear rhythm in the atmosphere unrelated to diurnal or annual variations, though its regularity is upset occasionally by volcanic eruptions like that of Mt Agung (at 8°S in Bali) in 1963. The change of wind direction occurs simultaneously round the entire tropical belt, beginning at 30 km altitude and extending to 20 km within a year or so. Below that, the oscillation becomes less evident.

The QBO is presumably associated with the tendency for alternate years to be relatively wet (Section 10.4). A similar alternation has been seen in an approximately two-year variation of temperatures in America, noted first in 1885. The explanation involves increased uplift within the atmosphere above Australia and South Africa during the *westerly* phase of the QBO, and therefore more rain, fed by evaporation from the Indian ocean. Years when the upper equatorial winds are from the *east* are likely to be relatively dry because of descending air, warming and evaporating of any cloud. But this effect on rainfalls is feeble compared to that of the El Niño (Section 11.2), which appears to be independent of the QBO and much more whimsical.

12.4 THE UPPER WESTERLIES

Strong westerly winds extend over most of the upper troposphere just below the tropopause (Figure 12.10). They are esentially *thermal winds* (Note 12.F), due to the meridional gradient of near-surface temperatures at midlatitudes. The westerlies are strongest near the polar front (Figure 12.12), where the temperature gradient is steepest. They are not found higher than the tropopause because the latitudinal gradient of temperature is actally reversed at such elevations, i.e. it is colder at lower latitudes (Figure 1.9 and Figure 12.10), especially in the summer hemisphere. In short, the belt of strongest winds, called the *jet stream*, is above the polar front and just below the tropopause.

The speed and direction of the jet stream are evident in the path of a balloon launched from New Zealand and tracked for 102 days as it was carried along at 200 hPa (**Figure 12.13**). It travelled about 1,000 km/day. Another balloon flight in the upper westerlies is described in **Note 12.I**. Airplane flights from Sydney to Santiago (Chile) at a level of nearly 11 km take about an hour less than the return flight in summer, and two hours in winter, on account of the upper westerlies.

Rossby Waves

Figure 12.13 shows that the upper westerlies do not flow steadily towards the east, but sway from side to side as *Rossby waves*, named after the Swedish meteorologist Carl-Gustav Rossby. He explained them in 1939 in terms of the Coriolis effect (**Note 12.J**). The waves are bends in the path along which the winds blow, most evident in the jet stream. If there are six such waves in circling the globe, we say that the *wave number* is six. The waves travel against the wind direction, at speeds which depend on their size.

Rossby waves may form on account of horizontal variations of low-atmosphere temperature. As an example, relative warmth over a peninsula in summer leads to vertical expansion of the air, causing a local raising of the level at which pressures are, say, 200 hPa (Note 12.E; **Figure 12.14**). Thus, there is an increased pressure over the land at any stipulated elevation in the upper atmosphere; we say there is a *ridge* of high pressure. This promotes a 'thermally direct circulation', like a Hadley cell (Section 12.3) or sea breeze (Chapter 14), as shown in Figure 12.14. The upper-level ridge also affects the flow of upper winds, which flow geostrophically, following the isobars around the region of high pressure, anticlockwise in the southern hemisphere. Conversely, an adjacent cooler surface has the effect of creating a clockwise bend in a jet stream in the southern hemisphere, around a *trough of low pressure*. So there is a series of alternately left and right loops in the wind's path (**Figure 12.15**). This is an example of a surface condition affecting upper-level winds. We shall see in the next chapter that the two levels are closely linked, with interactions in both directions.

The initial deflection forming a Rossby wave might have been a coastal difference of temperatures, but the cause could be a mountain range, discussed later. However, it should not be inferred from the fixed positions of coasts and mountains that the Rossby waves are tied to particular locations. There is some tendency that way (which we discuss in connection with 'blocking' in Section 12.5 and Chapter 13), but the dominant feature of the waves is their mobility.

The sharpness of the turning, i.e. the amount of rotation (or *vorticity*) created by the ridge or

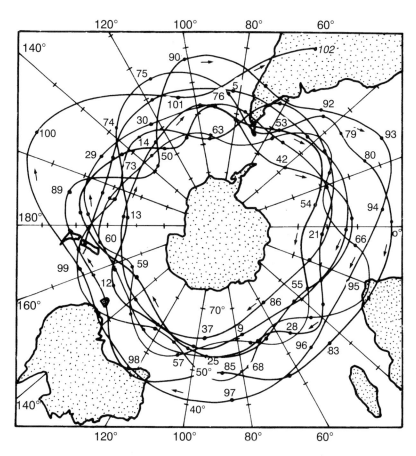

Figure 12.13 Trajectory of a balloon released from Christchurch (NZ) and carried along at a level of 12km. The numbers indicate the days elapsed from the time of launch.

trough, depends on both the strength of the wind through the wave and the length of the wave (**Note 12.K**). Vorticity is a useful concept because it is a property that tends to be 'conserved', to persist. Thus, whirls that form behind an obstacle in a river and then are carried away by the flow do not disappear as soon as they are shed from the obstacle. The vorticity which is conserved is the *absolute vorticity*, which has two components from separate sources – the turning of the wind over the Earth, and also the turning of the Earth in space. The former contributes *relative vorticity*

and the latter *planetary vorticity*. These will be discussed later.

Planetary Waves

Rossby waves are of two kinds, short and long. The latter are known as *planetary waves*. They are almost stationary and last from a few weeks to a season. They usually have a wave number of two in the northern hemisphere (because of the two land masses, Eurasia and North America), and one in the southern hemisphere because of the asymmetry of Antarctica about the South

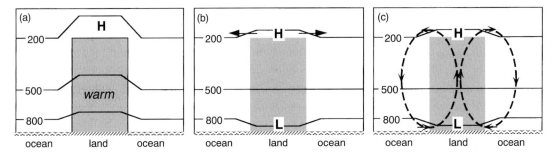

Figure 12.14 The effect of warm land on atmospheric pressures. The land heats the air above, which therefore expands lifting the higher atmosphere, so that the level at a pressure of 200 hPa, for instance, is raised (a). In other words, pressures over the land are greater than at the same height over the sea, especially at higher levels. For example, the pressure on top of the shaded block of warm air in (a) exceeds the 200 hPa of adjacent air at that level. The pressure difference leads to an outwards flow at the upper levels. This reduces the weight of air above the land, lowering the surface pressure there (b). That causes an inwards flow near the ground. The contrary flows at different levels create a convective circulation (c).

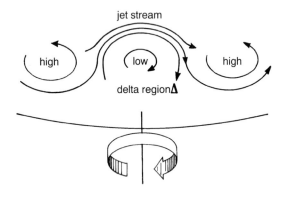

Figure 12.15 The upper-troposphere winds in the vicinity of a shortwave trough or low.

Pole; Antarctica bulges towards the Indian Ocean. (This asymmetry is one reason why Perth at 32°S in west Australia receives 865 mm/a of rain, whereas Santiago at 33.5°S in Chile receives only 318 mm/a.) There is also a simultaneous weaker undulation of wave-number three in the southern hemisphere, due to South America (where much of the Andes is above 3,000 m), Africa (where most of the land in the south is above 1,000 m), and the 'island continent' consisting mainly of Australia

and its Dividing Range, as well as mountainous New Zealand.

Shortwaves

The co-existing short Rossby waves have wave-lengths of a few thousand kilometres at most and are transient, developing and decaying within a week or two. Their short length means rapid twisting, i.e. considerable vorticity (Note 12.K). They travel *eastward* at a varying pace, typically 1,000 km/day, slightly slower than the winds travelling through them.

Shortwaves are associated with disturbances at the polar front, when a tongue of cold air extends towards the equator, for instance. This causes a lowering of isobaric surfaces in the upper troposphere, i.e. a trough of low pressure (Figure 12.15), and therefore a clockwise turning in the southern hemisphere. Shortwaves in the upper westerlies are linked with frontal disturbances beneath, which cause weather. This is the reason for weather forecasters focusing attention on upper-level charts of winds and vorticity.

The short Rossby waves and the associated frontal disturbances can play an important role in the redistribution of heat across the globe

(Section 5.2). That is because large amounts of sensible and latent heat are advected poleward ahead of a frontal disturbance (Chapter 13), and the disturbance is followed by an outbreak of polar air towards the equator. Either way, there is a lessening of the temperature difference between equator and pole.

12.5 JET STREAMS

A jet stream is a narrow channel of strongest winds near the tropopause (Section 12.4). A typical example is a few thousand kilometres long and a kilometre or two deep within the upper westerlies, with winds faster than 30 m/s (108 km/h). It is only about a hundred kilometres wide at any moment, but meanders from high latitude to low and back within the Rossby waves, and covers a range of latitudes within a month, so that monthly mean averages of wind speed show a broad band of strong wind (Figure 12.10). The instantaneous position of a jet stream is often indicated by a characteristic long band of cirrus.

Jet streams are discontinuous and vary with the weather. They may slow down, split or join, and contain patches, called *jet streaks*, where winds exceed 50 m/s (180 km/h), sometimes reaching twice that. Jet streams were first discovered in the course of high-altitude flights to Japan during wartime in the early 1940s. A pilot going in the same direction tries to catch a ride for extra speed, whilst one flying in the opposite direction steers well clear.

Subtropical Jet Streams

Two jet streams can sometimes be distinguished in the westerlies aloft. One is the *subtropical jet* (STJ), a chain of jet streaks at about 12 km altitude. The core velocity of a STJ averages 70 m/s (250 km/h) at 25°S over Australia in winter, but only 30 m/s at 31°S in summer. The average latitude and the mean speed of STJs over Australia vary in alternate years, with years of stronger jets around 27°S taking turns with years with weaker jets around 29°S. Presumably this is connected with the QBO (Section 12.3).

The STJ is partly due to the acceleration (relative to the ground) of upper westerlies, as the air moves polewards in the upper part of the Hadley cell. (Air from the equator moves eastward at 490 m/s, whilst the Earth's surface at 30 degrees latitude rotates 65 m/s slower.) Also, the troposphere is much colder at latitudes above 30°, and the STJ is partly a thermal wind resulting from the temperature gradient (Note 12.F).

Polar Front Jet Streams

Polar-front jet streams (PFJ) occur at about 50°S and 8 km altitude, directly above the polar front, whose position changes with season and from day to day. The PFJ is a thermal wind due to the temperature difference across the polar front. It often contains a series of rapidly evolving shortwaves, whereas longwaves are more common in the STJ.

Sometimes the PFJ and STJ combine into a single jet, as in Figure 12.10. This fusion is common over large continents in winter. At other times, the PFJ ridges far to the south (e.g. to 65°S), at the same time as the STJ forms a broad trough near 20°S. Such a pattern obstructs frontal disturbances which are travelling from the west, and sends them southward around the ridge. This is known as *blocking*. It happens when the shifting pattern of upper ridges and troughs locks onto a large high at the surface, located south of its normal subtropical position (Figure 12.7). Such a coincidence may arrest the eastward movement of the waves for days or weeks, causing settled weather at ground level, so weather forecasters are keen to detect incipient blocking. It is most common in winter, and may lead to drought in places that receive their rain from frontal disturbances, e.g. south-western Australia and Tasmania.

Blocking is associated with large-amplitude Rossby waves, swinging over a wide range of latitudes, whereas a low amplitude corresponds to a more even westerly flow. The two cases are distinguished by the difference between the heights (averaged over all longitudes) at which pressures are 500 hPa, at 35° and 55° latitudes, respectively. This difference is called the *zonal index*. A high index implies a fairly straight, strong jet stream. A *low* value corresponds to large loops of the Rossby waves, which equalise conditions at the two latitudes, and implies a low zonal wind speed and (in the extreme) blocking. The index tends to wax and wane irregularly, sometimes over periods of 3–8 weeks, and this irregular *vacillation* is called the *index cycle*.

In addition to the westerly jets there is sometimes in mid-year an *easterly* jet stream high above the ITCZ affected by the QBO (Section 12.3). This is due to the elevation of equatorial air by convection to a height of 14 km or so. The air at ground level rotates eastwards with the Earth's surface at a velocity of 463 m/s, but moves about 2 m/s slower at a height of 14 km to maintain a constant 'angular momentum', in the same way that a skater spins more slowly on stretching out to increase his/her radius. This small westward flow adds to the zonal average easterly to produce an equatorial jet stream of about 4 m/s. But it is patchy, reaching 10 m/s over the Indonesian archipelago but is non-existent over South America and the eastern Pacific.

Vertical Motions

Jet streams are important in controlling temperature, cloudiness and precipitation at mid-latitudes because they induce vertical motions in the troposphere; subsidence usually means fine weather, while uplift can lead to rainfall. The place of greatest uplift is on the poleward side of the exit of a jet streak, called the *delta region* (Figure 12.15) where two causes of upper-level divergence combine. First, there is that due to acceleration from cyclonic to anticyclonic rotation at the exit of the jet streak, and, second, that caused by the momentum of the jet's air at the exit which generates divergence on the right-hand side because of a temporary excess of leftwards Coriolis acceleration (**Note 12.L**). The 'delta region' is seen in satellite pictures of clouds to be about 1,000 km across and triangular, like the Greek letter delta.

Uplift due to a jet causes low-level convergence and hence a surface low which may grow into a frontal disturbance and then a storm (Chapter 13). The frontal disturbances are responsible for alternations of cold and warm, wet and dry weather in midlatitudes. The storms have led to the belt of highest jet-stream activity being called the *storm track*. It is centred at about 47°S in both winter and summer, which is clear of Australia, South Africa and (just) New Zealand, but not South America, which extends to 56°S. Slight movement of the storm track, due to changes in ocean circulation for instance, can significantly alter climates locally.

Jet streaks are also linked with Clear Air Turbulence, a little-understood hazard to aviation (**Note 12.M**).

12.6 MODELS OF THE GENERAL CIRCULATION

At this point it is useful to summarise the previous sections in terms of a single coherent model of the world's circulation overall. The model must account for the distribution of pressures (Figure 1.8), the meridional transfer of heat (Note 5.F) and the latitudinal variations of rainfall (Figure 10.6) and winds (Figure 12.5).

Various models have been suggested in the past. Edmund Halley proposed in 1686 that the easterly Trade winds were following the Sun, flowing towards the part of the Earth that is warmed by solar radiation, like the draught to a fire. But that would imply a daily reversal of winds.

A better model was advocated by George Hadley in 1735. He explained the Trades as due to a lag of the wind on the rotation of the Earth: the ground moves eastwards faster than the atmosphere does, as the air is drawn towards the equator by the warmth there. Then there is thermal convection upwards from the equator, followed by subsidence at higher latitudes. This explains the pattern within the Hadley cells (Section 12.3) and contains an early interpretation of the Coriolis effect, but fails to account for surface westerlies at higher latitudes.

That objection was later considered by William Ferrel in the light of the Coriolis effect (Note 11.D). He suggested that the Hadley cell meshes with a midlatitude cell rotating in the reverse direction, which in turn interlocks with a polar cell beyond, like three cog-wheels in a row. Such a three-cell model of the general circulation was more clearly described by Tor Bergeron in 1928, and was used in Section 12.3 in considering Figure 12.10 and Figure 12.11. It has the advantage of being simple, but has at least three difficulties. It implies a boundary between the Ferrel and polar cells at latitudes much higher than is observed in practice; polar air actually meets low-latitude warm air at fronts nearer the equator than 60°. Secondly, the three-cell model implies upper easterlies above the midlatitudes (as the counterpart of the surface westerlies), which is incorrect (Figure 12.10). Thirdly, the circulation known as the Ferrel cell proves to be insignificant. In fact, it is now realised that circulations in midlatitudes are not regular flows around *horizontal* axes (as in the three-cell model), but are largely the outcome of sporadic, asymmetric eddies around *vertical* axes.

So we arrive at a more complex version (**Figure 12.16**), following the ideas of Rossby (1941), Palmen (1951) and Newton (1969), and incorporating what has been learnt about the upper winds. This model almost omits the Ferrel cell (with a horizontal axis) and instead involves slantwise convection within vast horizontal Rossby waves. But the Palmen–Newton model retains the ITCZ and the Hadley cell, and there are vestiges of a polar cell on the polar side of the circumpolar westerlies. The subtropical jet (STJ) lies at the edge of the Hadley cell, above the interface between descending equatorial air and cold air from higher latitudes. Similarly, the polar-front jet (PFJ) is above the interface between subpolar and subtropical air masses (Chapter 13). There is no well-defined jet above the weaker and more shallow Antarctic front.

Even the model in Figure 12.16 has the disadvantage that it is essentially static, understating the atmosphere's inherent unsteadiness. One way of demonstrating its dynamic character is to play a movie loop of the observed wind, temperature and moisture contents at thirty levels, say, and points about 70 km apart horizontally, with data for each twelve hours over a decade. This has provided detailed estimates of the meridional movements of energy and moisture within the Hadley cell, and in transient and stationary eddies. It has also given insights into the characteristics of storm tracks and teleconnections.

Alternatively, we simulate the global circulation on a large computer, creating a *General Circulation Model* (GCM). GCMs were first developed by Newton Phillips in 1956 and Joseph Smagorinsky in 1963, on lines pioneered by Lewis Richardson in 1922, before suitable computers were available. A GCM ignores concepts like circulation cells, jet streams and large-scale winds. Instead, it involves the physics of atmospheric processes using fundamental equations of motion (Chapter 15) and derives the temperature change, for instance, of each unit volume of the atmosphere from the advection of heat into the volume, the

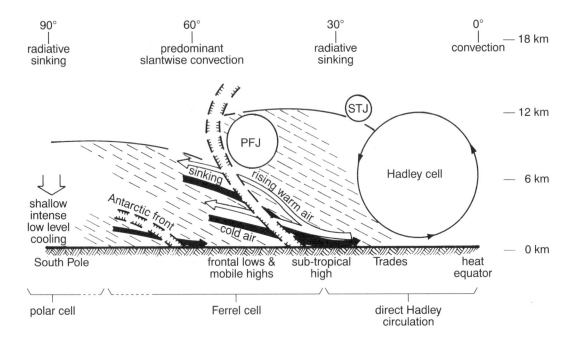

Figure 12.16 The Palmen–Newton model of the meridional winds of the general circulation. PFJ is the polar-front jet and STJ is the subtropical jet. The shallow front poleward of the polar front is the Antarctic front.

net radiation input and any release of latent heat there. Likewise for changes of wind speed or moisture content during any time-step. The calculations are repeated in each successive time-step for heat, motion and moisture in each of thousands of unit volumes, starting from a description of the initial conditions (e.g. those of today) and carrying on to deduce the situation hours, days, months or years ahead. The trillions of calculations involved have become practicable only since the recent advent of very large, very fast computers. Unfortunately, the atmosphere is still represented by data from points 100 km apart, for example, so that smaller features like clouds are ignored, except indirectly. Nevertheless, GCMs are the basis of modern weather prediction, leading to clear improvements in the accuracy of forecasting (Chapter 15). They are also essential tools in estimating climate change. This

requires allowing for SST fluctuations, which can be determined by a separate model of ocean movements. Preferably, both the atmospheric and ocean models are combined (i.e. 'coupled'), and this is done in studies of the ENSO phenomenon.

12.7 ENSO

There is a pattern of zonal flows over the equator across the Pacific Ocean named the *Walker circulation* after Gilbert Walker, who discovered it in the 1920s (**Figure 12.17**). The strength and direction of the circulation are measured by the difference between sea-level pressures (in hPa) at Papeete (17°S in Tahiti in the central Pacific) and Darwin (12°S in northern Australia), 8,500 km away. Tahiti is under the influence of the South Pacific high (Figure 12.1) and

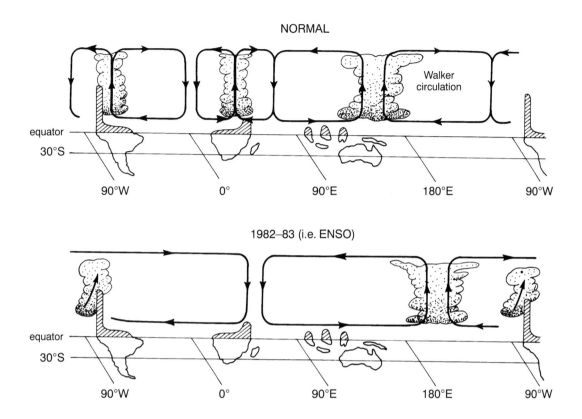

NORMAL

Walker
circulation

equator

30°S

90°W   0°   90°E   180°E   90°W

1982–83 (i.e. ENSO)

equator

30°S

90°W   0°   90°E   180°E   90°W

Figure 12.17 The Walker circulation in terms of zonal winds in the tropical troposphere during a normal and during an ENSO year, respectively.

experiences easterly Trades most of the year, while Darwin is near the west equatorial Pacific warm pool (Section 11.2) and has a distinctly monsoonal climate. The mean difference in the present month between the MSLP values at the two places is compared with the long-term average difference at this time of year, to obtain the current *MSLP anomaly*. (An 'anomaly' is a difference from the normal.) The month's anomalies are calculated for all past years to derive the standard deviation (a measure of the scatter – Note 10.L) for that month of the year. Dividing the relevant standard deviation into the current MSLP anomaly, and then multiplying by ten, gives the *Southern Oscillation Index* (SOI) for the present month. Values either

over 20 or below −20 are found to occur only 4.6 per cent of the time, although the SOI has varied between +33 and −39 during the last century. It is usually smoothed by taking a five-month running mean (Note 10.H), to remove some of the short-term scatter.

The SOI value is connected with the rainfall, as shown in the following examples:

1 The greater the SOI value, the stronger the westwards Trade wind (Figure 12.17), since winds near the equator blow directly from places of high to those of low pressure, unaffected by the weak Coriolis effect at low latitudes. A strong westward flow (i.e. a highly positive SOI) implies more uplift

over Darwin, for instance, and hence heavier rainfall over Australia (**Table 12.1**).

2 Fluctuations of the SOI match differences in the flow of the Burdekin River in Queensland and hence in the thickness of annual coral deposits in the sea at the mouth of the river.

3 **Figure 12.18** shows a connection between SOI and rainfall in terms of the flow along a river draining western New South Wales.

4 There has been a correspondence between Australian annual wheat yields and the June–August SOI during the period 1948–91. The coefficient of correlation was 0.47, which is impressive but insufficient to be useful in predicting yield.

5 A negative SOI value implies possible drought over northern Australia (Figure 10.16).

The SOI fluctuates every few years, due to a see-sawing of pressures between Papeete and Darwin. A rise at one place is accompanied by a fall of pressure at the other, and so an enhanced change of the difference between the two. This fluctuation is called the *Southern Oscillation*, from which we derive the name of the SOI.

Teleconnections

It became clear after the collecting of weather data during the International Geophysical Year of 1957 that variations like that of the Southern Oscillation are not confined to the Pacific ocean (Figure 12.17). That year happened to be a major El Niño year (Figure 10.16) and the IGY involved collecting data worldwide. The data showed that the Walker circulation in the Pacific intermeshes with similar east–west circulations right round the globe at low latitudes, as well as with the meridional Hadley cells. So pressure anomalies at Darwin coincide with anomalies far away, especially in the tropical region of the southern hemisphere. The rela-

Table 12.1 Association of high values of the Southern Oscillation Index * with large areas of high rainfall in the eastern states of Australia during the period 1933–87

Range of annual average SOI values	Number of years with such SOI values	Average SOI over those years	Mean during those years, of the percentage of eastern Australia with the following rainfall:		
			Low †	Normal ‡	High §
Below −5	14	−9.6	**47** ‖	41	11
Between −5 and +5	30	+0.5	27	**46**	27
Above +5	11	+9.2	6	39	**56**

Notes:
* The annual SOI is the average of the monthly SOIs, as defined in Section 12.7
† 'Low' rainfall means that the annual total at a place was within the lowest three deciles of measurements there (Section 10.4). The deciles were obtained by ranking the annual rainfalls in ascending order to determine the smallest 30 per cent of the fifty-five values.
‡ 'Normal' rainfall here means that the annual total at each place fell in the middle four deciles
§ 'High' rainfall means that the annual total at each place fell within the highest three deciles
‖ This figure was derived from fifty-five annual totals of rainfall at each of many places within the easternstates of Australia. For each place, the fifty-five values were ranked and divided into deciles, so that a decile could be allotted for each year. In any particular year the appropriate decile value for every place was mapped, allowing calculation of the average decile for the whole region for that year. In the fourteen years with low SOI values, 47 per cent of the region, on average, had low rainfall, 41 per cent had normal rainfall, and 11 per cent had high rainfall. The most likely rainfall regime is highlighted in bold.

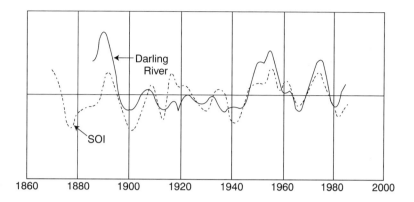

Figure 12.18 The parallelism of fluctuations of the Southern Oscillation Index and flows of water along the Darling River in western New South Wales. Each vertical unit represents 20 SOI units. The curves show ten-year running averages.

tionship is given in terms of the *correlation coefficient*, a statistical measure of the degree to which a change (in this case of the pressure at Darwin) is accompanied by a similar anomaly at any other place on the map. **Figure 12.19** shows that when the MSLP is anomalously low in Darwin (i.e. the SOI is high and therefore Darwin is relatively wet), the MSLP tends to be high in Tahiti, where rainfall is consequently unlikely. But the correlation is slightly positive in central Africa and in the Amazon Basin, suggesting that *wet* periods there tend to accompany rain at Darwin.

The global relevance of the phenomenon is shown in **Figure 12.20**, indicating simultaneous but various changes in the rainfall at the time of negative SOI values.

Relationship to SST

It was pointed out by Hendrik Berlage in 1957, and by Jakob Bjerknes in 1966, that the Southern Oscillation is related to the occurrence of El Niño (Section 11.2), since both occur within the Tropics, where anomalies of pressure are closely associated with alterations of sea-surface temperatures. The connection is seen in **Figure 12.21**. An association arises from an anomalously high SST in the central equatorial Pacific, creating atmospheric convection and hence a release of latent heat into the atmosphere which lowers its density and hence the surface pressure there, which implies a negative SOI. Another association between pressure and SST works the other way; a decreased MSLP at Tahiti reduces the force which drives the Trades, so there is less cooling of the surface by upwelling. Either way, we say that the tropical atmosphere and ocean are 'tightly coupled'.

As an example, the negative SOI from June 1982 till March 1983 coincided with an abnormally strong El Niño off Peru. Other long periods of negative SOI were from May till December 1940, and June to October 1941, again associated with periods of strong El Niños (Figure 10.16). In other words, low values of the SOI imply an El Niño. In fact, El Niños and the Southern Oscillation are simply aspects of the same global *ENSO episodes*, where this title is compounded from **El Niño** + Southern Oscillation.

The global average SST is higher when the SOI is negative, so it is sometimes referred to as a 'warm phase'. Within that period, an *ENSO warm episode* involves both an El Niño and a low

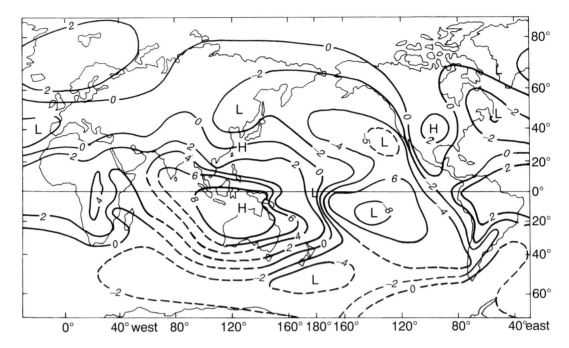

Figure 12.19 The correlation of annual mean pressures with those at Darwin, in terms of the 'correlation coefficient'. The coefficient is +1 (shown as 10 in the diagram) if changes are the same as those at Darwin, zero if unrelated, and −1 (i.e. −10 in the diagram) if exactly opposite. Thus, −8 in the diagram, for example, indicates a strong tendency towards opposite changes.

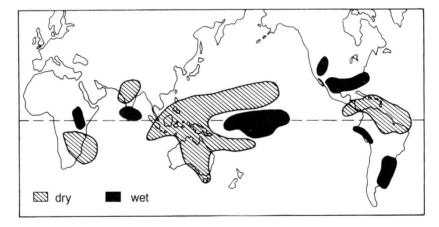

Figure 12.20 Regions experiencing changes of rainfall during an ENSO warm episode, showing which have an increase ('wet') and which a decrease, 'dry'.

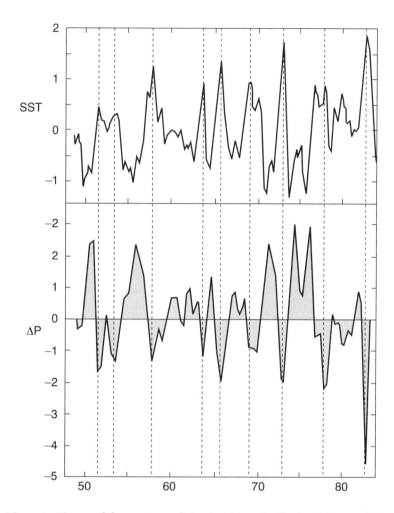

Figure 12.21 The coincidence of fluctuations of the Southern Oscillation Index and the sea-surface temperature in the central equatorial Pacific (between 150–90°W and 5°N–5°S).

SOI as the extreme set of conditions. Tropical cyclones (Chapter 13) are more common in the South Pacific during an ENSO warm episode. Contrariwise there are 'ENSO cold episodes', which include a La Niña and a high SOI. Details are given in **Note 12.N**.

ENSO Events

The occurrence of ENSO events is quasi-cyclic, with at least two rhythms beating against each other. One involves a period of 2–3 years, though it is apparently unconnected with the stratospheric Quasi-Biennial Oscillation (Section 12.3). The other rhythm is more important and takes 3–5 years for each cycle. Despite this, the SOI was continuously negative for more than five years between January 1990 and September 1995. No two El Niños are the same.

There might perhaps be a link to sunspots, since 'strong' ENSO events since 1710 at least have been more frequent in years with fewer sunspots. Another clue comes from the similarity of the dates of El Niños and those of Nile floods in recent decades which suggests the possibility of using the long record of the floods to examine ENSO frequency since AD 622; it seems they were less common during the Medieval Warm Period, between AD 900–1200 (Chapter 15).

In view of the connection between SOI and rainfalls, it is not surprising that ENSO events also coincide with variations of precipitation. Examination of layers of ice on top of Quelccaya (Section 3.2) shows that 30 per cent less was deposited from the easterly winds during five recent ENSO events. Trujillo (at 8°S in South America) normally receives less than 25 mm of rain annually but 400 mm fell in 1925 on account of an El Niño. However, twelve of the driest twenty years between 1875 and 1978 in south-east Africa were El Niño years, and twenty out of twenty-six El Niño episodes in the last 120 years were associated with droughts in Australia. The relationships are not simple. Connections between El Niño and droughts (or abnormal rainfalls in the case of Santiago, for instance) are shown in Figure 10.16 to be only approximate, and the strength of the connection between rainfalls in eastern Australia and the SOI seems to change from decade to decade.

In summary, we now know enough about the progress of an ENSO episode to permit the following few months' events to be predicted with modest confidence (Note 12.N) once it has started, but we still cannot foretell its onset. One problem is that so many feedbacks complicate the process, and another is our ignorance of the interaction of the ocean with relatively weak winds.

It is not only the ENSO phenomenon that is becoming better understood. Recent decades have also seen enormous advances in explaining the synoptic-scale events which constitute weather. These are dealt with in the next chapter.

NOTES

12.A   Streamlines
12.B   Trade winds
12.C   The geostrophic wind and isobaric surfaces
12.D   The gradient wind
12.E   Thickness
12.F   Thermal wind
12.G   Convergence, divergence and vertical circulations
12.H   Baroclinic and barotropic conditions
12.I   Balloon flight across Australia
12.J   Rossby waves
12.K   Vorticity
12.L   Jet streams and weather
12.M   Clear Air Turbulence
12.N   El Niño, part 3

13

SYNOPTIC-SCALE WINDS

13.1 INTRODUCTION

The global circulations discussed in Chapter 12 are evident only after averaging the fluctuating winds that are actually measured (**Note 13.A**). In this chapter we consider some of the detail which was overlooked in focusing on year-long averages over the whole globe. In particular, we will consider winds on the scale of a thousand kilometres or so – the 'synoptic scale' (Table 1.1) – and look at day-by-day snapshots instead of long-term patterns.

The word 'synoptic' (i.e. 'together seen') implies that we observe a combination of measurements from a wide area – of the size of Australia, for instance. It is the scale of *regional* weather, uncomplicated by local effects like surface friction, slope or local differences of surface temperature. All the measurements refer to the same moment in standard time, the Greenwich Meridian Time (GMT), also known as Universal Time and signified by UTC or Z, e.g. 1300Z means 1 p.m. at Greenwich in London. Meteorological offices around the world use this convention, irrespective of local clocks.

Figure 13.1 shows mean sea-level pressure (MSLP) isobars over Australia at a particular moment, i.e. the map of pressures after each measurement has been corrected for elevation. It indicates the weather at that time, in three ways. Firstly, isobars at middle and high latitudes show the direction and strength of the geostrophic winds. The winds are shown blowing anticlockwise around the high-pressure regions (the highs) and clockwise around the lows, in accordance with Buys-Ballot's Rule (Section 12.2). Secondly, the MSLP reflects what is happening aloft, because it indicates the weight of air in the entire column above (Note 1.G). So changes of pressure demonstrate the overall inflows and outflows from the column at every level. Thirdly, mobile highs and lows determine most aspects of the weather, notably temperature, precipitation and cloudiness. For instance, lows or troughs on the MSLP map show where air is ascending and may form cloud, with rain as a possible sequel, while subsidence typically occurs where there are low-level highs or *ridges*.

The various conditions around a place of low pressure amount to what we call a *cyclonic system*. Likewise for an anticyclonic system associated with a region of high pressure. These systems are not to be regarded as independent whirls within an otherwise steady atmosphere; they

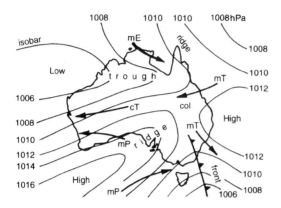

Figure 13.1 A typical pattern of sea-level pressures and therefore surface winds over Australia, showing the air masses involved and hence a front between mT and mP air masses, with different temperatures and wind directions.

interact with each other and are essential ingredients of the global circulations. It is only for convenience that we separate the various systems and their characteristics, to examine the life cycle of each system's formation, maturity and decay, which lies behind the local variabilities of weather.

13.2 AIR MASSES

Synoptic-scale winds can be thought of as distinct streams of air, which may emerge from large regions of uniform air temperature, humidity, stability, wind speed and direction. Then the atmosphere comes to be regarded as consisting of discrete '*air masses*' and this approach to meteorology became customary in the middle of the twentieth century.

An 'air mass' is a fairly uniform body of air, hundreds or thousands of kilometres across, with surface dry-bulb and dewpoint temperatures within a few degrees of the respective averages. Alternatively, and preferably, we characterise air masses by the values of 'conserved' variables, such as the mixing ratio

(Note 6.B), the equivalent potential temperature (Section 7.2) or an even more completely conserved variable called the *potential vorticity*, which is discussed in more advanced texts. It combines both air mass stability (Section 7.2) and vorticity (Note 12.K).

The concept of an air mass is used both near the surface and aloft. For instance, ozone concentrations are used to characterise stratospheric air masses. Here we will focus on ground-level conditions, where the air masses are separated by fronts (Section 12.3).

Air masses are considered in meteorology in much the same way as an air parcel in discussing stability and convection (Section 7.3). But air mass is a much larger body of air, whose movements and changes help us explain the weather.

The characteristics of an air mass are acquired when winds linger for a few days over a large uniform surface, like an ocean or extensive land areas more than about 500 km from the sea, such as a great desert. The required light winds occur where the atmosphere is slowly subsiding in the region of a high (Section 12.3), for example. Such regions are called *source areas* and give air masses their names (**Table 13.1**).

Classification

An initial categorisation of air masses was made by Tor Bergeron in 1928. Primarily they are classed according to the latitude of the source area (i.e. its temperature) and secondarily according to whether the source area was continental or maritime. For instance, mP refers to an air mass of marine polar origin, coming from the southern ocean. There is sometimes a third subdivision in terms of the stability of the air mass. The last is indicated by the direction of movement: an air mass travelling to higher latitudes, for instance, is warmer than the surface and therefore labelled 'w'; such an air mass becomes increasingly stable as its base becomes cooled. Conversely, the label 'k' (for '*kalt*', Ger-

Table 13.1 Kinds of air mass in the southern hemisphere, using two-letter labels: 'c' refers to continental and 'm' to maritime air masses, from the equator 'E', temperate region 'T', polar region 'P' (i.e. high latitude) or Antarctica 'A'. Characteristic surface daily mean temperature (T°C), mixing ratio (r) and stability are listed for winter/summer

Approx latitude of source	Label	T (°C)	r (g/kg)	Stability
Equatorial (0–10°S)	cE	25/25	18/18	moist neutral
	mE	25/25	19/19	moist neutral
Subtropical (30°S)	cT	15/25	4/6	stable/dry neutral
	mT	18/22	14/17	stable
Polar (50°S)	cP*	0/10	3/5	stable/dry neutral
	mP†	4/8	5/8	moist neutral
Antarctic	cA	−40/−20	0.1/0.3	stable

* *Found only in Patagonia.*
† *Called the maritime Southern in the southern oceans.*

man for 'cold') means an increasingly unstable air mass.

Dominant air masses in the southern hemisphere are labelled mP and mT, arising from subtropical highs over the oceans (Figure 12.1). The two kinds differ appreciably in temperature (Table 13.1). Areas south of about 35°S obtain most of their rain from northward excursions of mP air, while those north of 35°S receive it from mT air, except that in monsoonal areas, such as Darwin (Section 12.1), it comes from mE or cE air. A wintertime cP/mP air mass in South America occasionally penetrates north of 20°S in the lee of the Andes (Section 13.3).

Air masses change character according to the surface they traverse. They are affected by surface heating or cooling, by wet or dry surfaces, by mixing with other air masses and by radiative cooling. In fact, the susceptibility to change is a weakness of the notion of definable air masses, and accounts for the reduced interest in the concept since the 1960s. Another reason is the fact that the atmosphere does not move *en bloc*, because the upper air travels faster, so that the stability of an air mass can change even in the absence of any changes at the surface. Also, there is the difficulty of categorising air whose properties do not match those in Table 13.1.

Nevertheless, the concept remains helpful in describing climates (Chapter 15) and in explaining atmospheric 'fronts', for instance.

13.3 FRONTS

The concept of 'fronts' arose after the 1914–18 war from the similarity of the interface between different air masses to the battle-front between opposing armies in France. The idea was introduced by a handful of meteorologists working in a spare room of the home of Vilhelm Bjerknes in Bergen (Norway). He developed the idea in co-operation with his son, Jacob, and Tor Bergeron, Carl-Gustav Rossby and others, who became known as the 'Bergen School'. No group in history has had a larger impact on the way we think about weather today.

It can be seen in Figure 13.1 that adjacent winds blow in contrary directions over the south-east of Australia; to the left, an mP air mass is advected from the south-west, and, to the right, much warmer mT air enters from the north. So a line with triangular protuberances has been drawn on the map at the boundary between the two air masses (Chapter 15). This line represents a *cold front*, advancing in the direction of the triangles.

Criteria for a front vary, but typically a meteorologist will look for a horizontal temperature gradient of at least 3 K/100 km in subtropical regions (more at higher latitudes), and a difference of wind direction by at least 60°. The whole pattern of temperatures, winds, uplift, humidity, clouds and precipitation around a front constitutes a *frontal system*, including a *frontal (transition) zone*, where the differences of temperature etc. are most abrupt. The frontal boundary is a 'cold front', when a cold air mass moves into a warmer area. A *warm front* arises when a warm air mass advances into a colder region, repelling and riding over the cooler air mass. Conventional symbols are shown in **Figure 13.2**.

Cold Fronts

The basic feature of a cold front is the insinuation of a heavy, cold air mass under a lighter, warm one. The result of the cold air's advance is often the pattern of uplift, subsidence, clouds and rainfall shown in **Figure 13.3**, the classical 'Norwegian' or 'Bergen' model. There is a tilted

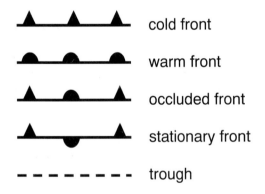

Figure 13.2 Conventional depiction of the most common types of fronts and a trough on weather charts. The half-circles and/or triangles are plotted on the forward side of the front.

frontal zone which is 20–200 km wide, intersecting the ground at the front

The zone slopes at only about 1 km in 100 km, unless there is an *active cold front* (or *anafront* – from the Greek word 'ana' for upward) when the zone may be two to four times as steep. A front is termed 'active' if it is preceded by a warm air mass which is already unstable and being slowly forced to rise by a jet stream above (Note 12.L). The instability and the jet stream promote the air's ascent, and usually trigger heavy rain and sometimes thunderstorms (Note 7.H). Without these stimuli, the front is a *passive front* or *katafront* (from the Greek word 'kata', meaning downward), which is only 1–2 km deep and brings cooler air and stratus cloud but little rain. Such fronts commonly occur along the south-east coast of Australia in summer, when the air is too dry to generate enough instability for cumulonimbus and there is no lifting by a jet stream.

Details of the winds around a front are shown in **Figure 13.4**. Moist, warm air is drawn from the north-east ahead of the front and slowly rises over the frontal surface. It is eventually deflected to the east by the upper westerlies. This flow is called the *warm conveyor belt*, which carries sensible and latent heat poleward (Section 12.3). The rising creates clouds, so the warm conveyor belt is often visible from satellites. Similarly, cold air follows the cold front and pushes it eastward. This is the *cold conveyor belt*, which slowly subsides under the frontal surface.

The approach of a cold front is usually heralded by a rapid movement of cirrus cloud across the sky. The cloud thickens to cirrostratus, then altostratus, followed by nimbostratus. The last brings rain, which may persist for hours, even after the passage of the cold front. Cumulonimbus may occur if the atmosphere is unstable. There is also a strengthening of the warm wind (northerly in the southern hemisphere) and thus a rise of temperature by a degree or two, causing an elevation of the freez-

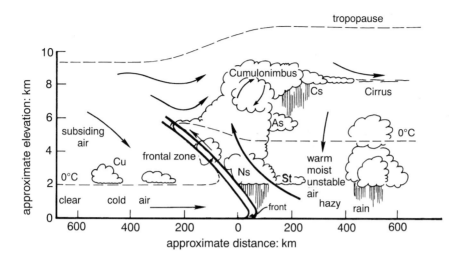

Figure 13.3 Idealised cross-section of an active cold front, showing cumulus cloud (Cu), stratus (St), nimbostratus (Ns), altostratus (As) and cirrostratus (Cs).

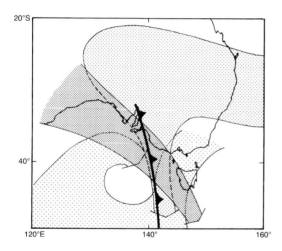

Figure 13.4 Three distinct airstreams involved in a typical cold front. There is a shallow flow of warm air near the ground from the east, called the 'warm conveyor belt', which turns south and ascends before the front. A mid-level flow, called the 'cold conveyor belt', approaches from the south, turning eastwards as it subsides behind the front. A jet stream blows from the north-west at high levels, either slowly descending or slowly ascending, depending on the strength of the frontal disturbance. The coastline of south-east Australia indicates the scale.

ing level just ahead of the front. In addition, there is a fall in atmospheric pressure, due to the front lying in a trough of low pressure, caused by the lightness of the air in the warm conveyor belt. The front lies like a stream in a valley, with opposite-facing pressure gradients on the two sides, this being the cause of the opposing winds and differing air masses. The low-pressure centre at the end of a front is like the lake at the end of the stream.

The immediate proximity of a front is shown by a pressure minimum, an overcast sky, backing of the wind in the southern hemisphere from north-westerly to south-westerly, and a fall of dry-bulb temperature by several degrees. It fell 10 K in 20 minutes on one occasion in Melbourne, for example. There is also a change of dewpoint, according to the kinds of air mass. Commonly, there is a pulse of strong wind (e.g. over 28 m/s) and maybe rain, as shown in Figure 13.3. The rainfall eases once the front has passed, and then low cloud tends to clear, visibility improves and the weather becomes bright and cool. In addition, the tropopause lowers as the cold front passes (Figure 13.3), in accordance with the Palmen–Newton model (Figure 12.16).

The situation is different at sea, where the incoming cold air mass over a surface of warmer temperature creates an unstable atmosphere in which cumulonimbus clouds can arise, with showers and gusts of wind. This is a dangerous time for small boats.

Rain and thunderstorms can occur well ahead of a cold front, as shown by the pattern of clouds in Figure 13.3. For instance, a cold front crossed Western Australia on 8 November 1995 and the associated band of cloud is easily seen in **Figure 13.5**. There was a trough ahead of the front, called a *prefrontal trough*, where warm air converges and may trigger severe thunderstorms. So it is of concern to weather forecasters. There was another front to the south-west (Figure 13.5), and the cloudiness over New Zealand indicates a non-frontal trough.

Southerly Changes

A passive cold front of importance in south-east Australia is the *southerly change*. It occurs frequently in spring and summer, bringing welcome relief from the heat. Initially, there is an eastwards, shallow front south of Victoria. The front is then arrested on its northern flank by the mountains of the Dividing Range, which lie parallel to the east coast. This swings the more southerly flank forwards, so that the front now travels northwards, following the coastline. The driving force is the narrow and intense thermal gradient along the coast. It peters out at 100–500 km from the south-east corner of mainland Australia.

The arrival of a southerly change is usually sudden, with a shift of wind direction, an abrupt drop in temperature and the develop-ment of low stratus. Particularly powerful squalls of cool southerly wind accompany the change if there are strong westerlies south of Victoria and the coastal areas of New South Wales are hot. Sometimes the southerly wind lasts several hours, especially in the afternoon.

The change on the New South Wales coast is known locally as a *Southerly Burster*. Similar fronts occur along the east coast of New Zealand's South Island (**Figure 13.6**), between São Paulo and Salvador in Brazil, and near Durban in South Africa.

North-west Cloud Bands

Cold frontal troughs sometimes stretch across the subtropical highs in the southern hemisphere to connect to the ITCZ. In this case, the band of clouds associated with a cold front continues north-westward towards low latitudes, to form a *north-west cloud band*. These mainly upper-level clouds are due to uplift into divergence in the subtropical jet (Note 12.L). They are usually found either (a) in the south-west Pacific at the SPCZ (Section 12.1), (b) across south-east Brazil, (c) across Madagascar, or (d) across Australia (as in Figure 13.5). They may bring rain in the desert.

Frontal Movement

About a hundred cold fronts track along the southern coasts of South Africa and Australia annually, i.e. about two a week on average. Most derive from low pressures at about 60°S, extending into the troughs between subtropical highs (Figure 12.1 and Figure 12.7), as in Figure 13.1 for a particular day. They are typically oriented north-west–south-east and tend to move eastward at about 10 m/s (**Figure 13.7**), i.e. at about the same speed as the mid-

Figure 13.5 The correspondence of cloud seen from a satellite and the position of a front, both at noon GMT on 8 November 1995. The dashed line indicates the position of a prefrontal trough (Figure 13.2).

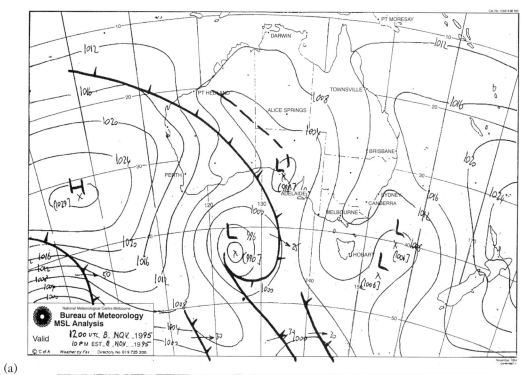

(a)

(b)

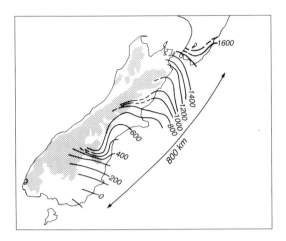

Figure 13.6 The position of the front of the Southerly Change that traversed the south island of New Zealand on 2 February 1988. The lines are *isochrones* showing the boundary of the cold air at the given times of day.

latitude westerlies in the middle troposphere (Figure 12.10). These winds are weaker nearer the equator, so the northern end of a front lags behind the southern end. The northern end

may extend well towards the equator, especially in winter. For instance, there is a cold front through Mt Isa (at 20°S in Queensland) several times a year in the form of a shallow wedge of cooler air, travelling as a density current (Note 8.C) through the PBL. Ripples form at night as the front ploughs through the stable air, and they can run ahead on top of the PBL to create a Morning Glory in the Gulf of Carpentaria (Note 8.L).

Cold fronts in South America can travel as far as 5°S in the lee of the Andes (**Figure 13.8**). Such an incursion of polar air, known as a *friagem*, can greatly harm Brazil's coffee crop (Section 3.6).

Warm Fronts

A warm front occurs where warm air advances on colder, as may be seen in Figure 12.12 in the places where warm northerly winds strike the polar front. Such a front is drawn on a weather chart as a line with half circles (Figure 13.2). A section across a warm front is similar to that

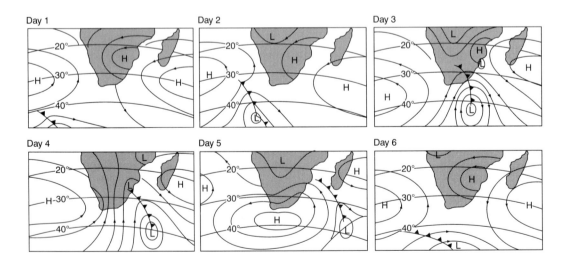

Figure 13.7 The daily shift of fronts across South Africa. (The contours do not match across the coastline because the MSLP is shown over the oceans and the 850 hPa height over southern Africa.)

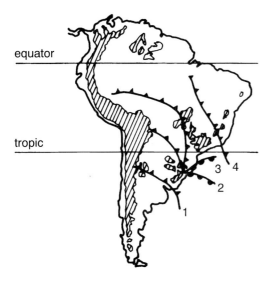

Figure 13.8 The progress of a cold front northwards over South America on successive days.

through a cold front (Figure 13.3), except that the lighter warm air moves over a retreating wedge of cold air. Warm frontal zones are even less steep than in the case of cold fronts, so the front is less evident and uplift more gradual. As a result, the first cirrus clouds may be 1,000 km ahead of the front at the surface. Commonly, the clouds gradually thicken and slowly obscure the Sun, the cloud base lowers, and eventually light rain falls.

A warm front typically advances clockwise down to the south and lies at 45–55°S, where there is little land, so they are encountered infrequently. One place where they are found is Patagonia, to the east of the southern Andes, where they occur in winter after a calm period has allowed a cold air mass to accumulate in the lee. This is called *cold air damming*, as the Andes block the inflow of warmer air from the west. A subsequent disturbance from the west drives warmer air from the north over the dammed air, with a warm front between the two air masses. Cold air damming also occurs on the south-east side of New Zealand's southern mountain range in winter, when warmer mT air from the north-west flows over colder, heavier mP air, deposited there a few days earlier and locked behind the mountains.

Occluded Fronts

More common is an *occluded front*, where cold and warm fronts overlap, so that the lower-level cold front shuts off (i.e. 'occludes') the upper warm front. This situation is illustrated in **Figure 13.9**. It is triggered by a poleward kink in the roughly east–west polar front (Figure 12.12), the boundary between a relatively warm northwesterly moving at 7 m/s, say, on the equatorward side, and colder southwesterlies on the poleward side blowing at 13 m/s, for instance (Section 12.3). The two differing air masses ruffle each other, amplifying the kink. The Bergen School explained what happens next by regarding the kink, in effect, as the pivot of scissors, with an advancing cold front as the curved blade to the west, and a slower warm front also swinging clockwise to the east of the kink. The faster cold front catches up on the warm front, closing the scissors, and then overtakes it, as shown in the cross-section AB in Figure 13.9. The occluded front lies at point C. The depth of warm air, i.e. of lightweight air, is shown as greatest above that point, so the surface pressure is lowest there in this cross-section.

An occluded front involves a tongue of relatively warm, moist air lifted on both sides by cold air (Figure 13.9), with heavy rainfalls nearby as the warm, moist air rises. There is eventually a mixing of the warm and cold air masses, which diffuses the temperature difference across the polar front locally and therefore the fronts. Dissipation is complete some four to seven days after the original kink. The regularity of this pattern of events makes midlatitude weather usefully predictable over a period of a few days (Chapter 15).

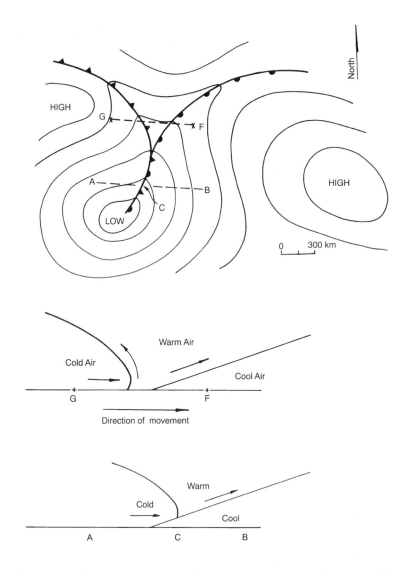

Figure 13.9 The pattern of fronts in the southern hemisphere at the stage of occlusion. The top diagram is a plan view of surface pressures, showing a cold front on the left overtaking the warm front on the right, and increasingly overlapping at the bottom, as shown in the cross-sections below.

Fronts and Jet Streams

It is hard to exaggerate the importance of that account by the Bergen School of the evolution of a *frontal disturbance* from a trivial kink in the polar front to an occluded front. Nevertheless, we now know about Rossby waves, jet streams and the complex nature of fronts (Figure 13.4) and realise their significance in the growth and decline of midlatitude cyclones (Note 12.L). Surface and upper-level winds are now thought of as separate but interacting closely, and we regard the growth of a kink in the polar front as due to the waviness of the upper westerlies.

This occasionally causes an eastward jet stream to lunge towards the equator and back, thereby making it move clockwise (in the southern hemisphere), as shown in Figure 12.15. Such cyclonic rotation implies an upper-level trough of low pressure, since a reciprocal association between rotation and pressure is implied in Buys-Ballot's Rule (Section 12.2). At the same time, cold air at the surface is advected towards the equator behind a cold front, and there is warm advection towards the pole ahead of the wave. (This is explained in **Note 13.B**.) Detailed consideration then shows that the effect of these cold and warm flows is to amplify the wave, which deepens the low pressure at the surface and shifts its centre, until eventually it is below the upper-level trough. Then the trough's convergence prevents uplift from the surface low, so that the latter is filled by surface convergence and consequently disappears, restoring the *status quo*.

Comments

Unfortunately, our attempt to clarify the complexity of the polar front results in too tidy a picture. The reality on any particular day is more complicated, as shown in Figure 13.5 and **Figure 13.10**. Every front is different, and few frontal disturbances develop exactly

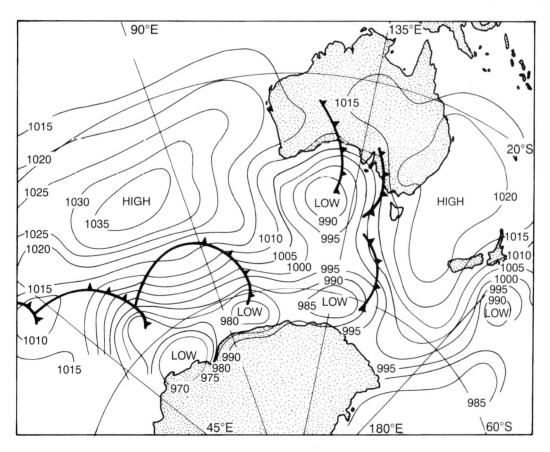

Figure 13.10 The pattern of pressures (hPa), lows, highs and fronts south of Australia on 28 July 1963.

as shown in the ideal cases discussed so far. Also, emphasis on fronts is vulnerable to the weaknesses of the related air mass concept (Section 13.2), and critics point to the subjectiveness of drawing fronts on maps, so that various meteorologists sometimes have different ideas about where to draw them. There are no fronts involved in modern numerical modelling of the atmosphere on computer for weather forecasting (Chapter 15). They are replaced by bands where the horizontal gradient of temperature happens to be steep – which is the reality.

13.4 LOWS

A *low* (or *depression*) is a pattern of reduced pressure, leading to rings of isobars about the point of lowest pressure. The circular pattern was recognised by Heinrich Dove in 1828 and led to the name '*cyclone*', which comes from the Greek for a coiled snake.

We will discuss various kinds of low in this section, at the risk of seeming to imply that they are distinct bodies of air. They are not. Air masses and winds are real, but a low is simply part of a pattern. The movement of a low in the atmosphere is like a ripple across a wheatfield: the wheat does not shift position, except temporarily. As a low moves within the westerly winds, its rotation drives air ahead towards the pole, air behind in the direction of the equator, it accelerates air on the equator-ward side and slows it down on the poleward side.

Lows occur at any level. For instance, they occur automatically within a clockwise meander in winds at 300 hPa level in the southern hemisphere (Figure 12.15). Any low, aloft or near the surface, becomes a *cut-off low* once the meander has become so extreme that the rotation forms a complete whirl.

Here we are primarily concerned with *surface* lows, i.e. minima in the MSLP pattern. They are caused by a reduced weight of air above

(Note 1.G), usually because of warmth. There are several possible arrangements:

1 There is warm air just above the surface in the case of *heat lows*. These form within cT air masses over the southern continents in summer, and remain almost stationary over the hot land. They are more shallow and are weaker than midlatitude lows, i.e. the lowering of pressure below normal is relatively slight. Heat lows are not associated with any front or with a jet stream aloft. Typically the tropopause above them is as high as 16 km, and flat.

There are often two distinct heat lows over northern Australia in summer, helping form part of the ITCZ and driving moist air and monsoonal rains inland from the Timor Sea, lying to the north (Section 12.1). The heat lows are, respectively, the *Cloncurry low* over Queensland and the *Pilbara low* at about 22°S in West Australia (**Figure 13.11**). The Pilbara low directs hot dry winds from inland towards south-west Australia, which is why Perth experiences hot arid summers. The lows may either weaken or amplify, and they move around, depending on the tracks of fronts to the south and tropical cyclones to the north, but their preferred positions can be seen in the December diagram of Figure 13.11. They are generally connected together into a single elongated trough across northern Australia. Sometimes it extends along the west coast of Australia, bringing extremely hot easterlies towards Perth, exceeding 40°C on occasion. Troughs of this kind are not found along the west coasts of Southern Africa and South America.

2 A frontal disturbance produces a deep low in its mature stage, normally between 45–60°S. Such *frontal lows* (or *extra-tropical lows*) are unusually deep in the southern hemisphere (Figure 1.8) and result from a lowering of the tropopause and consequent raising of the air column's average temperature (Note 13.B).

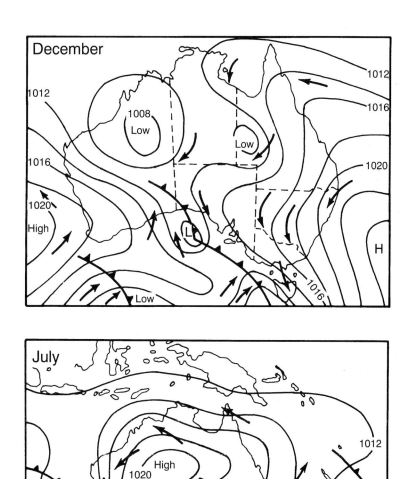

Figure 13.11 Pressure patterns (and hence winds) for Australia in December (summer) and July (winter), showing heat lows in the north in summer and a high over the continent in winter. A complex frontal disturbance affects south-east Australia in the July chart. The low in the Great Bight in December is unusual: a high there is more common.

3 *Polar lows* or 'comma' lows, are like frontal lows except for being much more shallow, with little cyclonic circulation above 500 hPa so that there is no interaction with any jet stream. They result from the temperature difference across the Antarctic front and the strong surface winds at high latitudes. They often occur in the Southern Ocean, especially within an outbreak north of cold air, in the wake of a major frontal low.

4 *Subtropical lows* between 25–40°S are due to a combination of warm air throughout the troposphere and a weak depression at the tropopause (**Note 13.C**). Such lows are far less common than frontal lows but cause most floods between 25–40°S. They often form beneath the poleward part of an unusually wide swing of the subtropical jet (Section 12.5), and may occur along the east coasts of the southern continents, in which case they are called *east coast lows*. A subtropical low lingers a day or more, under a cut-off low at 300 hPa level, while *frontal* lows at the surface always move along with the short-waves in the jet stream.

5 An *orographic low* occurs in the shelter of a mountain range, partly as a result of the warming due to subsidence of the wind on the lee, and partly because of the conservation of vorticity (**Note 13.D**). An example is a depression by as much as 4 hPa on the south-east coast of South Africa, offshore from the 1,200 m escarpment, whenever north-westerly winds blow towards the sea. Such an orographic low (or *coastal low*) and its resulting cyclonic circulation hardly extend above the escarpment, but the onshore winds on the equatorward side of the low may produce light rain, as happens in Durban a few times a month in winter. The low also brings great temperature changes, firstly due to the subsiding north-westerly winds, bringing warm, dry air to Durban (Day 2 in Figure 13.7), then cool cloudy weather as the orographic low moves eastward up the coast (Day 3). This is often followed by even cooler south-westerly winds, due to the passage of the cold front (Day 4), which was the cause of the north-westerly winds in the first place.

Similarly, a north-westerly wind often creates troughs along the south-east coast of New Zealand.

6 Warm air extends right through the troposphere in a tropical cyclone, creating an intense low (Section 13.5).

Rapid Cyclogenesis

'Cyclogenesis' means the formation of a low, which sometimes happens rapidly, e.g. a decrease of pressure by more than 24 hPa in a day. In this case, the resulting low is called a *bomb* which brings destructive winds and heavy rains. Some frontal lows and east-coast lows become bombs. They appear at an early stage as a triangle of cloud on satellite images (Section 12.5), which gradually deforms into an inverted comma shape (Figure 13.5).

Factors causing rapid cyclogenesis include the following:

1 upper-level divergence due to the coincidence of a Rossby wave trough and a jet streak (Note 12.L),
2 a low-level region of steep temperature gradient, i.e. a baroclinic zone (Note 12.H),
3 a warm, moist air mass ahead of this zone, and
4 an orographic low.

Some bombs attain the intensity of a tropical cyclone.

13.5 TROPICAL CYCLONES

A *tropical cyclone* is an especially intense low-pressure system at low latitudes, away from any front, including a ring of particularly strong winds around the centre. Tropical cyclones

(TCs) are called *hurricanes* or *typhoons* in the west Atlantic or north-west Pacific, respectively. The man in the street commonly calls them simply 'cyclones', but this is wrong because they differ from the cyclones discussed in Section 13.4, which are larger, weaker and encountered only at higher latitudes. Also, TCs are individually named (**Note 13.E**).

Description

A TC is a circular system, whose cross-section is shown schematically in **Figure 13.12**. There is a central *eye* of cloudless, calm, warm air, first described by the pirate William Dampier in 1687 when exploring parts of the Pacific. The eye is typically 25 km in diameter, but can be half or twice that. Around it is a wall of strong winds, rotating cyclonically, i.e. clockwise in the southern hemisphere. The air inside the eye is subsiding, and that is why it is cloudless, calm and warm. That is surrounded by a wall of cloud within a raging vortex of updraught. This in turn is encompassed by weaker updraughts further from the eye, creating spirals of convective rainclouds, easily seen in satellite photographs. Between the eye wall and the central subsidence there is a thin cylinder of descending air cooled by evaporation from the wall. This cooled air becomes entrained into the ascending wall near sea-level (Figure 13.12).

The updraught in the eye-wall is fed by a clockwise (i.e. cyclonic) spiralling inflow at sea-level, felt over a radius of up to 1,000 km. On

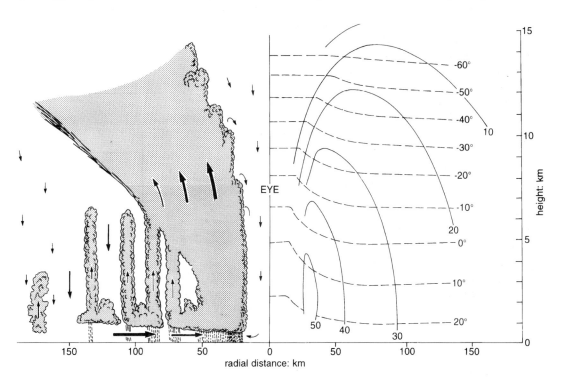

Figure 13.12 Radial cross-section of an idealised tropical cyclone. The solid lines to the right of the diagram are isotachs (m/s) showing the primary cyclonic circulation *around* the eye. The dashed lines on the right are isotherms (°C). The secondary, vertical circulation is shown on the left, with radial flow aloft and subsidence in the surrounding environment.

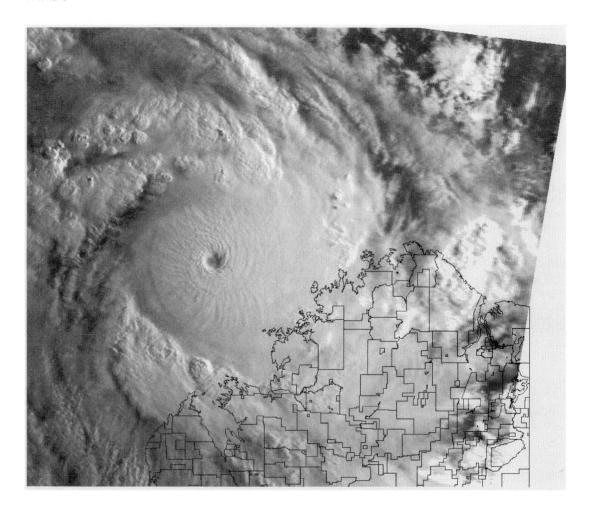

Plate 13.1 Tropical cyclone Chloe viewed from above, when located off the north-west coast of Australia, in the Kimberley region. The photograph was taken from the NOAA-12 satellite at 7.19 a.m. local time on 7 April 1995. Notice the eye of the cyclone, and the swirl of cloud from it in the upper troposphere. The distance across the solid disk of cloud around the eye is about 300 km.

the other hand, convective rainclouds extend only 500 km or less, and winds of 10–20 m/s up to about 200 km from the eye. The updraught is surmounted by an anticyclonic outflow of cirrus near the tropopause, which itself is lifted by the force of the updraughts to as much as 18 km.

Warming in the eye by subsidence from near the tropopause leads to a tall column of low-density air, and hence a very low sea-level pressure, e.g. below 950 hPa in severe cyclones. The record minimum in the Australian region is 914 hPa, measured in 1899, whilst a global record of 876 hPa was observed in the north-west Pacific in 1975. So the sea-level pressure may fall by 50 hPa in eight hours as a TC approaches.

The steep horizontal gradients of sea-level

pressure imply strong surface winds (Section 12.2; **Note 13.F**). In fact, TCs are conventionally distinguished from tropical storms by wind speeds above 25 m/s for at least ten minutes (**Table 13.2**). A rough rule is that a central pressure of 950 hPa means winds up to 39 m/s at 30°S, 46 m/s at 20°S and 56 m/s at 10°S (Note 13.F).

An analysis of TCs affecting Fiji shows that the wall of the eye characteristically involves gusts in excess of 44 m/s. The highest gust recorded at the surface in the Australian region was 69 m/s (i.e. 250 km/h) but there are even higher speeds at about 2 km elevation within the eyewall.

The energy for these winds comes from the surface of the warm ocean, collected directly as sensible heat and as latent heat in the rapid evaporation that the high speed of the surface winds induces. This heat is released in the condensation caused by the adiabatic expansion of surface air entering the central zone of low pressure, and then the consequent warming and convection within the eyewall powers the immense updraught. That lifts the heat to the upper limb of the Hadley cell, where it is exported to higher latitudes (Figure 12.16). This export of heat is important in limiting temperatures near the equator.

Formation

A TC has a life of several days, from the time of the first evidence of a centre of intense low pressure until its disappearance. Typically, formation takes 2–3 days while the core is still cool, then 1–2 days while the core warms and the central pressure falls, followed by a few days of maximum intensity, with extension of the cyclone's radius, and finally a dying away over one day or more. Factors which promote TC formation are the following:

(a) There must be sufficient Coriolis effect to deflect winds to the left (in the southern hemisphere), so that they rotate clockwise around a low (Figure 12.9; Note 13.F). This requires a latitude of more than about 5 degrees from the equator (**Figure 13.13**)

(b) TCs form over the sea where the SST is high. Comparison of Figure 11.2 and Figure 13.13 shows that at least 27°C is necessary, which occurs only at latitudes below about 20°S (or 30°N) and mainly in the summer hemisphere, i.e. January and February in the vicinity of Australia and Madagascar. They arise over the west of the oceans, where surface temperatures are highest (Figure 11.2), after the currents of the great gyres have traversed the equator

Table 13.2 Classification of tropical-cyclone severity

Class	Central pressure (hPa)	Max. sustained wind* (m/s)	Storm surge† (m)	Damage
1‡	>990	18–25	< 1.0	Minor
2	990–966	25–35	1.0–2.4	Moderate
3§	966–940	35–46	2.4–3.8	Extensive
4	940–890	46–63	3.8–7.0	Extreme
5	< 890	> 63	> 7.0	Catastrophic

* Winds are here measured over ten minutes or more at 10 m height
† The raising of the sea-level above normal, taking tides into account. The figures are only indicative for a straight coastline, and may be quite different elsewhere.
‡ Class 1 concerns tropical storms. An estimated 60 per cent of them later develop tropical-cyclone intensity.
§ Less than half of TCs are in Class 3 or higher

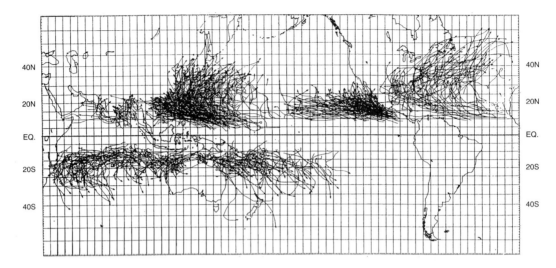

Figure 13.13   Tracks of tropical cyclones with winds above 17.4 m/s during the period 1979–88.

(Figure 11.15). Less than a third of TCs develop in the southern hemisphere, where the summers are about 2 K cooler than in the northern hemisphere (Section 3.2), and where SSTs above 20° latitude tend to be lower (Figure 11.2). The most common source in the south is just east of northern Madagascar. They do not form over land, for lack of moisture to provide latent heat.

The frequency of TCs might be affected by any future rise of SSTs (**Note 13.G**). Years with many TCs onto Australia have been preceded by high SST around the north coast, e.g. three tropical cyclones during a year with local SSTs 0.6 K less than normal, but seventeen in a year with SSTs 1.0 K above normal.

(c) The mid-troposphere has to be moist and conditionally unstable, without any PBL inversion to prevent warm and moist surface air from mixing with the mid-troposphere. Such conditions prevail at the western end of the equatorial segment of the gyres and quasi-permanent anticyclones (Figure 12.1). Herein lies the explanation for the absence of TCs over the South Atlantic, even though there is an area east of Brazil where the sea-surface temperature exceeds 27°C in March; there is insufficient space between Africa and South America for creating a moist, conditionally unstable troposphere, and there is the Trade-wind inversion extending from south-west Africa to Brazil (Figure 7.10).

(d) The troposphere has to be free of strong wind shear vertically, e.g. no more than 10 m/s difference between winds at 2 km and 12 km. Otherwise there is rupturing of the updraughts within any incipient TC.

(e) The stratospheric jet stream is preferably in a weak phase of the Quasi-Biennial Oscillation (Section 12.3). It has been observed that TCs are less frequent and less intense during the strong phase, presumably because the stronger easterlies shear off the top of any updraught column, preventing its full development.

(f) There has to be a tropical depression as a trigger, usually a trough in the Trade winds as part of an *easterly wave* (**Note 13.H**). Convergence occurs in the trough of this wave, leading to uplift which deepens the

PBL and erodes the Trade-wind inversion (Section 7.6), so that convective updraughts can penetrate the entire troposphere. The resulting latent heating may reduce the surface pressure further, which produces even more cyclonic rotation and convergence.

Mature Stage

The tracks of tropical cyclones are shown in Figure 13.13. Their movements are irregular and difficult to predict, especially within 15° of the equator. Generally they move with the average wind of the troposphere, i.e. westward north of about 15°S, and eastward south of that latitude (Figure 12.10 and **Figure 13.14**). Alternatively, they may loop, meander or stall. They usually move away from the equator, come under the influence of the midlatitude westerlies and then accelerate eastwards to about 15 m/s, before decaying over cooler waters. As a result, most of the tropical cyclones affecting Fiji (18°S) come from the north-west, like that shown in Figure 13.14.

The passage of a TC leaves the SST lowered by as much as 3 K in a swath about 100 km wide. This cooling is partly due to the transfer of heat to the atmosphere within the TC, and partly to upwelling induced by the TC, since the circling winds create Ekman transport of the ocean surface outwards from the cyclone. Consequently, a stationary TC automatically dies away, by lowering the SST below the critical 27°C.

The chances of encountering tropical cyclones are about equal on the two sides of Australia, the greatest likelihood being around 20°S. The part of the coast most frequently crossed by cyclones is a stretch of 100 km around Cairns at 17°S in Queensland, with fifteen making landfall there over seventy-one years, i.e. one each five years on average. In the South Pacific as a whole, TC frequency peaks within the South Pacific Convergence Zone (Section 12.1), which is a spur from the ITCZ, stretching from the Coral Sea (to the north-east of Australia) to the Tropic of Capricorn at 160°W, near New Caledonia. There has been a TC nearly every year (i.e. fifteen in twenty years) within a 200 km square just west of Fiji, at about 18°S, 170°E.

Tropical cyclones happen more often (especially in the central Pacific and between 5–15°S) during an ENSO warm phase, when the Southern Oscillation Index (Section 12.7) is low (**Figure 13.15**). But there are fewer tropical cyclones in the *south-west* Pacific area (including Australia). This is because tropical depressions that otherwise would have developed into cyclones in the west have already formed TCs further east because of the higher SST there, and these mature and recurve towards the south-east before reaching Australia.

Decaying Stage

A tropical cyclone decays for several reasons:

(a) it moves inland, where the cyclone's inflow is no longer made humid by the surface, and surface friction is greater than over the sea,

(b) it moves to an area of the sea which is too cool,

(c) the TC remains stationary, steadily cooling the sea beneath, until it is too cold to supply the required heat,

(d) it shifts to higher latitudes, where the ground's vorticity is greater (Note 12.K), reducing the cyclone's spin relative to the ground,

(e) the upper divergence (which sucks the central core upwards) becomes detached by the tug of upper winds, allowing upper westerlies to encroach into the system.

Attempts have been made to use cloud seeding to promote the decay of tropical cyclones which threaten coastal areas (Note 9.E). For instance, seeding outside the radius of strong winds might encourage cloud growth and deep

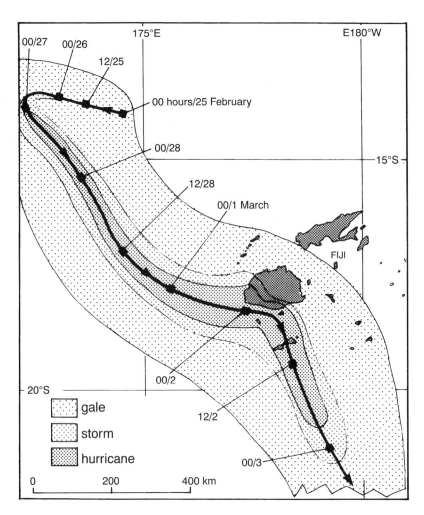

Figure 13.14 The track of tropical cyclone Oscar in February 1983, showing the areas near Fiji swept by storm winds, gale-force winds and hurricane winds, respectively.

convection there. The latent heat thus released at the periphery of the tropical cyclone would lessen that in the eyewall, and hence weaken its updraught. Unfortunately, this does not seem to work.

Damage

Tropical cyclones bring so much damage from strong winds, flooding rains and 'storm surge' of the ocean surface that they have to be care- fully tracked by means of satellite pictures, radar, weather stations, buoys and reconnaissance flights, to enable adequate warning of the TC's approach. The power of a wind at 50 m/s is a thousand times that of a more normal 5 m/s, creating huge waves at sea. Winds are strongest on the left side of the eye, where the cyclonic winds around the eye are augmented by the speed of advance of the eye itself. There is great danger to small boats in the left-forward quarter, where the circling winds

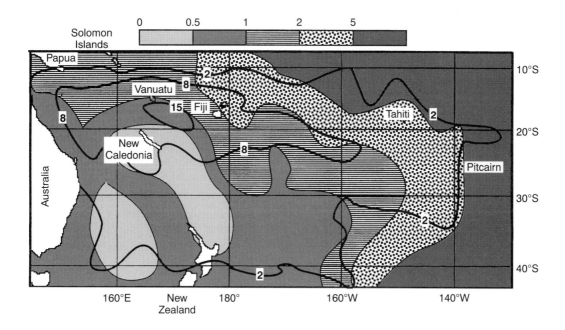

Figure 13.15 The frequency of tropical cyclones and the effect of an El Niño. The dashed lines show the annual number through each 2 × 2 degree box of latitude and longitude during the period 1969–89, e.g. over ten a year around Fiji. The shading shows the probability of a tropical cyclone during El Niño events (when the SOI exceeds zero), as a fraction of what is normal. For instance, a tropical cyclone is about four times more likely to strike Tahiti in an El Niño year.

blow the craft into the path of worse conditions. Sometimes tornadoes form in this quarter, within the spiralling rainbands (Figure 13.12).

The winds were responsible for the destruction of Darwin in Australia's Northern Territory on Christmas Day in 1974, with the loss of fifty-five lives and a billion dollars' worth of damage.

Rains due to TCs can be heavy, particularly as the hurricane crosses the coast, where the greater friction of land surfaces causes deceleration and hence increased local convergence and updraught. For instance, a TC affecting Mackay (a port at 21°S) caused precipitation of 1,400 mm within 72 hours. The effects are also felt inland and over a wide area, so that there is considerable flooding of rivers (Section 10.6 and Note 10.Q). About a quarter of a million people drowned in such floods in Bangladesh in

1970, for instance. Precipitation of 750 mm fell in one day on Whim Creek (21°S in Western Australia), which received only 4 mm in the whole of 1924. Even TCs well to the north of New Zealand bring heavy rains to parts of the north island in late summer and autumn, though less if the TC passes quickly.

A *storm surge* is the coastal wave of high seas created by an offshore TC. The suction of the central low pressure lifts the sea's surface by about a centimetre for each lowering by a hectopascal, e.g. by 0.5 m in a typical cyclone. But strong onshore winds can heap shallow seas onto a beach by several metres (Table 13.2), according to the slope and shape of the shore. For instance, by 2.8 m when Althea struck Townsville (19°S) in 1971. Such surges flood low-lying coastal land if the TC's landfall coincides with the time of high tide.

The authorities broadcast a 'tropical cyclone advisory' warning when conditions favour the development of a cyclone within 800 km of the Australian coast, and a 'cyclone warning' when the TC is confirmed and named. These are widely broadcast and posted on the Internet. Despite this, it is estimated that TCs globally have caused almost 15,000 deaths each year, or far more if storm surges are included (Table 10.5).

13.6 HIGHS

Centres or ridges of high pressure at the surface imply a relatively cold atmosphere (Note 1.G) and regions with subsiding air. So they tend to be found over continents in winter, when the land is colder than the surrounding seas. Thus, a large anticyclone sits over Siberia every winter (Figure 3.4 and Figure 12.1) and a pressure has been measured there equivalent to a record MSLP of 1,084 hPa (Section 1.5). This is a *cold high*. There is one permanently over Antarctica. Also, there tends to be one over southeast Australia in winter, whereas highs are located south of the continent in summer, when it is the sea that is colder (Figure 13.11 and **Figure 13.16**)

Cold highs are shallow and often stationary, although a mobile cold high follows any mid-latitude frontal disturbance (Note 13.B), forming below the equatorward part of the jet stream, where upper-level convergence takes place (Note 12.L).

Another type is the *subtropical high* (or *warm anticyclone*) due to cold air at the tropopause, not near the surface. In this case, the tropopause is higher than usual, i.e. colder, so there is cold air even above the 300 hPa level. In other words, subtropical highs are associated with a high or ridge at that level, as well as at sea-level, unlike the situation with cold highs, which occur below an upper-level *trough*.

A ring of highs lies around the southern hemisphere at 30–35°S (Figure 12.1), resulting

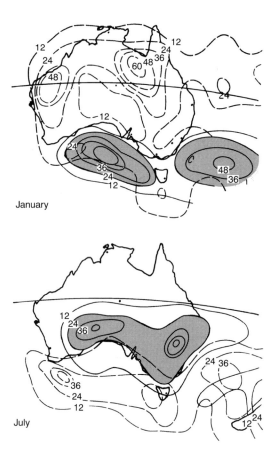

Figure 13.16 The positions of highs and lows in summer and winter around Australia. The continuous lines show the number of hours in a month when a high's centre is within the indicated 5–degree square, i.e. the *anticyclonicity* of the region. The dashed lines show the corresponding *cyclonicity* (Section 13.4). There is a high centred for more than 24 hours each month in the areas shown shaded.

in an average pressure at that latitude higher than elsewhere (Figure 1.8). The precise latitude of these subtropical highs corresponds to the subsiding part of the Hadley cell, so it alters in response to the seasonal shift of the ITCZ (Figure 12.11), but only over 5–10 degrees. On average, highs cross the east coast of Australia south of Sydney in summer (Figure 13.16), so that the anticlockwise rotation of winds brings easterly maritime breezes in that season, whereas dry westerly winds prevail in winter when the centres of highs pass further north.

Subtropical highs tend to lie over the oceans between the southern continents, especially in summer, when there are heat lows over the continents. One subtropical high is anchored over the eastern Pacific by an anticyclonic swirl induced by the Andes when they deflect westerly winds north (Figure 12.1). The centre of this South Pacific high shifts from 32°S in January to 23°S in July, in response to the Sun's declination (Section 2.2). The high is particularly strong because of the cold ocean surface (Figure 11.2), except during an El Niño, when it is weaker and displaced to the south. Another semi-permanent high lies over the Indian ocean, moving nearer Australia in summer and towards Africa in winter.

Highs are usually elliptic in shape, with a zonal diameter of 2,000–4,000 km and a meridional diameter of 1,000–2,000 km. In other words, they tend to be larger than lows. Therefore they involve smaller pressure gradients, so that winds are lighter, with calm conditions at the centre of any high (Note 12.D).

The belt of subtropical highs is intersected by cold fronts, located in troughs which connect to frontal lows to the south. As a result, it appears that the highs themselves are moving eastward at the same speed as the frontal disturbances. One study showed that sixteen large highs with central pressures over 1,024 hPa travelled at about 30 km/h (the range being 6–72 km/h) across Australia, whilst fifteen smaller, less intense highs moved at about 50 km/h. They tend to move more slowly in winter than summer. A typical speed of 40 km/h, and an east–west dimension of 4,000 km, implies that they pass across in four days if they keep moving.

Blocking

An anticyclone sometimes moves south (e.g. to 45°S) and becomes a *blocking high*. This means that its movement is stalled, and it travels less than 20 degrees of longitude in a week. Its place at normal latitudes is taken by a subtropical low. Blocking is connected with a parting of polar and subtropical jet streams (Section 12.5; Note 12.L), which appears to be associated with either instability in the flow of upper winds or patches of unusually warm sea.

Blocking in the southern hemisphere is only half as common as in the northern, where there are larger land masses and more mountain ranges to disturb patterns of windflow. A blocking event may last a few days or a few weeks. During that time, oncoming cold fronts are deflected to the south.

Features of northern hemisphere weather, including blocking, are discussed in Notes 13.I and 13.J.

Effects

Highs (or ridges) at the surface imply subsidence at a few hundred metres a day, or less. This slow rate allows warming due to subsidence to be offset by cooling by radiation loss and by the evaporation of clouds. Also, the subsidence leads to an inversion on top of the boundary layer at about 1,000 m or so (i.e. a PBL inversion, Section 7.6), especially with cold highs in winter over continents. Where there is low-level moisture and air pollution it is trapped by the inversion, which leads to the sky becoming covered by persistent stratus cloud and thus to *anticyclonic gloom*. This occurs in Melbourne and Santiago in winter, for instance.

Generally, the subsidence characteristic of a subtropical high makes cloud and precipitation unlikely, yet it can occur in two ways. Firstly, the slight lowering of MSLP within a shallow trough moving across a subtropical high may be sufficient to trigger thunderstorms, especially in summer. Secondly, a turning of winds to become southerly or south-easterly, after the passage of a trough across a high, can induce light rain or drizzle along a coast facing south-east, even though the atmosphere is stable and subsiding. The rain is the result of coastal uplift and happens along south-east coasts of Brazil, South America and Australia, where it is an important source of rain in winter for places sheltered from westerly frontal rain by mountains. The case of Durban on the south-east coast of South Africa is shown on Figure 13.7 (Day 5).

Arid climates result from a prevalence of highs, as in the subtropics (Figure 10.3b). North-east Brazil is arid, even at a latitude of only 8°S or so, because it protrudes far enough into the south Atlantic to be dominated by the high there. The same is true for the Galapagos Islands, dominated by the South Pacific high, even though they are at the equator. Droughts in midlatitudes are caused by a prevalence of highs, sometimes blocking highs, which deflect rain-bearing lows poleward.

Thus we end our consideration of the aspects of winds of the scale important in weather forecasting. These form the background to surface winds actually experienced at particular sites, discussed in Chapter 14.

NOTES

13.A Scales of winds
13.B Frontal disturbances
13.C Subtropical lows
13.D Vortex spreading and stretching
13.E Naming of tropical cyclones
13.F Winds around a tropical cyclone
13.G Global warming and tropical cyclones
13.H Easterly waves
13.I The Coriolis effect in the northern hemisphere
13.J Weather in the northern hemisphere compared with that in the south

14

LOCAL WINDS

14.1 GENERAL

The general circulation (Chapter 12) is the sum of the synoptic-scale winds (Chapter 13), averaged over space and time, and these in turn contain local surface winds, which are the topic of this chapter. The flow of these local winds around surface irregularities generates swirls which eventually cause frictional heat, i.e. increased vibration of the air molecules. So there is a chain of descending scale and increasing irregularity of motion, as the Sun's radiation (which fundamentally energises all the various circulations) degenerates to the least useful form of power: low-temperature heat.

There are four main factors which create a surface wind. They are (i) the synoptic-scale wind, which is usually close to the gradient wind (Note 12.D) in speed and direction, (ii) a horizontal difference of temperature in the PBL (Section 14.2), (iii) the topography, which makes cold air flow downhill and warm air upwards (Section 14.3), and (iv) storms, especially thunderstorms. If none of these operates, the air is 'calm', i.e. it has a speed below 1.5 m/s (5.4 km/h) and standard anemometers become less accurate.

Wind Profile

Synoptic-scale winds are those blowing at least 1 km from the ground, above the PBL (Section 12.2) and beyond the influence of the ground's irregularities. They equal the local gradient winds if there is no acceleration or slowing up, so we will call them 'quasi-gradient winds'. They drag surface air along by transferring energy downwards through turbulent *eddies*, which are circulations in all directions including the vertical, lasting for seconds or minutes. They are smaller in scale closer to the ground. Strong winds and atmospheric instability increase their intensity. The descending part of an eddy carries brisk quasi-gradient air downwards, to replace low-momentum surface air in the rising part, previously slowed by friction with the ground. In this way, eddies transfer momentum downwards into the PBL, creating average speeds at each level which vary logarithmically with height from the ground (**Note 14.A**).

The fact of lower wind speeds close to the ground's friction is illustrated by birds flying over a wide beach or the sea; those flying against the wind skim the surface, whilst birds going with the wind fly many metres above. A practical consequence is that comparing winds at different places requires measurements at a standard height, e.g. 10 m, else it is necessary to adjust measurements to the 10-metre equivalent. Also, the strong vertical wind shear near the ground explains why shouted messages carry further downwind than upwind; the wind profile bends sound waves from downwind down to the listener on the ground, focusing them, whereas upwind sound is deflected overhead (Note 7.M).

The downward sharing of a gradient-wind's energy is prevented by any inversion layer, since an inversion inhibits vertical movement. Therefore, a ground inversion (Section 7.6) decouples the gradient wind from the surface air, which releases the upper wind from the braking effect of the ground's friction. Hence, for instance, the average 1,000 m wind at Sydney in winter is 7.5 m/s at 3 p.m., but 9 m/s at 3 a.m. On the other hand, detachment from the driving force of the gradient wind is associated with the calm conditions at the surface at night (**Figure 14.1**).

A rough surface creates eddying within the atmosphere, on a scale proportional to the roughness. It increases the frictional retardation and spreads it over a greater depth (**Figure 14.2**), according to the wind speed. The increase of wind with height extends to 200 m if the wind is light, but 1,500 m if it is strong. Speeds measured near the relatively smooth surface at sea are about 65 per cent of the quasi-gradient wind's speed, while surface winds over rough ground are less than 50 per cent. These percentages are greater when either the atmosphere is unstable, the gradient wind light or the latitude high. In each case, the surface friction makes the surface wind flow more directly towards the low-pressure region than the gradient wind does (Figure 12.9c).

Of course, it makes little sense to think of average wind profiles between the tall buildings of a city, where the eddies are not transient or mobile but locked to particular buildings, so that some places are sheltered and others subject to funnelled winds. The same would apply to any extremely rough surface.

Measurement

There are several kinds of *anemometer* for measuring the surface wind. **Figure 14.3** shows a simple device used by dinghy sailors, and at some weather stations. The cup anemometer has been commonly used since its invention in 1846; cups on each of three radial arms from a vertical axis are driven by the wind, and their rotations are counted. The number of rotations multiplied by the distance around the cups' circle is proportional to the *wind run*, the distance that a parcel of air would travel. International agreement in 1956 fixed the *knot* as the unit of wind speed, though subsequent metrication of units leads to the use of kilometres per hour or, preferably, metres per second (Note 1.J).

Alternatively, one can use a landlubber's version of the Beaufort Scale, devised in 1896 by a

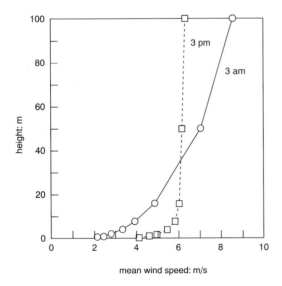

Figure 14.1 The effect of a nocturnal ground inversion on wind-speed profiles.

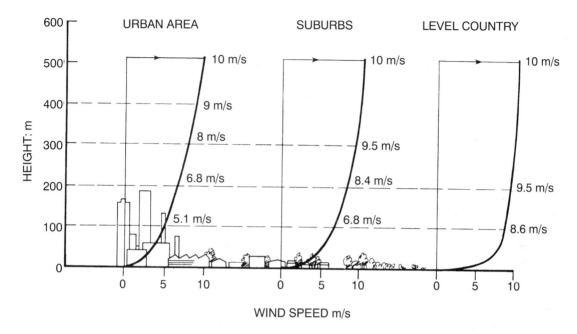

Figure 14.2 The effect of various degrees of surface roughness on the wind-speed profile.

British admiral to determine wind speed from the appearance of waves at sea (**Table 14.1**). (It is hard to measure the wind speed from a small boat at sea, because of its rocking and the eddies caused by the superstructure.) Beaufort scale 4 (a moderate breeze) is enough to make a dinghy 'plane', while 8 on the Beaufort scale is a gale, which is too strong for dinghy sailing, so a red triangular pennant is often flown as a warning. Two such pennants mean a strong gale.

A new method of determining the surface winds anywhere at sea involves an orbiting satellite which sends a radar beam onto the waves and then measures the back-scatter. The character of this depends on the waves' size, being different when waves are large, i.e. winds are strong. In particular, the back-scatter of radar at wavelengths of 2 cm responds rapidly to changes in wind speed and direction.

Nowadays, there are also 'Doppler radar' and 'acoustic profile' equipments, which detect wind by its effect on the echoing of pulses of radiation or sound sent from the instruments. For instance, air approaching the equipment returns an echo at a slightly higher frequency, just as the sounds of a train when it is coming towards us are at a higher pitch than when it is departing. Other methods of measuring winds aloft were mentioned in Section 12.3, including observing the sideways deflection of rising balloons. This is still common, partly to check more modern methods.

Variations of Winds

The speed and direction of measured winds can be indicated on a chart by the symbols in **Figure 14.4**. Repeated measurements can be summarised by a *'wind-rose'*, which indicates the frequency with which the wind has a particular strength and direction (**Figure 14.5**).

Surface winds vary annually and daily, and **Figure 14.6** shows the outcome in the form of

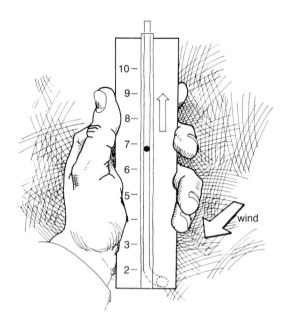

Figure 14.3 A 'Dwyer wind meter', which is used to measure the wind speed by means of a lightweight ball made of pith, inside a slightly conical tube, whose wider end is at the top, and whose lower end is connected to an opening which is faced into the wind. The stronger the wind, the greater the lifting force on the pith ball, and so the higher up the tube it can be lifted, despite the wider diameter there.

hodographs for Sydney, for instance. This diagram shows a south-easterly breeze on January afternoons, but winds are more westerly in July. In both months the wind *backs* during the day, i.e. it changes direction anticlockwise (Section 12.2). Figure 14.6 also shows that the wind at Sydney is generally stronger during the daytime than at night, though 9 p.m. winds in January are stronger than those at 9 a.m. Hodographs like those in Figure 14.6 are especially useful in considering which areas are vulnerable to air pollutants after they have

been emitted into the boundary layer (Section 14.7)

There is a clear variation of windiness latitudinally about Australia and out to sea. The 'annual mean daily wind run' (i.e. the distance that a balloon floating in the wind would be carried in a day) is greater offshore than on the mainland (**Figure 14.7**), whilst the wind run inland is lower in the north and east. On the coast, it is greatest along the west and in Tasmania, so these would be the best places for wind turbines to generate electricity (Section 14.5). **Table 14.2** shows that once-in-five-years extreme winds in Australian cities are similar, but once-in-a-century winds are strongest in Darwin and Brisbane, which are vulnerable to tropical cyclones.

Comfort

The surface wind influences personal comfort in cold climates in terms of the windchill (Note 3.E). Even indoors, a cold draught of only 0.3 m/s can be uncomfortable, though up to 0.6 m/s is reckoned reasonable ventilation in moderate climates. Higher velocities lead to papers being blown about. The achievement of comfortable ventilation indoors depends on appropriate building design, which is considered in **Note 14.B** and Chapter 16.

A pleasant breeze outdoors has a speed of about 2 m/s, but over 6 m/s can be annoying, disturbing the hair and making your clothes flap, with dust and litter blown about if the wind is gusty. The force of a strong wind can be considerable (Note 14.B). The elderly may find it hard to walk against a wind above 7 m/s, and an opposing wind of 9 m/s is equivalent to walking up a hill with a slope of 1 in 20. It is necessary to lean at 20 degrees into Antarctic winds of 24 m/s, and a gust of that speed will knock people over.

Table 14.1 The Beaufort scale of wind speeds

Beaufort Scale	Description	At sea	On land	Speed Knots	Speed M/s
1	Calm	Flat sea	Smoke vertical	0	0
2	Light air	Ripples	Smoke drifts	2	1.0
3	Light breeze	Wavelets	Leaves rustle	6	3.1
4	Gentle breeze	Breaking wavelets	Wind felt on face	9	4.6
5	Fresh breeze	Moderate waves	Small leafy trees sway	17	8.7
6	Strong breeze	Spray, white foam	Large branches sway	23	12
7	Moderate gale	Heaped sea	Whole trees move	29	15
8	Gale	Long crests and blown foam	Twigs break off, walking impeded	37	19
9	Strong gale	10 m waves and reduced visibility	Removes tiles	43	22
10	Storm	Heavy rolling seas, overhanging crests	Trees blown down	50	26
11	–	Spray obscures	Much damage	58	30
12	Hurricane *	Sea white with foam	Extreme damage	64	33

* The threshold peak wind speed in a tropical cyclone (Table 13.2)

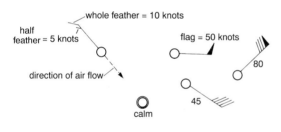

Figure 14.4 Symbolic representation of the wind and its direction at any moment, at the place indicated by the location of the circle at the end of the arrow.

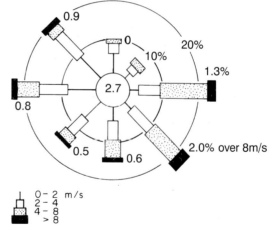

Figure 14.5 Wind rose of measurements each three hours during the period October 1976–March 1977 at Silverwater in Sydney. The length of each segment is proportional to the frequency of winds of the indicated direction and speed. There is a calm during 2.7 per cent of the time. Also, easterly and southeasterly winds occur about half the time, with 60 per cent of them over 4 m/s.

14.2 SEA BREEZES

These coastal winds are due to sea-surface temperatures (SST) varying each day by only a degree or so, whilst surface air temperatures onshore change by around ten times as much (Section 3.4). The result is that daytime temperatures inland are appreciably warmer than the SST, and the warming spreads throughout the planetary boundary layer. Also, the onshore warmth leads to thermals which ascend to the top of the PBL and gradually extend it upwards

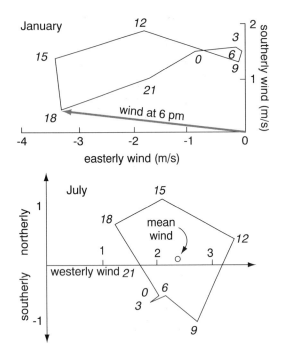

Figure 14.6 Hodographs of surface winds at Sydney. Each month's diagram shows the average wind direction and strength each three hours, by the positions of the eight corners. For example, the wind at 6 p.m. in January (shown by the corner labelled '18') is on average easterly, with a slight southerly component. The monthly mean wind in July is westerly at nearly 2.5 m/s.

Table 14.2 The maximum gust experienced at 10 m height at places in Australia once each *R* years (i.e. *R* is the return period)

Place	R = 5 years	25	100
Adelaide	33 m/s	39	45
Darwin	30	44	55
Brisbane	34	45	54
Canberra	32	37	39
Giles	29	34	38
Hobart	34	39	44
Melbourne	32	37	41
Perth	31	40	45
Sydney	34	41	46

(Figure 7.1). The warming of a column of 1 km by 5 K, for instance, reduces the MSLP by 2 hPa (Section 13.4, Note 1.G). This reduction does not occur offshore, so a surface-pressure difference develops, which drives marine air onshore – the *sea breeze* (**Figure 14.8**). This slides inland under the warmer PBL there.

The cool breeze is shallow at first, perhaps 100 m, and becomes deeper during the day, typically to 200–500 m in temperate climates and 1,000–1,400 m in the tropics. The wind causes atmospheric divergence over the water, and hence a subsidence of air offshore, which in turn creates a return flow from the air ascending over the land, completing a circulation. The return flow is perhaps twice as deep and half as fast as the sea breeze, but is often masked by the quasi-gradient wind. **Figure 14.9** is the result of pioneering measurements; it now appears that the return flow is less prominent and less common than once thought. There is an inversion between the cool sea breeze and any warmed return flow above (Section 7.6).

Prerequisites for a sea breeze include a clear sky, to allow sufficient radiation to heat the land surface (**Note 14.C**). The greater radiation of summer facilitates sea breezes, so that they are more common, involve stronger winds and start earlier in the day in that season (**Figure 14.10**). Sea breezes are less common in autumn, and if they do occur they are generally weaker, start later, and penetrate less far inland, because the SST has continued to rise (Section 11.2) while daytime warming of the land declines. The breezes are rare in winter, when the land is usually cooler than the ocean. For example, nine sea breezes, on average, reach Renmark (290 km from the West Australian coast) in February, but only one in July.

The fundamental mechanism driving a sea breeze is the same as that for a monsoonal circulation or a Hadley cell (Section 12.3), being a 'thermally direct circulation' (Figure 12.14). The difference is that a sea-breeze circulation is confined to the PBL and lasts only

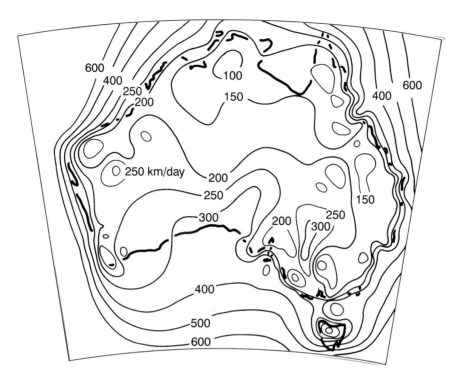

Figure 14.7 Variation of annual-mean daily wind run across Australia and the adjacent seas.

6–12 hours. The same process operates around large lakes, where there are miniature sea breezes (i.e. *lake breezes*) on land, within a kilometre or two of the shoreline. Such a wind is often observed in the afternoon along the shores of Lake Victoria, at about 2°S in Africa. Similarly, there may be a cold breeze along the edge of a large area of melting snow or ice, or a cool wind blowing towards the sunny region outside the shadow of stationary stratus clouds or fog. Likewise, there might be a *country breeze* of up to 3 m/s blowing in the afternoon towards the centre of a large city, when there is appreciable urban heating (Section 3.7). In each case, the wind is driven by a temperature difference. But a 'direct circulation' is not a thermal wind (Note 12.F). The latter blows at right-angles to the difference and at a level above it, whereas a sea breeze, for example, blows at a low level

and *directly* towards the area of higher temperature.

An established sea-breeze circulation has a certain momentum which maintains its orientation whilst the Earth turns, so that a midday easterly sea breeze at Sydney (on a roughly north–south coast) becomes a north-easterly by the evening. This Coriolis effect was noticed in the seventeenth century by William Dampier, who observed that shore winds turn with the Sun each day, i.e. counterclockwise in the southern hemisphere. A similar backing of the sea breeze is observed on the desert coast of Namibia.

Sea-Breeze Front

The leading edge of the sea breeze is called the 'sea-breeze front', which propagates inland

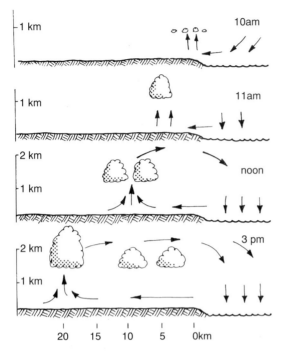

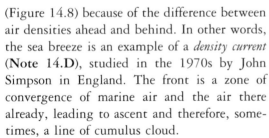

Figure 14.8 The growth of a sea-breeze cell during the day.

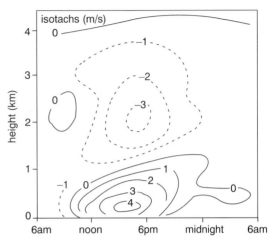

Figure 14.9 The diurnal variation of the winds at Jakarta (6°S) at different elevations. Wind speed is shown in units of km/h. The diagram shows onshore surface winds (solid lines) from about 9 a.m. till 9 p.m., though the strongest winds occur around 4 p.m. at about 200 m. The return flow (dashed lines) is fastest at 2 km around 5 p.m. The sea-breeze flow deepens during the daytime until well after 4 p.m.

(Figure 14.8) because of the difference between air densities ahead and behind. In other words, the sea breeze is an example of a *density current* (**Note 14.D**), studied in the 1970s by John Simpson in England. The front is a zone of convergence of marine air and the air there already, leading to ascent and therefore, sometimes, a line of cumulus cloud.

The front moves inland as continued heating of the land enlarges the cell, advancing at a fraction of the sea-breeze speed and generally accelerating during the day, from below 3 m/s to over 6 m/s, for instance. The result is that a sea breeze may be felt well inland. An extreme example is shown in **Figure 14.11**. Inland penetration of sea breezes is especially notable in Australia, because of its aridity, high temperatures and flatness. A sea breeze which starts at the coast near Perth in Western Australia might reach 400 km inland by the evening and last there for 2–3 hours, having already died away at the coast. Similarly, a sea breeze from the Gulf of Carpentaria in the north of Australia has been observed from 2 a.m. to 9 a.m. at Tennant Creek (20°S), which is more than 500 km inland.

The arrival of the front is indicated by a switch of the wind to the onshore direction, a drop of air temperature, a rise of surface pressure by a hectopascal or so, and an abrupt decrease of the air's wet-bulb depression (Section 6.3). There is often a considerable increase of wind speed and of turbulence (**Figure 14.12**), especially where a dry surface allows rapid heating, and a cold ocean current along the coast accentuates the land–sea difference of temperature. The arid coast of northern Chile

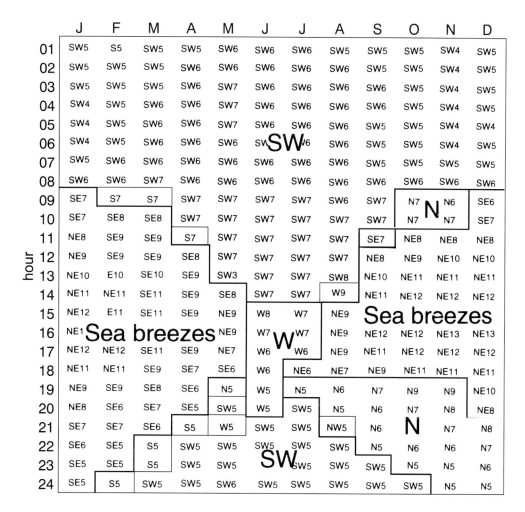

Figure 14.10 Prevailing surface winds at Brisbane. The numbers indicate the mean speed (km/h). Daytime winds from the north-east, east and south-east are sea breezes, which are fostered at Brisbane in summer by easterly gradient winds resulting from the shift southwards of the highs across Australia (Section 13.6).

has sea breezes which approach gale force, and those on the coast of Western Australia at Geraldton (at 29°S, where the total rainfall is only about 30 mm during the period October–March) are sufficiently strong to distort trees growing 16 km inland. The sea breeze on the desert west coast of South Africa typically reaches 10 m/s.

A sea breeze brings welcome relief in hot weather in summer, especially if the front arrives before mid-afternoon, thus preventing temperatures reaching their normal maximum. That happens only within a few tens of kilometres of the beach, depending on the time of the breeze starting and the speed of the front's advance. This limit to the area benefiting from sea breezes affects real-estate values.

There are other effects too. A sea breeze spoils the waves for surf-riding by creating a bumpy surface called 'chop'. Separate sea breezes on

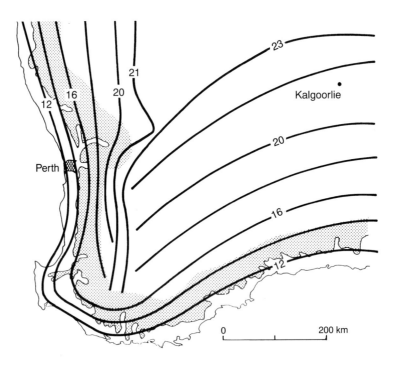

Figure 14.11 The position of the sea-breeze front in south-west Australia at different hours of a day. The shading highlights the edge of the inland plateau, which is only a few hundred metres high. The sea breeze from the west was arrested by the prevailing easterly winds of summer.

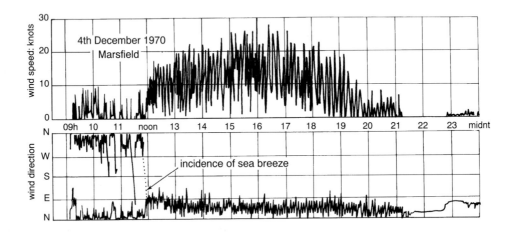

Figure 14.12 The fluctuations of wind speed (upper diagram) and direction (lower) during a summer day in Sydney. The arrival of a sea breeze at about noon was followed by a great increase of speed as well as a shift in wind direction.

opposite sides of Cape York Peninsula in the north of Queensland approach each other and collide, creating a Morning Glory (Note 8.L). A similar confluence of sea breezes from opposite sides of tropical islands such as Viti Levu (Fiji) or Bathurst Island (north of Darwin) leads to ascent inland and then rainfalls there in the afternoon. Sometimes the arrival of a sea-breeze front may trigger deep convection if the air ahead is unstable, so that there are thunderstorms, e.g. in moist low-latitude environments, such as those of Brisbane in summer and Port Moresby (9°S).

Land Breeze

The opposite to a sea breeze happens at night, when the land has cooled below the local SST. On shore, such 'land breezes' are slower than 1 m/s and less deep than the daytime sea breezes, because the stability of the atmosphere at night confines the flow to a shallow layer close to the ground's friction.

Land breezes are usually strongest offshore, and may propagate as a density current more than 100 km out to sea, possibly triggering nocturnal thunderstorms over the relatively warm waters. Nocturnal storms of this kind are common off the east coast of Australia in winter. Thunderstorms at night are also provoked by the convergence of land breezes from the shores of Lake Victoria in Africa, or within large bays (e.g. the Gulf of Carpentaria to the north of Australia) or between the islands of the Indonesian archipelago. Likewise, there is convergence offshore from an ocean coast on nights when the land breeze meets an onshore gradient wind which is weak (and moist), again creating uplift and the possibility of rain. In fact, most thunderstorms in the tropics are initiated by sea breezes, land breezes and mountain winds, unlike the situation in midlatitudes, where cold fronts are usually responsible.

The daily alternating between a sea breeze and a land breeze produces a circular hodograph in Sydney, for instance (Figure 14.6).

14.3 MOUNTAIN WINDS

Mountains have several effects on winds. Firstly, there is generally an increase of velocity at higher levels, towards the speeds characteristic of the upper troposphere (Figure 12.10). Secondly, a strong wind perpendicular to a high and long range will undulate on the lee side if there happens to be a slightly higher inversion layer to bounce against. These undulations (called *lee waves*) yield lines of cloud fixed parallel and downwind of the mountains wherever the upper part of an undulation is above the lifting condensation level (Section 8.1). Between them are separated bands of strong surface winds, at the lower parts of the undulations. Also, there may be *downslope windstorms* over the downwind foothills of the mountain, due to the strong winds prevailing at mountain-crest level being carried down in a lee wave. Lee waves are felt in the upper troposphere too, up to a height perhaps five times that of the mountain range itself. These high waves can help induce Clear Air Turbulence (Note 12.M).

Thirdly, there is the foehn effect, the warming of winds blowing down mountains when there has been rainfall on the windward side. The customary explanation (Section 7.2) provides an instructive exercise in the use of an aerological diagram but applies only to long mountain ranges. Surface winds onto an isolated mountain are normally deflected sideways around it, and do not flow upslope unless the atmosphere is almost neutral or unstable. A slight pressure reduction on the lee side of the mountain draws dry air down from the upper levels of the slope, and the air warms at the dry-adiabatic lapse rate as it descends. This particular explanation of the foehn effect does not necessitate precipitation on the windward side of the mountain.

Foehn winds are most evident in winter, when their warmth contrasts most sharply with prevailing conditions. Sometimes their onset is sudden, leading to a rapid rise in temperature. There is a detectable effect in the lee of the Blue Mountains near Sydney when westerlies blow in winter.

Fourthly, there are the strong winds caused by the channelling of airflows within narrow valleys. Such *gully winds* are important at Adelaide in South Australia, for instance, formed within the Lofty Range behind the city.

All four effects occur when a mountain acts as a topographic barrier to winds. But now we will consider winds caused rather than obstructed by the mountain. In particular, there are thermally direct circulations due to temperature differences on mountains, as follows.

Katabatic and Anabatic Winds

The name of *katabatic winds* comes from the Greek word for 'down', as these are downhill flows of heavy cold air, driven by gravity and sometimes called 'cold-air drainage'. Initially, these flows slide down the hillsides on either side of a valley, but then they turn down-valley to become *valley winds*. A *fall wind* is a cold large-scale katabatic wind from an elevated plateau. All katabatic winds behave like density currents (Note 14.D).

The winds are unaffected by the air's humidity or the surface roughness and they are shallow – typically about 5 per cent of the descent. So the wind is only 10 m deep at the bottom of a slope 200 m high, for example. Nocturnal cold-air drainage over Sydney is commonly a flow about 100 m deep moving at about 4 m/s. But there are katabatic winds about 300 m deep at the coast in Antarctica, of remarkable strength and persistence (Chapter 16). Katabatic winds blow at Mawson (67°S) on about a hundred days in a year, with an average speed of 11 m/s,

equivalent to a strong breeze (Table 14.1). As a result, winds flow out from the central ridges of the Antarctic plateau in such volume that they induce the polar subsidence which is part of the global circulation (Section 12.3).

The daytime counterparts of katabatic winds are called 'anabatic' winds. They flow up sunny slopes, providing lift for glider pilots and for hang-gliding. Anabatic winds are generally deeper and more gusty than katabatic winds. Speeds of 6 m/s have been measured in Papua New Guinea, in flows more than 150 m in depth.

Anabatic winds are not like density currents but arise when the PBL over mountains is warmer than the adjacent layer of free atmosphere. This causes a surface-pressure reduction over the mountains, and hence winds down the pressure gradient up the side of the mountain. They flow up both sides of broad valleys in South America, for instance, causing a central downdraught which dissipates clouds, so that the middle of a valley is more arid than on the slopes. Also the upslope anabatic winds may trigger thunderstorms, which helps explain why thunderstorms are more common around mountains in summer, especially in the tropics.

All these various kinds of wind can be found in hilly terrain. Depending on the time of day, there may be a toposcale katabatic or anabatic flow near the ground, surmounted by a mesoscale wind such as a country breeze or sea breeeze, with another quite different layer above that containing the synoptic-scale quasi-gradient wind. Thus, for example, afternoon measurements in a South African valley showed a surface anabatic wind of 1 m/s of 50 m depth, with a different wind of 3 m/s between 50–200 m above ground, and a quasi-gradient wind dominant above 600 m.

Daily Pattern

Another example of the various kinds of wind near mountains is illustrated in **Figure 14.13**,

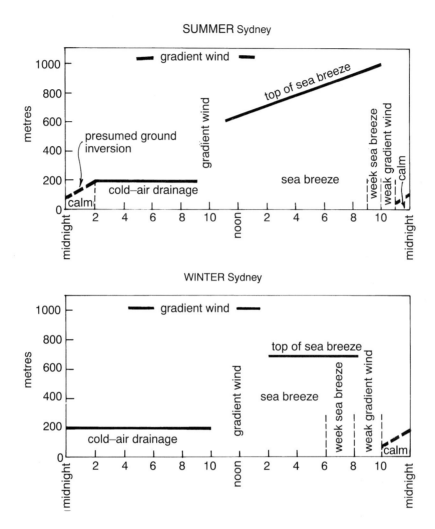

Figure 14.13 Typical sequences of surface winds and inversion layers on cloudless days with weak gradient winds in Sydney, in terms of the causes. Cold-air drainage corresponds to a westerly drift, whilst a sea breeze in Sydney is a brisk easterly.

which shows the sequence of winds in the Parramatta Valley, which opens out into Sydney. There is cold-air drainage downhill during the early morning, with an inversion layer between the cold air and the stationary air above. Once the Sun's heat has warmed the surface sufficiently, there is convection which links the surface air to the quasi-gradient wind, which may be in any direction. However, this period ends once the sea breeze arrives from the coast, with an inversion above the cool maritime air. That dies away sometime after sunset, and the sequence repeats itself, unless there is a change of cloudiness or a strong gradient wind.

14.4 TURBULENCE

Up to this point in the book we have been considering winds averaged over five minutes or so. In reality, both the wind speed and direction may vary widely during those five minutes. The irregularities constitute *turbulence*, defined as 'the complex spectrum of fluctuating motion imposed on the average flow'. It is due to the eddies mentioned in Section 14.1. The fluctuations lead to bumpy aircraft flights, ripples across wheat crops and isolated patches of ruffled surface on a lake, called 'cats' paws'. More importantly, they are the means by which water vapour, sensible heat and friction are transferred from the ground to the free atmosphere. Also, turbulence is associated with *gusts* of high speed and *lulls* of low.

Wind Gusts

A 'gust' is defined as the 'wind-speed deviation from the mean which, on average, is exceeded once during the reference period'. Such extreme winds are important in the design of buildings, bridges and windmills, for instance, even if they are only short-lived. Very strong winds have been recorded at places such as these:

(a) An hourly average of 43 m/s at Cape Denison at 68°S in Antarctica.

(b) A gust of 75 m/s lasting three seconds has been measured on a 450 m hill at Wellington (NZ).

(c) There was a gust of 68 m/s at Onslow in Western Australia during a tropical cyclone in 1975.

(d) A speed of 89 m/s was measured in a tornado near Melbourne in 1918 (Section 7.5).

These high winds cannot be measured easily: anemometers would be blown away. Instead, extreme speeds are estimated from the resulting damage (**Table 14.3**).

Winds above 30 m/s occur about once each two years around the south coast of Australia, and above 23 m/s along the north coast. At Sydney, the frequency of strong winds during the period 1938–62 is indicated in **Figure 14.14**. For instance, there was a gust faster than 28 m/s once a year on average, over 31 m/s once each two years, and hence, it is estimated, more than 46 m/s once a century (**Note 14.E**). In other words, the return period (Section 10.2) for winds exceeding 46 m/s in Sydney is a hundred years. Winds exceeded on average once in fifty years (which is assumed to be the life of a building) are shown in **Figure 14.15**, indicating the particular hazard along coasts exposed to tropical cyclones, which are most violent off the north-west coast. The

Table 14.3 The F scale for extreme winds, devised by Theodore Fujita in the late 1960s to classify tornadoes

Scale	Speed (m/s)	Expected damage
F0	18–32	*Light*: tree branches broken, sign boards damaged
F1	32–50	*Moderate*: trees snapped, windows broken
F2*	50–70	*Heavy*: large trees uprooted, weak structures destroyed
F3	70–92	*Severe*: trees levelled, cars and mobile homes overturned
F4	92–116	*Devastating*: frame-house walls levelled, roofs lifted
F5	116–142	*Incredible*: brick homes levelled, cars and trees moved over 100 m

* Only a handful out of about 1,000 tornadoes reported in Australia and a similar number of recorded tropical cyclones have had winds exceeding those of an F2 tornado

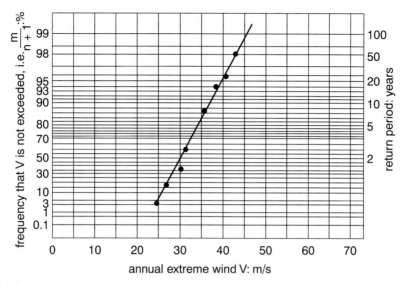

Figure 14.14 The frequency of high winds at Sydney.

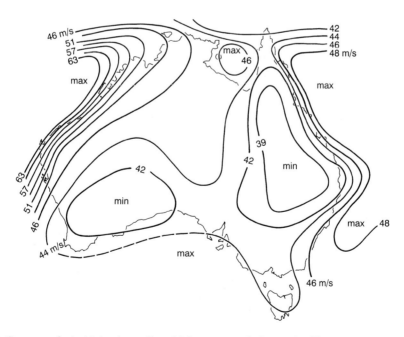

Figure 14.15 Gust speeds (m/s) in Australia which are exceeded once in fifty years on average.

frequencies of extreme gusts at some other places are shown in Table 14.2.

It is the extra strength of gusts during a storm that causes most damage. It was found after the tropical cyclone Tracy that demolished Darwin in 1974 that the cost of repairing houses, as a fraction of the initial cost of building them, was zero where gusts were below 30 m/s (i.e. F0 in Table 14.3), but 0.2 where they reached 42 m/s (i.e. F1), and 0.6 where 56 m/s (F2). These were houses built on stilts to catch cooling sea breezes; the fractions were about halved for houses built on the ground.

Numerical measures of *gustiness* compare the mean wind speed during a short-period gust with the average over an hour or ten minutes, say. The *Gust Factor* is the ratio of gust and average speeds, and the value depends on the selected gust period. For example, data from hurricanes yield factors of 1.2 for two-minute gusts and 1.5 for three-second gusts, compared with hourly averages. In other words, there are three-second pulses of wind which are 50 per cent faster than the hour-long average. Alternatively, gustiness may be described by the swing of wind direction, which is larger in turbulent conditions (Table 7.1; **Figure 14.16**). In either case, values are enhanced by the extra stirring created by the irregularity of a surface such as that of a city.

Gusts are due to volumes of air being mixed by eddies from parts of the atmosphere where the winds have quite different speeds and directions. Some of the agitation may be due to atmospheric instability (Section 7.4). The fluctuations are greater if nearby winds differ considerably, i.e. if there is strong wind shear. This is most likely in the vicinity of discontinuities such as inversions or fronts, and near obstacles such as hills.

There is also strong wind shear causing turbulence in association with thunderstorms and near *low-level jets*. The latter are like upper-troposphere jet streams (Section 12.5), but occur at only about 2 km above the ground.

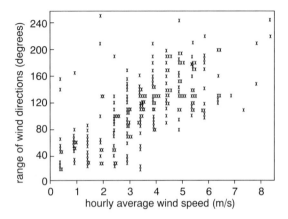

Figure 14.16 The difference between the most and least clockwise directions of the surface wind during an hour, plotted against the average speed during the hour, at Marsfield, Sydney.

They are fairly common in Australia on clear nights in winter or spring, and arise in the course of forming the nocturnal radiation inversion which detaches the gradient wind from the ground's friction. Also, there is often a low-level jet ahead of a cold front, blowing parallel to it from the north or north-west, at a speed of up to 30 m/s.

Thunderstorm Gusts

Thunderstorms (Section 9.5) may cause strong wind gusts near the surface in three ways:

1 Severe thunderstorms occasionally spawn vortices of extreme wind, such as tornadoes (Section 7.5).
2 Strong downdraughts within thunderstorms may carry parcels of air down from the jet stream to the surface within no more than fifteen minutes, so that the air still contains its original momentum.
3 A subsiding parcel of air may accelerate downwards under the weight of its water content, and as a result of the cooling caused by evaporation of drops within the parcel. In extreme cases, this leads to a *downburst* of cold

air, which spreads in all directions near the surface up to a few 100 km away. Downbursts have caused several airplane crashes. The smaller downbursts, called *microbursts*, with a radius of a few 100 m, are a special danger to aircraft because of the powerful downdraught within the microburst, and because of the strong wind shear at each end. A plane flying into a microburst near the surface feels a sudden change from headwind to tailwind, causing a disconcertingly abrupt loss of lift. Microbursts can be either dry or wet; the wet kind are due to a downpour, while the dry kind may emerge from apparently harmless thunderstorms with a high cloud base.

The leading edge of the cold outflow from a thunderstorm is known as a *gust front* (Section 9.5) which spreads like a density current (Note 14.D). One in the Port Moresby area of Papua New Guinea is known as a 'Guba'. It occurs occasionally during the early morning as a sudden wind of up to 30 m/s, and lasts for about half an hour. It is a gust front associated with nocturnal thunderstorms over the Gulf of Papua, often begun by convergent land breezes from the surrounding land.

14.5 WIND ENERGY

Winds can be harnessed to provide power, though extreme winds may damage structures (Note 14.B), and some of the wind's energy goes into eroding the land, which is the other aspect we will consider in this section.

Wind Power

The power of wind at velocity V (m/s) through an area of a square metre equals $\rho.V^3/2$ watts (**Note 14.F**), where ρ is the air's density (about 1.25 kg/m^3 at sea-level). For instance, a breeze of 5 m/s blowing onto the rotating blades of 3 m radius of a *wind turbine* contains 78 W/m^2 of power (i.e. $0.5 \times 5^3 \times 1.25$), so the blades (sweeping an area of 28 m^2) receive 2.2 kW. Such a wind turbine with an efficiency of 40 per cent could power fifteen 60W lightbulbs (i.e. $2{,}200 \times 0.4/60$).

The dependence on the cube of the wind speed means that a small change of velocity makes a large difference of power. If the wind were 10 m/s in the example above, instead of 5 m/s, the collected power would be eight times as much. So it is worth while taking trouble to find the windiest spot, and erecting a tall mast to benefit from the stronger winds away from the ground's friction (Section 14.1).

Unfortunately, the strongest winds occur at sea, where it difficult to mount a wind turbine. Daily average winds across the Atlantic and Indian oceans at 40°S exceed 15 m/s on 30 per cent of days. The long-term average is over 12 m/s in the gap at about 56°S between South America and Antarctica.

Figure 14.7 and Figure 14.15 show that winds are relatively modest inland, bearing in mind that 200 km/day, for instance, averages only 2.3 m/s. The world's windiest place onshore appears to be at Commonwealth Bay at 67°S, 141°E, where three different stations have measured annual mean winds of 11–18 m/s.

Critics of wind power complain that wind farms are noisy, kill birds, spoil TV reception locally and blight areas of the upland or coastal wilderness, where the strongest winds tend to be found. There is also the economic problem of the variability of winds, between seasons and between times of day, so that the output from any place is fluctuating. The effect of this can be reduced by linking widely separated wind farms, where there are different patterns of wind. In Britain, for instance, there are more than eighteen wind farms connected to the national grid, generating up to 30 megawatts each, and thereby reducing the dependence on fossil fuels, with their undesirable outputs of carbon dioxide and suphur dioxide (Chapter 15).

Blowing Particles

Winds disturb loose materials on the ground and blow them around. A speed of 7 m/s is usually sufficient to lift fresh powdery snow and reduce visibility. Piles of stored coal have to be sprayed with water to prevent clouds of dust when winds exceed 10 m/s.

Australia has occasional *dust storms*, when visibility is reduced to less than 1 km by a cloud of red soil. They occur especially in the arid centre (**Figure 14.17**), where Alice Springs averages over ten annually, mostly in summer. A dust cloud covering 3,000 km^2 to a height of 3 km and containing 0.2 grams of particles per cubic metre, removes 2 million tonnes of topsoil and the cloud may be blown to New Zealand and even Fiji, some 4,000 km downwind.

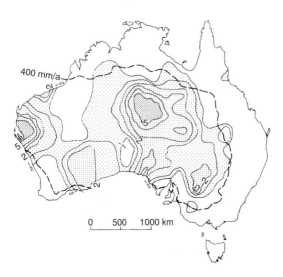

Figure 14.17 The frequency of dust storms in parts of Australia. The darkest shading represents over 5 dust storms annually, the next lightest 2–5, the next 0.5–2, and the unshaded part has less than one dust storm in two years, on average. The dashed line is the 400 mm/a isohyet.

Dust consists of particles of 1–10 microns diameter, and dust storms usually need winds of at least 12 m/s or so, along with a strongly unstable atmosphere. In general, conditions for dust storms are the same as for heat waves (Section 3.2), drought (Section 10.7) or an extreme risk of bushfire, i.e. prolonged, hot and dry weather.

Sand storms involve surface particles about a hundred times larger in diameter, so winds need to be stronger, the threshold depending on the particles' dryness, shape and density. Winds of only 3 m/s can move the smaller grains of dry sand across the surface in a hopping motion called *saltation*, where each dislodged grain jumps some centimetres into the air and then falls to the ground and thereby loosens another one or two grains, as well as dust. Indeed, bombardment by saltating sand is probably the main process raising dust from the ground in dust storms. But most movement of sand *dunes* is caused by winds above 12 m/s.

Soil erosion is caused by wind drying the surface (Chapter 4) and then lifting particles into the air. The rate of 'aeolian soil erosion' (i.e. erosion by wind) is proportional to the wind's power, i.e. to the cube of the wind speed, so it is greatly reduced by decreasing the surface wind. The decrease caused by the friction of even a partial cover of vegetation reduces soil erosion considerably, and it is the rare high wind that does most of the damage.

Water in the surface soil reduces aeolian erosion by holding the grains together, as well as by promoting the growth of a vegetative cover. Even 2 per cent of moisture in bare soil typically raises the threshold wind speed for erosion by more than 2 m/s.

Windbreaks

Winds across a field are commonly reduced by a *windbreak*, consisting of a wall or hedge, or a *shelter belt* of a row of trees. These lessen evaporation and soil erosion downwind, and give

Plate 14.1 An unusual dust storm over Melbourne on 8 February 1983.

shade. The wind protection that is provided by a windbreak of height H is indicated by **Figure 14.18**; it depends on the porosity of the windbreak and on the distance downwind. About 10H away, crop yields tend be 10 per cent more than elsewhere, but the yield nearer to the windbreak is reduced by the windbreak's own demand for sunshine, moisture and nutriment.

14.6 SEA WAVES

More of the energy in the winds at sea goes into creating waves than into driving ocean currents. As a result, sea waves contain enormous power.

Ripples form on water when winds are only 1 m/s or so (Table 14.1). But strong winds drive the waves accordingly, and their speed is inherently related to the eventual wave height and to the distance between crests – the *wavelength*. For instance, a wave driven to a speed of 5 m/s is finally 0.5 m high from crest to trough and has a wavelength of 16 m, whilst a 12 m wave in the vicinity of a tropical cyclone is 400 m long and travels at 25 m/s. (These speeds do not mean that water actually travels along, it is simply the wave *pattern* that moves, like the undulations along a fixed rope that is shaken.) Usually the wave speed is slightly less than the speed of the wind over the ocean surface.

Waves do not reach their full height, wavelength and speed in immediate response to changes of wind speed. The degree of adjustment depends on the duration of the wind regime, or, in a confined body of water, the distance upwind to land – the *fetch*. **Figure**

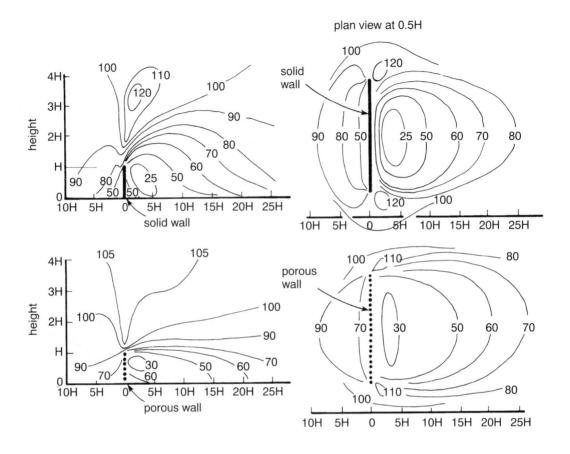

Figure 14.18 The wind speeds around a windbreak, as percentages of the speed at the height H of the top of the windbreak, and 20 times H upwind, showing elevation and plan views, with either a solid wall or one through which almost half the air can flow.

14.19 illustrates that the fetch required for the sea to adjust to a wind of 6 m/s, for instance, is about 80 km, and the time needed about five hours. After that, waves are about 0.7 m high and have a wavelength of 12 m and a speed of 4 m/s, so the *period* of the waves is three seconds (i.e. 12/4). The fetch and time to adjust fully are shorter with strong winds.

Long waves are called *swell*, and originate in distant major storms. They travel faster than the storm, so their arrival can give useful warning. Swell reaching Australian coasts comes mostly from midlatitude storms, and waves

higher than 7 m are occasionally experienced on the south coast.

What is called a 'moderate sea' is one with waves 1–2 m high, whereas a 'heavy swell' has waves over 4 m high. Often there is a combination of swell from distant storms and smaller waves due to local winds, and the occasional synchronisation of swell and local waves leads to unusually large waves from time to time.

The power in kilowatts in each metre along the crest of a wave is about $H^2.P$, where H is the wave height (m) and P the period (seconds). Thus, for example, waves which are 0.7 m

Plate 14.2 The night-time collision of sea breezes from both east and west coasts of Cape York (in the north-east of Australia) causes parallel, low-level, long rolls of circulation, subsequently carried westwards in the Trade winds, over the Gulf of Carpentaria. The forward rising edge of each roll lifts moist air from sea-level, forming a long cloud, producing the 'Morning Glory'. This photograph was taken at 7.45 a.m. and shows the first two of about five rolls oriented approximately north-west to south-east. The Sun in the east casts a shadow ahead of the clouds as they advance east of Burketown.

high and have a period of three seconds (from a wind of about 5 m/s) contain 1.5 kW per metre length, which is similar to the figure for a wind turbine with 3 m propellors in the same wind (Section 14.5). A doubling of the wind speed leads to an approximate quadrupling of the wave height (Figure 14.19), and wave power is proportional to the square of the wave height, so the power is very sensitive to the wind speed, e.g. doubling the wind speed increases power about sixteenfold, if the wind speed is maintained over a sufficient time and fetch. Short-lived winds with a short fetch, like sea breezes, yield little wave power.

Such sea-wave power is unleashed in the course of coast erosion. It would be good to harness the energy, sustainably available to generate electricity close to coastal cities.

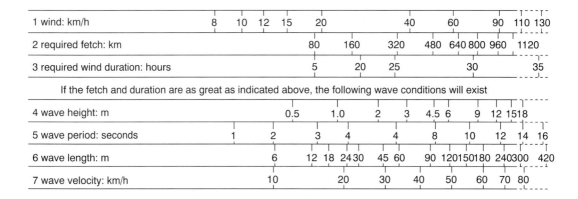

1 wind: km/h					8	10	12	15	20			40		60		90	110	130
2 required fetch: km									80	160		320	480	640	800 960		1120	
3 required wind duration: hours									5	20		25		30				35

If the fetch and duration are as great as indicated above, the following wave conditions will exist

4 wave height: m						0.5		1.0		2		3	4.5	6		9	12	15	18
5 wave period: seconds			1		2			3	4			4		8		10		12	14 16
6 wave length: m					6		12	18	24 30		45	60		90	120 150 180		240 300		420
7 wave velocity: km/h					10			20		30		40		50		60	70	80	

Figure 14.19 Diagram for the estimation of the eventual wave height, *period* (i.e. time between crests), length and speed, for a given wind, when the fetch and duration are sufficient.

Unfortunately, the practical problems of tides, corrosion, the vagaries of wave conditions, reduced wave height inshore and the awesome force of the worst storms have so far prevented our using the energy in sea waves.

14.7 URBAN AIR POLLUTION

The surface wind is a major factor controlling the distribution and concentration of air pollutants in urban atmospheres. Other factors are the rate of emission of the pollutants and the stability of the lowest part of the troposphere.

Emissions

Most urban pollutants come from either chimneys or automobiles. The former involve relatively slow combustion with plenty of oxygen. The fuels may contain sulphur, in which case the gas *sulphur dioxide* is created, along with carbon dioxide, water vapour, nitrogen dioxide and particulate matter. Particles less than 10 μm in diameter are referred to as 'PM10', and are dangerous to human health. They are so small as to remain in the air for hours or days, just like cloud droplets. Sulphur dioxide combines with moisture when the RH is over

80 per cent, forming cloud droplets of sulphuric acid. This is one reason why a humid atmosphere is usually hazy, especially in cities. The droplets eventually yield acid rain (Section 10.1). Nitrogen dioxide (NO_2) is a poisonous reddish-brown gas and it too forms an acid in combination with water. The carbon dioxide resulting from combustion is implicated in global warming.

Combustion in a vehicle engine is too rapid for complete oxidation of the fuel, so that not all the carbon forms carbon dioxide (CO_2) and some makes carbon monoxide (CO) instead, with only one atom of oxygen in each molecule. It is a poisonous gas, which later turns to carbon dioxide. There is also some unburnt hydrocarbon emitted, again depending on the design, speed and condition of the engine, and some monoxide of nitrogen – i.e. 'nitric oxide' (NO) – because nitrogen is the main constituent of air (Table 1.3). The NO converts to NO_2 in reaction with the air's oxygen, and the various nitrogen oxides are collectively called 'NO_x', pronounced 'nox'. It affects air passages in the body, so that they become sensitive to allergens which cause asthma, for instance. Also, NO_x combines with the emitted hydrocarbons to form ozone when temperatures and solar radiation are sufficient, e.g. in summer at the latitude of Sydney (34°S), Santiago (33°S) and Los Angeles at 34°N (**Note 14.G**). This ozone is referred to as *tropospheric ozone*, to distinguish it from the desirable ozone in the stratosphere (Section 1.4). Concentrations of tropospheric ozone have been rising in most cities in recent decades, on account of increased automobile traffic (**Note 14.G**). It harms plants and can cause fatal damage to the human heart and lungs.

Emissions in the open air are diluted in two ways – vertically and horizontally. The first depends on the amount of atmospheric stirring, which increases in faster winds (Section 14.4) and greater instability (Section 7.4). The stirring is confined beneath the lowest appreciable

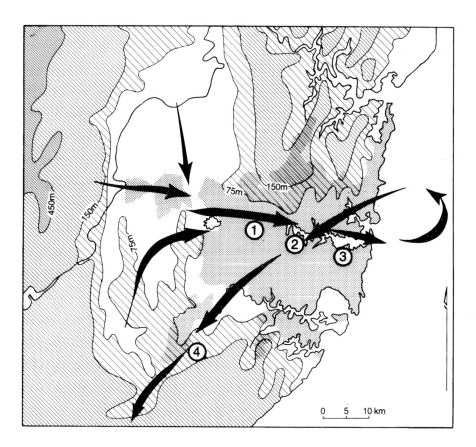

Figure 14.20 Air movements during the course of the morning and early afternoon in summer, carrying air pollutants over Sydney. The city's extent of about 35 × 35 km in 1986 is shown by shading. Initially there is eastwards cold-air drainage from the hills, which picks up effluent from the vehicles and industries along the Parramatta River (1), the pollution becoming increasingly concentrated until the air flows over the Central Business District (3) at the mouth of the river. The sea breeze starts at about this time, gradually becoming a northeasterly which drives the pollutants towards the south-western suburbs. By now the initial pollutants have reacted in the midday sunshine to form ozone, whose concentration is consequently highest in the south-western suburbs (4). The point marked (2) is Homebush, the site of the Olympic Games in the year 2000.

stable layer, whose height depends on the time of day, etc. (Section 7.6). Horizontal dilution is proportional to the surface wind speed (Note 14.G).

The smoke and gases from vehicles and bush fires, for instance, come effectively from ground level, and vertical dilution depends on the stability of the surface air. The dilution of chimney emissions depends on the temperature of the emergent gases (they rise further if they are hot), on their chimney-top velocity, and on the atmosphere's temperature profile. An inversion layer below the height of the plume actually protects people on the ground from the pollution (Note 7.L). The plume fans out sideways as a thin layer if it is in a stable layer, but loops in vertical eddies downwind if the atmosphere is unstable.

The daily maximum concentration of a pollutant can be often be predicted with useful accuracy by means of numerous previous measurements at the same spot. For instance, today's highest carbon-monoxide measurement (parts per million in the air) might be related to *yesterday's* values of the maximum concentration (CO_x) to allow for persistence, the expected wind speed (V) at the time of heaviest traffic, the day of the week D (i.e. the likely traffic density) and the forecast cloudiness (and hence the solar radiation R at that time of year, which governs surface temperature and therefore atmospheric stability). By collecting sets of values for dozens of days, one can derive statistically the appropriate constants a, b, c, d and e in the following equation:

$$CO_x = a + b.CO_x + c.V + d.D + e.R \quad ppm$$

Thereafter, tomorrow's concentration can be predicted by inserting appropriate values for CO_x, V, D and R. The same sort of equation can be developed for any pollutant.

Ozone Pollution

Maximum ground concentrations of *primary* pollutants occur just downwind of the sources (Note 14.G). However, ozone is a *secondary* pollutant, which takes time to form from NO_x and hydrocarbons (the 'precursor' ingredients), so that its highest concentrations are found some hours downwind of the precursor sources. Thus, the early morning drainage flow eastwards down the industrialised Parramatta Valley into Sydney (Figure 14.13) collects NO_x and hydrocarbons, so that their concentrations increase in the shallow flow to the sea. A sea breeze in the late morning and afternoon then returns the air towards the south-west of the city (Section 14.2), and ozone has formed by that time, given adequate midday temperatures and solar radiation (**Figure 14.20**). Hence the maximum NO_x concentration may occur at 8 a.m., whilst most ozone is measured in the afternoon. Figure 14.20 implies that the worst ozone pollution in Sydney is experienced to the south-west, not where the precursors were emitted, upwind in the western suburbs. This is an example of how an understanding of surface winds is relevant to city planning.

NOTES

14.A The wind profile
14.B Winds and housing
14.C Sea breezes
14.D Density currents
14.E The return period
14.F Dimensions of wind's power density
14.G Air pollution

Part V

CLIMATES

15

WEATHER AND CLIMATE CHANGE

15.1 WEATHER DATA

Weather data come chiefly from *weather observing stations* on land, and from ships at sea (**Figure 15.1**). Measurements are made of pressure (Section 1.5), temperature (Section 3.1), humidity (Section 6.3), rainfall (Note 10.B) and wind (Section 14.1). Other readings are taken of visibility, lightning and thunder, and cloud cover at three levels of the troposphere. In addition, there were about 600 buoys drifting at sea by 1992, and another 200 or so moored, measuring air and sea-surface temperatures and pressure, and then transmitting the data to passing satellites for later relay to ground receivers. Weather radar is now widely used, especially near cities, to monitor rainfall, wind and temperature (**Note 15.A**).

The number of places where weather data are collected has increased steadily (**Note 15.B**). There were over 13,000 weather stations worldwide by 1994, where observers were taking readings at the same moment, each three or six hours. But only 17 per cent of the places were in the southern hemisphere, where the network of observations remains inadequate because of the vast areas of ocean, ice and desert, and lack of finance (**Table 15.1**).

Weather forecasting requires information on winds and temperature aloft; so wind, temperature and humidity profiles are measured daily at about a thousand weather stations. Wind and temperature are also reported by most large civil aircraft, producing several thousand soundings of the troposphere every day in the vicinity of airports.

Increasing use is made of satellites to fill the large gaps in observations over the oceans and unpopulated land (Figure 15.1). Instruments on the satellites measure cloudiness (Section 8.8), rainfall (Note 10.C), upper-level winds (Section 12.3) and surface winds over the ocean (Section 14.1). Such measurements now outnumber those from weather stations, but the latter remain important: (i) to calibrate satellite instruments, (ii) to provide more accurate data, and (iii) for obtaining guidance in interpreting satellite data.

Measurements are also taken at *climate stations*, where instruments indicate the daily extreme temperatures, twice-daily humidity, daily rainfall and, in some cases, hours of sunshine (Section 2.2), soil temperatures (Section 3.5), pan evaporation (Section 4.5) and dew (Section 4.7). These data are mailed to headquarters at the end of the month for eventual analysis, whereas information from weather stations is

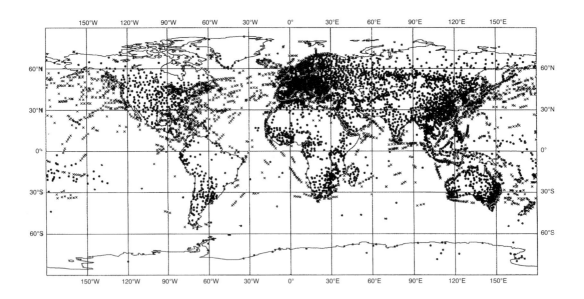

Figure 15.1 Typical daily coverage of surface observations at weather stations and ships.

Table 15.1 Numbers of daily weather stations active in 1994. These stations measure eighteen elements, such as daily mean temperature, extreme temperatures, dewpoint, mean wind speed, maximum wind speed, mean pressure, visibility, total precipitation and snow depth

Area	Number
South Africa, Namibia, Botswana and Lesotho	168
Argentina	129
Brazil	342
New Zealand (plus islands)	319
Australia (plus islands)	666
Southern hemisphere	2,369
Northern hemisphere	11,225

sent immediately for use in forecasting, and subsequently is passed on as climate data.

In Australia, for instance, there are about sixty weather stations staffed by the Bureau of Meteorology, 125 automatic weather stations (eighteen of which are offshore, on reefs and islands), 560 co-operative stations and hun-dreds of nearby ships sending data. Upper atmosphere soundings are made from about fifty places regularly. Ozone is measured at five stations, solar radiation at nineteen, and rainfall-intensity measurements are taken at 600 places. In addition, there are over 6,000 voluntary observers of daily rainfall (Note 10.B).

Data Sets

The longest continuous set of daily data comes from Kew near London, begun in 1773. The longest sets in Australia began at Parramatta in Sydney in 1821 and Perth in 1830, in South Africa at Cape Town in 1841, in New Zealand at Dunedin in 1853, in Brazil at Rio de Janeiro in 1851. Daily measurements have been taken at the Argentine base at Orcadas in Antarctica (at 61°S) since 1903, and at the South Pole since 1957. Unfortunately, almost half the 610 southern-hemisphere stations in 1991 had records for less than twenty years, mostly in South America, and many stations in Africa have closed or record only intermittently. Likewise, there are only about 60–70 places in the southern hemisphere where upper-atmosphere measurements are taken regularly, as against more than 600 in the northern hemisphere.

Handling Weather Data

Forecasters compress the information from a weather station by means of an internationally agreed code, which allows data to be sent rapidly by cable or radio, and shared with other weather bureaux. The code is a series of five-figure numbers in a standard sequence agreed in 1982. The information can subsequently be displayed in a standard fashion (**Figure 15.2**) on the corresponding point on a map. Such a map, with figures from many places, is called a *synoptic chart*, providing a snapshot of the weather at the time of measurement. A synoptic chart reveals what weather systems affect the region. For instance, the data in **Figure 15.3** indicate a cold front along a line across which there is a sudden drop in temperature from east to west by about 8 K, a rise in dewpoint by about 6 K and a backing of the wind from

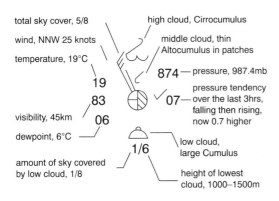

total sky cover, 5/8

wind, NNW 25 knots

temperature, 19°C

high cloud, Cirrocumulus

middle cloud, thin Altocumulus in patches

874 — pressure, 987.4mb

pressure tendency
07 — over the last 3hrs, falling then rising, now 0.7 higher

visibility, 45km

dewpoint, 6°C

amount of sky covered by low cloud, 1/8

low cloud, large Cumulus

height of lowest cloud, 1000–1500m

19
83
06
1/6

Figure 15.2 Coded information for a report from Christchurch (New Zealand) as displayed on a synoptic chart. The central circle is plotted at the location of Christchurch on the map. Cloud symbols are discussed in Figure 8.11 and wind symbols in Figure 14.4.

north-westerly to south-westerly. A series of daily synoptic charts like this shows the trends common in the region, and was the best tool available until the 1970s for forecasting tomorrow's weather.

15.2 WEATHER FORECASTING

A weather forecast is a statement of what seems probable, not a prediction of what is certain. It can be done in several ways, as follows. Whatever the method, the aim is to do better than either tossing a coin (which gives a 'random forecast') or simply guessing, which depends on the oddities of human prejudice and experience.

Folklore

Useful guidance is sometimes given by the experience distilled into folklore. An example is a traditional method of forecasting in Peru, for determining when conditions are propitious for planting crops. The method shows remarkable success. It is based on the brilliance of stars (i.e. the air's moisture content) and the occurrence of lightning, the taste of rain, etc. A similarly complicated method is used in Nigeria, based on the behaviour of chameleons, hawks, doves and grasshoppers, the leafing and fruiting of certain trees and selected calender and astronomical events.

Unfortunately, many weather sayings are worthless. For instance, a belief that can be traced back twenty-five centuries in Europe, that the coming year's weather copies that of the twelve days after Christmas. One reason for folklore being disappointing is its use in places remote from its origin. For instance, a saying about a red sunset promising fine weather tomorrow, common in Britain and fairly reliable there, is less useful in southern continents. The reason is that red skies in Britain result from Rayleigh scattering (Section 2.3) caused

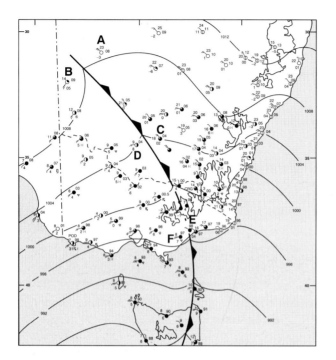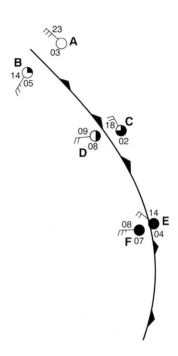

Figure 15.3 A synoptic chart of south-east Australia at 6 UTC (i.e. 4 p.m. Eastern Summer Time) on 23 August 1991. It shows only the wind, temperature, dewpoint, pressure ('04' means 1,004 hPa, '98' means 998 hPa), cloudiness (oktas) and precipitation, according to Figure 15.2. The part on the right shows only the temperature and dewpoint for six points near the cold front.

by numerous ice particles in the upper troposphere ahead of a *warm* front approaching from the west, whereas such warm fronts are rare at populated latitudes of the southern hemisphere (Section 13.3).

Persistence Forecasting

The easiest method of forecasting is to assume a continuation of the present – the *persistence forecast*. It is successful where the weather is dominated by processes which last longer than the period of prediction. For instance, it is easy to forecast the rainfall over the next week in a monsoonal area, where rains over several months alternate annually with dry periods of more months; if it is dry now, we are in a dry

period, which will probably continue beyond the seven days we are concerned about. Similarly, there appears to be a 60 per cent chance of a relatively dry month ahead in New Zealand if this month's rainfall is less than average. The chance of thunder tomorrow at Nelson in New Zealand is almost eight times greater if there is thunder today. Other examples of persistence are given in Section 10.4.

The accuracy of persistence forecasting in one country is illustrated in **Table 15.2**, in terms of the 'correlation' between recent and future daily mean temperatures. The shorter the time ahead of forecasting, the stronger the connection, i.e. the more accurate a persistence forecast will be.

Table 15.2 The correlation between the mean of the daily average temperatures over the past 'n' days, and the mean over the coming 'm' days, in Norway; the tabulated values show the correlation coefficient as a percentage

Number of recent days (n)	Average over the coming m days				
	m = 1	m = 3	m = 7	m = 15	m = 30
n = 1	70	59	51	43	35
n = 3	59	55	49*	44	35
n = 7	51	49	48	46	35
n = 15	43	44	46	47	31
n = 30	35	35	35	31	21

* That is, the correlation between the mean temperatures of the last three days and the next seven days, respectively, is 49 per cent

Climatological Forecasting

Whereas persistence forecasting is most accurate over short periods (before factors for change have had time to operate), the best estimate of the weather a long time ahead is the average value of past measurements there at that time of day and year – the *climatological forecast*. Such an estimate evens out the effects of processes which take a shorter time than the period of prediction. This way of averaging-out disturbing processes complements that of ignoring them, which is involved in persistence forecasting, and the average of the persistence and climatological forecasts proves to be notably accurate, as well as simple. In fact, the expense of other methods of forecasting always has to be justified by demonstrating better accuracy than this combined method.

Incidentally, there is no so-called 'Law of Averages', no truth in the idea that a series of above-normal temperatures, for instance, somehow increases the chance of below-normal values in the future in order to maintain the past average. Tossing a series of heads suggests a double-headed coin, rather than the inevitability of tails soon.

Statistical Forecasting

A statistical forecast uses past records of relevant factors at a place to find equations relating them to the weather on the following day, and then uses the equations for forecasting. An example is frost forecasting, described in **Note 15.C.** However, the risk of frost is very dependent on the locality (Section 3.6), especially in valleys, so relationships worked out in one place do not apply elsewhere. Regional forecasts of this kind are useful only for radiation frosts (Section 3.6). Another example of statistical forecasting is the prediction of rainfall from values of 500–1,000 hPa thickness (Note 12.E).

Approximate 24–hour forecasts have also been based on sea-level pressure (indicating the degree of uplift, i.e. of cloud formation), the change of pressure (i.e. the approach or departure of a front), the wind direction (which determines the advection of heat and moisture), and the cloudiness, i.e. the amount of solar heating.

A related statistical technique involves a *contingency table* of past observations, relating the frequency of occurrence of certain conditions at a place to earlier measurements at the same place or elsewhere. For instance, there is a strong tendency for heavy rain in northern Victoria (at about 35°S) in the period September–October if air pressures at Darwin (at 12°S) were low during the previous July–August. Likewise, the prediction of the season's number of tropical cyclones around Australia (Section 13.5) may be based on a prediction of the

ENSO cycle (as there tend to be more cyclones during a La Niña, Figure 13.15), the Quasi-Biennial Oscillation (more cyclones when the lower stratospheric winds are easterly, Section 12.3), and the SST around Australia (more cyclones when the SST is above-normal). Since these three factors are all either predictable or varying slowly during a season, tropical-cyclone frequency is fairly predictable.

Statistical relationships between conditions at widely separated places are known as tele-connections (Section 10.7). They can be either simultaneous or lagged, in the latter case they can be used for forecasting. For instance, it is relatively wet in Indonesia and New Guinea during the latter half of most years in which there has been a La Niña episode off Peru (Figure 10.17). In addition to the ENSO cycle, there are other, weaker connections between conditions at different latitudes, e.g. central Chile tends to be cooler and wetter when westerly winds strengthen over the south-eastern Pacific ocean. Also, relationships between conditions at different longitudes (such as the eastwards migration of weather systems, Section 13.3) lead to a tendency for Adelaide's weather to be experienced 12–24 hours later in Sydney, a thousand kilometres to the east.

Statistical methods are much used in long-range forecasting. One problem with statistical forecasting is that it applies only to the place where the data were gathered. Even there, relationships may change, so they need regular updating.

Analogue Forecasting

A further method of forecasting over two or three days involves comparing today's synoptic chart with thousands of charts drawn in the past to find those most similar, and then assuming that the consequences will be the same. The synoptic charts used may be for the surface or for 300 hPa height, or, preferably, both. Unfortunately, exact matches are not possible, and the sequels to the nearest approximations to today's chart turn out to differ from each other, so that there is no clear indication of what now to expect. The sequels differ because changes of the atmosphere are essentially *chaotic* (**Note 15.D**). So analogue forecasting has been largely abandoned.

Periodicity Method

The daily rhythm of warm days and cooler nights, and the annual cycle of rainfall in most places, leads us to look for other regularities of weather. Several were discussed in Section 10.7 in connection with the occurrence of droughts. The Madden–Julian Oscillation was mentioned in Section 12.1. If any were to prove reliable, it would allow prediction. For instance, if there were a 26-week repetition of some feature of weather and if twenty weeks have elapsed since the previous occasion, one can expect another in six weeks' time.

Sometimes there may be several rhythms in combination, creating occasional outstanding maxima and minima. Indeed, detection of four periodicities in parallel within the records of rainfalls in New Zealand since 1900, and then extrapolation into the future, allowed successful prediction in 1980 of the dry period from 1982–85.

It has often been suggested that the weather varies in accord with the eleven-year fluctuation of the annual number of sunspots (**Note 15.E**). The QBO has some influence on tropical cyclone frequency and annual rainfall at various places (Section 10.7) and there may be some effect of the phase of the Moon (**Note 15.F**). But none of these (except perhaps the QBO) is sufficiently regular or pronounced to be useful in weather forecasting. A graph of rainfalls looks remarkably like a graph of random numbers; similar apparent but unreal regularities occur occasionally in both.

Dynamical Forecasting

Next we consider the method of forecasting currently used by meteorological services around the world, based on calculations of the changes that will occur in each part of the whole atmosphere, starting from as complete a statement as possible of present conditions. This consists of the information available on a synoptic chart of recent surface measurements (Figure 15.3) and on charts of conditions aloft, at the standard levels of 850, 700, 500, 300 and 200 hPa. Deriving these charts is known as the *analysis*. Dynamical forecasting then involves using the analysis to derive a *prognosis*, i.e. charts of the situation to be expected at some specified time in the future.

Until the 1970s, the prognosis was based on empirical rules for modifying the current synoptic chart, and on human judgement. A key feature was the identification of the positions of air-mass boundaries, i.e. the fronts. It was then possible to use the Bergen model (Section 13.3) to estimate subsequent frontal development and movement, followed by inferences of the resulting wind directions and atmospheric uplift, which determine temperatures, cloudiness and rainfall. Such forecasts were reasonable up to about 24 hours ahead, but serious errors were common.

Numerical Weather Prediction

Nowadays, high-speed supercomputers are used instead to calculate changes to the synoptic chart. As a result, analysis of the weather has become objective, and the prognosis is based on equations which predict the changes of temperature, humidity, velocity, etc. at each point of an imaginary three-dimensional lattice (**Figure 15.4**). The lattice may consist of perhaps nine layers (representing nine levels of the atmosphere), and a rectangular grid of points in each layer for places separated by 500 km, for instance. Then a simplified set of equations

called the *primitive equations* (**Note 15.G**) is used to describe the basic laws of fluid motion and to calculate changes of conditions. This method of forecasting is called *Numerical Weather Prediction* (NWP) (**Note 15.H**), providing fresh prognoses each twelve hours, for instance, to show conditions up to five days ahead.

It has to be assumed in NWP that conditions are uniform around each grid point (**Figure 15.5**), a regrettable simplification necessitated by the limitations of even the largest compters. With point separation (i.e. a 'resolution') of 500 km, a model is unable to allow for the very different climate conditions on opposite sides of the southern Andes, for instance. More importantly, such a 'coarse-mesh' model cannot detect the mountain range itself, though it affects the weather for thousands of kilometres downstream (Note 12.K). And, most importantly, it cannot allow for atmospheric processes smaller than the grid size, such as thunderstorms. To cope with these problems, it is becoming increasingly common for a global model of widely spaced points to be supplemented by an embedded 'fine-mesh model' for a region, of points only 60 km apart at eighteen levels of the atmosphere, say, describing the region's atmosphere in more detail, to obtain more refined prognoses there.

The advantage of NWP is that it avoids errors of human judgement in deriving the prognosis, and can be steadily improved by enlarging the amount and reliability of input data, by new understanding of the physics of atmospheric change, and by faster, larger computers. The speed of computer systems used in NWP has increased tenfold every three years for the last thirty. As a result, errors of four-day forecasts in 1995 were no more than those for 24–hour forecasts in 1980.

Nowcasting

Regional forecasts for up to 24 hours ahead are now possible, using a computer model with a

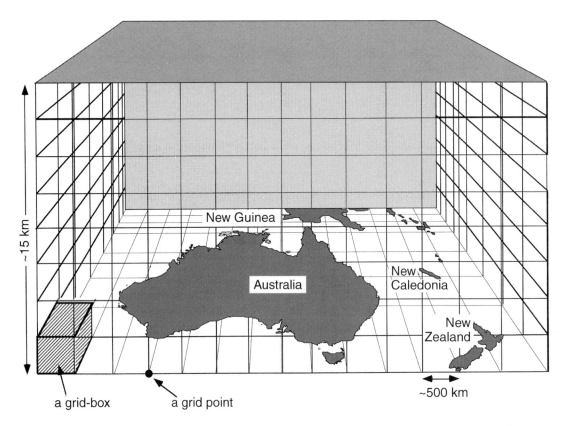

Figure 15.4 Part of a model used for Numerical Weather Prediction, representing a lattice of regularly spaced points which sample the troposphere to 15 km, say. It should be regarded as continuing sideways to cover the whole globe. This is an eight-layer model, but some models have more layers for greater accuracy, if a faster computer is available. The horizontal dimension of a grid box here is about 500 km, but some models have a closer spacing of grid points over the region of particular interest to the forecasters.

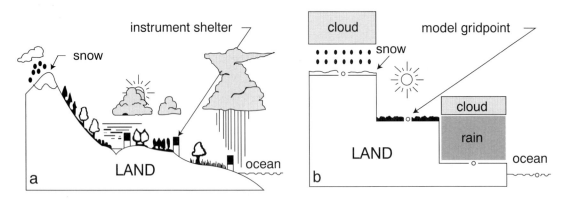

Figure 15.5 Schematic difference between (a) surface conditions in the real world, and (b) the equivalent in a computer model, showing the spatially stepwise description adopted in Numerical Weather Prediction.

local resolution of only 20 km, for instance. Such models can predict the onset of a sea breeze or the time that a cold front passes by, or a squall line (Section 9.5). The accuracy of such 'nowcasts' is limited mainly by the availability of frequent, closely spaced measurements for updating the model. This problem is being tackled by increasing use of data from satellites, aircraft and ground-based radars.

Short and Medium-range Forecasts

The dynamical NWP method is used for 'short-range forecasts' of a day or two and also for *medium-range forecasts* of 3–6 days, but there remains an essential role for weather forecasters. They have first to compare the prognoses from the models of different organisations (e.g. from the European Centre for Medium Range Weather Forecasts, at Reading in southern England, and from the Australian Regional model in Melbourne), in the light of past success in forecasting local movements of small and large highs and lows at this time of year. Having chosen a prognosis, the forecaster must interpret it in terms of the local weather, which is on a smaller spatial scale, in view of local experience of sea breezes, geography, current satellite pictures of clouds and so on. This interpretation often involves reckoning the positions of fronts; NWP models simulate well the evolution of frontal disturbances (Section 13.3), but are unable to pinpoint where the fronts are, because of their limited resolution. The whole procedure leads to estimates of the likelihood, amount, and type of rain, and daily extreme temperatures. Finally, the forecaster determines the need for warnings of tropical cyclones, thunderstorms, strong winds, bushfire risk, floods, hazard to exposed animals in cold and wet conditions, and so on.

Medium-range NWP models are similar to those for short-range forecasting, but they are global because fast-travelling disturbances, such as short waves in the jet stream, can circle the Earth in six days. The range of short and medium-range forecasts, especially in midlatitudes, is limited by the lifetime of frontal disturbances being 3–7 days (Section 13.3). It is difficult to predict the condition of a disturbance not yet created.

Longer-range Forecasts

Extended-range forecasts deal with conditions 6–10 days ahead. They are produced by the same NWP models that yield medium-range forecasts, but involve more uncertainty, usually consisting merely of a statement about the rainfall and temperature being above, about or below normal. Similar descriptive forecasts are made for times of 10–30 days (a *long-range forecast*) or 1–4 months (a *seasonal outlook*). These result from a combination of the persistence, climatological, statistical, analogue or periodicity methods described above. Also, use is made of a dynamical NWP model which allows for oceanic processes, which are too slow to be important in short-range weather forecasting.

Meteorological bureaux now regularly provide seasonal outlooks, with an accuracy notably enhanced by our increased understanding of the relevance of the Southern Oscillation, indicated by the sea-surface temperatures, the strength of the Trade winds, the location of areas of deep convection across the tropical Pacific ocean, and the depth of the thermocline (Notes 11.C and 12.N).

Accuracy

There are several measures of forecasting skill (**Note 15.I**) used to monitor the success of the agencies concerned. The forecast accuracy depends on (a) the feature of concern (such as the rainfall, daily maximum temperature, wind speed, the location of a tropical cyclone, or the occurrence of a storm, etc.), (b) the length of the *lead time* (the time between the forecast statement and the expected event), (c) the season of the year, (d) the location and (e) the forecasting method used. We will consider these in turn.

(a) In general, an unusual or a localised event, such as a tropical cyclone or a thunderstorm, is harder to foretell than the ordinary or the extensive, like a high-pressure system. In the case of occasional tropical cyclones, for example, it is inherently difficult to detect them in the early stages, but once a TC is mature the location of its eye and the strength of its circulation can be estimated by satellite. This information is manually entered into NWP models, in order to forecast the TC's future course. This deliberate injection of specific local information is called 'bogussing'. When a TC poses a threat to populated areas, planes are flown into the eye of the storm to obtain more information for bogussing.

Rainfall is the most difficult to forecast because it is patchy in time and space; the 'skill' in three-day forecasts in one American study published in 1981 was 45 per cent for daily maximum temperatures but only 18 per cent for the incidence of rainfall. A common yardstick in assessing the accuracy of prognostic charts is a comparison of estimate against measurement of the height of the 500 hPa level in the atmosphere, or else the pressure at sea-level.

(b) Obviously, the accuracy of forecasting falls off as the lead time increases. There is a doubling of error for each two or three days of numerical forecasting, and it outgrows the error of climatological forecasts after 10–15 days. The average error in predicting the daily maximum temperature at Melbourne is 1.7 K for a lead time of 24 hours, 2.4 K for 48 hours, 2.9 K for 72 hours and 3.1 K for four days, compared with 2.9 K for a climatology-plus-persistence forecast.

(c) Forecasting is easier in any place with a highly seasonal climate, as in a Mediterranean climate (Chapter 16) or in the north of Australia (except during the transition from the Wet to the Dry).

(d) It is easier to forecast the development of a disturbance where there is a sharp contrast between adjacent air masses. For this reason, forecasting in midlatitudes is more accurate than in the tropics, where steep temperature gradients are rare. Also, there is less difficulty in predicting conditions over a large plain than those amongst the irregularities of mountains or a coastline.

At the coast, errors are less in forecasting the minimum than the maximum temperature, because the latter is affected by the occurrence or not of a sea breeze (Section 14.2), whilst the minimum is stabilised by the ocean nearby. Inland, the possibility of cold air flowing onto a low-lying weather station at night makes forecasting the minimum the more difficult (**Figure 15.6**).

(e) A test in 1989, of six methods of forecasting thunderstorms within nine hours in Colorado, showed accuracies no better than that of persistence or climatological forecasting.

There have been dramatic improvements in long-range forecasting during the last decade or two, due to our increased understanding of ENSO (Section 12.7). In December 1982, for instance, the New Zealand authorities were able to predict correctly an unusually cool summer, an 80 per cent chance of drought in the following January–March, and abnormal rains on the west coast of the South Island. Seasonal outlooks of the rainfall in early spring for Australian farmers are now correct 70 per cent of the time.

Of course, accuracy is not the only criterion of successful forecasting. Timeliness, lead time and manner of presentation are also important, and all have improved in the last twenty years.

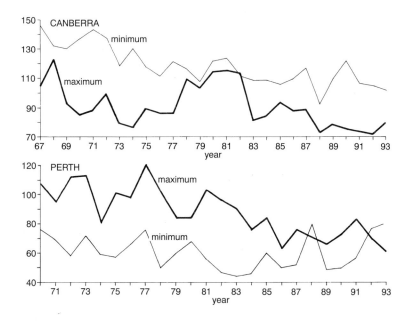

Figure 15.6 Changes in the numbers of days annually when forecast maximum or minimum temperatures were in error by at least 3 K, at coastal Perth and inland Canberra.

15.3 PAST CLIMATES

Information on remotely past climates is obtained by means of considerable ingenuity ('Table 15.3). As an example, layers in 7.6 metres of sediment in a lake near sea-level at 42°S in Chile can be individually dated as far back as 43,000 BP, and the type of pollen in a layer indicates either rainforest (with over 4,000 mm/a of rain) or dry conditions, with less than 1,000 mm/a, compared with the current 2,600 mm/a. (It is notable that the Chilean climates seem to have varied in parallel with those in Tasmania and New Zealand, judging by pollen data there also.)

All such evidence needs careful evaluation. Most of the techniques listed in Table 15.3 are only indirect and inaccurate, and even instrument measurements before about 1900 warrant caution because of differences of equipment and site. Also, the evidence may apply only locally; a high rainfall at one latitude does not necessarily imply wetness everywhere, but perhaps a change of ocean circulation (Section 11.5), a shift in the global circulation pattern (Figure 12.17) or a change in the track of frontal disturbances (Section 13.3). Another example concerns indications of a fall in sealevel. This might mean less ocean water due to the locking up of water in polar ice in cold periods, or could have been due to rising of the land locally. Likewise, evidence of a dwindling glacier (implying a rate of accretion by precipitation less than the rate of loss by sublimation and melting) might mean either reduced precipitation or more warmth or both, or may be associated with an interlude between periodic surging of the ice. Proof of global changes requires the concurrence of several lines of evidence from several locations.

Earliest Climates

Section 1.2 refers to the origin of the atmosphere. Since then, fossil algae in the oldest sedimentary rocks (Table 15.3) and evidence

Table 15.3 Some methods of assessing past climates (BP means 'before present', i.e. before 1950)

Data	Variables measured	Region	Time (years BP)*	Climatic inferences‡
Sedimentary rocks†	Appearance and fossil content	–	At least 100 million	Rainfall and sea-level
Geomorphic features	Shape and elevation of terrain	–	10 million	Temperature, rainfall, and sea-level
Ocean sediments	Types and isotopes of plankton fossils§	Oceans	10 million	Sea-surface temperature
	Ash and sand	Shallow oceans	200,000	Wind direction
Ice cores‖	Depth and isotopes of layers	Antarctica and Greenland	200,000	Temperature, precipitation and solar activity
Lake sediments	Varves¶	Midlatitudes	About 100,000	Temperature and rainfall
Pollen type**	Species amount	50°S–70°N	100,000	Temperature, rain
Ancient soil type	Composition	Low and midlatitudes	100,000	Temperature, rain
Glaciers	Length	Global	20,000	Temperature, precipitation
Archaeology	Various	Global	Over 10,000	Various
Boreholes††	Temperature	Various	About 10,000	Temperature
Tree rings‡‡	Ring width	Mid- to high latitudes	8,000	Temperature, rain
Proxy records§§	Phenology, sailing logs etc.	Europe and Asia	Over 1,000	Various
Instrument measurements	Various	Global	300	Various

* This is the earliest time that can be assessed by means of the given technique. See **Note 15.L** about radiometric dating of evidence.

† Sedimentary rocks are those deposited initially as grains of sand, dust, etc., turning over the course of time into shale, etc.

‡ The sea-level is an indirect indication of global temperature, since a low level means low temperatures when water is locked up in polar ice.

§ Columns of sediment drilled from the sea bed contain shells, including those of microscopic snail-like creatures called *foraminifera*. Various species flourish near the surface of the sea according to the temperature there. Also, they contain oxygen, which occurs in two isotopes – ^{16}O is most common, ^{18}O is rare. The ratio of $^{18}O/^{16}O$ is greater when the water vapour (which eventually deposits as ice) forms over a warmer sea surface.

‖ Ice cores display the annual cycle, through variations in acidity and concentrations of dust (there is more acid and dust in winter), especially in Greenland. Extremely cold years whose dates are known from other evidence act as markers in the ice-core record. Cores have been drilled through the Antarctic ice cap as deep as 3 km, indicating conditions over 200,000 years. Shorter cores have also been retrieved from the ice on Mt Kilimanjaro in Africa and some high peaks in the Andes.

¶ Varves are layers seen in lakes fed by meltwater, examined by a technique developed in Sweden. A layer of relatively coarse texture is deposited in spring and summer, from material brought in streams from the melting snow and ice. A thin layer of clay settles each autumn/winter when the melting stops, there is no streamflow and the lake freezes over. The various sediments deposited in one year constitute a varve. The layer's thickness and coarseness are greater if extra warmth increases the rate of melting and hence the streamflow. In one example, a sediment 16 m thick contained 250 varves, showing conditions over that number of years. Sediments from various lakes can be correlated by finding similar sequences of thin and thick layers, and overlapping records provide an extended history of the climate.

** The typical habitat of the dominant species of plant suggests the type of climate at the time.

†† See Section 3.5

‡‡ The tree ring is wider in a wet year for a tree growing in an arid climate, but for a warm year for one in a cold climate. The temperature may also be inferred from the ratio of ^{13}C (i.e. the carbon isotope with seven neutrons, Note 15.L) to normal ^{12}C in the wood.

§§ Proxy records are a substitute for climatic data, i.e. historic records that reveal climatic fluctuations. For instance: the wheat price in Europe (since AD 1200), the height of the Nile in Cairo (since AD 622), the blooming date of cherry trees in Kyoto, Japan (since AD 812), the occurrence of sea-ice off Iceland (since AD 860).

Plate 15.1 Evidence on past climates can be derived from the analysis of ice, and the bubbles of air within it, from various depths in Antarctica. The photograph shows a rod of ice being handled in an ice cave, after having been extracted by means of a vertical hollow drill mounted at the surface. The drill may be many hundreds of metres long, allowing the examination of ice of great age.

from later times all suggest that the climate of the globe *as a whole* has never differed by more than a few degrees from what it is nowadays. Despite this, there have been important changes of climate, such as the *Ice Ages* when ice sheets covered north-western Europe and much of Canada, and the locking up of water as polar ice lowered sea-levels by as much as 150 metres. The Ice Ages occurred around 700 million years before the present (i.e. 700 mBP), 300 mBP, and during the last 2 mBP (**Figure 15.7**).

The climates of places changed greatly when the Earth's crust shifted and cracked apart, millions of years ago. Australia was in the 'tropics' 340 million years ago (**Note 15.J**) and

grew the lush vegetation which became coal. Africa was over the South Pole in 300 mBP. What is now the middle of Australia was at 50°S by 280 mBP, and cold enough for considerable glaciers. Australia separated from the Indian subcontinent around 130 mBP, and the present Simpson Desert was under water between 110–65 mBP. New Zealand separated off around 50 mBP and Antarctica some 20 million years later, deflecting the ocean currents which affect climates. Australia is currently drifting northwards at a rate of about two centimetres annually.

The global mean temperature around 3.5 mBP was about 3 K higher than now. This period (the 'Pliocene Climatic Optimum') was

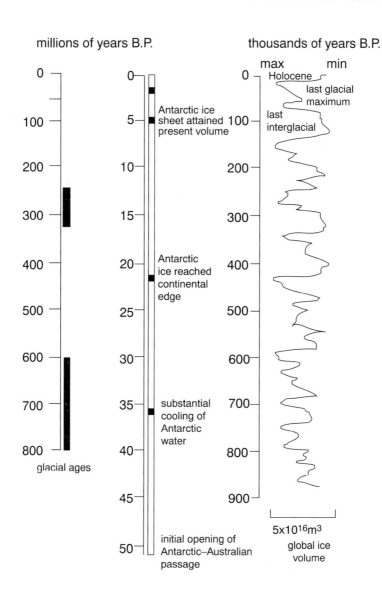

Figure 15.7 Variations of global climates since 800 mBP.

followed by a gradual cooling, culminating in the latest Ice Age. Temperatures in the southern hemisphere during the coldest part of this Ice Age were 3–10 K lower than now, depending on location.

Pleistocene

The 1.8 million years since the last Ice Age constitute the *Quaternary period*, a time too brief for continental drift to be an explanation of considerable variations of climate. The period is divided into the *Pleistocene* until 10,000 years ago (which more or less coincided with the evolution of human beings since *Homo erectus* in Africa in 1.9 mBP), and then the more recent *Holocene*.

There have been several major cold periods called *glaciations* (Figure 15.7) in the last 900 millenia, i.e. since 900 kBP. Each lasted about a hundred millenia and culminated in a notably cold time, along with discernible minor coolings each forty and twenty-two millenia, attributed to the Milankovic variations of the Sun's orbit (Section 2.2). The glaciations have alternated with warmer *interglacial periods*. Some of the switches between the alternative regimes appear to have been remarkably rapid, e.g. 5 K in a hundred years. As far as we can tell, our present era, the Holocene, is just another interglacial period.

The interglacial previous to the current one is called the *Eemian interglacial* and lasted some 20,000 years, until about 120 kBP. Temperatures in Europe were around 2 K warmer than now. There was more rain, and hippopotamus wallowed in the Thames. The increase of Antarctic temperatures was closely parallelled by an increase of carbon dioxide in the atmosphere from 190 ppm to 280 ppm. Also, Antarctic ice was greatly reduced in area, so that sea-levels were about 6 m higher than nowadays. The abrupt end of that warm period was possibly triggered by a change in the direction of the ocean conveyor belt in the North Atlantic (Figure 11.19).

The subsequent most-recent glaciation involved cooling from 120 kBP until about 20 kBP (**Figure 15.8**), with a parallel reduction of carbon dioxide, suggesting a greenhouse effect (Sections 1.3 and 2.7). The overall lowering of temperature by about 8 K did not progress steadily, but consisted of six minor coolings, each followed by a smaller warming. The eventual cooling at 20 kBP froze so much water on glaciers and at the poles that the sea-level had

fallen to about 120 m below what it is now. This facilitated human migration across the globe as early as 40 kBP, in particular into South America via a land bridge between Asia and America (now the Bering Strait) and into Australia across what is now the Torres Strait. New Zealand was a single island.

The cooling had several other consequences. Glaciers were probably active in the Snowy Mountains in south-east Australia in 30 kBP, and South Africa seems to have become wetter after 32 kBP. Global-average temperatures were about 5 K lower than at present by 20 kBP, but 6–8 K lower in South America, 5–8 K in the southern half of Australia and about 10 K lower in Antarctica, causing polar ice to extend as far north as 45°S at some longitudes, i.e. to much lower latitudes than nowadays (Figure 11.7). Ice covered much of Tasmania in 18 kBP. Even in the tropics the average cooling was about 4K, or yet more in the tropical highlands, so that the treeline in Papua New Guinea was about 1,000 m lower than now.

At the same time, there was extensive aridity in South Africa and Australia; much of the Simpson Desert of sand dunes in central Australia was formed around 18 kBP and lake levels were low. Most of South America also had less rain. The general aridity during the cold period is attributed to a reduced area of ocean and reduced evaporation from a cooler water surface (Note 4.C).

The Earth's orbit around the Sun gradually changed between 18–10 kBP, causing a 6 per cent decrease of summertime radiation and a similar increase in winter, notably at high latitudes. So polar mean temperatures had increased by about 11 K around 15 kBP. South Africa was initially wetter than now (during 17–15 kBP), but the climate became arid during 12–10 kBP, when there was a global cooling by about 1.5 K for 500 years or so (a period called the 'Younger Dryas', **Figure 15.9**). Australia was also drier than now (except inland in the south-east), probably on account of a shift

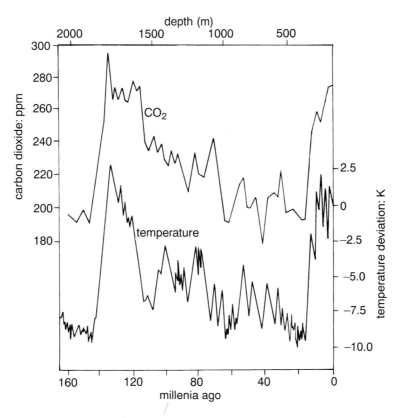

Figure 15.8 Changes in the carbon-dioxide concentration in air bubbles within ice from various depths (i.e. times since 160,000 BP) beneath Vostok, Antarctica, along with the temperature during bubble formation. The temperature is estimated from the ratio of the amount of 'heavy' oxygen (with a molecular weight of 18) to that of normal oxygen, with a molecular weight of 16 (Note 15.L). The ratio depends on the global sea-surface temperature at the time the bubbles were trapped.

southwards in the latitudes of the subtropical anticyclones (Section 13.6) and the midlatitude westerlies, in addition to weaker year-end monsoons in northern Australia. The sea was around 90 metres below present levels in 15 kBP.

Holocene

The relatively warm times since 10 kBP are known as the Holocene, the era of humanity's domination. The warming led to a rise of sea-level, so that only the northern tip of Queensland was joined to Papua New Guinea by 8 kBP.

At that time, New Zealand was wetter on the west side than now, while the east side was drier. Lake levels worldwide were high during 8–6 kBP, South Africa was relatively wet, Australia became wetter than now and global temperatures continued to rise. The time of highest global temperatures is known as the *Altithermal* (or Climatic Optimum). It occurred during 5–6 kBP in the northern hemisphere, but may have been a thousand years or so earlier in the southern. Temperatures during the Altithermal were about 2 K higher than now in New Zealand and Papua New Guinea, for instance, but

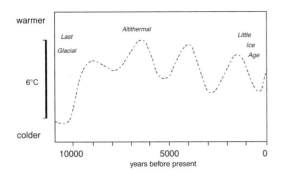

Figure 15.9 Greatly generalised variation of global climates during the Holocene, showing the Younger Dryas cold spell between 11–10 kBP, and a general warming after 10 kBP, except for four cool spells of which the last was the Little Ice Age.

tropical sea-surface temperatures were no higher than now. (Climate changes have generally been greatest at high latitudes.) The sea had risen to 3–10 m below the level nowadays.

Western Australia was wetter than at present in the later part of the Altithermal, most lakes in Australia were relatively full, and rainforest replaced drier vegetation over much of northern Australia. Similarly in New Zealand, the south-east coast of South America and the South African coast opposite Madagascar. Simultaneously, there was *dry* warmth in Argentina and parts of south-east Australia.

There was cooling after the Altithermal until about 3,000 BP, and then temperatures were about 2 K lower than now for the next two millenia, at least in south-east Australia.

The Latest Two Millenia

Relative warmth prevailed in Europe between AD 900–1200, with temperatures a fraction of a degree above those now. Stalagmites in New Zealand caves dating from AD 1200 indicate an average temperature of 10.2°C, compared with 9.4°C now, and tree rings in Tasmania also indicate this *Medieval Warm Period* (or 'Little Climatic Optimum').

Annual layers within 160 m of ice at 5,670 m on top of Quelccaya in South America (Section 3.2) indicate little of the normal November–April deposition of snow around AD 700, and during AD 1050–1500, but wet conditions from AD 1500–1700 followed by dryness till 1850. Conditions were colder than now during the period 1540–1880, but then there was an abrupt warming within a couple of years.

A worldwide cooling occurred between about 1450 and 1850, called the *Little Ice Age* (LIA). It appears to have been the fourth of similar cool periods, spaced almost equally apart since the last glacial period (Figure 15.9). The LIA happened to include the time of the Maunder Minimum, when there were hardly any sunspots, and the end of the LIA coincided with the termination of the second period of few sunspots, the Dalton Minimum (Figure 2.8). There was an increased difference between summer and winter on top of Quelccaya, i.e. less moisture in the colder air of winter along with more melting in summer. Tree rings in Chile confirm that the LIA occurred there at about the same time as in the northern hemisphere, though the evidence of cooling is less striking. New Zealand stalagmites from that period indicate temperatures only about 0.7 K cooler than now, and glaciers there were longer than usual. Some parts of the world were drier and some wetter during this time of cooling. Nowhere was the LIA continuously cold: it was simply a period which included many cold episodes.

Indications

This brief survey of the patchy and confusing evidence on past climates leads to the following provisional summary:

1 The temperature of the globe as a whole has varied within at most 10 K, for millions of years. Climates during recent centuries are amongst the warmest during the Quaternary period.

2 However, conditions at any spot have varied considerably. The climate of a place is not fixed, if we look beyond the experience of a single generation.

3 Temperatures (and by implication rainfall) can change rapidly from those of an Ice Age to those of an interglacial, or vice versa. Ice-core data from Greenland imply a switch in less than a hundred years, or perhaps only thirty. There is much to be explained about this process.

4 Changes of climate have not been uniform around the globe. They appear to have been greater at high latitudes than at low, and in the northern than the southern hemisphere.

5 Cool times tend to mean dry times in most places, presumably because of less evaporation from the oceans (Section 4.2). Thus, buried desert sand-dunes in tropical Africa and Australia extend beneath the present sea-level, so they were formed when the sea was low during a glaciation but when the land was dry. Nevertheless, the relationshp between aridity and temperature is not simple; inland dryness could also arise in warm periods because of increased evaporation from the ground.

Possible Causes of Change

There appear to be several factors causing alterations of climate, all acting together:

1 There is the random element inherent in the atmosphere and in the occurrence of volcanic eruptions.

2 There are the regular rhythms due to the Earth's spin and its orbit around the Sun, which account for daily and seasonal changes, modified by persistence. Milankovic variations of solar radiation (Section 2.2) are unlikely by themselves to cause much climate alteration but they may have triggered positive feedbacks sufficient to cause change (e.g. Note 2.J and Note 7.A). There are also other processes not quite so regular, like sunspot fluctuations (Section 2.2), the rotation of oceanic gyres (Section 11.5), the Southern Oscillation (Section 12.7) and the continuous processes of mountain building and erosion. In addition, there are occasional surges of enormous amounts of ice from the Antarctic glaciers into the sea, which might account for sudden coolings in the southern hemisphere, lasting for years.

3 There may be alternative patterns of energy flows between the atmosphere, hydrosphere, cryosphere and biosphere, each stable within limits but triggered into another regime by a sufficient perturbation. The Walker circulation (Figure 12.17) is an example of a system with two alternative, almost self-maintaining, sets of wind and ocean temperature conditions. If this analogy is applicable to the atmosphere as a whole, it would be useful to know how great an excursion from the normal can be accommodated without setting off a catastrophic change, such as a run-away greenhouse effect due to more of the Earth's oceans being converted to water vapour, which is a greenhouse gas.

4 In addition to chance, rhythmic processes and the possible onset of an abrupt acceleration of existing trends as a result of positive feedbacks, there is now another factor affecting climatic change. This is the influence of human activities, such as urban heating (Section 3.7), alteration of the surface albedo and roughness by deforestation and agriculture, and modification of the air's chemical composition by urban or industrial air pollution (Section 14.7).

15.4 CLIMATES IN THE TWENTIETH CENTURY

There appears to have been erratic global warming between 1900–40 (**Figure 15.10**), unlikely to have been due to any enhanced greenhouse

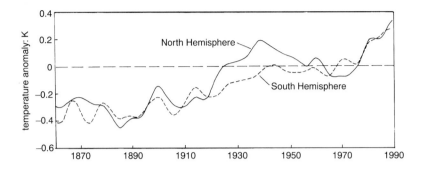

Figure 15.10 Recent changes of hemispheric average temperatures, showing departures from the 1951–80 average.

effect, as fossil-fuel consumption was modest compared with present rates and the CO_2 concentration was hardly changed from about 310 ppm. Warmth around 1920 may have been associated with a reduction of the atmospheric 'dust veil' caused by volcanoes (Note 2.G). But New Zealand experienced a relatively cold period from 1900–35, so changes were not uniform.

There followed a cooling by about 0.3 K between 1940 and 1970 in the northern hemisphere, probably due to increased pollution of the air by sulphates from the burning of coal. Sulphates convert to sulphur aerosols, which act as cloud condensation nuclei (Section 8.2), leading to more cloud droplets, i.e. a higher cloud albedo, so that more solar radiation is reflected away. This explanation is supported by the absence of any cooling trend between 1940 and 1970 in the southern hemisphere (Figure 15.10), where much less sulphate was created. Another explanation is that the apparent cooling is not real, but due to the relocation of many weather stations to airports during the 1950s, from within cities, which are often warmer (Section 3.7).

Frosts were more frequent at Quito (on the equator in Ecuador) during the period 1940–60, and temperatures remained steady or fell at Punta Arenas (53°S in Chile) until 1972 (**Figure 15.11**). Tree rings in Tasmania show a decline of summer temperatures during the period 1900–46 and then an equal rise by 1970, which continues (Note 10.D).

Recent Global Warming

Surface temperatures have increased lately at most places on Earth, especially since 1979. From that date, the rise has averaged 0.09 K/decade globally, and in eastern Australia about 0.2 K/decade between 1950 and 1990. The rise seen in **Figure 15.12** for Sydney, especially since 1966, may be due partly to urban growth (Section 3.7).

The average warming during the period 1951–93 was 0.15 K/decade in the southern Pacific region, being more in winter than summer, and at night than during the day. The annual mean daily minimum rose over the forty-two years, by 0.4 K at places in Queensland away from the coast, and by more than 0.2 K over half the continent. The result is that daily ranges of temperature are now less, as in the case of South Africa (Figure 3.15) and elsewhere.

There has been a falling number of frosts within Australia, especially in outback Queensland. Tree rings in west Tasmania show unprecedented growth since 1965. Also, there was a latitudinal shift during the period 1975–92 of the subtropical *jet* in the upper troposphere,

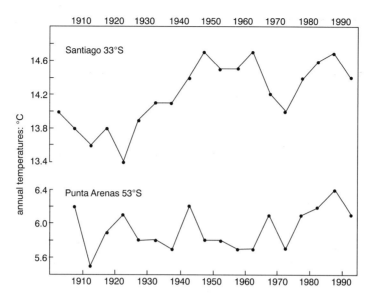

Figure 15.11 Annual mean temperatures at Santiago (33°S) and Punta Arenas (53°S) in Chile.

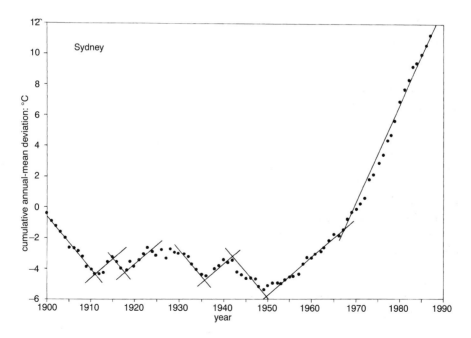

Figure 15.12 The variation of the 'cumulative deviation' of the annual-mean temperature from the long-term average of 17.6°C at Sydney, as in Figure 10.10.

from 26°S to 28°S, indicating an expansion of (warm) low-latitude climates. In accordance with this is the increase of summer rainfall over eastern Australia since 1953.

Reliable indications of global warming come from outside Australia too. New Zealand's surface temperatures show a rise of about 0.7 K since 1900. Sea-surface temperatures at 43°S off Tasmania have risen steadily since 1949, and a similar rise has been observed off Auckland in New Zealand.

Almost all the world's glaciers are in retreat. For instance the Franz Josef glacier in New Zealand shrank rapidly between 1935 and 1980, except for a few short-lived advances (**Figure 15.13**). A glacier at nearly 5 km elevation on Mount Jaya near the equator in Irian Jaya has almost disappeared, with a rise of the snowline from 4,400 m to 4,750 m between 1936 and 1993. The sea-level rose by 13 cm between 1910 and 1980, chiefly as a result of a rise of global sea-surface temperatures by about 0.5 K, with consequent thermal expansion (Note 11.B). There have been increased temperatures at Santiago in Chile, though not at Punta Arenas (Figure 15.11). Thirteen of fifteen weather stations around Antarctica have shown

warming, the overall figure during the period 1956–88 being about 0.3 K/decade.

Unfortunately, establishing long-term trends is still complicated by year-to-year fluctuations. Apparent changes of climate during the past century have to be judged against the background of normal inter-annual variation. A typical standard deviation of annual mean temperatures of about 0.5 K (Section 3.2) makes it difficult to be confident about trends of smaller magnitude. Also there is the confusion caused by much larger warming temporarily in some places, as a result an El Niño, e.g. by 6 K along part of the South American Pacific coast in 1982/83, raising the global mean temperature in 1983 by 0.2 K above values in the four surrounding years. Conversely, the eruption of the volcano on Mt Pinatubo in the Philippines in June 1991 produced a veil of dust in the lower stratosphere, reflecting more sunlight than normal and therefore cooling the Earth during the following twelve months or so (Note 2.G), once more obscuring any warming trend.

Cloudiness and Rainfall

There has been an increase of cloudiness in many places. For example, average cloudiness over Australia increased from 39 per cent at the beginning of the century to 49 per cent in 1980 (**Figure 15.14**). Such an increase globally could be explained as due to more evaporation from warmer oceans. The effect of increased cloudiness (at low levels) would be to offset some of the greenhouse warming by reflecting solar radiation away to space, though increased humidity at high levels acts as a greenhouse gas, enhancing the warming. The matter is receiving much study.

There have been erratic changes of rainfall over the last century (Figure 10.8), so that the standard deviation of annual rainfalls is generally much more than any trend. Nevertheless, some changes are discernible. Much of southern

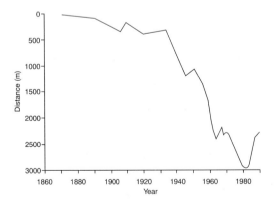

Figure 15.13 The position of the snout of the Franz Josef glacier in New Zealand, showing the distance of retreat since 1868.

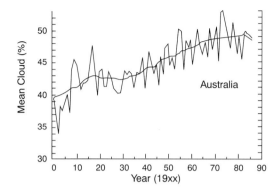

Figure 15.14 The increase of cloud in Australia.

raindays has increased in south-eastern New South Wales (**Table 15.4**).

Part of the explanation of recent changes of rainfall is the abrupt alteration in the character of ENSO events since the 1970s. Prior to that, La Niña episodes lasted about as long as El Niño episodes, but El Niño episodes since 1977 are more frequent and more persistent, with only occasional excursions into the La Niña phase. The continuously negative Southern Oscillation Index from 1990 to 1995 was unprecedented in 120 years of record.

Africa has experienced a drying trend since 1950, whereas South America has received more rain (**Figure 15.15**). Summer precipitation in south-east Australia increased from 1895 for the next fifty years, with an opposite trend of winter rainfall. The annual number of

15.5 FUTURE CLIMATES

Estimates of climates in the future depend on the relative significance of the factors causing past changes (Section 15.3), including the random element. It appears that random events

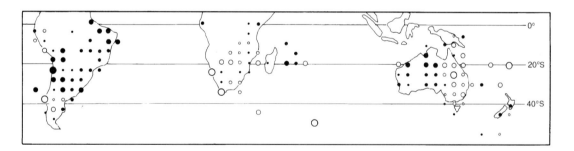

Figure 15.15 'Relative trends' in precipitation between 1950 and 1993, i.e. the change expressed as a percentage of the average precipitation during that period. For instance, if the average rainfall between 1950 and 1993 was 1,000 mm/a and a gradual decrease of 100 mm/a occurred during that period (e.g. from 1,050 to 950 mm/a), then the relative trend is about 10 per cent. The largest black circles mean a relative trend of 200 per cent, the next largest 100 per cent, the next 50 per cent, the next 25 per cent and the smallest 10 per cent. Solid rings imply increases and hollow rings decreases.

Table 15.4 Changes of the annual number of raindays at places on the southern tablelands of New South Wales

Intensity (mm/day)	1880–1900	1901–20	1921–40	1941–60	1961–80	1981–90
>0	89 days/a	87	93	101	109	109
>30	3.5	3.1	3.7	3.9	3.8	3.0

such as volcanic eruptions have an appreciable effect on the atmosphere (Note 2.G), but only for a year or two. Cyclic processes such as the Milankovic variations operate slowly. The impacts of human society are of increasing importance.

Effects of Human Society

People are likely to determine future climates in various ways. An extreme instance is nuclear warfare, which would entail the horrors of airborne radioactivity, possibly damage the stratospheric ozone layer, and maybe force enough aerosols into the stratosphere to exclude the sunshine to the extent that temperatures fall and crops are seriously depleted (Note 2.G). More certain will be the impacts of population growth and industrialisation, producing greater urban heating in the swollen cities and more atmospheric pollution by chemicals and dust. Sulphate pollution from the burning of coal is particularly threatening, because of the impact on cloud formation and hence global temperatures (Sections 8.9 and 15.4). It also leads to acid rain (Section 10.1). So it is a matter of concern that increasing amounts of coal are being burnt, especially in developing countries.

More profoundly, there is a fear that the carbon dioxide and similar gases (Section 2.7) that we produce in increasing amounts (Figure 1.2) will eventually create a dangerous degree of enhanced greenhouse heating (Note 2.L). Emissions are likely to be three times the 1990 rate by the year 2100, if the world population doubles, as seems probable, and if there is moderate economic growth without strong pressure to reduce the emissions. In the meantime, the effect on the atmospheric concentration of carbon dioxide seems likely to be a doubling (compared with 1900) by the middle of the next century. To prevent such an increase, it was resolved at an international conference in Rio de Janeiro in 1992 that emissions should be cut back to 1990 levels by the year 2000. The chances of that being achieved seem slender,

especially in developing nations, though the increase of emissions had been cut back from 1.5 ppm/year in the 1980s to just below 1 ppm/year in 1995, and a similar slowdown has been measured for methane.

The effects of the expected increase of carbon dioxide can be estimated in various ways. Firstly, consider the remarkable dependence of global temperature on CO_2 concentration during the last 160,000 years (Figure 15.8), implying future warming. Secondly, extrapolate twentieth-century changes, which have shown warming recently (Figure 15.10). Thirdly, calculate the change of temperature from the expected effect on the loss of longwave radiation to space (**Note 15.K**), which again suggests global warming. Fourthly, note that computer simulations of future climates by means of GCMs (Section 12.6) all indicate a rise of global temperatures.

GCMs

A general circulation model (or *climate model*) is basically the same as a NWP model except that the GCM is set to follow developments over many years, not a few days, at the expense of spatial and temporal detail. (A wide spacing of the points which sample the climate, and a long time step between recalculation of changes of temperature, etc., are both needed to reduce the number of calculations, to permit working out climates decades hence, in a reasonable time.) A climate model uses the same equations as a weather model, starting from present January-average conditions, for instance, and particular attention is paid to processes which are too slow to be important in weather forecasting, such as changes of land or ocean-surface conditions. Modern models (there are about a score of different GCMs in the USA, Australia, Europe and elsewhere) are much improved on those used by pioneers in the 1970s. They now allow for a *gradual* increase of CO_2 concentration, for the other greenhouse gases, for sulphate aerosols, for the daily cycle of solar radiation, for the interaction between atmosphere and ocean, etc.

The models are used for 'what-if?' questions, e.g. what would the general circulation be like *if* the carbon-dioxide concentration were doubled? The answers achieved are made credible by the success of GCMs in the following ways:

(a) in representing current patterns of pressure, temperature and rainfall (**Figure 15.16**), and their variability,
(b) in simulating the climates of about 9,000 BP, when the seasonal variation of radiation was different because of the altered orbit around the Sun (Section 2.2), and
(c) in reproducing the global response of the atmosphere to perturbations such as El Niño and volcanic eruptions.

It is notable that every GCM shows the inevitability of global warming from a doubling of carbon dioxide. Though estimates of the amount of warming vary within the range 1.5–5 K, the range is being narrowed, converging towards 3 K or so. This is approximately equivalent to the difference between the annual

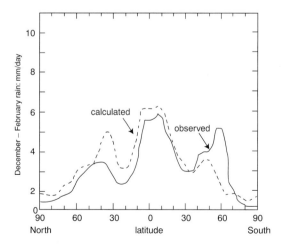

Figure 15.16 The degree to which the output of a modern GCM reproduces the actual variation of zonal-mean rainfall with latitude.

means of Wellington and Auckland, or Canberra and Adelaide, for example.

The various models differ chiefly in their estimates of future rainfalls in particular regions, because of uncertainty about the effects of changes of cloudiness at either low or high levels. Some models, but not all, indicate that twice the carbon dioxide implies fewer raindays around 30°S in Australia, but more rain on each rainday, leading to a 10 per cent increase overall. Indeed, one would expect an increase of precipitation as a consequence of more evaporation from warmer oceans.

Impacts

Higher average temperatures are likely to increase the frequency of days hot enough to affect mortality (Note 3.C). The increase in the case of Alice Springs, for instance, can be estimated by comparing the number of hot days in past years of different average temperature (**Figure 15.17**). The increase would be less at places by the sea, where daily maxima are limited by sea breezes (Section 14.2). So a general warming by 3 K at Brisbane would increase the number of hot days by only 5.4 annually, and at Melbourne would increase the annual number from the present eight, to fifteen.

Higher sea-surface temperatures might reduce the subsidence in the north Atlantic which drives the global oceanic conveyor belt (Section 11.5). In that case, there would be considerable alterations to the distribution of heat around the world, with consequences hard to foresee, but possibly comparable to the switching of climate at the end of past Ice Ages.

Evidence in Sections 15.3 and 15.4 indicates that warming in the past has gone hand in hand with increased rainfall at many places. Other clues to future rainfalls can be obtained by comparing rainfalls in the five warmest years during the period 1925–74, for instance, with the pattern in the five coldest; it appears that some places get *less* rain, notably in summer in

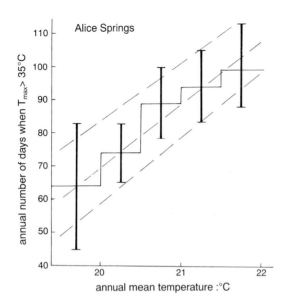

Figure 15.17 The connection between annual average temperature and the number of days when the daily maximum exceeds 35°C, at Alice Springs (24°S).

important grain areas in central USA and much of Europe and Russia. Another method of assessment is to consider rainfalls during the Altithermal period, some 6,000 years ago, when temperatures in Europe were 2–3 K warmer than now (Figure 15.9). This, too, indicates relatively dry conditions in North America but wetter conditions in some other areas, including western Australia. It is clearly unsafe to plan future water supplies, irrigation schemes, hydro-power engineering, etc. on recent climate data alone.

Sea-levels

Sea-levels were about 5 m higher than now during the previous interglacial period 120,000 years ago, and over 100 m lower at the depth of the Ice Age at 18 kBP (Section 15.3). So future global warming must lead to the sea rising, chiefly as the result of the increased melting and calving of icebergs from Greenland and the West Antarctic ice-cap, and, more immediately, thermal expansion of the sea above the thermocline. Sea water expands by roughly 0.02 per cent per degree (Note 11.B), so a layer of 500 metres warming by 1 K on average would rise by 100 mm, perhaps at a rate of about 1 mm/year. This approximates the rate measured at Wellington over the last century. However, any rise may be offset initially by the accumulation of snow in Antarctica due to increased precipitation following more evaporation from warmer oceans. The exact rate of rise is still uncertain, though it is important to people living on coral islands and in Bangladesh and Holland, and eventually to the vast populations living in coastal cities.

Effects on Agriculture

The patchy warming and either increase or decrease of precipitation that seem to lie ahead will affect agriculture, again in an irregular way. Some high-latitude areas, where greenhouse warming is expected to be most dramatic, will have enhanced yields because of greater warmth and fewer frosts, and some semi-arid areas because of additional rain. C3 crops (e.g. wheat and rice) will be stimulated by the higher carbon-dioxide concentration (Note 1.B). But the enhanced evaporation that results from warmth removes soil moisture, tending to reduce crops and extend the deserts. Also, higher temperatures promote insect attack, weeds and disease, and accelerated crop development in warm conditions allows less time before maturity for collecting the radiation which determines the harvest (Note 2.I).

Comparisons of the crops of warm and cool years in the last few decades, calculations based on computer models of crop growth and experiments on plants grown in controlled conditions, all indicate that global warming due to twice the carbon dioxide might *reduce* yields of wheat and maize by 5–10 per cent in northern

America, Europe and New Zealand, for example. It has to be remembered though that such figures ignore the impacts on crops of possible changes in the frequency of extreme events, like droughts, floods and strong winds, and also the mitigation achieved by crop adaptation, selection and breeding.

In short, global warming has to be taken seriously. There are still gaps in our understanding of the process, and uncertainties about its consequences, though rapid progress is being made. Even with the caution traditional in scientific investigation, we can say now that the evidence of the last few decades is 'not inconsistent' with the prospect of considerable changes due to the enhanced greenhouse effect.

In the next chapter we turn from speculations about the future to consideration of the present climates at places in the southern hemisphere.

NOTES

15.A Weather radar

15.B Places of weather measurement

15.C Frost forecasting

15.D Feedback, chaos and unpredictability

15.E Sunspots and forecasting

15.F Effects of the Moon's phase

15.G Primitive equations for weather forecasting

15.H Numerical Weather Prediction

15.I Forecasting skill

15.J The 'tropics'

15.K Radiative equilibrium and global warming

15.L Radiometric methods of dating past climates

16

SOUTHERN CLIMATES

16.1 INTRODUCTION

The purpose of this chapter is to illustrate how climates in the southern hemisphere can be 'explained' (to quote the book's title) in terms of what has been discussed in previous chapters, mostly concerning weather. Climate is the product of prevailing weather, as mentioned in Section 1.1, i.e. of the shifting highs and lows which occur at particular latitudes and linger in particular regions (Figures 12.1 and 13.16), creating average patterns of pressure (Figures 1.8 and 12.7) and winds (Figures 12.1–2, 12.4–6 and 12.12).

As regards geographical factors, we have seen that the climate of any place depends chiefly on the following six:

1 the hemisphere, which determines the warm season outside the Tropics, or the wet season between them;
2 the latitude, which controls daylength (Table 2.1), annual mean temperature (Section 3.2), seasonal range (Section 3.3), rainfall (Table 10.1), and prevailing winds (Section 12.1);
3 the elevation, which influences the amount of

UV radiation (Section 2.6), the net radiation (Section 2.8), mean temperature (Section 3.2) and, to a lesser extent, its daily and annual range (Sections 3.3 and 3.4), as well as the precipitation (Section 10.3), whilst the location upwind or downwind of a mountain range determines rainfall and affects temperature (Note 7.E);
4 the ocean circulation (and hence the pattern of sea-surface temperatures), which affects conditions at the coast (Table 11.2);
5 the distance downwind of an ocean, which governs annual and daily temperature ranges (Section 3.4) and rainfall (Section 10.3); and
6 the local topography, which influences the temperature (e.g. frost hollows, Section 3.6) and local airflow (Section 14.3).

These relationships are summarised in **Table 16.1**.

We will now consider climates in general, in terms of their classification, and then the effects of the six factors mentioned above on the climates of the main land areas of the southern hemisphere.

Table 16.1 The effects of geographical factors on climate elements. For instance, an increase of elevation lowers the temperature except in a valley bottom at night. '(S3.2)', for instance, means that further information is given in Section 3.2. '(T1.1)' refers to Table 1.1.

Climate scale (T1.1)	Geo-graphical factor	Radiation (S2.4)	Mean temp. (S3.2)	Annual range (S3.3)	Atmos. uplift (S7.4)	Precipitation (S10.3)	Water vapour pressure (S6.4)
Global	Latitude	Various	Less *	More	Various	Various	Less
Synoptic	Elevation	More	Less	–	More	Various	Less
	SST upwind	–	More	–	More	More	More
	Distance inland	More	Various	More	–	Less	Less
Meso and topo	Landform†	Various	Various	–	Various	Various	–
Micro	Surface condition	–	Various	Various	–	–	Various

* That is, an increase of latitude is associated with a lower temperature
† That is, slope, orientation, albedo, wetness, runoff

16.2 CLIMATE CLASSIFICATION

Surface data collected as described in Section 15.1 allow us to summarise the climate of a place in terms of average conditions and deviations from them. Particular attention is usually paid to monthly mean values of the daily-mean temperatures and daily extremes, along with the monthly rainfall.

The next step in condensing the flood of numbers that arise in continuously measuring the weather everywhere is to group *homoclimes*, places with similar climates. This imposes orderliness on the information, and stimulates wondering about the reasons for differences. Climate classification is also directly useful, e.g. in choosing crops for a particular climate – one selects from those grown in homoclimes. Or, to take a converse instance, there was the problem in Colombia of finding areas suited to the growing of tea, which became the problem of finding topoclimates in Colombia which resemble (in terms of monthly rainfall and mean temperature) those of tea-growing regions elsewhere in the world.

There are several ways of grouping similar climates, according to how we define 'similar'. Which criteria to use depends on the problem. If you are concerned with human comfort (Section 6.5), you would group places in terms of temperature and humidity. But rainfall would be more relevant if you are a farmer in an arid land. We will consider some of the criteria that have been used.

Latitude as the Criterion of Climatic Similarity

This is the oldest system, dating from the origin of the word 'climate', which is related to 'incline', as in the 'declination' of the Sun (Section 2.2). A tropical climate is found where the noonday Sun is inclined high in the sky.

Figures 3.4 and 10.3 indicate the effects of latitude on temperature and rainfall, by and large. But the effects of altitude and proximity to the sea (Sections 3.2 and 10.3) are ignored in using latitude alone as the criterion for classification.

Temperature as Criterion

Grouping places according to temperature was done in effect by annual-mean isotherms on maps of the world by Alexander von Humboldt in 1817, Alexander Supan in 1879 and Wladimir Köppen in 1884. An alternative is to categorise by the number of months when temperatures exceed the lower limit for plant growth, or the number of frost-free months, or the number of growing-degree days (Note 3.I). But this overlooks the importance of rainfall to plants.

Rain as Criterion

Alexsander Voeikov classified climates in 1874 according to the seasonal incidence of rain, leading to a world map in 1884, identifying areas of various degrees of wetness. Such a classification is useful in warm dry countries, where moisture is the main factor limiting growth. (Thus the preoccupation with rainfall in Australia, whereas Europeans are concerned about temperature and radiation.) An example is the Goyder Line in South Australia, which demarcated parts suited to growing wheat (Section 16.6). Elsewhere, the ratio of months with rainfall less than 60 mm to the number with over 100 mm has been used as a criterion for deciding where rice can be grown without irrigation.

An analagous criterion is *aridity*, a vague concept which takes in evaporation as well as rainfall. It may be expressed by the ratio of rainfall to the potential evaporation, P/E_o. A climate is 'arid' (i.e. the soil is dry) when the ratio is low. For instance, a comparison of Figure 4.12 and Figure 10.12 indicates that the ratio is less than 0.1 in much of Australia's interior.

The temperature is often taken as proxy for the evaporation rate in assessing aridity, since T and E_o are closely related (Section 4.3). So P/E_o is replaced by the ratio of rainfall to temperature P/T, where T is in degrees Celsius. But there are several other variants of either P/E_o or E_o/P, using net radiation or saturation deficit as a proxy for E_o. Categorisation of climates more explicitly in terms of soil moisture was introduced by Warren Thornthwaite in 1948, though it involved an unsatisfactory method of estimating the evaporation.

Vegetation as Criterion

Natural vegetation reflects the climate as a whole, and has been used as an indicator of it. Of course, vegetation also depends partly on the soil type, but that too is influenced by the climate. So coconut palms grow only where the monthly mean temperatures always exceed 18°C, pasture exists only where annual mean temperatures are above −2°C and trees where it is over +2°C, and the boundary of 'saltbush country' in Australia coincides with the isohyet of 200 mm during April to November. The association between vegetation and climate has led to the diagram in **Figure 16.1**. Temperature decreases vertically (a measure of increasing latitude or altitude) and rainfall increases diagonally, towards the lower right. As a result, T/P (or E/P, i.e. soil dryness) increases along the other diagonal, towards the lower left. Thus 'desert scrub' is found where rainfalls are between 125–250 mm/a and the E/P ratio is above unity, i.e. the soil is dry on average.

The disadvantage of classifying climates according to the vegetation is that plants depend on other things also (competition, soil type, nutrient level, slope and so on), not only on climate. As a result, the classification is only approximate. **Table 16.2** shows what a wide range of climates is associated with each kind of vegetation found in Australia. Thus, a climate with January/July rainfalls of 100/10 mm and temperatures 30/20°C can sustain either savanna woodland or tropical rainforest.

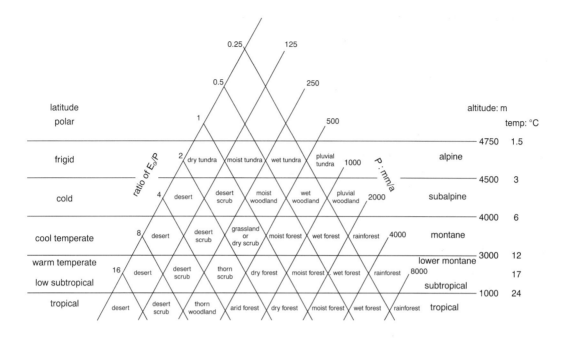

Figure 16.1 Stratification of vegetation with altitude as a function of annual rainfall P. The ratio E_o/P is a measure of aridity.

Table 16.2 January and July conditions associated with various kinds of vegetation found in Australia, in descending order of January rainfall. The range shown in each box results from about ten values, whose rounded-off median is shown bold

	Rainfall (mm/month)				Monthly mean temperature (°C)			
Natural vegetation	January		July		January		July	
Tropical rainforest	45–529	**290**	6–128	**35**	21.7–32.3	**27**	10.2–22.5	**18**
Savanna woodland	81–430	**220**	1–39	**8**	22.4–30.8	**28**	9.0–25.5	**23**
Shrub savanna	63–265	**130**	0–36	**3**	26.9–32.2	**31**	11.8–22.2	**19**
Mallee	63–265	**130**	23–104	**55**	18.5–28.6	**24**	9.5–14.3	**11**
Temperate rainforest	47–147	**90**	84–320	**200**	12.1–15.4	**13**	2.1–9.4	**4**
Dry sclerophyll forest	10–166	**75**	42–174	**70**	16.7–24.3	**22**	5.1–13.0	**9**
Savanna grasslands	45–134	**70**	2–22	**10**	29.6–32.3	**31**	15.1–22.0	**17**
Wet sclerophyll forest	17–116	**60**	38–185	**60**	14.9–21.3	**20**	6.3–13.7	**10**
Temperate woodland	11–69	**50**	28–93	**45**	14.5–26.8	**23**	4.8–10.2	**9**
Alpine	37–133	**50**	48–258	**100**	13.3–16.9	**15**	−2 to +8.4	**6**
Desert	20–89	**35**	6–46	**15**	26.7–32.3	**30**	10.9–18.1	**13**
Temperate semi-arid steppe	10–78	**25**	13–25	**15**	25.5–30.3	**28**	10.2–13.0	**11**
Shrub steppe	11–28	**20**	9–34	**15**	23.8–31.3	**25**	8.7–13.2	**12**

Köppen's Classification

Wladimir Köppen (1846–1940; his name is pronounced 'kerpen') first classified climates at the age of 24 and continued to refine his system until he was 90. His 1918 version is probably the most significant, and the most widely used nowadays. It involves grouping climates according to the kinds of vegetation present, using conditions at the boundaries of trees, for instance, as limits for the various categories (Note 16.A). As an example, South America's climates are shown in **Figure 16.2**.

About 20 per cent of the world's land has climates within class A (including 9 per cent as rainforest in 1987), 26 per cent in B, 15 per cent in C, 21 per cent in D and 17 per cent in E. D climates do not occur in the southern hemisphere; they characterise the climate on the large land masses between 45–65°N. Seventy-seven per cent of Australia's population

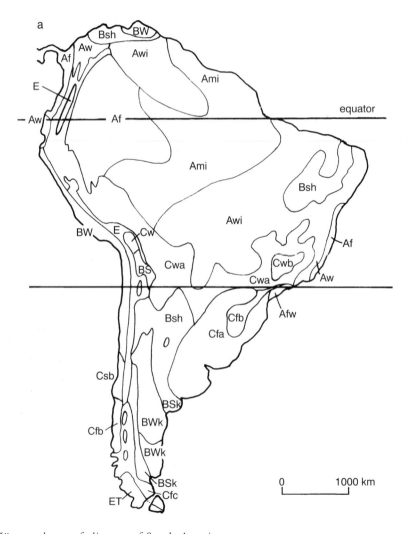

Figure 16.2 Köppen classes of climates of South America.

Plate 16.1 The strength of the Antarctic katabatic wind at the coast (in December 1991) is shown by the angle of lean in this photo, taken in the Vestfold Hills at 68°E.

live where the climate is labelled Cf, affecting 10 per cent of the continent's area, and another 15 per cent live within Cs areas, occupying 3 per cent of the land, where Cf and Cs are parts of the C category (Note 16.A).

Air-mass Frequency as Criterion

The climate of a location is the aggregate of the kinds of weather that prevail. So Tor Bergeron proposed in 1928 that places be classified according to the frequency with which they are affected by various air masses (Section 13.2). This is exemplified in **Figure 16.3**, which shows, for example, that Perth (in Western Australia) is governed by maritime polar air masses from June through September. The logical advantage of this method of classifica-

tion is that it is based on a cause of climate, not an aspect, a description or a symptom. Nevertheless, it is little used, because the definition of air masses is somewhat arbitrary.

Agglomerative Classification

Nowadays there are sophisticated statistical procedures for grouping places with similar climates. One is *'cluster analysis'*, based on the numerical differences between climatic variables at different places, such as the annual extreme temperatures, seasonal rainfalls, frequency of hail, etc. Dozens of such climatic characteristics of each place may be considered. Classifying then involves grouping the places to minimise differences between the variables of any pair of them within each group. The arbi-

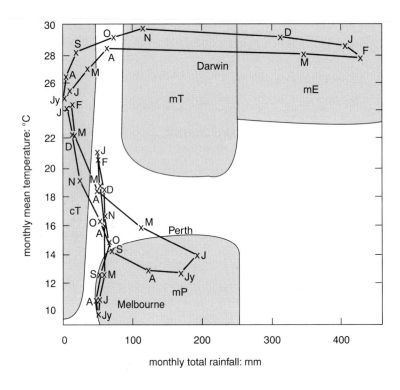

Figure 16.3 Thermohyet loops for Darwin, Perth and Melbourne, showing principal air masses influencing climates in each month.

trariness of the selecting of which climatic variables to consider can be reduced but not avoided by another procedure called *principal component analysis*, which has been used widely since about 1980. The groupings that result depend on which procedure is adopted.

Problems

Classifying climates has several of the problems common to the whole science of classification, *taxonomy*. They include the following:

1 It is necessary to make an arbitrary decision about the number of categories to use. Too few and there are more frequent problems in allocating odd cases. Too many and you lose the advantage of simplification.
2 There is a suggestion of abrupt differences at the lines on a map defining the zone of each group. A way round this is to express similarity as a number, rather than in terms of yes/no criteria (**Note 16.B**).
3 Any hierarchical system (like that of Carl von Linne in 1735 for classifying plants, and that of Howard for clouds – see Section 8.3, and Köppen's climate classification) involves judging which attributes are of first rank of importance and which of second, etc.
4 No allowance is made for the variability and extremes which are important in many fields.
5 Insufficient distinction is made between the mesoclimate sampled by a climate station and the microclimate which affects crops and people.
6 Students of climatology often mistake allotting a class label to a climate as somehow explaining it. Köppen's classification, for instance, is merely descriptive, not an explanation.

Homoclimes

The problems just listed make some looseness unavoidable when matching homoclimes. Places within the same class do not have precisely the same climate. Nevertheless, it is at least interesting that central Chile has some resemblance climatically to the area around Cape Town in South Africa, and to the south-western corner of Australia, and that south-east Brazil is a homoclime of Madagascar. A knowledge of the climate at one place provides a feeling for what to expect at corresponding places in the same class.

The practical usefulness of the concept of homoclimes is evident in the following examples.

1 Beetles specialising in the burial of pellets of sheep dung in Australia were sought and found in homoclimes in southern Europe and the south-west of South Africa.
2 Correlations between conditions at fifty-four stations in Colombia and those in eleven tea-growing areas around the world, showed that five stations in Colombia have climates like those in part of Malaysia. So those five places were identified as possibly suitable for growing teas introduced from that area in Malaysia.
3 The transfer of bananas and sugar-cane from their origin in south-east Asia, and potatoes from Peru, has required an initial searching for homoclimes and then breeding to adapt the plants to the new circumstances.
4 Rubber originated in the Amazon valley and was prevented from spreading naturally by the quite different climates which surround it. Now it flourishes in homoclimes in south-east Asia where the daily mean temperature remains a little above 24°C or so, and the rainfall exceeds 1,750 mm/a.

In view of these examples, one concludes that climate classification is worth while, despite the difficulties.

16.3 ANTARCTICA

Antarctica is a vast island (**Figure 16.4**), with an area roughly the same as that of South

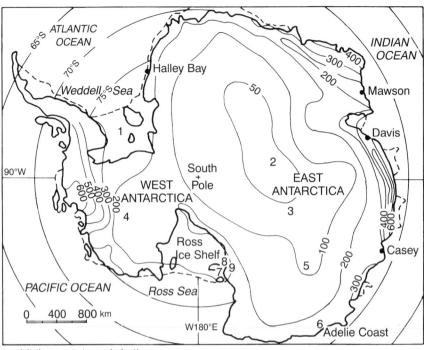

precipitation: mm water equivalent/year

Figure 16.4 Places on Antarctica and isohyets showing the annual precipitation in terms of the water equivalent, i.e. mm/a. The numbered places refer to the following: 1. Filchner ice shelf, 2. the highest point on the plateau (3,570 m), 3. Vostok, 4. Byrd, 5. Dome C, 6. Dumont d'Urville, 7. Mt Erebus, 8. Lake Vanda and 9. McMurdo Sound.

America (south of the equator), twice that of Australia (Note 1.A) and three times the area of permanent ice in the Arctic. It is the world's highest continent, with an average elevation of 2,450 m. There is an eastern part with a coast at about 68°S and containing most of the high land, and a much smaller western part, only 850 m high on average, with a coast at about 75°S, facing the south-east Pacific ocean. So the continent is not symmetric about the Pole. The parts might be thought separated by a line through the Pole, between two broad inlets, the Weddell Sea and the Ross Sea. Each inlet is covered by an immense shelf of partly floating ice, hundreds of metres thick. The larger is the Ross ice shelf (Figure 16.4), whose area is about

530,000 km^2 (twice the size of New Zealand) and thickness 700–250 m (thinner at the seaward edge).

There is a steep coast around the continent, rising to an interior plateau at 3,000–3,500 m above sea-level. Most of the area above sea-level is ice, which is up to 4,500 m thick, so that bedrock is below sea-level in some places. At other places, there are mountains rising to a peak 5,140 m above sea-level, including the active volcano Mt Erebus (at 3,743 m – Figure 16.4). The point furthest from the sea (the so-called 'Pole of Inaccessibility') is Vostok, at 78°S and 3,450 m elevation.

Antarctica carries 90 per cent of the world's glacial ice, and melting of it all would raise the world's sea-level by about 70 m. Glaciers bear the ice slowly towards ice shelves or directly to the ocean, where they crumble off as icebergs (Figure 11.7). The Lambert glacier on the edge of East Antarctica (at 70°E) is 60 km wide and 400 km long, the world's largest.

Sea-ice a few metres thick surrounds the continent (Figure 11.7). It covers an area which fluctuates during the year (Section 11.2), and it is the retreat in late summer, which allows ships to reach McMurdo Sound in the Ross Sea. The sea-ice acts as a giant insulator, blocking heat from the ocean. If it were absent, temperatures in Antarctica would be about 10 K higher.

Winds

The cold (i.e. heavy) air over the Antarctic plateau creates a high pressure at the surface, which leads to cold diffluent winds down to the sea as katabatic winds (Section 14.3). The divergence leads to slow subsidence of the polar atmosphere, as part of the polar cell (Section 12.3). The Coriolis effect is particularly strong at high latitudes, so geostrophic winds flow as southeasterlies from the anticyclone which prevails over Antarctica (Figure 12.7).

The katabatic winds are shallow and strong, especially at the steep coast (**Figure 16.5**). There is an annual average of 11.5 m/s at Casey,

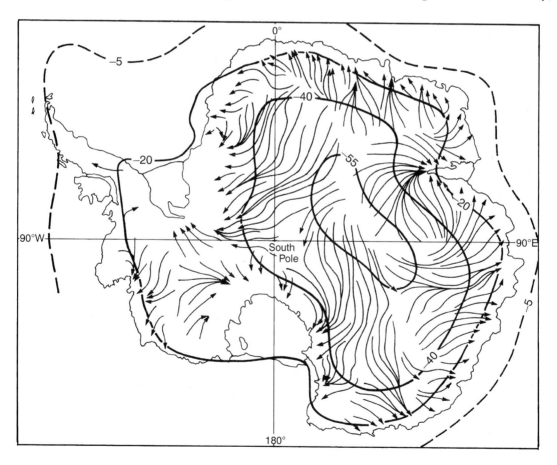

Figure 16.5 Isotherms of annual mean temperature (°C) in Antarctica, and the directions of katabatic winds.

and winds at Dumont d'Urville (at 67°S, 140°E) are typically 11 m/s, but averaged 29 m/s over March 1951, for instance, and peaked at 89 m/s over two minutes. The winds are usually strongest in winter, but rarely extend beyond 10 km from the shore. Such katabatic winds tend to start and end suddenly, which is characteristic of density currents (Note 14.D). When the winds exceed some threshold, they abruptly become gusty, picking up loose snow and giving rise to blizzards.

The surface wind is much less on the inland plateau. For instance, the average wind speed at the South Pole is 5.3 m/s. There is most movement in summer when the ground inversion is weakest, and so there is more coupling with winds aloft.

Frontal disturbances and deep depressions prevail over the seas around Antarctica. These are followed by cold-air outbreaks which pull air northward from the plateau, forming small polar lows (Section 13.4), mainly at the edge of the sea-ice. These lows occasionally cause winds reaching the strength of those in tropical cyclones, though they are much more shallow.

Temperatures

Average temperatures in Antarctica are around 3 K lower than at the same latitude in the northern hemisphere, because of the altitude (for inland locations) and the insulating effect of the sea-ice. (The warm Gulf Stream in the Atlantic penetrates the Arctic to 80°N, and the large land masses surrounding the North pole warm up considerably in summer.) **Figure 16.6** implies a cooling by about 12 K per km of ascent, and more recent measurements give a value of 13 K/km. These values are far greater than the average 4 K/km found elsewhere (Figure 3.5); the difference is due to extra distance from the sea and the strong ground inversion which affects all surface temperatures in Antarctica (Section 7.6). The inversion means that measurements only 10 m above screen height

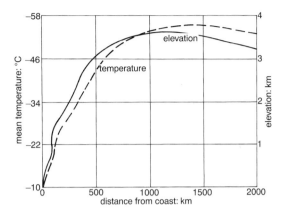

Figure 16.6 The connection between annual mean temperature, elevation and distance inland in Antarctica, around 100°E longitude.

are often 4 K warmer, and screen measurements are greatly affected by even slight vertical winds bringing warmer air, which sometimes leads to rapid fluctuations of temperature during the day. It may be noted that a temperature gradient of 12 K/km exceeds the dry adiabatic lapse rate of 10 K/km (Section 7.2), so that air descending 1 km is 2 K colder than the atmosphere around, creating a positive feedback which amplifies the katabatic wind.

Daily mean temperatures at the South Pole show a 'summer' of up to −25°C, lasting only from mid-December to mid-January, and a 'winter' of almost constant −60°C, from April to September. There is no clear minimum, i.e. the winter is described as 'coreless'. These temperatures are much lower than the annual range from zero to −35°C at the North Pole, where heat comes from the sea beneath the ice, and from the more frequent south–north winds. Even lower temperatures are encountered at Vostok (Figures 16.4 and 16.6), where the world record minimum was measured (Section 3.2).

Low temperatures mean that the air holds little moisture (Section 6.4). For instance, there is only 0.1–0.4 mm of precipitable water (Note 6.B) on the plateau, and the vapour pressure at the surface is below 1 hPa. As a result, skies over the Antarctic Plateau are usually clear and cloudless, making the area attractive to astronomers (**Note 16.C**). The clear skies and lack of water vapour also allow unimpeded loss of terrestrial radiation (Table 2.6), which is the explanation for the extremely low temperatures and a negative net-radiation balance (Table 5.2, Figure 5.5). By the same token, the long daylight hours in summer lead to significant warming, notwithstanding a high albedo, which accounts for the large annual range of temperature.

The Earth is nearer the Sun at year's end (during the Antarctic summer) than at midyear, so that the maximum extra-terrestrial radiation reaching the South Pole is 7 per cent more than that reaching the North (Section 2.2). The clear skies and the elevation of the South Pole mean that sunshine (including its UV component) is almost unattenuated, shining all day for months.

Precipitation

Cold air and clear skies make it the driest continent on Earth. Figure 16.4 shows that the water-equivalent of the annual accumulation of snow is about 400 mm/a around most of the coast, but less than 50 mm/a over the majority of eastern Antarctica. The overall average is about 160 mm/a (Section 10.5).

There are a few so-called *dry valleys* near sea-level, notably Wright Valley on the east side of McMurdo Sound (Figure 16.4). It is rocky and ice-free because of sublimation into katabatic winds, which often exceed 28 m/s. After descending 3,000 m or so from the central plateau, the air is relatively warm and so dry that the relative humidity is below 10 per cent (Note 7.E). One of the dry valleys contains Lake Vanda (Figure 16.4), which lies under a permanent layer of clear ice 4 m thick. Most of the lake's water is very salty, so that, whenever ice around the lake melts, the fresh meltwater

(which has a lower density) floats on top, forming a solar pond (Note 7.I). As a result, the salty water in the lake can reach temperatures above +25°C, heated by sunshine through the layers of ice and meltwater.

Precipitation tends to be most in summer, but falls are too light to allow the visual discernment of annual layering of ice which is possible where snowfalls exceed about 500 mm/a.

About two-thirds of any depletion of Antarctic ice is by calving of icebergs from the ice shelves and (to a minor extent) from glaciers. Because the ice shelves are flat, most icebergs in the southern hemisphere have a table-like top, unlike those in the northern hemisphere. The volume of calving icebergs totals 1,300 km³ per annum, which is enough to provide water for the entire world population at the current average consumption of 600 litres per head daily.

Apart from icebergs, roughly 6 per cent of the total loss of ice from Antarctica occurs as sublimation into the dry air, and another 13 per cent melts along the coast. The remaining 14 per cent, is blown out to sea as snow in a surface layer a few metres deep during katabatic wind storms, making visibility very poor.

In summary, strong coastal winds and ground inversions are among the main features of Antarctic climates. Others are aridity and extremely low temperatures.

16.4 SOUTH AMERICA

This continent covers almost 18 million square kilometres, compared with Antarctica's 14 Mkm² and North America's 24 Mkm². It stretches from 12°N almost to Antarctica, and all along its western coast is the Andes, up to 6,960 m high, so there is a wide range of climates, with sharp contrasts (Figure 16.2). Near the equator, the Amazon Basin contains the largest tropical rainforest in the world with about 2,500 different species of tree, whereas for about 600 km around Buenos Aires there are treeless plains which provide grazing, and at the frigid tip of the continent there is Tierra del Fuego, with only six species of tree. The capital of Tierra del Fuego is Ushuaia, at 55°S the most southern city in the world, with a winter average temperature just above freezing. There are glaciers nearby, prevented from melting in summer by the prevailing cloudiness.

Winds and Air masses

Climates in South America are conveniently explained in terms of the winds, which in turn depend on the patterns of pressure. An almost stationary anticyclone occurs over the Pacific ocean at about 90°W and another over the Atlantic at 15°W, both at about 30°S (Figure 12.7). The South Pacific high sends cold southerly winds along most of the west coast, bringing rains in winter to central Chile at 30–40°S.

The atmosphere is stable west of the Andes, between the equator and 30°S. A subsidence inversion there separates the cool boundary layer (due to southerly winds and low SST) from warm, dry air aloft. However, the Andes are a major barrier, so that air masses, and therefore climates, are very different on the opposite side.

On the east side of the continent, the South Atlantic high produces the easterly Trade winds at 3°N-15°S (Figure 12.4) and northwesterlies along the Argentine coast (Figure 12.1). The anticyclone extends in winter to cover the southern half of Brazil, reducing the rainfall there. But in summer there is a heat low over Paraguay (at about 20°S), linked by a badly defined spur to the global Intertropical Convergence Zone (Figure 12.1) stretching across the Amazon basin. This pattern of pressures leads to weak northerly winds, bringing moist equatorial air masses over the low-latitude part of the continent, with heavy summer rains (**Table 16.3**).

Winds tend to be westerlies at places above either 5,000 m between 15–30°S, or 2,500 m further south. Strong winds occur only at high elevations and latitudes, e.g. there are gales on about thirteen days annually along the southern coast of Brazil.

Tropical cyclones have never been observed around the continent (Figure 13.13), because the low-latitude oceans nearby are too cool (Figure 3.4) and the fetch across the warm equatorial Atlantic is too short to generate unstable Trade winds. Also, southern Africa does not produce the easterly waves (Note 13.H) needed to trig-

Table 16.3 Air masses occurring over South America east of the Andes, to be compared with the details in Table 13.1

Kind of air mass	Symbol	Nature	Unstable?	Occurrence
Equatorial	mE	Humid	Moist neutral	North Brazil in summer and fall
	cE	Weak winds	Moist neutral	Upper Amazon
Temperate	cT	Dry	Unstable due to heat low	23°S in summer
	mT	Lower 2 km is cool and humid, with subsiding dry air above	Stable above the PBL	Forms over Atlantic, in winter
Polar	mP	Cold southerly following cold frontal passage	Stable, but showers at coast	South of 30°S in winter and 45°S in summer
	cP	Cold and dry	Stable	Patagonia in winter

ger tropical cyclones. Despite this, cyclonic tropical storms of less intensity have been recorded near Brazil's east coast, and it is conceivable that global warming might make tropical cyclones a possibility there.

Temperatures

Screen temperatures in South America depend on the same geographical factors as elsewhere (Section 3.2) – the latitude (Figure 3.4), elevation (Figure 3.5) and distance from the sea. Other factors are the amount of cloud, wind direction, season and time of day. Peculiar to South America is the large difference between the east and west coast temperatures, from 40°S to the equator (Table 11.2). Lima, at 12°S on the west coast, is 7 K cooler on average than Salvador at 13°S on the east. The lower temperatures on the west side are caused mainly by a lower SST due to upwelling and northward ocean currents. A similar east–west difference is found in southern Africa (Section 3.2, Table 11.2 and Figure 11.3), but not as far equatorward.

A layer of maritime polar air invades South America in the lee of the Andes two or three times a year, when the South Atlantic high weakens and shifts eastwards. The air mass comes behind a cold front (Figure 13.8), as an outbreak which typically lasts about four days and approaches the equator as a layer only 500 m thick. It causes an abrupt cooling of surface temperatures by perhaps 10 K.

The daily range of temperature is small in the Amazon basin because of the surface wetness and the cloudiness (**Figure 16.7**). The Amazon basin evaporates about as much as an ocean (Section 10.5), which reduces daytime warming, whilst the cloud reduces cooling at night. The daily range at Manaus (3°S) is only 8 K, and it is small along the arid west coast also, mainly because of persistent stratus clouds. The range increases southward to the Gran Chaco, a vast lowland plain at 20–28°S in central South America, where the daily range is about 19 K in August and 13 K in February, because of the aridity and distance from the sea. Further south, the daily range is smaller again, partly on account of proximity to the oceans (Figure 3.10).

Annual ranges of monthly mean temperatures are only 2 K at Manaus but over 16 K in the Gran Chaco (Figure 3.9). Temperatures in the Gran Chaco range from frosts in winter to an absolute maximum of 47°C.

The effect of elevation on the average temperature may be seen by comparing data in Table 11.2 for Antofagasta and Rio de Janeiro at the coast, i.e. about 23°C in January and 17°C in July, with those from La Quiaca (at 22°S and 3,4358 m). The latter has temperatures about 12 K lower, implying an average lapse rate of surface temperatures of 3.5 K/km (Figure 3.4). The annual range at La Quiaca is almost 10 K, whilst the daily range is 15 K in January and 24 K in July, compared with daily and annual ranges of about 6 K near the coast. So the ranges increase with height (and therefore distance from the ocean), as shown in Figures 3.14 and 16.4, mainly because the lack of atmospheric water vapour at high altitudes allows greater cooling at night.

Winters are notably cold in the 'altiplano', the windswept plains at about 3,650 m in south-east Peru and western Bolivia. The coldness is despite the low latitude, and is due to the altitude and aridity. For instance, the mean temperature of the warmest month is only 9.5°C at La Paz (at 16.5°S and 4,103 m) and the rainfall about 555 mm/a. This means a 'polar' climate denoted by E in Köppen's classification (Note 16.A). The coldest month (July) is only 2 K colder on average, yet there is a frost on 85 per cent of mornings.

Precipitation

South America is the wettest continent on Earth, with an average of 1,630 mm/a. At the extreme, rainfall averages 13,000 mm/a at

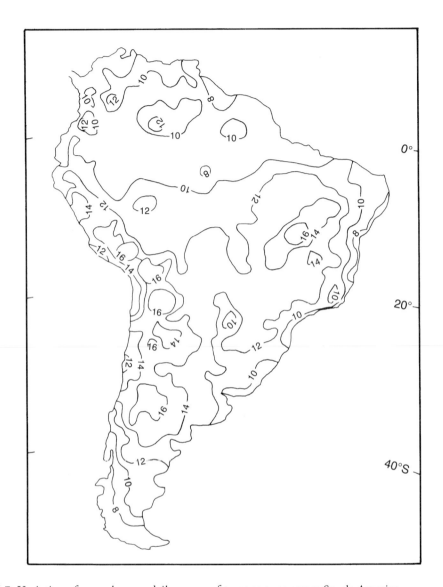

Figure 16.7 Variation of annual mean daily range of temperature across South America.

Andagoya (6°N) in western Colombia. Such heavy precipitation gives rise to the great rivers which are a major feature of South America. The Amazon discharges 42 per cent of the rainfall received in its basin, which amounts to 17 per cent of the world's river flows and is about eighteen times the total of all Australian rivers.

Figure 16.8 shows that rainfall is highly seasonal over much of the continent, according to the location and to movements of the South Atlantic high and the ITCZ (Section 12.1). The ITCZ over the Amazon basin leads to its receiving about 2,500 mm/a, about a quarter of which comes from water vapour previously evaporated locally. Rainfall is spread fairly uniformly throughout the year in most of the

Figure 16.8 Patterns of monthly rainfall at places in South America.

region, with a thunderstorm almost every late afternoon at Belem (at 2°S on the coast). In the southern parts of the basin there is more rain in the period November–April.

Not all South America is wet; there are great regional variations (Figure 10.3 and **Figure 16.9**), with considerable aridity in some parts. All the central north coast of South America is dry, especially in mid-year (which is unusual for places of similar latitude). **Figure 16.10** demonstrates that annual totals of rainfall are less than 500 mm/a in three parts of the continent, south of the equator. One is north-east Brazil, second is the Patagonian desert, south of 38°S in Argentina, and third is the coast of Peru and Chile. The last includes the Atacama

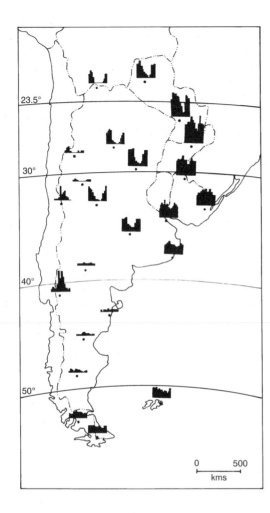

Figure 16.9 Average annual rainfall in South America.

desert in northern Chile, which is the driest desert in the world. These are shown as B climates in Figure 16.2. They will now be considered in turn, while the characteristics of deserts in general are discussed in **Note 16.D**.

North-east Brazil (i.e. the Nordeste)

The moisture in the Trade winds striking the coastal hills of eastern Brazil at 5–10°S is pre-

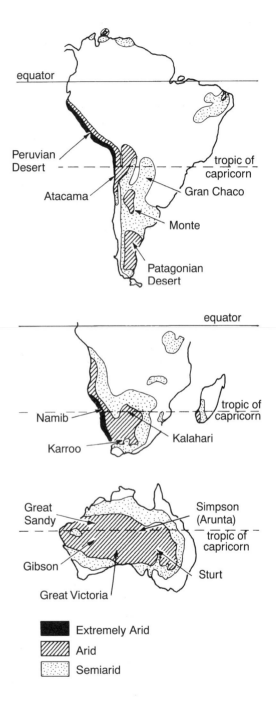

Figure 16.10 Deserts of the southern hemisphere.

cipitated immediately, with annual totals around 1,600 mm/a. Most of the coastal rain falls during the morning, as the result of convergence of (i) nocturnal katabatic winds from the eastern slopes, and (ii) the prevailing Trade winds. But the rainfall is reduced to less than 500 mm/a at 300 km inland, for an area approaching 100,000 km². The part with less than 400 mm/a is known as the 'drought polygon'. The dryness is due to atmospheric stability caused by the location of eastern Brazil within the influence of the South Atlantic high (Section 13.6). Most rain comes from occasional thunderstorms in summer and, particularly, March–April. There are also gentle rainfalls around October, called 'caju' rain after the fruit which buds then.

The annual rainfall is highly variable, with a relative variability (Note 10.L) which is over 50 per cent in some places (Figure 10.9). The South Atlantic high shifts south in some years, allowing the incursion of moist equatorial air with more rain. There are also extreme droughts (Section 10.7), which cause social distress to the substantial population of the Nordeste. For instance, there was no rain whatsoever in the town of Cabrobo (9°S) during the years 1951–53.

Rainfall variability in the Nordeste is not well understood, but three factors appear relevant. Firstly, the region is often dry during a time of negative SOI (Section 12.7), e.g. in 1915, 1919, 1932, 1936, 1942, 1951 and 1983 (Figure 10.16), when convection in the eastern Amazon was suppressed (Figure 12.17). But the ENSO cycle explains only 10 per cent of the variability in the Nordeste. A second factor seems to be unusually cold winters in North America east of the Rockies, these correlating well with wet summers in the Nordeste. Occasional continental polar air masses come down east of the Rockies, like a north-hemisphere friagem, and proceed along the western edge of the Gulf of Mexico, pushing the ITCZ south over the Nordeste, so that there is rain there. Thirdly, there is a strong correlation between summertime rain in the Nordeste (e.g. at Fortaleza, at 4°S) and the SST in the south-equatorial Atlantic (**Figure 16.11**). The increased SST moistens the air and raises and weakens the Trade wind inversion (Section 7.6), allowing for more active growth of cumulus clouds as the winds blow westwards over Brazil.

Patagonia

The Patagonian desert is the largest in South America, extending in the lee of the Andes from 37–51°S, with vast plains, rising from the coast to about 1,000 m. The rainfall in the semi-arid northern part is 90–430 mm/a, mostly in summer thunderstorms, while rain and snow in the southern part amounts to only 110–200 mm/a. The region is protected by the Andes from the moisture of westerly winds, whilst easterlies are made stable by the cold Falklands Current up the west coast (Section 11.5).

The rain is insufficient to rinse salts away from the surface soil, so that only clumps of wiry grass can survive. Poplar trees are planted extensively as protection from the strong cold winds from the south-west.

The Patagonian desert continues north into the Monte desert (Figure 16.10) between 30–37°S in the lee of the Andes, and the semi-arid Gran Chaco in Paraguay.

The Western Littoral

A great range of precipitation is measured along the western edge of South America. At one end is the mountainous coast of Colombia (7°N– 0°), where moist winds within the ITCZ (Figure 12.1) deposit more than 10,000 mm/a in the Choco region. To the south there is a narrow chain of deserts from 5–27°S, and then a wet coast beyond about 36°S.

The desert from the equator to about 10°S is limited to a narrow coastal strip. For instance,

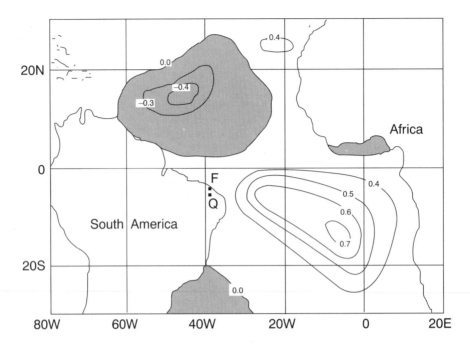

Figure 16.11 The correlation between the SST in March and the March to May rainfall at Fortaleza (F) and Quixada (Q) in Brazil's Nordeste. Areas with a negative correlation (e.g. a cold SST anomaly and more rain at F and Q) are shaded.

there is 260 mm/a at Manta (1°S) and only 36 mm/a at Lima (12°S, see Note 11.E), because of the stability of both easterly winds subsiding down the Andes and westerly winds cooled by the Peru ocean current, which turns west and leaves the coast near the equator (Figure 11.15). It is this departure which governs the difference between climates to north and south, respectively. There is a rapid increase of rainfall inland from the coast, e.g. there is rainforest at Pichilingue (at 1°S and 73 m elevation) only 120 km inland. Rainfall there is due to thunderstorms which develop on the Andes foothills on summer afternoons, triggered by a combined sea breeze/anabatic wind (Sections 14.2 and 14.3). But there can be heavy rains even on the coastal strip during an El Niño, and subnormal rains inland during a La Niña (Note 11.C).

South of 10°S, the dry coastal strip broadens out to include the Andes foothills and then the extremely arid Atacama desert and even the altiplano between 16–26°S. The Atacama desert is several hundred kilometres long, at around 24°S (Section 10.3 and Figure 16.10). What little rainfall there is comes mostly during the period May–October, as the result of occasional northward penetrations of cold fronts and midlatitude westerly winds. Normally the Andes block moist air from the Amazon basin, whilst westerly winds are stable (i.e. dry), because of oceanic upwelling and the Humboldt Current, which yields an inshore sea-surface temperature some 6 K colder than elsewhere at these latitudes (Section 11.4). Another influence on the region's aridity is the anticyclone fixed in the eastern part of the South Pacific (Section 13.6). Coastal weather stations between 17–23°S have measured no more than a 'trace' (i.e. 0.2 mm) of rain for years, except on a few days with brief downpours. Calama (22°S) held the record for no more than traces of rain since records began over a century ago, until February 1972 (an El Niño year), when a fall of 28 mm caused flashfloods.

There is a third demarcation around 36°S in Chile. Just north of that, Santiago (at 34°S) receives 317 mm/a, whereas 2,486 mm/a falls in Valdivia, just to the south at 39°S. Almost all the latter precipitation occurs between April and October as the result of frontal disturbances and uplift by the Andes. Then south of 47°S there is a different regime again, where the consistent westerlies bring rain evenly throughout the year.

Other Features

The rainfall in the Andes depends on the latitude and season. There are two rainy seasons (in April and October) at the equator, because the Sun is overhead twice, at the times of the equinoxes (Section 2.2). This applies at Quito (at 0°S and 2,800 m), for instance. There is mostly winter rain on the western side of the Andes between 25–45°S and on the mountain ridge (Figure 16.8), because westerly winds are stronger in winter. But there is mostly summer rain on the east side, due to thunderstorms. Some thunderstorms can be severe, especially in late spring, when moist air from the Amazon basin flows below strong westerlies aloft.

High rainfalls are strikingly related to a small daily range of temperature (Figure 16.7). Ranges of over 16 K occur in the drier parts of the continent, but less than 10 K where rainfall exceeds 2,000 mm/a. This is due to the effects of rainclouds in reducing the range (Section 3.4).

About five tornadoes occur annually in northern Argentina (mainly between 30–35°S), 16 per cent of them with an intensity of F2 or more (Table 14.3). Tornadoes have also been reported in Uruguay, southern Brazil and Paraguay.

Pacific Islands

One of the most equable climates in the world occurs at 52°S, on the island of Los Evangelistas, off Chile. The annual range of monthly mean temperatures is only 4 K, and between 200–300 mm of rain falls every month, with rainfall on at least twenty days monthly.

Another part of Chile is Easter Island (27°S), in the Pacific Ocean. There the daily range of temperature is no more than about 7 K and the annual range of monthly mean temperatures 6 K, because of the ocean's influence. Rainfall is only 850 mm/a because of the south-east Pacific anticyclone above. The rain falls fairly evenly through the year, mostly on the south-east side of the island which faces the Trades.

The Galapagos Islands are on the equator but nevertheless arid and relatively cool, i.e. 288 mm/a and 24°C on average. This is due to the westward continuation of the cold Peru current (Figure 11.15) and upwelling along the equator (Section 11.4). The islands experience extreme interannual variability, being about 4 K warmer and four times wetter during El Niño years than during La Niña years.

Islands far to the west of Easter Island receive more rain, some places over 2,000 mm/a (Figure 10.3). This is explained by the 'warm pool' in the western equatorial Pacific (Figure 11.2) and by the South Pacific Convergence Zone, stretching from Papua New Guinea to 140°W, 30°S (Figure 12.1). The SPCZ is similar to the ITCZ (i.e. there is a belt of low-level convergence, with updraughts in thunderstorms and upper-level divergence) but it is unique in its orientation, which is away from the equator. This is due to the strong south-east Pacific high and the cold Humboldt current. The SPCZ can be discerned year-round but is most clearly defined and active in causing rain in summer.

16.5 SOUTH AFRICA

About a third of Africa is south of the equator, and most of that is above 900 m in elevation (**Figure 16.12**). Consequently, the customary sea-level synoptic charts were generally replaced by charts of pressures at a height of 850 hPa (e.g. Figure 13.7) until 1992. (Sea-level charts have been used more recently, to knit better into the charts from other countries.) There is a sharply defined plateau but no high range of mountains to deflect winds or create a rainshadow. Mount Kilimanjaro (3°S) rises to 5,895 m, with a cap of isolated large blocks of ice and the Penck Glacier down to 4,500 m. Gradation of climate is gentle across the continent, except near the escarpments of the plateau, which are 100–500 km from the coast.

Winter Winds

Gradient winds south of 20°S are dominated by the permanent high over the south Atlantic (Figure 12.1), a more mobile high over the Indian ocean (it moves eastwards in summer), and by the annual fluctuations of the Intertropical Convergence Zone. In winter, high pressures settle over the southern plateau, often connecting with the ocean anticyclones, which are at about 33°S. Consequently, westerlies blow onto the southern coast (Figure 16.12b). These are turned northward over the cold Benguela current (Figure 11.15) by the influence of the South Atlantic high, and hence are stable, creating the Namib desert at the coast (Note 16.D). North of 22°S are easterly Trade winds.

The westerlies along the south coast give rise to typical midlatitude frontal weather, as illustrated in Figure 13.7. On the first day in the series illustrated, the weather is dominated by subtropical highs, with unsettled conditions confined to the east coast north of 25°S. Then a frontal disturbance approaches from the south-west (days 2–3) and plateau air is drawn south, ahead of the cold front. This leads to *berg winds* along the coast, which are offshore winds

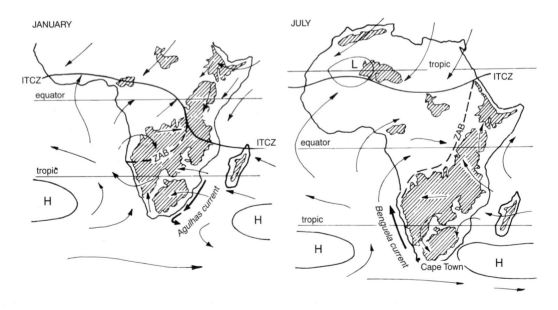

Figure 16.12 Generalised near-surface winds over Africa in summer (January) and winter (July). ZAB is the Zaïre Air Boundary, a region of low pressure. The shaded areas are higher than 900 m.

heated by subsidence from the plateau. The onset of a berg wind can be sudden and produce a temperature near 30°C even in mid-winter. The cessation of a berg wind can be even more abrupt than the onset, due either to the beginning of a sea breeze or to an onshore flow behind a coastal low (Section 13.4) The passage of the cold front causes a further temperature drop (day 4), occasionally involving an outbreak of cold air from the south. In this case, the temperature hovers around 10°C along the coast and light snowfalls occur on the Drakensberg range, about 160 km inland at 31°S. Passage of the cold front (day 5) restores settled weather to the south coast.

Summer Winds

Trade winds occur in summer as far south as the tip of South Africa, making fronts less common there and bringing warm moist air all along the east coast. The ITCZ is pulled south in January, into the heat low over Botswana. This creates the *Zaïre Air Boundary* (ZAB), a region of converging air masses (Figure 12.1 and Figure 16.12), which leads to a deep unstable mass of humid air and hence heavy rainfall. Northeasterly monsoon winds dominate eastern Africa as far south as Johannesburg at 26°S.

Temperatures

Table 16.4 shows that January mean temperatures vary remarkably little with latitude across southern Africa, except at the coast south of 30°S. Such uniform conditions in summer are typical of a wet monsoon, but July mean temperatures do fall with latitude, as expected.

Coastal temperatures are affected by the ocean currents offshore (Figure 11.15). Thus, monthly mean temperatures at Walvis Bay at 23°S on the west coast are only around 17°C because of the cold Benguela current. The difference between summer maxima and winter minima is small along the coasts and towards

the equator, but large over the South African plateau (**Figure 16.13**), where frosts are common in winter, especially in the highlands of Lesotho.

There can be large differences of temperature from one day to the next along the south coast, especially during the months April–September, due to the berg winds, coastal lows and cold fronts, discussed earlier.

Rain

Several factors control the patterns of rainfall at various latitudes and distances from the sea. Coastal rainfall depends on the stability of the onshore winds (i.e on the temperature of coastal ocean currents), on tropical cyclones at low latitudes, and on fronts further south. The Benguela Current causes a rainfall of only 30 mm/a at Walvis Bay on the west coast, whereas it is 760 mm/a at Maputo at a similar latitude on the east coast, which is affected by the warm Agulhas Current (Figure 11.15). Concerning tropical cyclones, about ten form in the southwest Indian ocean each year (Figure 13.13) and most affect Madagascar, but only a few reach the mainland, mainly between 15–25°S. Damage from these in South Africa is mostly due to flooding rains, rather than strong winds.

Inland, there is convective uplift on the plateau, causing thunderstorms along the ITCZ (Figure 16.12) and orographic uplift at the scarp on the edge of the plateau. The increase is 110 mm/a per 100 m elevation on the eastern scarp between 23–26°S. Elsewhere in the southern part of the continent the increase is about 30 mm/a per 100 m extra height, up to a height of about 1,300 m.

South of 20°S, Africa is generally arid (**Figure 16.14**), except along the south and east coasts, whereas the annual rainfall at lower latitudes exceeds 1,000 mm/a, except at the Angolan coast and in eastern Tanzania. The east coast of Africa between 10–26°S is slightly drier than comparable coasts in either South America or

Table 16.4 Effects of elevation and latitude on the January and July mean temperatures *T* (°C) and rainfalls *P* (mm/month) in Africa south of the equator

Latitude	Place	Jan T	July T	Jan P	July P
Places at 0–100 m elevation, i.e. near the coast					
4	Mombasa	27	25	25	89
7	Dar es Salaam	28	24	66	31
9	Luanda	25	21	25	0
15	Moçamedes	22	17	8	0
18	Tamatave	27	21	366	302
20	Sofala	28	21	277	31
23	Walvis Bay	19	15	0	0
26	Moputo	26	19	130	13
31	Durban	24	17	109	28
34	Port Elizabeth	21	13	31	48
34	Cape Town	21	12	15	89
Places at 100–1,200 m elevation, i.e. inland					
0	Kisumu	23	22	48	58
3	Buyumbusa	23	23	94	5
4	Brazzaville	26	23	160	0
4	Kinshasa	26	23	135	3
5	Kigoma	23	23	122	3
6	Dadoma	23	19	152	0
14	Lilongwe	22	15	208	0
16	Zumbo	27	21	208	0
16	Tete	28	21	152	3
21	Francistown	25	15	107	0
26	Mbabane	20	13	254	23
Places above 1,200 m in elevation, i.e. on the plateau					
1	Nairobi	19	16	38	15
1	Kabala	17	15	58	20
2	Rubona	19	19	111	7
10	Kasama	21	17	272	0
12	Lubumbashi	22	16	267	0
13	Ndola	21	14	142	0
15	Lusaka	21	16	231	0
15	Huambo	20	17	221	0
18	Harare	21	14	196	0
19	Astananarivo	21	15	300	8
20	Bulawayo	21	14	142	0
23	Windhoek	23	13	76	0
26	Johannesburg	20	11	114	8
26	Pretoria	21	11	127	8
29	Bloemfontein	23	9	91	10

Australia, because the south-easterly Trade winds have lost much of their moisture over Madagascar.

Most rain near Cape Town (34°S) falls in winter (**Figure 16.15**), and is due to cold fronts. Thunderstorms are rare. As a result, there is a dry-summer 'Mediterranean climate' (**Figure 16.16**). Such a pattern differs from that over most of the continent, where most rainfall is derived from summertime thunderstorms.

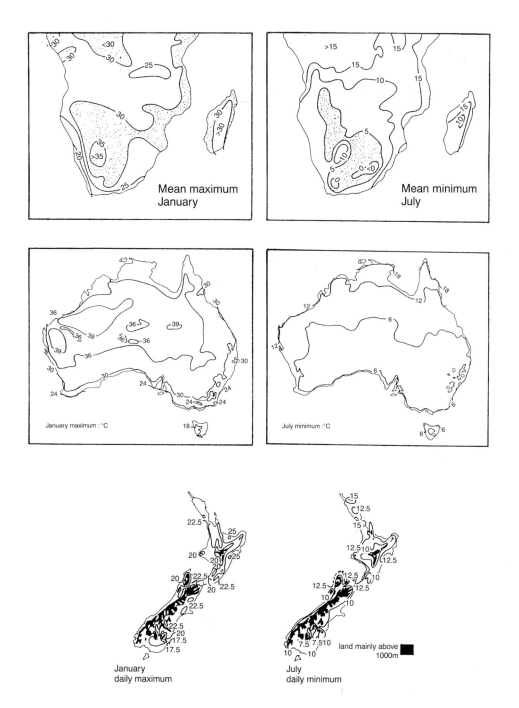

Figure 16.13 The mean daily minimum temperatures in the coldest month and the mean daily maximum in the hottest, in (a) South Africa, (b) Australia, and (c) New Zealand.

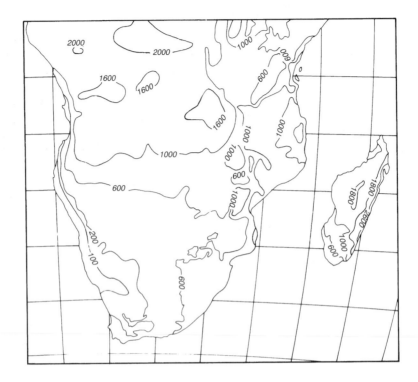

Figure 16.14 Annual rainfall (mm/a) in southern Africa.

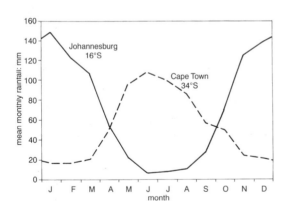

Figure 16.15 Seasonal variation of rainfall at Johannesburg and Cape Town.

Two rainy seasons tend to occur in the equatorial region, the main one shortly before the Sun crosses the equator towards the Tropic of Capricorn, and a second one shortly after it recrosses. There is a mid-year dominance of rainfall along the East African coast down to 6°S, presumably because the easterlies due to the Asian monsoon circulation are strongest then. Year-end monsoon westerlies lose much of their moisture over the high plateau of Kenya.

Rainfall variability (Figure 10.9) increases towards the dry south-west. There the annual rainfall was 3,027 mm in 1917 at Broederstroom (24°S at 1,554 m) but only 1,033 mm in 1941. Along the coasts of Namibia and Angola, the variability exceeds 50 per cent. Wet years there tend to correlate with weaker-than-normal easterly winds in the equatorial Atlantic and higher-than normal SST (Figure 10.18).

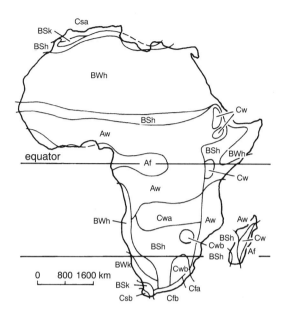

Figure 16.16 The Köppen classes of climates in Africa.

In summary, most of the African plateau south of the equator has a moderate winter-dry climate (Cw in Köppen's classification, Table 16.A.1), not a tropical A climate, as might have been expected from the latitude.

The Deserts

The greatest part of southern Africa suffers drought ocasionally (Figure 10.16), partly on account of variations of SST nearby (Section 10.7). But some areas are so consistently short of rain as to be deserts. There are two in particular, the coastal Namib (17–29°S) and the adjacent Kalahari, inland (Figure 16.10). The former is like the Atacama (Section 16.4) but less extensive and less extreme. There are aridity, small ranges of daily and annual temperature at the coast and frequent fog or low stratus,

with fine drizzle called 'moth rain', all resulting from the cold currents on the west coast. Also, the marine surface air is capped by an inversion at about 500 m (Figure 7.10). The air above the inversion usually originates over the Kalahari plateau, so it is dry and warm, and subsidence causes further warming and drying. This inversion can be as much as 12 K, especially in summer, when surface maxima on the Kalahari plateau are about 35°C (Figure 16.13).

The Kalahari desert covers about 260,000 km^2, a sandy plateau flattened by extensive erosion. It is not totally sterile, since there are thorn bushes and salt-tolerant succulents in shallow depressions as a result of about 200 mm/a of rain in the western part and 430 mm/a in the east, almost all falling in summer. The dryness and distance inland result in an annual range of temperature which is considerable. In some places the July mean minimum is below freezing and the January maximum above 35°C, with extremes of −13°C and 47°C.

Madagascar

Madagascar (12–26°S) is the world's fourth largest island (after Greenland, New Guinea and Borneo), with an area over twice that of New Zealand's two islands. There is a central mountain range, rising above 2,000 m in some parts. The ITCZ is centred over the northern end of the island in summer (Figure 16.12) bringing heavy rain there. The whole island is generally exposed to the moist Trade winds, causing orographically enhanced precipitation on the east throughout the year, of 2,000–3,700 mm/a. Most people live on a central plateau at 800–1,500 m elevation, where rainfalls are 1,300–2,000 mm/a, and the monthly mean temperatures 15–21°C (i.e. a Cw climate, Figure 16.16).

The western side of the island is dry in winter, being in the lee of the central range, but wet in summer because of tropical cyclones and the bend of the ITCZ. There are strong sea

breezes in summer. On average, the west coast is about 2 K warmer than the east, on account of the foehn effect (Note 7.E).

The south-west corner is semi-arid, with less than 400 mm/a, because it lies under the south Indian ocean high in winter, and is protected by the mountains from the northern monsoon wind in summer.

16.6 AUSTRALIA

This is the smallest and flattest of the continents, with a mean elevation of about 300 m. The mountains are chiefly within the Dividing Range, which stretches along the eastern coast. They are about 1,000 m high, higher to the south and lower to the north.

The country stretches from 11°S to 44°S, which places most of it in the zone of subtropical highs (Figure 12.7), with their descending air, cloudlessness and consequent aridity. The ample west–east dimension of about 4,000 km allows the development of continental tropical air masses (Section 13.2), and considerable modification of air from the oceans, so that cold fronts entering from the west are stirring up dry desert air by the time they reach the Nullarbor plain downwind, and Trade winds from the east are dry when they reach the interior of Queensland. In contrast, polar air from the south is unmodified by intervening land, and dominates climates in the south of the continent.

The mainly coastal population experiences both the devastating and the moderating effects of the oceans, such as tropical cyclones and sea breezes. The country is outstandingly vulnerable to droughts induced by El Niño (Section 10.7), to floods and strong winds due to tropical cyclones, and to bushfires (**Note 16.E**).

Winds

There is a seasonal shift of the pattern of surface pressures which determines the gradient winds, with the overall highest pressures at about 36°S in summer and 30°S in winter (Figure 13.16). Individual anticyclones south of the Tropic are remarkably mobile – this is a unique feature of Australian weather. They drift from the west at 500 km/day, for instance, sometimes linger over the continent as blocking highs, and then continue eastwards. Any blocking lasts a much shorter time than in the northern hemisphere, presumably because of the smaller and flatter land mass. The mobility implies that the wind alternates regularly between north-west and south-west (to the south of the axis of the highs) and between south-east and north-east (to the north).

The movement of surface highs can alternatively be regarded as the passage of troughs across a fixed subtropical band of high pressure. These mobile lows are the result of divergence in the vicinity of the jet streaks associated with active Rossby shortwaves (Note 12.J). The troughs are associated with surface cold fronts, which may penetrate as far north as 15°S in Queensland, as shallow intrusions of cold air.

Figure 13.11 shows typical pressure patterns in summer and winter. A high dominates the continent in winter, but covers the Australian Bight to the south in summer (Figure 13.16), changing the direction of winds prevailing over the southern coast. Cold fronts across the south are followed by cold marine southerlies, which become unstable over the relatively warm land in winter and hence yield rain in the form of showers.

In summer, a heat trough is found across the northern part of Australia, often with two centres – the Pilbara low and the Cloncurry low (Section 13.4). The trough draws the ITCZ into northern Australia. The north-westerly winds on the equatorward side of the trough bring monsoonal rains between December and April, a period called the 'Wet' (Sections 3.3, 6.5 and 12.1). At the same time, northern coasts are also vulnerable to tropical cyclones (Figure 13.13). About two cyclones a year strike the western coast, sometimes as far south as Perth. This is the only region in the world where tropical cyclones strike a western coast, due to the warm current down the west coast instead of the normal cold current (Figure 11.15). The TCs bring occasional heavy rains to the north-western desert.

Surface ventilation at the coast is governed by sea breezes and land breezes (Figure 14.13). These make Perth the windiest capital city, with an average of 4.4 m/s (**Table 16.5**). Canberra is the least windy (i.e. 1.7 m/s) because it lies inland, and usually near the centre of a high in winter (Figure 13.16). Extreme wind gusts (Table 14.2) may occur both inland and at the coast, usually in the vicinity of thunderstorms (Section 14.4).

About a dozen tornadoes are reported each year, the majority in the southern half of the continent, outside the dry interior (Section 7.5). The hardest hit area seems to be the Sydney metropolitan region, with about two tornadoes annually. Most tornadoes in Australia are spawned by severe convection in late spring and occur within 6 degrees latitude of a jet stream or 14 degrees longitude of an upper trough.

Temperature

Temperatures range from occasionally over 35°C to below freezing in the Snowy Mountains

in the south-east in winter. Temperatures are over 30°C at Brisbane for about 150 hours annually (**Figure 16.17**), but almost never above 35°C, which is critical for mortality amongst the aged (Note 3.C). For comparison, Canberra is hotter than 35°C for about 40 hours annually. The places differ because Brisbane experiences sea breezes and is more cloudy than Canberra in summer (Figure 8.16). However, Canberra's heat is more bearable because it is drier (Note 6.F), and the nights cool off more (**Table 16.6**).

Temperatures at Perth normally exceed 40°C at least once each summer, when the Pilbara

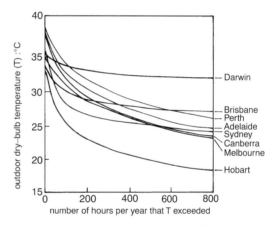

Figure 16.17 The number of hours each year when various temperatures are exceeded.

Table 16.5 Features of the climates of seven places in Australia

Place	Latitude (°S)	Elevation (metres)	Cloud (oktas)		Sunshine (hours/d)		Solar radiation (W/m²)		Dewpoint (°C)		Wind speed (m/s)	
			Jan	July	Jan	July	Jan	July	Jan	July	Jan	July
Darwin	12	30	5.9	1.3	5.9	9.8	213	224	24.7	15.5	2.6	3.4
Alice Springs	24	545	2.3	0.7	11.0	9.5	310	186	10.6	1.8	2.6	1.9
Perth	32	19	2.3	4.5	10.5	5.3	317	109	12.8	8.2	4.9	3.9
Sydney	34	42	4.7	3.5	7.2	6.2	261	121	16.5	6.4	3.4	3.2
Canberra	35	577	4.1	4.4	8.9	5.2	300	110	11.0	1.0	1.8	1.4
Melbourne	38	35	4.1	5.2	8.1	3.7	289	73	11.0	5.3	3.6	3.6
Hobart	43	54	5.0	4.8	7.9	4.3	269	64	8.4	3.0	3.5	3.0

low extends along the west coast and directs north-easterly desert winds onto the city, blocking the sea breeze (Section 13.4). The hottest month north of 20°S is November, during the 'build-up' prior to the monsoon (Section 6.5).

Table 16.6 shows that winter temperatures are notably low inland, e.g. at Alice Springs and Canberra, and that the daily range is greater there than at places on the coast (Figure 3.10).

Precipitation

Australia as a whole has an average rainfall of only 419 mm/a, so it is a dry continent (Figure 10.3) dominated by deserts (Figure 16.10). Areas which receive 375–750 mm/a in northern Australia or 250–500 mm/a in the south, are sometimes called *semi-arid* and occupy about 30 per cent of the whole country (**Figure 16.18**). A further 40 per cent is conventionally termed *arid*, with a rainfall of less than 375 mm/a in the north or 250 mm/a in the south. A place inland near Lake Eyre at 28°S in South Australia has had an average of only 81 mm/a over fifty-seven years.

An isohyet of historic importance in South Australia was the 'Goyder Line', drawn in 1865 after a series of disastrous droughts to define the limit to wheat farming. It corresponded roughly to the modern-day 350 mm/a isohyet, or (more importantly for wheat farming) 200 mm between April and November.

Variations of rainfall within the continent and during the year are shown in Figure 16.18. The highest average rainfalls in Australia are about 3,500 mm/a, measured on coastal hills in Queensland, facing the Trade winds and tropical cyclones. The record at Bellenden Ker there was 11,251 mm in 1979 (Section 10.2).

Rainfall is seasonal, according to the latitude. In the north, the rain comes from thunderstorms due to intense convection during summer, e.g. 1,668 mm/a in sixty days at Darwin (12°S). By contrast, rain falls at Cradle Valley in Tasmania (42°S at 914 m elevation) on about 237 days each year and totals 2,774 mm/a, resulting from the vast upwind fetch over the sea, and orographic uplift or fronts. Rainfall intensities are generally greater in the north (Figures 10.1 and 10.2).

The main rainfall regimes in Australia are shown in **Table 16.7**. Precipitation along the south-west coast of Australia varies as in central Chile and South Africa's south-west coast (Figure 10.3), with wet winters and dry summers south of about 30°S and arid conditions to the north. Along the east coast there is a variation from a well-defined wet summer in Queensland

Table 16.6 Monthly mean daily maximum and minimum temperatures (°C) at places in Australia, and the annual means

Place	Latitude (°S)	January		July		Annual mean
		Max	Min	Max	Min	
Darwin	12	32	25	31	19	28
Wyndham	15	36	26	31	19	30
Alice Springs	24	36	21	19	4	21
Brisbane	27	29	21	20	9	20
Perth	32	29	17	17	9	18
Sydney	34	26	18	16	8	17
Adelaide	35	30	16	15	7	17
Canberra	35	28	13	11	1	13
Melbourne	38	26	14	13	6	15
Hobart	43	22	12	11	4	13

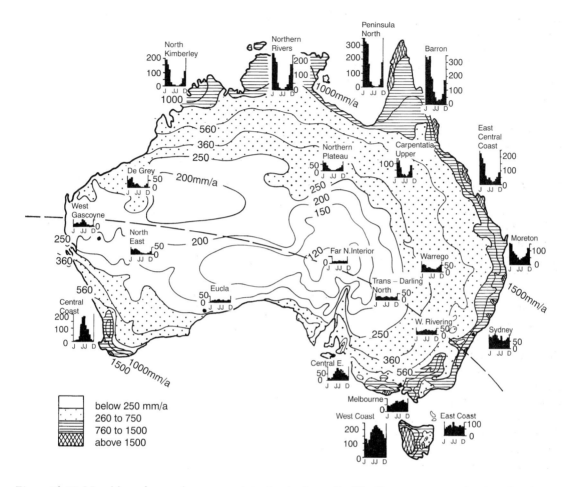

Figure 16.18 Monthly and annual mean precipitation in Australia. The line separates predominantly winter rain (to the south) from mainly summer rain (to the north).

to winter dominance in Victoria to the south (Table 10.3). The wet summers, which occur from 30°S on the east coast, and around the top and down to 15°S on the west coast, are due to both convective uplift caused when the Sun is high, and to winds from off warm seas, drawn inland by heat lows. A slanted line across Australia in Figure 16.18 separates areas with mostly winter rain to the south (due to cold fronts) from areas with predominant summer rains to the north, due to convection and the ITCZ. Similar, but even more slanted lines can

be drawn across South America (from 10°S on the west coast, to 45°S on the east coast) and southern Africa (from 20°S to 33°S).

Australia's interior is dry in summer, apart from occasional thunderstorms. This occurs for two reasons: (i) the Dividing Range along the east coast extracts moisture from the onshore winds and shelters places downwind, and (ii) heat lows in the north and the high south of Australia prevent southward penetration of wet monsoonal winds. Most of the rain in the arid interior north of 26°S comes from mesoscale

Table 16.7 Rainfall regions of Australia

Region	Approximate latitudes	Main cause of rain	Period of most rain
North	10–20°S	Thunderstorms, tropical cyclones	Dec–April
North-west	25–15°S	Tropical cyclones	Jan–April
Queensland coast and ranges	10–28°S	Trade-wind cumulus and tropical cyclones	Summer (weakly)
NSW coast and ranges	29–37°S	Easterly troughs and frontal convection	Nearly uniform (autumn)
South-east Australia	30–45°S	Cold fronts and summer thunderstorms	Winter (weakly)
South-west Australia	25–35°S	Cold fronts	Winter (markedly)
The interior		MCCs* and isolated thunderstorms	Summer (weakly)

* See Section 9.5

convective systems (Section 9.5), either arising within easterly waves (Note 13.H) or left as remnants of tropical cyclones to the north. Parts of the western interior receive most rainfall in March (Figure 16.18), when tropical cyclones are most common to the north-west. These storms travel inland from the north coast down almost to Kalgoorlie (at 31°S) and may deposit large amounts of rainfall, causing flash floods. In general, much of the rain falling from isolated storms in the desert evaporates before reaching the ground, because the clouds are so high and the air so dry.

The interannual variability of rainfall in Australia is high, but not as extreme as in either Brazil's Nordeste (Section 16.4) or the Namib desert in Africa (Section 16.5). The variability in eastern and northern Australia is largely explained by ENSO events (Section 12.7), and governs the kind of vegetation (**Note 16.F**) and the frequency of bushfires (Note 16.E). Rainfall variability in western Australia is less well understood, but appears to be affected by the SST in the Indian ocean.

Snowfall on mountains in south-east Australia (Figures 10.20 and 10.21) is associated with the cold winds directed north by intense anticyclones over the Australian Bight, south of the continent. Strong winds on the eastern side of

such a high bring maritime polar air from 50–60°S, where sea-surface temperatures are within a few degrees of freezing.

Climates

Figure 16.19 shows the Köppen classification of Australia's climates. Note the Mediterranean climates Cs near Perth and Adelaide, and the small strip of tropical rainforest climate (Af) just south of Cairns on the north-east coast. B climates clearly dominate. Some homoclimes are shown in **Table 16.8**.

New Guinea

New Guinea (consisting of Irian Jaya and Papua New Guinea) is located between 1–11°S. It is essentially mountainous, and the highest peak (Mt Jaya at 5,040 m) even bears a small glacier.

Its climate can be largely explained by the movement of the ITCZ (Figure 12.1). Its shift to the south at year's end leads to copious rains on the north coast, because the ITCZ draws north-easterly Trades from warm seas in the northern hemisphere onto the mountains (Figures 11.2, 12.4 and 12.6). For instance, Madang on the north coast receives 2,891 mm from

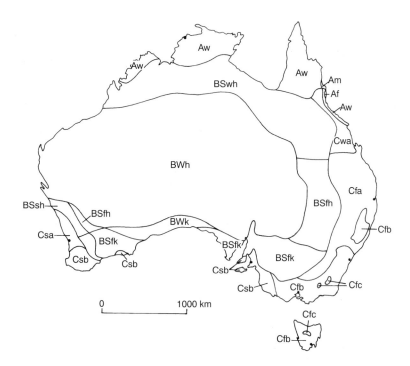

Figure 16.19 Köppen classes of climates in Australia.

Table 16.8 Homoclimes of towns in Australia

Place in Australia	Latitude	Köppen class	Southern homoclime	Northern homoclime
Innisfail	17°S	Af	Salvador, Brazil	Miami, USA
Cairns	17°S	Am	Brasilia, Brazil	Lagos, Nigeria
Darwin	12°S	Aw	Rio de Janeiro	Calcutta, India
Bourke, NSW	30°S	BSh	Gabarone, Botswana	Kartoum, Sudan
Griffith, NSW	34°S	BSk	La Pampa, Argentine	Denver, USA
Alice Springs	24°S	BWh	Moçamedes, Angola	Aswan, Egypt
Broken Hill	32°S	BWk	Mendoza, Argentina	Las Vegas, USA
Sydney	34°S	Cfa	Buenos Aires	Milano, Italy
Brisbane	28°S	Cfa	Durban, S. Africa	New Orleans, USA
Canberra	35°S	Cfb	Port Elizabeth, S. Africa	Paris, France
Melbourne	38°S			
Cradle Valley	42°S	Cfc	Punta Arenas, Chile	Reykjavik, Iceland
Perth	32°S	Csa	Santiago, Chile	Sevilla, Spain
Adelaide	34°S			
Mt Gambier, SA	38°S	Csb	Cape Town, S. Africa	San Francisco, USA
Mackay, Qld	21°S	Cwa	Belo Horizonte, Brazil	Hong Kong

October to May, which is about three times what falls on the south coast during the same period. Most of the south coast remains dry in mid-year, when the ITCZ draws south-easterly Trades from Australia which provide little moisture. The east coast is always exposed to maritime Trade winds, so rain falls on eight days out of ten during June to August at Lae (7°S), depositing about 1500 mm, mostly from cumulus clouds.

Most summer rain is from thunderstorms, especially over the mountains, resulting from afternoon convection triggered by sea breezes and mountain winds. Thunderstorms are generally after midnight over the Gulf of Papua, west of Port Moresby, occasionally producing a strong gust front, locally called the 'guba' (Section 14.4).

Steady temperature of around 26°C and high humidity (except in winter along the south coast) make the coastal area much less comfortable than the mountains, which are traditionally more inhabited.

16.7 NEW ZEALAND

The factors which govern New Zealand's climates are its latitude between 34–48°S, its being surrounded by vast oceans and the range of mountains along much of its length of 1,900 km, up to 3,764 m high on Mount Cook at 44°S. (This is far higher than the 2,228 m of Australia's Mt Kosciusko.)

Winds

The latitude puts the country across a regular succession of anticyclones and cold fronts. The highs usually pass over the North Island, especially in spring. There are intervening cold fronts, when warm north-westerlies back to become cold southerly winds (Section 13.3). Sometimes the anticyclones are blocked in winter over the Tasman Sea, to the west of New Zealand, directing polar air masses onto the country (e.g. Figure 13.10). Single large anticyclones, or a series of them separated by only weak troughs, lead to fine weather in summer and frosts in winter.

Frontal disturbances often form over the Tasman Sea, especially in winter (Figure 13.11), but may become occluded (Section 13.3) by the time they reach New Zealand. Cold fronts are often associated with vigorous storms, and sometimes tornadoes in the North Island.

The range along the South Island tends to steer lows further south, or else block them. The result is two distinct tracks for lows, either south of the country or irregularly across the North Island. In the second case, a low upwind of the island gradually fills, whilst a new low forms over the ocean to the south-east. This lee cyclogenesis (Note 12.K) can take forecasters by surprise and cause a sudden windshift from warm, dry north-westerly to much cooler, wet southerly winds in Christchurch, for instance.

The mountains deflect the westerly winds which prevail for about 40 per cent of the time. The winds are funnelled by the gap of Cook Strait, making Wellington a notably windy city (Table 16.9). Speeds exceed 25 m/s (90 km/h) in Wellington on about thirty days each year, ten times the frequency at Auckland to the north or Christchurch to the south. Winds tend to be slightly stronger in summer than in winter.

Temperatures

The numbers of hours of sunshine each day at Auckland, Wellington and Christchurch (Figure 8.15, Table 16.9) about equal those at the same latitudes in Australia, and so daily maximum and minimum temperatures are also similar. Table 16.9 indicates a change of mean temperature of about 0.5 K per degree of latitude. The change with elevation is around 7 K/km.

No part of New Zealand is more than 130

Table 16.9 Features of four coastal cities in New Zealand

Feature	Auckland (37°S)		Wellington (41°S)		Christchurch (44°S)		Dunedin (46°S)	
	Jan	July	Jan	July	Jan	July	Jan	July
Sunshine (h/day)	7.6	4.2	7.6	3.4	6.8	4.1	5.7	3.3
Daily max (°C)	23	13	21	12	21	10	19	9
Daily min (°C)	16	8	13	6	12	2	10	3
Dewpoint (°C)	13	8	13	5	11	2	10	2
Rainfall (mm)	79	145	81	137	56	69	86	79
Wind (m/s)	2.8	2.5	8.1	6.9	4.7	3.3	2.8	2.8

km from the sea, which reduces both the annual and daily ranges of temperature to 9 K or there-abouts. The highest temperatures are recorded east of the mountain ranges, usually in association with a north-westerly foehn wind. But temperatures depend greatly on local circumstances; there was only one frost in fifty years at Albert Park in Auckland, and about eight each year at a nearby aerodrome.

Fronts generally bring only small changes of temperature. An exception are changes of over 10 K around Cook Strait, whenever air heated by warm land or by a foehn effect is replaced by polar winds.

Precipitation

The incident winds are moistened by the surrounding oceans, so that there is considerable orographic cloud, notably along the South Island range. This is the 'long white cloud' for which New Zealand is famous. Cloudiness is greater in winter and at higher latitudes (Table 16.9).

In general, the mountains cause orographic precipitation on the west, and a rain-shadow and foehn effect (Note 7.E) on the east (Figure 10.4). Heavy rains are brought by moist north-westerlies before a cold front, resulting in an estimated 10,000 mm/a or more in some parts of the Alps. The record amount of 559 mm in one day was measured at Milford Sound (at 45°S on the west), where the annual average is 6,350 mm. In contrast, the only part of New Zealand with less than 600 mm/a is on the east of the range; some places in Central Otago receive only 300 mm/a.

The particularly strong westerlies of spring increase the rainfall on the west coast but decrease precipitation in the lee on the east. Inland showers arise in summer from convection and from convergence of sea breezes from opposite sides, especially on the North Island.

There is rain over most of the North Island on at least 150 days each year. Rain in winter comes from the lows which form to the west or north-west, whilst anticyclones in summer reduce the rainfall in that season. The remoteness of the lows lessens their influence on the rainfall in the South Island. As a consequence, there is a *northwards* increase in the proportion of rain during winter, which contrasts with the pattern in Australia (Section 16.6).

The number of thunderdays in New Zealand is shown in Figure 9.13. They are most common on the west of the South Island, triggered by orographic uplift.

Precipitation falls as snow on the highest parts of the Southern Alps, and lies briefly down to 700 m above sea level in Otago. Permanent snow lies above 2,400 m in the North Island and 2,100 m in the South Island. Glaciers between 43–45°S cover 5 per cent of South Island, and the Fox and Franz Josef glaciers descend to within 300 m of sea-level. The glaciers retreated with accelerating speed until about 1985 (Figure 15.13), presumably on account of more frequent blocking highs, reducing cloudiness, so that skies are clearer and rainfall less. On the other hand, recent advancing of the glaciers is attributed to stronger westerly winds, increasing precipitation onto the snowfields.

Climates

There is a remarkable range of climates, but most of New Zealand falls within the Cfb category in Köppen's classification. A more detailed classification is described in **Table 16.10** and displayed in **Figure 16.20**.

16.8 CONCLUSIONS

The foregoing can be augmented by discussing Indonesian climates and also north-hemisphere climates (Notes 16.J and 16.K). From all this and from the previous parts of the book we reach the following conclusions:

1 Weather and climate are different aspects of the atmospheric condition – the first dealing with processes taking a day or so, while the other describes the overall character at a particular place over a period such as thirty years. The climate is a composite of the weather.
2 Weather and climate in the southern hemisphere are different from what is observed in

the north. There is the obvious reversal of the Coriolis force affecting all large-scale rotation of lows, highs, tropical cyclones, tornadoes, ocean currents and jet streams. But there is also the importance of the oceans, the sub-

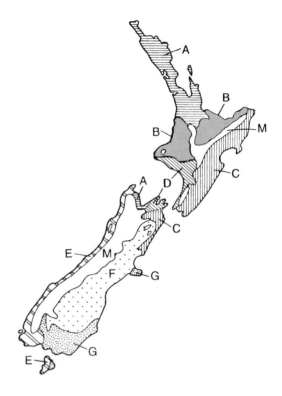

Figure 16.20 The distribution of climates in New Zealand, as defined in Table 16.10.

Table 16.10 A climate classification for New Zealand. The distribution is shown in Figure 16.20.

Class	Summer	Winter	Annual rain (mm)	Wettest months	Rain-bearing wind
A	Warm	Mild	1,100–2,500	July–August	North-west
B	Very warm	Mild	1,000–1,500	Any	North-west
C	Very warm	Mild	650–2,000	Any	South
D	Warm	Mild	900–2,000	May–July	Westerly (often gale strength)
E	Mild	Mild	1,000–3,000	November–May	North-west
F	Warm	Cold	330–1,500	March–May	South
G	Warm	Cold	650–1,250	December–June	South-west
M	Mountain climate		1,000–3,000	Any	West

tropical position of some continents, the extreme coldness of Antarctica, and the mainly north–south orientation of mountain chains in the south.

3 Explaining the weather is difficult because numerous factors are involved. In brief, weather (and consequently the climate) depends on three factors – (i) atmospheric processes (e.g. wind, the advection of energy and moisture, radiation, cloud physics, instability and turbulence), (ii) surface characteristics (albedo, roughness, soil moisture, evaporation, ocean currents, etc.) and (iii) features of geography (the Earth's turning, the latitude, altitude, proximity to the sea, etc.). These do not act independently but interact, with feedback loops of various scales of time and space, all complicating the problems of weather prediction, for instance. The interrelatedness of the various aspects of our atmospheric environment is indicated by the considerable cross-referencing within the book.

4 Several of the Notes attached to the chapters illustrate how relevant the study of weather and climate is to everyday life. Other examples include the forecasting of crop yield (**Note 16.G**), house design (**Note 16.H**) and preparations for outdoor sports (**Note 16.I**).

5 Comparison of the text with any similar book written only a few decades ago indicates what great progress is being made in observing, understanding and forecasting, despite the complexity of the subject. Considerable contributions have been made by satellite observations and computer modelling. Advance has been fostered by the importance of problems associated with droughts, tropical cyclones, acid rain, agricultural production and climate change, for instance.

6 Many aspects remain to be explained satisfactorily, including the mechanism of ENSO

events, the future development and implications of the Antarctic ozone hole, the rate of global warming in the coming century, the interaction between atmosphere and ocean on time-scales ranging from a few days to a few years, and the effect of deep ocean circulations on climate. In addition, weather forecasting promises to continue to improve into the twenty-first century, especially nowcasting (e.g. the prediction of severe thunderstorms) and extended-range forecasting.

7 Finally, this survey of what is known about weather and climate demonstrates what a fascinating subject it is. It combines theory, experiment and practical application, it involves microscopic, local and global viewpoints, it links ideas of conditions millions of years ago to a concern for the future, it draws nations together in co-operative endeavour. In view of this, we hope that the reader will feel encouraged to pursue the study of weather and climate in more detail.

NOTES

16.A Köppen's classification of climates
16.B The 'Canberra metric' of similarity
16.C Selecting a site for a telescope
16.D Deserts
16.E Australian bushfires
16.F Kinds of vegetation in Australia
16.G Estimating crop yield from climate information
16.H Climate and housing
16.I Climate for the time of the Olympic Games in Sydney
16.J Indonesian climates
16.K A comparison between northern and southern climates
16.L European climates
16.M North America climates

Part VI

SUPPLEMENTS

17

ACKNOWLEDGEMENTS

17.1 ASSISTANCE

We are grateful to many people. It would have been impossible to prepare this book without data from several members of the Australian Bureau of Meteorology, and without the skilled preparation of the diagrams from Kevin Cowan and Val Lyon of the Geography Dept, Australian National University, Canberra, by permission of Professor Diana Howlett, head of the department. We have benefited from the computer skills of Tim Gilbert (Purdue University, USA), Steve Leahy (Geography Dept, ANU, Canberra) and Jenny Edwards (Forestry Dept, ANU, Canberra).

17.2 ADVICE

In addition, the book would have been impoverished without the comments of the following experts on points in the indicated chapters:

Chapter 1. Dr Andrew Glikson (Australian Geological Survey Organisation, Canberra), Dr Helen Cleugh (CSIRO Division of Environmental Mechanics, Canberra), Jenny Kesteven (Centre for Resource & Environmental Studies, ANU, Canberra), Assoc. Prof. Howard Bridgman (Newcastle University, NSW), Assoc. Prof. Jack Hobbs (University of New England, NSW), Ian Galbally (CSIRO Division of Atmospheric Research, Melbourne).

Chapter 2. Prof. Jetse Kalma (Newcastle University, NSW), Dr Manuel Nunez (University of Tasmania), John Evans and David de Pury (Research School of Biological Sciences, ANU, Canberra).

Chapter 3. Jenny Kesteven (Centre for Resource & Environmental Studies, ANU, Canberra), Dr Lawrence Truppi (US Environmental Protection Agency, North Carolina).

Chapter 4. Ian McIlroy (previously of the CSIRO Division of Atmospheric Research, Melbourne).

Chapter 6. Dr Richard deDear (School of Earth Sciences, Macquarie University, Sydney).

Chapter 8. Dr Martin Platt (CSIRO Division of Atmospheric Research, Melbourne), Prof. Steven Warren (University of Washington, USA).

Chapter 9. Dr Keith Bigg (previously of the CSIRO Division of Cloud Physics, Sydney).

Chapter 10. Dr William Gibbs (previously of the ABM, Melbourne), Christopher Robertson (John Oxley Library, Brisbane), David Morrison (Civic Centre, Grafton), D. Ingle Smith (Centre of Resource & Environmental Studies, ANU, Canberra), James Irish (NSW Dept of Water Resources, Sydney), Prof. Calvin Rose (Griffith University, Brisbane), Dr Vincent Kotwicki (South Australian Dept of Environment & Natural Resources, Adelaide).

Chapter 11. Dr Stewart Godfrey (CSIRO Division of Oceanography, Hobart), Dr Anthony Hirst (CSIRO Division of Atmospheric Research, Melbourne).

Chapter 12. Prof. Michael Fritsch (Pennsylvania State University, USA), Prof. David Karoly (CRC for Southern Hemisphere Meteorology, Monash University, Melbourne).

Chapter 13. Ian Forrest and Mike Rosel (ABM, Melbourne), Dr Chris Landsea (NOAA Hurricane Research Division, Miami, USA), Andrew Slater (Macquarie University, Sydney).

Chapter 14. Roger Nurse (School of Earth Sciences, Macquarie University, Sydney), Prof. Jorg Hacker (Flinders Institute for Atmospheric and Marine Sciences, Flinders University, Adelaide).

Chapter 15. Clem Davies and Keith Colls (ABM, Canberra), Dr Barrie Pittock (CSIRO Division of Atmospheric Research, Melbourne), Dr Geoffrey Hope (Dept of Archaeology & Natural History, ANU, Canberra), Pieter Visser (South African Weather Bureau).

Chapter 16. Dr Janette Lindesay (Geography Dept, ANU, Canberra), Dr Blair Fitzharris (Geography Dept, University of Otago, NZ), Prof. William Budd (University of Tasmania, Hobart).

17.3 TABLES, NOTES AND ILLUSTRATIONS

The following includes references to the souces of figures and notes in the supplementary CD. Most of the plates came from the collection of the Australian Bureau of Meteorology, Melbourne, and we are grateful for the help of Esther Amot in obtaining these.

The illustrations were mainly drawn by Kevin Cowan of the Geography Department of the Australian National University, Canberra. Most are adaptations of diagrams published by the following:

Note 1.D Lovelock 1986, Graedel and Crutzen 1989: 32, Houghton *et al*. 1990, Wuebbles and Edmonds 1991: 115, Hidore and Oliver 1993: 378.

Note 1.L Hartmann 1994: 370.

Table 1.1 Hess 1974: 649, Linacre 1992: 12.

Table 1.2 Houghton 1986, Wayne 1991: 3.

Plate 1.1 Courtesy of the Australian Bureau of Meteorology.

Figure 1.1 Kasting 1993: 923, Budyko 1982: 43.

Figure 1.2 (a) Gribbin 1988b: 3, Keeling *et al*. 1989; (b) Ekdahl and Keeling 1973, Machta 1977; (c) Denmead 1991: 76 (by permission of Kluwer Academic Publishers); (d) Denmead 1991: 76 (by permission of Kluwer Academic Publishers).

Figure 1.3 Sundquist 1993: 935, Bolin *et al*. 1994: 9.

Figure 1.5 (a) Jones and Shanklin 1995: 410 (curve of October ozone change over Halley Station: by permission from *Nature*, Macmillan Mag. Ltd); (b) NOAA 1993: 62; (c) Australian Bureau of Meteorology, from NASA/Goddard Space Flight Center.

Figure 1.8 Peixoto and Oort 1992, Oort 1983.

Figure 1.11 Oke 1988: 474.

Note 2.D Oliver 1973: 254, Griffiths 1976b: 100, Miller 1981: 32.

Note 2.K Sasamori *et al*. 1972: 19.

Table 2.2 Fitzpatrick and Armstrong 1972: 15, Paltridge and Proctor 1976: 242.

Table 2.4 Hartmann 1994: 66.

Table 2.5 Gay 1979: 353 (by permission of Springer-Verlag).

Table 2.6 Schwerdtfeger 1984: 258.

Plate 2.1 Thanks are due to Periplus Editions, Singapore, for this photograph from *The Periplus Guide to Bali*.

Figure 2.1 By permission of Elsevier Science.

Figure 2.2 Weyl 1970, Oliver 1973: 15, Fleagle and Businger 1980.

Figure 2.8 Waldmeier 1961, Schneider and Moss 1975, Lockwood 1979: 27, Hartmann 1994: 288.

Figure 2.11 Budyko 1974: 1, *World Survey of Climatology* 12: 36 and 183 (by permission of Elsevier Science); 13: 42; 15: 336 and 582, Barry and Chorley 1992: 25.

Figure 2.12 Chang 1970, Oliver 1973: 264, Linacre and Hobbs 1977: 219.

Figure 2.13 Monteith 1973: 64 (by permission of the author).

Figure 2.14 Nunez *et al.* 1987: 9.

Figure 2.15 Neiburger *et al* 1981: 78.

Figure 2.16 Robertson 1972: 278.

Figure 2.17 Budyko 1982: 213 (by permission of Kluwer Academic Publishers).

Figure 2.18 Williamson 1973: 116, after Von der Haar and Suomi 1971: 305.

Figure 2.19 Paltridge 1975: 38 (by permission of the Australian and New Zealand Association for the Advancement of Science)

Table 3.1 Linacre and Hobbs 1977: 27.

Table 3.2 Redman and McCrae 1975 (courtesy of Dr Mary Redman).

Table 3.3 Truppi 1976: 17.

Table 3.4 Fairbridge 1967: 987.

Table 3.6 Okoola 1992.

Table 3.F.1 Edey 1977, Angus *et al.* 1981: 365.

Plate 3.1a Dozy 1938, Hope *et al.* 1976. Photo supplied by Dr I. Allison of the University of Tasmania, with the agreement of Professor J.J. Dozy.

Plate 3.1b By permission of the Zeitschrift Für Gletscherkunde & Glazialgeologie; photo taken in 1991 by Peter Sedgwick, chief surveyor of Freeport Indonesia.

Figure 3.4 Blüthgen 1966, Weyl 1970: 78, Lamb 1972: 149.

Figure 3.5 Pearce and Smith 1984: 211 (by permission of Hutchinson).

Figure 3.6 Maejima 1977: 125, Navarra 1979: 476, Leffler 1980, Berry 1981: 32.

Figure 3.7 Kalma and Crossley 1981.

Figure 3.8 Lieth and Whittaker 1975: 243 (by permission of Springer-Verlag).

Figure 3.9 Dr Peter Jones, Centro Internacional de Agricultura Tropical, Cali, Colombia.

Figure 3.10 Dick 1966: 1.

Figure 3.13 Oliver 1973, after Trewartha 1968.

Figure 3.14 Strahler 1963: 215, after M. Jefferson.

Figure 3.15 Jones and Lindesay 1993: 360.

Figure 3.16 Oke 1987 (by permission of Methuen).

Figure 3.17 Shields 1965.

Figure 3.18 Carlsmith and Anderson 1979: 341 (by permission of the American Psychological Association).

Figure 3.C.1 Keig and McAlpine 1977 (by permission of the University of New South Wales Library).

Figure 3.D.1 Ingram and Mount 1975: 147.

Figure 3.D.2 Roberts 1982: 47 (by permission of the International Society of Biometeorology).

Figure 3.E.1 Smith 1975: 167, Munn 1970: 190, after Wilson 1967.

Figure 3.E.2 Dixon and Prior 1987: 9 (British Crown copyright. Reproduced by permission of the Controller of Her Majesty's Stationery Office).

Figure 3.I.1 McMahon and Low 1972: 40.

Table 4.2 Peixoto and Oort 1992: 170–1, after Baumgartner and Reichel 1975.

Plate 4.1 Courtesy of the Australian Bureau of Meteorology.

Figure 4.5 Greacen and Hignett 1976: 18 (by permission of the CSIRO Division of Soils).

Figure 4.9 Clemence and Schulze 1982.

Figure 4.11 Peixoto and Oort 1992: 169 (by permission of the American Institute of Physics), Barry and Chorley 1992: 44, after Budyko *et al.* 1962, Baumgartner and Reichel 1975.

Figure 4.12 Jenny Kesteven, Centre for Resource & Environmental Studies, ANU, Canberra.

Table 5.1 Sellers 1965: 105, Budyko 1974: 220, Edelstein 1992: 265.

Table 5.2 Weller 1980: 2011.

Table 5.3 Miller 1965: 250.

Table 5.4 Oke 1978, Oliver and Fairbridge 1987: 417.

Table 5.F.1 Newton 1972b: 246, Hastenrath 1985: 89 (by permission of Kluwer Academic Publishers).

Figure 5.2 Budyko 1974: 166, Peixoto and Oort 1992: 235, Barry and Chorley 1992: 45.

Figure 5.3 Frohlich and London 1985.

Figure 5.4 Crowe 1971: 47, after Budyko 1958.

Figure 5.5 Flohn 1978, after Schwerdtfeger 1970.

Figure 5.6 Hoy and Stephens 1977.

Figure 5.7 Greenland 1973: 298 (by permission of Elsevier Science).

Figures 5.8a, 5.8b Lockwood 1974: 34 (by permission of the author).

Figures 5.8c, 5.8d Budyko 1974: 196 and 205.

Figure 5.9 Denmead 1972: 168.

Figure 5.10 Deacon 1969: 86.

Table 6.1 Linacre 1992: 86.

Table 6.2 Australian Bureau of Meteorology 1973.

Table 6.3 Crowe 1971: 332 (by permission of Addison Wesley Longman).

Plate 6.1 Courtesy of Dr J. Lindesay, Geography Dept, Australian National University, Canberra.

Figure 6.2 Houghton 1984: 148, Riviere 1989: 50, Eagleson 1991: 37, Chahine 1992: 373.

Figure 6.7 Okolowicz 1976: 314.

Figure 6.8 Dr Peter Jones, Centro Internacional Agricultura Tropical, Cali, Colombia.

Figure 6.9a Gentilli 1978: 45 (by permission of the Department of Geography, University of Western Australia).

Figure 6.9b Booth 1981.

Figure 6.10 Lindesay 1994, after Jackson 1961.

Figure 6.12 Dunsmuir and Phillips 1991: 90.

Figure 6.13 Tuller 1968: 789.

Figure 6.G.1 McIntyre 1980: 186.

Table 7.1 Oke 1987, Reiquam 1980: 804, Hanna 1982.

Table 7.2 Luna and Church 1972, Williamson and Krenmayer 1980: 780, Branzov and Ivancheva 1994: 68

Plate 7.1 Courtesy of the Australian Bureau of Meteorology.

Figure 7.1 Unpublished work by Dr R. Hyde and his colleagues of Macquarie University, Sydney.

Figure 7.7 Webb 1977.

Figure 7.8 Geiger 1966: 471, after Woodcock and Stommel 1947.

Figure 7.9 Day and Sternes 1970: 291.

Figure 7.10 Hastenrath 1991: 145 (by permission of Kluwer Academic Publishers).

Figure 7.L.1 Tucker 1993: 167, after Sawford *et al.* 1990.

Table 8.1 Rogers and Yau 1989, Cotton and Anthes 1989.

Table 8.2 Mason 1975, Oddie 1962, Parker 1980: 98.

Table 8.3 Loewe 1974: 20.

Plate 8.1 Courtesy of the Australian Bureau of Meteorology.

Plate 8.2 Mitchell *et al.* 1990 (courtesy of the CSIRO Division of Atmospheric Research, Melbourne).

Figure 8.2 Wallington 1977: 209, Petterssen 1969: 86.

Figure 8.4 Trewartha 1968: 144, Harvey 1976: 26.

Figure 8.5 Pedgley 1962: 72.

Figure 8.6 Maher 1973.

Figure 8.7 Hess 1974: 359, Baumgartner *et al.* 1982, after Blüthgen 1966.

Figure 8.10 Linacre 1992: 171.

Figure 8.12 Clem Davies, Australian Bureau of Meteorology, Canberra.

Figure 8.13 Bradley *et al.* 1991: 543.

Figure 8.14 Okolowicz 1976: 325.

Figure 8.15 Garnier 1958.

Figure 8.16 Gaffney 1975: 11.

Figure 8.18 Clem Davies, Australian Bureau of Meteorology, Canberra.

Plate 9.1 Courtesy of the NOAA/National Geophysical Data Archive, Boulder, Colorado.

Figure 9.1 Atkinson 1971: 6–7.

Figure 9.2 Jones 1991: 183.

Figure 9.3 From data supplied by the Tasmanian Hydro-Electricity Commission and analysed by Dr Keith Bigg.

Figure 9.5 Critchfield 1974b: 122.

Figure 9.6 Emanuel 1994: 234.

Figure 9.7 Garstang *et al.* 1990: 26 (courtesy of the American Meteorological Society).

Figure 9.8 Velasco and Fritsch 1987: 9608.

Figure 9.9 Gentilli 1972: 116.

Figure 9.10 Clem Davies, ABM, Canberra.

Figure 9.11 Australian Bureau of Meteorology 1967, Atkinson 1971: Ch. 9, p.2, Griffiths 1972: 29, Boucher 1976: 39, Griffiths and Driscoll 1982: 172, D.D. Houghton 1985: 146.

Figure 9.12 Okolowicz 1976: 252.

Figure 9.13 Tomlinson 1976: 320 (by permission of the New Zealand Science Information Publishing Centre).

Figure 9.14 Neuberger and Cahir 1969: 90.

Figure 9.16 Schulze 1972: 523.

Figure 9.17 Crop Insurance Services of Australia, Sydney, courtesy of Heather McMaster, Natural Hazards Research Centre, Macquarie University, Sydney.

Table 10.1 van Loon 1972: 107, after Moller 1951.

Table 10.2 Watterson and Legg 1967: 4 (by permission of the Australian Bureau of Meteorology).

Table 10.3 Australian Bureau of Meteorology.

Table 10.4 Boyd and Bufill 1988.

Table 10.5 Obasi 1994: 1655.

Table 10.6 David Morrison of Grafton City Council, and Smith *et al.* (1979: 244) for the Lismore data.

Plate 10.1 Thanks are due to the Japanese Meteorological Agency.

Figure 10.1 Australian Bureau of Meteorology.

Figure 10.2 Jennings 1967.

Figure 10.3 (a) Longwell *et al.* 1969: 38, Riehl 1979: 87, Parker 1980: 373, Hartmann 1994: 122, (b) Jaeger 1983: 137.

Figure 10.4 Garnier 1958, after Kidson.

Figure 10.5 McAlpine *et al.* 1983: 64.

Figure 10.6 Newton 1972b: 230, Riehl 1979: 84, Hastenrath 1985: 95 (by permission of Kluwer Academic Publishers), Peixoto and Oort 1992: 168, after Wust 1954.

Figure 10.7 Griffiths and McSaveney 1983 (by permission of the New Zealand Science Information Publishing Centre).

Figure 10.8 Data supplied by the Australian Bureau of Meteorology, Dr Janette Lindesay (Geography Dept, ANU, Canberra) and Dr Patricio Aceituno of Santiago, respectively.

Figure 10.9 Lutgens and Tarbuck 1992, Atkinson 1971: 6–20.

Figure 10.10 Carter 1990: 18.

Figure 10.11 Zucchini *et al.* 1992: 103 (by permission of the South African Society for the Advancement of Science).

Figure 10.12 Australian Bureau of Meteorology.

Figure 10.14 Instn Engineers Aust. 1977: 40.

Figure 10.16 The dates in row *a* came from Dr Tom Smith (Climate Analysis Center, National Meteorological Service, Maryland) and refer to years when the average sea-surface temperature in the eastern Pacific (between 5°S–5°N, 90°W–150°W) was at least 1 K ('strong') or 0.5 K ('moderate') above normal for at least two consecutive months. Slightly different years are quoted from Diaz and Markgraf (1992: 18) in Note 10.M. The years given in row *b* had at least four months ('moderate') or seven months ('strong') when the normalised SOI (Chapter 12) was more negative than −10. The strong and very strong ENSO warm episodes indicated in row *c* are those listed by Quinn 1992. The drought dates in row *d* came from Gibbs and Maher 1967, Maher 1973 (taking years when there were droughts in at least two of the eastern states of Australia), Coughlan *et al.* 1976, and an analysis of the years when the percentage of Australia's area with subnormal rainfall exceeded 70 per cent (Streten 1981: 490, and data from the National Climate Centre, ABM, Melbourne). The dates in row *e* were supplied by Dr Blair Fitzharris of the University of Otago, showing the beginnings of the worst droughts until 1992. Brazilian drought data in row *f* came from Caviedes 1973: 48, Flohn and Fleer 1975: 97 and Magalhaes and Reboucas 1988: 286. The American information in row *g* came partly from Currie 1984: 7227, and partly from Dr Tom Petersen of the US National Oceanic and Atmosphere Administration, referring to March–August rainfalls during 1895–1993 in the primary maize and soybean belt of the US. The South African drought data in row *h* refer to years at Durban when rainfalls were less than 800 mm, and were supplied by Dr Janette Lindesay of the Australian National University. The Santiago rain data in row *i* were supplied by Dr Patricio Aceituno of that city.

Figure 10.17 Nicholls 1973: 9.

Figure 10.18 Hirst and Hastenrath 1983.

Figure 10.19 Heathcote 1991: 222 (by permission of Kluwer Academic Publishers).

Figure 10.20 O'Connell 1986.

Figure 10.21 Dr Alan Duus, Canberra, 1994.

Figure 10.A.1 Lieth and Whittaker 1975: 243, da Mota 1977: 112.

Figure 10.A.2 Nix 1975: 209.

Table 11.1 Streten and Zillman 1984: 404.

Plate 11.1 Courtesy of the CSIRO Division of Environmental Mechanics, Canberra.

Figure 11.1 Hartmann 1994: 16.

Figure 11.2 Sverdrup 1942.

Figure 11.3 Joubert 1994.

Figure 11.4 Neal 1973: 14 (courtesy of the Australian Bureau of Meteorology).

Figure 11.5 Sverdrup *et al.* 1942.

Figure 11.6 Pickard and Emery 1990: 45, after Tabata 1965.

Figure 11.7 Dietrich *et al.* 1980: 245, after Budel 1950 and the US Oceanographic Office 1957 and 1968.

Figure 11.8 Oberhuber 1988 (by permission of the Deutsches Klimarechenzentrum GmbH).

Figure 11.9 Dr Stuart Godfrey; after Leutus 1982.

Figure 11.15 Budd 1993: 276.

Figure 11.16 Priestley 1977: 162.

Figure 11.18 Duxbury 1974: 223, Hastenrath 1985: 66 (by permission of Kluwer Academic Publishers), Tomczak and Godfrey 1994: 86, after Sverdrup *et al.* 1942.

Figure 11.19 Gribbin 1991, Held 1993.

Figure 11.E.1 Hastenrath 1991: 158 (by permission of Kluwer Academic Publishers).

Table 12.1 White 1989: 5.

Plate 12.1 Courtesy of the NASA Johnson Space Centre, Houston, Texas, with the assistance of O.W. Vaughan.

Figure 12.1 Gribbin 1978: 214, Webster 1981, Lindesay 1994, after Taljaard 1972 and Nieuwolt 1977, Battan 1984.

Figure 12.2 Manabe *et al.* 1974: 119, after Mintz 1968.

Figure 12.3 Riehl 1979: 16 (by permission of Academic Press).

Figure 12.4 Barry and Chorley 1992: 121.

Figure 12.5 Riehl 1979: 4 (by permission of Academic Press), Peixoto and Oort 1992: 201.

Figure 12.6 Niewolt 1977: 52.

Figure 12.7 Guymer and Le Marshall 1980: 26 (courtesy of the Australian Bureau of Meteorology), Preston-Whyte and Tyson 1988: 183.

Figure 12.10 Ludlam 1980: 311.

Figure 12.13 Dyer 1975: 30.

Figure 12.16 Palmen and Newton 1969: 569, Hastenrath 1985: 119 (by permission of Kluwer Academic Publishers).

Figure 12.17 Flohn and Fleer 1975, Neal and Holland 1978: 73, Lighthill and Pearce 1981: 17, Wyrtki 1982, Streten and Zillman 1984: 356, Climate Monitoring System 1985, Hastenrath 1985: 192 (by permission of Kluwer Academic Publishers), Allan 1988: 316, Peixoto and Oort 1992: 419.

Figure 12.18 Whetton 1988: 176.

Figure 12.19 Trenberth and Shea 1988: 3079.

Figure 12.20 Hunt 1991: 92, Enfield 1989, after Ropelewski and Halpert 1987.

Figure 12.21 Hirst 1989: 102, after Trenberth 1984 and Vallis 1986.

Table 13.2 Frank Woodcock, ABM, Melbourne.

Table 13.G.1 Frank Woodcock, ABM, Melbourne.

Plate 13.1 This image from the NOAA-AVHRR satellite was processed by John Adams of the Remote Survey Sensing Applications Centre, Dept of Lands Administration, Western Australia.

Figure 13.3 Linacre and Hobbs 1977: 130.

Figure 13.4 Browning 1972, Ryan 1986: 33, Houze 1993.

Figure 13.5 Clem Davies, ABM, Canberra.

Figure 13.6 Smith *et al.* 1991: 1279 (courtesy of the American Meteorological Society).

Figure 13.7 Preston-Whyte and Tyson 1988: 211 (by permission of Oxford University Press, Southern Africa).

Figure 13.8 Renner 1972: 24, Ratisbona 1976: 227.

Figure 13.9 Australian Bureau of Meteorology.

Figure 13.11 Wallace and Hobbs 1977: 253, Emanuel 1994: 478.

Figure 13.12 Neumann undated, Ch. 1, p.25.

Figure 13.13 Krishna 1984: 15 (courtesy of the Fiji Meteorological Service).

Figure 13.14 Basher and Zheng 1995.

Figure 13.15 Karelsky 1961.

Note 14.G Gifford and Hanna 1973.

Table 14.2 Oliver 1976.

Table 14.C.1 McGrath 1972.

Plate 14.1 Courtesy of the Australian Bureau of Meteorology.

Plate 14.2 Courtesy of Dr Roger Smith of the Meteorological Institute, University of Munich.

Figure 14.7 Kalma and Hutchinson 1981: 11 and 16.

Figure 14.9 Riehl 1979: 266, after van Bemmelen 1922.

Figure 14.10 Auliciems 1979: 42, after Shields.

Figure 14.11 Clarke 1955.

Figure 14.13 Linacre 1992: 208.

Figure 14.15 Whittingham 1964, Oliver 1983: 249.

Figure 14.17 McTainsh and Pitblado 1987: 418 (by permission of John Wiley and Sons).

Figure 14.18 Aynsley 1973: 144.

Figure 14.19 Neal and Holland 1978: 255.

Figure 14.20 Michael Johnson, NSW Environmental Protection Authority, Sydney.

Note 15.E Hines and Halevy 1977.

Note 15.F Hanson *et al.* 1987

Table 15.1 National Climatic Data Center, Asheville, N.C., USA.

Table 15.2 Eriksson 1966: 108.

Table 15.3 Kutzbach 1975: 124.

Table 15.4 Yu and Neil 1991: 656

Plate 15.1 Courtesy of Dr David Etheridge, CSIRO Division of Atmospheric Research, Melbourne.

Figure 15.1 WMO 1994 (by permission of the World Meteorological Organization).

Figure 15.6 From data supplied by I.R. Forrest, ABM, Melbourne,

Figure 15.7 Australian Academy of Science 1976.

Figure 15.8 Barnola *et al.* 1987: 410, Houghton *et al.* 1990: 11, Budd 1991: 285, Houghton 1994: 50.

Figure 15.9 van Andel 1985: 46 (by permission of Cambridge University Press).

Figure 15.10 Gordon 1992: 2 (courtesy of the American Meteorological Society).

Figure 15.11 Burgos *et al.* 1991: 231, with additional data from Dr Patricio Aceituno.

Figure 15.13 Fitzharris *et al.* 1992.

Figure 15.14 Jones and Henderson-Sellers 1992: 261 (courtesy of the American Meteorological Society).

Figure 15.15 Nicholls *et al.* 1996: 152 (by permission of Cambridge University Press).

Figure 15.16 Whetton *et al.* 1993: 295.

Note 16.B Cook and Russell 1983: 27.

Table 16.2 Unpublished work by Peter Shoebridge in 1981, from a map of natural vegetation by Leeper 1970: 44, after R.J. Williams 1959.

Table 16.3 Ratisbona 1976.

Table 16.4 Pearce and Smith 1990.

Table 16.5 Oliver and Fairbridge 1987: 155.

Table 16.6 Pearce and Smith 1990.

Table 16.9 Linacre and Hobbs 1977: 171, Pearce and Smith 1990.

Table 16.10 Coulter 1975: 98.

Table 16.A.1 Munn 1970: 278, Lamb 1972: 509.

Table 16.E.1 Skidmore 1988: 234.

Table 16.F.1 Fowle 1934: 327, Barton 1969: 4, Givoni 1969: 106, Saini 1973: 35, Koenigsberger *et al.* 1974: 287, Crowther 1977: 121, Muncey 1979: 15, Evans 1980: 84.

Plate 16.1 Courtesy of Dr Michael Bird of the Research School of Earth Sciences, Australian National University.

Figure 16.1 Holdridge 1947: 367, Oliver 1973: 163, Henderson-Sellers 1991: 154.

Figure 16.2 Renner 1972: 9, Evans 1980: 48, Jiminez and Oliver 1987: 793.

Figure 16.3 Oliver 1970: 625.

Figure 16.4 Schwerdtfeger 1979: 63, after Budd *et al.* 1971, Parish 1980: 4, Parish 1992: 150.

Figure 16.5 Rubin 1962: 6, Parish 1980: 27, Parish 1992: 151, after Parish and Bromwich 1987.

Figure 16.6 Rubin 1962: 7.

Figure 16.7 Dr Peter Jones, Centro Internacional de Agricultura Tropical, Cali, Colombia.

Figure 16.8 Dr Peter Jones, Centro Internacional de Agricultura Tropical, Cali, Colombia.

Figure 16.9 Prohaska 1970: 61.

Figure 16.10 McGinnies *et al.* 1968.

Figure 16.11 Moura and Shukla 1981.

Figure 16.12 Griffiths 1972: 10, Taljaard 1972: 197, Nicholson *et al.* 1988.

Figure 16.13 (a) Dr Janette Lindesay, Geography Dept, Canberra, (c) Coulter 1975: 123.

Figure 16.14 Tyson 1969: 1, Nicholson *et al.* 1988.

Figure 16.16 *World Survey of Climatology* 10, p. 13 (with permission of Elsevier Science).

Figure 16.17 Pescod 1976.

Figure 16.18 Australian Bureau of Meteorology.

Figure 16.19 McBoyle 1971: 1, Dick 1975.

Figure 16.20 Coulter 1975: 98.

Figure 16.H.2 Anon 1971: 3, Evans 1980: 72.

PLATES

FIGURES

TABLES

NOTES

The following are mentioned in the text of this book and will be found on the supplementary CD-ROM.

NOTES FOR CHAPTER 1

1.A   Features of the Earth's surface
1.B   Photosynthesis and respiration
1.C   The densities of air and water vapour
1.D   Ground-level concentrations of gases
1.E   The chemistry of the destruction of ozone
1.F   Mass, density, weight and pressure
1.G   The hydrostatic balance
1.H   Height, altitude and elevation
1.I   Effects of the rarefied atmosphere at high elevations
1.J   SI units
1.K   Scales of temperature
1.L   Mean properties of the atmosphere
1.M   The 'ideal-gas' law

NOTES FOR CHAPTER 2

2.A   Electromagnetic radiation
2.B   Shortwave and longwave radiation
2.C   The Stefan–Boltzmann equation
2.D   Effects of the various components of solar radiation
2.E   The inverse-square law of radiation
2.F   The monthly mean extra-terrestrial radiation
2.G   Aerosols and volcanoes
2.H   Effects of the atmospheric windows
2.I   Radiation and crop growth
2.J   Effect of an albedo change on global warming

2.K   Annual mean longwave radiation
2.L   The greenhouse effect
2.M   Simple estimation of net radiation

NOTES FOR CHAPTER 3

3.A   The transfer of sensible heat
3.B   Effects of latitude and elevation on mean temperature
3.C   High temperatures and human mortality
3.D   Acclimatisation and adaptation
3.E   Windchill
3.F   Temperature and crops
3.G   The annual range of monthly mean temperatures
3.H   Cold nights
3.I   Growing-degree-days and agriculture
3.J   Degree-days and comfort
3.K   The conduction of heat
3.L   The thermal belt

NOTES FOR CHAPTER 4

4.A   Water molecules
4.B   Protection of crops from frost
4.C   Saturation vapour pressure and temperature
4.D   Rates of evaporation
4.E   Dalton's evaporation equation
4.F   Effect of drop radius on its evaporation rate
4.G   Crop evaporation and yield
4.H   The Relative Strain Index of comfort

NOTES FOR CHAPTER 5

5.A   Why doesn't the world get hotter?
5.B   Does a car's colour influence its temperature?
5.C   Factors governing the daily minimum temperature
5.D   Estimation of evaporation
5.E   Sol-air temperatures
5.F   Energy balances of the southern hemisphere

NOTES FOR CHAPTER 6

6.A   Aspects of the hydrologic cycle
6.B   Alternative ways of stating the air's humidity
6.C   Saturation deficit and crop growth
6.D   Psychrometer measurements
6.E   The weather-stress index (WSI)
6.F   A thermal sensation scale
6.G   The Standard Effective Temperature
6.H   Evaporative coolers
6.I   The skew $T - \log p$ diagram, part 1

NOTES FOR CHAPTER 7

7.A   Feedback
7.B   The dry adiabatic lapse rate
7.C   The saturated adiabatic lapse rate
7.D   The skew $T - \log p$ diagram, part 2
7.E   Calculation of the foehn effect
7.F   Non-local instability
7.G   Indices of instability
7.H   How an atmosphere becomes unstable
7.I   Solar ponds
7.J   Tornado damage
7.K   Dispersion of ground inversions by fans
7.L   Atmospheric instability and air pollution
7.M Temperature profiles and sound

NOTES FOR CHAPTER 8

8.A   The formation of cloud by mixing
8.B   The Lifting Condensation Level and the Convective Condensation Level
8.C   Atmospheric density currents which create uplift
8.D   Formation of cloud droplets
8.E   The water content of clouds
8.F   The evolution of cloud classification
8.G   Motoring in fog
8.H   Formation of advection fog
8.I   Formation of steam fog
8.J   Weather satellites
8.K   Effect of clouds on global climate
8.L   The Morning Glory

NOTES FOR CHAPTER 9

9.A   Monthly mean cloudiness and rainfall in Australia
9.B   The rainfall rate from stratiform cloud
9.C   The Bergeron–Findeisen process
9.D   Rainfall intensity and raindrop size
9.E   The early history of rain-making
9.F   The effectiveness of cloud seeding
9.G   Electrification within cumulonimbus cloud
9.H   The gradient of electrical potential in the lower atmosphere
9.I   Temperature and the frequency of hail
9.J   Hail cannon

NOTES FOR CHAPTER 10

10.A   Typical effects of rainfall in agriculture
10.B   Rain gauges
10.C   Remote rainfall measurement
10.D   Indication of seasonal rainfall by tree rings
10.E   Acidity and alkalinity
10.F   Soil erosion
10.G   Estimation of rainfalls for long recurrence intervals
10.H   Defining the 'typical' rainfall
10.I   The Bradfield Scheme
10.J   The possible effect of forests on rainfall
10.K   Dependable rainfall
10.L   Indices of rainfall variability
10.M   El Niño, part 1
10.N   The chance of a second dry day after a first
10.O   Desert runoff
10.P   Water budgets of soil moisture
10.Q   Flooding of the Brisbane River in 1893
10.R   Droughts in New South Wales
10.S   Droughts and sunspots

NOTES FOR CHAPTER 11

11.A   Effects of the oceans on climates
11.B   Buoyancy in the oceans
11.C   El Niño, part 2
11.D   The Coriolis effect
11.E   The climate near Lima
11.F   Traverse measurements

NOTES FOR CHAPTER 12

12.A   Streamlines
12.B   Trade winds
12.C   The geostrophic wind and isobaric surfaces
12.D   The gradient wind
12.E   Thickness
12.F   Thermal wind
12.G   Convergence, divergence and vertical circulations
12.H   Baroclinic and barotropic conditions
12.I   Balloon flight across Australia
12.J   Rossby waves
12.K   Vorticity
12.L   Jet streams and weather
12.M   Clear Air Turbulence
12.N   El Niño, part 3

NOTES FOR CHAPTER 13

13.A   Scales of winds
13.B   Frontal disturbances
13.C   Subtropical lows
13.D   Vortex spreading and stretching
13.E   Naming of tropical cyclones
13.F   Winds around a tropical cyclone
13.G   Global warming and tropical cyclones
13.H   Easterly waves
13.I   The Coriolis effect in the northern hemisphere
13.J   Weather in the northern hemisphere compared to that in the south

NOTES FOR CHAPTER 14

14.A   The wind profile
14.B   Winds and housing
14.C   Sea breezes
14.D   Density currents
14.E   The return period
14.F   Dimensions of wind's power density
14.G   Air pollution

NOTES FOR CHAPTER 15

15.A Weather radar
15.B Places of weather measurement
15.C Frost forecasting
15.D Feedback, chaos and unpredictability
15.E Sunspots and forecasting
15.F Effects of the Moon's phase
15.G Primitive equations for weather forecasting
15.H Numerical Weather Prediction
15.I Forecasting skill
15.J The 'tropics'
15.K Radiative equilibrium and global warming
15.L Radiometric methods of dating past climates

NOTES FOR CHAPTER 16

16.A Köppen's classification of climates
16.B The 'Canberra metric' of similarity
16.C Selecting a site for a telescope
16.D Deserts
16.E Australian bushfires
16.F Kinds of vegetation in Australia
16.G Estimating crop yield from climate information
16.H Climate and housing
16.I Climate for the time of the Olympic Games in Sydney
16.J Indonesian climates
16.K A comparison between northern and southern climates
16.L European climates
16.M North American climates

ABBREVIATIONS

ABM	Australian Bureau of Meteorology	ICAO	International Civil Aviation Organisation
ANU	Australian National University, Canberra	IGY	International Geophysical Year
BP	before the present	IR	infra-red (radiation)
cA	a continental Antarctic air mass	ITCZ	Intertropical Convergence Zone
CAPE	convective available potential energy	LCL	Lifting Condensation Level
CCL	convective condensation level	LFC	level of free convection
CCN	cloud condensation nuclei	LIA	Little Ice Age
cE	a continental equatorial-climate air mass	LNB	level of neutral buoyancy
CFC	chloro-fluoro-carbon	LW	longwave radiation
cP	a continental polar-climate air mass	MCC	mesoscale convective complex
CRC	Co-operative Research Centre	mE	a marine equatorial-climate air mass
CSIRO	Commonwealth Scientific and Industrial Research Organisation, Australia	μm	micrometre, i.e. 10^{-6} metres
cT	a continental temperate-climate air mass	mP	a marine polar-climate air mass
DALR	dry adiabatic lapse rate	MSE	mean square error
DLR	dewpoint lapse rate	MSLP	Mean Sea Level Pressure
EGE	enhanced greenhouse effect	MT	a marine temperate-climate air mass
ELR	environmental lapse rate	nm	nanometre, i.e. 10^{-9} metres
ENSO	El Niño + Southern Oscillation	NOAA	National Oceanic and Atmospheric Administration
ESU	equivalent sunburn unit	NSW	New South Wales
ET	Effective Temperature	NWP	Numerical Weather Prediction
GaBP	thousand million years before present	NZ	New Zealand
GCM	General Circulation Model	PAL	present atmospheric level
gdd	growing-degree-day	PAR	photosynthetically active radiation
GMS	Geostationary Meteorological Satellite	PBL	planetary boundary layer
GMT	Greenwich Meridian Time	PDSI	Palmer Drought Severity Index
GtC	a thousand million tonnes of carbon	PFJ	polar-front jet stream
GWP	global warming potential	pH	a measure of acidity or alkalinity
hdd	heating degree-day	PNP	potential net photosynthesis
		ppm	parts per million
		QBO	Quasi-Biennial Oscillation
		QG	quasi-geostrophic

RH	Relative Humidity		svp	saturation vapour pressure
RMS	root mean square		SW	shortwave radiation
RSI	Relative Strain Index		TAW	total available water capacity of soil
SALR	saturation adiabatic lapse rate		TC	tropical cyclone
SE	south-east direction		US	United States of America
SET	standard effective temperature		UTC	Coordinated Universal Time
SMR	saturation mixing ratio		UV	ultra-violet radiation
SOI	Southern Oscillation Index		WMO	World Meteorological Organisation
SPCZ	South Pacific Convergence Zone		WSI	weather-stress index
SST	sea-surface temperature		ZAB	Zaïre Air Boundary
STJ	subtropical jet stream			

BIBLIOGRAPHY

Adebayo, Y.R. 1992. Urban climatology in Africa. *African Urban Quarterly* 5 (February and May). Published by World Meteor. Organ. 160 pp.

Allan, R.J. 1988. El Niño Southern Oscillation influences in the Australian region. *Prog. Phys. Geog.* 12, 313–48.

Angus, J.F., R.B. Cunningham, M.W. Moncur and D.H. MacKenzie. 1981. Phasic development in field crops: I. Thermal response in the seedling phase. *Field Crops Res.* 3, 365–78.

Anon. 1971. House design for hot climates. Notes on Sci of Building 63 (Aust. Exptl Building Stn) 4 pp.

ASHRAE. 1993. Handbook: *Fundamentals* (Amer. Soc. Heating, Refrigerating and Air-conditioning Engineers).

Atkinson, G.D. 1971. *Forecasters' Guide to Tropical Meteorology.* Tech. Rept 240 (Air Weather Service, US Air Force) 347 pp.

Auliciems, A. 1979. *Spatial, Temporal and Human Dimensions of Air Pollution in Brisbane* (Dept of Geography, Univ. of Queensland, Brisbane) 89 pp.

Auliciems, A. and J.D. Kalma. 1979. A climatic classification of human thermal stress on Australia. *J. Appl. Meteor.* 18, 616–25.

Aust. Acad. Sci. 1976. *Climate Change.* Report 21 (Australian Academy of Science) 92 pp.

Aynsley, R.M. 1973. Wind effects on high and low-rise housing. *Archit. Sci. Rev.* 16, 142–6.

Barnola, J.M., D. Raynaud, Y.S. Korotkovich and C. Lorius. 1987. Vostok ice core provides 160,000 year record of atmospheric CO_2. *Nature* 329, 410.

Barry, R.G. and R.J. Chorley. 1992. *Atmosphere, Weather and Climate* (6th edn) (Routledge) 392 pp.

Barton, I.J. 1969. *Estimating the Heat Requirements for Domestic Buildings* (Newnes-Butterworths) 144 pp.

Basher, R.E. and X. Zheng. 1995. Tropical cyclones in the southwest Pacific. *J. Climate* 8, 1249–60.

Battan, L.J. 1984. *Fundamentals of Meteorology* (Prentice-Hall) 321 pp.

Baumgartner, A., G. Enders, M. Kirchner and H. Mayer. 1982. Global climatology. In Plate 1982: 125–78.

Berry, M.O. 1981. Snow and climate. In Gray and Male 1981: 32–59.

Blüthgen, J. 1966. *Allegemeine Klimageographie* (de Gruyter, Berlin) 720 pp.

Bolin, B., J. Houghton and L.G.M. Filho. 1994. *Radiation Forcing of Climate Change* (Intergov. Panel on Climate Change, World Meteor. Organ., Geneva) 28 pp.

Booth, T.H. 1981. Prediction of mean monthly 9am dewpoint temperature for any site in mainland eastern Australia. *Aust. Meteor. Mag.* 29, 1–8.

Boucher, K. 1976. *Global Climate* (John Wiley) 326 pp.

Boyd, M.J and M.C. Bufill 1988. Determining the flood response of urbanising catchments. *Search* 19, 286–8.

Bradley, S.G., R.G. Grainger and C.D. Stow. 1991. Some satellite-derived cloud statistics for the New Zealand region. *NZ J. Geol. and Geophys.* 34, 543–8.

Branzov, H. and I. Ivancheva. 1994. On the determination of Pasquill stability classes. In Brazdil and Kolar 1994: 67–71.

Brazdil, R. and M. Kolar (eds) 1994. *Contemporary Climatology.* Proc. Commission on Climatology, Brno (Internat. Geog. Union) 620 pp.

Browning, K.A. 1972. Radar measurements of air motion near fronts. Part II: *Weather*, 26, 320–40.

—— 1990. Organisation of clouds and precipitation in extratropical cyclones. In Newton and Holopainen 1990: 129–53.

Budd, G.M., R.H. Fox, A.L. Hendrie and K.E. Hicks. 1974. A field survey of thermal stress in New Guinea villages. *Phil. Trans Roy. Soc. B* 268, 393–400.

Budd, W.F. 1993. Antarctica and global change. *Climatic Change* 18, 271–99.

Budyko, M.I. 1974. *Climate and Life* (Academic Press) 508 pp.

—— 1982. *The Earth's Climate: Past and Future* (Academic Press).

—— 1986. *The Evolution of the Biosphere* (Reidel, Dordrecht) 423 pp.

Bunting, A.H. (ed.) 1987. *Agricultural Environments* (Commonwealth Agric. Bureau Internat.) 335 pp; or *Agroecological Zonation* (Cambridge University Press) 335 pp.

Burgos, J.J., H.F. Ponce and L.C.B. Molion. 1991. Climate change predictions for South America. *Climate Change* 18, 223–39.

Byers, H.R. 1974. History of weather modification. In Hess 1974: 3–44.

Carlsmith, J.M. and C.A. Anderson. 1979. Ambient temperature and the occurrence of collective violence. *J. Personality and Soc. Psychol.* 37, 337–44.

Carlson T.B. 1991. *Mid-latitude Weather Systems* (Harper-Collins Academic).

Carras, J.N. and G.M. Johnson (eds) 1982. *The Urban Atmosphere – Sydney, A Case Study.* (Aust. Commonwealth Sci. Indust. Res. Organ.) 655 pp.

Carter, M.W. 1990. A rainfall-based mechanism to regulate the release of water from Ranger uranium mine. *Tech. Memo. 30* (Supervising Scientist for the Alligator Rivers Region, Aust. Gov. Publ. Service) 23 pp.

Caviedes, C.N. 1973. Secas and El Niño: two simultaneous climatical hazards in South America. *Proc. Assoc. American Geog.* 5, 44–9.

Chahine, M.T. 1992. The hydrological cycle and its influence on climate. *Nature* 359, 373–80.

Chang, J.H. 1970. Potential photosynthesis and crop productivity. *Annals Assoc. Amer. Geographers* 60, 92–101.

Clarke, R.H. 1955. Some observations and comments on the sea breeze. *Aust. Meteor. Mag.* 11, 47–68.

Clemence, B.S.E. and R.E. Schulze. 1982. An assessment of temperature-based equations for estimating daily crop water loss to the atmosphere in South Africa. *Crop Production* 11, 21–5.

Climate Monitoring System. 1985. *The Global Climate System* (World Meteor. Organ.) 52 pp.

Cole, J.E., G.T. Shen, R.G. Fairbanks and M. Moore. 1992. Coral monitors of ENSO dynamics across the equatorial Pacific. In Diaz and Markgraf 1992: 349–75.

Colls, K. and R. Whitaker. 1990. *The Australian Weather Book* (Childs & Associates, Sydney). 175 pp.

Cook, S.J. and J.S. Russell. 1983. The climate of seven CSIRO field stations in northern Australia. *Tech. Paper 25* (Div. Tropical Crops & Pastures, Commonwealth Sci. & Indust. Res. Organ.) 38 pp.

Cotton, R. and R. Anthes. 1989. *Cloud and Storm Dynamics* (Academic Press) 880 pp.

Coughlan, M.J., C.E. Hounam and J.V. Maher. 1976. *Drought: A Natural Hazard.* Proc. Symp. Natural Hazards in Australia, Canberra (Aust. Acad. Sci.) 33 pp.

Coulter, J.D. 1975. The climate. In *Biogeography and Ecology in New Zealand*, G. Kuschel, Dr W. Junk (eds) (B.V. Publishers, The Hague), pp. 87–138.

Critchfield, H.J. 1974a. Climatic maritimity of midlatitude Pacific littorals: a mirror for perception. *Proc. Internat. Geog. Union Regional Conf., Palmerston North* (New Zeal. Geog. Soc.) 241–5.

—— 1974b. *General Climatology* (Prentice-Hall) 446 pp.

Crowe, R. 1971. *Concepts in Climatology* (Longmans) 589 pp.

Crowther, R.L. 1977. *Sun Earth: How to Apply Free Energy Sources to our Homes and Buildings* (Crowther/Solar Group, Denver) 232 pp.

Currie, R.G. 1984. Periodic (18.6 years) and cyclic (11 years) induced drought in western North America. *J.Geophys. Res.* 89, 7215–30.

Currie, R.G. and R.W. Fairbridge. 1985. Periodic 18.6-year and cyclic 11-year induced drought and flood in northeastern China and some global implications. *Quatern. Sci. Reviews* 4, 109–34.

da Mota, F.S. 1977. *Meteorologica Agricola* (Livraria Nobel SA, São Paulo) 376 pp.

Day, J.A. and G.L. Sternes. 1970. *Climate and Weather* (Addison-Wesley) 407 pp.

Deacon, E.L. 1969. Physical processes near the surface of the Earth. In Flohn 1969: 39–104.

Denmead, O.T. 1972. The microclimate of grass communities. In *The Biology and Utilisation of Grasses* (Academic), pp. 155–70.

—— 1991. Sources and sinks of greenhouse gases in the soil–plant environment. *Vegetatio* 91, 73–86.

Diaz, H.F. and V. Markgraf (eds) 1992. *El Niño; Historical & Paleoclimatic Aspects.* (Cambridge University Press) 476 pp.

Dick, R.S. 1966. The influence of major climatic controls on the pattern and character of Australian climates. *J. Geog. Teachers' Assoc. Queensland* 1, 1–10.

—— 1975. A map of the climates of Australia: according to Köppen's principles of definition. *Qld Geog. J.* 3, 33–69.

Dietrich, G., K. Kalle, W. Kraus and G. Siedler. 1980. *General Oceanography* (Wiley & Sons) 626 pp.

Dixon, J.C. and M.J. Prior. 1987. Windchill indices – a review. *Meteor. Mag.* 116, 1–16.

Dobson, G.M.B. 1968. *Exploring the Atmosphere* (Clarendon Press) 209 pp.

Dozy, J.J. 1938. Eine Gletscherweit in Niederlandisch – Neuguinea. *Zeitschrift für Gletscherkunde* 26, 45–51.

Dunsmuir, W.T.M. and D.M. Phillips. 1991. Modelling of annual variation of tropospheric moisture in the Australian region from radiosonde and satellite data. *Aust. Meteor. Mag.* 39, 87–94.

Duxbury, A.C. 1974. *The Earth & Its Oceans* (Addison-Wesley) 381 pp.

Dyer, A.J. 1974. The effect of volcanic eruptions on global turbidity. *Quart. J. Roy. Meteor. Soc.* 100, 563–71.

—— 1975. An international initiative in observing the global atmosphere. *Search* 6, 29–33.

Eagleson, S. 1991. Global change: a catalyst for the development of hydrologic science. *Bull. Amer. Meteor. Soc.* 72, 34–43.

Eddy, J.A. 1981. Climate and the role of the Sun. In Rotberg and Rabb 1981: 145–67.

Edelstein, K.K. 1992. The global hydrologic cycle and its continental links. *GeoJournal* 27, 263–8.

Edey, S.N. 1977. *Growing Degree-days and Crop Production in Canada.* Publ. 1635 (Canada Dept of Agric.) 62 pp.

Ekdahl, C.A. and C.D. Keeling. 1973. Atmospheric carbon dioxide and radiocarbon in the natural carbon cycle. In Woodwell and Pecan 1973: 51 *et seq.*

Emanuel, K.A. 1994. *Atmospheric Convection* (Oxford University Press) 580 pp.

Enfield, D.B. 1989. El Niño, past and present. *Rev. Geophys.* 27, 159–87.

Eriksson, B. 1966. Simple methods for statistical prognosis. In WMO 1966: 87–114.

Evans, M. 1980. *Housing, Climate and Comfort* (Architectural Press, London) 186 pp.

Fairbridge, R.W. (ed.) 1967. *The Encyclopedia of Atmospheric Sciences and Astrogeology* (Reinhold) 1200 pp.

Fitzharris, B.B., J.E. Hay and P.D. Jones. 1992. Behaviour of New Zealand glaciers and atmospheric circulation changes over the past 130 years. *The Holocene* 2.2, 97–106.

Fitzpatrick, E.A. and J. Armstrong. 1972. The bioclimatic setting. In Nix 1972: 7–26.

Fleagle R.G. and J.A. Businger. 1980. *An Introduction to Atmospheric Physics* (Academic Press) 346 pp.

Flohn, H. (ed.) 1969. *World Survey of Climatology* 2 (Elsevier) 266 pp.

—— 1978. Discussion. In Pittock *et al*. 1978: 351.

Flohn, H. and H. Fleer. 1975. Climatic telecommunications with the equatorial Pacific and the role of ocean/atmosphere coupling. *Atmosphere* 13, 96–109.

Fowle, F.E. 1934. *Smithsonian Physical Tables* (Smithsonian Institution) 686 pp.

Frohlich, C. and J. London. 1985. *Radiation Manual* (World Meteor. Organ., Geneva) 132 pp.

Gaffney, D.O. 1975. Rainfall deficiency and evaporation in relation to drought in Australia. Paper to 46th Ann. Conf., Canberra (Aust. New Zeal. Assoc. Advance. Sci.) 17 pp.

Gagge, A.P. *et al*. 1971. An effective temperature scale based on a simple model of human physiological regulatory response. *Amer. Soc. Heating, Refrigeration and Air-conditioning Engineers Trans*. 77, 247–62.

Garnier, B.J. 1958. *Climate of New Zealand* (Edward Arnold) 191 pp.

Garstang M., S. Ulanski, S. Greco, J. Scala, R. Swap, D. Fitzjarrald, D. Martin, E. Browell, M. Shipman, V. Connors, R. Harriss and R. Talbot. 1990. The Amazon Boundary-Layer experiment (ABLE 2B): a meteorological perspective. *Bull. Amer. Meteor. Soc*. 71, 19–32.

Gay, L.W. 1979. Radiation budgets of desert, meadow, forest and marsh sites. *Archiv. Meteor. Geophys. Bioklim. B* 27, 349–59.

Geiger, R. 1966. *The Climate Near the Ground* (Harvard University Press) 611 pp.

Gentilli, J. 1972. *Australian Climate Patterns* (Nelson) 285 pp.

—— 1978. *Physio-climatology of Western Australia*. Geowest (Dept of Geog., Univ. of WA) 105 pp.

Gibbs, W.J. and J.V. Maher. 1967. Rainfall deciles as drought indicators. *Bull*. 48 (Aust. Bureau of Meteor.).

Gifford, F.A. and S.R. Hanna. 1973. Modelling air pollution. *Atmos. Environ*. 7, 131–6.

Givoni, B. 1969. *Man, Climate and Architecture* (Elsevier) 364 pp.

Gordon, A.H. 1992. Inter-hemispheric contrasts of mean global temperature anomalies. *Internat. J. Climatol*. 12, 1–9.

Graedel, T.E. and P.J. Crutzen. 1989. The changing atmosphere. *Sci. Amer*. (Sept.), 28–47.

Gray, D.M. and D.H. Male (eds) 1981. *Handbook of Snow* (Pergamon) 776 pp.

Greacen, E.L. and C.T. Hignett. 1976. A water balance model and supply index for wheat in South Australia. *Tech. Paper 27* (Soils Division, Aust. Commonwealth Sci. Indust. Res. Organ.) 33 pp.

Greenland, D.E. 1973. An estimate of the heat balance in an Alpine valley in the New Zealand alps. *Agric. Meteor*. 11, 293–302.

Gribbin, J. (ed.) 1978. *Climatic Change* (Cambridge University Press) 280 pp.

—— 1988a. The ozone layer. *New Scientist* 118 (5 May) 1–4.

—— 1988b. The greenhouse effect. *New Scientist* 120 (22 Oct.), 1–4.

—— 1991. Climate change – the solar connection. *New Scientist* 132 (1796), 14.

Griffiths, G.A. and M.J. McSaveney. 1983. Distribution of mean annual precipitation across some steepland regions of New Zealand. *New Zeal. J. Sci*. 26, 197–209.

Griffiths J.F. (ed.) 1972. *World Survey of Climatology* 10 (Elsevier, Amsterdam).

—— 1976a. *Climate and the Environment* (Elek) 148 pp.

—— 1976b. *Applied Climatology* (Oxford University Press) 136 pp.

Griffiths, J.F. and D.M. Driscoll. 1982. *Survey of Climatology* (Merrill) 358 pp.

Guymer, L.B. and J.L. Le Marshall. 1980. Impact of FGGE buoy data on southern hemisphere analysis. *Aust. Meteor. Mag*. 28, 19–42.

Hanna, S.R. 1971. A simple method of calculating dispersion from urban area sources. *J. Air Pollution Control Assoc*. 21, 774–7.

—— 1982. Review of atmospheric diffusion models for regulatory applications. *WMO Tech. Note 177* (World Meteor. Organ.) 42 pp.

Hansen, J. and S. Lebedeff. 1897. Global trends of measured surface air temperature. *J. Geophys. Res*. 92, 13345–72

Hanson, K., G.A. Maul and W. McLeish. 1987. Precipitation and the lunar synodic cycle. *J. Climate Appl. Meteor*. 26, 1358–62.

Hartmann, D.L. 1994. *Global Physical Climatology* (Academic) 408 pp.

Harvey, J.G. 1976. *Atmosphere and Ocean* (Artemis, Sussex) 143 pp.

Hastenrath, S. 1985. *Climate and Circulation of the Tropics* (Reidel) 455 pp.

—— 1991. *Climate Dynamics of the Tropics* (Kluwer Academic Publishers) 488 pp.

Heathcote, R.L. 1991. Managing the droughts? *Vegetatio* 91, 219–30.

Held, I.M. 1993. Large-scale dynamics and global warming. *Bull. Amer. Meteor. Soc*. 74, 228–41.

Henderson-Sellers, A. 1991. Developing an interactive biosphere for global change models. *Vegetatio* 91, 149–66.

Hess, W.N. (ed.) 1974. *Weather and Climate Modification* (John Wiley) 842 pp.

Hidore, J.J. and J.E. Oliver 1993. *Climatology: An Atmospheric Science* (Macmillan) 423 pp.

Hines, C.O. and I. Halevy. 1977. On the reality and

nature of a certain Sun–weather correlation. *J. Atmos. Sci.* 34, 382–404.

Hirst, A. 1989. Recent advances in the theory of ENSO. *Bull. Aust. Meteor. Ocean. Soc.* 2, 101–13.

Hirst, A. and S. Hastenrath. 1983. Atmosphere–ocean mechanism of climate anomalies in the Angola–tropical Atlantic sector. *J. Phys. Ocean.* 13, 1146–57.

Holdridge, L.R. 1947. Determination of world plant formations from simple climatic data. *Science* 105, 367–8.

Hope, G.S., J.A. Peterson, U. Radok and I. Allison (eds) 1976. *The Equatorial Glaciers of New Guinea* (Balkema) 244 pp.

Houghton, D.D. (ed.) 1985. *Handbook of Applied Meteorology* (Wiley) 1461 pp.

Houghton, H.G. (ed.) 1984. *The Global Climate* (Cambridge University Press) 233 pp.

Houghton J.T. 1985. *Physical Meteorology* (MIT Press, Cambridge, Mass.) 442 pp.

—— 1986. *The Physics of Atmospheres.* 2nd edn (Cambridge University Press) 271 pp.

Houghton J.T., G.J. Jenkins and J.J. Ephraums (eds) 1990. *Climate change: The IPCC Assessment* (Cambridge University Press) 365 pp.

Houghton J.T. 1994. *Global Warming: The Complete Briefing* (Lion Publ., Oxford) 192 pp.

Houghton, J.T., L.G. Meira Filho, B.A. Callander, N. Harris, A. Kattenberg and K. Mashell. 1996. *Climate Change 1995: The Science of Climate Change.* Contributions from the Working Group I to the Second Assessment Report of the Intergovernmental Panel on Climate Change (Cambridge University Press) 572 pp.

Houze, R.A. Jr. 1993. *Cloud dynamics* (Academic Press) 573 pp.

Hoy, R.D. and S.K. Stephens. 1977. The estimation of missing net radiation data. Appendix A In Field study of lake evaporation: analysis of data from Eucumbene, Cataract, Manton & Mundaring. *Tech. Paper 21* (Aust. Water Resources Council) 154–8.

Hunt, B.G. 1991. The simulation and prediction of drought. *Vegetatio.* 91, 89–103.

Hutchinson, M.F. 1987. Methods of generation of weather sequences. In Bunting 1987: 149–57.

Hyde, R., H.R. Malfroy, A.C. Heggie and G.S. Hawke. 1982. Nocturnal wind flow across the Sydney basin. In Carras and Johnson 1982: 39–60.

Ingram, D.L. and L.E. Mount. 1975. *Man and Animals in Hot Environments* (Springer) 185 pp.

Instn Engineers Aust. 1977. *Australian Rainfall & Runoff; Flood Analysis and Design* (Instn Engnrs Aust., Canberra) 159 pp.

Jaeger, L. 1983. Monthly and areal patterns of mean global precipitation. In Street-Perrott *et al.* 1983: 129–40.

Jennings, J.N. 1967. Two maps of rainfall intensity in Australia. *Aust. Geog.* 10, 256–62.

Jiminez, R. and J.E. Oliver. 1987. Climates of South America. In Oliver and Fairbridge 1987: 789–95.

Jones, A.E. and J.D. Shanklin. 1995. Continued decline of total ozone at Halley, Antarctica, since 1985. *Nature* 376, 409–11.

Jones, P.A. 1991. Historical records of cloud cover and climate for Australia. *Aust. Meteor. Mag.* 39, 181–9.

Jones, P.A. and A. Henderson-Sellers. 1992. Historical records of cloudiness and sunshine in Australia. *J. Clim.* 5, 260–7.

Jones, P.D. and J.A. Lindesay 1993. Maximum and minimum temperature trends over South Africa and the Sudan. Preprint for 4th Internat. Conf. Southern Hemisphere Meteor. and Oceanog., Hobart (Amer. Meteor. Soc), 359–60.

—— 1994. Hemispheric surface air temperature variations: a re-analysis and an update to 1993. *J. Clim.* 7, 1794–1802.

Joubert, A.M. 1994. General circulation model simulations of Southern African regional climate. Unpub. M.Sc. thesis, Univ. Witwatersrand.

Kalkstein, L.S. and K.M. Valimont. 1986. An evaluation of summer discomfort in the US using a relative climatological index. *Bull. Amer. Meteor. Soc.* 67, 842–8.

Kalma, J.D. 1968. A comparison of methods for computing daily mean air temperature and humidity. *Weather* 23, 248–52, 259.

Kalma, J.D. and D.J. Crossley. 1981. Inequities in climatic energy use: some determinants. Paper to Ann. Conf., Brisbane (Aust. & N. Zeal. Assoc. Adv. Sci.), 280–3.

Kalma, J.D. and M.F. Hutchinson. 1981. Spatial patterns of windspeed and windrun in Australia: implications for network design. In *Proc. Workshop on Solar and Wind Data Networks for Australia* (Solar Energy Res. Inst. West. Aust.), ch. 16, pp. 1–11.

Karelsky, S. 1961. Monthly and seasonal anticyclonicity and cyclonicity in the Australian region. *Meteor. Study 13* (Aust. Bur. Meteor.) 11 pp.

Kasting, J.F. 1993. Earth's early atmosphere. *Science.* 259, 920–6.

Keeling, C.D., R.B. Bacastow, A.F. Carter, S.C. Piper, T.P. Whorf, M. Heimann, W.G. Mook and R. Roeloffzen. 1989. A three-dimensional model of atmospheric carbon dioxide transport based on observed winds. Part I: Analysis of observed data. In *Aspects of Climate Variability in the Pacific and Western Americas*, D.H. Peterson (ed.), Geophysical Monograph 55 (Amer. Geophys. Union, Washington, DC) 165–236.

Keig, G. and J.R. McAlpine. 1977. Mortality and climate in Adelaide. Paper to Ann. Conf., Melbourne (Aust. & N. Zeal. Assoc. Adv. Sci.).

Kiddle, I.B. 1965. Inland water; natural desalination research is necessary. *Sci. Australian*, 6–11.

Koenigsberger, O.H., T.G. Ingersoll, A. Mayhew and S.V. Szokolay. 1974. *Manual of Tropical Housing and Building.* Part I: *Climatic Design* (Longman) 320 pp.

Krishna, R. 1984. *Tropical Cyclones.* Publ. 4 (Fiji Meteorol. Service) 23 pp.

Kutzbach, J.E. 1975. Diagnostic studies of past climates. In *Physical Basis of Climate & Climate Modelling.* Publ. 16, GARP series (World Meteor. Organ., Geneva) 119–26.

Lamb, H.H. 1972. *Climate: Present, Past and Future. 1 Fundamentals and Climate Now* (Methuen) 613 pp.

Lazenby, A. and E.M. Matheson (eds) 1975. *Australian Field Crops* (Angus & Robertson) 535 pp.

Lee, D.H.K. 1963. Physiological objectives in hot weather housing. (US Dept Housing & Urban Devel., Washington) 79 pp.

Lee, D.O. 1984. Urban climates. *Progress in Physical Geog.* 8, 1–31.

Leeper, G.W. (ed.) 1970. *The Australian Environment* (Melbourne University Press) 163 pp.

Leffler, R.J. 1980. Using climatology to estimate elevations of alpine timberlines in the Appalachian Mtns. *Environ. Data & Info. Serv.* (Washington) 11, 19–22.

Lieth, H. and R.H. Whittaker (eds) 1975. *Primary Productivity of the Biosphere* (Springer-Verlag) 339 pp.

Lighthill, J. and R.P. Pearce (eds) 1981. *Monsoon Dynamics* (Cambridge University Press) 700 pp.

Linacre, E.T. 1973. A simpler empirical expression for actual evapotranspiration rates – discussion. *Agric. Meteor.* 11, 451–2.

——— 1992. *Climate Data and Resources* (Routledge, London) 366 pp.

——— 1993a. Data-sparse estimation of lake evaporation using a simplified Penman equation. *Agric. & Forestry Meteor.* 64, 237–56.

——— 1993b. A three-resistance model of crop and forest evaporation. *Theoret. Appl. Climatol.* 48, 41–8.

Linacre E.T. and J.E. Hobbs. 1977. *The Australian Climatic Environment* (Jacaranda Wiley) 354 pp.

Lindesay, J. 1994. Private comm.

Lockwood, J.G. 1974. *World Climatology: An Environmental Approach* (Arnold) 330 pp.

——— 1979. *Causes of Climate* (Arnold) 260 pp.

Loewe, F.P. 1974. The total water content of clouds in the southern hemisphere. *Aust. Meteor. Mag.* 22, 19–20.

Longwell, C.R., R.F. Flint and J.E. Sanders. 1969. *Physical Geology* (John Wiley) 685 pp.

Loomis, R.S. and W.A. Williams. 1963. Maximum crop productivity: an estimate. *Crop Sci.* 3, 67–72.

Lovelock, J.E. 1972. Gaia as seen through the atmosphere. *Atmos. Environ.* 6, 579–80.

——— 1986. Gaia: the world as a living organism. *New Scientist* 112, 25–8.

Ludlam, F.H. 1980. *Clouds and Storms* (Penn. State University) 405 pp.

Luna, R.E. and H.W. Church. 1972. A comparison of turbulence intensity and stability ratio measurements to Pasquill stability classes. *J. Appl. Meteor.* 11, 663–9.

——— 1974. Estimation of long-term concentrations using a 'universal' wind speed distribution. *J. Appl. Meteor.* 13, 910–16.

Lutgens, F.K. and E.J. Tarbuck. 1992. *The Atmosphere*, 5th edn (Prentice-Hall) 430 pp.

McAlpine, J.R., G. King and R. Falls. 1983. *Climate of Papua and New Guinea* (Aust. Nat. University Press) 200 pp.

McBoyle, G.R. 1971. Climatic classification of Australia by computer. *Aust. Geog. Studies* 9, 1–14.

McGinnies, W.G., B.J. Goldman and L. Paylore (eds) 1968. *Deserts of the World* (University of Arizona Press) 788 pp.

McGrath, C.A. 1972. The development of the sea-breeze over Sydney and its effect on climate and air pollution. M.Sc. thesis for Macquarie University, Sydney.

Machta, L. 1977. Monitoring solar radiation for solar energy. In WMO 1977: 1–35.

McIlveen, D. 1992. *Fundamentals of Weather and Climate* (Chapman and Hall) 497 pp.

McIntyre, D.A. 1980. *Indoor Climate* (Applied Sci. Publ., London) 443 pp.

McMahon, J. and A. Low. 1972. Growing degree days as a measure of temperature effects on cotton. *Cotton Grow. Rev.* 49, 39–49.

McTainsh, G. and J.R. Pitblado. 1987. Dust storms and related phenomena measured from meteorological records in Australia. *Earth Surface Processes & Landforms* 12, 415–24.

Maejima, I. 1977. Global pattern of temperature lapse rate in the lower troposphere – with special reference to the snowline. *Geog. Reports 12* (Tokyo Metrop. University) 117–26.

Magalhaes, A.R. and O.E. Reboucas. 1988. Drought as a policy and planning issue in north-east Brazil. In Parry *et al.* 1988: 279–304.

Maher, J.V. (ed.) 1973. *Fog risk at Canberra*, Special Rept 5 (Bureau of Meteor.) 11 pp.

Manabe, S., J.L. Holloway and D.G. Hahn. 1974. Seasonal variation of climate in a time-integration of a mathematical model of the atmosphere. In WMO 1974, 113–22.

Mason, B.J. 1975. *Clouds, Rain & Rainmaking*, 2nd edn (Cambridge University Press) 189 pp.

Matthews, C. and B. Geerts. 1995. Characteristic thunderstorm occurrence in the Sydney area. *Austr. Meteor. Mag.* 44, 127–38.

Miller, D.H. 1965. The heat and water budget of the earth's surface. *Advances in Geophysics* 11, 175–302.

——— 1981. *Energy at the Surface of the Earth* (Academic Press) 516 pp.

Mitchell, R.M., R.P. Cechet, P.J. Turner and C.C. Elsum. 1990. Observation and interpretation of wave clouds over Macquarie Island. *Quart. J. Roy. Meteor. Soc.* 116, 741–52.

Monteith, J.L. 1973. *Principles of Environmental Physics* (Arnold) 241 pp.

Moura, A.D. and J. Shukla. 1981. On the dynamics of drought in northeast Brazil. *J. Atmos. Sci.* 38, 3653–75.

Muncey, R.W. 1979. *Heat Transfer Calculations for Buildings* (Applied Sci. Publishers, London) 110 pp.

Munn, R.E. 1970. *Biometeorological Methods* (Academic Press) 336 pp.

Navarra, J.G. 1979. *Atmosphere, Weather and Climate* (Saunders) 519 pp.

Neal, A.B. 1973. *The Meteorology of the Australian Trades*. Tech. Rept 5 (Aust. Bur. Meteor.) 29 pp.

Neal, A.B. and G.J. Holland 1978. *Australian Tropical Cyclone Forecasting Manual* (Aust. Bur. Meteor.) 274 pp.

Neiburger, M., J.G. Edinger and W.D. Bonner. 1981. *Understanding Our Atmospheric Environment* (Freeman).

Neuberger, H. and J. Cahir. 1969. *Principles of Climatology* (Holt, Rinehart & Winston) 178 pp.

Neumann, C.J. undated. *Global Guide to Tropical Cyclone Forecasting*. WMO Tech. Doc. 560, Report no. TCP-31 (World Meteor. Organ.) 43 pp.

Newton, C.W. (ed.) 1972a. *Meteorology of the Southern Hemisphere*. *Meteor. Monog. 13* (Amer. Meteor. Soc.) 263 pp.

—— 1972b. Southern hemisphere general circulation in relation to the global energy and momentum balance requirements. In Newton 1972a: 215–46.

Newton, C.W. and E.O. Holopainen (eds) 1990. *Tropical Cyclones* (Amer. Meteor. Soc., Boston) 262 pp.

Nicholls, N. 1973. The Walker circulation and Papua New Guinea rainfall. *Tech. Rept 6* (Aust. Dept of Sci., Bureau of Meteor.) 13 pp.

—— 1981. Sunspot cycles and Australian rainfall. *Search* 12, 83–5.

Nicholls, N., G.V. Gruza, J. Jonzel, T.R. Karl, L.A. Ogallo and D.E. Parker. 1996. Observed climate variability and change. In Houghton *et al.* (eds): 132–92.

Nicholson, S.E., J. Kim and J. Hoopingarner. 1988. *Atlas of African Rainfall and its Interannual Variability* (Dept. Meteor., Florida State University) 237 pp.

Nieuwolt, S. 1977. *Tropical Climatology* (John Wiley) 207 pp.

Nix, H.A. (ed.) 1972. *The City as a Life System?* (Proc. Ecol. Soc. Aust. 7) 279 pp.

—— 1975. The Australian climate and its effects on grain yield and quality. In Lazenby and Matheson 1975: 183–226.

NOAA 1982. *Proc. 6th Ann. Climate Diagnostics Workshop, Palisades, N.Y.* (Nat. Oceanic and Atmos. Admin. Dept of Commerce) 341 pp.

—— 1993. *Fourth Annual Climate Assessment 1992* (National Oceanic & Atmospheric Admin., US Dept Commerce) 90 pp.

Nunez, M. 1990. Solar energy statistics for Australian capital regions. *Solar Energy* 44, 343–54.

Nunez, M., W.J. Skirving and N.R. Viney. 1987. A technique for estimating regional surface albedos using geostationary satellite data. *J. Climatol.* 7, 1–11.

Obasi, G.O.P. 1994. WMO's role in the International Decade for natural disaster reduction. *Bull. Amer. Meteor. Soc.* 75, 1655–61.

Oberhuber, J.M. 1988. The budgets of heat, buoyancy and turbulent kinetic energy at the surface of the global icean. *Report 15* (Max Planck Institut für Meteorologie).

O'Connell, D. 1986. *Guide to the Determination of Snow Loading on Roofs in N.S.W.* Report G.2/Si (Commonwealth Dept Housing & Construction, NSW Region) 41 pp.

Oddie, B.C.V. 1962. Clouds. In *Encyclopaedic Dictionary of Physics* (Pergamon) vol. 1, 706–11.

Oke, T.R. 1987. *Boundary-layer Climates*, 2nd edn (Methuen) 435 pp.

—— 1988. The urban energy balance. *Prog. Phys. Geogr.* 12, 471–508.

Okolowicz, W. 1976. *General Climatology* (Polish Sci. Publishers, Warsaw) 422 pp.

Okoola, R.E. 1992. The influence of urbanisation on atmospheric circulation in Nairobi, Kenya. In Adebayo 1992: 69–75.

Oldeman, L.R. 1987. Characterisation of main experimental sites and sub-sites and questions of instrumentation. In Bunting 1987: 101–12.

Oliver, J. 1976. Wind and storm hazards in Australia. *Proc. Symp. Natural Hazards in Australia*, Canberra, 26–29 May 1976 (Aust. Acad. Sci.).

—— (ed.) 1983. *Insurance and Natural Disaster Management* (Centre for Disaster Studies, James Cook Univ., Townsville) 396 pp.

Oliver, J.E. 1970. A genetic approach to climatic classification. *Annals Assoc. Amer. Geographers* 60, 615–37.

—— 1973. *Climate & Man's Environment* (John Wiley) 517 pp.

Oliver, J.E. and R.W. Fairbridge (eds) 1987. *The Encyclopedia of Climatology* (Van Nostrand Reinhold) 986 pp.

Oort, A.H. 1983. *Global Atmospheric Circulation Statistics, 1958–73*. NOAA Paper 14, 180 pp.

Palmen, E. and C.W. Newton. 1969. *Atmospheric Circulation Systems* (Academic Press) 603 pp.

Paltridge, G.W. 1975. Net radiation over the surface of Australia. *Search* 6, 37–9.

Paltridge, G.W. and D. Proctor. 1976. Monthly-mean solar-radiation statistics for Australia. *Solar Energy* 18, 235–43.

Parish, T.R. 1980. *Surface Winds in East Antarctica* (Dept of Meteor., Wisconsin) 121 pp.

—— 1992. On the interaction between Antarctic katabatic winds and tropospheric motions in the high latitudes. *Aust. Meteor. Mag.* 40, 149–67.

Parker, S.P. (ed.) 1980. *McGraw-Hill Encyclopedia of Ocean and Atmospheric Sciences* (McGraw-Hill) 580 pp.

Parry, M., T.R. Carter and N.T. Konijn (eds) 1988. *The Impact of Climate Variations on Agriculture. 2: Assessments in Semi-arid Regims* (Kluwer Academic) 764 pp.

Pearce, E.A. and C.G. Smith. 1990. *The World Weather Guide* (Hutchinson) 480 pp.

Pedgley, D.E. 1962. *A Course in Elementary Meteorology* (HM Stationery Office, London) 189 pp.

Peixoto, J.P. and A.H. Oort. 1992. *Physics of Climate* (Amer. Inst. Physics) 520 pp.

Penman, H.L. 1948. Natural evaporation from open water, bare soil and grass. *Proc. Roy. Soc. A* 193, 120–45.

Pescod, D. 1976. *Energy Savings and Performance Limitations with Evaporation Cooling in Australia*. Tech. Rept TR5 (Div. Mech. Engrg, Aust. Commonwealth Sci. Indust. Res. Organ.) 16 pp.

Peterson, J.A. and L.F. Peterson. 1994. Ice retreat from the neoglacial maxima in the Puncak Jayakesuma area, Republic of Indonesia. *Zeit. Glet. Glaz.* 30, 1–9.

Petterssen, S. 1969. *Introduction to Meteorology* (McGraw-Hill) 333 pp.

Philander, S.G.H. 1990. *El Niño, La Niña and the Southern Oscillation* (Academic Press) 289 pp.

Pickard, G.L. and W.J. Emery. 1990. *Descriptive Physical Oceanography* (Pergamon, Oxford) 320 pp.

Pittock, A.B., L.A. Frakes, D. Jensen, J.A. Peterson and

J.W. Zillman (eds) 1978. *Climatic Change and Variability* (Cambridge University Press) 455 pp.

Plate, E.J. (ed.) 1982. *Engineering Meteorology* (Elsevier) 740 pp.

Preston-Whyte, R.A. and P. Tyson. 1988. *The Atmosphere & Weather of South Africa* (Oxford University Press) 375 pp.

Priestley, C.H.B. 1977. Flinders 1976 lecture on winds and currents. *Aust. Acad. Sci. Records* 3, 143–65.

Prohaska, F. 1970. *Agricultural Meteorology*. Publ. no. 310 (World Meteor. Organ.).

Quinn, W.H. 1992. A study of SO-related climatic activity AD 622–1900 incorporating Nile River flood data. In Diaz and Markgraf 1992: 119–49.

Ratisbona, L.R. 1976. The climate of Brazil. *World Survey of Climatol.* 12 (Elsevier) 219–93.

Redman, M.E. and J.A. McRae. 1975. *High Temperatures in Australia*. Rept 625 (Materials Res. Labs, Aust. Dept Defence).

Reiquam, H. 1980. Stability climatology from on-site wind data. *Applics. of Meteor.* (Amer. Meteor. Soc.), 803–8.

Renner, J. 1972. *Geography of South America: Climate* (Hicks-Smith) 32 pp.

Riehl, H. 1979. *Climate and Weather in the Tropics* (Academic Press) 626 pp.

Riviere, J.W.M. 1989. Threats to the world's water. *Sci. Amer.* 261, 48–55.

Roberts, D.F. 1982. The adaptation of human races to different climates. *Biometeor.* 8, 39–52.

Robertson, D.F. 1972. The prophylaxis of ultraviolet radiation damage: a physicist's approach. *Proc. Internat. Cancer Conf., Sydney* (Aust. Cancer Soc.) 273–91.

Rogers, R.R. and M.K. Yau. 1989. *A Short Course in Cloud Physics*, 3rd edn (Pergamon Press, Oxford) 293 pp.

Rotberg, I. and T.K. Rabb (eds) 1981. *Climate & History* (Princeton University Press) 280 pp.

Rubin, M.J. 1962. The Antarctic and the weather. *Sci. Amer.* (Sept.) 12 pp.

Ryan, B.F. 1986. Cold fronts research. *Search* 17, 32–4.

Saini, B.S. 1973. *Building Environment* (Angus & Robertson) 148 pp.

Sasamori, T. 1982. Stability of the Walker circulation. *J. Atmos. Sci.* 39, 518–25.

Sasamori, Y, J. London and D.V. Hoyt 1972. *Radiation budget for the Southern Hemisphere*. Metor. Monograph 13 (Amer. Meteor. Soc.), 9–23.

Schneider S.H. and C. Moss. 1975. Volcanic dust, sunspots and temperature trends. *Science* 190, 741–6.

Schulze, D.A. 1972. South Africa. *World Survey of Climatology* 10, edited by J.F. Griffiths (Elsevier) 508–86.

Schwerdtfeger, P. 1979. On icebergs and their uses. *Cold Regions Sci. & Technol.* 1, 57–79.

Schwerdtfeger, W. 1984. *Weather and Climate of the Antarctic* (Elsevier) 261 pp.

Sellers, W.D. 1965. *Physical Climatology* (Chicago University Press) 272 pp.

Shields, A.J. 1965. *Australian Weather* (Jacaranda).

Simmonds, P.L. 1843. Climate of New South Wales. *Colonial Magazine* (London) p. 238.

Skidmore, A.K. 1988. Predicting bushfire activity in Australia from El Niño/Southern Oscillation events. *Aust. Forestry* 50, 231–5.

Smith, D.I. *et al.* 1979. *Flood Damage in the Richmond River Valley, New South Wales* (Centre for Resource and Environmental Studies, Australian National University, Canberra).

Smith, K. 1975. *Principles of Applied Climatology* (McGraw-Hill) 233 pp.

Smith, R.K., R.N. Ridley, M.A. Page, J.T. Steiner and A.P. Sturman. 1991. Southerly changes on the east coast of New Zealand. *Mon. Weather Rev.* 119, 1259–82.

Steiner, J.T. 1989. New Zealand hailstorms. *N.Z. J. Geol. & Geophys.* 32, 279–91.

Strahler, A.N. 1963. *The Earth Sciences* (Harper & Row) 681 pp.

Street-Perrott, A., M. Beran and R. Ratcliffe (eds) 1983. *Variations in the Global Water Budget* (Reidel), 518 pp.

Streten, N.A. 1981. Southern Hemisphere sea-surface temperature variability and apparent associations with Australian rainfall. *J. Geophys. Res.* 86, 485–97.

Streten, N.A. and J.W. Zillman. 1984. Climate of the South Pacific Ocean. *World Survey of Climatology* 15 (Elsevier) 263–427.

Sundquist, E.T. 1993. The global carbon dioxide budget. *Science* 259, 934–41.

Sverdrup, H.U. 1936. The eddy conductivity of the air over a smooth snow field. *Geofysiske Publikasjoner* 11, 1–69.

Sverdrup, H.U., M.W. Johnson and R.H. Fleming. 1942. *The Oceans, their Physics, Chemistry, and General Biology* (Prentice-Hall) 1087 pp.

Taljaard, J.J. 1972. Synoptic meteorology of the southern hemisphere. In Newton 1972a: 139–213.

Tomczak, M. and J.S. Godfrey. 1994. *Regional Oceanography: An Introduction* (Pergamon) 422 pp.

Tomlinson, A.I. 1976. Frequency of thunderstorms in New Zealand. *New Zeal. J. Sci.* 19, 319–25.

Trenberth, K.E. 1983. What are the seasons? *Bull. Amer. Meteor. Soc.* 64, 1276–81.

—— 1984. Signal versus noise in the Southern Oscillation. *Mon. Weather Rev.* 112, 326–32.

Trenberth, K.E. and D.J. Shea. 1988. On the evolution of the Southern Oscillation. *Mon. Weather Rev.* 115, 3078–96.

Trewartha, G.T. 1968. *Introduction to Climate*, 4th edn (McGraw-Hill) 406 pp.

Truppi, L. 1976. The Environmental Protection Agency's mortality data bank. In *Climate and Health Workshop: Summary and Recommendations*. Research Triangle Park, N. Carolina (US Dept Commerce), 11–17.

Tucker, G.B. 1993. New skills in predicting atmospheric pollution. *Aust. Meteor. Mag.* 42, 163–74.

Tuller, S.E. 1968. World distribution of mean monthly and annual precipitable water. *Mon. Weather Rev.* 96, 785–96.

Tyson, P. D. 1969. *Atmospheric Circulation and Precipitation over South Africa*. Occasional Paper 2 (Dept of Geog. & Environ. Studies, Univ. Witwatersrand, Johannesburg) 22 pp.

Vallis, G. 1986. El Niño; a classical dynamical system? *Science* 232, 243–5.

van Andel, H. 1985. *New Views on an Old Planet* (Cambridge University Press) 324 pp.

van Loon, H. 1972. Cloudiness and precipitation in the southern hemisphere. In Newton 1972a: 98–138.

Velasco, I. and J.M. Fritsch. 1987. Mesoscale convective complexes in the Americas. *J. Geophys. Res.* 92, 9591–613.

Waldmeier, M. 1961. *The Sunspot Activity in the Years 1610–1960.* (Schulthess, Zurich) 171 pp.

Wallace, J.M. and V. Hobbs. 1977. *Atmospheric Science* (Academic Press) 467 pp.

Wallington, C.E. 1968. A method of reducing observing and procedure bias in wind-direction frequencies. *Meteor. Mag.* 97, 293–302.

—— 1977. *Meteorology for Glider Pilots* (John Murray) 331 pp.

Watterson, G.A. and M.P.C. Legg. 1967. Daily rainfall patterns at Melbourne. *Aust. Metor. Mag.* 15, 1–12.

Wayne, R.P. 1991. *Chemistry of Atmospheres*, 2nd edn (Clarendon) 447 pp.

Webb, E.K. 1977. Convection mechanisms of atmospheric heat transfer from surface to global scales. *2nd Aust. Conf. on Heat and Mass Transfer, Sydney* (ed. R.W. Builger) 523–39.

Webster, P.J. 1981. Monsoons. *Sci. Amer.* 245, 109–18.

Weller, G. 1980. Spatial and temporal variations in the South Polar surface energy balance. *Mon. Weather Rev.* 108, 2006–14.

Weyl, K. 1970. *Oceanography* (John Wiley) 535 pp.

Whetton, P.H. 1988. A synoptic climatological analysis of rainfall variability in southeast Australia. *J. Climatol.* 8, 155–77.

—— 1990. Relationships between monthly anomalies of Australian region SST and Victorian rainfalls. *Aust. Meteor. Mag.* 38, 31–41.

Whetton, P.H., A.M. Fowler, M.R. Hayleck and A.B. Pittock. 1993. Implications of climate change due to the enhanced greenhouse effect on floods and droughts in Australia. *Climatic Change* 25, 289–317.

White, D.H. 1989. *A Study of the Feasibility of Establishing a Short-term Moisture Stress Evaluation Service and a Long-term Climate Forecasting Service to Farmers.* Working Paper no. 16/89 (Australian Bureau of Rural Resources) 41 pp.

Whittingham, H.E. 1964. *Extreme Wind Gusts in Australia.* Bull. 46 (Aust. Bureau Meteor.) 133 pp.

Williams, M.A.J. 1994. Some implications of past climatic changes in Australia. *Trans. Roy. Soc. South Aust.* 118, 17ff.

Williamson, H.J. and R.R. Krenmayer. 1980. Analysis of the relationship between Turner's stability classifications and wind speed and direct measurements of net-radiation. *Applic. Meteor.* (Amer. Meteor. Soc.) 777–80.

Williamson, S.J. 1973. *Fundamentals of Air Pollution* (Addison-Wesley) 472 pp.

WMO 1966. *Statistic Analysis and Prognoses in Meteorology.* WMO Tech. Note 71 (World Meteor. Organ.) 197 pp.

—— 1974. *Physical & Dynamical Climatology: Proc. Symp., Leningrad, 1971.* WMO Publ. 347 (World Meteor. Organ.) 400 pp.

—— 1977. *Solar Energy.* Symposium, Geneva 1976. WMO Publ. 477 (World Meteor. Organ.) 654 pp.

—— 1994. *Observing the World's Environment.* WMO Publ. 796 (World Meteor. Organ.) 41 pp.

Woodwell, G.M. and E.V. Pecan (eds) 1973. *Carbon and the Biosphere* (Tech. Info. Center, Office Info. Services, US Atomic Energy Commission).

Wuebbles, D.J. and J. Edmonds. 1991: *Primer on Greenhouse Gases* (Lewis Publishers) 230 pp.

Wyrtki, K. 1982. El Niño outlook for 1982. In NOAA 1982: 221–2.

Yu, B. and D.T. Neil. 1991. Global warming and regional rainfall. *J. Climatol.* 11, 653–61.

Zachar, D. 1982. *Soil Erosion* (Elsevier) 547 pp.

Zucchini, W., P. Adamson and L. McNeill. 1992. A model of southern African rainfall. *S. Afric. J. Sci.* 88, 103–9.

INDEX

SINGLE USER LICENCE AGREEMENT

We welcome you as a user of this Routledge CD-ROM and hope that you find it a useful and valuable teaching and learning tool. Please read this document carefully. **This is a legal agreement** between you (hereinafter referred to as the 'Licensee') and Routledge which defines the terms under which you may use the Product. **By opening the package containing the CD-ROM you have agreed to these terms and conditions outlined herein.** If you do not agree to these terms, return the Product to Routledge intact, with all its components as listed on the back of the package, within ten days of purchase and the purchase price will be refunded to you.

1. DEFINITION OF THE PRODUCT

The product which is the subject of this Agreement consists of either:
Climates and Weather Explained (the 'Product'), which comprises:

1.1   Underlying data comprised in the Product (the 'Data')

1.2   A compilation of the Data (the 'Database')

1.3   Software (the 'Software') for accessing and using the Database

1.4   The accompanying textbook (the 'Textbook')

1.5   A CD-ROM disk (the 'CD-ROM')

or

Climates and Weather Explained: Instructors' Resource Pack (the 'Product'), which comprises:

1.1   Underlying data comprised in the Product (the 'Data')

1.2   A compilation of the Data (the 'Databases')

1.3   Software (the 'Software') for accessing and using the Databases

1.4   The accompanying textbook (the 'Textbook')

1.5   Two CD-ROM disks (the 'CD-ROMs')

2. COMMENCEMENT AND LICENCE

2.1　This Agreement commences upon the breaking open of the package containing the CD-ROMs by the Licensee (the 'Commencement Date').

2.2　This is a licence agreement (the 'Agreement') for the use of the Product by the Licensee, and not an agreement for sale.

2.3　The Publisher licenses the Licensee on a non-exclusive and non-transferable basis to use the Product on condition that the Licensee complies with this Agreement. The Licensee acknowledges that it is only permitted to use the Product in accordance with this Agreement.

3. INSTALLATION AND USE

3.1　The Licensee may provide access to the Product only on a single personal computer for individual study. Multi-user use or networking is only permissible with the express permission of the Publisher in writing and requires payment of the appropriate fee as specified by the Publisher, and signature by the Licensee of a separate multi-user licence agreement.

3.2　The Licensee shall be responsible for installing the Product and for the effectiveness of such installation.

4. PERMITTED ACTIVITIES

4.1　The Licensee shall be entitled:

4.1.1　to use the Product for its own internal purposes;

4.1.2　to download onto electronic, magnetic, optical or similar storage medium reasonable portions of the Databases provided that the purpose of the Licensee is to undertake internal research or study and provided that such storage is temporary;

4.1.3　to make a copy of the Databases and/or the Software for back-up/archival/disaster recovery purposes.

4.2　The Licensee acknowledges that its rights to use the Product are strictly as set out in this Agreement, and all other uses (whether expressly mentioned in Clause 5 below or not) are prohibited.

5. PROHIBITED ACTIVITIES

The following are prohibited without the express permission of the Publisher:

5.1　The commercial exploitation of any part of the Product.

5.2   The rental, loan (free or for money or money's worth) hire purchase of the product, save with the express consent of the Publisher.

5.3   Any activity which raises the reasonable prospect of impeding the Publisher's ability or opportunities to market the Product.

5.4   Any provision of services to third parties using the Product, whether by way of trade or otherwise.

5.5   Any networking, physical or electronic distribution or dissemination of the product save as expressly permitted by this Agreement.

5.6   Any reverse engineering, decompilation, disassembly or other alteration of the Software save in accordance with applicable national laws.

5.7   The right to create any derivative product or service from the Product save as expressly provided for in this Agreement.

5.8   The use of the Software separately from the Databases.

5.9   Any alteration, amendment, modification or deletion from the Product, whether for the purposes of error correction or otherwise.

5.10   The merging of the Database or the Software with any other database or software.

5.11   Any testing, study or analysis of the Software save to study its underlying ideas and principles.

6. GENERAL RESPONSIBILITIES OF THE LICENSEE

6.1   The Licensee will take all reasonable steps to ensure that the Product is used in accordance with the terms and conditions of this Agreement.

6.2   The Licensee acknowledges that damages may not be a sufficient remedy for the Publisher in the event of breach of this Agreement by the Licensee, and that an injunction may be appropriate.

6.3   The Licensee undertakes to keep the Product safe and to use his/her best endeavours to ensure that the Product does not fall into the hands of third parties, whether as a result of theft or otherwise.

6.4   Where information of a confidential nature relating to the Product or the business affairs of the Publisher comes into the possession of the Licensee pursuant to this Agreement (or otherwise), the Licensee agrees to use such information solely for the purposes of this Agreement, and under no circumstances to disclose any element of the information to any third party save strictly as permitted under this Agreement. For the avoidance of doubt, the Licensee's obligations under this sub-clause 6.4 shall survive termination of this Agreement.

7. WARRANT AND LIABILITY

7.1   The Publisher warrants that it has the authority to enter into this Agreement, and that it has secured all rights and permissions necessary to enable the Licensee to use the Product in accordance with this Agreement.

7.2   The Publisher warrants that the CD-ROMs as supplied on the Commencement Date shall be free of defects in materials and workmanship, and undertakes to replace any defective CD-ROMs within 28 days of notice of such defect being received provided such notice is received within 90 days of such supply. As an alternative to replacement, the Publisher agrees fully to refund the Licensee in such circumstances, if the Licensee so requests, provided that the Licensee returns the CD-ROMs to the Publisher. The provisions of this sub-clause 7.2 do not apply where the defect results from an accident or from misuse of the product by the Licensee.

7.3   Sub-clause 7.2 sets out the sole and exclusive remedy of the Licensee in relation to defects in the CD-ROMs.

7.4   The Publisher and the Licensee acknowledge that the Publisher supplies the Product on an 'as is' basis. The Publisher gives no warranties:

7.4.1   that the Product satisfies the individual requirements of the Licensee; or

7.4.2   that the Product is otherwise fit for the Licensee's purpose; or

7.4.3   that the Data is accurate or complete or free of errors or omissions; or

7.4.4   that the Product is compatible with the Licensee's hardware equipment and software operating environment.

7.5   The Publisher hereby disclaims all warranties and conditions, express or implied, which are not stated above.

7.6   Nothing in this Clause 7 limits the Publisher's liability to the Licensee in the event of death or personal injury resulting from the Publisher's negligence.

7.7   The Publisher hereby excludes liability for loss of revenue, reputation, business, profits, or for indirect or consequential losses, irrespective of whether the Publisher was advised by the Licensee of the potential of such losses.

7.8   The Licensee acknowledges the merit of independently verifying Data prior to taking any decisions of material significance (commercial or otherwise) based on such data. It is agreed that the Publisher shall not be liable for any losses which result from the Licensee placing reliance on the Data or on the database, under any circumstances.

7.9   Subject to sub-clause 7.6 above, the Publisher's liability under this Agreement shall be limited to the purchase price.

8. INTELLECTUAL PROPERTY RIGHTS

8.1 Nothing in this Agreement affects the ownership of copyright or other intellectual property rights in the Data, the Database, the Software or the Manual.

8.2 The Licensee agrees to display the Publisher's copyright notice in the manner described in this clause 8 and in the Product.

8.3 The Licensee hereby agrees to abide by copyright and similar notice requirements required by the information provider, details of which are as follows: copyright in the Product is held by Routledge and the authors.

8.4 This Product contains material proprietary to and copyrighted by the Publisher and others. Except for the licence granted herein, all rights, title and interest in the Product, in all languages, formats and media throughout the world, including all copyrights therein, are and remain the property of the Publisher or other copyright owners identified in the Product.

9. NON-ASSIGNMENT

This Agreement and the licence contained within it may not be assigned to any other person or entity without the written consent of the Publisher.

10. TERMINATION AND CONSEQUENCES OF TERMINATION

10.1 The Publisher shall have the right to terminate this Agreement if:

10.1.1 the Licensee is in material breach of this Agreement and fails to remedy such breach (where capable of remedy) within 14 days of a written notice from the Publisher requiring it to do so; or

10.1.2 the Licensee becomes insolvent, becomes subject to receivership, liquidation or similar external administration; or

10.1.3 the Licensee ceases to operate in business.

10.2 The Licensee shall have the right to terminate this Agreement for any reason upon two months' written notice. The Licensee shall not be entitled to any refund for payments made under this Agreement prior to termination under this sub-clause 10.2.

10.3 Termination by either of the parties is without prejudice to any other rights or remedies under the general law to which Termination by either of the parties is without prejudice to any other rights or remedies under the general law to which they may be entitled, or which survive such termination (including rights of the Publisher under sub-clause 6.4 above).

10.4 Upon termination of this Agreement, or expiry of its terms, the Licensee must:

10.4.1 destroy all back-up copies of the Product; and

10.4.2 return the Product to the Publisher.

11. GENERAL

11.1 *Compliance with export provisions*
The Publisher hereby agrees to comply fully with all relevant export laws and regulations of the United Kingdom to ensure that the Product is not exported, directly or indirectly, in violation of English law.

11.2 *Force majeure*
The parties accept no responsibility for breaches of this Agreement occurring as a result of circumstances beyond their control.

11.3 *No waiver*
Any failure or delay by either party to exercise or enforce any right conferred by this Agreement shall not be deemed to be a waiver of such right.

11.4 *Entire agreement*
This Agreement represents the entire agreement between the Publisher and the Licensee concerning the Product. The terms of this Agreement supersede all prior purchase orders, written terms and conditions, written or verbal representations, advertising or statements relating in any way to the Product.

11.5 *Severability*
If any provision of this Agreement is found to be invalid or unenforceable by a court of law of competent jurisdiction, such a finding shall not affect the other provisions of this Agreement and all provisions of this Agreement unaffected by such a finding shall remain in full force and effect.

11.6 *Variations*
This Agreement may only be varied in writing by means of variation signed in writing by both parties.

11.7 *Notices*
All notices to be delivered to: Routledge, 11 New Fetter Lane, London EC4P 4EE, UK.

11.8 *Governing law*
This Agreement is governed by English law and the parties hereby agree that any dispute arising under this Agreement shall be subject to the jurisdiction of the English courts.

Important Note: see previous pages for Licence Agreement.

INSTALLATION INSTRUCTIONS FOR STUDENT CD-ROM

Macintosh

To view the text contained in the *Climates and Weather Explained CD-ROM* you will need Acrobat 3 (or higher) software. If you do not have the software, double click the 'Install Acrobat 3.0' icon in the acroread folder and follow the on-screen instructions. To initialise *Climates and Weather Explained CD-ROM*, double click the 'climates.pdf' icon.

Windows PCs

To view the text contained in the *Climates and Weather Explained CD-ROM* you will need Acrobat 3 (or higher) software. To install Acrobat reader software in Windows 3.1, from Programme Manager, choose File, then Run 'setup.exe'. This is in the '16bit' directory which is within the reader directory on the CD-ROM. To install Acrobat in Windows 95/NT, run 'setup.exe' in the '32bit' directory which is within the reader directory. To initialise *Climates and Weather Explained CD-ROM*, simply run Acrobat 3.0 (or higher), and open the 'climates.pdf' file on the CD-ROM.

MACHINE SPECIFICATIONS

Windows PC

Windows 3.1 (or later)
MS-DOS 6.2 (or later) and 8 megabytes of free RAM
or Windows 95 and 8 megabytes of free RAM
13″ VGA colour monitor
CD-ROM drive (double speed or faster)

Apple Macintosh

Macintosh system 7
68040 or higher recommended
8 megabytes of free RAM
13″ colour monitor (256 colours minimum)
Quicktime 2.0 or later plus Apple Media Tuner (supplied on disk)
CD-ROM drive (double speed or faster)

To access the Internet links on *Climates and Weather Explained*, you need to have access to the World Wide Web with a browser such as Netscape.

All trademarks acknowledged